Jonathon Green

NEWSPEAK

A DICTIONARY OF JARGON

Routledge & Kegan Paul

London, Boston, Melbourne and Henley

First published in 1984
First published as a paperback in 1985
by Routledge & Kegan Paul plc
14 Leicester Square, London WC2H 7PH, England,
9 Park Street, Boston, Mass. 02108, USA,
464 St Kilda Road, Melbourne,
Victoria 3004, Australia, and
Broadway House, Newtown Road,
Henley-on-Thames, Oxon RG9 1EN, England
Set in Linotron Plantin
by Input Typesetting Ltd, London SW19 8DR
and printed in Great Britain by
T.J. Press Ltd

British Library Cataloguing in Publication Data

Green, Jonathon

Newspeak
1. English language—Jargon
I. Title
427'.09   PE1449

ISBN 0-7100-9685-2 (c)
ISBN 0-7102-0673-9 (p)

NEWSPEAK

For Pearce Marchbank

CONTENTS

INTRODUCTION

George Orwell coined 'Newspeak' for his novel *1984*; its purpose 'was not only to provide a medium of expression for the world-view and mental habits proper to the devotees of Ingsoc, but to make all other modes of thought impossible'. It was designed to shrink vocabularies, to eliminate subtlety, to destroy nuance and to let loose a verbal holocaust upon the English language. In Orwell's nightmare future, where totalitarian simplicity had been stamped upon a world once less black and white, this continuing reduction of language was the perfect verbal extension of the social process. In the event, the chronological 1984 appears along lines very different from Orwell's grim blueprint. Yet no-one would deny that a form of 'newspeak', however altered, is all too prevalent. Where Orwell's society was governed by the stick, we are offered the carrot. The truncation of the language on 'Airstrip One' was a logical response to the harsh social engineering that engendered it. The soothing, delusory world of 'equality', of much-touted 'democracy', has created a 'newspeak' all its own. Rather than shorten the language it is infinitely broadened; instead of curt monosyllables, there are mellifluous, calming phrases, designed to allay suspicions, modify facts and divert one's attention from difficulties. Thus *doubleplusungood* becomes 'negative evaluation', *sexcrime* 'interpersonal relationship', *rocket bombs* 'systems', and their effects fall neither on proles nor on Party, but are simply 'collateral damage'. The new newspeak is of a different tone from its fictional predecessor. Orders have been modified into persuasion. Ignorance, desired or not, is made to seem bliss.

The intention of this Dictionary is to amass a selection of this latter-day newspeak, as well as a selection of allied jargons – the slangs and specific vocabularies of a number of trades, professions, occupations and interests. As the first part of a two-volume work, it has concentrated on the more immediate of such areas: the media, the military, economics and finance, advertising, the new therapies, and so on. A further collection will embrace that great quantity of words and phrases that have evolved amongst the workers in the countless occupations in which we all make our livings. Of course, not all the entries in this Dictionary will have quite the sinister import of Orwell's famous coinage. Many of those who use this 'trade slang' do so as much out of a desire to make themselves understood (and accepted) by their peers as to confuse the uninitiated. But the lure of the 'in-group' is undeniable, and simple language is a painless way of stating one's elite status. On the other hand, many of these words are aimed to obscure. The calming tones of soldiers and civil servants connive at glossing over the unpalatable facts of our possible nuclear demise. Politicians mask the facts that catch no votes in some fluent polysyllable. Criminals talk in the most genteel of euphemisms to pass off murder and mayhem. The vagaries of the economic and financial community are bowed beneath a set of terms that differ only in the geography of their use from those of the race track and the casino. And so the list goes on.

Any dictionary must inevitably be unfinished, especially one that seeks to chart the ever-increasing vocabulary of obfuscation. I am fortunate, with entries for a further volume already on file, to be allowed a second attempt at all-inclusiveness. To that end, while I have already thanked elsewhere everyone who has made a generous contribution to this volume, I appeal once more for any help and suggestions that readers might offer. As I have found to my mingled delight and horror, there are as many 'professional slangs' as there are occupations in which they might evolve. I can only hope to cover as wide an area as possible and thus would be grateful for any expertise that those who know such professions far more intimately than I do, might feel able to offer.

JONATHON GREEN

ACKNOWLEDGMENTS

Very many people were concerned in the research and compilation of this book. Some gave one word, others offered several and the replies to my appeals in magazines both in Britain and in America were generous and beyond my more optimistic hopes. Many of those replies, and the jargon they included, have not been used in this, first, volume of my Dictionary of Jargon; I can only ask them to await their proper acknowledgment until its successor appears. As regards this volume, I would thank everyone who made their contribution, and would like to specify certain individuals who offered particular encouragement and aid throughout this project: Phillippa Brewster, Nick Cole, Angela Coles, Karen Durbin, Susan Ford, Leslie Gardner, Harriet Griffey, Colin MacCabe, Heather Page, Dick Pountain, David Rattray. Also: J. E. Begley, Nigel Burwood, Andrew Cockburn, Lesley Cockburn, Sidney Cohen, MD, Christopher Cory, Peter Davies, Felix Dennis, Ron Dorfman, Quentin Falk, Mick Farren, Dr. Rodney Foale, Col. J. E. Greenwood, USMC (Retd.), Philip Hodson, Thomas S. Holman, David Jenkins, Ted Klein, David L. Lockhard, Derek Lovell, Donald Macintyre, Dennis MacShane, Pearce Marchbank, Alan Marcuson, Dr. Guy Nield, Andrew Payne, Norman A. Punt, FRCS Ed., DLO, Prof. Gerald J. Schiffhorst, PhD., Mike Seabrook, David Walsh, Nicholas Weaver.

ABBREVIATIONS

a:	adjective	**medic:**	medical
abbrev:	abbreviation	**milit:**	military
acro:	acronym		
advert:	advertising	**n:**	noun
aka:	also known as	**nb:**	note well
appx:	approximately		
archit:	architecture	**obs:**	obsolescent
		orig:	originally
cf:	compare		
cp:	catch phrase	**pols:**	politics
		public relats/PR:	public relations
d:	died		
D&D:	Dungeons & Dragons	**qv:**	which see
edn:	edition	**RAF:**	Royal Air Force
educ:	education	**RM:**	Royal Marines
eg:	for example	**RN:**	Royal Navy
esp:	especially	**Rus:**	Russian
ex:	from		
		SE:	standard English
fl:	flourished	**sl:**	slang
Fr:	French	**sociol:**	sociology
fr:	from	**Sp:**	Spanish
		spec:	specifically
Ger:	German		
govt:	government	**UK:**	United Kingdom
		US:	United States
ie:	that is	**USAF:**	United States Air Force
indust relats:	industrial relations	**USMC:**	United States Marine Corps
Ital:	Italian	**USN:**	United States Navy
		usu:	usually
Lat:	Latin		
lit:	literally	**v:**	verb
lit. crit:	literary criticism		
		Yid:	Yiddish

A & P repair (medic) (abbrev) surgical tightening of the Anterior and Posterior muscles between the vagina and rectum.

A & R man (record business) (abbrev) Artistes and Repertory (US), Repertoire (UK). Company executive who deals with the contracted performers and their material.

ABC (airline) (abbrev) Advance Booking Charter. aka *alphabet fares*. Cheap air fares available to those who book a certain number of days before flying and contract a stay of a certain length.

ABC (medic) (abbrev) Airway, Breathing, Circulation: major areas of concern in a medical emergency. 'Watch your ABCs'.

ABC Art (art) see *Minimal Art*.

ABC warfare (milit) (abbrev) Atomic, Biological and Chemical weaponry. (cf: *integrated battlefield*)

AB, C1, C2, D (market research and statistics) Social groups/classes: AB: Upper and professional middle class; C1: white collar; C2: skilled working class; DE: unskilled and below plus pensioners.

ABD (educ/US) (abbrev) All But Dissertation. Describing a doctoral candidate who has all the necessary academic credits for a PhD but has yet to write the required dissertation.

ability gap (sociol) an alleged inherent difference in ability between blacks and whites. Coined for a survey published October 1982 by the National Opinion Research Center, U. of Chicago.

ability grouping (educ) teaching fast or slow learners in their respective intelligence groups.

able (educ) clever, or at least up to the required academic level. (thus) *less able*: below the average intelligence.

ABM (milit) (abbrev) Anti-Ballistic Missile. Capable of destroying hostile missiles inside or outside the atmosphere.

abort *n, v* (aerospace) an unsuccessful mission that has to be cut short; to cut short a mission at any stage of launch or flight; (spec.) the emergency separation of the spacecraft from its rocket booster.

above (gambling) the earnings of any gambling enterprise that are listed for tax and other legal purposes.

above (horse-racing) overfed, under-exercised horse; one that has not been adequately trained for a specific race.

above (theatre) stage direction implying 'behind' a person or item of stage furniture. (thus) *below*: in front of. (cf: *upstage, n*, and *downstage, n*)

above the line (TV) the basic budget of a production including both direct and indirect costs of the programme, other than unusual expenditure.

above the market (stock market) at a price in excess of the normal market quotation. (thus) *below the market*: at a price beneath the normal market quotation.

abreaction channels (indust relats) from psychiatric *abreaction* 'emotional discharge' for the purpose of ridding oneself of a trauma rather than brooding on it. A management technique to allow dissatisfied employees to let off steam either through surveys or in conversation with special counsellors.

absolute address (computers) the specific location for the storage of an item of information within the computer.

absolute architecture (arts) a proposed system of architecture that would be dictated not by utilitarian requirements, but by the taste of the individual architect. The antithesis of functionalism (qv), these buildings would be 'pure', non-objective and purposeless.

absolute dud (milit) a nuclear weapon that fails to explode on target.

absolute music (arts) self-dependent instrumental music without any literary or other external influences. (cf. *programme music*)

abstauben (milit) (Ger.) Used in French Foreign Legion to denote anything acquired by irregular means.

abstract expressionism (art) movement in US painting in late 1940s, early 1950s. Many adherents in varied styles but overall characteristics include the large scale, generally abstract subjects with some figurative/symbolic elements, asymmetrical composition, dramatic colour or tonal contrasts. (cf: *drip painting, all-over paintings, calligraphic painting, tachisme, action painting*)

abstract expressionist sculpture (arts) work produced by a number of US artists in late 1950s, early 1960s who rejected traditional materials in favour of new media that would reflect the spontaneity and techniques of

A

abstract expressionism (qv) (cf: *junk art, assemblage art*)

abstract illusionism (art) the tendency of American painting in the mid-1960s to return to illusionism: the use of pictorial devices, orthographic drawing, cool/warm colour contrasts, etc.

abstract impressionism (art) paintings with a uniform pattern of brushstrokes which retained the optical effects of impressionism while dispensing with its representational content. This contrasted completely with contemporaneous schools such as *action painting*, etc.

AC (rock music) (abbrev) Adult Contemporary, aka *soft rock*. Music purportedly for grown-up former fans of 1960s groups such as Beatles, Rolling Stones, etc.

academic (educ) the basic subjects of the traditional curriculum: 'the Three Rs' plus science, history and geography.

academic socialism (pols) aka *armchair socialism, socialism ex cathedra*. The socialism of words not deeds, primarily enjoyed by academics within their secure and ivory towers. Neither fast nor aggressive enough for hardliners.

academy leader (movies) the length of film numbered 12 to 3 that is attached to a spool of film so as to ensure perfect cueing during projection.

Acapulco Gold, Acapulco Red (drugs) see *drug names*.

accelerated history (aerospace) the testing of a component by artificially 'ageing' it with machine induced stresses or 'work' that condense its potential life-span into a conveniently abbreviated period.

accelerated motion (movies) the effect obtained by running the camera slowly: when the film is projected the movement filmed will seem faster since it occupies less frames that it would normally.

acceleration (educ) the speed at which a child learns and the progress he or she makes through a school career.

acceptable casualties (milit) the percentage of casualties that can be suffered in combat without forcing a retreat, defeat or similar military reversal. Applicable to all levels of combat up to nuclear exchange (when casualties would include civilian populations).

acceptance house (commerce) a financial house, especially a merchant bank, which lends money on security of bills of exchange or adds its name as the endorser of bills drawn by another party. In UK the leading acceptance houses are merchant banks linked in the Acceptance House Committee.

accepted pairing (advert) aka *pre-emption*. The concept of using one of the competition's advantages and using it to boost your product. Epitomised in Avis Cars 'We Try Harder' campaign which played on their undeniable second place in car rental statistics.

access *v* (computers) to retrieve information from a memory store.

access (TV/UK) the concept of offering time on state or independent TV networks to minority or special interest groups to state their own cases, usually with some professional guidance. (thus) *access broadcasting, access programmes*.

access program (TV/US) programme shown by network affiliates (qv) during specific hours every week. Often updated versions of former hit shows.

access time (computers) the period between 'asking' for the information and the computer's producing it for the user.

accessible television (TV/US) programming aimed at lowest level of audience appeal: 'fewer words, more white space, and many more pictures, especially of entertainment figures' (Michael J. Arlen, *The Camera Age*, 1981).

accessorise (advert) to provide with accessories; also popular in fashion context.

accidental delivery (milit) the shelling of one's own troops. (cf: *friendly fire*)

accommodation collar (police/US) an arrest made to satisfy the public that police are on the job and filling up crime statistics. During highly publicised crack-downs on crime, such arrests are even pre-arranged between gangsters and the police department when lowly figures are sacrificed to keep the real criminals secure.

accommodation payment (business) aka *kickback*. A method of high-level bribery in which a customer is knowingly overcharged – to keep the books straight – and subsequently returned the surplus money for personal use.

accord and satisfaction (commerce) the agreement between two parties to alter the terms of an original contract. Both the accord – the change itself – and the satisfaction – the performance of the contract as changed – must take place before the old contract is fulfilled, unless both parties agree that the changes mean in themselves that all previous contracts are henceforth cancelled.

according to Hoyle (gambling) on the highest, most expert authority. Used in card games and more generally. From *A Short Treatise on the Game of Whist* by Edmund Hoyle (1742).

account (advertising) aka *A Piece of Business*. The client.

accountability (educ) the holding of schools and teachers as responsible for the performance of their pupils by allotting school funds and teachers' salaries on the basis of student achievement.

accounting package (computers) the computer program that takes care of routine machine operations, particularly in the scheduling and analysis of the workload.

account sale (finance) a statement of purchase and sale issued by commodity broker to a customer after a futures (qv) transaction is closed out (qv) itemising the profit or loss, the commission and any other charges applicable.

accumulation (pols) the socialist equivalent of capitalist 'investment': that part of the national income that is produced but not consumed within the same year.

accumulator (horse-racing) the carrying forward of the money won on one bet to be used as stake money for the next one and so on as long as possible or desired.

accuracy (computers) the number of bits (qv) required to define a number; the more bits required, the greater the accuracy.

AC/DC (sex) from the two forms of electrical current: bisexual, 'swinging both ways'.

ace (sport) 1 (golf) *n*, a hole in one. 2 (tennis) *n*, *v*, an unreturnable shot; to play an unreturnable shot.

acey-deucey (horse-racing/US) a rider who sets his stirrups at different lengths.

A check (airlines) a regular 60 hour check on civil airliners. Landing and anti-collision lights, landing gear, doors, oil level and tyre pressure all checked; wings and fuselage given external visual assessment; water system and coffee makers drained, refilled; oxygen masks and escape systems and liferafts checked. (cf: *B check*)

achieve a solution (milit) to lock electronically onto a target in one's sights and to fire and (theoretically) destroy that target.

achievement motive (business) the desired motivation of an executive who should value success for its own sake rather than simply for the acquisition of a larger salary. Work should be seen as 'meaningful' in its own right.

acid (drugs) see *drug names*.

acid fascism (drugs, sociol) pathological state of mind usually associated with heavy users of hallucinogens (especially LSD25 – 'acid') and epitomised in the Manson 'Family' murderers of 1969 who based their homicidal crusade on a philosophy fuelled by psychedelic drugs.

ACL (business) (abbrev) Action Centred Leadership. The concept in management training that assumes that one can create leaders irrespective of natural abilities. Originated by Dr. John Adair, formerly an advisor on leadership to the British Army.

acoustical excitation (milit) sound.

acoustic perfume (audio) aka: *white noise*: an overlay of 'background' noise intended to have no specific character of its own to but drown out a selection of irritating sounds that would otherwise prove distracting.

acquisition (milit) the meeting of possible hostile airplanes by a fighter pilot during his flight.

across the board (indust relats) from the betting vocabulary for backing one horse either to take first, second or third place (US 'win, place or show'): a wage deal in which a bargain is accepted that embraces all classes and categories of workers without exception within a union. Formerly (1950s) the 'flat-rate'.

across the board (horse-racing) placing a bet that any one horse might appear in any of the first three places. Known in US as win, place or show.

acting out (sociol) from the psycho-analytic concept of a subject, in the grip of unconscious wishes and fantasies, reliving these same wishes without acknowledging their source: used by social workers to describe those who cause trouble, especially for social workers, by releasing their own emotional tensions in their dealing with those who most probably have nothing directly to do with them.

action *n* 1. (entertainment); the commercial potential of any place, be it single shop, cinema, street, town, whole area or country, etc.
2. (gambling) the volume of betting, intensity of play.
3. (drugs) the availability of supplies.

action *v* (business) to perform one's job emphatically, purposefully; particularly to act as the corporation for whom one works would desire.

action architecture (arts) the concept of creating architecture 'on site' with materials 'as found', using sketches rather than detailed drawings, and depending on the continuing presence and inspiration of the architect throughout the building. An optimistic concept, enjoyed by few clients and fewer contractors.

actioner *n* (movies) thrills, spills, sex and violence all contained in one type of eternally popular film.

action house (movies) the opposite of *art house* (qv), a cinema where ultra-popular all-action films are shown to their mass audiences. Often sited in poor areas and aimed straight at non-discriminating viewers.

action level (govt/US) the level of concentration in a food of such poisonous/dangerous substances that the public health authorities demand a ban on the sale of such food.

action painting (art) the loosely painted, highly gestural works of such artists as Jackson Pollock. Action stresses the essential act of painting – the process of making having a greater importance than the finished work – and is an extension into oil painting of the Surrealists' technique of automatic writing.

action research (management, educ, sociol) the concept of implementing static 'desk research' with field work to create new ideas; then the continuous monitoring of the practice of these ideas and the possible updating of them while they are being put to use.

active defence (milit) the use of weapons systems to defeat enemy troops; with the implication that the enemy will have made the first hostile move.

active listening (new therapies) in 'Rogerian' (client-centred) therapy, the therapist 'reflects back' what he/she hears the client saying instead of analysing or commenting on it. Unlike the traditional Freudian analyst, the Rogerian presumes the basic goodness and worth of his client.

active money (commerce) money that is in circulation or otherwise being used for business purposes rather than simply invested or on deposit.

activism (pols) high-level political zealots, more concerned with the correct ideology than many of the rank and file members, and simultaneously maintaining pressure on their fellows to accentuate their political struggle whenever and wherever possible. Similar to *militant* but implying the extent of political involvement rather than merely the depth of one's radical stance.

activity programme (educ) extra-curricular activities such as clubs, sports, etc.

actor proof (theatre) said part-jokingly of a script that should guarantee the management a hit, no matter how grotesque the ineptitude of those performing it.

actor's bible (theatre) *Variety* magazine (US); *The Stage* (UK).

actual (milit/US) the radio code for the commander of a force; used at all levels and meant to distinguish the officer from his radioman who would actually put through the call.

actual *n* (TV) the real, final cost of a programme, calculated at the end of the production; as opposed to the projected cost, optimistically set out before work began.

actual money (econ) see: *real money*.

actualise *v* (new therapies) to fulfil the potentials of something or somebody, (thus) *actualiser* one who so performs; one who makes active and supposedly beneficial decisions for themselves and others. (Possible use in business sense).

actuality (TV) method of reimbursing expenses based on the *actual* costs incurred rather than on some agreed allowance claim.

actuality, actualities (TV, radio) from Fr. *actualités*, on the spot reporting of events, especially violent/dramatic ones, but including any live reporting such as a press statement from a government source. Supposedly, in its more dramatic versions, the ideal style of news reporting, boosted perhaps by its absolute unavailability to print media.

actuals (commerce) the opposite of *futures* (qv), commodities that are physically available for transfer when deals concerning them have been concluded.

act well *v* (theatre) a play that is both easy to produce and to perform; filled with plenty of good lines and 'business' for the actors to indulge.

ad (press) (abbrev) additional copy, extra material for a story. *ad one*: the first page of extra material; thus *ad two*, *ad three*, etc.

ada from Decator (gambling) pron. *eighter* . . . the point 8 in craps (dice).

add *n* (rock music) (abbrev) addition of a new record – single or album – to a radio station's playlist.

added money (horse-racing) extra money added to the basic stakes awarded to the victor in a race which thus bulks up the prize.

add-on (computer) anything that can be added to the basic machine that will improve or expand its performance.

add-on sales (commerce) continuing sales to an already satisfied customer.

address *n, v* (computers) the location of a specific piece of information within a computer; to indicate or to find that location within the memory.

address bus (computer) the physical connection between the processor, the computer memory and the rest of the system. (cf: *bus*)

adhocery (govt, business) decisions, rules, agreements that are made on the spur of a moment and for the specific problems involved.

adhocism (archit) the concept of creating a building in which one part is designed by a specialist who takes little or no regard of the overall project. By extension the architect needs no longer invent new forms but can select the best available from a suitable catalogue and collage the parts together for his whole.

adhocracy (govt, business) Coined by Alvin Toffler in *Future Shock* (1970): the concept that in place of monolithic and thus static institutions for decision-making, there should evolve temporary organisations which deal with specific problems and are then dissolved. An 'action group' to fit each circumstance. Ideally the management of the future.

adjusting the contract (movies) 'which means paying (a writer) a few weeks salary under the threat of keeping his idea until his next option comes up, with everyone knowing that he has no assignment and that no producer on the lot wants him' (*The Selected Letters of Raymond Chandler*, ed. F. MacShane, 1981).

adjustment (law/US) in the US Family Court, the dismissal of charges by a Probation Officer.

adjustment centre (prisons/US) part of the prison where mentally unstable and dedicatedly rebellious prisoners are kept isolated from main prison population in solitary confinement.

admass (soc sci) coined by J. B. Priestley 1955: the economic, social and culture system that is dominated and controlled by the desire to acquire and consume material goods, an ideology that is expanded and intensified by a barrage of seductive advertising.

administrative loading (milit) the loading of a

transport vehicle in which priority is given to the volume of material loaded rather than to tactical need or convenience. (cf: *tactical loading*)

admiralty sweep (navy) extravagantly wide sweep of a boat as it approaches a gangplank or jetty.

adoption process (marketing) the process whereby customers come to accept new products.

adshel (advertising) from trade name of a specific poster contractor: shorthand for a four-sheet poster in a High Street or shopping precinct. (cf: *sheet*)

adult (sex) euphemism for pornographic; adult bookstore, adult cinema, etc.

adult (TV) reasonably, by the standards of television, sophisticated; in UK this implies those programmes shown after 9pm, the cutoff point at which it is assumed children are in bed.

adult contemporary (rock music) mainstream, soft rock music, aimed at those whose lifestyle and tastes have moved beyond the excesses of 'real' rock 'n' roll.

advance *n, v* (pols) the preparing in advance of a live audience or the briefing of radio or TV stations in order to obtain the maximum vote-catching exposure for a political candidate. Such activities are performed by the *advance man* whose job includes having 'spontaneous' demonstrations with banner-waving supporters ready for the cameras, writing 'local' inserts for his boss's speech, and generally geeing up the local party activists. Advance can be *good advance* or *bad advance*, depending on quality. The concept supposedly originated with carnival or circus hucksters who sent a man on ahead to whip up enthusiasm for the show. (cf. *black advance*)

adventurism (pols) derogatory term used by both US and USSR to imply an aggressive foreign policy especially as regards the amassing of large nuclear arsenals, the military sabre-rattling that is backed by such 'deterrents', and the involvement (Vietnam, Afghanistan) in neo-imperialist campaigns.

adverse selection (business) the concept in insurance terms of disproportionate risks; those who are poorer or more prone to suffer loss or make more claims than the average risk.

advertise (gambling) in gin rummy the discarding of one card in the hope of luring an opponent into believing that this, in fact your strong and desired suit, is one in which you have no interest and which he, in turn, may discard.

advertorial (public relations) advertising by large companies in which editorial copy is used to present themselves in a self-justifying light when dealing with areas – such as pollution, energy saving, the environment – in which they are more generally cast as the villains.

advice and consent (pols/US) the Senatorial power, written into the US Constitution Art. II, Sec. 2, to act as a check on the appointive and treaty-making powers of the President.

advocacy *n* (sociol) the action of social workers in representing their clients before tribunals and similar services whose requirements and organisation may prove too complex for the client to understand and thus use to his/her own benefit.

advocacy *a* 1. advocacy advertising: partisan advertising, both of minority groups and of major companies wishing to counter adverse publicity.
2. advocacy journalism: journalism that eschews the traditional non-involvement of the writer/paper; aka *campaigning journalism*.
3. advocacy planning: urban planning by specialists each of whom attempts to ensure that the group whom they represent – disparate sections of the community for whom the buildings are being created – will have their interests remembered in the overall scheme.

aerobics (medic/sport) currently fashionable keep-fit exercise regime which depends on increasing oxygen intake in order to stimulate the activity of the heart and lungs.

aerospace plane (aerospace) a space vehicle – ie the Shuttle – that can be launched beyond the atmosphere, and can then re-enter the atmosphere and there be manoeuvred and landed on the Earth's surface like a conventional jet or airliner. Such vehicles are presumed to be manned and to use some form of airbreathing (qv) propulsion.

aesthetic surgery (medic) plastic surgery, usually on the face, that is carried out purely for cosmetic reasons.

affectional preference minorities (sociol) homosexuals, either male or female.

affiliates (TV/US) those local stations that operate independently of the three major US networks, although they are forced to take much of their programming from them. (cf: *o & o, webs*)

affirmations (new therapies) positive self-enhancing statements that accompany the rebirthing process of Theta training seminars. This baptism-like rebirthing takes place complete with snorkel and nose-clips in a bath of water heated to 99°F – the temperature of the womb's amniotic fluid.

affirmative action (pols) the hiring of minority/disadvantaged/poor individuals for jobs that might require higher credentials than they can offer, on the principle that their poverty, etc has made it impossible for them to obtain such credentials. Unfortunately, despite the basic worthiness of such a scheme, those credentials are still missing and it may be that those so employed still can't do the required job.

Afghanistanism (press) from the remoteness of that country from the US: the practice of

A

concentrating investigations on far off places for which some 'answers' can be put forward, rather than looking at problems closer to home, for which no such simple solutions are available. This concept has naturally suffered somewhat since the 1979 USSR invasion.

aft (TV/US) the end of a piece of tape that contains one news item. (cf: *fore*)

after market (stock market) the market for a share after its issuer has made the initial sale through the underwriters.

after market *v* (computer) to begin buying accessories for a machine after purchasing the basic equipment.

afternoon bath (TV) urgent order for developing film. Film is usually developed and put through its 'bath' overnight. If an 'afternoon bath' is required, the film will be developed the same day.

AFV (milit) (abbrev) armoured fighting vehicle.

agate (press/US) 5½ point typeface, as used for small ads in US papers.

age *n* (gambling) in poker, the player immediately to the left of the dealer, aka the *ante-man*, whose task it is to provide the ante payment into the pot before betting and dealing begin.

age cohorts, age peers (educ) those in the same age-group.

age-ism (pols) one of the various pressure-group suffixes that emerged after the popularisation of *sexism* (qv). The discrimination against the old on the grounds of their being old. Pressure groups against ageism include the 'Grey Panthers', modelled on the 'Black Panthers' of 1960s. (thus) *ageist* derog. *n* or *a*.

agent (gambling) a player-cheat who works in collusion with the staff of the casino – croupiers, pit bosses etc – but not with the owners.

agent (espionage) spies who are employed as freelances by the CIA but who are not actual, permanent employees of the organisation.

age the accounts *v* (commerce) to take the various accounts which concern a firm and arrange them according to date and to which payments are owed, which due, etc etc.

aggress (sport) to play aggressively. (spec) *aggress the ball*.

aggressive portfolio (stock market) a group of stocks chosen specifically with the likelihood of their increasing in price.

aggressive pricing (commerce) aka: *competitive pricing*: pricing one's goods cheaper than those of one's rivals, thus launching a price war.

AGI (milit) (acro) Aliens Gathering Intelligence: code for Russian 'trawlers' and other vessels that track NATO fleets or anchor near major land-based military bases.

agitprop (pols) ex Dept. of Agitation and Propaganda (Odtel Agitatsi i Propagandy) est. 1920 by Central Committee of USSR Communist Party. Bureaucracy has changed but the concept still exists to influence and propagandise both USSR and the world with communist ideology.

agonal (medic) immediately prior to death.

agony column (press) originally the personal columns of the daily press, especially *The Times* (London), which were often used for illicit assignations, requests for communications from missing persons, etc. Now implies those columns used to answer the pains and problems of the lovelorn, the sexually perturbed and the generally unhappy. The advisors who run such columns are *agony aunties*.

agribusiness, agrobusiness (business) those wide-ranging enterprises which produce, process and distribute farm products, as well as their ancillary suppliers and other businesses. The prefix *agri-* has been used recently for such compounds as *agribusinessman, agricorporation, agricrime* (the stealing of farm machinery), *agripower, agriproletariat*, etc.

agricultural (cricket) a brutally clumsy swipe of the bat; aka *cowshot*.

aha reaction (psychol) the sudden realisation of an ideal insight or similar illumination that seems to make clear a complex and painful problem. The analytical eureka!

ahead (gambling) winning; ahead of the house in one's pile of cash.

AI (computers) (abbrev) artificial intelligence. The continuing research into making machines more like human beings – with thought, speech, intuition, etc. – will theoretically develop the first real androids, the exemplars of AI.

aided recall (market research) an interviewing technique in which subjects are asked for their response to a question and allowed to give an answer chosen from a pre-selected list.

aids (sport) in horse-riding, the correct and combined applications of hands and legs.

air *n* (TV) space in the framing of the television picture.

air *v* (radio) to broadcast.

air art (art) aka *blow up art, gonflable art, inflatable sculpture*: a broad category of art which comprises many different structures, all with the common purpose of exploiting the possibilities of compressed air or the natural force of the wind, usually by inflatables. The artists claim such works are both public and participatory.

airborne alert (milit) policy of maintaining bomber force permanently in the air around the clock in order to make an offensive quicker and to keep planes from being destroyed on the ground. This was dropped by USAF in 1968, but is put into operation at any level of crisis warning.

air breather (aerospace) a jet engine that requires the intake of air for the combustion of its fuel.

airburst (milit) a nuclear explosion that is detonated sufficiently far above the ground to ensure that none of the fireball actually touches the ground and thus none of the effect of the explosion is lost; an airburst ensures the maximum product and dissemination of radioactive fallout.

airdale (USMC) an aviator.

air date (TV) the date on which any of the various television transmitter masts went into operation.

air defence warning conditions (milit) 1. yellow: attack by hostile aircraft and/or missiles is probable; hostile aircraft and/or missiles are en route; unknown aircraft/missiles suspected to be hostile are en route toward or within an air defence division/sector.
2. red: attack by hostile aircraft and/or missiles is imminent/in progress; hostile aircraft and/or missiles are within an air defence division/sector or are in its immediate vicinity with high probability of entering that division/sector.
3. white: attack by hostile aircraft/missiles is improbable. (this may be issued before or after yellow or red conditions).

airline nicknames Pandemonium Scareways (Pan Am), Try Walking Airways (TWA), Queer & Nice Types of Stewards (Qantas), Can't Promise Anything (Canadian Pacific) Sweet & Sexy (SAS).

air miss (aerospace) the official description of a narrow escape from collision by two airplanes flying too close to each other.

airplay (rock music) the radio broadcasting of a record. (cf: *needle time*)

air time (TV) the time during a schedule available to advertisers.

aisle sitter (theatre) the critic (who can thus escape to write his/her review rather than battle along a crowded row).

alarm threshold (tech) in nuclear research laboratories and energy plants, the level of lost nuclear material (MUF, qv) that is considered dangerous – terrorists could have stolen the material, other nations might have had it delivered for making their own bombs, etc.

albatross (sport) in golf, a hole played in three strokes under *par* (qv).

ALBM (milit) (abbrev) air launched ballistic missile; fired from a plane at ground, water or other plane.

ALCHEM (milit) from ALCM (air launched cruise missile) thus: Slickem (SLCM: sea launched cruise missile) Glockem (GLCM: ground launched cruise missile).

alert crew *n* (milit) five-man USAF teams who man SAC (qv) missile launch facility at Offutt AFB and in the Cover All flying command post (qv).

alert levels (airlines) regular inspection times set up for repair and replacement of defective parts on civil airliners.

ALGOL (computers) algorithmic language: computer language designed by a committee of European academics and still more popular in Europe than US. Intended for programming in higher maths and complex technology.

algorithm (computer) a set of well defined rules for solving a problem in a finite number of steps.

alibi copy (press) duplicate copy of the original story and notes; kept in the morgue (qv) and filed against any possible challenges, libel suits and other recriminations.

alienation 1 (Marxist) the estrangement of the worker from his true 'social' being – his family, friends and useful work – for the production of meaningless and unnatural work; the feeling of being unable to influence one's own life and environment, becoming not a person but a thing.

alienation 2 (theatre) ex Ger. *Verfremdungseffekt*, an effect desired by Bertolt Brecht (1898–1956) whereby his plays would place the audience at a discernible distance from the events related, in direct opposition to the cosy involvement and identification encouraged by 'bourgeois' theatre.

alignment *n* (D & D) a capsule description of a character's behaviour in terms of the basic designations of law, neutrality and chaos.

alimony drone (sociol) a divorced woman who deliberately refuses to remarry in order to continue receiving alimony.

all (TV) a scheduling term within commercial TV: this denotes the use of a programme by all the IBA companies without exception.

all commodity volume (market research) the accumulated turnover of everything sold in a shop, chain or multiple group.

Allen charge (law/US) an instruction or charge to a hung jury in which the judge suggests that they reconsider their views in deference to whatever majority already prevails and to do their best to reach a verdict. From Allen vs US (1897) in which this 'charge' was first used.

Allende principle (pols) from the late Chilean President Salvador G. Allende (1908–73) who developed the concept of international compensation for the poorer nations whereby less developed nations have the right to deduct all profits above 10% that are otherwise owed to the foreign owners of nationalised firms. The principle was first introduced by Allende in 1971.

on all fours (law) the existence of direct legal precedent for the case now under consideration.

Alliance for Progress (int'l relats) the financial links between the US and Latin/South America whereby the US attempts to buy off revolutionary fervour by bolstering right-wing governments, ie: El Salvador; on a more extreme level, the Alliance extends into active destabilisation of left-wing governments, ie Allende in Chile.

A

all-in (TV) a special breakfast sandwich provided by location caterers for TV crews: it comprises bacon, sausage, egg and tomato.

allonge (commerce) a piece of paper attached to a bill of exchange which provides space for extra endorsements once the space available on the original bill is used up. fr. Fr. *allonger*: to lengthen.

all-over paintings (art) works that avoid all kinds of central composition or grouping of forms into areas of special interest to create a figure/ground effect. Usually painted in a uniform manner, or with accents distributed evenly across the surface of the canvas, filling it right up to the framing edges.

allowance (horse-racing) deduction from the weight a horse has to carry.

all singing, all dancing version (business) super-glamorised, gimmicky, flashy version of any stock product. No guarantee other than the superficial saleability that there have been any real improvements on the basic model.

all standing (RN) 1. come to a sudden stop (of a ship); cut short an activity (of a person). 2. fully equipped. (thus) to *sleep all standing* to sleep with your clothes on.

alpha-beta approach (stock market) Wall Street j. for mathematical ways stocks differ from the movement of the market as a whole. A *beta* coefficient tries to work out in advance what will happen to any one stock or portfolio of stocks when considered against the overall market shift; the *alpha* measurement accounts for a stock's performance in ways that cannot be put down to the beta.

alpha stage (finance) the initial seed money required in venture capital financing. *beta stage* the second stage of venture financing, the financial commitment to an idea that still has no backlog of financial data on its performance. *gamma stage*: expansion financing stage, based on the examination of the records over a reasonable period of time.

also rans (theatre) from the runners up in a horse race: the support, the bit parts.

alternates (aircrew) other airports than the stated destination which are listed on the flight plan in case engine malfunction or inclement weather force the plane to land other than as intended.

amateurs (pols) citizens otherwise successful and powerful who help out in political campaigns much to the scorn of professional politicians. Not like envelope licking volunteers, amateurs use their own real power/status to enhance the professionals' electoral chances. Implies a quality of open, honest dealing as opposed to hard-bitten cynical 'pols'.

ambivalent *n* (sex) a bisexual person.

ambulance chaser (law/police) a lawyer who makes a business out of persuading accident victims to take legal actions over personal injuries. Metaphorically pursues the sirens right into the emergency room.

AMF (US medic) (abbrev) Adios Motherfucker!: note written on file of a patient considered to be malingering and taking the space of some more deserving case.

amp (drugs) (abbrev) ampoule (of methedrine). See *drug names*.

anamorphic art (art) paintings or drawings containing images that appear distorted or 'stretched' but which become normal when viewed in a mirror with a curved surface or from a particular vantage point.

anamorphic lens (movies) lens by which an image is 'squeezed', ie a wide picture onto a standard film. The projector is equipped with a reverse system which 'unsqueezes' the picture back onto a wide screen.

anarchism (Marxist) a revisionist political movement which with its complete condemnation of the organised State, is condemned utterly by orthodox USSR ideologues ... 'petty bourgeois, reactionary, social political current, hostile to the proletarian scientific socialism' (*Soviet Encyclopedia*, 1950).

anarcho-communism (pols) dedicated to the elimination of the state and the establishment of free collectivism. Society to be made up of 'associations of working people' and there would be distribution according to needs rather than as any form of 'reward' for work performed.

anarcho-co-operativism (pols) version of anarchism that would base all economic and social life on small co-operative ventures.

anarcho-individualism (pols) version of anarchism which advocates a return to free, natural and competitive economy, operated by small, independent owners.

anarcho-syndicalism (pols) version of anarchism which takes the trades unions as the source of all social and economic organisation, its management and pursuits.

anarchy of production (pols) in Marxist terms a description of unrestricted laissez-faire capitalism, cut throat competition and the in-built destructive instability that such a system supposedly must promote.

anchor light (RN) a white light visible all round the horizon that must be shown fore and aft by all vessels over 150' long when anchored at sea.

anchor man/woman (TV) newscaster who actually reads the news and co-ordinates the reports of specialists and remote reporters in and out of the studio. UK equivalent is *presenter*, but US usage is taking over. Two or more anchor persons/people are *co-anchors*.

anchor man (gambling) a player in black jack who sits to the dealer's extreme right and is thus the last player to play his hand.

anchor tenant (business/real estate) a 'celebrity' tenant (most probably a successful, well-known business) which will encourage other firms to rent leases in a shopping area.

and cakes (theatre) a supplementary allowance that may be part of the actor's main contract. It means that management either supplies or pays for board and lodging.

Andrew n (RN) the Royal Navy; originally the name for a man o'war or the government authorities in general. Both terms from one Lieut. Andrew Millar (or Miller), who allegedly forced so many recruits into the Navy that it has borne his first name ever since.

Andromeda strain (science) any strain of virus, bacteria or similar microorganism the release of which from a research laboratory into the outside world might lead to devastating effects because it was a basically unknown biological makeup. From Michael Crichton (1942–), *The Andromeda Strain* (1969).

anecdotal (educ, soc work) backed up by example.

anfo (milit) a type of home-made explosive used for terrorist bombs in Ulster.

angel n v (theatre) the backer of a show; the action of so investing.

angel (milit) 1. (RAF) measurement of height above ground in 1000′ distances. Thus 'Angels one-five' = 15,000′.
2. (radar) an otherwise unattributable electronic signal on the screen. Possibly caused by unusually strong humidity or atmospheric pressure that causes an 'echo' to be shown up on the screen.
3. (general) a helicopter who rescues seamen from possible drowning.

angel dust (drugs) see *drug names*.

animals (gambling) professional 'heavies' on the casino payroll to collect outstanding debts and make sure no-one falls out of line on the premises.

animatic (advertising) 1. moving, animated element within a television commercial.
2. rough commercial made from a storyboard (qv).

ankled vt, vi (movies) 1. to be fired from a job. 2. to resign, with implication of instant departure leaving everyone in the lurch.

Annie Oakley (theatre) a free pass to the theatre. Named for the markswoman Annie Oakley (Phoebe Ann Mozee Butler 1860–1926): the holes punched in the tickets supposedly resembled those aces out of which Ms Oakley had shot the pips.

annual (theatre) the regular Christmas pantomime production.

annuals (public relations) the annual report to the stockholders; these days this once basic profit and loss document has turned into a massive piece of self-justifying promotion and as such is unsurprisingly more often than not the task of a PR firm to put together for maximum effect.

anomalous water (science) aka *polywater, orthowater, superwater, water II*: type of water that behaves more like a non-crystalline material (ie glass) than a crystalline one (ie ice) at sub-zero temperatures. Opposing views see it as something totally unknown or alternatively merely water with ionic impurities.

anomaly switch (stock market) in reference to the gilt-edged (qv) market, an anomaly means that the prices of two stocks have moved out of their normal relationships. When this situation occurs an 'anomaly switch' is carried out: one stock is sold and the other bought with the intention of reversing the process once the price relationship returns to normal.

anomie (sociol) lit. 'without law' (Gk.) Resurrected by Fr. sociologist Emile Durkheim in *Suicide* (1897) to denote a society which had lost its sense of generally accepted social values and standards. Increasingly used for an individual who has lost his traditional moorings and is subject to psychic and social maladjustment and disorientation.

anonymous sculpture (art) coined by Bernhard and Hilla Becher in 1970 to describe certain types of industrial building (ie gasometers) which they feel exhibit sculptural qualities.

another place (pols/UK) formal reference by members of the House of Lords or House of Commons to the opposite chamber.

another pretty face (TV/US) derogatory putdown by network anchormen of their less famous peers who work on affiliate news shows.

answer print (movies) the first print of a film to contain both the pictures and the sound. Colour values, etc, are still to be added before the *release print* (the one which will be shown in the cinemas) can be manufactured.

ant (aerospace) (abbrev) antennae, aerial.

antagonistic conditions of distribution (pols) Marx's view of the inequalities of financial distribution in non-socialist and especially in capitalist countries.

anti-art (art) the fundamental concept of the Dada movement which totally repudiated bourgeois art and culture. But however shocking and destructive of traditional 'art' Dada might have been at its inception, the inevitable historical paradox has caught up with it and now 'anti-art' is as collectable and highly priced as any 'respectable' artefact.

anticipation (commerce) aka: *cash discount* (UK): a deduction taken off his bill by the customer if he pays up before the due date. The UK cash discount differs only in that here the bonus is *given* by the firm, as it were a favour rather than a right.

anticipatory reaction (milit) aka: *pre-emptive strike* (qv): a surprise attack.

anticipatory retaliation (milit) a surprise attack.

anti-dumping (commerce) measures to discou-

A

rage the importation of cheap goods that undercut the home country's products.

anti-economism (pols) according to Marx, the revolutionary belief that politics – not just economic improvement – will improve the lot of the workers.

anti-form (art) sculptures of the late 1960s that focus on materials, the force of gravity and the production process, and by so doing react against the geometric, predominantly rectangular form of previous abstract sculpture.

anti-object art (art) aka: *post-object art*: art that attempts to minimise the art itself in favour of the personality of the artist, his or her ideas, theories and beliefs.

anti-psychiatry (psychiatry) a movement in therapeutic practice, pioneered by R. D. Laing, which rejects traditional concepts of psychiatry – and especially such treatments as ECT, leucotomy, major tranquillisers and any authoritarian psychiatry – in favour of the properly self-directed resolution of personality disorders. Psychiatrists and mental hospitals were seen as socially repressive and 'madness' was quite possibly a healthy response to a sick world.

anti-social attitudes (pols) in doctrinaire left terminology, the condemnation of any beliefs that fail to accord with the socialist party line.

AON (business) (acro) All Or None: a lot of goods up for sale that must be bought complete and unopened or not at all.

AOR (rock music) (abbrev) Adult Orientated Rock, or Album Orientated Rock: like adult contemporary (qv), music aimed at the teenagers of the 1960s, now mortgaged and parents themselves. Lacks rock 'n' roll's gut appeal and retains only the banality of its lyrics.

APB (police/US) (acro) All Points Bulletin: an emergency call that alerts all available officers and vehicles to the identity and description of a wanted suspect.

ape *v* (theatre) to steal lines from another actor during the performance.

aperturismo (pols) in Spain, the opening out of the formerly fascist political system after the death of General Franco in 1975. From the Ital, which used aperturismo to refer to new trends in Catholic ecumenism.

APEX (airlines) (abbrev) Advance Purchase Excursion tickets. Cheap fare booking for advance reservations for holidays of a declared length, usually 22/45 days. *Backdated APEX*: cheap tickets on APEX scheme but sold illegally through *bucket shops* without regulation 21 day advance booking or minimum stay requirements.

apollo suit (aerospace) an integrated suit of four layers of garments which insulate and warm an astronaut for space travel, extra-vehicular activity, moon walks etc.

appearance money (sport) thinly disguised

bribes paid to star athletes as 'expenses' but in fact a way of ensuring that these 'amateurs' will turn up to the big races and attract the paying crowds with them. (cf: *boot money*)

apple (citizen's band) Citizen's Band enthusiast.

applebox (TV) a small podium hidden from the camera which raises the height either of short actors or of props.

apple jack (milit) lowest level of US military preparedness for war.

appliance computer (computer) a prepackaged microprocessor designed for over the counter sales just like any other home appliance. Take it home, plug it in and, given an adequate manual, the owner will be computing.

application (sex) the first 'interview' by a black pimp of a prospective prostitute in order to assess her 'qualifications'.

application program (computer) what the computer actually does, rather than the technology that determines how it does it.

appointment (crime) a meeting between members of the US Mafia; a business only conversation between a *capo* (qv) and one of his *buttonmen* (qv).

approach (sport) 1. (golf) the shot that puts a player's ball on the green.
2. (bridge) a style of bidding in which the suit rather than the no-trump is to be preferred in a biddable hand.

APV (business) (abbrev) Administrative Point of View: the management/corporate 'party line' which lays down the firm's orthodoxy.

Arakcheyevism (pols) from Arakcheyev (1769–1834), chief of police for Tsars Nicholas I and Alexander I. His regime of arbitrary, crude and militaristic policing left a name that characterises many of his successors. Now the name includes any Soviet boss who intimidates his critics with threats and violence.

arbitrage (finance) simultaneous trading in two markets in order to profit by the difference in prices.

arbitrary (printing) an extra character, supplementary to the normal fount of type, used for extra letters, accents, technical signs, etc.

arc (movie) a high powered lamp used for projectors and in studio lights; its illumination consists of an electrical discharge between two carbon rods.

arc light (milit) a bomb strike delivered by B-52 bombers; the flash and explosion of the massive payload gives the bright light that earned this name.

arc out (movies) an order to an actor to cross in front of the camera by walking in a slight arc: this will appear on screen as a straight line, whereas an actual straight line will seem like someone approaching and then retreating from the camera.

archaeopsychic relics (new therapy) in the terminology of TA (transactional analysis, qv) the child that remains in us all; as manifested in the adult, our excitements and fantasies.

arch it (sex) gay prostitutes who solicit from alleyways or archways.

architecture (computer) the internal design of a computer, the linkage of its components. A concept of the theory behind the design, not the actual silicon chips, *buses* (qv), etc.

architecture without architects (archit) aka *non-pedigreed, anonymous, vernacular, spontaneous, indigenous, rural, rude, exotic* architecture: shelters and structures (caves, earthworks, tents, tree houses, villages) used or built by people with no professional training in architecture: early man, ancient and primitive tribes, nomads, peasants.

arcology (archit) (*architecture* plus e*cology*) a completely integrated planned city or environment within a singular structure; i.e. Paolo Soleri's Arcosanti in the Arizona Desert. The concept of a vast, vertical megastructure housing several million inhabitants and solving 20th century urban problems.

arctic smoke (aerospace) surface fog found in arctic regions when very cold air is drifting across warmer water.

area defence (milit) measures to defend great centres of population by ensuring that fighting is carried out at great distances from them.

arg (computer) (abbrev) argument. The number that a function works on to produce its results.

Arica (new therapy) from a city in N. Chile where the system was first used in late 1960s by Oscar Ichazo. Intends to raise one's consciousness and 'transform your ability to experience living' through an electric set of mind/body training techniques.

A ring (milit) the circle of complete destruction that surrounds the detonation point of a major nuclear device.

arisings (milit) the various parts created from a large piece of war material that is broken down for scrap.

armourers (milit) the ground crew on land or carrier who arm the planes.

arms length price (stock market) the initial price stated as a basis for the detailed negotiations that follow.

arms stability (diplomacy) a temporary pause in the arms race when neither side feels that it requires new military programmes to ensure it is not being placed at a strategic disadvantage.

Army (pols) in Catholic areas of N. Ireland, the Irish Republic Army, usually its Provisional wing. (cf: *troops*)

around the world (sex) licking and sucking the client's entire body, probably including fellatio, possibly also the anus.

arrest *v* (medic) to suffer a heart attack – a cardiac arrest.

arrière-garde (sociol) the opposite of the chic avant-garde: those intellectuals who maintain the old values and standards in the face of no matter what advances by their more fashionable peers.

arrogance of power (pols) from a lecture by Senator J. William Fulbright in 1966, one of a series to criticise the US involvements abroad, particularly in Vietnam and the Dominican Republic. His theory was that the US needed such involvement only to make sure everyone remembered just how powerful a nation she was, and how necessary it was to foist the American way of life on the world, like it or not.

art (press) illustrations. (thus) *leg art*: pictures of pretty girls and in particular their legs.

art (advert) all the graphic parts of the advertisement, as opposed to the *copy* (qv).

l'art brut (art) Fr.: raw art. Coined by Jean Dubuffet in 1949 for any crude, unsophisticated work by a non-professional artist, especially children or primitives. Dubuffet admired this work for its innocent vision, directness of technique and use of unconventional materials and tried to emulate these qualities in his own work. In turn his work has come to be called l'art brut.

art deco (art) from Exposition Internationale des Arts Decoratifs et Industriels Modernes, held in Paris in 1925. Revived briefly in late 1960s, early 1970s, a style that offered ornateness, asymmetry, geometrical shapes and bold colours.

art house (movies) up-market cinema which shows 'intellectual' and 'cult' films, very often from Europe with or without subtitles. (cf: *action house*)

ARTHUR (aerospace) sl. for automatic flight control system.

articulation (educ) the process of helping a child move into a new school and, latterly, through the various groups that will be encountered on the progress through that school.

artificial intelligence (computers) see *AI*.

art of the possible (pols) from Otto von Bismarck (1815–98) who stated that politics was 'the doctrine of the possible, the attainable . . . the art of the next best'. Adlai Stevenson called President Lyndon Johnson 'a master of the art of the possible in politics' and LBJ claimed to accept the necessity of compromise, but only as a step on the road to complete success in one's wishes.

artology (art) the science and theory of art. Not aesthetics, since it is not concerned with questions of beauty in nature but with art itself. Artologists study art and are knowledgeable about it, but like many scholarly experts, they do not practise that which they preach.

art povera (art) aka *anti-form, conceptual art, earth art, matter art, minimal art.* Ital: 'impoverished art'. Art povera contains several 1960s trends all of which stress 'unworthiness' of the

A

materials used – ie, not canvas and oils of 'fine art' – such as twigs, newspaper, coal. Art povera is de facto temporary and often created far from galleries or even cities and thus seen only second hand through photographs or sketches.

artspeak (art) term devised to describe the tortured, convoluted and obscure jargon of the art critic.

art trouvé (art) lit. Fr. 'found art'. Art that is not created from scratch but taken by the artist as it is found and adapted as an art object by virtue of its intrinsic qualities.

as built drawings (archit) drawings that are made on completion of a building to show exactly what was built, rather than the initial plans which showed what was originally supposed to be built.

ascension, make an (theatre) to forget one's lines which 'fly up' out of one's head.

ascots (security) UK Customs code for all members of the Royal Family, other than H. M. the Queen and Prince Philip, when they pass through Heathrow Airport.

A shares, A stock (stock market) common, rather than preferential stock.

ashcan (theatre, TV) aka *can*: footlight unit in a compartment; an open reflector with two 1 kilowatt bulbs fitted with a frosted glass diffuser.

ashore (USMC) 1. not on the ship.
2. anywhere that is neither Marine Corps nor other US government property. *go ashore:* to go on leave.

asia dollar (econ) US currency based in Singapore, controlled by Monetary Authority of Singapore. (cf: *eurodollar*)

asiatic (USMC) slightly mad or eccentric after serving too lengthy a time on a far east posting.

A side (rock music) the more important side of a 45 rpm single. Supposedly that which carries the 'hit' song. *Double A side:* has two 'hit' songs, eg. 'Strawberry Fields Forever' c/w 'Penny Lane' (1967).

assemblage art (art) aka *combine painting, junk sculpture, object art, neo-Dada, emballages*: a concept that embraces all forms of composite art – three dimensional constructions – created from natural or manufactured objects and materials. There are no theoretical limits to what items may be used.

assembler (computer) a program that produces a machine language program that the machine can understand and work from.

assembly language, assembly code (computer) a programming language which is comprehensible to the machine.

asset (espionage) any resource – human, technological, environmental, etc – at the disposal of an intelligence agency for use either in operational or as a support role. Often means someone who works with the CIA on a secret mission but is not employed directly by the agency.

asset management (business) a style of management which ensures that all the assets of a group or institution – material and otherwise – are all manipulated towards furthering the aims and intentions of that group or institution.

asset-stripping (business) process whereby a financier buys up companies not to expand them but sell off their assets, often sacking all those who were previously employed there, and keeping the money thus gained for use in his original enterprises, possibly to buy another company for more stripping.

assist *n.* (sport) in American-style soccer a point awarded for passing the ball to the man who actually scores the goal.

assured destruction (milit) the ability to inflict unacceptable (qv) damage on the enemy, even after suffering his first strike (qv) (cf: *MAD*)

A staff (milit) those staff working for the Adjutant-general, the Army's chief legal officer.

as-told-to (press, publishing) euphemism for ghosted (qv); a celebrity 'confession' of greater or lesser quality and revelation purportedly written by the star with help from a professional writer or journalist.

astutau (crime) lit. Ital 'extinguished'. Snuffed out, murdered.

asymmetrical joking relationship (sociol) a joking relationship in which only one of the two partners has the right to practise joking towards the other.

AT (science) aka *soft technology* (abbrev) appropriate technology. Alternative forms of technology that rely not on coal, gas, nuclear power but solar energy, the waves, the wind etc.

at it (police/crime) involved in crime.

at liberty (theatre) out of work; mainly US use. (cf: *resting*)

atmos (TV, theatre) (abbrev) atmosphere. The background noises of a scene, barely recognisable but glaring in their absence if they are overlooked: cars passing, doors slamming, snatches of radio or TV sound.

atom (computers) aka *node*: the basic 'building block' of a data memory; one atom corresponds to one record in a paper file.

atomistic competition (business) aka *perfect competition, pure competition*: a market in which neither buyers nor sellers have any preference as to whom they do business so long as the prices are the same.

at rise (theatre) the position of those actors who are on stage when the curtain goes up for the start of a new act or scene.

attack options (milit) varieties of methods and targets available to a US President under the SIOP (qv); these include *MAO*s (major attack options), *SAO*s (selected attack options), *LNO*s (limited nuclear options, aimed specifically at fixed enemy military or industrial targets), *RNOs* (regional nuclear options, to destroy the milit. command of a given area). Also one special category for US pre-emptive strike; plus LOW/LUA (launch on warning/launch under attack: all out retaliation on the warning or the actuality of an attack).

attentioner (press, wire services) a note on the telex to call the editor's attention to dubious language – obscenity, profanity – in a story in case anyone feels it has to be cut before the story is run.

attention getter (aerospace) prominently displayed warning sign in the cockpit or on the flight deck of military or civil planes that flashes amber or red to indicate a malfunction.

attitude (marketing) a predisposition towards an object or a concept; ideally the predisposition towards buying, or the act of buying.

attitude management (public relations) the concept that the individual's 'free choice' can be manipulated, that there is no hard and fast 'reality' but simply, as in the most efficient propaganda, what people can be persuaded to believe is 'reality'.

attrit *v* (milit) current use is simply death, particularly in a nuclear war: attrits per second.

attrite *v* (milit/business) to wear down, or be worn down by friction; thus the gradual erosion of resources, human or otherwise, by action of various forces.

attrition *n* (business) the process whereby the average salaries paid in an organisation decline as new, younger staff are hired to replace older personnel and are paid less money to perform the same jobs.

attrition out *v* (indust relats) the reduction of the number of jobs/employees by failing to hire replacements for those who have retired or resigned.

at zero (milit) to have a hostile fighter on one's own tail.

audible *n* (US football) play called out by quarterback at line or scrimmage and thus audible to opposition, unlike plays told in the isolation of the huddle.

audience proof (theatre) a production that cannot fail to succeed, no matter how obtuse the audience, thanks to excellent acting, words, costumes, etc. (cf: *actor proof*)

audio (radio) a fuzzy, poor-quality interview fed through a telephone line to the studio tape recorder and thus less than ideal for broadcasting.

audit (aerospace) comprehensive, detailed overhaul and examination of a plane (especially after one of the type has been involved in a crash) to search out any structural faults.

audit trail (computer) inbuilt system that checks automatically on the functioning and working accuracy of the machine.

Audley it *v* (theatre/UK) to abridge a play or suddenly to cut it short irrespective of the stage of the plot. From the supposed habit of one Shuter, an 18th century travelling showman, who would stretch out each matinee performance until the queue for the next house seemed sufficiently long. At this point he would shout 'Is Audley here?' and audiences would find the play brought to a near instant conclusion.

auger in *v* (aerospace) to crash land one's airplane. From the idea of boring a hole in the ground.

august (circus) a type of clown who wears the battered bowler, tattered clothes, a back-to-front jacket. Allegedly from this costume's initiation in a German ring during the 19th century. The audience, seeing the new clown, are supposed to have shouted 'August!' (Ger. 'crazy'). (But the OED Supp A–G (1972) calls this story 'unsubstantiated').

Aunt Edna (theatre) slightly derogatory description of traditional theatre-goer of safely conservative tastes.

Aunt Emma (sport) in croquet, a typically unenterprising player, or play.

Auntie (sex) an ageing homosexual; if rich as well, then a *sugar daddy* (as used by heterosexual prostitutes).

Auntie (TV, radio) reasonably affectionate if slightly derogatory term used by commercial TV (IBA) of the state medium (BBC).

Aunt Tabby, Aunt Tomasina (feminism) a woman who refuses to accept every excess preached in the name of women's liberation.

austere cantonment (milit) military installation set up by a superpower in a client state, 'prepositioned' there for the purpose of waging a possible austere war (qv).

austere wars (milit) current (1983) concept of *winnable* nuclear engagements, fought between the client states of the superpowers and as such both geographically distant and considered, despite the use of nuclear weapons, fully controllable.

autarky (econ) a national policy of economic self-sufficiency in food, technology, etc. usually based on stringent import controls. This found its greatest popularity in the depression years of 1930s and given the current world economic situation may seem once more appealing to the more beleaguered nations.

auteur, auteurism (movies) lit. Fr. 'author'. Film term beloved of French critics in the *Cahiers du Cinema* which preached that the great directors who both wrote and directed their films were 'authors' who transformed any scripts they were given into vehicles for their own preoccupations and creative genius. An acceptable theory in moderation, it led too often to the canonisation of third rate and the arrogant dismissal of any other contemporary talents contributing to the films under discussion.

authenticator (movies) a studio researcher

A

responsible for establishing the accuracy of all script detail; the anonymity of any addresses or phone numbers used, etc etc.

authenticity (new therapy) honesty, sincerity, the dismissal of false values, as epitomised by 'bourgeois' traditional hypocrisies and social mores. Thus creating a personality and atmosphere conducive to such brandishment of the ego as 'letting it all hang out' (qv), 'going with the flow' (qv) and so on.

auto-destructive art (art) Coined by Gustav Metzger in 1961 to describe his own work: instead of canvas and pigment he took sheets of nylon, spraying them with acid and creating rapidly changing shapes until the sheet was completely burnt away. This made for a work that was simultaneously auto-creative and auto-destructive.

automatic art (art) aka *automatism*: paintings, drawings or writings produced while their creators are in a distracted state, ie day dreaming or subject to a light trance. An everyday eg: doodling. The supposed freedom of such artworks is claimed as a direct key to the artist's subconscious.

autopsy (aerospace) the detailed examination of a crashed airliner in the hope of discovering the cause of the disaster.

autoscopy (medic) the moment immediately before death when a person becomes detached from their own body and, if they survive, may well report an 'out-of-body experience'.

auxiliary chair (new therapy) the use in psychodrama (developed by Jacob Moreno from Freud's 'cathartic method') of a chair which can augment the variety of roles the subject is already taking on: thus it can be a soapbox for the subject to use to feel sentiments of power; or left empty for the subject to use as a 'ghost' with whom he/she can interact, exchange roles, etc.

auxiliary egos (new therapy) in a psychodrama (qv) the other group members alongside the subject whose drama is being enacted: both trained assistants of the therapist and 'amateurs', themselves future clients, all of whom help by playing out the required roles in the subject's drama.

available (theatre) temporarily out of work. (cf: *at leisure, at liberty, between engagements, resting*)

availability (pols) one who has the hallmarks of a successful candidate; derogatory use for one who is over-desperate to become a candidate. The ideal possessor of 'availability' would offend no interest group, either social or geographical, but would offer widest possible appeal to all potential voters.

avails (business) 1. the remaining balance of a legacy, an auction sale, etc after all debts, commissions, expenses and so on have been deducted.
2. The net proceeds of a loan after the discount has been deducted in advance.

avant-garde art (art) aka *vanguard art*: that art of the current moment in history that is more advanced in concept, more extreme in technique than all the art of present times. The features it requires are activism, antagonism, nihilism, agonism and futurism.

averager (milit) one of two opposing viewpoints on the hazards of post-nuclear radiation. The averager looks at the general population and works out the average effects on the basis of millions of people affected. (cf: *hot spotter*)

aviary (theatre) chorus girls' dressing room – for the 'birds'.

avoidable costs (business) costs incurred to pay for specific actions, rather than the basic costs that come with the day to day running of the company, irrespective of any special projects.

AWACS (milit) (acro) Airborne Warning and Control System. Aircraft-carried early warning radar system. By working high over the earth AWACS has the advantage of a range far greater than static, ground based radar.

away (sport) in golf, the first player to start a hole.

away (prison) serving a sentence in prison.

axe *n* (gambling) the extraction of a cut from a player's bet by whoever is running the card or dice game.

axe *v* (TV) to stop before completion; either before broadcasting or even editing a production or to cut off a series before every episode has been seen.

axe *n* (rock music) a performer's musical instrument; usually guitar. (cf: *lick, chops*)

Ayatony (press) in *Private Eye*, the nickname for Tony Benn, implying a similar wild-eyed fanaticism and potential for tyranny to Iran's former saviour Ayatollah Khomeini.

B

baby (TV, movies) small spot light, 750W. Used at a short distance from the subject or object, to light up a specific actor or area of the set.

babykicker (TV, movies) aka *inky dinky*, *pup* a small keylight (qv).

baby legs (TV, movies) a low tripod to support a film camera.

baby sitter (USN) a destroyer that accompanies an aircraft carrier.

baby-sitting (espionage) controlling operatives or any potential risks with other, 'secure' operatives. (cf: *mole*, another word used in the spy fiction of John Le Carré and popularised within the 'real' espionage world)

back anno (radio) (abbrev) back announcement: an extra snippet of information at the end of a tape. Read from the *cue* (qv) by the studio producer.

backchannel *n, v* (US govt) secret lines of communication within the government, unknown to the public and to other members of the same government; to make use of those secret lines for one's communications. From the long-time CIA clandestine cable network that runs in parallel to normal cable traffic from worldwide US embassies.

backcloth star (theatre) second rank performer who is out of the limelight but still manages to steal the show from the star by persisting in extraneous business that diverts audience attention.

back door (sport) in golf, the back or side of the hole into which the ball falls.

backdoor entry (milit) entering the army with an officer's commission by any means other than through the Royal Military Academy at Sandhurst.

back end *n* (movies) the money that is paid after a film has been made and exhibited, often referring to the percentage 'points' (qv) that are paid out of the gross profits to certain favoured individuals.

back end (commerce) in mail order selling, the ultimate response to an offer, especially after a continuity series (qv).

back end (science) that part of the fuel cycle of a nuclear reactor in which the used fuel is reprocessed to separate usable materials – uranium and plutonium – from radio-active waste.

background (computer) less important compu-ting tasks that can be performed in the milli-seconds that separate the foreground (qv) tasks.

backgrounder (press/govt) aka *thumbsucker* press conferences or one-on-one interview in which lengthy and possibly detailed information is handed out by senior government figures, up to and including presidents, but which can never be attributed to anyone but 'a senior White House source', etc.

backing (movies) a huge backdrop – of a city or landscape – made from enormously blown up photo. (cf: *cyclorama*)

backloading (milit) the rearward movement of supplies, troops, casualties, etc within a theatre of war.

back lot (movies) see *lot*.

back of the book 1. (print) general interest material, rather than current affairs, news, etc, which is given low priority treatment at back of a paper, magazine. 2. (TV) from (1) the division of network news shows into the hard news in the early part of the show, and the less immediate material towards the end.

back of the/an envelope (science) from the cliché portrait of genius/absent-minded professor scribbling great notions on a scrap of paper: simple and speedy calculations.

backout (aerospace) the reversed number sequence that runs down a missile or rocket launch countdown, ie: 10, 9, 8. . . .

back projection (movies) technique for saving expensive backgrounds or set-ups: actors perform in front of translucent screen onto which the required background, often in motion, is projected.

backscatter radar (milit) radar system that uses the energy reflected from ionised sources to pick up information from over the horizon, an area formerly barred to conventional radar.

backselling (commerce) indirect sales promotion which stimulates the usual manufacturer/ wholesaler/retailer sales chain in reverse. The campaign hits the retailers who will then agitate their wholesale suppliers. An equally common version is for the manufacturer or wholesaler to aim a campaign at the consumer who is then intended to start asking the retailer for more goods.

backshop (aerospace) the first part of a manufac-turing plant to be shut down as a production programme draws to its conclusion.

backstopping (espionage) the provision of suitable background for a 'cover' story in case of any inquiries as to whether an operative 'is' what he claims to be.

back tell (milit) transfer of information from senior to junior levels of command.

back to back (gambling) aka *wired* in stud poker to have two cards of the same denomination; such as one's hole card (the face-down card) and the first face-up card one receives.

back to back (TV, movies) the making of two or more films which use an overlap of budget, actors, crew, etc. Productions may be either concurrent or consecutive.

backwardation (commerce) a commodities market situation whereby future prices are progressively lower as the delivery time recedes further away.

backward integration (commerce) the taking over by the retailer of a major supplier or the manufacturers of his most important stock in order to ensure full and continuous supplies. Also when the manufacturer takes over his source of raw materials. (cf: *forward integration*)

backwash effect (commerce) the discrepant trade balance between developed and under-developed countries. The manufactured goods of developed nations are more attractive to under-developed customers than are their own offerings – low productivity mining and agricultural commodities – to the developed world.

bad actor (technology) any chemical, plant, etc found or considered to be harmful.

badge reader (computers) a machine specially equipped for reading credit cards and debiting the owner accordingly.

bad laugh (theatre) when the audience choose to laugh at the wrong – ie: not deliberately funny – lines in a play.

bafflegab (pols) confusing, obfuscating political jargon, based perhaps on President Truman's dictum 'If you can't convince them, confuse them'. Coined in 1952 by Milton Smith, then asst. general counsel to US Chamber of Commerce, who had toyed with burobabble and gabbalia before going with his own particular synonym for gobbledegook.

baffy (sport) in golf, the traditional name for the Number 4 wood.

bag (drugs) a measure of drugs which comes in a small glassine bag or, occasionally, in a rubber contraceptive (a *balloon*) Bags can be *dime bags* ($10) or *nickel bags* ($5). Given the fluctuating cost of drugs the payment remains the same, but the quantity of one's 'dime' may vary considerably. Its quality, in so small an amount, varies even more.

bag (new therapy) one's personal preference, state of mind, way of life, emotional standpoint, 'where you're at' (qv). Bag can be qualified variously as to the current feelings: 'a heavy bag', 'a weird bag', etc. It is nearly always preceded by 'in . . .' or 'into'.

bag *v* (medic) to apply an oxygen mask to a patient's face.

bagbiter (computers) aka: *loser, barfucious, cretinous*: 1. *n* equipment for a program which fails, usually intermittently. 2. *a* describing hard- or software that fails to work. May also be used adjectivally as an obscenity. (cf: *bletcherous, chomper, chomping*)

baggage (gambling) 1. an observer of a game who does not himself play (aka *kibitzer* (qv)). 2. anyone who does not earn sufficient to pay his own way.

baggage (box) boy (sex) homosexual prostitute who offers only active intercourse or fellatio to his clients.

bagged (gambling) a crook or cheat who has been caught in the act.

baggies (surf) loose-fitting 'boxer' shorts worn for surfing, often over a pair of tighter swimming trunks. Also known as *board bags* in Australia.

bagman (pols) 1. the intermediary in any form of political payoff or corruption – the man who actually carries the bag of money from A to B. Directly from criminal use, but always carrying the implication that one user of the bag is allegedly 'honest' – politician, policeman, etc. 2. the officer who accompanies the President and carries the *football* (qv) which lists the nuclear *go-codes* (qv).

bagpipe *v* (sex) *coitus in axilla*: sexual intercourse between the penis and the armpit, considered to be the province of the homosexual world.

bag the patient *v* (medic) to attach a clear container to the patient's penis in order to conserve his urine.

bait advertising (advert) the vendor touts some item that he is not actually interested in selling but which will attract the interest of the potential buyer sufficiently for the vendor to offer something that he *does* wish to sell. (cf: *bait and switch selling, switch selling*)

bait and switch selling (US), switch selling (UK) (advert, commerce) scheme whereby a customer is persuaded by the appeal of a low-priced item to enter store where he will be sold a higher-priced item. The 'bait' is heavily advertised, the 'switch' is carefully worked.

bake (into) *v* (indust relats) see *consolidate*

balance (TV) the concept of equal time for opposing opinions that dominates all UK current affairs broadcasting. Intended, laudably, to avoid any overt propagandising, it often means the dilution of an otherwise powerful statement or investigation when the balance is there only for form's sake.

balcony stalls (theatre/UK) seats in the front few rows of the dress circle.

bald-headed row (theatre) the first few rows of the orchestra stalls. These were traditionally occupied by ageing roués and sugar daddies who leered up at the chorus girls and leg shows.

bald-tyre bandits (police) inter-force nickname for traffic patrol units.

bale (drugs) a measure of marijuana: either one pound (aka one *weight* (qv)) or half a kilo.

balloon 1. (theatre) *v* to forget one's lines or business. (cf: *go up in the air*, *make an ascension*) 2. (drugs) a contraceptive filled with some form of drug, usually powdered. (cf: *bag*)

balloon *v* (airlines) aka *porpoise*: for a plane to bounce badly on landing when the pilot has failed to master either his controls or the state of the runway.

balloon (finance) the lump sum payable at the end of a loan.

ball park (commerce, pols) a large, rough assessment of numbers – based on the cursory glance a commentator might give around an arena before giving his estimate of those watching a particular sports match. Thus *ball park figure* is the number estimated to be 'in the ball park'. Used for people, budget figures, material, prices, etc etc.

baloney (pols/US) nonsense, rubbish; a reasonably strong alternative, in the eyes of its devotees, to actual obscenity.

Baltic *n* (commerce) The Baltic Mercantile and Shipping Exchange, found in the 18th century at the Baltic Coffee House, London. The Exchange specialises in the chartering of ships, and now takes on air freighting; its members are stockbrokers, shipbrokers and general merchants.

Baltimore chop (sport) named for the Baltimore baseball team of 1890, who brought its use to perfection: a batted ball that bounces too high for an infielder to catch it cleanly and thus make an out at 1st base.

BAMBI (milit) (acro) Ballistic Missile Boost Intercept: an orbiting armed satellite intended to target and destroy hostile ground installations.

bamboo curtain (pols) created by US publicists in the 1950s, this hypothetical barrier between the West and communist China parallels Winston Churchill's 'iron curtain' between the West and the Soviet bloc.

banana (milit) a line, curving slightly at each end, that appears on certain high-level radar screens and indicates the presence of ships or planes.

bananas (milit) nickname for the Kalashnikov AK-47, brandished in myriad revolutionary posters, and so named for the shape of its curving ammunition clip. In Mexico this shape has the gun called *goat's horns*.

banana shot (sport) a golfer's extreme slice which sends the ball on a fruit-like curve off the required straight line.

bananas on bananas (movies) a description of what is thought to be a complete excess of whatever is currently under discussion.

banco (finance) bank money on account as distinguished from actual currency.

band *v* (educ/UK) to group pupils according to their academic ability so as to spread the various levels equally around secondary schools.

banded (radio/UK) when an interview splits into several parts the engineer will splice in pieces of yellow leader tape – bands – to indicate the changes.

banding (indust relats) the rationalisation of pay by creating artificial groupings into which all workers can, at various levels, be fitted conveniently.

bandit (police/UK) general term for a villain, but on the whole a slightly ironic description of a lesser type of criminal. Often qualified as to occupation: *piss-hole bandit* – man who hangs around outside public lavatories, *gas-meter bandit* – a small-time thief who, figuratively, only manages to break into the gas meter, etc.

bandits (milit) hostile aircraft.

bandwidth (pavlov) the environment or milieu. Taken from electronics where it means the difference between highest and lowest frequencies of a communications channel. Used in phrases like 'change bandwidth' to give a spurious technological feel to the concept of altering one's current physical position.

bang *v* (stock market) to depress prices.

bang (print/US) exclamation mark. (cf: *interrabang*)

bang time (milit) the period between sighting an explosion and actually hearing it, caused by the discrepancy between the speed of light and of sound.

bang to rights (police) caught in the act; no doubt whatsoever.

bang up 1. (gambling) to close up a game or casino voluntarily. 2. (prison/UK) aka *dub up* to lock up a prisoner in his cell.

bang valley (milit) any overland training area which supersonic planes traverse and which therefore suffers bangs when they go through the sound barrier.

banjo *v* (milit/UK) to hit, (spec) to shell.

bankable (movies) the financial aspect of 'star quality'; an ability to guarantee large profits on a film in which he or she appears. Thus a performer whose name alone will help a producer gain the required financial backing for a new venture.

banker (gambling) 1. in football pools, a result which one forecasts consistently over a series of entries. In gambling banker has the implication of solidity, security, and, theoretically, cash gains. 2. the operator of a *banking game* (qv).

banking game (gambling) any betting scheme that gives the operator or a player some percentage or odds advantage over his opponents; ie: lotteries, casino games, sporting 'books', etc.

banner *n v* (press) large headline that runs across the full width of a page. (cf: *flag*)

baraka (milit) Fr. Foreign Legion: luck.

barber (sport) 1. a talkative baseball player; both from the cliché of the chatty barber, and the commentator 'Red' Barber. 2. pitcher who fires balls at batter's head and forces them away from the plate, named for the prime exponent of this art Sal 'The Barber' Maglie.

barbs (drugs) (abbrev) barbiturates: see *drug names*.

bare (business) in insurance, to be without a covering policy; thus *to go bare* is to carry no insurance against claims for malpractice, malfunctioning products, etc.

bare boat (commerce) form of naval charter in which the boat alone, without crew or gear, is chartered.

barefoot (radio) operating a Citizen's Band radio on a legal basis; so-called as reverse of the CB slang for an illegal transmitter: *boot* (qv).

bare navy (RN) any activity involving the bare minimum outlay; living on 'bare Navy' would be to eat only the basic service rations.

barf (computers) 1. *interj.* a term of disgust. 2. *v* to choke, as in to malfunction when machine is faced with a function it cannot handle and thus 'barfs'. Both uses stem from 1950s student use of barf as 'vomit'.

bargain (stock exchange) any deal put through on the Exchange.

bargaining chip (pols) derived from gambling chips, of which the more one has the better off one ought to be, bargaining chips gained verbal prominence during the SALT I (anti-nuclear proliferation) talks c1973. Took over from 'trade-off' as concept of concessions and compromises one might offer were the other side to lay their own chips on the (negotiating) table.

bargaining creep (indust relats) the gradual erosion of a company's bargaining position by the offering of piecemeal concession to individual shop stewards rather than putting across a wholesale wages deal based upon full company/union collective bargaining.

bar hustler (sex) prostitute, male or female, who solicits in bars.

barn (science) coined in 1942 as the measurement in nuclear physics of the cross section of a nucleus as 10^{-24} square centimetres. From the saying 'as big as a barn'.

barnburners (pols) individuals who will forward their own cause no matter what the cost. Allegedly based on the story of a man who burnt down his barn so as to destroy the rats inside it. Current uses tend to refer to anti-Establishment radicals.

barn burner wizards (commerce) a variety of 'whizkid' who is so dedicated to his goals that

he 'burns down the barn' around him with the heat generated by his efforts. An approving use of *barn burner* as opposed to the political use (qv).

barn doors (TV, movies) adjustable flaps fitted to lamps in order to channel or otherwise adjust the beam; *to barn door*: to adjust flaps on a light.

barney (TV, movies) aka *blimp* a padded, flexible cover that encloses the film camera and is intended to muffle the noise of its mechanism. *heater barney*: a heated cover that is used during outdoor shots in cold weather.

barnstorm 1. (theatre) a touring company of no great talent that played the undemanding rural areas, often in rented barns. 2. (pols) by extension of (1), a campaign tour that works the rural areas, stopping briefly and often. (cf: *whistlestop*)

barometer stock (stock exchange) a widely held stock of a major corporation, whose ups and downs may be construed as an average of the general market conditions.

baron (prison/UK) a powerful prisoner inside the prison, usually one who is well supplied with money and/or tobacco. (cf: *daddy*)

baroud (milit) French Foreign Legion: a fight.

barrack stanchion (RN) a sailor who has stayed on shore for a long time without a sea posting: thus 'holding up the barracks'.

barratry (commerce) the stirring up of unnecessary law suits and quarrels; from the naval term of the wilful misdemeanour of a ship's captain against the interest of his owner.

barrel (TV) a metal tube that suspends lights from a studio ceiling.

barricuda (TV) telescopic light support, made from lengths of alloy pole.

barring clause (movies) part of an exhibitor's contract with a renter preventing him from showing new films before any other specified cinema in the same area. Eg: exhibiting a film in London may preclude its appearing anywhere within a 50 m. radius until the renter so decides.

basal (educ) derived from the medical use 'basal metabolism' etc, teachers use basal as a jargon form of 'basic', as in 'basal reader' to describe primary level reading material, etc.

base (pols) Stalin, *Marxism in Linguistics* (1950): 'the base is the economic structure of society at the given stage of its development. The superstructure is the political, religious, artistic, philosophical views of society and the political, legal and other institutions corresponding to them'.

baseline aircraft (aerospace) the basic, no-frills design of a type of aircraft on which all developments and additions are based and which, in performance, can be used as the yardstick of comparison for later and other models.

baseload (business) the minimum amount of

goods, services, etc, required or produced to stay in business.

basher (milit/UK) covered makeshift sleeping bay, often a depression dug out of the ground, adjacent to a firing trench.

basher (TV, movies) small floodlight: 200–500W

bashing/on the bash (police, sex) soliciting as a prostitute. Fell out of use after Street Offences Act 1959, but currently returning, as are street prostitutes.

BASIC (computers) (acro) Beginners All-purpose Symbolic Instruction Code. Simple, though rather lengthy and inelegant (to programmers) computer language for learners. Usual starting language for microprocessors. *Tiny BASIC*: special form of BASIC designed specifically for micro-computers.

basic encyclopedia (milit) compilation for military use of all local military installations and points of similar importance to be known and considered in the case of an attack.

basic material (movies) the source material for a film: the original play, short story, newspaper article, novel or whatever. It rarely survives intact or even recognisable in the final shooting script.

basis (commerce) the difference in commodity trading between the spot (cash) price of a commodity and the future price of the same or a near related commodity. This difference may represent other time periods, quantities, locations and forms of the product.

basket (govt, econ) a group of inter-related issues, especially when these are to be discussed at a conference. *A basket of currencies*: a selection of currencies related to the central one under discussion, ie the pound, and against which the performance of that one can be assessed.

baskets are in (theatre) a full house; from the one-time practice of leaving the prop baskets as security against the income of a touring company. If the house didn't guarantee the payment of the theatre's rent, the props were theoretically forfeit.

bas-offs (milit) French Foreign Legion: the lower ranks.

bath (TV) the developing tank in which film is processed. (cf: *afternoon bath*)

bathtub (milit) 1. the heavier armour around the base of a fighter's cockpit to protect against ground fire. 2. in aircraft manufacturing, a temporary recession: the dip and then rise of sales figures resembles the outline of a bathtub on the sales graph.

bathtub theorem (econ) the total stock of goods (the bath) is equal to the production (the tap flow) less the consumption (the drain flow). Ie: the rate of accumulation equals the excess of inflow over outflow.

baton rounds (milit/UK) official nomenclature for plastic bullets.

batphone (police/UK) a policeman's personal walkie-talkie radio; from an ironic reference to the superheroic Batman.

batsman (RN) officer on flight deck of carrier who guides in landing aircraft by manipulating two hand-held 'bats'. Gradually disappearing as replaced by technological aids. (cf: *meatball*)

batter (sex) to work as a male prostitute.

batters (advert/print) damaged or broken letters in print work.

battleship model (aerospace) a development model made to size but constructed from cheap and speedily assembled material for use in statistical assessment and similar, often repeated trial runs.

baud (computers) a variable unit of data transmission speed, reckoned at one bit (qv) per second. Measuring the baud will define the capacity of a communications line.

baulk (aerospace) 1. *v* to obstruct the runway and thus impede an intended landing. 2. *n* to abort (qv) a landing.

Bayreuth hush (opera) aka *Glyndebourne silence* the moment of silence when the conductor raises his baton prior to commencing the performance.

B check (airlines) a rigorous overhaul and full-scale examination of every system on a civil airliner carried out at the end of each 400 flying hours. (cf: *A check*)

beach (sport) used in cricket to refer to the standard of play and of pitch one might expect to find on the seashore. *beach wicket*: very slow, dry and dusty, a spinner's paradise.

beach ball (aerospace) aka: *personal rescue enclosure*: a compact, sealed sphere designed to surround an astronaut in the event of an emergency transfer from an orbiting spacecraft into a rescue vehicle.

beach energy (science) from the post-World War III film *On the Beach*: a unit of fission energy named by UK mathematician F. J. Dyson. One Beach = 3×10^6 megatons. The planetary fallout from 1B would kill 50% of the Earth's population by fallout alone.

be afraid (new therapy) a command in primal therapy that calls on the patient to surrender to whatever fear and pain is being experienced, on the principle that one fear leads to a deeper one and thence, as intended, to the climactic *primal* (qv).

beanball (sport) in baseball, a fast pitch aimed directly at the batter's head ('bean').

bean rag (milit) in the US Navy a flag hoisted to denote that the ship's company is eating.

beanstalk (TV) hydraulically extending platform rising to 20′ high for use in erecting lights on location.

bear (milit) 1. NATO definition for all types of Soviet bomber. 2. general military description of Soviets 'the bear'.

bear (stock market) one who believes prices will

fall and operates according to this supposition by selling shares in the hope of repurchasing them when they reach lower levels.

bear-cat (sport) a style of wrestling ('all-in' US) with minimal rules or 'fouls'.

Beard, the (espionage) US intelligence nickname for Fidel Castro, President of Cuba.

bearding (TV, video) the overflow in one's picture of black tones into the adjacent white areas.

bearer (bonds) (stock market) securities that are transferable without the need for registration; ownership is transferred simply by handing them on.

beat (press) a piece of news discovered and published ahead of rivals; from concept of 'beating' the rest of the press, and replacing, almost completely, the use of 'scoop' for the same activity.

beatout (sport) a baseball play in which a batter makes a run to 1st base by outrunning the fielder's throw to stop him.

beauty (science) a property of a sub atomic particle known as a *bottom quark* (qv). (cf: *quark, charm, truth*)

beauty shot (advert) a close up shot (either still or on film) of the product to be advertised, inside its packaging. (cf: *pack shot*)

beaux arts (archit) a rigid, highly composed, often symmetrical style based on the criteria encouraged by the Ecole des Beaux Arts of Paris and as such generally conservative and pitted against any avant-gardism.

beckets (milit) Royal Navy sl. for pockets in trousers: from its use as a 'means of holding and securing', loops on ropes, handles for buckets, etc.

bed, go to, bed, put to (press) to finish writing and editing the newspaper and consign it to the printing presses.

bed and breakfast deal (stock exchange) a method for investors to establish tax losses against possible capital gains by selling shares and then repurchasing them in unconnected deals.

bedsheet ballot (pols/US) aka *blanket ballot*: a ballot with a lengthy sheet of candidates, the length of a bedsheet, and as such confusing to voters. From the US practice of using presidential elections not merely to vote for the president, but for a multiplicity of lesser, local officials as well.

beef (prisons) from rhyming slang *bully beef, corned beef* (eaten more generally in recent years): chief officer.

beef *v* (aerospace) the strengthening of a plan's structural parts; the modification of current designs and hardware.

beef chit (milit) menu in ship's wardroom; beef stands for all types of meat in RN.

beef it up *v* (archit) to darken up the lines on a drawing.

beg (crime) the method whereby the telephone con-man will plead with a victim to send him a subscription to the (quite legitimate) charity event that he has persuaded its sponsor to let him organise. In the event, while some of the subscriptions *will* go to charity, the vast majority will vanish, as will the con-man, long before anyone realises what has happened.

beggar's communism (pols) coined by N. S. Khrushchev who derided Mao Tse Tung's belief in the excellence per se of subsistence living which Mao was forced to tout in a pragmatic attempt to make palatable the facts of China's economy.

behavioural art (art) an art form based on the principles and techniques of cybernetics and the behavioural social sciences and assuming that the function of art is to alter behaviour. The projects involve members of the public and are aimed to increase participants' awareness of their physical and social environment.

behind (new therapy) in respect of, concerning, about. 'I got off behind. . . .'

Belgian block (milit) a tank testing course designed for the US Army and comprising cobblestones and rainfilled hollows.

beliefs (marketing) an individual's view of the existence of something; in particular the association of one advertised concept with another: that such and such a product possesses such and such a property and that on these grounds it is worthy of purchase.

bells (milit) in the RN bells are rung every 30 mins. while at sea to denote the time. The day is divided into 4 hr. watches each of which comprises one to eight bells, as the half hours pass. Thus 3 bells = 1½ hrs. of watch, 8 bells = the end, etc etc.

belly cut (medic) abdominal surgery.

below the gangway (pols/UK) for an MP to sit among the general members of the House of Commons rather than with 'the front bench' of either the government or the opposition – the ministers, ex ministers and 'shadow ministers'.

below the line (TV) special budget for 'extra-mural' expenditure – outside construction, a freelance director, etc. (cf: *above the line*)

below the line (advert) aka *sales promotion* publicity of all types except for direct advertising. Giveaways, store displays, special offers, etc.

bench (sport) in soccer and US football, the shelter where the manager, trainer and substitutes can watch the game; usu. adjacent to the touchline.

benched (sport) in US football, the retaining of a player on the bench (qv) rather than permitting him to play; this decision can keep a player out of the playing team for one game or anything up to a full season's games.

benchmark (computers) 1. *n* a standard which serves as a reference and testing point.
2. *v* to test a machine against a standardised

problem, or set of achievements which place it in the context of its peers.

bench scientist (science) a scientist who works in the laboratory, a research scientist; slightly derogatory when used by those scientists who have moved into govt. or milit. advisory posts which pay more and grab the headlines.

bench warmer (sport) athlete who fails to make the team – either through incompetence or failing to fit the coach's plans – and spends most of the season sitting on the bench.

bend (sport) understated euphemism for crashing a car in racing. Groomed, no doubt, for devil-may-care image of those who drive. (cf: *shunt*)

bender n (prison/UK) a suspended sentence.

benefit segmentation (marketing) a form of market segmentation which bases its divisions on the differences in the benefits sought from a product by its potential purchaser.

benevolent capitalism (pols) Marx's alternative description of paternalism: the status quo remained absolutely unaltered while the sensible capitalist, under the auspices of 'benevolence' papered over the cracks and threw sops to his workers in the form of charity and welfare.

benny (crime) an overcoat used to mask the goods one is engaged in shoplifting.

benny (drugs) (abbrev) benzedrine; see *drug names*.

benny squad (sport) the special team used in US football for the most savage, desperate plays with maximum and dangerous physical contact. The name is derived from the theory that such aggression may or may not be fuelled by large pre-match doses of benzedrine (a drug often prescribed for soldiers on the verge of entering a battle).

bent (police) crooked, corrupt, often with implication of a policeman who has 'gone wrong'.

bent spear (milit) US emergency code to denote an incident (less potentially dangerous than an *accident* (qv) involving a nuclear device. This ranks below all 'accidents' as well as any possibility of 'war risk detonation.'

be off (theatre) to miss one's entrance.

bertie, doing a (police) turning Queen's Evidence, 'grassing' on one's erstwhile partners in crime. Named, one assumes, for some earlier informer.

best boy (movies) film crew member who is assistant to gaffer (qv) or key grip (qv).

best case scenario, worst case scenario (milit, pols, etc.) planning theories designed to offer ideas of the most and the least favourable outcomes, events, possibilities, results and general unknown quantities.

best efforts *adj* (stock market) of an underwriter: not involving a firm commitment to take up any unsold shares or bonds of any issue being underwritten.

bets (gambling) the major horse-racing (and dog-racing) bets include: *yankee* six horses backed for first place in six different races; *nap*(oleon) the horse that a tipster – on TV or in press – offers his viewers or readers as a 'best bet', a 'certainty'; *trixie* or *treble* half a yankee, three horses backed in three races; *double* two horses backed in two races. (cf: *across the board*)

bevels (gambling) crooked dice on which one or more sides are slightly rounded instead of correctly flat, thus forcing the dice to roll off the rounded face more than it will off the flat.

BFT (new therapy) (abbrev) Bio Feedback Training see: *biofeedback*.

bible (milit) in RN, a large holystone, a piece of sandstone used to polish the deck. By extension, a smaller stone is a *prayerbook*.

bicycle n (aerospace) a form of landing gear in which the main wheels and their supports are set one behind the other (like bicycle wheels) along the centreline of the aircraft.

bicycling (media) taking one source – a programme, feature, etc – and using it for extra pieces which are attributed to various members of the original production team and are disseminated through fellow media outlets.

bicycling (TV/US) a method of passing round syndicated programmes: each affiliate in an established order will air (qv) a show one week, then send it on to the next station in line, meanwhile receiving its own new segment for that week's schedules. Circuit known as the *bicycle route*.

bicycling (movies) the involvement of an actor or director in two projects, either concurrently or consecutively.

bid n, v (stock market) an offer to purchase shares at a specified price, or to make such an offer.

Bids and Proposals (milit) R. W. Howe, *Weapons* (1980): 'the expenses incurred by defense contractors or would-be contractors in response to official requests for proposals concerning weaponry and weapons technology. . . .' Such expenses are used as a convenient cover-all to hide additional defense expenditure over and above the regular weapons spending sanctioned by Congress.

Big Board (stock market/US) the New York Stock Exchange (cf: *Wall Street*).

big bourgeoisie (pols) Marx's definition of the top strata of the bourgeoisie who own and run the multinationals and the conglomerates, and control raw materials and all the most vital means of production; super-capitalists.

big character poster (pols) lit. Chinese: *dazibao*. large government-authorised propaganda posters; for a short while following the demise of the Gang of Four (qv), the public were permitted, even encouraged, to write and exhibit such posters themselves. But this freedom was short-lived and ended in a spate of arrests to muzzle the over-enthusiastic.

big Dick (gambling) in dice craps, the point 10.

B

big eight (gambling) in dice craps a large space on a crap table layout which allows players to place bets there and thus signify they feel an 8 will be thrown before a 7.

big feeling, the (new therapy) in Theta rebirthing seminars, the sought after sensation of re-experiencing one's birth, enhanced, or at least aided, by immersion in a 99°F bath with a snorkel and noseclips, to approximate the sensation of being back in the womb.

big inch (tech) an oil or natural gas pipeline of minimum 20″ diameter.

big lie (pols) the premise, advanced *inter alia*, by Adolf Hitler in *Mein Kampf* (1925), that the greater and more audacious the lie, the more chance there is of the masses believing it. A popular philosophy of dictators and demagogues, and indeed, on a more subtle level, of supposedly 'democratic' governments, who tend to gild the process by explaining that 'what you don't know won't hurt you' when it comes to concealing affairs of state from those who elected them.

big nickel (gambling) racing and sporting gamblers' term for $500.

big noise (milit) US government level six state of war readiness.

big one (milit) US strategic intelligence sl. for a USSR missile test.

big order (gambling) a large bet, which may have to be shared around a number of bookies so that, in the case of a victory for the punter, none is absolutely wiped out.

bigot list (espionage) using 'bigot' strictly in the sense of 'narrow', lists of those who have access to particularly restricted and highly classified information. For more conventional, if inverted lists of 'bigots', one might recall Richard Nixon's 'enemies lists' of 1973.

big science (tech) scientific research that requires massive capital investments, but which should yield concomitantly 'big' results.

big six (gambling) in craps dice a bet in which the player reckons that a 6 will be thrown before a 7. (cf: *big eight*)

big tent (pols/US) the belief that a political party should shelter many various and argumentative viewpoints beneath its overall political umbrella, rather than adopt a narrowly ideological point of view that forces out all but the acceptably doctrinaire.

big triangle (commerce) a merchant navy expression to describe the trade routes taking in UK to Australia to South America and back to UK.

billback (stock market/US) a charge made to members of the exchange when a commodity on which they were advanced money sells for a sum less than which they were initially advanced.

billboard (radio) an hourly list of available news and feature tapes fed (qv) down the audio line to all subscribing Independent Local Radio stations (UK) to show what programmes are on offer.

billboard (radio) extra large antennae that consist of a series of long poles set up in front of a large vertical metal reflector, supposed to resemble a 'billboard'.

billboard *v* (TV/US) to announce the name of the anchorman and/or the various 'editors' prior to a news programme or the individual reports included in it.

billboard (TV/US advert) the announcements during a programme that explain 'The programme comes to you thanks to . . .'

billboard pass (theatre) free tickets issued to trades people who allow posters for a show to be put up in their shops.

bill from the hill (police) from 'old bill', cant for police: the police who work at Notting Hill Gate station.

billing (advert) the total amount of business done by an advertising agency in a given period, probably a working year.

billy board (sport) a surfboard less than 3′ long.

billyboy dolly (TV, movies) heavy duty dolly (qv) with pneumatic wheels for ease and silence of movement.

Billy Williams' Cabbage Patch (sport/UK) Twickenham Rugby Football Ground, named for William Williams (1860–1951) who established 'the head-quarters of rugby union' in 1907. In 1970 a local pub was renamed 'The Cabbage Patch'.

bin (aerospace) all space is divided for radar surveillance purposes into three-dimensional 'bins' which are based on a chunk of space sufficiently large for one plane to occupy it safely at any one time. No bin should contain, except for a brief movement in and out of a bin, more than one plane.

bin (TV, movies) a container that holds sequences of film during editing; *binstick*: a stick (probably metal) suspended over the bin holding a number of clips which suspend short sequences of film ready for editing.

bin *v* (milit) to discard a weapons system from the inventories after it has been tried in battle and proved to be inadequate.

binary weapon (milit) shell or bomb filled with two chemicals that remain harmless while separated but which mix on impact to provide a highly toxic chemical for use in biological warfare.

bindle (drugs) small quantity of drugs, usually narcotics, prepared for sale and wrapped in a specially folded square of paper or card.

Binet, the (sociol) the Binet-Simon personality test named for psychologists A. Binet (1857–1911) and T. Simon (1873–1961).

bingo (milit) US Dept. of Defense code:
1. aircraft to proceed to an agreed alternative base other than that from which it took off.
2. aircraft to return to base since fuel has fallen

below a critical level and mission must be cut short.

binnacle list (USMC) list of marines placed on light duty under the surgeon's orders.

bio-energetics (new therapy) a therapeutic system that draws on the theories of Wilhelm Reich to use physical exercises to 'loosen' the body which in turn should 'loosen' mental blocks.

bioenvironmental integrity (aerospace) the area around an embarking or newly returned astronaut which must be kept free from germs for the safety of both the astronaut and those meeting him.

biofeedback (new therapy) the use of electronic monitoring and measuring equipment, such as a portable electroencephalograph, to teach people to exert conscious control over otherwise un-noticed body functions: heart beat, blood pressure, stomach acidity, mental state, physical tension, etc.

biographic leverage (espionage) the use of personal indiscretions, whether voluntary or the result of a deliberate entrapment, to blackmail a subject for espionage purposes – either for recruitment as a spy, or simply to nullify the subject's usefulness to his own side.

biorhythms (new therapy) a method of analysing and predicting personal performance on the basis of three body/brain cycles: 23 day physical cycle, 28 day emotional cycle, 33 day intellectual cycle. By charting these cycles one can forecast highs, lows, peaks, valleys and plan one's life accordingly for maximum efficiency and benefit.

bird (TV) 1. *n* satellite for international TV transmissions.
2. *v* to transmit programmes via satellite. *bird feed*: programmes that come via satellite, often abbrev. to *bird*.

bird (milit) aka *fowl, skate* a sailor in the RN who is rarely out of disciplinary trouble.

bird (milit/US) the eagle that denotes senior military rank in US forces. (cf. *crow*)

bird (aerospace) jocular reference to rockets, missiles, aircraft.

bird dog (gambling) small time or novice gambler who hangs around experienced professional gamblers to pick up tips.

bird dog (commerce) in US real estate business, a salesman or broker who scouts the real estate listings to pick up extra business by cutting into a rival's sale.

birdie (sport) in golf, a score of one under par for a hole.

bird's nest (theatre) the crepe wool used to construct false beards.

birdwatcher (aerospace) from 'bird' meaning rocket: anyone who makes a habit of watching rockets launched.

birdwatchers (govt, business) derogatory reference by politicians or businessmen to the more dedicated ecologists and environmentalists whose worries as to the destruction of natural resources stand in the way of vote-catching or money-making schemes.

birthmarks of the old society (pols) according to Marx, in *Critique of the Gotha Programme* (1875), those surviving features of capitalism which might linger on for a while even after the Proletarian Revolution.

bishop *v* (horse-racing) to disguise the age of a horse by tinkering with its teeth. Allegedly from the name of an early practitioner of this fakery.

bit (computer) the basic unit of computing, an abbreviation of binary digit. All data can be expressed in binary form – combinations of Os and Is – which is clumsy in normal use, but extremely simple and fast for electronic processing, in which it becomes merely an on/off switching action.

bit (part) (theatre) a very small speaking role. aka *walk-on*.

bitch (sex) black pimp's description of his working woman/women. Given the relationship, this has all the predictable and negative connotations.

bit diddling (computers) trying to pack extra storage into a machine memory, but taking so much time to work this out that the time expended makes the small gain worthless.

bite (TV/US) aka *snatch* short piece of news film inside a voice wrap (qv).

bit fiddler, bit tweaker (computers) a computer programmer more fascinated by the machine itself than by what it can actually do on a practical and useful level. Just 'fiddles' with all the 'bits' (of information).

bit of mess (police, sex) a prostitute's male lover, neither a ponce nor a paying customer but a completely non-financial relationship. (cf: *tin soldier*).

blabbermouths (airlines) turret-mounted foam guns used for airport fire-fighting.

blab-off switch (TV) a device to enable a viewer to cut out the volume during the commercial breaks.

black *n* (theatre) the forestage, the apron; usually painted black. (cf: *the green*)

black *v* (indust relats) the boycott of a firm's goods in furtherance of an industrial dispute.

black (finance) in credit, from former habit of handwritten bank statements or accounts in which debts were written in red, and credit in black ink.

black advance (pols/US) the disruption of a political opponent's campaign by 'dirty tricks'. An inverted version of the advance (qv) that a candidate sends out to prepare a favourable reception for his campaigning appearances, in which legal and illegal methods are used to harass and confuse the candidate's supporters and alienate potential voters.

B

B

black agent (espionage) illegal operative.

black and whites (police) 1. (UK) official paperwork, warrants, receipts, notes, etc.
2. (US) police vehicles that are so painted.

black bag job (espionage) illegal entry by Federal or intelligence personnel in order to obtain otherwise inviolate information against a subject. Used generally as cover description of all illegal activities by supposedly law-abiding agencies of the state.

black beauty, black bomber, black widow (drugs) high-strength amphetamines available in black capsules.

black body (tech) a body whose surface absorbs all the electromagnetic radiation incident upon it.

black book (finance) a privately circulated prospectus used in investment banking to offer special information to favoured clients that would never be included in a normally circulated public prospectus, such as projections of profit and sales.

black box (business, govt, tech) based in technology where it applies to an instrument or component that can be dealt with as an entity; extended in government or business use as a separate area of knowledge within a larger system which can be dealt with as it is without having specialist understanding of its mechanism or internal structure.

black box (recorder) (airlines) the ostensibly indestructible flight data recorder which contains on wire a record of everything that happened during a journey. Invaluable aid to reconstruction of events immediately prior to a crash. From orig. RAF slang to denote any navigational aid.

black box syndrome (govt/US) 'we break systems down into sub-systems, and sub-systems into electronic entities, or black boxes. Then we assign to each of these black boxes an obscure name that has at least five words in its title. Finally . . . we refer to them with an unpronounceable acronym' (Gerald P. Dineen, US govt. official, *New York Times*, 1979).

black crush (TV) method of electronically reducing the black level in TV so as to produce a contrasty white for captions.

black economy (econ, pols) the parallel economy of those who perform their usual jobs but outside the normal hours and without admitting to such earnings for tax purposes. Such work also called *moonlighting*; *black money*: money not declared for tax, but tends to imply money earned by casino operators.

black flag *v* (sport) to signal a racing driver to leave the course by waving a black flag as he passes the pits.

black gangsters (pols) Chinese propaganda description of anti-Maoists who operate in fields of literature and culture.

black hole (science) a hypothetical hole in space which acts as an all-powerful ever 'hungry' vortex into which all matter is sucked. (cf. *white hole*)

black international (pols) communist party description of the Roman Catholic church.

black jack (aerospace) a special tool for manual forming of sheet metal: made of tiny lead shot in a tubular, usually leather container, it resembles the weapon of this name.

black light *v* (milit) the failure to ensure that the light in the signalling lantern is working properly prior to flashing a ship-to-ship message.

black matzo (rock music) the saying that 'if you can't sell them, you'd better eat them'. From the shape of an album which might just resemble a circular black matzo, the unleavened bread eaten at Passover.

black mist (pols) fr. Jap. kuro kiri – black fog; phrase used in Japan to describe scandals and corruption within government: 'black mist affairs'. Implication of the cover-up that tends to mask such events.

black operations (espionage) activities such as assassinations, blackmail, smear campaigns – none of which are admitted by an intelligence agency, but all of which are carried out regularly.

black out skit (theatre) a skit that climaxes with a black-out, the shutting off of the lights on stage.

black radio (milit) broadcasts by one side that are disguised as broadcasts by the other; putting out disinformation and psywar (qv) distortions. (cf: *white radio*)

black rock (TV/US) nickname for CBS-TV headquarters at 52nd Street and 6th Avenue, New York City.

blacks (TV) 1. any black drapes, black painted flats, etc.
2. the darkest areas of TV pictures. (cf: *black crush*)

black shoes (milit) in US Navy those members of an aircraft carrier who sail and service the carrier and planes but are not involved with flying.

blade (medic/US) a surgeon.

blag, blagger (police, prison) robbery with violence, one who carries out these robberies.

blah (movies) unsatisfactory sales at the box office.

blank *v* (police) to ignore, reject, turn down. (cf: *KB, knockback*)

blank (gambling) in some card games, unsupported by another card of the same suit.

blanketing (aerospace) the distortion or suppression of a desired radio signal by an unwanted one, whether through deliberate jamming or not.

blanking (TV) period during transmission of a TV picture when the scanning spot (which creates the picture) returns to the top of the screen. Spare lines thus created used for Tele-text etc.

blaster (sport) in golf, a sand wedge, which 'blasts' the ball out of sand-filled bunkers.

blat (pols) in Russia the basic currency of influence; the ability to induce the right person to produce the particular privilege, not always legal, that happens to be sought after, whether great or small.

blaxploitation (movies) aka *blackploitation*, *blacksploitation* series of films featuring black stereotypes, albeit as heroes, that dominated the production schedules for a while in early 1970s. *Shaft, Superfly* etc. In the event, for all the sex, money, and similar vestiges of white liberal guilt/fear, these films made little advance on the age of Stepin Fetchit.

blaze (gambling) in poker, a hand of five court cards, in no particular suit or sequence, but which beats two pairs.

bleachers (TV) from the use in sports for the seats (originally uncovered, and in the sun, where people watching would get 'bleached'): seats for the audience at a TV show. By exten-sion 'bleachers' means the people who sit there, the masses, 'Joe Public'.

bled (milit) French Foreign Legion: the desert, the open country.

bleed *v* (press, ads) to run visuals right to the edge of the page, ignoring any border or gutter (qv) *bleed space*: the extra charges made to advertisers for running advertisements that take up the additional white space that is covered by the bleed.

bleed the monkey (milit) RN practice of clandes-tine tapping of a cask of liquor, or swilling out an otherwise empty cask with water to get the much diluted dregs.

blender (theatre) a wig with a flesh coloured band at the front which is covered in the same makeup as in the forehead and should thus blend in as naturally as possible.

bletch (computers) interj. expression of distaste. adj. *bletcherous*: implies any negative, especially as to design or function. (cf: *barf*)

blimp (TV, movies) soundproof cover for a film camera (cf: *barney*) *self-blimped*: a camera which requires no special housing since its own covering minimises noise.

blind *n* (espionage) a complex security arrange-ment used by secret services for laundering (qv) money, to hide illicit payments or expenditure, etc.

blind *v* (gambling) in poker to bet without looking at the cards. In some schools this means that opponents have to double their bets as long as the blind player keeps risking his luck without looking at cards.

blind (theatre) to work an auditorium 'blind', either in theatre or night club, is to start one's act without having first checked out the exits, position of the bar and so on.

blind *a* (sex) homosexual use for uncircumcised.

blind bidding (movies) when an exhibitor is forced by a distributor to put in bids to rent a picture without even the opportunity to see a preview. Forbidden in some states, but a quick way of raising some extra funds while a film is actually still in production.

blind bombing (milit) the dropping of bombs on targets that are invisible to those who are dropping them.

blind envelope (advert) a mail order shot (qv) which uses plain envelopes with no opaque 'window' in them.

blinder (horse-racing) a doped horse.

blinders (theatre) bright lights next to the proscenium arch which are focussed on the audience in order to blind them during a quick scene change on a blacked out stage.

blind figure (commerce) when a book-keeper writes a figure so badly that it might be another one: 3 for 8 etc. A declining problem in the era of the micro-computer.

blind pool (commerce) a group of speculators who operate in secret, revealing to the market in which they are working only the name of their spokesman.

blindside *v* (sport) to tackle a player after approaching from out of his line of sight and thus leaving him no time to prepare himself for the physical shock. Such 'surprise' attacks are much more likely to cause serious injury.

blind trust (econ) a trust that manages an individ-ual's assets, usually so as to ensure that there is no professional conflict of interests between the individual's job as a public official with responsibilities to the voters, and his private business interests.

blip (TV) to censor out possibly offensive conver-sations, libellous references, obscenities from a TV programme.

blip (milit) the electronic signal on a radar screen that reveals the presence of a plane, ship, etc. *blip driver*: a radar operator.

blitz (milit) to concentrate maximum effort on: the original use of blitz, *blitzkrieg*, seems to have no further place in military vocabularies other than historical.

blitz *n v* (sport) in US football a concerted attack on the passer by the opposing linemen; to perform this tactic.

blob (aerospace) local atmospheric disturbances.

blob (sport) a score of zero. (cf: *duck*)

blobocracy (management) coined 1971 by Prof. Albert Shapero: the concept that management, especially in its middle levels, becomes bloated with an excess of techniques and structures for performing what ought to be less over-complex tasks.

block *n* (prison/UK) the segregation (solitary confinement) and punishment unit of a person.

block (drugs) measurement of a cube (qv) of

morphine. There are approx. 125 blocks per ounce of morphine.

block (press) an illustration, either halftone or line, which is engraved into metal for printing. *single column block*: usually a head and shoulders portrait, is a block the width of one column.

block booking (movies) the method whereby the distributors force the exhibitors to purchase a job lot of their product and thus take on a number of third-rate movies, which they must show willy nilly, in order to have the automatic profits from showing the one blockbuster.

blockbusting (pols) originally, a population shift in cities whereby the black population began moving into formerly white areas, gradually turning them into ghettos as the whites fled the inner cities. In last decade the process, after thirty years of one-way traffic, has started to reverse. Young, reasonably affluent white bourgeoisie are moving back to ghetto/working class areas. The first one to buy up a house, formerly under mass occupation and probably still in its original unconverted plan, is a *blockbuster*.

blockers (salesmen) people a salesman encounters in firms who set out to block access to a potential deal – receptionists, secretaries, etc.

blocks (computers) regularly sized pieces of information that can be transferred as they are from one component of the system to another. The transfer is checked by the IBG – the interblock gap – which ensures that the various blocks stay together as separate units while they are on the move.

bloke (milit) RN: the executive officer, the second in command.

blonde (TV, movies) 2KW quartz iodine lamp.

blood *v* (sport) the daubing of a novice, often a child, with the blood of a freshly killed fox as an initiation right to hunting.

blood chit (aerospace) 1. the indemnity form signed by any passenger in a civil or military aircraft who has paid no fare or holds no official rank. Thus he can make no claims in case of accident or death.
2. a military flier's plastic cloth or message written in several languages which offers money to a possible helper or rescuer in case he crashes outside friendly territory.

blood money (gambling) money that has been hard and painful to earn.

bloop *v* (TV) to cover a joint in the sound-track, usually by using thick 'blooping ink' or 'blooping tape'.

blooper (pols/US) a verbal faux pas by a politician that can be exploited to their advantage by the opposition.

blooper's syndrome (TV) the unsophisticated hard-selling of a product on TV commercials.

blow *n* (US/TV) aka: *button*: the joke or punchline

which is necessary to permit any character to leave a scene.

blow *n* (drugs) cocaine.

blow (sex) to lose a whore from your string of girls.

blowback (espionage) aka *fallout, domestic replay* disinformation and black propaganda spread by one's own agents abroad that sometimes makes its way back to information services at home and confuses those who do not appreciate the truth.

blowdown *n* (science) the sudden, explosive breaking open of a cooling pipe, especially in a nuclear reactor.

blowdown *v* (TV) to spray a studio set with dark paint to create 'shadow' effects or the illusion of decay.

blower (gambling) the Tannoy in bookmakers' shops that broadcasts commentaries on the races, the results, the changing odds, etc.

blow the meet (drugs) for the dealer, or possibly the customer to fail to arrive at an arranged meeting to sell/buy drugs.

blowtorch (milit) USAF use for jet fighter.

blue (TV) 1. the final script, amended and corrected for shooting: derives from the colour of the paper on which it is typed. Previous drafts typed on pink or green paper.
2. (movies) earliest rewrites of a script, later versions are on pink or yellow.

blue blazers (medic/US) hospital's administrative staff who do not have medical duties but deal with complaints, bureaucracy etc and wear blue blazers, brass buttons etc for a uniform.

blue bloater (medic) fat patient suffering from emphysema whose skin turns blue.

blue book (TV) a company's weekly internal production schedule.

blue book (govt/UK) official documents that come before Parliament which are bound together as books when their number reaches sufficient size for a volume to be made. Once reasonably candid explanations of policy, their frankness has diminished as the numbers of the electorate have increased.

blue button (stock market/UK) an unauthorised clerk, once identified by a circular blue badge worn in the buttonhole, now replaced by a blue badge that bears the name of his firm.

blue chip (stock market) stock considered to be of above-average reliability as an investment, bested only by gilt-edged issues (qv).

blue collar (indust relats) manual workers.

blue collar computer (computer/business) a computer that is used within the factory, rather than a *white-collar* computer which is used only to provide the data needed by management.

blue 'flu (indust relats/US) organised absence of policemen or firemen, ostensibly through illness, when wages negotiations are under way.

blue force (milit) in Western military exercises

and war games, blue force represents 'the goodies'. (cf: *orange force*)

blue heaven (drugs) see *drug names*.

bluenose (milit) in USN, a sailor who has crossed the Arctic circle; from the general slang for a native of Nova Scotia.

blue on blue contact (milit) one friendly patrol meets another from the same side.

blue pipe (medic/US) a vein.

blue room (airlines) the toilet on an airliner.

blues (milit) the blue dress or undress uniform worn by enlisted men in the USMC.

blue sky (stock market/US) fake bonds and stocks: one might as well have bought a piece of the wide blue yonder.

blue sky bargaining (indust relats/US) the start of wages negotiations by stating completely unrealistic demands from which compromises will eventually be found.

blue sky laws (stock market/US) local laws passed by the various states to control dealing in stocks and shares and try where possible to outlaw the selling of fake bonds. (cf: *blue sky*)

blue slip (pols/US) each individual senator's courtesy personal approval of a Presidential nomination. Blue slips are sent out to all senators by the Majority Leader. A failure to return the slip implies that the Senator is blackballing the nomination. Sufficient blackballs could result in the cancellation of a nomination. In that case a candidate has been *blue-slipped*.

blue suits (milit) the military personnel on an airbase, as opposed to the civilian contractor's employees who may be working on their firm's planes, the *white suits*.

blue water navy (milit) naval forces committed to operating in the blue water: the open sea. (cf: *brown water ships*)

blunting mission (milit) retaliatory action, presumably employing nuclear weapons, designed to destroy enemy materiel. (cf: *counterforce strike*)

blurb (press) the announcement, in a suitably titillating form, of upcoming features and stories in a newspaper.

blurb (TV/US) advertising spots on television.

blurb (publishing) brief, invariably laudatory comment about a book. In UK this is written in-house and contains facts on the book and its author; later editions may include such good reviews as there may have been. In US the blurb comes from 'celebrity' comments, canvassed prior to first publication.

blushing (aerospace) the surface of an aeroplane that has been badly doped or varnished.

B.M. (rock music) (abbrev) beautiful music: banal rearrangements of former hits. Like Muzak, to be found doubling as wallpaper in lifts, waiting rooms, coming through phones that have left the caller on 'hold', etc.

boa (econ) a proposed system of jointly floated currencies whose rates are allowed to fluctuate against each other but within limits that are wider than those which make up the snake (qv).

boarder baby (medic/sociol) a baby or young child who has to be kept in hospital indefinitely because the parents are either unable or not legally responsible to take adequate care of the child. Ie: a child born to a junkie mother and addicted to drugs itself.

board of honour (pols) a Soviet internal propaganda technique: a board featuring such workers as have exceeded the norms and similarly covered themselves with socialist glory. Supposedly a sufficient substitute for the less idealistic incentives preferred under capitalism.

boat race (gambling) a crooked horse race, the result of which only the suckers do not know long before the start.

boat truck (TV) a wheeled platform for the transport of sets, flats, stage furniture and so on.

bodice-rippers (publishing) the traditional 'woman's romance' set in a fantasised 18th or 19th century but with the added sales potential of a salting with sex and violence: the ripping of those once chaste bodices, before, as ever, Mr. Right triumphs once again. (cf: *hysterical historicals*; *sweet savagery*)

body (police) a person; especially one who can be charged with a crime.

body art (art) aka *body sculpture, body works, corporal art* a late 1960s vogue which combined aspects of sculpture, performance art and conceptualism, and above all elements of narcissism, masochism and sexuality.

body bag (milit) specially made zippered rubber containers in which battlefield corpses could be removed and stored prior to burial.

body count (milit) the totalling up, after a battle or a raid, of the numbers of enemy dead. Commanders tended to exaggerate their successes, since a good body count proved to their superiors that, as far as Vietnam went, the 'good guys' were winning.

body shop (business) a firm that specialises in providing 'bodies', people who will fill halls, stage demonstrations, etc. Such people were known in UK as *rentacrowd*.

bodywash *v n* (TV) in TV makeup, the covering of the entire body with a removable stain to create a darker appearance.

body work (new therapy) such modern physical therapies – jogging, the consumption of herbs – that are an adjunct to psychological ones.

boff (theatre, movies) 1. any form of entertainment that succeeds at the box office, also as *boffo*.
2. a big laugh, esp. in form *boffola*; all uses, like the sl. meaning of sexual intercourse, stem from the essential idea of a boff, a smack, thus the idea of action, of stirring things up.

bogey (sport) in golf, to score a par for the hole;

B

the number of strokes a good player ought to require to complete a hole, or a round.

bogeys (milit) USAF description of hostile aircraft. (cf: *bandits*)

bogus (computers) non-functional, false, incorrect, useless, silly.

boiler plate (business) standard legal covenants used by large institutions when drawing up the legal papers on their investments; also means any standard language used for contracts or specifications.

boilerplate (media) nationally syndicated wire service material – news stories, features, strips, pictures, etc – that are run unchanged in hundreds of local papers across US.

boiler room (stock market) high pressure selling of stocks done by salesmen each of whom sits in a cubicle surrounded by phones and attempts to talk potential investors into following his advice.

boiler-room (crime) on the model of the stock market boiler-room (qv), the action centre for the telephone con man who has a number of phones installed in his rented or hotel room and uses this to con as many victims as he can before removing their money and running.

bolter *v* (milit) an incoming airplane that misses the arrester cables that should slow it down and secure it to the flight deck of its carrier.

B.O.M. (press/US) (abbrev) Business Office Must: a note attached to a story which the business office of the paper wishes to be published without question and in a specific place.

bomb *n* (sport) 1. US football: a long pass.
2. basketball: a long shot into the basket.

bomb *v* (theatre) 1. (US) to flop completely.
2. (UK) to do very well. These contrasting meanings can wreak havoc with transatlantic congratulatory cables.

bomb *v* (computer) on the model of the (US) theatrical definition, a computer bombs when the programmer deliberately writes it a program that will disrupt its system.

bomfog (pols/US) (acro) coined by Gov. Nelson Rockefeller's stenographer Hy Sheffer who thus abbreviated his boss's oft-repeated phrase 'the brotherhood of man under the fatherhood of God'. Fortuituous combination of 'bombast' with 'fog', the essence of so many political speeches, has given the word general currency beyond its acronymic base.

bon-bon (theatre) a 2KW spotlight that is directed onto one performer's face.

bond (sex) (abbrev) bondage: any pornography that features men or women tied, chained or otherwise restrained for sexual purposes.

bond-washing (stock market) 1. the operation whereby the owner of shares sells them at a price which covers the accrued dividend and then repurchases them ex (qv) dividend.
2. the conversion of (taxable) dividend income into (tax-free) capital gains.

bonedome (aerospace) a padded, rigid, protective helmet worn by aircrew.

boneyard (aerospace) the dumping ground for obsolete, useless, cannibalised aircraft; also store for those new aircraft that the recession has left on their manufacturer's hands, unsold to an airline.

bongs (TV/UK) the sonorous, portentous chimes, purportedly from Big Ben, that herald the headlines on ITN's News at Ten.

bonk *n* (sport) cyclists' feeling of being devoid of energy. *bonk-bag*: small satchel to carry emergency rations to stave off bonk.

boojum (science) coined by Prof. N. David Mermin to describe a specific vanishing pattern of lines that can sometimes be seen in the flow of superfluid liquid helium.

book (stock market) the operation of a jobber (qv) in dealing in one specific stock is termed 'making a book'.

book *n* (advertising) 1. the portfolio of completed ads carried by a copywriter or art director when seeking a new job. (cf: *reel*)
2. a magazine (cf: *back of the book*)

book *n* (sex) the oral tradition of street wisdom handed down from one black pimp to another. Contains advice on setting oneself up as a pimp, handling the women, avoiding trouble, etc.

book *n* (sex) 1. a supply of tricks' (qv) names, addresses, etc held by a black pimp and often traded between them for high prices.
2. *working from a book*: conducting one's business from such a book, and thus avoiding the pitfalls of streetwalking. Thus working as a *call girl*.

book (theatre) 1. the script used for prompting; thus *on the book*: taking the prompter's job during rehearsals and performances.
2. the story and the dialogue of a musical comedy, as opposed to the lyrics.

bookends (TV) the first and last episodes of a TV drama series.

booking spots (TV) one-on-one interviews with celebrities who are in that day's news. The time for such interviews has to be 'booked' in advance.

boom *n* (TV, movies) extension from the camera unit which carries a microphone above the actors and theoretically out of shot to pick up remote dialogue. If the boom comes between the lights and the shot, a shadow, *boom shadow*, may be seen in the completed picture. *camera boom*: high moveable platform that can support the entire camera unit.

boom, lower the (milit) USN: severely punish or reprimand.

boom carpet (aerospace) aka *boom path* the strip of ground over which supersonic jets pass and which suffers the audible booms they make in flying.

boom corridor (aerospace) a restricted route along which supersonic aircraft must fly to minimise the effect of their boom path on the people living below.

boomerang (theatre) usually *boom*, the mounting for lights along the cyclorama (qv) and at the sides of the stage.

boomers (milit/US) nickname for strategic submarines, such as Poseidons and Trident Is.

boondockers (milit) heavyweight combat boots worn in USMC; for trekking through the boondocks (qv).

boondocks (milit) aka *boonies*: woods, jungle, marshes, dense and unhospitable undergrowth (fr. Tagalog: *bundak* = mountain).

boondoggle (pols/US) from a word meaning odds and ends or gadgets; orig. a project to create work for the otherwise unemployed but currently any project on which government funds are wasted through inefficiency or government corruption.

boost (crime/US) to shop lift. Thus *booster* is a shoplifter.

boot (audio) an illegal linear amplifier used by Citizen's Band radio enthusiasts.

boot (milit/US) recruit undergoing training for either USMC or USN. Thus *boot camp*: basic training camp for these two services.

boot (stock market) 1. the common stock that can be sold as a bonus with other corporate securities.
2. cash or another consideration paid to make up the imbalance between two commodities: i.e. a large machine that is paid for by a smaller one plus a boot of £100.

boothmen (movies) cinema projectionists who occupy their special booth.

bootie (milit/UK) a basic private soldier. Possibly akin to US *boot* but with no implication of training.

bootleg (rock music) from the Prohibition use for illegally distilled or imported liquor: illegally produced and distributed record or tape of a session or a concert. Invariably expensive, often of less than first quality, deplored by legitimate record business.

boot money (sport/UK) the payment of bribes, either in cash or in kind to the supposedly amateur players of Rugby Union. The money often comes from sports equipment manufacturers whose trade increases if rugby stars are persuaded to wear their boots, etc. for major, and thus televised matches. (cf: *appearance money*).

bootneck (milit/UK) aka *buffalo, bullock, turkey* RN slang for members of the Royal Marines.

boot one (sport) in baseball, to make an error or blunder.

boots (milit/UK) the junior ship of a squadron, a role based on the seniority, or lack of it, of its captain.

bootstrap (computer) a set of inbuilt instructions within the computer's machinery which tell the machine how to load a program. Once loaded, this program will then take over the task of instructing the machine.

bootstrap (science) the theory, in nuclear physics, that all nuclear particles are composed of each other, as opposed to the theory that all particles are built from a limited number of elementary particles. The theory suggests that physics can thus 'pull itself up by its bootstraps'.

bootstrap exploration (aerospace) a concept of space exploration whereby the results and gains of each mission are used as the basis for the store of information on which its successor can be launched.

bootstrapper (milit/US) a career military man who is released from his usual duties in order to obtain an academic degree.

borax (design) an Americans sl. term dating from 1920s (meaning gaudy, shoddy knicknacks) to denote the artificial, flashy decorations that characterise 1940s/1950s design: bogus streamlining, blubbery inflations or curves as seen in the period's cars, jukeboxes, etc.

borrow *n v* (sport) in golf, to compensate for any idiosyncrasies in the slope of the green by altering one's putting accordingly.

borscht belt (entertain) a show business circuit based on a number of Jewish (hence borscht, a Russian beetroot soup beloved of the patrons) family hotels in the Catskill mountains in upstate New York.

bosh lines (theatre) the violin strings used by puppeteers to control their characters.

bosie (sport) aka *the wrong 'un* Australian cricketers' description of the googly (qv): a ball bowled with an apparently leg break action but which actually breaks in the opposite direction, i.e. an off break. fr. UK bowler B. J. T. Bosanquet, its creator.

boss (crime) Ital: *capo* head of a Mafia family (qv).

bossism (pols/US) a pejorative description for (usually) big city party corruption in which one major figure, through graft, violence, patronage and other tactics, gains control of his party's machine and thus, irrespective of the actual candidates at a local level, will be able to deliver vast numbers of votes to the national candidate he favours.

boss player (sex) a star in the world of black pimping. Such a star might even be able to move out of pimping into a more lucrative and more 'respectable' racket.

Boston version (theatre/US) a show excised of any possibly offensive lines in order to satisfy the puritan censors of any local authority; Boston, the home of puritanism, is used to characterise all such authorities.

bottle (milit/UK) in the RN, a reprimand.

bottleneck inflation (econ) coined by the Japanese to describe the inflation that results

B

B

from a rise in prices without a parallel rise in the overall demand for goods.

bottom line (econ, commerce) the final figure on a balance sheet; the net profit or loss after all deductions, including tax. By extension (in and out of financial use) the ultimate standard for making a judgement, the facts without frills. 'What's the bottom line on. . .?'

bottom out *v* (stock market) for a slump or fall in the market to reach as low a point as possible and to start improving once more.

bottom power (pols) from the plump market women of Ghana: the power in Ghana of middle-class black marketeers who profit from their own corruption in the face of a declining legitimate economy.

bottom quark see *quark*.

bottom-up management (business) the viewing of corporate responsibility and relations as proceeding from bottom to top of the management ladder; usually viewed as coming from the reverse direction.

bottom woman (sex) the member of a pimp's stable of prostitutes who is considered the most reliable, efficient and profitable.

bounce *n* (business) the illegal altering of invoices, order forms, receipts, price tags, etc so as to disguise the theft of goods by employees or by accomplices, not actually employed by the firm, who do the stealing for them.

bounce *v* (medic) for a patient who has been successfully turfed (qv) onto another ward or hospital department to be sent back to the doctor who had first arranged to have him moved.

bounce *v* (movies) to fire, give the sack.

bounce-back (commerce) the offering of a new purchasing incentive – sometimes on the same goods, sometimes for a related product – with an initial offer made to a consumer in the form of a free gift or self-liquidator (qv).

bourgeois (pols) from the medieval description of a member of a free city (*bourg*) and thus neither peasant nor lord, bourgeois is essentially middle class. Marx praised them in the *Communist Manifesto* but currently bourgeois is revolutionary short-hand for reactionary, selfish, culturally, socially and politically conservative. For many radicals, the word also means their parents.

bourgeois reactionary line (pols) in China, the opponents of Chairman Mao.

bourgeois realism (art) the work of turn of the century academic painters, salon artists implacably opposed to all modern movements. Their paintings were a precise reflection and celebration of bourgeois society at the height of its prosperity.

bourgeois revolution (pols) 1. the bourgeois/democratic revolution is against the aristocracy but not in favour of the proletariat.

2. the ceaseless drive of capitalism to maximise its profits by research, reorganisation, advancing technology, etc.

bourgeois socialism (pols) weak, utopian socialism propounded by those who would probably not wish to see it made a fact; socialism with little bearing on 'real life' as lived by the masses. (cf: *academic socialism*)

boutique agency (advertising) a small agency, high on the creative (copywriting and art directing) fields but without the ancillary departments (market research, space buying, etc) that make up the services of the major agencies.

bouzbir (milit) French Foreign Legion: a brothel.

bovrilise *v* (advert) from ad. for Bovril 'the best of the meat': to omit all inessential matter from an advertisement.

bow *v* (entertain) from a performer's 'taking a bow': to launch a new show.

bowler-hat *v* (milit/UK) the British Army sl. for 'a golden handshake'; retirement from the service before one has reached the statutory age, with a compensatory financial bonus.

box (TV) the control room from which a show is produced, over-looking the studio. (cf: *gallery*)

box (aerospace) a tight diamond-shaped formation of four aeroplanes.

box *n* (sport) in cricket:
1. a protector, either of metal or plastic, for the batsman's genital area.
2. a close-fielding position to the off side of the batsman and slightly behind the stumps, aka *gully*.

box (sex) the crotch, mainly homosexual use, thus *box-lunch*: fellatio.

box cars (gambling) in dice: double 6, allegedly from the similarity to the wheels of freight cars.

boxed (medic) from box: coffin (undertakers' sl.): dead. Thus *box out*: to die.

box Harry (commerce) a commercial travellers' term for avoiding the expensive *table d'hote* lunch or dinner and making up with the cheaper food at teatime. From 'box a tree, to cut a tree to draw off the sap': extended to 'draining' the landlady of her cheap tea.

boxman (gambling) the casino employee who runs the craps table. In the Australian game of two-up, the *boxer* is in charge of the apparatus and the stake money.

box up *v* (gambling) in craps, to mix up a set of five or six dice so that a gambler may choose his preferred pair from the selection.

Boy *n* (theatre) the Principal Boy (invariably an actress) in the annual Pantomime season.

boy (milit) any nuclear device that explodes successfully.

boy (drugs) heroin.

boylesk (entertain) from burlesk (burlesque), US abbrev. for third-rate variety shows, dependent mainly on striptease: homosexually orientated burlesk, featuring male performers.

B picture (movies) low budget pictures, originally designed as the second feature in a double
bill and often of much the same content as
their 'literary' peers, the pulp magazines. Now
mainly defunct, and replaced in studio budgets
by 'made for TV' pictures which share similarly
low production values and banal plots.

bracket creep (econ) the tendency of inflation
to push individuals into higher tax brackets as
their inflation-fuelled income increases,
although in real terms they are no better off.

brady (theatre/US) a seat saved by the management for a personal friend. From the late
William A. Brady (1863–1950) a theatrical
manager.

brahmin (pols/US) from the highest Hindu caste:
an elite both social and intellectual who make
up a political aristocracy whose influence perv-
ades the highest levels without any member
suffering the hurly-burly of an actual election.
Often characterised as *Boston Brahmins* from
their power base in the blue-blood families of
Boston, Mass. (cf: *mandarin*)

brail breasted (theatre/UK) to move a suspended
piece of scenery and then fasten it with a special
rope (the *brail rope*).

brain candy (TV/US) escapist programming –
game shows, banal 'thriller' series, etc. Equivalent of 'light entertainment' in UK.

brain-damaged (computers) both the operator
and his machine are in a useless condition; the
operator should have known better than to start
work, the machine may well be beyond repair.

brains (police/UK) ironic reference to the detectives of the CID; the same department is
known to criminals as *the filth*.

brainstorming (business) intensive group
sessions aimed at thrashing out a problem with
the help of all those capable and interested in
dealing with it. Sessions initiated c1953 in US;
free association and 'thinking aloud' are encouraged as means of solving the problem.

brake-up (aerospace) when an airplane tips up
onto its nose on landing because the pilot has
applied the brakes too harshly and the tail is
forced to flip up.

branch *v* (indust relats) to bring a union member
before a branch union meeting to face disciplinary investigation and punishment.

brand awareness (commerce)
1. from the consumer or retailer's point of
view, the belief in the excellence or value of
the product.
2. from the manufacturer's point of view, faith
in the product he makes.

brand mapping (marketing) aka *perceptual
mapping:* a diagram or 'map' of the perceptions
that consumers claim to have of a product
gleaned from market research interviews.

brandstanding (advert) pun on grandstanding:
short term brand promotion.

brass (police/UK) a prostitute.

brass collar Democrat (pols/US) those voters
who slavishly follow the party line.

brass hat (milit)
1. top ranking officers; from the gold leaves
(scrambled egg, qv) on their hats.
2. *v* to promote an individual into the higher
ranks.
Often abbrev. to *the brass, top brass.*

brassie (sport) in golf, the traditional name for
the Number 2 wood.

brass up *v* (milit/UK) to shell; from the brass
shell casings that are ejected after firing the
projectile.

bread and butter (TV) long running
programmes, ie. soap operas (qv), that cost
relatively little to produce, require a modicum
of ability to perform or present, and bring in
high ratings and (in commercial TV) regular
advertising income.

breadboard (computer) an experimental arrangement of circuits set out on a flat surface. Thus
to breadboard, breadboarding.

break (sport) in golf, a sideways slope on the
putting green.

break *v* (press) to publish or reveal an item of
news; a *breaking story* is one that continues over
a number of issues/days with the continuing
addition of new developments to be *broken.*

break *v* (entertain, esp. rock music) to make an
individual, an act, esp. a record successful in
the required outlets of venues. A record or act
thus succeeding is a *breaker,* aka *prime mover*
(with reference to ascending the Top 40 record
charts).

break (gambling)
1. (horse-racing) the start of a race.
2. (cards, dice) to take one's opponents' money.

break *v* (theatre/US) to close the run of a play or
show.

break *n v* (stock exchange) the sudden fall in
the prices of shares on the market; for prices
suddenly to decline.

break *n* (press) in US press, the continuation of
a story on a following page. Thus *break page,*
the page where that story is continued, aka
jump, jump page.

break *n* (music) in jazz, a performer's improvised
addition to a scored piece of music, often
specified as *guitar break, horn break* etc.

break a leg! (theatre) traditional good luck wish;
it is considered bad luck actually to say 'Good
luck', or even to address an actor prior to his/
her first entrance of the night. Also *I hope it
keeps fine for you.*

breakaway (UK) *n, break up, collapse* (US) *n*
(theatre) a piece of scenery or a costume that
is deliberately designed to alter its shape or to
self-destruct on the stage.

breaker (audio) in Citizen's Band radio usage, a
formal request by one broadcaster to employ
the channel. By extension, those who use CB.

break-even (theatre/US) the total weekly cost of

B

B

a production; the ability of a touring company to pay the rent of the theatre and other overheads. (cf: *get-out*)

break figure (movies) a specified amount of weekly takings after which the exhibitor, subject to a pre-arranged contract, must start paying a higher percentage to the renter, based on the volume of business.

break luck *v* (sex) to turn the first trick (qv) of the day for a prostitute.

break-out *n* (aerospace) the first visual references a crew can make after a plane has been flying 'blind' through clouds.

break-out (milit) in RN: to leave the ship without permission; equivalent of Army's AWOL (absent without leave).

breakout (record business) for a record to become a hit. The size of this hit is modified geographically as a *national breakout* or a *regional breakout*.

break squelch *v* (milit) USMC: to break radio silence.

breakup *v* (TV) a makeup process that enhances the highlights and shadows of an otherwise bland face.

breeder (science) a nuclear reactor that creates more fissile material than is consumed in the chain reaction; this material is used as a source of power supplies.

breezing (horse-racing) a brisk pace, but one in which the horse is still under some restraint from its jockey.

Brezhnev doctrine (pols) from Leonid I. Brezhnev (1908–1982): as epitomised in the Soviet invasions of Czechoslovakia and Afghanistan, and the continuing pressure on *Solidarity* in Poland, the concept that if a country is turning against socialism, then this is a problem for *all* socialist countries to help deal with, not merely internal. Thus invasions by the supreme socialist nation are justified. Paralleled ironically by Henry Kissinger's backing of the CIA's destabilisation (qv) of Chile with the words 'We're not going to stand by and let a country go communist just because that's what its people want'.

brick (milit) in RN: any projectile, a rocket, shell, etc.

brick (gambling) a dice that has been specially cut so that it is no longer a true cube. Dice that have been shaved on one or more sides are *flats*.

brick (finance) a bundle of brand-new notes.

brick areas (marketing) sales areas broken up for research purposes into those which have similar sales potential by virtue of their population, amenities, etc.

brick by brick forecasting (marketing) the rough averaging out of views canvassed from a selection of salesmen and consumers.

bricks and mortar (theatre) a dull, heavy, leaden acting style.

bridge *n* (prison/UK) the gallery in many of the UK's Victorian prisons that joins two of the landings that run at various levels around the cells that make up each wing.

bridging (theatre) the insertion by a director of extra explanatory words into the script for use in rehearsals.

bridle (TV) a rope brace used to help distribute the weight of hanging drapes.

Bridlington (indust relats) from the Bridlington Conference, 1939: the principles established at this conference set up a TUC disputes committee for arbitrating inter-union disputes between such unions as were competing for the registration of the same workers.

brief (police)
1. a barrister (who has a criminal's brief).
2. any form of police identification, esp. the warrant card.

brief treatment (sociol) treatment planned deliberately within set limits, rather than long-term; treatment/inter-relationship between a social worker and client that lasts, either through design or through the exigencies of the situation, a matter of weeks rather than years.

brig (milit/US) a military gaol, either on a ship (USMC) or at a shore camp. thus *brig time*: the duration of sentence; *brig rat*: habitual offender.

brigadier (pols) in Soviet use, a working foreman or the leader of a Production Brigade. Usually a skilled senior worker with an excellent production record.

bring in (theatre) to switch on a particular stage light or lights at a particular cue.

brinkmanship (pols) from the declaration by John Foster Dulles (US Secy. of State) in 1956: 'if you are scared to go to the brink, you are lost. . . . We walked to the brink and we looked it in the face': a method of conducting international relations (esp. with Soviets) on a level only marginally short of declared war. The Cuban Missile Crisis of 1961 was probably the supreme instance of brinkmanship since the word was coined.

Brixton shuffle (police) shuffling gait peculiar to old criminals who have had to make their repetitive way around the confines of the exercise yard at Brixton Prison.

broad (TV, movies) small, box-shaped floodlight.

broadband (business) the system of combining several categories of employees under a single title in order to facilitate wider methods of selection and promotion.

broad-based (govt) taxes that are levied on all tax-payers, irrespective of whether one receives any indirect benefit from the levy or not.

broad-brush *adj* (govt) roughly outlined, lacking detail, incomplete; used for characterising policy or planning.

broad masses (pols) aka: *simple toilers*: communist definition of those workers who are not actually party members, but who take their orders and their standard of living from the conduct of the party.

broad-mob (police) from broads = cards: any form of cardsharps, esp. practitioners of three card monte (qv) (the three-card trick/find the lady).

broads (gambling) (police) orig. (c1780) playing cards; still occasionally so used, but by extension: all forms of 'plastic money', credit cards, cheque cards, cash machine cards, other valuable identification.

broadsheet (press) newspaper size equivalent to that of a full size rotary press plate, ie: *The Times, Guardian, D. Telegraph.* (cf: *tabloid*).

broadtape (stock market) financial news and figures carried on the general wire services; as opposed to the exchanges' own price transmission wires which use narrow 'ticker-tape'.

broken (computers)
1. not working properly (of a program).
2. behaving strangely, exhibiting odd symptoms or extreme depression (of people).

broken arrow (milit) US Dept. of Defense Nuclear Accident Code:
1. unauthorised/accidental detonation; no war risk.
2. non-nuclear detonation of nuclear device.
3. radioactive contamination.
4. seizure, theft or loss (incl. emergency jettisoning) of the weapon.
5. any public hazard, actual or implied.

broken-backed war (milit)
1. (nuclear) such fighting as might continue assuming that first, second and retaliatory strikes (qqv) had failed to settle the conflict and that any survivors still wanted to fight on.
2. (conventional) the continuing resistance by a guerilla force after their main army has been defeated.

Brompton cocktail (medic) a pain-relieving mixture of narcotics, usually based around heroin, and often supplied in an alcoholic drink (hence cocktail) administered to alleviate the pain of terminal cancer sufferers. From the Brompton Chest Hospital, London, where it was first created and used.

brown *n* (sport) in hunting, *to fire into the brown* implies an indiscriminate blast into the heart of a covey of passing birds.

brown bar (milit) USMC: second lieutenant, from the single bar that denotes his rank.

brown book (business) the annual report published by the Dept. of Energy for the government, listing details of the nation's petroleum, gas and oil industry, its current state, future requirements, etc.

browncoat (police) a junior examiner at London's Police Public Carriage Office – which administers London's cabs – who tests potential taxi drivers on their Knowledge (qv). (cf: *white coat*)

brown goods (commerce) TVs, hifi systems; dating from 1950s when such items invariably came clad in boxes of ubiquitous wooden veneer.

browning shot (milit) RN use taken from hunting use of *the brown* (qv): a shot fired with no specific target into the middle of a group of ships with the hope of hitting one of them.

brown job (milit) RAF sl. for a soldier, or the entire Army; from the khaki uniforms.

brown shoes (milit) USN use for navy fliers. (cf: *black shoes*)

brown water ships (milit) ships used for coastal or river work. (cf: *blue water navy*)

bruch (pols) originally Ger, adopted by Russia since 1920s: a production reject which has to be scrapped.

brushback (sport/US) in baseball, a pitch thrown deliberately straight at the batter's head in order to force him to retreat off home plate.

brushfire operations (milit) skirmishes, improvised conflict on a small scale.

brushfire wars (milit) small wars which, like brushfires, flare up and then die down again quickly. They do not involve the superpowers directly – although the armaments will almost certainly come from one or the other of them – but like brushfires, they can spread and grow.

brutalist (archit) a movement that emphasised the basic elements of architecture – space, materials and structure – in their most basic, unadorned or altered form. The main practitioners were Le Corbusier and Mies van der Rohe both of whom offered buildings with rough brickwork, open service ducts, exposed floor beams etc.

brute (TV, movie) large, focussing arc lamp. 15KW-22.5KW. *brute shutters*: a 'Venetian blind' type of diffuser fixed in front of the brute; *brute spud*: a vertical stand for the brute; *brute turtle*: a low 3-legged stand for the brute.

B share, B stock (stock market) a preferred stock, rather than the common, or A stock.

B side (rock music) aka *flip side*: the less featured side of a 45rpm single. Intended merely as a makeweight for the featured A side, some B sides do manage to make the music charts, sometimes even displacing the purported 'hit' A side.

BTA (advert) (abbrev) Best Time Available: an instruction attached to an advertisement space/ time order; no specific place or date is required as long as the newspaper, magazine, radio, TV places it somewhere. (cf: *ROM*).

bubble (TV)
1. any bulb for TV lighting.
2. overtime; thus *double bubble, triple bubble* etc.

bubblegum (rock music) extra-banal, easily memorable (and equally easily forgotten) pop music aimed at pre-teen market; supposedly the chewers of bubblegum.

B

bubble memory (computers) faster, more sophisticated memory system aimed to supplant floppy and hard discs (qqv) by using 'bubbles' of magnetic technology.

bubble pack (commerce) a bubble of rigid, transparent plastic attached to a product package and which holds and protects some form of free gift or sample.

Buchmanites (pols) from Frank Buchman (1878–1961), the founder of the Oxford Group Movement and Moral Re-Armament: 'Buchmanites advocate the repudiation of the class struggle and preach racism and other fascist theories ... through the notorious MRA organisation'. (*Tass* 1953).

buck *n* (movies) a rare understatement for Hollywood, from usual sl. for $1: $100,000.

buck *a* (milit) used in US military for *buck private* – the basic military rank – and *buck general* – a brigadier general. In both cases the implication is that the man in question is 'bucking' for promotion.

buck the tiger (gambling) playing against the faro bank.

bucket (medic) a bedpan.

bucket broad (sex) a prostitute who will allow anal intercourse.

bucket gaff (crime) aka *bucket job*: from bucket shop (qv): a con man's description of a fraudulent company.

bucket shop
1. (stock market) office where illegal, worthless or at best highly speculative stocks are sold by telephone by dealers who actually own no shares but speculate with victims on the possible rise/fall of actual shares.
2. (airlines) an unlicensed travel agent with no bonds to a trade association, who buys bulk lots of aircraft seats and sells them, cheap, to the public. They are not, de facto, criminal, but the public has no redress if they do blunder, and naturally, and with increasing success, the legitimate operators are campaigning to have them put outside the law.

buckwheats (crime/US) US Mafia description of a man who is being gradually stripped of his powers within the organisation; from sl. for foolishness.

buddy pack (aerospace) refuelling hose and drogue carried on certain planes to facilitate in-flight exchange of fuel between two planes of the same type, 'buddies'.

buff *n* (movies) specialist, enthusiast, whose knowledge and involvement in film exceeds that of the average fan.

buff *a* (movies) for specialists, enthusiasts only. 'The buff National Film Theatre. . . .'

buff *v* (medic/US) to check out and smarten up a patient; run all necessary tests, put charts in perfect order, prescribe drugs, insert intravenous drips, etc. Preparation both for impressing a consultant on his rounds and for a possible turf (qv) to another ward.

buffer (milit) RN use: the chief bo'sun's mate.

buffer (TV) a permissible over-run, usually no more than 60 secs, which is automatically built into the running time of longer programmes.

buffer (computer) the temporary storage area between parts of a computer which helps to cushion differences between the operating speed and efficiency of the various components and lets them all work optimally.

bug (indust relats/US) the official union label put on publications to guarantee legitimate union printing has been carried out.

bug (press/US) an asterisk.

bug (horse-racing) the five pound weight allowance for apprentice jockeys; derived from the * that appears next to their names in the racing sheets and morning papers, which is known to printers as the bug (qv).

bug (gambling) in poker, the joker.

bug *n* (tech) an external welder used for oil pipelines.

bug *n v* (espionage) a clandestine eavesdropping or wiretapping device; to eavesdrop or wiretap.

bug (gambling)
1. a steel gimmick placed inside the mechanism of a slot machine to make sure that some (highly lucrative) combinations never come up.
2. a clip that can be attached to the underside of a table to hold cards that have been secretly taken out of the pack.

bug (computers) an unwanted and unintended property of a program. From telephone engineers' use of bug: interference on the lines with no apparent source.

bug (aircrew) moveable white pointer that is set on the airspeed indicator to mark required speed limits.

buggers' grips (milit) RN sl. for the short tufts of hair over each temple, often found in the smooth, well-barbered tonsures of distinguished elderly men: coarse reference to 'handles' by which a bugger might hold his victim in place.

bugle bag (aircrew) the in-flight sick bags provided for relief of queasy passengers.

build-up (gambling) aka: *pitch*, *con act*: the performance put on by the proprietor of a gambling game to arouse the betting spirit of the punters (qv).

Bukharinites (pols) from N. I. Bukharin (1888–1938): the first Bukharinites were supporters of Bukharin's foolish decision to interpret Lenin's qualified permission of some private trade (in the NEP) as a full freedom of trade. For this Bukharin was executed in 1938 as having exposed the Revolution to 'the revival and development of capitalist elements'. Today's Bukharinites are generally 'right wing deviationists', including the late Josef Broz Tito, President of Yugoslavia.

bulge (stock exchange) a rise in prices or shares.

bulk *v* (commerce) the putting together for economy and efficiency two or more consignments of goods for different addresses in the same town and thus charged for freighting purposes as only one lot.

bulkhead (milit) in accordance with the USMC usage of naval terms even when on land: the walls.

bull (stock market) a speculator who expects a rise in prices, and thinking on these lines buys stocks in the hope of selling them again at a higher level. *Bull market*: a market in which prices are rising. (The opposite of bear (qv)).

bulldog (press/US) the first morning edition of an evening paper; the first night edition of a morning paper. (cf: *pups*)

bulldog (theatre) an iron grip used to fasten one cable securely to another.

bulldogging (sport) in rodeo, to leap off a horse and then wrestle with a steer, the intention being to twist it by the horns and force it over onto the ground.

bullet (gambling) the ace in cards.

bullet (rock music) a notation on the Top 40 charts that implies that the given record is climbing higher. Thus 'number 10 with a bullet'; *super-bullet*: a record has progressed at least 10 places that week.

bullet vote (pols/US) applicable mainly to those voters who have little grasp of or interest in mainstream politics: the intention of voting for one candidate, the one whom one knows and approves, with no interest in any other, either of one's own or of a rival party. The vote is registered direct and fast – like a bullet.

bullpen (sport) in baseball, the warm up enclosure for pitchers and batters just off the diamond (qv) and near the dugout (qv).

bullpen (advert) as an extension of the baseball use (qv): an area in an agency where the pasteups and mechanicals (qvv) are assembled ready for the printer.

bull ring camp (sex) a brothel for homosexual prostitutes only.

bull week (indust relats) a week of exceptionally low absenteeism at a factory and, therefore, high productivity. (cf: *Monday morning model*)

bumblepuppy (sport) in bridge, a game played at random, with neither rhyme, reason nor sensible planning.

bump (science) in chemistry, to give off vapour intermittently and with almost explosive violence.

bump *v* (airlines) to cancel passenger's flight due to mistaken over-booking. A passenger is bumped onto the soonest available flight.

bumping (business)
1. downgrading a previously senior employee by giving him the job of a junior who has resigned or been sacked.
2. Improving one's own job by using your seniority to grab the job of a junior and adding it to your own.

bunco (police) fraud, often card-sharping or a similar confidence trick. *Bunco-steerer*: a shill who persuades a victim to join in the con-game or illegal scheme.

bundleman (milit) RN use: a married man going ashore for the night.

bung *n v* (police) a payment, almost always from a criminal to a policeman, a bribe. *To bung X* is to bribe someone. (Interestingly Powis, see Bibliog., writing as a policeman, states 'a gratuity of an almost legitimate nature, not quite a bribe').

bunker *n* (pols) from the hard-core coalition of ultra-right wing supporters of General Francisco Franco of Spain (1892–1975): now those diehards who wish to see the return of fascism to Spain.

bunny dip (sex) a special method of serving food, drinks, etc employed by the 'bunny girls' of Hugh Hefner's Playboy Clubs, which necessitated passing everything backwards onto the table so as to ensure that the girls' exaggeratedly cantilevered costumes did not spill their breasts onto the customer's table.

burn (aerospace) a means of changing course in midflight by an exact firing, both as to time and duration of ignition, of the spacecraft's rockets.

burn *n* (sport/medic) in aerobics (qv) the pain barrier through which the cultist devotees must masochistically pass. *Go for the burn!* is the accompanying exhortation/slogan.

burn *v* (espionage)
1. to pressure the victim by his weak spots and use this pressure for gain; blackmail. (Used in fiction by John Le Carré, cf: *mole, babysitter*).
2. to expose deliberately the identity and allegiance of an agent using a cover story, thus *burned* – to be exposed, to have one's cover blown.

burn *v* (drugs) to sell poor quality, adulterated drugs. Thus *to be burnt* – to be a victim of such a sale.

burn *v* (press) to scoop, to conspicuously embarrass the professional opposition.

burn bag (espionage, govt) a special bag kept for holding such official documents that must, either routinely or in the case of invasion or similar crisis, be burnt.

burner (aircrew) a second rate airliner, so called from its capacity to 'burn' fuel usually restricted to short haul flights where consumption of fuel is less critical.

burn in *v* (computer)
1. a method of using heat testing to weed out dud electronic components.
2. programs that are 'burned in' to PROM (qv) chips.

burn notice (espionage) an official statement from one intelligence agency to its peers, either domestic or foreign, that a specific individual or organisation is unreliable for any of a number of reasons.

burn out (govt) an occupational ailment of frustrated or exhausted government employees; essentially a state of depleted mental faculties, it may well be accompanied by ulcers, high blood pressure, heart attacks, etc.

burn-up (tech) the total amount of heat released in a nuclear reactor per kilogram of the fuel; usually assessed in megawatt days per kilogram.

Burolandschaft (archit) Ger. lit. 'office landscape' sophisticated office planning schemes originated in Germany in 1950s/1960s. An open plan office was created, with the various departments and their furnishings disposed according to the flow of paper and the movement of individuals. All of this gave maximum flexibility for any necessary re-organisation.

burzhuanost (pols) a phenomenon much disliked in the Soviet Union. 'Bourgeois-mindedness', entailing the use of 'Mr.' rather than 'Comrade', etc.

bus (computer) aka: *highway*
1. a set of electrical connections between various parts of the computer's hardware.
2. a power line that conveys information to a number of devices. (cf: *trunk*)

bus (milit) the final stage of a nuclear MIRV (qv) missile, containing guidance systems and directional jets as well as the missiles themselves.

bus stop (aircrew) holiday charter route; from the type of passengers and the shortness of the flights.

business (theatre)
1. plenty of movements, gestures, both bodily and facial that make a role more 'dramatic'.
2. the day's or week's box office takings.

business art (art) art based on Andy Warhol's philosophy: 'Business Art is the step that comes after Art. Being good in business is the most fascinating kind of art . . . making money is art and working is art and good business is the best art.'

businessman's risk (stock market) an investment with a moderately high risk factor that is bought with an eye to its growth potential and capital gains or tax advantages rather than a simple, short-term profit.

bust *v* (press) a headline that is too long to fit the available space 'busts' out of the page.

bust *v* (drugs) although a general word for being arrested on any charge, it is not a mainstream criminal word (more likely 'to get a pull' etc) but used nearly invariably by those who are arrested for drug sales/possession.

bust caps (milit) USMC usage: to fire rapidly; by extension, to make a great fuss over something.

busted pilot (TV) a pilot show that never succeeded in graduating to launching an actual series.

buster (aerospace) a radio command: fly at maximum continous power.

busters (gambling) a pair of dice that are marked only with certain numbers that will thus only produce a limited number of combinations. aka *tops, Ts, mis-spots*.

bust off (radio) notation on the teleprinter printout when the operator has made sufficient errors to wish to start again. This shows that the story will be starting again because of the error.

bust-out man (gambling) a dice mechanic (qv) whose speciality is switching crooked dice, usually busters (qv) in and out of the game.

busy (TV) a scene or single shot that is too full of action or visual distractions to make it easy viewing or successful as action.

busy (police) the CID, aka: *the Busies*.

butch game (sex) from butch: lesbian; a technique where a lesbian prostitute will persuade a man to give her money but will not then permit him intercourse.

Butskellism (pols) from R. A. Butler (1902–1981) and Hugh Gaitskell (1906–1963): a political situation whereby purportedly opposition parties achieve some large area of common ground despite the necessities of mutual party antagonisms. Coined for the two politicians cited during 1950s.

butter-boy (police) a fresh young constable, 'butter wouldn't melt in his mouth'.

button (aerospace) the extreme downwind end of a usable runway.

buttoner (crime) in three card monte (qv), the assistant who 'steers' the punters (qv) into the game; anyone who persuades suckers to put up their money. (cf: *bunco*).

buttonhole (medic) a small, straight opening in either an organ or other part of the body.

button-man (crime) in US Mafia, a rank and file member of a family (qv). A 'private' in a criminal 'army'.

button mob (police) a large group of uniformed officers deployed in the street, at a demonstration, riot etc.

button on (milit) armament or equipment that can be fitted onto a vehicle subsequent to its being issued to the troops; i.e. a machine gun that fits onto a helicopter, etc.

button up *v* (milit) to seal off, with three-ton anti-blast doors, the NORAD (qv) Combat Operations Center at Cheyenne Mt., Colo. Though it was formerly a hardened (qv) site, today's more accurate missiles have rendered even this site vulnerable.

buy (gambling) to lay heavy odds on a favourite horse.

buyer (police) the receiver of stolen goods. aka *fence*.

buy in (stock market) to cover or close out (qv) a short (qv) position, a procedure used in order to obtain the delivery of securities which have not been forthcoming after a reasonable time.

buy in (milit) a contractor 'buys in' to a contract by deliberately making a bid he knows to be too low. Once this bid has been made, it is rarely difficult to persuade the Pentagon to reassess the costs onto a realistic, or even grossly profitable level. Thus possible for a firm to obtain a contract with a bid for $1.9 bn, when the final costs reassessed at $3.9 bn.

buy-off (business)
1. the act of purchasing all rights to a product or a service. Often because it rivals one's own equivalent and it is easier to buy it outright and remove a potential rival from the market than to chance the public preferring it over one's own product.
2. a person who has been paid in full: an actor or writer who prefers a flat fee at once to the opportunity of making more in royalties, but over a longer period.

buy off the page (theatre) to buy a script as such, simply on its own merits, before any angel (qv), star or director has shown any particular interest in it. Not, on Broadway or in the West End, a very common occurrence.

buy on close (stock market) to buy at the end of the trading session at a price within the closing range. Thus *to buy on opening* is exactly the opposite.

buy-out (business) the purchase of the entire stock of a product.

buy the rack (gambling) in horse-race betting to bet on every possible combination of horses that might make up the 'daily double' (qv). From the era when tickets for each of these combinations were printed up before the race and placed in racks by bookmakers for the bettor to choose. The bettor buying the rack could take one of each ticket. Only figurative in present days of machines.

buzz (computer) a program that runs into very tight loops, endlessly reduplicating itself with no apparent chance of escaping the repetition.

buzzard (sport) in golf, two strokes over par for a hole.

by (sport) Horse B *by* Horse Y, denotes the horse's sire. (cf: *out of*).

by-line (press) the name of a story's writer/reporter set above/or below the story in the newspaper. 'By . . .'

byte (computer) a group of 8 consecutive bits (qv) which are operated as a unit. (cf: *nybble*).

B

C (govt) (abbrev) CBE, Commander of the British Empire.

C (drugs) see *drug names*.

cab (airlines) the visual control room overlooking the runways at an airport.

cabbage (commerce) in fashion, the manufacturer's extra on the wholesaler's order. Cut from the same length of cloth as ordered with great and economic skill; then made up into extra garments by the cutters and sold to street markets for pin money. From c1660 to denote tailors' perks, bits of spare cloth, offcuts etc.

cabling up (TV) the linking up of a cameraman and his sound recordist for outside broadcast news reporting.

cabo (milit) French Foreign Legion: corporal.

cabotage (airlines) the reservation to any one country of controlling the air traffic whilst over its own territory.

cab-rank patrol (aerospace) close air support technique: instead of taking off and flying straight to a predestined target which should be destroyed and then abandoned, the planes loiter (qv) in the air, waiting for targets of opportunity which are sent to them by ground control.

cabtyre (theatre) thick rubber insulated stage cables.

ca'canny (indust relats) fr. Scottish dialect: moderation, caution; deliberate policy of the go-slow in furtherance of industrial disputes.

cache memory (computer) a method of speeding up the access to the (relatively slow) disc memory. The cache is a buffer (qv) which attempts to work out whatever material the program requires next and have it ready from the memory for instant use. Cache memory tends to achieve 70—90+% 'hit rate' accuracy in so doing.

cacklebladder (espionage) aka *catsup*: a means – usually chicken blood which, even after being exposed to the air still remains red and fresh and resembling human blood – of bloodying up the body of someone whom an opposition target has been forced to shoot. He may not have actually managed to kill his victim, but to have him believe he has is excellent blackmail material, especially backed by pictures of a gory corpse.

cackle the dice (gambling) to pretend to shake up the dice when actually they are held in a special grip that stops their free movement within the hand.

cadre (milit)
1. a small body of troops assembled for specific instructional purposes.
2. *cut down to cadre*: reduced to key personnel only.

cadre (pols)
1. 'A man who is able to understand the guiding principles (of communism) and carry them out honestly' (Stalin).
2. (Chinese) a full time functionary of the Party of government; anyone who exercises leadership in an everyday work or political situation. From Chinese *kan-pu* or *gan pu* (pinyin).

caesar (milit) code for underwater sonar anti-submarine warning system positioned at edge of US continental shelf.

caesar (medic) (abbrev) the delivery of a baby by Caesarean section.

cafeteria system (indust relats) aka *compensation cafeteria*: the opportunity for executives (and, very rarely employees) to choose how they are paid. They can select from a 'menu' of methods: salary plus fringe benefits, deferred payments, insurances, etc etc, in their own preferred way.

cake and wine (milit) in USN: bread and water punishment

cake mix solution (govt) a pre-created, ready made solution to a problem, available to all those who are interested in an effort by government agencies to standardise their programme activities.

calk off (milit) in USMC, to take a nap, laze about while supposedly performing a task.

call (theatre)
1. advice to an actor that an entrance is coming up.
2. any notice for the company to assemble. Thus treasury call (qv), *train call*: catching the train for travel to the next town in a tour.
3. *curtain call*: taking a bow at the end of a performance.

call (stock market)
1. the right to demand payment of additional money due on 'partly paid' securities.
2. the option to buy a security or designated commodity at a specific future date for a given price.

call a cab (horse racing) the jockey's action in

waving one arm to hold his balance when he and the horse are taking a fence.

call a taping (TV) the creation of a programme onto a master tape by a director who is monitoring and editing live material, video tape, slides, credits, telecine, etc, etc.

callback (manufacturing) the recall or total withdrawal of a new model (usually of a car) after the manufacturer has discovered, or angry purchasers have pointed out, that it possesses some potentially dangerous fault.

call-bird (commerce) a lure used by a salesman to promote sales; in shops it is an extraordinary bargain set in the window to drag the buyers inside to where prices are more realistic.

calligrams (art) visual puns: words drawn or printed in such a way as to form a picture or an image in an attempt to create a verbal/visual effect.

calligraphic painting (art)
1. those painters who acknowledged the direct influence of Oriental artists in their own style.
2. those Western painters who arrived independently at an approach comparable in many ways to that of Eastern calligraphers.

call over (gambling) in betting, the reading through of the current list of odds available.

call over (stock market) the procedure of fixing opening and closing prices in those stock exchanges where auction markets are operated.

call rate, call norm (commerce) the 'call rate' denotes the numbers of times a salesman manages to visit his customers; the call 'norm' is the optimum number of visits, which due to various adverse circumstances, he will probably not be able to make.

cambodian red (drugs) type of marijuana.

Camelot (pols) an idealisation of the administration of President John F. Kennedy (1961–63), now used only with irony as the only golden boy President stands revealed increasingly as one more self-seeking corrupt mortal. Refers to the supposedly halcyon years of the mythical court of King Arthur and his Round Table.

cameo (movies) an important but by no means starring role played by a major performer. The cameo is probably short, possibly only a single appearance, but the performer will be well paid and the company can put another big name on the poster.

campaign *v* (sport) to prepare a racehorse for a race.

campaign basis (aerospace/business) the solution of an aerospace problem on a campaign basis implies an all-systems-go, ultra-intense community effort to deal with the hitch; when extended to a business context, the meaning is one of plunging ahead on a project without actually waiting to see how it fits into the overall scheme of things.

can (sport) in golf:
1. the hole.

2. to hole the ball.

can (drugs) a measure of approx. 8oz. marijuana. (cf: *lid*).

can *v* (science) to cover the fuel element in a nuclear reactor with a protective jacket.

can, in the (movies) the completed sequence, scene or entire film is *in the can*.

candle (business) to check for quality; from the method of candling eggs to check for freshness.

candle *v* (medic) a method of treating arthritis by bathing the hands in a paraffin wax bath.

candy store problem (business) a situation which offers a multiple choice of options similar to a child choosing how best to spend limited pocket money in a lavishly stocked sweet shop, where no one sweet/solution suggests itself as particularly better than the rest.

candy-striper (medic/US) teenage girls who offer volunteer work in hospitals where, dressed in red and white striped jumpers, they help deliver papers and flowers, escort new admissions to their ward, help visitors with directions, etc, etc.

cannon (police/US) a pickpocket or a thief – both skilled in their trade.

cannon (espionage) the use by intelligence agencies of professional thieves (cannons, qv) for special jobs: i.e. the retrieving by theft of an object used to obtain information from a target – e.g. a bribe – or to obtain some compromising material. Cannons are often used when agency funds are low or there is a 'moral' crackdown on in-house criminality.

canoe (gambling) in roulette one of the thirty-six winning slots into which a ball may fall to denote which number pays off.

can opener (crime) any tool required for opening a safe.

cans (audio) headphones; so called in movie, TV, video, radio, CB, advertising, recording business use.

cap (drugs) (abbrev) capsule. To *cap up*: to divide any powdered drugs – opiates, tranquillisers, amphetamines, etc – into capsules prior to selling them. The dealer may well cut (qv) his wares before capping them.

capability (milit) the possession of a range of weaponry by a nation or military force.

capain (milit) French Foreign Legion: mate, pal, buddy; derived from general; Fr. sl. copain.

capcom (aerospace) (abbrev) capsule communicator: the audio link between the ground and the men in space.

caper (movies) genre of film involving mix of comedy/thriller; often sympathetic to criminals – bankrobbers, conmen – but no blood is ever shed and no-one, other possibly than the self-righteous or kill-joy, is seen to suffer. And if, by chance, the script has the heroes heading for jail, it can be assumed their wacky adventures will not long be arrested.

capitalisation (stock market) 1. the amount and structure of the capital of a company; 2. the market value of a company's share capital, ascertained by multiplying the current quoted market price of its shares by the number of shares that have been issued.

capitalism in one country (econ) the concept, voiced in 1975 by an American writer, T. McCarthy, that there was a possibility of the entire world, except for the US, turning socialist. This refers to Stalin's concept of 'socialism in one country' whereby Russia was to perfect its own socialism before moving onto international revolution. McCarthy suggests the US should perfect *its* own system and let the rest of the world fend for itself.

capitalist roader (pols) fr. Chinese 'Ziben zhuyi daolu' – a term from the Chinese Cultural Revolution (qv) attacking those who persisted in Soviet-style policy and practice: a governmental elite, 'private', elements in industry, bonuses for production, etc.

capitulationism (pols) in China, the act of capitulation, i.e. weakness and a falling away from the party line, be it negating the principles of the Revolution, currying favour with the West, etc.

capo (crime/US) Ital: chief. Head of a Mafia 'family' (qv) in US. *capo-regime*: second in command, lieutenant to the capo, responsible for the discipline and maintenance of 40–60 buttonmen (qv) or soldiers.

Captain Armstrong (sport) in horse-racing, a cheating jockey who pulls his horse back with his 'strong arm', to stop him drawing ahead.

Captain Queegs *n* (medic) aka *pill rolling* from the mad naval captain in *The Caine Mutiny* (film, 1954): nervous symptoms that feature twitching, twisting hands, playing constantly with imaginary steel ball-bearings.

captain's cloak (milit) the metaphorical 'cloak' with which an RN captain may wrap himself in disciplinary matters; the immensely far-reaching powers a captain has aboard ship, dating almost unchanged from the Naval Discipline Act 1966.

captain's mast (milit) in the USN, a daily muster at which the captain deals with defaulters, hands out commendations, answers requests and generally takes care of ship's business.

captive candidate (pols/US) a candidate who is supposedly under the domination of others; a phrase usually brought out when the opposition man is too popular for a frontal attack to have any effect, instead one challenges his immediate entourage.

captors (milit) encapsulated torpedoes secured to the ocean floor which can be activated to zero in on a target once their sensors pick up the signature (qv) of a hostile submarine.

capture *v* (computer) to retrieve information from the storage unit of a computer.

caramel (science) lightweight reactor fuel, developed by French nuclear scientists, using only 8% enriched plutonium, well below the 20% required for weapons use, and thus ideal to be given to countries who really do wish to use plutonium for peaceful purposes, not military development.

carbolic soap operas (TV) soap operas (qv) based in hospitals.

card (pols) a specific gambit or tactic used in bargaining; the 'human rights card', the 'inner cities card' etc. (cf: *bargaining chip*).

card *v* (sport) in golf, to register one's score on the score-card after playing a hole, or round; 'he carded 86. . . .'

cardboard bomber (aircrew) a detailed, fullscale mockup made of cardboard and drawn up with every dial, level and needle in place to perfect crews of civil airlines in full 'cockpit familiarisation' before they even see a real simulator, in which they can 'fly', let alone an actual airplane.

care and control (social work) a balance between using care to control or using control to care – dependent on character of the individuals involved.

career *adj* (milit) an officer who intends to make his career in the Army and remain there for his entire working life.

careerism (pols) communist party description of left-wingers who put themselves before the party; if convicted of such blatant opportunism, they can be purged from the party.

caring professions (sociol) those professions that have arisen as ancillaries of the welfare state and especially the National Health Service to 'care' for those whom, it is felt, cannot care for themselves. Aka the *helping professions*. There are those among their clients who feel that for all the earnest ideology, the whole concept is little advanced on traditional patronising, middle-class do-gooders who only help 'the poor' in an attempt to suppress their individuality.

carl rosa (police) (rhyming sl.) a poser (from the opera star of the same name). Used generally to refer to a fraud, either the conman or his scheme.

carp(s) (theatre/US) (abbrev) carpenter.

carpark job (TV) a short insert which needs to be shot after the main filming is over; to save time and money it is not shot on location but somewhere near the company's head office and all too often looks like (and may well be) the carpark. Such efforts bring back the traditional Hollywood slogan: 'a tree is a tree, a rock is a rock – shoot it in Griffith Park!'.

carpet (sport) in cricket the surface of the pitch and the outfield. Thus *along the carpet*, and *carpet shot*.

carpet (prison) three months sentence; from

rhyming slang for carpet bag: drag (sl. for 3 mths sentence).

carpet (sport) in golf,
1. the fairway.
2. the putting green.

carpet (milit) an electronic device used to jam radar reception.

carpetbagger (pols/US) from the influx of northerners to take advantage of the devastated South in 1865, travelling light – with only a carpetbag – and looking for what he could get; now used for the politician who moves into a new area to gain power or position at the expense of the local politicians, often a celebrity who finds his own patch too crowded and wants easier pickings.

carpet joint (gambling) a well-appointed gambling venue with carpets on the floor. aka: *rug joint*.

carry the bat *v* (sport) a member of a cricket team who is still not out when the rest of his team have been dismissed; applied to early or middle order batsmen, for whom this is an achievement, rather than tailenders, who have fewer peers to wait out.

cart (radio) (abbrev) cartridge: the tape cassettes on which commercials, jingles, station identification and signature tunes, etc. are recorded.

cartoon (computer) a computer printout that forms a visual image or display.

case-ace (gambling) in poker, the fourth ace to appear, after players have seen the other three dealt out.

case card (gambling) in poker, the one remaining card in the deck which will improve a player's hand.

case officer (espionage) the intelligence agency officer in charge of running an operation.

case the deck (gambling) the ability of a card expert to recall exactly every card that has been dealt and work out his bets and odds from that recall.

casting *n* (movies) one shade less starry than bankable (qv), but well worthy of investment. (cf: *tickets*).

castle (sport) in cricket, a slightly flowery description of the wicket – which is defended by the batsman.

cast off (advert, press) from the calculation of stitching in knitting: to assess the space occupied by a given piece of copy when it is set into type.

casual water (sport) in golf, 'any temporary accumulation of water (whether caused by rainfall or otherwise) which is not one of the ordinary and recognised hazards of the course' (*Rules of Golf*, 1899).

CAT (airlines) (abbrev) clear air turbulence; a severe hazard to aircraft.

catalogue (espionage) a dossier, first developed by the STB (the Czech equivalent of the KGB) of compromising pictures of VIPs using prosti-

tutes, entering and leaving massage parlours and 'bookshops' and so on. Intelligence thus gathered by help from assistants and owners of such establishments as well as agents. All useful when planning to burn (qv) a target.

catalytic war (milit) a war between two nations which is brought about by the actions of a third who precipitates it by acting as the catalyst.

catastrophe theory (soc sci) a system in mathematics proposed for describing a discontinuity or phenomenon of sudden change in a continuous process by fitting the attributes of the change into a geometric model consisting of dimensional planes that describe the change.

catatonia (computer) a condition of suspended animation when the system is wedged (qv) and will not work although it is not actually broken.

catch *v* (police/US) to be assigned to the station complaints desk, where one 'catches it' from the public.

catch a cold (theatre) to do badly during provincial tour.

catch flies (theatre/US) to steal scenes by continuing facial and/or bodily movement that distracts audience from the main action. (cf: *backcloth star*).

catch line (advert) note put at the top of a page or above a piece of type to indicate its place in the overall ad., paper, magazine, etc.

catch-up (aerospace) a steering manoeuvre by which a pilot shortens the distance between his craft and a target.

categorically needy (soc work) people who fall into the various categories that entitle them to some form of welfare aid.

catenaccio (sport) in soccer, a 'sweeper' defence: one player is used at the back of the defence to 'sweep up' forward attacks and loose balls.

caterpillars (airlines) people who are scared of flying.

cat films (sex) porno/violence films featuring two women fighting.

cat scene (theatre/UK) in a pantomime, the last but one scene in which the cavern/prison transforms into a fairy grotto or woodland dell.

cats (rock music) 1980s teenagers who enjoy 1950s rock and roll. They wear the college styles of the 1950s to look like vintage US high school students rather than Teds, who still dress as they, or their parents, did in the 1950s.

cats and dogs (stock exchange) low priced stocks that yield only low returns.

cattle call (movies) a mass audition, bearing out Alfred Hitchcock's admonition 'actors are like cattle'.

caught in the rain (milit) for a member of the USMC to be caught outside when the colours (the US flag) are being lowered and thus compelled to stand at attention and salute.

caveman *adj* (computers) a machine, program or programmer who is badly behind the times; an antique.

C³CM (milit) command, control and communications counter-measures: aspect of electronic warfare which aims to discover the hostile C³ and take electronic counter-measures – jamming, etc – and plan a systematised method of attack and destruction. Friendly (qv) C³ should be able to defend itself with superior technology.

ceiling (aerospace) the maximum height at which an aircraft can maintain horizontal flight or at which the rate of climb falls beneath 100'/minute. *zero ceiling*: clouds or mist at ground level.

ceiling (commerce) the highest price a market can reach.

cement (drugs) wholesale illicit narcotics.

cemetery network (milit) NATO code: the main nuclear command link, based on an HF radio network.

cemetery vote (pols/US) voter corruption effected by using the vote of someone recently dead but still on the voter registration lists.

centage (theatre) the % paid to local theatres from the receipts of a touring company.

central processing unit (CPU) (computers) the part of a computer system which controls all its operations and performs the arithmetical and logical functions.

centre *v* (new therapy) to be calm and relaxed, and simultaneously physically energised and psychologically balanced. *uncentred*: the opposite.

centrism (pols) the adopting of a middle way between various extremes.

CEP (milit) Circular Error Probable: the radius of a circle in which it is computed that all the missiles of a particular weapons system ought to land and explode.

certainty equivalent (stock market) an investment that offers a guaranteed return which, though a smaller sum, does compensate for the uncertainty of more dramatic financial gambles.

chad (computer) the piece of paper that is punched out of the holes in a perforated paper tape.

chaff (milit) strips of metal foil released to jam radar and/or guidance systems of missiles, etc. (cf: *window*).

chaining (computer) a method of dealing with large programs that might otherwise have exceeded the machine's storage capacity: the task is split into several lesser programs which are then run in sequence.

chair warmers (theatre) an unresponsive audience.

chalk eaters (gambling) horse race punters who bet only on favourites. From their following the bookie as he writes (in chalk) the current odds. (cf: *chalk players*).

chalk number (milit) reference number given to a complete load of troops and to the carrier that transports them. Thus *chalk commander*, *chalk troops*.

chalk player (gambling) a horse-racing bettor who wagers only on favourites.

challenged (sociol) social euphemism for crippled. (cf: *the caring professions*).

chamois down *v* (TV) makeup term for mopping a face free of sweat.

change (sport) in horse-racing, the fractions – fifths – of seconds that are used in declaring the time of the winner, second, third and fourth horses.

change agent (business) an individual consultant, or firm of consultants brought in to effect efficient changes in the structure of a corporation. A *personal change agent* is employed to help the executives shift careers or re-orientate their personal goals.

change-over (movies) the transition from one reel of film to the next during projection. There are approx 20–30 mins/reel. A set number of seconds prior to the end of a reel a series of cue dots appear on top right of screen to warn the projectionist.

change-up (sport) a baseball pitcher's disguised ball which appears to be fast – with a big windup, etc – but is actually delivered slow and thus confuses the batter.

channel money (commerce) interim payments to merchant seamen when they reach port, calculated against their actual wages, which are computed when the whole voyage is over.

chapel *n* (press, indust relats) the alternative name for a trade union 'branch' that is used in all print-related unions, both of journalists and printers (the NUJ, NGA, SLADE, NATSOPA) in the UK.

character, go out of (theatre) forget one's accent, business, etc – either through dozing off or corpsing (qv).

character disorder (soc wk) problems that stem primarily from a person's behaviour but which are neither psychotic nor neurotic; a condition that can best be approached by some form of ego-building. (cf: *acting out*).

character merchandising (advert) using TV/movie/entertainment or similar celebrities as the basis for a special offer or competition.

character part (theatre) any stock role – wicked uncle, fallen woman, etc – other than the lead or juvenile lead.

charge *v* (sport) in golf, to approach a round aggressively, playing each hole with maximum energy, force, etc.

charger (milit) from hard-charger: member of USMC who is 'highly motivated'. (cf: *gung-ho*).

charity goods (sex) a homosexual prostitute who is persuaded to give his services free.

charlie (drugs) see *drug names*.

charlie bars (TV) small flaps fixed in front of a lamp to break up the light.

Charlie Moore (milit) in RN: honest, above

board: from an advertisement in 1850 for a public house in Malta 'Charlie Moore: the fair thing'.

charlie noble (milit) in RN, a galley funnel; from Charles Noble, a merchant navy captain who prided himself on the spotless condition of his galley.

charlie regan (pols/US) a non-existent but highly valuable personality used during political campaigns to keep questioners at bay and generally accept that passed buck. (cf: *George Spelvin*).

charm (science) see *quark*.

chart (rock business)
1. ratings of successful records – 45s, LPs – listed weekly as Top 20/30/40.
2. musical arrangements, the 'chart' is a sheet of music.

chart *v* (rock business) to appear on a record industry chart – Top 40 etc. 'This one's sure to chart soon. . . .'

charter (air lines) essentially an aircraft chartered by a group organiser for that group's exclusive use; but latterly the 'charter' has been stretched to include *part charter*: blocks of seats of an otherwise scheduled flight are saved for the charter fliers: (the agent who buys them receives a large discount from the company): *half charter*: flights that are not really charter in any way, but can be so termed by obtaining the correct official permission.

chartist (stock market) an individual who studies the movements of shares and similar prices by charts, usually graphs.

chase *n* (music) a jazz style whereby a number of musicians take turns to play solo, during which time each plays several bars of improvisation before passing on the turn.

chase *v* (gambling) in stud poker, to play against a better hand which you can already see exposed on the table, thus requiring good bluffing skills.

chase eighths (stock market/US) a speculator who is satisfied with only the smallest of profits – just $⅛.

chaser (milit) USMC prisoner's escort.

chaser (theatre/US) music played by the orchestra to accompany the audience's leaving the theatre.

chase the dragon (drugs) the smoking of heroin; a portion of the drug is placed on silver foil, this is heated from below and the resultant smoke sucked into the lungs through another tube of foil. The liquefied heroin runs along the foil, thus 'the chase'.

chassis (computer) the metal base of the computer machinery on which the various parts of the electronic assembly are fixed.

a chat with Susan (pols) phrase used by interrogators in Argentina to denote a session of torture by an electric shock machine. A descendant, perhaps, of the 15th century British

description of the rack as being 'wedded to the Duke of Exeter's daughter': John Holland, Duke of Exeter, introduced the rack to England in 1447.

Chats (milit) RN abbreviation of Chatham, former home of the RN Dockyard.

cheat *v* (TV) to move something or someone within the frame of a shot when it or they are spoiling the composition, even though such a movement works against continuity (qv). In films this is known also as *cheat the look*.

cheat (film) the procedure of concealing part of the action necessary to the taking of a shot by excluding it from the camera's field of view.

cheat shot (advert) the use in a commercial of a faked up picture.

check cop (gambling) a light glue that a cheat puts on the palm of his hand so as to steal chips ('check'). He casually rests his hand on a pile of chips, when he removes it, the top one is stuck to his palm.

checker (gambling) an employee of a casino or gambling enterprise who checks luggers (qv) to see how many players they have brought to the game.

checking (stock market)
1. the agreement between a broker and a jobber (qv), normally on the first business day after a deal, on the details of that deal.
2. *checking the market*: to enquire of a number of jobbers as to the price and amount of shares in a given security.

checkoff
1. (indust relats) the system whereby the employer withholds all union dues and other payments from the employee and pays them directly to the union.
2. (US farmers) a system for livestock producers to contribute an agreed levy to a central body which then uses it for general promotion of their trade.
3. (govt) a method whereby a taxpayer can indicate to the Revenue whether or not he wishes to have a certain % of his taxes put towards financing an election campaign.

checks and balances (pols/US) the essential failsafe mechanism of the US government system, built into the Constitution: the means whereby each of the three branches of US government – legislative, judiciary, administrative – can be limited by mutual interdependence.

cheeseburger (milit) aka *daisy-cutter*: the BLU/82/B11 concussion bomb. 11' long, 4.5' wide, weighing 7.5 tons and containing over 6 tons of gelled aqueous slurry of ammonium nitrate and aluminium powder. Only a nuclear weapon is more powerful than this bomb which sends a mushroom cloud 6000' into the air and, exploded 3' above the ground, will kill *everything* (including the worms beneath the surface) in a surrounding area of 755 acres and *most things* within 2000 acres.

C

cheesecake (sport) in ten pin bowling, a lane where high scores can be made easily.

chemical architecture (archit) a proposed novel form of architecture whereby a variety of chemicals – powders and liquids – could be activated by the addition of catalyst agents to expand into pre-determined shapes.

chemigrams (art) a form of art based on chemistry and chemical processes, using photographic paper or film.

chequebook journalism (press) the payment of large sums of money either to celebrities or, more usually, to figures currently notorious and newsworthy – royal lovers, mass murderers – in order to 'scoop' one's rivals.

chequerboard (TV) the favourite method of cutting negative film; it guarantees no visible joins and is the best way to make opticals (qv).

cherries (gambling) from rhyming slang: cherry hogs: dogs. Greyhound racing tracks.

cherry picker (aerospace) a mobile crane with a platform that can be placed alongside a free-standing rocket or missile as working scaffold or as an escape route for an astronaut.

cherrypicker (TV) a hydraulically operated tower for high lighting or for high angle camera work.

cherry picking (publishing/US) making trips for on-the-spot entrepreneurial research of persons or ideas, then taking one's findings back to base (probably New York) for consideration and possible action.

cherry soda circuit (show business/US) a system whereby US soft drink companies, then selling drinks in bottles, not cans, would pay touring acts a small fee to accept the caps from their bottles instead of money for admission to their shows. (cf: *borscht belt*).

chew the scenery (theatre) to overact. One who so performs is a *scenery-chewer*.

Chicago boys (econ) a group of monetarist economists, including the current, if tarnished, guru Milton Friedman, whose theories stem from their work at the University of Chicago.

chicane (sport) in bridge, the condition of holding no trumps; *double chicane*: neither partner holds a trump.

chicken button (aerospace) aka *chicken switch*:
1. a switch or button that can destroy a malfunctioning rocket in mid flight.
2. a switch or button that an astronaut or jet pilot can use to eject his capsule from a malfunctioning rocket, or his seat from a potentially crashing plane.

chickenhawk (sex) an older homosexual who prefers his sex with young boys, the 'chickens'.

chicken soup (aerospace) a solution of amino acids, vitamins and other nutrients in a 'broth' that was used to check the possibility of life on Mars. Any living organism would ingest the nutrients and expel gases that could be picked up by sensors and relayed to Earth.

chicks (milit) friendly fighter aircraft.

child-centred (educ) built around the needs, ability and interest of the child. In progressive education, this means that pupils are able to decide what they learn and when they choose to learn it. On a more general level, the meaning implies an attempt to make lessons as appealing as possible to those who must endure them.

chili-dip (sport) in golf (US), this means a weak, lofted shot that follows a mis-hit that has managed to hit more ground than ball. From the image of taking a taco and scooping up a helping of chili.

chiller (movies) a horror film.

Chiltern Hundreds (pols/UK) the stewardship of the Chiltern Hundreds of Stoke, Desborough and Burnham was established to rid the Chiltern Hills of their many predatory bandits. This requirement fell into disuse, but since 1707 the taking of this stewardship has been used as a legal fiction to permit the resignation of an MP. To hold an office for profit under the Crown – such as the Chiltern Hundreds – automatically disqualifies an MP from sitting in the House. Thus a member may supply and will be granted the stewardship, although no such office exists nor is it ever held.

chin (aerospace) the area, logically, right beneath the aircraft's nose.

chinaman (sport) in cricket, the opposite of the googly (qv): an off-break bowled out of the back or side of the hand by a left-handed bowler. Possibly from Ellis Achong, a Chinese player for the West Indies c. 1940, but he was by no means the first man to bowl thus.

China syndrome (science) a catastrophe in a nuclear reactor whereby the cooling system fails and the resultant meltdown (qv) would create a nuclear lava flow of unassailable intensity. From the concept of the nuclear flow 'burning all the way through to China'.

Chinese (TV) when the barn doors (qv) are adjusted to diffuse light through horizontal slits; from the racial cliché of narrow, slitted, oriental eyes.

Chinese cut (sport) aka: *Staffordshire cut, Surrey cut*: a glancing stroke, in cricket, quite possibly meant to go in another direction, which edges the ball behind the stumps and between the fielders.

Chinese money (stock market) 'paper' (qv) rather than cash; a payment made in a mix of stock certificates and debts.

Chinese snooker n (sport) in snooker, a position whereby the white ball is in front of another ball and a shot on the object ball is open, but the white and the adjacent ball are so near (but not touching) that it is extremely hard for the player to use his cue safely. Such a position often necessitates the use of the 'half-butt'.

chippy (gambling)
1. a sucker.

2. a novice player.

chippy (drugs) a user – usually of narcotics – who buys only occasionally, rather than a regular addict.

chips (milit) in RN, the carpenter, joiner or any artificer.

Chi-square (press/US) a professor of journalism or communications whose teaching and/or research concentrates on the statistical determination of normative modes of sending and receiving messages as defined by the Chi-square test of significance.

chistka (pols) in USSR, periodic purges of the party. Translation of Rus: 'purification'.

chitlin circuit (entertain) the black equivalent of the borscht belt (qv). The food, naturally, caters for a different ethnic group, but the amenities and standards are equally as third-rate.

chleuh (milit) French Foreign Legion: the enemy.

choice (stock market) *having the choice* denotes the possibility of being able to buy or sell shares at the same price with different jobbers (qv).

choke (sport)
1. (golf) to shorten the swinging length of the club by adopting a lower grip on the shaft.
2. (baseball) as (1).

choke (sport) to fail to perform at one's best through nervous tension; the composure goes and with it all skill and success.

choke point (govt) an artificially created bottleneck created by an incumbent government whereby all valuable supplies – food, drugs, weapons, fuel, etc – are controlled and denied to those whom the government wishes to defeat or demoralise.

cholly (gambling) from black sl. for $1: folding money.

chomp (aerospace) to reset one's co-ordinates on a new direction/communications beacon during a flight after reaching the limits of the last one; airliners navigate by following a line of radio beacons that run along their route, moving from one to the next as they proceed.

chomp (computer) to lose; to chew off something bigger than that which one's teeth can deal with satisfactorily or efficiently.

chop *n* (milit) the change of operational control.

chopper (milit)
1. helicopter.
2. a machine gun.

chops (music) see *lick*.

chop-socky (movies) Oriental martial arts films; puns on chop-suey and sock: to hit.

chop the clock (commerce) in the auto trade, a method of improving a car's age by turning back the odometer and thus registering a false and lower than actual mileage.

chosen instrument (airlines) the national airline chosen and designated by a government to act as the country's representative in international flying.

chosisme (lit. crit) from Fr: 'thingism': the minutely detailed descriptions of every item in a given scene that feature in the New Wave novels of such authors as Alain Robbe-Grillet.

chow (milit) US forces: food. Either from allegedly insatiable appetite of chow dogs or from era of Chinese cooks dominating the railroad camps in US. Thus *chow hound*: greedy eater; *chow line*: queue for a meal in the mess hall.

christmas tree (movie) a small cart that transports pieces of lighting equipment which are strung around it like lights on a christmas tree.

christmas tree (aerospace) an indicator board showing radar traces, so called for its flashing lights.

christmas tree (milit) a combat uniform belt adorned with grenades, knife, flask, flares, and whatever else is required in a battle or assault.

christmas tree (milit) an indicator panel on a submarine which flashes red and green lights to show that all valves, hatches, etc are locked tight when the submarine dives.

christmas tree bill (pols/US) a bill, often aimed at improving life for special interest/minority groups, that is bedecked with a number of amendments which are 'hung on' to it, to satisfy those groups but which are only loosely tied into the main law.

christmas tree effect (science) the theory, in astronomy, that rather than some quasars actually moving, the 'blinks' that some scientists feel prove that movements are actually caused by an internal mechanism that causes them to flash 'on and off'.

chuck-up (milit) in RN, any kind of vocal support or similar sign of approval.

chuffing (milit) the characteristic of some rockets to burn intermittently and with irregular noises; conveys the image of an 'old banger' on the London to Brighton vintage car excursion.

chugging (milit) an irregular explosion of exhaust gases from a rocket motor; to move with the sound of a steam or electric engine, officially termed 'low frequency oscillations'. (cf: *chuffing*).

chumming (milit) a night attack strategy involving two planes: one keeps its lights on and draws fire from the target. Thus pinpointed, the target is open for the 'dark' plane to destroy it.

chummy (police) anyone, but by implication a villain or a prisoner.

chump change (music business) a pittance paid to an artist which will ensure his survival but little else. He is a 'chump' to accept what is little more than 'change'.

chunking (information) the process of re-coding information so as to reduce the number of independent symbols while increasing the actual kinds of symbols. A system that adapts best to the limited number of mental 'slots' we seem to have when dealing with matters for immediate attention.

churn (business) the process of generating more income by artificially increasing the amount of business carried out, even if, in fact, no more deals are made, clients aided, problems solved, etc. Creating heat but casting no more light.

churning (stock market) by extension of churn (qv): a marginally illegal method of pushing up the price of stocks one wishes to sell by making wash sales (qv) which create a falsely 'active' market, thus boosting prices as required.

C³I (milit) pron. 'c-cubed-i' Command, Control, Communications and Intelligence: the electronic 'nervous system' of a battlefield. C³I can be extended to a global level, including spy satellites, early warning systems and so on.

cigarette deck (milit) in USN, the casing of the submarine immediately abaft the conning tower (sail, qv).

cilop (aerospace) the conversion of old aircraft to increase one's materiel instead of scrapping them and building new ones for far more money.

cinderella liberty (milit) US forces' leave that must end at midnight.

cinderella sale (commerce) an occasional sale to get rid of a store's odds and ends.

cinematographer (movies) the lighting cameraman or the chief photographer.

cinetisations (art) images of contorted and distorted buildings which are produced by the simple device of removing key portions of the original photograph and then remounting them slightly askew – thus utterly shattering the building's stability.

cinniri (Mafia) lit: 'ashes': heroin.

circuit (movies) a chain of cinemas under the same ownership, often playing the same movie simultaneously across a state or country.

circuit slugger (sport) in baseball, a regular homerun hitter who has to run the circuit of the bases every time he slugs a home run.

circular file (govt/US) joking reference to the waste paper basket.

circus job (theatre/US) an extravagant pre-production publicity campaign, particularly lavish when the management fear they are facing a flop. From the excesses of circus ballyhoo of earlier eras.

citadel (milit) those enclosed areas of a warship without which it can neither sail nor fight. Made safe from gas and nuclear attack to the greatest possible extent.

citronella circuit (theatre/US) a circuit of small, local summer theatres. Named for a (necessary) insect repellent. (cf: *borscht belt, chitlin circuit*)

city-busting (milit) the targeting, and presumed 'busting' of cities in the case of a nuclear exchange.

civvy *n* (prison/UK) aka: *straight, tailor-made*: a

proprietary branded cigarette, as opposed to a 'roll-up'.

claim *v* (police/UK) to arrest.

claimer (horse-racing) a claiming race in which all contesting horses (none of which will be of a particularly high or desirable standard) may be claimed (purchased) for sums specified before the race.

clambake (audio) the possibility of two or three commentators all talking over/against each other and thus confusing the listeners.

clamp (aerospace) weather that makes it impossible to fly safely; it clamps planes to the ground.

clandestine cache (milit) secret supplies of fissionable material within the borders of a nation ostensibly party to a disarmament treaty.

clapperboard (movies) a hinged board that records the details of each shot. At the start of each 'take' it is held in front of the camera for identification and then clapped to ensure synchronisation of the sound track. *Clapperloader*: an assistant to the cameraman who doubles as clapper operator and loader of film into the camera.

clash (TV)
1. two commercials in same or adjacent breaks which employ the same actors, voice over themes, etc.
2. a commercial that seems too similar in style to the programme into which it has been inserted.

class (pols/sociol) originally based on the feudal, pre-industrial differences of *rank* within an intricately ordered world, modern class, based on differences of material possessions, evolved after the Industrial Revolution. Class has also been defined as an endless split between creditors and debtors, based around the 'life chance' (skill as well as property) of the individual.

class action (legal) a legal proceeding enacted to take into account not merely the specific defendant/plaintiff, but everyone to whom the case might actively refer.

class enemy (pols) that class which stands between the proletariat and its struggle for power; usually the bourgeoisie.

classical figure *n* (milit) that amount of special material that provides a critical mass for the manufacturing of nuclear bombs: 20 kilograms of highly enriched uranium.

classics (horse-racing) the five major British horse races: the 1000 Guineas, the 2000 Guineas, the Oaks, the Derby and the St. Leger.

classification at birth (govt) the concept that some ideas, which develop from or within classified areas – military, nuclear, intelligence, etc – are automatically classified as secret from the actual second of their being propounded. Thus a professor lecturing to students who offers such an idea quite spontaneously can be seen as *thinking classified thoughts*.

classification levels (govt) an ascending ladder of secrecy used to classify data: *confidential, secret, top secret, special intelligence*. (Special Intelligence covers a range of super-secret classifications hidden from most government and elected officials, let alone the public).

classified (espionage, govt) officially such material that is not of utmost secrecy but can only be circulated amongst a specified group. On the whole all secret material, of whatever level of importance, is termed classified.

classified mode (govt/US) any institution thus labelled has been shut to public inspection for an indefinite period.

class 'in itself' and 'for itself' (pols) two Hegelian concepts adopted by Marx to describe two stages of proletarian class consciousness: *in itself:* the workers become aware as individuals of individual grievances against other individuals, ie their own complaints against their own boss, *for itself:* the workers gain a consciousness of class identity and the overall struggle against the bourgeoisie; this should culminate in revolution.

class VI (milit) used in USMC to denote alcoholic drinks of any sort.

clastic art (art) sculptures consisting of ready-made units, such as bricks, wooden blocks, metal poles, etc., which can be taken to pieces and re-assembled if required. Alternatively the component elements may be returned to their original 'non-art' condition.

clause IV (indust relats) from the Constitution of the Labour Party: 'to secure for the workers by hand or by brain the full fruits of their industry and the most equitable distribution thereof that may be possible upon the basis of the common ownership of the means of production, distribution and exchange, and the best obtainable system of popular administration and control of each industry or service'. I.e. nationalisation; the perpetuation of the letter of Clause IV persists in dividing the left (pro) and the right (anti) of the British Labour Party.

claw-back (pols/UK) the decision by government to withdraw various advances in social benefits by direct cuts or by making them subject to extra taxation. Often proposed to 'keep benefits in line with inflation' (on those rare occasions that inflation drops).

clean (milit) a nuclear device that produces maximum blast and thermal effects but keeps radiation fallout to a minimum, thus, theoretically, producing most of the resultant deaths immediately rather than over the succeeding months.

clean *v* (milit) in RN, the changing into an appropriate uniform, suit of clothes for the job; thus if the job is dirty, there is no reason why 'cleaning' need require clean clothes.

clean (theatrical) all seats sold: 'the house went clean'. (cf: *SRO*)

clean (aerospace)
1. an aircraft with its landing gear retracted. (cf: *dirty*).
2. an aircraft carrying no external stores such as extra fuel tanks, above average armaments, etc.

clean (sex) a black pimp's description of his whores as smartly and fashionably dressed.

clean (stock market) the price of security after the deduction of any fixed interest.

clean (drugs)
1. not carrying any drugs.
2. free of addiction to narcotics.

clean bed (medic) bed for a patient needing surgery, the setting of broken limbs, or other non-infectious diseases.

clean entrance (movies) the making sure by an actor that neither his/her body nor its shadow should be visible prior to an entrance.

clean feed (TV, radio) for one station to transmit to another a programme without any local information – news, advertisements, station ID, etc.

clean float (econ) money exchange rates allowed to adjust themselves to the prevailing market without any government interference.

clean room (science) a special room in which precision objects are to be manufactured/assembled which has been completely disinfected and had all dust removed as well as having its temperature and humidity kept under static, artificial control.

clean wheels (police) a car, ideal for robbery/getaway driving, which has had no problems with the police.

clear (new therapy) in scientology, the ultimate state of scientological perfection, the ideal human being.

clear (milit, espionage) from Fr: 'en clair': neither in cipher nor code.

clearing (stock market) the settlement department to which brokers and jobbers (qv) submit a daily list of the transactions in certain stocks. Those securities which are handled by the Settlement Department are *clearing stocks*.

clearing house (stock market) an organisation that provides the market with a central body for all settlements, becoming 'buyer' for the seller and vice versa. Orig. established by bankers to adjudicate mutual claims over cheques and bills. *Clearing member*: organisation with access to the Clearing House for the purpose of dealing with its customers' business.

clearings (finance) cheques, drafts, and other paper (qv) presented by a bank for collection at the clearing house.

clearing the market (stock market) the satisfaction of all parties – buyers and sellers – by moving the price.

clear yourself (movies) instruction to an actor

to ensure that he/she is not covered from the camera by an object or person.

cleek (sport) in golf, the traditional name for the Number 1 iron or the Number 4 wood.

click (radio) local atmospheric disturbances caused by small activity within thunderclouds. (cf: *grinder*, *tray*).

clicker (theatre/US) free admission pass.

client (new therapy) a description that has taken over from the 'patient' of a classical therapist. Perhaps this helps all concerned remember the financial basis of the relationship: pay quickly, get 'cured' equally quickly.

client (pols) a nation whose economy, armed forces and political stability depend on one or other of the super-powers, or at least some other far more powerful country.

climate for learning (educ) the environment in which the child learns, with reference to the personality of the teacher, the architecture of the school, the mental and physical health of the child, etc, etc.

climb (police) cat burglary, thus *at the climb:* in the profession of cat burglary, a *climber:* one who works thus.

climb-out (airlines) the immediate post-take off flying phase of the aircraft (the first 50 secs of flight) during which it must gain full speed, lift its undercarriage and gain sufficient height to allow for local noise pollution regulations.

climb the rigging (milit) RN: to lose one's temper; the naval equivalent of 'going up the wall'.

clinching (computer) any wrinkling in the magnetic tape: this may be the cause of errors in running a program.

clipper (TV) anyone who makes a hobby of collecting 'Star Trek' film clips.

clip sheet (public relations) a one-page press release which combines a number of pictures, short items and small features all supposedly for easy use by newspapers.

clock (computer) an electronic circuit or set of components that generate a set of control signals which govern the overall speed at which a computer functions.

clock start (radio) an item that starts exactly to the second – reports, inserts, parliamentary question time, etc: anything that has its own set time.

clogger *n* (sport/UK) in soccer: a deliberately savage player, free with physical fouls.

close (stock market)
1. v to reverse an open (qv) position either by buying a security which has been sold short (qv) or by selling one which has been previously purchased.
2. adj a small fraction used in quoting prices for shares. *close to close:* that same fraction either side of a main number.

closed bed (medic) a made up bed. Thus *open bed* has been turned down for the night.

closed end (stock market) a closed end trust is an investment with a fixed capital as opposed to an open end trust whose issue of units can expand or contract.

closed out *v* (aerospace) the final sealing of a spacecraft prior to the launch.

close down *v* (sport) in soccer, to deny the opposition room to manoeuvre.

closed period (TV) that period on Sunday evenings dedicated by law and television charter to paying lip service to the 'Lord's day'. (cf: *God slot*).

closed season (TV) the summer holiday period which, on the assumption that everyone is on holiday, is bad for ratings and for scheduling of new programmes. (cf: *dog days*).

closed shop (computers) facility where outside programmers are not allowed to process or to oversee the processing of the programs that they have written.

closed visit (prison/UK) for prisoners who are currently undergoing punishment of some sort; rather than meet their visitor(s) across a normal table, they are placed in a booth behind glass and no physical contact is permitted.

close out *n v* (business) the closing of a successful deal or sale; the act of so doing.

closer *a* (stock market) when a stock or price is closer it implies that the margin between buying and selling prices can be narrowed.

close-up *n* (movies) a tight head-and-shoulders shot of a person or any close shot of an object. The first close-up was apparently on one Fred Ott who sneezed for Edison in an experimental film in 1900.

closing price (stock market) the price recorded during the period designated as the official close.

closing the books (stock market) the procedure carried out by the registrar of a company at the time of a dividend or similar distribution. Only those shareholders registered on the company books at the date of closing them will receive a part of the distribution.

cloth cap pensions (indust relats) aka *EPF* (excepted provident fund): a scheme whereby a worker can take his/her entire future pension as a lump sum on retirement; this scheme is usually non-contributory and is aimed at the hourly paid manual workers.

clothesline *v* (sport) a foul move in US football: one player jabs his forearm into the throat of an on-rushing opponent, a move that produces a similar effect to if he had run full tilt into a taut clothesline and hit it Adam's apple first.

clothespin vote (pols/US) a vote delivered with extreme reluctance, but for lack of any option; the image is of one placing a clothespin (peg, UK) over one's nose to banish disgusting smells when one is forced to venture among them.

cloud of title (commerce) in real estate (US): a

defect in the title to a property or piece of land, thus making it unmarketable.

clout v (crime/US) shoplift. (cf: *boost*).

clout n (pols) power, influence in politics and government whether or not one stands for election; indeed, sufficient clout makes the process of standing for election a waste of time and (in US) money, also an unnecessary risk. When applied to a politician it means power to see programmes carried through; when applied to his fellow citizens, it means the influence to rule what those programmes shall be.

club n (science) the organisation of the world's uranium producers, founded Paris 1972.

cluster (archit) a planning term that refers to a type of city that is laid out in a number of small centres rather than using a nodal point surrounded by concentric rings and a radial road plan.

clustering (computers) the process of grouping problems with similar characteristics together when preparing instructions for a program.

clutch n (milit) in USMC, a sudden and serious emergency.

clutch (sport) by extension from USMC use (qv): thus a *clutch team* is a tough team who can keep fighting from a poor position – used in all sports.

clutter (advert) the great mass/mess of advertising in all media and the problem for advertisers and their agencies in finding a message that will stand out from the rest.

Cmos (information tech) a type of complex semiconductor which features a low power requirement and high 'intelligence'. The Cmos chip is increasingly useful for watches and calculators and other small, portable electronics in which it is convenient not to have the worry or bulk of continual battery changes.

coaling a (theatre/UK) telling, 'meaningful' lines in one's part; possibly derived from *cole*: money, and thus implying a meaty part that should pull in the paying customers.

coalplex (tech) a theoretical type of industrial complex in which coal would be used to create a range of secondary fuels and chemical products; these would be used in the various industries sited at the complex and would thus achieve a far higher efficiency than a plant working purely on coal alone.

Coast n (movies) Hollywood, sited on America's West Coast.

coating (police) a reprimand, thus to *give a coating* is to reprimand a fellow officer.

coat-tail v (pols/US) to hang onto the power, influence and probably electability of a strong candidate in the hope of gaining election oneself despite one's own actual weaknesses.

COBOL (computers) (acro) Common Business-Orientated Language: the most popular and widely known of the high-level (qv) languages

developed for commercial (rather than technical) computer use.

cochealed (prison/UK) extremely well provided with a given commodity; (the spelling and origin of this common prison word are both unknown; possibly it originates in the Gaelic 'cashail': to have something hidden away for a bad time).

cockade (aerospace) the national insignia carried as coloured roundels on military aircraft.

cocked pistol (milit) US *defcon* (qv) 1 (maximum force readiness), the last step prior to actual war-fighting.

cocktail (medic/US)
1. a barium enema.
2. castor oil.

co-counselling (new therapy) aka: *re-evaluation counselling*: a therapy system whose adherents both offer and receive counselling from each other. No special skills are required except for the ability to listen usefully to another co-counsellor's talk and the ability to reverse this role within the mutually interdependent framework.

code 9 (medic/US) emergency code for broadcasting over hospital PA system and not alarm patients/visitors: everyone available is to rush to a cardiac arrest emergency. (cf: *Dr. Blue*)

coffee-and-cakes (theatre/US) a very small salary for a part. Just buys subsistence edibles.

coffee-and habit (drugs) a minimal addiction, requiring no more daily expenditure than would figuratively pay for snacks. Given the nature of heroin, this would seem to be a strictly temporary state.

coffee-and pimp (sex) third rate black pimp whose girls can barely keep him in coffee-and-doughnuts, rather than the desired pimp accoutrements of Cadillac, cocaine etc.

coffee grinder (sport) in gymnastics, a manoeuvre from a squatting position on the floor involving a circle of the leg while keeping both hands on the floor.

coffee-klatsch campaign (pols/US) a campaign approach in suburbs which takes the candidate on a round of coffee-klatsch (coffee morning, UK) meetings and addresses.

coffee queen (sex) aka: *hamburger queen, Hershey queen*: homosexual prostitute's derogatory reference to a third-rate rival who will offer his favours for food or drink instead of charging a proper fee.

coffin (science) a specially lead-insulated container used for the transport of radio-active substances.

cognate disciplines (educ) related, associated disciplines.

cognitive dissonance (marketing) from psychoanalytic concept of the holding of inconsistent or incompatible ideas which produce tension within an individual: in marketing terms, the feeling that the wonderful 'bargain' which the advertisements persuaded you to buy is infinitely less appealing once you have brought it home; a feeling of dissatisfaction with the purchase and the method of selling it ensues.

cokuloris (movies) a light diffuser punched with irregular holes which can be put between the light and the camera to give a 'real life' approximation of light and shadow. (cf: *cookie*)

COLA (econ) (acro) Cost of Living Adjustment.

cold-blooded (sex) amongst black pimps, a term of approbation; spec. reference to the ability to control one's sexual responsiveness toward one's women.

cold call (marketing) the appearance of a salesman at a shop or office without a prior appointment, thus 'cold', but intends through his own enthusiasm, to warm up the potential for a sale.

cold canvas (marketing) refers to the blank canvas an artist faces before he begins to create: for a businessman this becomes the open situation he can start to adopt when facing a new problem or series of decisions. For business consultants, cold canvas implies an assignment which has little or no prior outline and more than usually wide discretion as to creating both a view of the task and the methods of approaching it.

cold canvas (indust relats) a membership drive in which union recruiters wait outside a workplace to meet the workers as they change shifts.

cold deck (gambling) aka *cooler*: specially presorted deck of cards which will be substituted for the legitimate deck at a propitious moment during the play.

cold launch (milit) system proposed for launching a missile without igniting fuel but by using low pressure gas which leaves the launcher itself intact. The rocket ignites once it has cleared the launch site. This system is incorporated in, inter alia, the MX 'peacekeeper' missile.

cold player (gambling) a player on a losing streak.

cold ship (milit) aka *dead ship*: a ship without power.

collar *v* (police/US) to arrest.

collarette (marketing) a card punched with a die-cut hole which fits around the neck of a bottle and carries some advertising copy, news of a free gift, or similar promotional material.

collar the bowling (sport) for a cricketer to knock the opposition bowlers all over the field.

collateral damage (milit) civilian casualties caused by bombing.

colonise *v* (pols/US) the placing of political supporters in such areas as where their votes will be most useful. The opposite of gerrymandering, no longer feasible, whereby the people are taken to the areas, rather than attempting to fit the optimum areas around your strongest areas of support.

CO lot *n* (police) Metropolitan policemen's reference to the Special Patrol Group, who carried CO (Commissioner's Office) on their shoulder straps, where normal police exhibit the letter identifying their division.

colour (press) background facts, information, material that lends some brightness to the monochrome relentlessness of basic facts and figures.

colour (science) in nuclear physics, referring to the three hypothetical quantum states which combine to produce the strong force that binds quarks. From the idea of assuming three basic colours – red, yellow and blue, for the three basic quarks, then when they combine, they produce white, representative of the neutralised state of the perfect combined quark. (cf: *flavour, quark*).

colouration (pols/US) the ideological identification of a politician based on his/her past record of statements, votes for key bills, etc. The political position thus shown may have little to do with a man's actual extra-political point of view, but is based on that vital characteristic of all of his calling: expediency.

colourcaster (TV) background commentator, often a retired sports celebrity, who backs up the play-by-play commentators with reminiscence, biographical details, etc which enliven the basic facts of the sport.

colour field painting (art) colour-field painters replace tonal contrasts and brushwork by solid areas of colour extending, usually, across the canvas from edge to edge to imply that the fields of colour stretch beyond the confines of the canvas on to infinity. aka: *hard-edge painting, stain painting, shaped canvases*.

colour man (TV) aka: *colour announcer, colour babbler* (derog.) broadcaster who adds colour (qv) to commentary or backup/editorial material to news reports.

colour of title (commerce) in real estate, a situation whereby a title appears to be in order, but hides a defect which then emerges to colour the title and cause problems for the sale.

comb *v* (milit) of a ship, to turn into line of the tracks of an approaching torpedo in an attempt to avoid being hit.

combat loading (milit) loading a transport vehicle for the best tactical requirements, regardless of the volume of the load. (cf: *administrative loading*).

combat radius (milit) the distance an aircraft can fly, be of effective use in combat, and return safely to base.

combi (aerospace) an interchangeable passenger or freight aircraft.

combine paintings (art) Robert Rauschenberg's description of those of his own works that incorporate non-art objects with traditional pigments; such paintings are the logical and extreme extension of Cubist collages, stretching the accepted convention of the easel picture to its breaking point.

combined print (movies) print in which the soundtrack and pictures have been 'married' to produce the standard print which will be shown in the cinemas.

come-along *n* (milit) in USN the fairing that covers the deck and makes it secure for storing aircraft, vehicles, etc.

comebacker (sport) in baseball, a ball hit directly back along the ground from the batter towards the pitcher.

come-back money (gambling) money bet with bookies away from the track; the bookies then take it to the track where they bet it again in the hope of changing the odds on particular horses.

come back Tuesday (theatre) aka: *don't call us, we'll call you*: clichéd pieces of pseudo-friendly advice from theatrical directors and management to hopefuls; they all mean 'go away'.

come from (new therapies) usu. 'where are you coming from?' or 'where I am coming from', etc: the exposition of one's mental attitudes, philosophies, way of life, background to stated opinions, all in all an opportunity to sound off at length about the niceties of one's self-image.

come on (theatre/US) a mediocre actor whose attempt at performing is limited to walking on and possibly around the stage. Acting, as such, is not part of his/her repertoire.

come-out (gambling) the first throw of the dice after a shooter has named the point he is chasing.

come up with the rations (milit) British Army: those medals that are so common that they might have been given out at mealtimes, rather than actually and meritoriously earned.

come your cocoa (police) aka: *come your fat, come your lot*: various references to ejaculation, excretion and vomiting all of which mean to make a full confession.

comint (intelligence) (abbrev) *comm*unications *int*elligence: information derived from satellites, monitoring foreign radio and other broadcast media, listening in to foreign codes and telephone calls, etc. (cf: *elint, humint, sigint*)

command economy (pols/econ) an economy that is centrally planned and managed with targets imposed from above. Inflexible, bureaucratic. Once the norm in socialist states but recently they have achieved a small degree of flexibility. Command economies are imposed on all countries, irrespective of ideology, during an emergency, ie: war.

commandism (pols) the concentration of power at the centre. (cf: *command economy*)

commercials (sex) all usages by homosexual prostitutes:
1. tired old excuses which no-one believes to justify this choice of occupation.
2. a personal build up to attract clients.

3. advertising in those papers and magazines that will accept the copy to increase trade.

commission (finance) aka: *round turn*: the one-time fee charged by a broker to a customer when a position is liquidated whether by offset or delivery.

Committee of the Whole House (pols/UK) the Speaker leaves his chair, the mace is placed beneath the table and the house acts as a Committee under the chairmanship of the Chairman of Ways and Means. On this occasion only can a member speak more than once in a debate.

common learnings (educ) such education as it is considered should be the common experience of all pupils.

common site picketing (indust relats/US) the picketing of a subcontractor at a construction site by members of a union whose dispute is essentially with the main contractor.

communicated authenticity (new therapies) longhand for genuineness.

comp (press) (abbrev) compositor: the man who actually sets up the metal type on the stone (qv).

comp (theatre) (abbrev) complimentary: free tickets. (cf: *paper, orders*)

comp (music) in jazz, to play an accompaniment, esp. with irregular rhythmic chords.

comp (advert) (abbrev) comprehensive: a preliminary version of the artwork, giving the basic look of the ad. Thus *rough comp*: absolutely basic; *tight comp*: nearer the finished product.

Company *n* (espionage) euphemism for the CIA (Central Intelligence Agency).

comparability (indust relats) a theoretical means of working out pay levels by comparing one job with another. Easy to propose, almost impossible to carry out efficiently.

comparative spot (advert) a TV commercial which compares the client's product with that of a rival, invariably to the advantage of the one being touted.

compartmentalisation (govt) the restriction of knowledge (esp. of military or scientific developments) to the various 'compartments' in which this knowledge was being developed, giving only a very few people access to the overall picture; a participant should know sufficient to perform his job, but nothing extra.

compartmentalised (espionage) a method of running agents whereby each one is told exactly what he requires to discover for efficient working and nothing more. (cf: *need-to-know*).

compatible (computers) the ability of one computer to deal with material intended and designed for another: programs, peripherals, add-ons, etc. (qqv).

competitive parity (marketing) a method of setting the advertising budget by matching it to that of the opposition.

C

compiler (computer) a specialised program that translates the source (qv) program into a code that the computer can understand.

complimentary play (gambling) a gambling session indulged in by a casino manager in a rival casino, or by a professional gambler or racketeer as a gesture of friendship – since it is assumed he will lose money – to the casino bosses.

compo (milit) (abbrev) composite rations, as issued to British soldiers on manoeuvres or in battle. Supposedly of ideal nutritive value.

compositing the resolution (trades unions) collecting a variety of similar resolutions put forward for the annual conference and grouping them together to make one composite resolution to save time.

compound (horse-racing) for a horse to fail to keep up its speed and blow up during the race.

compound labour (pols) aka *complex labour*: skilled, especially trained labour. Such skills justify wages differentials on the principle of 'to each according to his work'.

comsymp (pols) (abbrev) Communist sympathiser: coined during the McCarthy era of early 1950s by ultra-right winger John Birch to brand fellow travellers. Reasonably rare these days, but still popular with the Right.

con (crime) the scheme of a telephone con-man whereby he sells tickets in the name of a legitimate sponsor, but pockets the subscriptions himself.

con (theatre) to memorise a role.

con (milit) aka *conn*: naval use meaning to direct the course of the vessel by giving specific orders to the helmsman who controls the wheel. USN uses *to have the con*: to be in control of the course.

con (TV) 'Star Trek' fans' convention.

concentrator (computers) a method of combining data from several local phone lines and sending it all down one special high speed data line and thus saving money when communicating with a distant and otherwise costly computer data bank.

concept tests (marketing) the use of a psychological testing panel to decide whether the concept of a product is feasible, prior even to deciding whether there is any market for that product.

concept video (TV/rock music) a promotional video linked to the idea behind an album or a song rather than simply pictures of its performer in concert or in the studio.

conceptual art (art) aka: *con art, idea art, impossible art, documentary art, begriff kunst, post-object art, anti-object art, dematerialised art, blind man's art, head art, project art*. an international idiom of the avant garde, fashionable in late 1960s/early 1970s which centred on its giving low priority to the art work as a physical object since that merely emphasised the artist's physical ability rather than his mental resources. Their aim was for a 'dematerialised art' which would produce works that were physical but not directly available to the human senses, eg: inert gases detectable only via scientific instruments.

conceptual difficulties (sociol) euphemism for stupidity both on an individual or, referring to local government decisions etc, on an organisational level.

concerti (crime) aka: *consigia*: intra-family (qv) courts for members of the US Mafia to sort out their mutual problems, punish offences, etc.

concessional exports (pols) exports of grain and similar vital commodities for which the recipient countries never pay. In effect consumer propaganda.

concrete art (art) term introduced to replace 'abstract', the latter being considered as unsatisfactory since it implied a separation from reality. The concrete artist does not abstract from nature, he constructs from the given elements of natural phenomena, 'the concretion of the creative spirit'.

concrete labour (pols) work that has actually been performed.

concrete poetry (poetry) aka: *audiovisual texts, constellations, evident poetry, kinetic poetry, machine poetry, objective poetry, optical poetry, poem paintings, poetry of surface, popcrete, process texts, publit, semiotic poetry, visual texts, word art*, the concrete poet arranges elements freely across a surface rather than restricting himself to linear syntax.

concurrency (aerospace) the meeting together of a number of scientific, technological, training and allied experts at a given time so as to consult together and if possibly accelerate their mutual progress towards a successful development of a given programme.

conditionality (govt) rules established by the International Monetary Fund to control those countries who need its aid but appear to be moving out of line: quite simply it is made clear that unless the government in question conducts itself in such a way that the IMF sees fit, there will be no loan.

condominium (govt) barbarism perpetrated by Henry Kissinger, apparently attempting to use a literal Latin translation to imply the ideas of the USSR and US linking together to rule as one: the word in fact is more usually known to describe a large co-operatively owned apartment house.

cone (movies) cone shaped light for soft lighting effects.

confab (movies) a conference. (cf: *take a meeting*)

conference (pols) the use of *conference*, bereft of definite or indefinite articles, appears to imply some greater statement of collective force than would the normal grammar. Much used by trade union and Labour party annual conference statements.

configuration (computer) the collection of parts that make up a computer system, and the way that they are arranged.

configuration management (aerospace/management) the management discipline and technology required for the building and design of such high-quality and precision products as spacecraft. Standards of excellence and customer satisfaction must be far greater than in a normal project and the configuration of the project – the way parts are made and put together on many and complex levels – must be precise and acceptable.

conflict spectrum (milit) all levels of hostility: from the first pre-crisis wrangling and sabre-rattling, through to full scale 1st and 2nd strike nuclear exchange.

conformer (indust relats) member of a piece work group who accepts the various fiddles that are established by the rest of the group. The conformity is to the group, not to the employer. Those who refuse to conform are classified, with the same irony, as *job spoilers*.

confrontation (sociol) the action of facing someone so as to describe their own behaviour and its likely effects in order to evoke a response from them. A particular use of confrontation is to bring home to alcoholics or drug addicts the reality of their situation.

conga (airlines) a chain of snow clearing vehicles – snow ploughs in a line – led by a high speed runway clearer.

connection (drugs) a supplier of narcotics; *to make a connection*: to find the dealer and buy drugs from him; thus *connection money*: money for drugs.

connectivity (milit) the making sure by nuclear planners that when a war actually begins, all plans and personnel will link up and work as required and intended.

connector conspiracy (computers) the alleged tendency of manufacturers to make sure that all their new products fail to connect with their previous ones, thus ensuring that the consumer must either start from scratch or buy expensive *interface* (qv) devices – all of which costs money.

conquest sales (commerce) sales that capture customers who had previously bought from a rival.

consciousness I, II, III (sociol) coined by Charles A Reich in his 1970 best-seller *The Greening of America*: I: the self-made man with 'traditional American' values; II: the verbal, college educated media man, representing the values of 20th century US society; III: what used to be called 'the alternative society' and 'youth culture'. Reich espoused con III with all the enthusiasm of the ageing convert. Time has shattered the myth, although one can see

certain parallels in another futurologist, Alvin Toffler, whose *The Third Wave* (1980) bears certain similarities, although from a very different standpoint.

consciousness raising (sociol) essentially the gaining of greater awareness of one's own position, one's needs, one's potential as a human being, but in fact swiftly co-opted by the women's movement to the exclusion of all else. Thus a risen consciousness means the fulfillment of one's true feminity and is not open for use by other groups.

conservatism (tech, govt) the philosophy of the Atomic Energy Commission (US) which claimed, in 1971 that although there might be some possible gaps in its understanding of reactor safety, in practice, the AEC's basic conservatism when designing and building the reactors would automatically ensure that no such problems would arise.

consideration (stock market) the cost of a purchase before adding expenses, calculated by multiplying the amount of stock or number of shares by the cost per unit.

consiglieri (crime) in US Mafia, the counsellor/advisor to the capo (qv) who advises on policy rather than takes part in any fighting.

consolidate (indust relats) to add the bonus and any other extra payments into the basic rates, so that this larger sum is that on which overtime (which multiplies the basic wage) is based.

constant wear garment (aerospace) a cross between ski-pants and long underwear, used by astronauts during their flights to and from the moon and while they are inside the artificial atmosphere of the capsule.

constipation (computers) see: *deadlock*

constructive dismissal (indust relats) a form of unfair dismissal when an employee, who has ostensibly left his job voluntarily, has in fact been forced out by management activity aimed to make his continued position untenable.

constructivism (theatre/art) the theatrical concept of using mechanical structures in theatrical settings, the theatrical parallel to industrial technique, demanding the exclusion of all useless decoration and the precise functional organisation of the stage; the movement had its heyday in the first flush of the Russian Revolution, the 1920s. Constructivist art was pioneered in Moscow in 1920 by Naum Gabo and later by the Hungarian Moholy-Nagy. It was the artistic equivalent of love of industry expressed in its stage counterpart.

consumer demand analysis (econ) the analysis by a government of what exactly it is that the people want.

consumer press (rock business) the specialist publications dealing with rock music and its ancillaries.

contact (aerospace) the state of flying within visual sight of the surface of the earth.

contact (milit) exchanging fire with hostile forces.

contact magazine (sex) a magazine where those seeking particular sexual pleasures can place advertisements or find others who are putting themselves on offer; often used by prostitutes for the legal advertisement of their services.

container premium (marketing) the use of the package itself – a fancy jar, a special re-usable container – as the marketing premium (qv) rather than offering something for which the consumer must apply, send box-tops, etc.

containment (pols) a policy, essentially defensive, of containing the expansion of a hostile power or its ideology beyond the boundaries that it has already established; at its inception containment implied a degree of positive opposition to such expansion, today it has declined into a wary maintenance of the status quo and an ineffectual theory in the face of an Afghanistan invasion.

contaminated runway (aerospace) a runway covered by snow, sludge, soil, sand, solid objects or anything that might hinder a safe landing.

contango (stock market) the percentage which a buyer of stock pays to the seller to postpone transfer to the next or future settling day. *Contango day*: a day on which all transactions of a merely speculative nature are held over for another fortnight.

continental seating (theatre) seating arranged without a centre aisle, but with sufficient space between the rows of seats to permit easy movement in and out.

contingency management (business) the ability of an executive to vary his attitudes and methods as to the task, the personalities, the technology and whatever other variables each different task brings with it. In short, a capacity for flexibility in handling various situations.

continuing education (educ) any form of education that continues after the compulsory formal education finishes (other than universities, colleges, etc): night schools, etc.

continuity (TV, movies, radio)
1. (TV, movies) the careful maintenance of all details from scene to scene – the right clothes, arrangement of furniture, etc – made more difficult since scenes are rarely shot in consecutive order of the script.
2. (radio) a series of linking announcements that maintain the flow of a radio broadcast.

continuity series (advertising) a promotion in which a number of products are sold and delivered over a period: a set of books, a series of records, etc.

contour-chasing (aerospace) flying close to the ground and following the shifting contours of the scenery.

contra-account (business) an account kept by a firm that both buys and sells from and to the same client so that in effect the transactions cancel each other out and exist only as paper entries.

contract (police) the hiring of a professional killer to murder a specific target.

contract (pols/US) an agreement to deliver a particular political favour; despite the parallel with the criminal use (qv), it is felt that political contracts are no longer especially corrupt.

contract (commodities) aka: *cars, lots*: each unit of trading in a specific futures instrument. The use of *car* stems from the time when most commodities (in US) were marketed at the major railheads and thus the commodity Exchanges fixed the contract size at whatever of that commodity would fit into a railway wagon, or 'car'.

contract agents (espionage) operatives recruited in the field by a regular intelligence agent who runs them himself without their ever meeting anyone else from the agency. He issues their orders and pays their wages, even though both orders and funds will come from higher ranking officers. Contract agents are short-term employees and are listed on no files.

contract in or out *v* (indust relats) legalities applied to trades union members who wish to give a subscription to the Labour Party. In essence members are 'in' unless they make a specific commitment 'out'.

contraction (econ) socialist governments' procurement of agricultural products from collective and, if they exist, private farms.

contract month (finance) the month in which futures contracts may be satisfied by making or accepting a delivery.

control (espionage) a rank beneath Case Officer (qv) and Handler (qv) in the chain of command of a clandestine operation.

controlled counterforce war (milit) a nuclear attack which will obliterate the enemy's troops but leave his cities and civilians unharmed. (cf: *counterforce*).

CONUS (milit) (abbrev) continental US.

conventional weapons (milit) weapons that have been sanctioned by agreement or usage and which conform to standard agreements on their acceptability; all weapons other than nuclear devices.

convergence *n* (govt) (abbrev): economic convergence: in the Common Market (EEC) the allying of all member countries but one against that errant one.

convergence theory (soc wk) the concept that in advanced industrial societies common patterns of behaviour emerge, which patterns approve the existence and pursuit of social welfare.

convergence thesis (pols) centrist (qv) theory that capitalism and socialism are each losing their more extreme aspects and gradually drawing together. Socialists reject this as merely an example of the capitalists attempting to worm their way into their ertswhile enemies' confidences as their own system, as confidently predicted, starts to collapse in earnest.

conversational *a* (computer) aka: *interactive*: a mode of operation in which the computer responds to each input from the user – vaguely similar to inter-human conversation.

convertible (stock market) a security of one corporation which can be converted to a security of another.

cook *v* (science) to make radioactive.

cookie (movies) (abbrev) cokuloris (qv).

cookies (sex) some sought after prize in the cosmos of the black pimp; either sexual or financial preferment.

cookie pusher (pols/US) a diplomat whose career is based more on the social niceties than the actual work of foreign relations; from the idea of exquisite young men sitting around passing cakes and making epigrams.

cook-off (milit) the spontaneous firing of a round of ordnance when the heat around a gun's breech sets it off.

cool (music) in jazz, relaxed, unemotional, a state to be desired and attained by those who favour such music.

cool art (art) a variety of styles of an art that exhibit detachment, rationality, austerity. Cool art is abstract, geometric with sharply defined forms of contours, comprising repetitive structures or units. There is much emphasis on precision and impeccability of execution.

cooler (medic) hospital morgue.

cool out (pols) in the jargon of Argentina's interrogators: to kill.

coop *v* (police/US) for an officer to sleep while on duty; such illicit rests are taken in motel rooms, etc.

cooper up *v* (business) from the trade of cooper, or barrel-maker, who uses a number of pieces to make his finished product: to take all the facets of a proposition and use one's own skills to make it into a feasible project.

co-op mix (pols) home-made bombs used in N. Ireland; so called from the availability of most of the materials at the local supermarket.

co-opt (pols) to absorb, to persuade into one's own ranks; tends to be used derogatively of attempts by far left activists to take over less virulent although still essentially socialist parties and individuals.

cop *v* (sex) the action of a black pimp in enrolling a fresh woman amongst his string of prostitutes.

cop (drugs) to buy drugs, usually in form *cop for* . . . (name of drug).

cop *v* (police) to accept a bribe.

cop and blow (sex) aka: *short-money game*: the exploitation by a black pimp of a woman to the greatest extent possible over a short period once he realises that she has little long-term future on his string.

copy *v* (govt) to send out copies; thus an individual is *copied* when he is sent a memo.

copy (press) the written 'story' that a reporter writes, an editor edits and the newspaper prints.

copy (advert)
1. a carbon copy, or any facsimile.
2. the words of an advertisement, rather than the pictures, the 'art' or 'graphics' (qqv).
3. the manuscript that goes off to the printer.
4. a complete advertisement (incl. the artwork) that is sent off to a printer.

copy strategy (advert) the 'message' of an advertisement and how best to get it across.

copy tests (advert) research to assess and improve one's current campaign – taking copy to mean the whole advertisement.

core curriculum (educ) an integrated programme which cuts across the divisions that make up traditional subjects.

core time (indust relats) that time of the working day, especially relevant to those firms where the work day is staggered, when all employees are present at the factory or office.

Corgi and Bess (TV/UK) commercial TV nickname for the Queen's annual Christmas TV broadcast.

coriolis effect (aerospace) named for its discoverer, Gaspard G. de Coriolis (1792–1843): the physiological effects upon a person moving in a rotating system, the complete loss of orientation caused by the rapid rotation of astronauts during parts of their flight.

corker (gambling) an unusual gambler – possibly good or bad.

corker (theatre) an actor who spoils a performance.

corned beef (prison/UK) aka: *bully beef*: the chief officer.

corner (stock market)
1. to secure such complete control of a commodity or security as to control its price at will.
2. to obtain more contracts requiring the delivery of commodities or securities than there are in existence such commodities or securities.
3. speculation whereby one obtains the whole of a security or commodity so as to force the market to accept one's own dictation of prices.

corner *v* (crime)
1. the selling of junk under the pretence of it being good, but stolen property.
2. selling stolen property to an honest, but gullible tradesman; just as they have passed over the cash, in comes the 'police' (actually the con-man's friend) who confiscates the goods and disappears, threatening the worst. Another 'friend' appears, promising to square the police

– for yet more money. (2) aka *lawing*. Sometimes a fake 'solicitor' is brought along, to blind the victim with legal complexities, and make sure he never tries to contact any real policemen.

corner-man (police) con-man, from use of the corner (qv).

corn-hog ratio (econ/US) a method whereby US farmers work out whether it is more profitable that year to sell their hogs or the corn that is used to help feed them. Based on the assumption that 11.5 bushels of corn are needed to put 100lb on a hog. The decision depends on the current price when that of 100 lb of live hog is divided by the price of 1 bushel of corn.

corporate metabolism (business) from 'metabolism': the consumption or 'burning' of food or fuel to maintain or replace living cells in the body: thus in a corporation the metabolism is the overall sum of everything that all employees – of every rank – contribute to 'fuelling' the organism (the corporation) and maintaining it in its accustomed style, values and professional and personal life.

corporate woodwork (business) all the bits and pieces that make a corporation work, its essential fixtures and fittings – policy, procedure, organisation, rules and regulations, PR, advertising, etc – everything, in fact other than its product and personnel that goes to create the overall image both internally and in customers' and competitors' eyes.

corporatism (pols) the concept of absorbing the business style of a corporation into the running of a state; the major example of this was Mussolini's Fascist Italy.

corpse *v* (theatre/UK) to forget lines, often by getting an on-stage fit of giggles.

corpsman (milit) a member of the US Naval Hospital Corps who provide medical assistance to USN and USMC.

correct *v* (pols) the concept of re-education that tends to follow speedily on successful revolutions as in Vietnam, Iran, etc.

corridor bashing (milit) the saturation bombing of hostile airfields, lines of communication and vital facilities.

corridor discussion (indust relats) off the record but vital part of wages bargaining when the leaders of both sides of the dispute can talk frankly 'in the corridor', or at least away from the main body of discussion, and admit to the realities of the situation – the actual compromises that can be made, and those that cannot be accepted, thus cutting through much of the rhetoric and bombast that rival supporters require to be permitted.

corset (finance) a restriction placed on British banks to control the money supply by reducing the profits on interest bearing deposits.

corvée (milit) French Foreign Legion: fatigue duties.

cosche (crime) in the Italian Mafia: a cell, into which the organisation is divided. From *cosca*: an artichoke, a plant with one heart surrounded by many tough and tightly gathered leaves.

cosmetic injury (sport) any injury that requires facial sutures.

cosmic (milit) NATO classification of material as top secret.

cosmopolitanism (pols) 'A reactionary, anti-patriotic, bourgeois outlook on things, hypocritically regarding the whole world as one's fatherland, denying the value of national culture, rejecting the rights of nations to independent existence . . . the ideology of US imperialism aspiring to world domination' (*Dictionary of the Russian Language*). Used of any manifestation in/out of Soviet world that might strengthen the US in any way. A useful theory that permits Soviets to ally with any ultra-nationalist groups (usually right wing and reactionary), claiming them as fellow bulwarks against US expansion. Cosmopolitanism also doubles as a means of attacking the Jews, who are deemed to reject Russia as their unique saviour.

cost-benefit (econ) an analysis which assesses the relationship of the actual cost of a project to the value of social and other benefits accruing or not on its completion.

cost-push inflation (econ) inflation in which rising costs of labour and production push up prices even when demand has not increased. (cf: *demand-pull inflation*).

costume *a* (theatre) *costume dramas* imply plays or films set in any era but the present in which the costumes, which any production demands by virtue of being acted, actually pertain to 'dressing up' rather than simply modern dress.

cottage (sex) a public lavatory frequented by homosexuals for assignations and sex.

cough and a spit (theatre) aka: *two lines and a spit* an easy, short part.

counselling (public relations) telling a client what he should best do for the optimum personal and corporate image.

counter (movies) the direction to an actor telling him/her to put more of themselves in front of the camera, or to allow space for another actor or object to be filmed.

counter-advertising (advert) advertisements specially written/designed to refute the claims of other advertisements broadcast or published by those groups who disapprove of the messages being put out by those against whom they are campaigning; eg: ecologists vs General Motors.

counterforce (milit) a nuclear strike against the enemy's weapons rather than at his centres of population. Thus *counterforce weapons, counter-*

force option, counterforce strike. (cf: countervalue).

counter trade (pols) aka: *revenge barter*: a deal where the importer forces the exporter to take his payments all or in part in goods rather than sacrifice his foreign exchange. Usually limited to 30% of the deal but can be 100%. Often forced on the West when trading with Warsaw Pact countries. To service this flood of unwanted goods a number of brokers, operating in Switzerland, have emerged to sell them off at a discount.

Countervailing Strategy (milit) a nuclear strategy developed in the Carter Administration (1976–80) that was to make any hostile aggression worthless to its perpetrator, since the US would guarantee a revenge strike of such utter devastation that the initial blow would be rendered pointless.

countervalue (milit) a nuclear strike against the enemy's cities. Thus *countervalue weapons, countervalue option, countervalue strike*. (cf. *counter force*)

count out of the house (pols/UK) the adjournment of the House of Commons when the Speaker can count less than 40 members present and thus a quorum for voting is not present.

country club at the top (management) the 'not what you know but who you know' of corporate management; exemplified by continuing to pay full salary to a board member even after he had been removed from the firm – often in the guise of a 'consultant'.

country damaged (commerce) damaged in the country of origin, prior to the goods being imported.

coup-de-bambon (milit) French Foreign Legion: a sudden physical or mental collapse with no apparent cause.

coupling (milit) usually known as strategic coupling: the linking of low-level conflict – Soviet/Warsaw Pact aggression in Europe – to US use of strategic nuclear weapons.

coupling up (indust relats) overlapping shifts in order to keep the factory's productivity moving without a break. Those employees involved in such overlaps are eligible for handover pay.

coupon (stock market) the promise to pay interest when it falls due; a printed form attached to a bond in coupon form and detached and submitted for payment at the correct time.

coupon candidate (pols/UK) a candidate who has been given the recommendation of his/her party leader. Coined by H. H. Asquith at the election of 1918.

courtesy announcement (TV) the reminder broadcast a few minutes after a channel has ceased its nightly programmes to tell viewers to switch off their sets.

courtesy of the profession (theatre/US) aka: *on

your card* (UK): free admission to theatres on production of an Equity card.

co-vary (sociol) a gratuitous amplification of the simple *vary* with no special or extra meaning, but beloved, like similar intensifiers, by the jargon coiners who are drawn to sociology.

cover *v* (TV/US) the replacement of one picture by another on the TV screen; eg: of a news anchorman by a reporter, or the reporter by a film clip, etc.

cover (finance) the purchase of sale of futures to offset a previously established long or short (qqv) position.

cover *v* (movies) for one actor to obscure another from the camera lens.

cover *v* (theatre) to understudy.

cover *n a* (espionage) a protective disguise taken on by an agent both to confuse others and infiltrate or survey a target, and to escape detection from hostile agents or forces.

cover *n* (milit) in USMC, any form of headgear worn by a Marine.

coverage (espionage) the putting in any area of a representative or representatives (up to a whole office of agents) of the CIA denotes that the area in question has been 'covered'.

Cover All *n* (milit) US code: converted Boeing 707 that acts as SAC (qv) flying command post in case of nuclear war. These planes patrol in 8 hr. shifts, covering the earth fr. 30,000'. (cf: *looking glass*).

covert *a* (espionage) any form of secret activity, often also illegal (either in US or abroad) taken for political, economic or social reasons to further the various aims of the CIA. The ostensible aim, and justification for covert operations/ actions is to influence those targeted in favour of US foreign policy. (cf: *destabilisation*).

cow (advert) the rubber based gum used for sticking paper to paper boards, a staple of advertising layout; not made of cows, but by the Cow Proofing Company, of Slough, Bucks.

cowabunga! (sport) Australian surfers' shout of elation as they surf down a superb wave.

cowboy (indust relats/US) aka *rate-buster*: one who ignores that rate (usually slower than necessary) set by his fellow piece-workers, but actually works sufficiently hard to make far more money than they do.

cowboy (milit) the term in N. Ireland for anyone who becomes involved with a sectarian gang.

cowcatcher *n* (radio/US) an advertisement inserted on a sponsor's programme which features one of the sponsor's products that is not being generally featured on that show. (cf: *hitchhike*).

cow-shot (sport) in cricket, a swipe across a straight, or any other ball, that with more luck than judgement, sends it off towards the legside boundary. (cf: *agricultural*).

cow sociology (indust relats) derogatory assessment of management experts' attempts to

C

bring out the 'human' side of work, ie, to lull the workforce into a sense of complacent passivity.

CPM (advert, marketing, etc) (abbrev) cost per thousand (where M = Latin for 1000). The estimated cost for the advertiser in reaching each 1000 houses through one of the media.

crab *n* (commerce) in the retail book trade, a book on sale or return that is returned, unsold, to the publisher.

crab *v* (TV, movies) to move a camera or a microphone sideways. (cf: *dolly*).

crab *n* (milit) a computer program used by the USAF for the flying and guidance of the F–16 fighter. This program frees the pilot's hands for weapons control; all other functions regarding direction, locking on to target, etc are 'crabbed' by the computer.

crac (milit) aka: *petto-fuori* French Foreign Legion: lit trans Fr./Ital: 'a loud fart', a brave, devil-may-care fighter. (cf: *gung ho*)

crackback (sport) an outlawed tackle in US football in which a pass-receiver blocks a linebacker or defensive back by smashing into him at knee level. A major cause of injuries, some of them permanent. (cf: *blindside*)

crack shorts *v* (crime/US) to break into (crack) automobiles (shorts).

crane *n* (TV) large, wheeled TV camera-mounting for giving the greatest variety of movement to a studio camera.

crane shot (TV, movies) a high angle shot in which the camera moves vertically or laterally while mounted on a crane (qv).

crap out (milit) aka: *goof off, flake out, fuck off*: USMC term for loafing around, or acting lazily.

crapule (milit) French Foreign Legion: a man who eats or drinks to excess.

crash *n* (theatre) an effect involving a sudden 'crash': breaking glass, slamming doors etc.

crash (computer) any greater or lesser failure of the system. From *head crash*: the accumulation of even a tiny amount (a few microns) of dust between the read/write head of the computer and the disc could destroy the information on that disc. The head had thus 'crashed'. (cf: *down*). Also used tr.: 'X just crashed the system'.

crash *v* (police/UK) write off or cancel enquiries into a complaint or a crime.

crash *v* (TV) desperately hurried work against a deadline; with the implication that the piece in question may in fact not meet that deadline.

crashworthiness (airlines) a plane's ability to withstand a crash and to protect the passengers from impact, fire and smoke.

cravata (milit) French Foreign Legion: a braggart.

crawl *n* (TV) the list of closing titles or credits, which 'crawls' across or up the screen. (cf. *creeping title*)

crawler way (aerospace) specially constructed roadway for moving heavy rockets or other heavy equipment from the construction sight to the launching pad.

crawling peg (econ) an economic system whereby the exchange rate can be frequently and marginally adjusted; used for international money markets, a basic credo of monetarism (qv).

creak *v* (theatre) the play being performed is beginning to seem outdated.

cream *v* (commerce) to steal from your employer in a careful, moderate, regular and ideally undiscovered manner.

cream-puff hitter (sport) in baseball, a weak, ineffective hitter.

creative (advert) working either as a copywriter or an art director rather than on the business or market research side of an agency; a job description, not necessarily a compliment.

creative Marxism (pols) forward thinking, flexible, controversial, constantly changing to suit the times; rather than an ideology which abides religiously by the dogmatic and doctrinaire letter of Marx's 19th century words.

creative strategy (advert) the whole style of a campaign, its theme.

credential *v* (educ/US) to award a certificate of teaching competence; coined in California where local teachers, claiming that the normal usage of 'certify' smeared them with madness, demanded a soothing neologism. Can be amplified to *credential the relevant competencies* and may extend outside education to any area where diplomas, certificates, etc are issued.

credibility (milit) the concept of making an enemy believe that you mean what you say, will do what you threaten, and to reassure an ally that you will do what you promise. *credible deterrent*: a weapons system (de facto nuclear) which the enemy believe you are ready and willing to use. (cf: *capability, credibility gap*)

credibility gap (govt) coined during the Vietnam War to underline the American public's growing inability to take the statements (as opposed to the actions) of the Johnson Administration at face value. An internal use of *credibility*, rather than the external, military one.

credits (movies) a list attached to a film – in brief at the start and at greater length at the conclusion – which names the actors, the technicians and the financiers involved in making that film.

credit squeeze (econ) a governmental method of clamping down on inflation by raising the bank rate, therefore making 'dearer' money (loans costing more in interest) and thus cutting down overdrafts, hire purchase agreements and similar inflatory borrowing and lending.

Creek Misty (milit) airborne reconnaissance flights carried out by NATO forces over Europe.

creep *n* (TV) the slight but gradual decline of any

electronic equipment away from its optimum performance standards.

creep (science) the continuous deformation of any material under operational stress, esp. at high temperatures.

creeper (sex) crooked homosexual hustlers (qv) who 'creep up' on clients to defraud them of their money.

creeper (sport) in cricket, a ball that 'creeps' along the ground, or at least keeps low after pitching in front of the stumps.

creepie peepie (TV) a hand-held TV camera, often used for live-action close-ups of sports.

creeping crud (new therapies) in Theta rebirthing (qv) the primal panic that is supposedly experienced due to the recalling of the sensations and memories of life in the womb; this is intensified by the rebirthing process being carried out immersed in 99°F water and might just stem from the fear in some people of being drowned.

creeping title (movies) aka: *roller title*: a title which 'rolls' up or across the scene at reading pace. (cf: *crawl*).

creepy weepy (publishing) a genre of popular fiction combining gothic horror with romantic melodrama. (cf: *bodice rippers, sweet savagery*).

crime *v* (milit) in British army, to put on punishment roster.

crimp *v* (gambling) to bend one or more cards in a deck so that a cheat will be able to cut the deck as he wishes, or to know that an innocent player will be cutting the deck at that same desired card.

crisis communications management (public relations) to relieve the pressure on a corporation or public individual when a massive blunder has been made which will ruin their image. The PR's job is not to undo the blunder, but to persuade the public of a more favourable perception of their client's role concerning it.

crisis intervention (soc wk) the involvement of a social worker with a client who is suffering a breakdown of adequate coping mechanisms, which problem entails great vulnerability and conflict. Early and informed intervention can have long-term beneficial effects.

crisis management (milit) coined after the Cuban Missile Crisis, 1961, by Robert McNamara, US Secy. of State 'there is no longer any such thing as strategy, only crisis management'. The concept that foreign relations is in essence a process of keeping such international crises that occur beneath such a point that actual conflict might be inevitable.

crisis theory (soc wk)
1. *v* work at speed, dealing with succession of urgent problems.
2. a comparatively long phase in psychological development, i.e. 'midlife crisis'.
3. see *crisis intervention*.

crispener (video) an electronic device for increasing the horizontal resolution of a picture.

crit (science, milit) (abbrev) critical:
1. (nuclear reactor) maintaining a self sustaining chain reaction; *to go critical*: to reach the critical stage.
2. (milit) the minimum mass or size of fissile material required to create a chain reaction in a nuclear weapon.

criteria-cued (sociol) the state of following critical criteria in such a way that one follows automatically and deliberately on from one criterion to the next. 'Cued' implies that preparedness and deliberateness.

crock (computer)
1. an awkward feature of programming technique that should be made clearer.
2. a programming technique that works acceptably but which is prone to failure at the least disturbance.
3. a tightly woven, almost completely unmodifiable structure.

crock (medic/US) a patient who complains long and often of multiple symptoms, many of which are pure hypochondria and all of which are far out of proportion to the actual seriousness of his illness.

crock in *v* (radio/UK) to send in one's story over the phone, using 'croc(odile)' clips which can cut into a phone line and thus transfer the material on tape through the public lines onto another phone linked into a tape recorder.

cross *v* (stock market) to make purchase or sale transactions in the same amount of the same securities which are matched within the broker's office and thus obviate the need to use jobbers (qv) or the Settlement Dept.

cross assembler (computer) used on one computer for the preparation of an object code (qv) which can be used on another. Eg: using a sophisticated, large machine to prepare a program for use on a microcomputer.

cross elasticity of demand (marketing) a means of determining the sensitivity of demand to competitive price changes by dividing the proportional change in sales 'demand' of one product by the proportional change in the price of another.

crosses (drugs) benzedrine tablets, from the crosses marked on them.

cross head (press) a centred subhead in the text, used to break up long columns of text and often created by taking one sensational word or phrase from the adjacent paragraphs.

crossover *n a v* (rock business) music that crosses over from one specialised area to another. Often used of black stars appealing to white fans, but also of country-and-western attracting a pop audience, etc.

crossover (movies) a movie that can attract a number of different specialist audiences. *cross* *over star*: a performer who can attain the same multiple success.

crossover vote (pols/US) the concept that in the primary elections some voters who will in fact vote for the party of their fundamental allegiance on national polling day, will for some mischievous reason vote against their own party at this earlier stage. A theory somewhat disputed but popular among politicians who show up poorly in primary contests.

cross ownership (business) the ownership by a corporation of more than one media outlet – TV or radio stations or newspapers.

crossroader (gambling) an itinerant card sharp who moves across the country in search of new victims for his cheating skills.

cross-roughing (govt/US) aka: *cross ruffing* (ex: bridge use 'to trump'): to take an idea, rub it against other, possibly opposing ideas, so as to refine and redefine the original concept.

cross talk (video) unwanted breakthrough between parallel channels of a programme chain.

cross trading (business) the business of a shipping line in which it conveys cargo between a variety of foreign ports.

crow (milit) USN usage for the eagle that is attached to an officer's cap. (cf: *bird*).

crows (crime) lookout men who check the street around a game of three-card-monte (qv).

crowsfoot (TV, movies) a three-legged floor brace for a lamp. (cf: *turtle*).

CRT (computers) (abbrev) *c*athode *r*ay *t*ube.

cru (finance) an international monetary unit designed to ease the strain on gold and hard-currency reserves in settling accounts between nations.

crud (milit) in US army, a real or imaginary disease.

crud (science) in nuclear physics, any undesirable residues, impurities that may arise in a system, esp. corrosion deposited on the surfaces of circulating water systems.

crudzine (TV) a poorly produced, badly written fan magazine for those who follow TV's 'Star Trek'.

crufty (computer)
1. poorly built, overly complex. Thus *cruft*: shoddy construction.
2. unpleasant, esp. to the touch; encrusted with some disgusting matter.
3. generally unappealing, unpleasant.
4. *a crufty thing*: anything that fails to fit satisfactorily into an overall plan or system.

cruise (milit) USMC: period of enlistment. *Hitch* (qv) is often used in error, but cruise, with its naval overtones is the only Marine usage.

cruise *v* (sex) for a homosexual hustler to look for clients on the street.

crumb (milit) USMC: a slovenly, dirty person. Thus *crummy* = adj.

crum up (milit) USMC: to tidy up, neaten and clean both a person and his uniform.

crunch (computer)
1. to process, usually in a time consuming or complicated way. An essentially trivial operation that is still painful to perform. (cf: *number cruncher*).
2. *file crunching* to reduce the size of a file by a complex scheme that produces bit (qv) configurations completely unrelated to the original data; the file ends up as the equivalent of a paper document that has been crumpled.

cruncher (milit) (abbrev) gravel cruncher: term used by the Marine Air Corps for those Marines who are assigned to ground duties.

crunchvid (entertain) highlights on film, TV or video of sport, public events, etc. The whole event has been 'crunched' together.

crusher (milit) member of a ship's police. (Used by John Le Carré in his fiction, but generally extended to imply Special Branch or similar clandestine disciplinary group).

crushing (TV) the foreshortening effect on the screen when a telephoto lens is used.

crutches (aerospace) padded and reinforced supports that brace a bomb or missile to prevent any shifting or involuntary dropping of the ordnance during flight.

cryppies (milit) fr. cryptology: those who work as decoding/coding experts.

cube (drugs) crude, illicit morphine for the wholesale trade; usually 120/140 cubes to 1 oz.

cuddy (milit) RN: the captain's cabin.

cues (radio) written material (yellow paper for studio presenter, pink for control room engineer and producer) so that those concerned can follow the schedule in the studio.

cuff *v* (medic) to take the blood pressure using a *blood pressure cuff* (sphygmomanometer).

cull *v* (milit) mercenary and white military use in Africa, esp. during last days of Rhodesia (Zimbabwe): to shoot blacks dead, on suspicion rather than on fact, and essentially for amusement.

cull *v* (commerce) in the fruit trade, to reject inferior fruit.

cultural art (art) a derogatory term, roughly equivalent to 'fine art' in progressive eyes, coined in 1949 by Jean Dubuffet. In cultural art the artist is impotent, his art is tame, exploited and controlled by the bourgeoisie.

cultural deprivation (govt) euphemism for poverty. Thus *culturally deprived environment* is the slums.

Cultural Revolution (pols) cultural, political and social upheaval in China between 1965 and 1969, launched by Chairman Mao to regain some of his depleted power, lost through the failure of the Great Leap Forward (qv). Intended to crush the bureaucracy and install true egalitarianism, the Cultural Revolution, with its massive purges, its violence and its growing personality cult around Mao, proved a major disaster for China and its people – and one from which it has yet fully to recover.

cultural script (sociol) a pre-established system of cultural rules, roles, codes and assumptions by which we supposedly live.

culture (milit) all names, legends, etc. on a map; the features of the terrain that are man-made, not natural.

culture-fair (sociol) making due allowance (often in examinations/tests) for the variety of cultural backgrounds of those involved. *Culture-fair testing* takes all such differences into consideration and attempts to ensure that the non-WASP is not penalised simply for his/her birth.

culture shock (sociol) the sense of confusion and alienation often experienced by those suddenly exposed to a culture and society which is totally outside their previous experience. Often it appears that the 'hosts' have no sense or logic to their way of living or communication.

cum and ex (stock market) cum: a word used in connection with dividends, rights, etc to indicate that shares so described are entitled to such dividends or rights. ex: the opposite of *cum*. 'Ex dividend' means that such shares are not entitled to the distribution of such dividends, rights.

cume (advert) (abbrev) *cumulative audience*. See: *reach and frequency*.

cumshaw (milit) USMC: anything free, gratis, buckshee. Thus *to get hold of cumshaw*, from Chinese *kan hsieh* 'with grateful thanks', which became 'a gift' in pidgin.

cumulative penetration (marketing) the build up of customers buying a brand a number of times over a measured period.

cunvittu (Mafia) fr. Ital 'convent': a prison.

cuppa (espionage) fr: 'not my cuppa char', ie: not my taste. Used by agents to denote the sister (qv) who will turn on a target sufficiently to place him in such compromising positions as will render blackmail simple. It may take a number of sisters' efforts before the target chooses his 'cuppa'.

curl (sport)
1. (surfing) a semi-hollow wave which allows the surfer to pick up speed on the top half and then, after it breaks, to move down to the bottom half and ride free of the white water, protected by the curl of water above.
2. (US football) a pattern of play in which two receivers cross each other.

currency cocktail (finance) a mix of foreign currencies used in international business deals.

current sheet (science) aka: *magnetodisk*:a cylindrical region of strong magnetic lines on the boundary of the area dominated by a planet's magnetic field.

curtain (press) aka: *hood*: a headline which is ruled off on three sides only.

curtain (TV) from theatrical 'curtain line' – the

last line of a play; the last line or scene of segments (qv) of a thriller series.

cushion (gambling)
1. money in the bank.
2. a reserve bank roll.

cusp (sport) in ice-skating, the point in a turn when the skater moves from one edge of the skate to the other.

cuspy (computer) from acro: commonly *used system program*, i.e. a utility program used by many operators. By extension, a functionally excellent and well-written program.

custom and practice (indust relats) set of beliefs and understandings, esp. in craft workshops and amongst pieceworkers, that have developed into hard and fast rules, and are administered as such by shop stewards.

customer service representative (airlines) non-flying airline personnel who work at check-in desks, etc.

cut *n* (sport) in US football, the regular sackings during pre-season practice, of those players who are deemed not to have made the current grade.

cut (music business)
1. *n* a track from an album.
2. *v* to record a song or piece of music.

cut *v* (TV, movies)
1. to edit film.
2. to make a quick transition from one shot to the next, an effect usually achieved by editing.
3. as interj. an order to stop filming.

cut *v* (drugs) for the seller to adulterate his wares – oregano into marijuana, mud for hashish, pain-killers for amphetamine or barbiturates, procaine or novocaine into cocaine, milk sugar into heroin, etc.

cut (press/US) an illustration.

cutability (commerce) in butchery: the proportion of saleable meat on a carcass.

cut and hold (movies) an instruction to the cameraman to stop filming but for the actors to hold their positions so that the director can check lights, angles, etc.

cutback (sport) in surfing: to turn one's board back towards the breaking part of the wave.

cut-in (movies) a leader (qv) inserted into a film sequence.

cut-ins (music business) if a singer would use a particular songwriter's material more than usually often, extra royalties were passed on as the reward for such extra publicity.

cut-off (press)
1. a full rule across one or more columns.
2. the depth of a rotary printed broadsheet (qv).

cut-off (TV)
1. a script that has been paid delivery money but has yet to go into production which is considered useless is dropped and 'cut off' from any further payments.

2. the small frame that surrounds a broadcast picture but never appears on the home screen.

cut-off man (espionage) a local intelligence network contactman who passes funds and messages for men in the field.

cut-out *n* (business) from espionage use: a person or business used as an intermediary between principals in a secret operation. Used for secret deals and similar operations that the corporations do not wish revealed at the given time, if ever.

cut-out (espionage) a middleman who establishes contact between the two main parties and enables them to keep conveniently apart and thus avoid suspicion.

cut-out *n* (advert) an illustration, often a figure cut out of its normal background and reprinted on white space.

cutter *n* (TV, movies) a film editor.

cutter (commerce) in butchery: an animal that yields an inferior grade of meat.

cut up big wins *v* (gambling) to reminisce over nostalgic glories.

cut up the score (gambling) to divide the winnings.

CYA (govt/US) (acro): *Cover Your Ass.* Whatever the blunder, make sure that you are in a position to pass the buck quickly and efficiently; the first rule of Washington bureaucrats.

cybercrud (computers) the blinding of gullible people with a flood of computer jargon and esoterica.

cybernetic art (art) the study of control and communication in animal and machine, and especially of messages as a means of controlling machinery and society. Feedback (in the form of information for correcting future behaviour of the system) is fundamental. Thus, cybernetic sculpture can respond to such stimuli as the proximity of the spectator.

cyc (theatre) (abbrev) cyclorama: a large back-cloth, frequently curved, which is stretched around the back of the stage, often to represent the sky.

cymatics (art) aka: *kymatics*: a term coined by Dr. Hans Jenny to describe his research into the structure and dynamics of waves/vibrations/periodic phenomena. Cymatics relates directly to kinetic art (qv).

dabs (police/UK) fingerprints.

dadcap (milit) (acron) *d*awn *a*nd *d*usk *c*ombat *a*ir *p*atrol.

daddy (theatre) stage manager.

daddy (prison) in Borstals, a heavy, powerful inmate who runs the institution by fear and threats. (cf: *baron*)

daemon (computer) a program that is not invoked implicitly but which lies dormant, waiting for certain conditions to occur. The perpetrator of such a condition may well not even know that the daemon is lurking – although a program may often commit a particular action simply because it is aware that such an act must invoke a daemon.

dagger (milit) RN: from † notation against the names of those officers who have taken a variety of advanced specialist courses: thus, those officers who are specialists in a subject (which will be marked after the dagger).

dailies (movies) the first, rough prints of the day's shooting on a movie. Viewed that same day by those involved or interested in the work done. (cf: *rushes*).

daily double (horse-racing) a bet that chooses the possible winners of each of the day's first two races.

dairymaid calculation (business) European business phrase based on the concept of an old-fashioned milk-seller touting her wares from house to house, pouring out the quantities desired, then totting up her sales at the end. Thus, any elementary calculation.

daisy-cutter (milit) aka: *big blue eighty-two* see: *cheeseburger*.

damage limitation (milit) the concept that judicious planning can limit the damage, and thus the virulence of the conflict, in a nuclear exchange; such theories are behind the current idea of 'winnable' nuclear wars.

damager (theatre) pun, meaning manager.

dancing (police) from sl. Fred Astaires: stairs, thus dancing image of those who specialise in robberies above the ground floor.

danger money (indust relats) aka: *dirty money, height money, plus payments, abnormal conditions payments, arduous conditions payments*. Extra wages paid for particularly difficult or dangerous work.

dangle *v* (medic) patient sitting on the edge of his/her bed: with dangling legs.

dangling the Dunlops (aircrew) lowering the undercarriage on a jet airliner.

danny (police) a 'plain-clothes' CID car for surveillance use. (cf: *nondescript*)

dark (TV, movies) an empty, non-functioning studio.

dark (theatre) a theatre that has closed, esp. one where the current production has had to be taken off.

dark blue (milit) British forces: a member of the Royal Navy.

dark objects (milit) satellites which are functioning but have never emitted regular traceable signals. Possibly missile-carrying space weapons.

dark satellites (milit) special satellites used for military or intelligence purposes, incorporating extra electronic counter-measures to reduce their 'visibility' to hostile sensors, radar, etc.

dart (milit) a target towed by one aircraft and used by others for training in artillery accuracy.

dart (milit) abbrev: Dartmouth: an RN officer trained at Royal Naval College, Dartmouth.

dash (govt) in Nigeria, that bribery which is officially condoned and accepted as part of national social/economic/political system.

data *v* (espionage) to compile a file of information on a targeted person or organisation.

data base (computers) any collection of information kept on an electronic file, though literally, even a file full of yellowing press cuttings could be termed a data base.

database management system (computers) a feature of the 'electronic office': a software (qv) package geared to arranging, sorting and retrieving and generally managing a database (qv).

data capture (computers) the simultaneous automatic recording and processing of information by means of equipment which connects local equipment with a remote central computer or processing unit.

date (entertainment) a theatrical or other entertainment performance, often as one stop on a tour.

daughter (science) a nuclide formed by the nuclear disintegration – either spontaneous or induced – of another nuclide. Orig. from *daughter atom* when the original nucleus is the 'parent atom' and the resulting atom either the 'decay product' or daughter atom.

dawn raid (stock market) a method of forcing a

take-over by the surreptitious purchasing of as many shares as possible of the company in which one is interested at 'dawn' – as soon as the stock exchange opens for business. One can purchase up to 29% of the company in such a raid before announcing the deal. All purchases of 30%+ must be declared.

day for night (movies) the use of special filters to obtain the idea of a 'night-time' sequence even though shooting in broad daylight. The point of this manoeuvre is to avoid massive union overtime demands for such late-night working.

day glow (aerospace) the visual effect seen from a spacecraft of the contrast between the earth's atmosphere above a sunlit section of the Earth and the void of space beyond.

day order (stock market) an order that is placed for execution, if possible, during only one trading session. If the order cannot be executed that day then it is automatically cancelled.

daypart (TV) a subdivision of the broadcasting day created for statistical, ratings and advertising purposes. (cf: *prime time*).

day player (movies) aka: *bit player*: an actor who has a small part and need only be hired for a single day's work.

day trading (stock market) the establishing and liquidating the same position (qv) or positions on the same day's trading. (cf: *day order*).

dazzle *n* (milit) the painting of large patches of irregularly shaped colour on warships in order to camouflage them during battles, air attacks, etc.

DB (TV/US) (abbrev) *delayed broadcasting*: the practice of some affiliates (qv) in putting off a network programme (qv) in favour of a programme that deals with events of local importance. The network show is taped for subsequent broadcasting.

DBs (police) (abbrev) *dirty books*: all pornographic material.

de-accession (art) aka: *de-acquisition*: the selling off by museums, galleries, collections of various valuable but low priority pieces or paintings, often to help fund the remaining collection.

dead (press) copy that has been set and used but can now be discarded.

dead (theatre) *on the dead*: a piece of curtain or a flat that lies properly flush with the stage floor.

dead (TV) a set that is no longer required and can be dismantled.

dead drop (espionage) aka: *dead letter box*: a place for the exchange of material, money, messages, etc.; one party deposits the 'letter' and the other appears later to collect it.

dead-ending (aerospace) from American fliers during World War II who refused to be grounded by even the worst weather and were

nicknamed 'the dead-end kids': flying through unusually bad weather.

dead fall (movies) a Western stunt rider; so-called probably from the content of such riders' most common stunt.

dead fish (sport) in baseball, a hit that goes fast for a few seconds then hits the ground and does not roll any further.

deadhead *n, v* (airlines) a pilot or other member of the crew who is flying merely for transport and not actually working; to take a free trip by virtue of one's being employed by an airline. (*deadheading* is by no means restricted as a usage to airlines; rail drivers, truckers, most employees of the many varieties of transport use the term when they are taking advantage of the transport but not on the job).

dead-head *v* (theatre) to gain a free admission to a performance.

deadhead agency (govt) a safe job for unenterprising civil servants who can while away their careers simply 'dead heading' or marking time.

dead horse work (indust relats/US) work for which payment has been received in advance.

deadlock (computers) aka: *deadly embrace*; a situation wherein two or more processes are each unable to proceed because each is interdependently waiting for the other to do something. When the cause of this 'embrace' is insufficient input, it is termed *starvation* and when excessive output, *constipation*.

deadly embrace (computers) see: *deadlock*.

dead man's hand (gambling) in poker, a hand made up of aces and 8s. From the hand held by Sheriff Wild Bill Hickok when he was shot in the back in 1876.

dead on arrival (computers) with ironic reference to police/medical use: an electronic circuit that fails to operate when new equipment is first turned on.

dead room (audio) an anechoic chamber, a room made absolutely sound-proof by being enclosed by non sound-reflecting surfaces which 'suck up' all sounds and permit no echo or reverberation.

dead stick (aerospace) a 'dead' engine, thus *dead stick landing*: a landing without engine power.

dead time (indust relats) unproductive time in a factory caused by plant malfunctioning or similar problem.

deaf aid (TV) the small earpiece used by newsreaders and other anchormen (qv) for hearing 'live' instructions from the director.

deaf-smack (milit) fr. acro Defense Special Missile and Aeronautics Center (def-smac) which monitors, fr. Washington DC suburb, US spy satellites.

dealer (drugs) a seller of drugs, either wholesale or retail. Thus *dealer's hand*: a method of holding small bindles (qv) of drugs under a rubber band so as to flick them away immediately if a policeman seems to be approaching with more than friendly interest.

dealer incentive (commerce) aka: *dealer loader*: any incentive or premium (qv) which is aimed at the retailer or wholesaler rather than at the consumer.

deal stream (business) concept within venture capitalism (qv) for those entrepreneurs with ideas but without adequate money who are seeking finance from a venture capitalist. They tend to outnumber the *dollar stream*, those entrepreneurs who have the money, but lack the right idea.

dead *n* (gambling) aka: *professor*: an experienced, successful professional gambler. Such nicknames come from his calm, intelligent demeanour and his ability to work out the odds.

de-architecturisation (archit) a term coined by SITE Inc. (a group of 'surrealist' US architects, Sculpture In The Environment) to denote a subversion or inversion of the established post-Bauhaus functional postulates of design, which ideas they regard as oppressive.

death (at the box office) (theatre) a piece that simply refuses to work. But *murder at the box office* and *this will slay them* both mean quite the opposite, a thoroughly successful performance or act.

death trail (theatre/US) touring circuit of Midwest small towns. (cf: *borscht belt, citronella circuit, chitlin circuit*).

de-bag (TV) a make-up term for the cosmetic removal of the bags from beneath a performer's or announcer's eyes.

de-boost (aerospace, milit) 1. the reduction of the thrust of a spacecraft or rocket in order to slow down the vehicle prior to altering course or impacting on target. 2. the reversing of the thrust of a rocket or artificial satellite for similar purposes as (1).

debug (espionage) to remove any bugs (qv) and render a room, building, car, etc. free from electronic surveillance.

debug *v* (computers) to isolate and iron out any errors in a program.

decapitation (milit) an attack which might be able to decapitate the US war effort, ie: to knock out the massively computerised US World-Wide Military Command and Control System (WWMCCS) which operates from thirty ultra-sophisticated centres all round the world. If this concept proved true, then the military 'torso' would be powerless once its 'head' was lopped off.

decay time (computers) the time it takes an electronic impulse – usually designated as a character appearing on a cathode ray tube (CRT) – to fade.

decertification (management/US) the cancellation by a company of its employees' affiliation to a union; the US is currently undergoing a huge and highly propagandised campaign to intensify nation-wide decertification.

decision-making unit (DMU) (marketing) the group of people who can most influence purchasing decisions; a DMU can operate in all areas, but it is a marketing concept mainly linked to largescale industrial marketing.

decision matrix (milit) computer program containing possible reactions to incoming hostile missiles.

decision tree (business) a flow chart or similar visual aid for the analysis of complex situations in which various alternative strategies are advanced and the possible outcome, profitability, problems and other desired data is made available.

deck (milit) USMC: the floor.

deck (theatre/US) the stage. Thus *deckhand*: stagehand.

deck (press) a separate portion or section of a headline, usually to denote the subsidiary headlines that follow the main one. A headline comprising two or more decks is a *-decker*, as in *triple decker, double decker*, etc.

deck (aerospace) the ground, spec. the landing runway at an airport or airfield.

deck (computers) 1. a means of storing information for future use, eg: magnetic tape. 2. a strip of material on which data can be recorded (magnetic tape, punched tape, optically sensitive material).

deck (drugs) a small folded paper container for passing powdered drugs.

deck (sport) in baseball, *on deck* refers to the player next up at bat.

declare *v* (horse-racing) to withdraw a horse from a race within the permitted period of such withdrawals.

decollage (art) the opposite of collage: the ungluing and taking off. Decollage was very popular in 1950s and can be seen in its natural state when posters on hoardings start to tear and several layers of previous advertisements start to show through beneath.

decouple (milit) the muffling of nuclear weapons tests by having them take place under ground.

decruit (business) as whizkid junior employees are recruited, so tiring senior ones are decruited: placed in a lesser position within the same firm, prior to being eased into less and less important jobs, or actually passed on, with glowing testimonials, to an unsuspecting rival.

decrypt *n* (espionage) signals that have been decoded.

ded (aerospace) (abbrev) deductive reckoning: aka *dead reckoning*: a method of aerial navigation based on the recognition of ground landmarks.

dedicated (computers) a machine or program, or one part of a machine that is completely given over to a specific task.

dedomiciling (business) to move the company's

D

parent domicile (its base for tax assessments) to some country where tax incentives and shelters are advantageous and the restrictions on foreign investment are minimal.

deep-basing (milit) nuclear defence strategy whereby a team of tunnellers accompany military personnel into a deep hardened shelter after the first phase of a war is over; possibly weeks or even months after the first and second and any other retaliatory strikes, these tunnellers drill their way up to the surface, create a makeshift silo and launch those missiles that they have kept in reserve and thus destroy the Soviets who will hardly expect the ultimate in surprise attacks.

deep cover (espionage) the assumption of a cover story and role so intensely and over so long a period that an agent almost 'becomes' his cover and truly lives in character rather than the mere taking on of a pose for a short-term operation. Such an agent, it is fondly hoped by all concerned, is in an impenetrable disguise.

deep creep (milit) naval term for an attack on a hostile submarine by a friendly vessel while both are at maximum depth below the ocean level.

deep engagement (milit) the strategy of hitting hostile forces well beyond the FEBA (qv, the contact zone of a head-on battle) and thus relieving one's own front-line forces and artillery: in other words, the traditional concept of hitting them behind their lines for confusion and diversion of troops.

deep feeling (new therapy) in primal therapy (qv) a moment of insightful truth that triggers off the primal (qv).

deepie (movies) a nickname for three-dimensional (3-D) films, on which principle, normal 2-D films are *flatties*.

deep six *v* (milit) USN, USMC: get rid of, lose deliberately, usually by tossing overboard into the 'deep six': the deep water. This term gained intense, if short-lived civilian notoriety during the Watergate Hearings (1973/74) when it was revealed that John Ehrlichman instructed John Dean to 'deep-six' some damaging material off the Potomac bridge.

de facto couple (sociol) a couple who live together, possibly have children, and generally act as man and wife without actually being married, yet *de facto*, if not *de jure*, they are married.

Defcon (milit) (abbrev) US code: defensive conditions; these range fr. 5 (normal readiness) to 1 (maximum force readiness).

defector in place *n* (espionage) an individual who signifies clandestinely to a foreign nation that they wish to defect but, for an indeterminate period, they will be willing to stay in their own country, amassing and/or passing on valuable information and material.

defence condition five (milit) US Dept. of Defense: the lowest possible condition of war readiness.

defence in depth (tech) a system of safeguarding against accidents in nuclear reactors which involves a series of back-up systems – *redundant safety systems* – to provide multiple levels of protection.

defender (govt, business) in game theory, that adversary who attempts to maintain in place the safeguards he has set up to defeat the incursions of the diverter (qv).

defensive industries (econ) those industries – food, utilities, insurance, etc – which provide the ultimate consumer with his basic needs and in which business activity is only marginally affected by even large-scale fluctuations in the market.

defensive medicine (medic) the practice by physicians who are faced with a highly complex and very highly publicised problem to order saturation testing on all levels so as to insure themselves against even the slightest possibility of a malpractice suit. In its most extreme form, some doctors have refused to treat highrisk patients in case a relation decides to sue if there is no 'cure'.

deferred futures (finance) the most distant months of a futures contract. (cf: *nearbys*)

definitise (business) general business use, deriving from aerospace industry term: to define a function or an action in precise and definite detail; a neologism for *specify*.

deformed workers' state (pols) a derogatory description of the Soviet Union by the Trotskyite far-left members of the International Socialists.

defund (govt) to deprive a government programme of funding and thus, in other words, to close it down.

degauss (milit) from K.F. Gauss (1777–1855), a Ger. scientist. To protect a ship against magnetic mines or any weapons relying on magnetism for guidance by using an electrically charged cable to demagnetise it on entering a battle zone. (cf: *deperm*)

degear (finance) to reduce the amount of a company's fixed-interest debt and to replace it by equity capital (qv).

degradation (computers) a machine working at a lower level than usual of efficiency because of some form of internal breakdown, although not one of such extent to render the machinery down (qv).

degrade gracefully *v* (milit) a concept inherent in positing a possibly 'winnable' nuclear war: for one's own command and control facilities and the weapons they administer to be destroyed less quickly, and to work to greater effect, than those of the enemy; that massive destruction/loss must occur even for the 'winner' is fully accepted.

deke (sport) in ice hockey, to deceive an

opponent and thus draw him out of his defensive position.

dekorier-dich (milit) aka: *demerdez-vous*: French Foreign Legion: get yourself moving, lit: 'get your shit together'.

del credere agent (business) an agent who sells on the risk of his own credit – having purchased the goods himself – rather than on that of a principal.

deliberate abstractor (educ) a slow learner; a phrase that mixes euphemism – deliberate = slow – with jargon – abstract = to take something out of, therefore to learn.

delinquency *n* (finance) credit card company use: late payments.

delivery (futures market) the actual settlement of a deal, whereby delivery is made to the Clearing House (qv) and thence to the buyer.

delivery (stock market) the transfer of securities between a seller and buyer or the documents concerned in the transfer. Thus *good delivery*: the documents concerned are all in order and the deal can proceed unimpeded. *Bad delivery* is the opposite.

delivery notice (futures market) the written notice given by a seller of his intention to make delivery against an open, short, futures position (qv) on a particular date. (cf: *delivery*)

delivery points (futures market) specific locations of delivery that suit the commodity – Swiss francs in Zurich, wheat in Kansas, etc.

delivery price (futures market) the price fixed by the Clearing House (qv) at which deliveries on futures are invoiced, also the price at which the futures contract is settled when deliveries are made.

Delphi technique (business) a method of forecasting which employs a group of experts who are initially polled singly for their opinions; they are then gathered together, the various theories revealed, and in further discussion these are all modified until a consensus can be reached.

demander (police) an extortionist, a protection racketeer.

demand-pull inflation (econ) inflation caused when the excessive demand for a limited amount of goods and services forces prices up. This demand usually caused through 'cheaper' money (more easily gained loans at lower interest) and tax cuts. (cf: *cost-push inflation*)

demarche (pols) from Fr. 'trample underfoot': any political or diplomatic manoeuvre.

de-marketing (advert) the selective providing of scarce goods; instead of actively marketing one's product when quantity is available, the process of holding back demand and attempting to make what there is go round.

demented (computers) a program which works perfectly well as far as it has been designed, but that design is in itself bad.

demo (rock business) (abbrev) *demonstration tape*: a tape made by a new band or singer or of a new song by an established band or artiste; in both cases the tape is used to promote the product to the record companies.

democratic centralism (pols) the principle by which, in theory, the world's communist parties take policy decisions and carry them out: after general discussion (democracy) the party line is laid out and everyone (centralism) must follow it, irrespective of any personal opinions. Lenin coined the phrase to imply the strengthened power of leadership when backed by such a group decision. In practice, it is a good euphemism for 'rubber stamp'.

democratism (pols) the process of democracy; the gradual assimilation of the exceptional and the eccentric by the mundane and the mediocre.

demographic targeting (milit) choosing population centres as targets for nuclear attack. (cf: *countervalue strikes*)

demote maximally (espionage) to kill by assassination. (cf. *terminate with extreme prejudice*)

denaderise (business) from Ralph Nader, US consumer advocate, whose activist 'Nader's Raiders' pursue companies whose products fall below the ideal standards of service and safety: to ensure that one's product or process is sufficiently good to keep Nader's criticisms at bay.

deniability (pols) the ability of any high official, esp. the US President, to disassociate himself from any illegal or improper activity performed by a subordinate. (cf: *CYA*)

denied areas (milit) those areas – USSR and satellites/allies – which are denied to simple intelligence gathering techniques and must be probed by more complex techniques and technology.

denounce (pols/US) a term used in the US Senate that stands midway between *censure* (the strongest condemnation of a fellow Senator) and *condemnation*, and used, like them, to show disapproval of alleged improper conduct.

dense pack (milit) a system of basing missiles, in particular the MX 'peacekeeper', in clusters so that even if hostile strikes do penetrate US defences, *some* of the retaliatory weapons will set off safely towards their targets. Dense pack is also intended to promote fratricide (qv) amongst incoming missiles – the idea that so many bombs exploding in such proximity must destroy their overall accuracy on the target.

dentology (milit) the 'science' of identifying otherwise anonymous black-painted submarines by the dents in a specific hull, the configurations of rivets, and other minor differences.

de-orbit (aerospace) to go out of orbit, to cause to go out of orbit.

deperm (milit) to demagnetise a ship to protect it from weapons that use magnetism for guidance onto their target. (cf. *degauss*)

deplane (airlines) to get off the plane.

D

deprivation (sociol) 1. the emotional deprivation of an individual, usually ascribed to the results of inadequate parenting and the unhappiness and social suffering that follows. 2. urban deprivation, a euphemism for slums, whether created by actual physical decay or the presence of an excess of the socially deprived.

depth polling (pols) voter research questions that go beyond the simple questions as to allegiance and into the ascertaining of why such allegiances have been formed and whether or not they will be maintained.

derived demand (marketing) where demand for one product depends on the demand for another one; industrial goods are demanded, in the long run, only insofar as they can supply the immediate demand for consumer goods.

derm (medic) (abbrev) *derm*atology: the study of skin and its related problems.

derrick (sport) in baseball, to remove a pitcher (with the image of lowering a hook and hauling him directly out of the ballpark).

deselect (govt) to discharge a trainee before he/she has concluded a programme.

desert dolly (TV, movies) a wheeled platform that is used to move the larger lights around a studio.

desert principle *n* (criminology) the concept that offenders should get exactly what's coming to them and should have no doubt that each particular crime brings with it a specific length of sentence. A simplification of the system already in use in Britain, but at odds with the US tradition of an indeterminate sentence between two extremes of minimum and maximum duration.

designer *a* (commerce) in the clothing trade, those garments ostensibly designed by a major couturier; unlike 'haute couture' which produces only a few of each design, these garments are deliberately made for mass production, on the assumption that a pair of jeans with a smart name will have a cachet, and thus a price, above a similar pair bereft of the chic label.

desk (press) the name used on newspapers for the various departments that contribute pages to the paper: the city desk, the sport desk, etc. Thus *desk-man*: a journalist who works mainly from his desk rather than spend time reporting in the field, the opposite of *leg-man*.

desk (rock business) the electronic control board for a synthesiser, upon which whole orchestras can be created by programming the machine correctly.

desk research (govt, business, etc) research that is carried out from one's desk, with necessary use of files, libraries, etc. Opposite of action research (qv).

desperado (gambling) ironic reference to a player who plunges heavily with bookmakers or in casinos but cannot pay off if he loses.

destabilise (espionage, pols) the use of clandestine methods to destroy a government and by extension to have it replaced with forces of one's preference. This process can include propaganda (both press and radio), the financing and advising of opposition parties, the arming of those same parties or their military wings, the assassination of heads of state.

de-stat *v* (commerce) the illicit methods of property speculators to buy or harass *statu*tory tenants out of a building that they wish to own, rent or sell without interference.

destination marketing (marketing) the process of persuading people to patronise specific places: resorts, countries, casinos, hotels, etc.

destruct *v* (milit) to destroy a faulty rocket or missile during its flight; destruct mechanisms are installed in the sensitive areas of such large military targets as ships, to ensure that no secret material is left available to an enemy in the case of a military defeat.

destructive art (art) aka: *actions, auto-destructive art, happenings, street art*: a term encompassing the work of several artists in all of whose work violence and destruction are used as modes of creation.

destructive read (computers) a memory element in which the act of reading the data that it contains automatically erases it from the files.

detailman (commerce) in the retail drug trade, a salesman who visits physicians and pharmacists in the hope of persuading them to prescribe or stock the company's latest products.

detank *v* (aerospace) to empty.

detente (pols) a policy of some form of mutual understanding and even de-escalation of the arms race between US and USSR that flourished for a while between 1972 and 1973 under the influence of Dr. Henry Kissinger. In the end even this little progress was vilified as 'a sellout' and has been replaced by an increasingly icy cold war, 1980s style. (cf: *linkage*)

deterrence (milit) the principle of making the cost of a nuclear war so devastating for either side that neither might ever wish to launch one. (cf: *MAD*)

deuce (theatre/US) a scenery flat 2' wide.

developing (pols, econ) a euphemism for poor nations which has replaced *under-developed* which in turn replaced *backward* and which, in its turn, is being rivalled by Third World (qv) or the South (qv). It is always assumed that 'developing' countries are gradually creating some form of wealth/stability along capitalist lines.

developmental (educ) geared to that which the child is ready to deal with: mentally, physically and emotionally.

deviation (pols) departure or divergence from the over-riding tenets and ideology of the ruling government, esp. as regards Communist countries; political heresy.

deviation (pols) in the British Labour Party: 1. straying from party policy. 2. subsequent to 1980: failing to act towards an agreed tactical objective.

devil theory (pols, econ, govt) when a man, an idea, a piece of legislation has been touted as the cure-all for a particular problem, and it fails to effect that cure, then that man, idea or Act becomes the *devil* for its opponents to decry. The concept of 'the wrong guys running the show', at least as far as the self-elected 'right guys' see it.

devised facility (espionage) a 'business' front behind which clandestine activities are carried out but which never attempts to perform any business even to maintain a cover.

DEW line (milit) (acro) *d*istant *e*arly *w*arning line: a system of radar stations on or around the 70th parallel of the N. American continent stretching from Alaska to Greenland, financed by the US with the co-operation of Canada and designed to alert US defences to missiles coming over the Pole from USSR.

dex (drugs) (abbrev) dexedrine: see *drug names*.

D-group (business) a management training group who aim to relate group behaviour to the personal work experience of each of the participants. (cf: *T-group*)

dhobi (milit) RN: a sailor's personal laundry; from Anglo-Indian use fr. 19th century.

dial back (govt/US) to play down, lower emphasis on, to have referred back until later; from the concept of moving the pressure dial back when too great a head of steam builds up in a boiler.

dialectical materialism (pols) the Marxist concept that explains the way in which events have, and therefore will continue to interact and develop; the general laws of motion that cover the evolution both of nature and society. Every stage of history contains the germ of its own destruction, the thesis provokes its own antithesis and from the clash between the two a new synthesis arises, formed from the best of the both; this process then repeats itself. Ideally these repetitions should lead to the classless, communist society, at which time the process will have achieved perfection and stop. (cf: *historical materialism*)

dialogers (radio/US) the scriptwriters of daytime series (soap operas).

dialoguing (new therapies) in Gestalt therapy, the subject recreates a conversation with two or more parts of his personality; this may be extended to parts of his body, objects in dreams, etc.

dial your weight (aerospace) a small computer into which is keyed the weight of all crew, the fuel, the payload and any other on-board items; it then calculates and displays the position of the plane's centre of gravity and its maximum take-off weight.

diamond (sport) in baseball, the diamond-shaped area within a baseball field which connects the four bases; sometimes extended to include the whole playing area.

dice mechanic (gambling) a professional cheat who is used to gee up the play, relieve a heavy winner of his gains, etc.

dichotomous question (marketing) a question designed to elicit one of the two basic replies: 'yes' or 'no'.

Dick Whittingtons (soc wk) individuals from the provincial cities and towns who come to London hoping for better work prospects, fail to find them, and join the unemployed homeless living in hostels or on the street.

dicky bird (theatre/UK) an actor who can sing too.

dictionary (computers) a list of code words used in a program and their meanings in that program.

die (theatre, entertain) for a comedian to fail to amuse.

differences (stock market) the balances due to clients and other member firms at the end of each account.

differentiated response (police/UK) when an enquiry isn't top priority, a policeman will make an appointment to call later.

differentiation (pols) treating Warsaw Pact countries separately, rather than as a homogeneous bloc.

diffusion (of innovations) (marketing) the gradual acceptance by the market of a new product.

dilution (finance) 1. the reduction in the proportion of the corporation still owned by its original share-holders after a new issue is made. 2. When the newly issued shares earn at a lesser rate than did the old ones at the point when the new issue was made.

dilution (indust relats) 1. the infiltration of unskilled labour into jobs where previously only skilled men worked. 2. a situation where skilled union members accept (1) and offer the new men union membership.

dinette (milit) USN: the mess hall in a submarine.

ding (sport) in surfing, a hole in the bottom of a surfboard.

ding *v* (govt/US) to prod into action.

dinged (sport) in US football, to suffer concussion after being hit on the head in a tackle.

dinged (milit) USMC: hit by a bullet, not necessarily killed.

dingleberries (business) from the metalworkers' sl. for splattered molten particles around a metallic weld on a pipe or vessel: an executive who makes a statement which still manages to leave a number of 'splattered' thoughts and ideas lying around that are by no means related to the main topic of discussion. Given the US origin of this use, one must assume that the coiner had no knowledge of the British rugby

D

players' colloquial use, which refers to pieces of excrement clinging to a poorly cleansed anus.

dink (sport) in tennis, a drop shot, one which barely clears the net and drops close by it on the other side.

dink (milit) pejorative blanket description of the Vietnamese natives.

Dior do (TV) the description of any particularly lavish and expensive costume.

dip (TV) a metal trap in the floor that covers electrical sockets.

dip (milit) the amount by which a naval mine, moored on the ocean floor, is carried under its set depth by the current or tidal stream.

dip-locker (airline) a special, secret, locked compartment for carrying diplomatic bags on the aircraft. Often used by cabin crew for transporting their own small specialities.

dipper (police) a pickpocket.

dipping (airline) the funnelling off by stewards of liquor from the free bottles of liquor that are available to first class passengers. This stolen drink is then decanted into empty miniature bottles and either taken home or more usually sold to regular cabin class passengers at the regular price, all of which is pocketed by the stewards. Thus *big dipper* a jumbo jet on which such illicit profits are commensurately massive.

direct access (computers) the ability of a computer to extract the required data at once; available only from discs which can be scanned. Cartridges, which have to be run through and are thus slower, can only offer *serial access*.

directive management (business) the opposite of a permissive, democratic style: an autocratic management style in which all decisions stem from the leader without any consultation.

direct response (commerce) high pressure, unsolicited telephone selling.

dirty (econ) (of a floating rate of exchange) manipulation by one country to influence the exchange rate of its currency in its own favour on the money markets.

dirty (milit) a nuclear explosion that creates the maximum radioactive fallout.

dirty (aerospace) an aircraft which has its undercarriage down. (cf: *clean*)

dirty (music) of jazz, to have a slurred or rasping tone.

dirty (milit) in bomb disposal units, any device that is still armed and has yet to be exploded or defused.

dirty bed (medic/US) a bed set aside for a patient with an infectious disease – usually found in isolation wards. (cf: *clean bed*)

dirty dozen (milit) USN: an unofficial but widely acknowledged list of the 12 most frequent reasons for the unserviceability of naval aircraft.

dirty feed (TV) in British commercial TV, an input to other stations in the network that includes all local information – station identifi-

cation, local announcements, advertisements, etc. Such a transmission requires exact 'outswitching' by local stations to slot in their own relevant equivalents.

dirty float (govt, econ) a currency cut loose from its fixed parity but still kept under a fixed ceiling, determined by its government or central bank. A term coined by German finance minister Prof. Schiller in 1971.

dirtying (espionage) when agents enter a house to place microphones, sneakies (qv) etc. for surveillance purposes they must make sure not to leave it too clean: thus it must be dirtied, made adequately messy so as to offer no suspicions to the owner.

dirty jacket (police/US) aka: *bad rap sheet, bad snitch sheet*: a bad police record.

dirty tricks (espionage) illegal activities by a political party or their hirelings which are designed to sabotage the smooth progress of their rival's political campaign; from the CIA's 'Department of Dirty Tricks' which specialises in covert operations, allegedly overseas only. (cf: *black advance*)

disabled (computers) a machine that has been given a signal that stops it from functioning.

disadvantaged (educ, sociol) poverty, inadequate parents, mentally backward, environmentally deprived, and all the other problems that put someone outside of an ideal social role.

disaggregated (business) the breaking of a sector of one's business into its component parts for detailed examination.

disappear (pols) as a translation of 'desaparacer': the arrest and subsequent disappearance of many alleged members of opposition groups in Argentina, El Salvador and other S. American countries. Once disappeared, it is assumed that those concerned are dead, imprisoned, suffering torture or perhaps a combination of all three.

disassociation tableau (espionage) a scene staged to make the opposition believe that one side's agent has become disenchanted and is thus willing to seek new employment.

disc (computers) a method of storing information by placing data on magnetic discs and making it retrievable by high speed read/write heads. Such discs, aka *floppy discs* or *diskettes* (qv) can be stored like gramophone records and used with equal facility. A development of the floppy disc is the *hard disc* or *Winchester* (qqv) which cannot be removed but stores approx 50× more information.

discharge (new therapy) the joyous outpouring of pent-up emotions by verbalising one's positive opinions of oneself; such outpourings are often heard as laughter.

discomfort index (econ) a measure of the fluctuating levels of economic discomfort, represented by the sum of the unemployment rate and the inflation rate.

discontinuities (milit) cracks in parts of tank bodies.

discotetic (econ) a situation which seems inescapably and progressively appalling and on which no efforts or changes seem to have any useful or positive effect.

discount (futures market) a deduction from face value, the opposite of premium (qv).

discovery centred (educ) teaching that is based on the pupils finding things out for themselves.

discovery method (educ) a method of teaching in which students pursue problems on their own and work out their own solutions under the guidance of a teacher. (cf: *open classroom, discovery centred*)

discretion (stock market) orders *at discretion* are those in which the broker is supposed to exercise his own judgement in the execution of a transaction.

discretionary account (finance) an account over which any individual or organisation, other than the person in whose name the account is carried, exercises trading authority or control.

discrimination (milit) the ability of an anti-missile weapon to tell the difference between a real weapon and the decoys it launches to confuse such weapons.

disideologisation (pols) the decline of both communist and capitalist ideological fervour, accelerating in 1960s and 1970s but possibly enjoying a respite in America under President Reagan's right wing backers.

disinformation (business) the spreading of inaccurate information about designs, sales, marketing etc. which is intended to confuse and worry trade rivals.

disinformation (espionage) distorted or false information specially put about to confuse foreign agents, or disseminated in a target country to worry its inhabitants.

disinformation (pols) as regarded by socialist nations, any statements that do not wholeheartedly support their stance; as such these facts are really 'deliberate distortions'.

disintermediate *v* (econ) to withdraw one's money from intermediate institutions – savings accounts, etc – for direct investment at higher interest rates in the stock market.

disintermediation (finance) a method for companies to avoid the mediation of banks by dealing directly with investors.

diskery (record business) a record store.

diskette (computers) floppy disc.

disorderly market (stock market) the erratic performances of prices on the stock market, when no buyers or sellers are willing to take a chance.

dispatchers (gambling) any pair of dice that are crooked or in some way loaded.

displaced home-maker (sociol) a married woman who has lost her means of economic support, either through divorce or the death or disability of her husband.

display *a* (music) a piece of music specially selected to display the performer's talents to their greatest advantage.

disposal centre (govt/US) euphemism for any dumping ground, junkyard.

dissolve *n* (movies) a scene that changes as the one that replaces it appears through gradual superimposition. (cf: *mix*)

distance *n* (sport) in boxing, *to go the distance* is to continue fighting through the scheduled length – ten rounds, fifteen rounds – of the fight.

distress merchandise (commerce) goods that have not sold as expected – over-ordered, shoddy quality, etc – and must therefore be disposed of cheaply and fast.

distress pattern (new therapies) in co-counselling (qv) the inner confusions and unhappiness which, in theory, will be removed by successful co-counselling.

distress selling (stock market) 1. the selling of stocks in a recession when the market is in fear of a sudden crash. 2. the selling off of assets after a firm has gone bankrupt.

distributive education (educ) a vocational scheme split between a school and an employer: the pupil mixes classroom lessons with on-the-job experience and training.

district *n* (medic/UK) *on the district* a midwife who covers a certain area, related geographically to a specific teaching hospital.

ditch (milit) 1. *n* (RN, RAF) the sea, esp. those adjacent to the UK. 2. (RAF) *v* to bring a plane down into the sea in an emergency/crash.

ditcher (sport) in bowls, a bowl which either runs or is knocked off the green into the surrounding ditch.

dittoanalysis (business) the process whereby consultants manage to arrive at a series of conclusions which were already determined prior to their starting to consult.

diversionist (pols) in communist terms, a saboteur, usually found in the phrase 'spies and diversionists' and meaning foreign espionage agents. On a domestic level, anyone who is deemed to be conspiring against the government.

diverter (govt, milit) in game theory, that adversary who attempts to destabilise the safeguard systems that are established by his opponent, the defender (qv).

dividend stripping (commerce) a method whereby a finance company offsets a dealing loss against tax reclaimed from dividends accumulated by the company which was the subject of the deal.

divisions (milit) RN: the parade of a ship's company according to its various divisions, once a daily event, now more likely to be weekly.

D

DJ copy (rock business) a special version of 45rpm single in which only the A side (qv) is pressed for radio play by the *disc jockey* and the reverse side is left blank.

DLP (theatre/UK) (abbrev) *direct letter perfect*: word perfect in a role.

D notice (govt, press/UK) (abbrev) *defence notice*. A voluntary system of self-censorship by British news media whereby the government cite a 'sensitive' piece of news as best left out of the public eye and trust to the editors to accept this restriction. Originated in 1912 as the prerogative of the Admiralty, War Office and Press Committee, now the Services, Press and Broadcasting Committee, the secretary of which signs the formal letter referring to the specific news item which is the actual 'notice'.

do a Brodie (theatre/US) aka: *take a Brodie*: to fail or flop spectacularly despite, or perhaps due to an excess of pre-show publicity. Named for one Steve Brodie who ballyhooed a forthcoming dive from the Brooklyn Bridge but then decided the stunt was too dangerous to perform.

do a Brodie (drugs) to exaggerate the symptoms of one's addiction – throwing a fit, fainting, etc – in front of a reluctant doctor in order to extract a narcotics prescription from him.

dobson *n* (TV) the final rehearsal of a shot on location filming. Especially when the shot in question involves complex dialogue and camera-work.

dock (theatre) 1. the space behind and at the sides of the stage where the scenery is stored. 2. the theatre basement, originally the scene dock in some theatres.

dock *v* (aerospace) the linking together of two vehicles in space. Thus *undocking* is the disengagement of those two vehicles.

dock asthma (police) the pretended gasps of 'surprise' by the accused when confronted with incriminating police evidence. By extension, the reaction to any unpleasant surprise, in or out of court.

doctor blue (medic/US) a radio code call put out over a hospital tannoy for all doctors and students available to rush to the site of a cardiac arrest: 'Dr. Blue to X floor'. Thus *Doctor Red*: a fire alarm; *Doctor Green*: all clear after an emergency.

docudrama (TV) a TV dramatisation based on facts – recreating an international crisis, etc – which is produced in the style of a factual documentary in order to lend extra authenticity. (cf: *faction*)

dog (movies) a flop.

dog *v* (milit) to split a watch with a friend.

dog (TV) a bad programme; *dog station*: a TV station which fails to please the viewers, draw advertising revenue, etc.

dog (horse-racing) a horse that is slow or difficult to handle.

dog and maggot (milit) UK forces: biscuits and cheese.

dog days (TV) the summer season when the viewers are supposedly on holiday and advertising revenues fall, new scheduling is held back and the current programmes gain only mediocre ratings. (cf: *closed season, silly season*)

dogface (milit) any US soldier, especially an infantryman in US Army. (cf: *grunt*)

dogger (sex) any military client for a homosexual prostitute; from dogface (qv).

doggie (milit) RN: a midshipman who attends a Captain or Commander.

dog heavy *n* (movies) the second or third rank villain in a Western.

doghouse (theatre/US) the theatre itself.

doghouse (aerospace) a cover over instrumentation, esp. on rockets; from the World War II sl. for the tail turret of a bomber.

dog it *v* (gambling) 1. to back down in an argument. 2. to be afraid to bet heavily even when your luck is in.

dog-robbers (milit) British forces: the mufti (civilian clothes) worn by officers going on leave.

dog's ballocks (press) the typographical sign :- thus *dog's prick* is !

dog ship (milit) USAF: a trial model of a new aircraft; from phrase 'try it on the dog'.

dog show (theatre/US) a show that is opened in the provinces before coming in to New York. From 'try it on the dog' (cf: *dog ship*)

dogtags (milit) stamped metal plates worn around a man's neck to indicate his name, blood group and religion.

dogwatch (press) the shift between 9pm and 12 midnight on newspapers.

dog watch (milit) RN: 1. the watches between 4 and 6am and 6 and 8am (the usual 4 hour watch is split in two). 2. a very short term of service.

doing the crazy dance (TV/US) the frantic efforts of a TV news team to beat a deadline with a specific piece. (cf: *go down in flames*)

doing the party (crime) in three card monte (qv): a ploy whereby one of the con-man's assistants pretends to have won heavily, thus encouraging the genuine suckers to lay down their money.

doll (horse-racing) a hurdle used as a barrier to mark out the sides of a gallop.

dollar-an-inch-man (sex) homosexual prostitute who claims to be so well-proportioned that even were he to charge clients 'a dollar an inch' he would still be richer than any rival.

dollar diplomacy (pols) the use of US economic power to further her interests abroad by offering material or financial incentives to allies or potential friends. Originally used 1910 when US businessmen were trying to open up the markets of Latin America; now a general term for such economic imperialism wherever it is practised.

dollar up *v* (commerce) US farming: to fatten up

one's cattle so as to get the best price when they are sold.

doll's eye (aerospace) a warning light in the cockpit that has a white bulb.

dolly (movies) any wheeled mounting for a camera, usually guided along tracks for backwards/forwards movement. Thus *tray dolly*: very low dolly; *scorpion dolly*: adaptable to various gauges of track; *crab dolly*: a nontracked mounting that can move in all directions (cf: *crab*); *to dolly* is to move a camera using such a mounting.

dolly (drugs) see *drug names*.

domestication (econ) the transfer of an overseas branch of a company into being a separate, non-resident (in UK) company.

domino (TV) light source to illuminate the cyclorama (qv).

domino (music) an error in performance.

domino theory (pols) the concept that were one nation in a specific area to turn Communist, then similarly placed adjacent nations would automatically follow suit, tumbling like a row of dominoes knocking each other down in turn. Coined by President Eisenhower in 1954 but used most commonly to justify the US presence in Vietnam.

Donald Duck effect (aerospace) the distortion of the voice up to a higher pitch which can be encountered during space flight. From Walt Disney's character who is known, inter alia, for his strangulated vowels.

donkey (milit) the chest in which a naval artificer keeps his tools.

don't block the key (movies) an instruction to an actor warning him/her not to cast a shadow over another actor. Refers to the key light (qv).

Doomsday Clock (milit, science) a clock that is printed on each issue of the Bulletin of the Atomic Scientists (founded 1945 by a group of physicists at the University of Chicago) which tells the 'time' left before nuclear doomsday. Originally set at 11.52, it has only been turned back once – in 1960, when Khrushchev appeared to be 'thawing' out the Cold War – and now stands at 11.58.

doomsday plane (milit) see *looking glass*.

doomsday scenario (milit) the 'war games' played by milit. planners in an attempt to evaluate possible ways in which a nuclear war might start.

door opener (commerce) a cheap giveaway item that a salesman offers his client, simply to 'get a foot in the door'.

doorstep *v* (commerce) the process of going from door to door soliciting sales; by extension anyone – politician, charity organisers, etc – can also doorstep for their own ends.

doorstepping (press) for a reporter to wait on a person's doorstep in order to attempt an interview when they come home or go out.

doorway state (science) in nuclear physics, a theoretical middle state between a simple and a more complex nuclear interaction.

dope (milit) USMC: 1. the sighting of a rifle, allowing for wind correction and any other conditions. 2. information, either *good dope* or *bad dope*.

dope sheet (TV) the breakdown of instructions for shooting each scene; usually prepared in advance by the director.

dope story (pols/US) a story leaked deliberately to a reporter and written up as his own investigation; a useful way of assessing public reaction to a plan or policy.

do protocol *v* (computers) to perform an 'interaction' as regards a person or an object that implies the use of a well- and clearly-defined procedure. (A pun on diplomacy's 'due protocol'?)

dormie (sport) aka: *dormy*: in golf, on a match play score, to stand as many holes up as there are holes left to be played – thus impossible to defeat.

Dorothy and Toto (sex) a homosexual client and his paid 'escort'.

DOT (medic) (abbrev) *death on the (operating) table*.

double *n* (advert) an advertisement of double column width, measured as to the relevant journal.

double *v* (espionage) to give, or to pretend to give information to each of two conflicting parties. Thus, a *double-agent* works for both sides at once.

double-bubble (aerospace) a fuselage cross-section consisting of two intersecting arcs with the floor forming their common chord.

double call *v* (commerce) for a manager to accompany a salesman on his visit to the client.

double-dabble *v* (computers) the process of converting decimal numbers into their binary equivalents.

double digit (inflation) (econ) aka: *double figure inflation*: inflation that exceeds 10% per annum. Thus *triple-digit*: any figure between 100 and 999.

double-dipping (milit, govt) the concept and the practice whereby a serving officer in the military can retire after 20 years with a full pension and then start a new career, often in government, which gives him a new income and, in time, a second pension. From the ice-cream cone with two scoops in it.

double exposure (movies) two or more images recorded on the same piece of film; often used to denote dreams or fantasies, or for trick shots involving 'twins' played by the same actor.

double headed print (movies) a print in which sound and vision are recorded on separate pieces of film, usually at the cutting copy stage (when a print is available for editing), or prior to giving approval for making the combined print that will go into the cinemas.

D

double-header (espionage) an agent who is working for two employers at the same time; *triple-header*: three employers. These employers are all essentially on the same side, but from different intelligence agencies.

double in brass (theatre) to play two parts in one performance; orig. for those performers who also helped out in the orchestra when they were not on stage. (cf: *George Spelvin, Walter Plinge*)

double take (milit) US Dept. of Defence: second level of war readiness.

double truck (advert, press) a feature or advertisement that runs across a double page spread.

doughnut (milit) 1. (RAF) an airplane tyre. 2. (RN) a circular inflatable life raft.

doughnut (science) in nuclear physics, a toroidal (dough-nut shaped) vacuum chamber placed between the magnet poles of a betatron or synchrotron, in which electrons or protons are accelerated.

dove (pols) anyone who prefers negotiation to armed conflict in international relations. Coined by Stewart Alsop and Charles Bartlett (US political writers) in 1962. (cf: *hawk*)

down (computers) for a computer to be out of action; (cf: *crash*). To *take down* or *bring down* implies the temporary turning off of a machine for repair work.

downer (indust relats) a brief work stoppage in which tools are 'downed' which ranks as the lowest level of strike action.

downer (movies) a story or film that ends sadly; unloved in Hollywood and if possible always altered for script purposes (other than in tear-jerkers like *Love Story*). From hippie sl. for a depressing experience.

downers (drugs) tranquillisers and barbiturates; see *drug names*.

downhill *adv* (aerospace) descending to the lowest point in a satellite's orbit.

down-market *a, v* (commerce) aimed at the lower-income consumer; or merchandise to alter a product so that it will appeal to the bottom end of the market. *Up-market*: the reverse.

downmouth *v* (govt/US) to use a compositely negative manner of speech, with elements of bad mouth, poor mouth, down in the mouth, down play and downside risk.

down quark (science) aka: *neutron quark*: a type of quark (qv) with a charge of −1/3 and a spin of +1/2. (cf: *up quark*)

downscale *v, a* (advert) 1. to make smaller; to reproduce in a smaller, though similar version. 2. lower income, or lower income than that previously mentioned (but not necessarily poor).

down-size (commerce) in the motor trade, the choice by (possibly less wealthy) car buyers of small vehicles – currently dictated by the economic recession.

downstage (theatre) at the front of the stage, nearest the audience. (cf: *upstage*)

down stream (commerce) in oil industry, all services related to processing, refining and distributing oil.

down the line (TV) transmitting a programme or part of a programme for internal use – recording or reviewing it – prior to the actual broadcast onto home screens.

down tick (stock market) a drop in the price of a share on the market (cf: *uptick*)

down time (business) a period when either people or equipment are idle through either human or technological error. (cf: *down*)

down time (milit) the time an aircraft is out of service and awaiting repair, replacement parts, etc.

dozens offer (commerce) a trade offer where the ordering of sufficient quantity of a product will enable the retailer to obtain some free bonus supplies.

drafting (sport) aka: *slipstreaming*: in motor-racing, the practice of driving so close to the car in front as to gain added momentum from his slipstream or draft (draught, UK).

drag (music) a drum stroke made up of two or more grace-notes preceding a beat.

dragger (police) a car thief.

dragon (computers) a subsidiary program similar to a daemon (qv) but in this case never invoked but used by the machine for the performance of necessary secondary tasks that do not appear on the main program.

dragon's tail (milit) USN: a sea thermistor towed behind a vessel to measure the temperature of the water.

drapes (theatre, TV) all studio curtains, fabrics and hanging materials.

draughtsman (police) a criminal specialist who plans the operation of major crimes – usually robberies – but takes no active part in their execution.

draw (prison/UK) aka: *blow*: marijuana, hashish.

draw (espionage) the method of placing a variety of lures in front of a target for blackmail so as to put him a position for the stable (qv) to start operating.

draw-down (milit) a reduction or cutback, either in spending or in men and material.

drencher (theatre/UK) a sprinkler pipe placed above the safety curtain for protection against fires.

dress *v* (theatre) to fill up otherwise empty seats by giving out free tickets. (cf: *paper*)

dress *v* (TV, movies) to prepare a set for filming – props, furniture, etc.

dresser (theatre) one who helps an actor or actress to put on their costume.

dress off (movies) an instruction to a performer to use a particular person or object as their mark (qv) in a shot.

dress out (medic) to dress a hospital out-patient

in a gown, mask, cap and special shoes before he is taken into surgery.

dress the house (theatre) 1. see: *dress*. 2. to allot such tickets as have been paid for in such a way as to make an otherwise empty theatre seem more full.

drift (audio) the variation in the speed of a recording medium that is not greater than one per second. (cf: *wow, flutter*)

drift *n* (TV) the gradually decreasing efficiency of a camera. A more serious decline than creep (qv).

drift *n* (movies) an imperceptible but still disastrous movement out of position by an actor which will ruin a take (qv).

drifter (milit) a parachute instructor who jumps before his pupils in order to ascertain wind speed/direction and similar variables.

drink *n* (police/UK) a bribe, blackmail payment, or payoff for help received (such as information, tipoffs) given by a villain to a policeman. Thus *does he drink?* is he corruptible? (cf: *can I speak to you?*)

drip *v* (milit) RN: to grumble, quietly, but steadily.

drip painting (art) a painting technique made famous by Jackson Pollock (1912–56) during late 1940s/early 1950s whereby liquid house-paint is flung across, or allowed to dribble (by puncturing the can) onto the surface of unstretched canvas. The formal significance of the style is that it compresses the problems of drawing and painting into a single action.

dripping (milit) British army condemnation of the weakening of morale; from 'drip' meaning weakling.

drive *v* (sex) the forcing of a woman to turn to prostitution.

driver *n* (computers) aka: *software driver*: a series of instructions followed by the machine in the process of transferring data to and from a particular peripheral (qv).

drogulus (philosophy) coined by A. J. Ayer in 1957 to represent an entity which one cannot see or touch and has no physical presence yet exists, even though the lack of such presence puts it beyond verification.

droop snoot (aerospace) aka: *droop snoop*: any aircraft with an adjustable nose or with an adjustable flap on the leading edge of a wing.

drop *v* (gambling) to drop out of the round of betting in a card game.

drop *n* (espionage) a term used to signify a team's success in a blackmailing operation. (cf: *sanctify*)

drop *n* (gambling) the total amount of money exchanged for chips at a casino in any one night's gambling.

drop *n, v* (drugs) 1. a sale of drugs, to sell drugs. 2. a receiver of stolen goods, to receive stolen goods.

drop (espionage) a 'letterbox' where information,

money, etc can be left by one person for another person, who has been informed of its position, to retrieve as required. (cf: *dead drop*)

dropby *n* (pols/US) a brief visit during a campaign to any possible vote-catching area: a factory, shopping centre, private home, etc. An elision of *drop by*.

drop dead *n* (aerospace) the final moment possible, the deadline.

drop in (sport) in surfing, 1. to obstruct a fellow surfer by starting to surf directly in his path. 2. to slide down the face of a wave directly after take-off.

drop-knee (sport) in surfing, a turn that involves bending both knees, with the trail-leg crossed behind the lead leg and nearer to the surface of the board.

drop-lock stock (stock market) stock in which the coupon (qv) floats in line with short term interest rates while their general level remains high, but locks into a predetermined rate once the general level of interest starts to drop.

dropout (TV) small white 'sparkles' on a TV picture, the result of impurities in the oxide coating of videotape.

drop-out (audio) a momentary drop in the signal from a tape due to some imperfection in that tape.

dropper (police/UK) one who passes dud cheques.

dropping the rubber jungle (air crew) lowering the oxygen masks into the passenger cabin of an aircraft.

drowned (gambling) someone who has lost heavily has been 'drowned'.

drug names *Cannabis*: (there are approx. 2,000 names for cannabis used around the world, these represent some encountered in the UK and US) ace, baby, bale, bar, black gunion, black russian, bomber, boo, brick, bush, charas, charge, dagga, djamba, djoma, dope, duby, esrar, gauge, ganga, ganja, gear, grass, grifa, griffo, gunga, hash, hay, hemp, herb, juanita, kif, locoweed, marijuana, mary jane, mary warner, mu, muggles, pot, reefer, root, sinsemilla, smoke, tea, twist, weed, wheat. Cannabis also goes under a variety of geographical 'trade names': acapulco gold (Mexico); acapulco red (2nd quality), Congo bush, temple balls (Nepal), black Pak (Pakistan), Thai sticks, red Leb (Lebanon), Turkish pollen, Afghani, Mexican green, Durban poison (Sth Africa), and homegrown (UK). *Opiates*: (heroin, opium, morphine, codeine and their various derivatives and synthetic substitutes). *Opium*: O, black, tar, mud, hop, high hat, button, yen pok, san lo, red smoker, green ashes, yen, card, canned stuff, sook nie, ah pen yen, green pill. *Morphine*: M, white stuff, morph, mary, junk, lent, white nurse, Dr. White, Miss Emma, mojo, cube, sweet Jesus. *Heroin*: H, horse, Henry, smack, scag, smeck, duji, shit, stuff. *Synthetics*: phy (abbrev: phyceptone). *Hallucinogens*: LSD, acid, hog, angel dust (Phencyclidine) plus various 'trade names': strawberry fields, windowpane, clear light, sunshine, Owsley (from Augustus Owsley Stanley III, a leading 'chemist'), etc. *Cocaine*: blow, C, fly, snow, leaf, lady, girl, flake, rock, Charlie, gonzo, ice, bowser. *Amphetamines*: most of these names come from the retail name, the size, shape or colour of the pill: speed (general for all amphetamines), uppers (ditto), whizz, Purple Hearts, Black Bombers, Bennies (benzedrine), dexies (dexedrine), sulfate (amphetamine sulfate), Meth (Methedrine). *Depressants/Tranquillisers*: like the amphetamines, other than a few general terms, most references specify a trade name or the packaging of the pill required: downers, barbs (barbiturates, but in non-specific use); reds, yellow jackets, blue heavens, Nembies (Nembutal), Mandies (Mandrax), ludes (Quaaludes), Moggies (Mogadon) etc.

drum (horse-racing) in Australian racing, a piece of reliable information, a tip.

drumming (police/UK) the practice of thieves who visit likely houses (sl: *drums*) to check if any are empty and thus ideal for breaking and entering. Thus *drummer*: housebreaker.

drunk funk (aircrew) aka: *Pilot Alert*: a situation in which the cabin crew have to ask the Captain to leave the cockpit and sort out a problem amongst the passengers; as the name implies, this is usually the presence of an obstreperous drunk whose tantrums, it is assumed, will vanish in the face of the Captain's authority.

dry (theatre) 1. to forget one's lines. (cf: *fluff*). 2. to make a fellow actor forget his lines.

dry (gambling) out of any available funds.

dual phenomenology (milit) the confirmation from more than one early warning radar source of the potential threat of a USSR missile launch.

dual satellitism (pols) the precarious foreign policy pursued by some small nations who attempt to use 'neutralism' as a guise in which to obtain benefits from both superpowers while still refusing to align with either.

dub (movies) 1. to add sound effects to a film. 2. the re-recording or replacing of original foreign dialogue. 3. to have a professional singer record onto the soundtrack such songs that the star is ostensibly performing in the film. (cf: *ghosting*)

dub (radio) to transfer a piece of recorded material onto another tape where it will be incorporated into a longer programme. Eg: to put an interview on a cassette tape onto a reel-to-reel tape for transmission.

dub (music) aka: *dub plate style* in West Indian reggae the improvising by a disc jockey against a dub version – only the drums and bass guitar – of a song. (cf: *toasting*)

dubok (espionage) from Rus. 'oak tree': a business or a person who acts as a front for spying activities and/or a drop (qv) for various communications.

ducat (theatre/US) aka: *ducket*: a ticket, whether issued free or as a paid admission.

duck (medic/US) a urinal for male patients, shaped like a bird with its long neck.

duck (milit) air intercept code: hostile forces or ordnance heading towards you.

duck (sport) a score of zero in cricket, so called from the resemblance of 0 to a duck's egg. A duck in each innings is a *pair of spectacles* (from the visual of 00) usually abbrev. to *a pair*.

duff *v* (sport) in golf, to top the ball after hitting the ground immediately behind it.

dugout (sport) in baseball, the enclosed shelter where the players of the batting team not actually facing the pitcher or on a given base wait for their turn to bat. (cf: *bench*)

dull sword (milit) US Dept. of Defense Nuclear Accident Code: any minor, insignificant nuclear incident (rating lower than an *accident*).

dumb terminal (computers) a remote computer terminal with no intelligence or computer faculties of its own.

dummy (drugs) fake or inferior drugs offered for sale.

dump (TV) aka *pass, push out*: pieces that have been prepared for a news programme but have not been transmitted. Such pieces then become *takeouts* and, if judged sufficiently useful, are *put on the shelf* for possible future use.

dump *v* (theatre/US) 1. to return to the Box Office any tickets that have not been sold through agencies. 2. to sell off remaining tickets cheaply at the last moment before a performance.

dump (computers) for a machine to react to a problem by printing out all the available data that it has on its files with relevance to that problem, much of which may not be required. To sort out such a dump requires debugging (qv).

dump (sport) in surfing, for a wave to knock a surfer off the board and into the water. A wave that does this is a *dumper*.

dump (commerce) the sale of imported foreign goods at prices far below those of the domestic equivalents.

dump bins (commerce) free standing display racks, usually to hold books.

dumper (gambling) a bettor who exercises no plan, skill or restraint but plays as if he were simply 'dumping' his cash onto the table, where he inevitably loses it.

dump on (new therapies) the laying of one's troubles on another person, quite possibly at a time when that person had no real desire to hear them; the speaker's implication is one of apology, but an over-riding necessity to speak out that cancels any possible social error.

dunker (milit) RN: a member of a helicopter crew who is lowered down above the surface of the ocean and operates a sonar buoy to search for hostile submarines.

dupe (advert) (abbrev) *dup*licate: any copy used in advertising, whether of an ad, a book, sheet music, a tape, etc.

dupey-dupe (police/UK) a singularly stupid member of the CID whose ineptitude will soon see him returned to the uniformed ranks. Usually a detective constable or temporary detective constable.

duplex (computers) the ability to communicate in two directions down the same line. *Full duplex*: two-way communication at the same time; *half duplex*: two way communication, but only one direction of message at a time.

dustbin check (marketing) aka: *home audit* a scheme which asks selected consumers to keep all empty packages in a special dustbin for later analysis of spending, eating, waste, etc. patterns. (cf: *pantry check*)

duster (sport) in baseball, a pitch deliberately aimed high and in the direction of the batter.

dust-off (milit, medic) aka: *medevac*: the picking up and ferrying by helicopter to hospital or aid stations of the wounded on a battlefield.

dutch book (horse-racing) a race bookmaker's or pricemaker's odds line that totals less than 100%.

dutchman (theatre) 1. a cloth strip used to conceal joins in the scenery flats. 2. a wooden batten or similar support that helps hold up a flat.

dutch roll (aerospace) from the supposedly rolling gait of Dutch sailors: the yawing from left to right of an aircraft's nose, which produces the same effect throughout the whole aircraft. If it becomes bad enough the plane begins to sideslip and go out of control. It is caused either by incorrect application of the rudder or by a lateral gust of wind.

dutch tilt (movies, TV) turning the camera off the horizontal in order to obtain supposedly dramatic effects.

dwarf (science) one of the group of smaller stars of greater density, as opposed to the larger, more diffuse stars called giants (qv).

dwarf dud (milit) a nuclear weapon that explodes as expected, but after so doing, fails to provide the degree of explosive yield that might be expected from its size. (cf: *absolute dud*)

dwindles *n* (medic, sociol) euphemism for those declining years when great old age moves inexorably towards death.

dymaxion (archit) coined by R. Buckminster Fuller (1895–1983) from 'dynamism' 'maximum' and 'ion' to mean the maximum efficiency and performance in the terms of the available technology.

eagle (sport) in golf, a score that is two strokes less than par (qv) for a hole.

E&E (espionage) (abbrev) *escape and evasion*: the infiltration of a specialist who will 1. help out or actually evacuate the field agents who are either blundering in their task or in danger of being arrested or 2. aid defectors and their families to escape from their own country to one where they are more welcome.

ear (gambling) the bent corner of a playing card so that a cheat can identify it whenever necessary.

ear (press) the small advertising space(s) to one or both sides of the front-page title of the paper. Thus *weather ear* (US) is a small box of weather information in the place of an advertising ear.

early fringe (TV) a segment of the TV day that runs from 3.30pm to 6.30pm, directly preceding prime time (qv). Named to facilitate scheduling, ratings, advertising pricing etc. (cf: *daypart, late fringe*)

earnest money (business) the money paid over at the time of entering into a contract as a deposit against the possibility of a buyer deciding after all to default on the deal – in which case that money is forfeit.

earnings drift (business) when a firm's salary payments rise above the national average, for local and corporate reasons.

earn out *n* (business) the assessment of a firm's future earnings when a price is being worked out for the take-over of a high-risk enterprise. The purchase price will be a minimum agreed value plus the *earn-out*.

ears (audio) a Citizen's Band radio transceiver. Thus *ears on*: the state of being tuned into the CB frequency and ready to receive/broadcast.

earth art (art) aka: *dirt art, earthworks, terrestrial art, site art*: a mid-1960s movement in which the artists rejected the traditional materials/methods of sculpture in favour of 'actual' materials – earth, rocks, turf, etc. Utilised either in a gallery or on site (often using bulldozers and similar plant). Like conceptual art (qv) great emphasis is laid on documenting the project.

easy (sport) in rowing, the order to the oarsmen to stop rowing.

easy listening (rock business) saccharine music,

exerting no emotional or intellectual demands on its listener; soft-rock, disco, MOR (qv).

ECC (TV) (abbrev) *electronic camera coverage*, a phrase coined by and used at CBS-TV in America.

eccentric abstraction (art) a label attached to a number of mid-1960s US sculptors whose work was outside the traditional geometric forms and thus 'eccentric', favouring ugly/vulgar synthetic materials with qualities of flexibility/limpness, evolving a style that mixed minimalism (qv) with surrealism.

ECCM (milit) (abbrev) *electronic counter-counter-measures*: an area of electronic warfare (EW) that is intended to outsmart the enemy's EW while keeping one's own equipment and methods functioning usefully and without interference.

echo (sport) in bridge, a means of showing your partner how many cards one holds in a specific suit.

echt (literary criticism) from Ger. 'genuine', 'true': genuine work that epitomises a style or an artist. The essential ingredient that makes that work what it is.

ecological architecture (archit) various projects designed to construct self-sufficient, self-servicing houses; as independent as possible of public utilities by using natural energy sources and recycling methods.

ecological art (art) aka: *environmental art, eco art, force art, systems art, bio-kinetic art*: an art that uses natural physical forces and chemical-biological processes. The artist aims to enhance the spectator's awareness of such natural processes by presenting microcosmic worlds of macrocosmic phenomena.

eco-museum (art) a French concept of late 1960s whereby a whole area of the countryside is declared a museum and everything contained therein becomes an exhibit.

economic crimes (pols) major crimes against property – pilfering, embezzlement, vandalism, bribery, black marketeering – in socialist countries.

economic determinism (pols) the Marxist concept that economic factors rule every other sector of society: politics, social life, arts, the intellect, etc.

economic man (econ) one who manages his private income and expenditure strictly and consistently in accord with his material interests.

economic normatives (pols) methods used in socialist economic plans to ensure that the state economy remains focussed on the plan both as to production and consumption.

economism (econ) a belief in the primacy of economic factors in every area of life. (cf: *economic determinism*)

economism (pols) 1. (Warsaw Pact) the concept that the workers must concentrate on the alleviation of their economic position, which will then automatically solve all other problems. 2. (China) the practice of 'bribing' workers with bonuses and similar incentives to promote productivity.

econuts (pols, sociol) those environmentalists who carry their worries about the world to an obsessional extent.

-ed (medic) a popular suffix that is added to various medical procedures to render them slang: *scoped*: to have undergone gastroscopy; *bronked*: bronchoscopy; *cathed*: catheterised, etc.

edge numbers (movies) serial numbers printed along the edge of film material to assist identification when dealing with various sections.

edge work (gambling) specially marked cards with a slight bevel or 'belly' drawn at crucial points along the edge to indicate to a cheat the value of that card.

edifice complex (archit) an obsession with large, imposing and costly buildings.

edit *n* (computers) one or more instructions to the machine to move data – either insert, delete or relocate. An edit can simply be a button on the computer that will perform such functions. Thus *editor*: a program which makes an edit.

edited American English (educ/US) the US equivalent of received standard English; a prescribed standard of American speaking and writing that rejects the modern kow-towing to various minority interest adulterations/ illiteracies.

EDR (prison/UK) (acro) *e*arliest *d*ate of *r*elease.

educated incapacity (business) corporate parochialism; the easy desire to do only that which one has already done, move along accepted ideologies and systems – whether or not they work or even if they work, are not outmoded – and to refuse above all to reassess any of these patterns in the light of experience, 'reality' or current needs.

educational visit (govt/UK) the mandatory visit to all those registered for value added tax by a VAT-man who explains exactly what the tax is about and the ways in which one should make one's way through its intricacies. This visit is less to educate than it is to make any subsequent prosecution legal, on the basis of 'don't say we didn't tell you'.

Edward Pygge (press) aka: *Edwina Pygge, Sir*

Edward Pygge, Bart; a house pseudonym used at the *New Statesman* for the compiling of competitions.

effectuate (educ) an unnecessary amplification of *effect* with no other meaning than greater appeal to those educators who enjoy such words.

efficiency *n* (commerce) in US real estate terms, an efficiency or *efficiency apartment* is one which offers only limited facilities for washing and cooking.

effie (advert) an award presented to advertising successes, on the lines of the Oscar (qv) or Emmy (qv) and taking its name from an abbrev. for *efficiency*.

eggbeater (sport) in yachting, an outboard motor.

eggbeater (aerospace) a helicopter.

eggcrate *n* (TV) a device put in front of a soft light source that stops the diffused light from spreading any further.

ego 1. (New Age (qv)): one's negative, ambitious, selfish, materialistic side. Ego is always a bad thing. 2. (New Therapies (qv)) based on Freud: the adult part of one's personality; the self. A large ego, ie: a strong self-image, is de facto a good thing.

ego- (new therapies) the pre-eminence of the ego in these therapies leads to various self-explanatory concepts: *ego-fulfilment, ego-protective, ego-enhancing, ego-transcending.*

ego state (new therapies) in TA (transactional analysis, qv): 'a coherent system of feelings related to a given subject and a set of coherent behaviour patterns'.

eight-ball (milit) USMC: a useless individual, a loser, one who is 'behind the eight-ball'.

eight-ball (aerospace) a spherical flight-path indicator – the same shape and colour (black) as an eight-ball in pool – on a spacecraft's instrument panel.

eightfold way (science) in nuclear physics, a symmetrical pattern among eight different elementary, interacting particles with similar mass, isospin and hypercharge.

eighth card (milit) US Dept. of Defense programme for the development of lasers for military use both in space and on the ground.

eighty-twenty rule (business) the concept that only a small proportion of all the items used in business – stock, shops, personnel, etc. – are really significant; 20% of these items generate 80% of the total business.

EJ (TV) (abbrev) *e*lectronic *j*ournalism: news-reporting based on portable electronic cameras which use videotape and require a minimal crew to operate them.

ekistics (archit) the science of human settlements. Ekistics collates the relevant information from many disciplines, incl. economics, anthropology, social sciences, urban planning, technology, etc. Coined by a Greek architect,

E

C. A. Doxiadis, it posits megalopolises of 50–100 million inhabitants as well as ecumenopolises that stretch from London to Peking.

elapsed time (computers) the actual time one takes to perform a specific computing task. The machine runs on *run time* (qv) or mill time, an infinitely shorter period.

elective admission (medic) scheduled admissions to a hospital, the opposite of emergency admission.

electrographic architecture (archit) aka: *autoscape architecture*: the building of largescale neon light advertising signs, whole constructions intended to be read from cars and designed primarily as pictures or representational sculptures.

electronic art (art) a variety of kinetic art (qv) which exploits the abstract patterns to be found on cathode ray tube or oscilloscope screens.

electronic journalism (TV) see: EJ.

electronic smog (audio) nonionising radiation – ie: radio or TV waves or radar – emitted into the air in such amounts as to threaten public health.

electronic sweetening (TV, radio) aka: *laugh track*: the addition of 'canned' laughter to the tape of a TV or radio show.

elephant ears (aerospace, milit) large, heavy metal discs added to a rocket or missile to reinforce it against the heat gained through friction in flight and to stabilise the flight orbit.

11 o'clock number (theatre) the finale of a musical or of a filmed musical: time for the audience to leave.

ELF (milit) (acro) extremely *low f*requency: communication frequency used for reaching strategic submarines, giving out only 2W radio power and thus, supposedly, inaudible to hostile tracking stations.

elint (espionage) (abbrev) *electronic intelligence*: all intelligence that is gathered from bugs (qv) and similar electronic surveillance. (cf: *comint, humint, sigint, telint*)

eliteness motivation (business) the desire of managers to identify with prestige organisations and the assuming, with this in mind, of a pose of great, if illusory, superiority.

elitism (pols, sociol) a current bugaboo concept which admits, against the prevailing egalitarian philosophies, that some people/things are actually and definitely superior to others. In pols. this means the rule of an aristocracy, of merit, power or simply wealth.

emanations (milit) electronic pulses from hostile bases, ships, forces, etc.

emballages (art) any art work that is centred on the act of tying, tangling, wrapping, concealing or disclosing and which uses to this end clothes, costumes, bandages, paper, cloth or found objects.

emblem (milit) USMC: the Marine emblem is the 'globe and anchor'; in the Marines the word insignia is utterly taboo.

emblematic art (art) paintings that use common emblems and thus, with a 'given' image that anyone understands, the painter can concentrate on technique – the application of brushstrokes etc.

embourgeoisement (pols) a derogatory left-wing description for any drift towards the ideals and practices of the bourgeoisie.

emergency action message (milit) the authorised launch instruction for firing US missiles.

Emmy (TV) television's equivalent of an Oscar: from image orthicon – immy – and thence *emmy*. Awarded annually by the US National Academy of Television Arts and Sciences.

emotionality (advert) advertisements that set out to play on people's emotions – nostalgia, home cooking, missing the family, pets, etc., etc.

empathy (social wk) the making of contact at a deep emotional level and the positive effects on a social work relationship that this can and should bring.

empty medium *n* (computers) any medium that is ready to record data: blank discs, paper tape with holes punched for feeding into the machine, etc.

empty nest syndrome (sociol) a form of depression that can assail those whose children have grown up and left home. Thus *empty nester* is one whose children have grown and departed.

emulate (computers) for a computer to perform the work of another machine without having to be modified as to mechanism or program.

enable (computers) to make the computer ready for operation.

enable (milit) to arm a weapon ready for use, esp. the arming of missiles with their nuclear warheads.

enarch (govt) in the French government, a member of the civil service chosen from the graduates of the *Ecole Nationale d'Administra*tion, the nation's elite training ground for highfliers (qv).

encierro (sport) in bullfighting, the driving of the bulls from the corral through the streets to the bullring. From Sp. 'enclosing', denoting the 'playing' of the bulls by the many amateurs who like to risk life and limb during this driving.

enculturation (sociol) those aspects of the learning experience which make man different from the other animals; a process of conditioning within the limits of a regularised and accepted body of custom.

endistancement (theatre) from Ger. *Verfremdungseffekt* 'alienation effect' coined by Bertolt Brecht. See: *alienation*.

endowments (finance) the current accounts of bank customers on which the bank pays no interest but which funds are available to the bank for its own investment.

end-state (sociol) the result, the goals achieved.

endurance (milit) the ability to fight and control a nuclear war over a period of time.

end-user (govt) those on the receiving end of all of the bureaucratically and politically engendered programmes and theories: the public.

end-user certificate (milit, commerce) a declaration of who will be using arms that must be filled out by those selling them as private arms dealers. This is supposed to stop such arms falling into terrorist hands, but in reality is of little use against the many methods of avoiding such restrictions.

energy bush (ecology) fast growing trees or other plants grown specifically for fuelling adjacent power plants.

energy park (govt) US concept of taking large tracts of land and installing a number of power-generating facilities on them so as to share resources and cut down on costs.

enforcer (sport) in ice hockey, a tough player who is used not to score or for his skills but to intimidate the opposition, often to the point of beating up rivals on the ice.

ENG (TV) (abbrev) *electronic news gathering*: current popular style of news reporting which depends on the use of cheap, lightweight, portable equipment and small crews.

engagé (literary criticism) aka: *engaged*: a writer of novels or plays who makes his/her political or social stance very clear; writers who are committed rather than producing art for art's or narrative's sake.

english (gambling) the sliding, spinning action that is typical of most throws controlled by a dice mechanic (qv).

english (TV, movies) when the barn doors (qv) are adjusted to give vertical slits over a lamp.

english (sport) in billiards or snooker, the spin imparted to the ball.

engrams (new therapy) in scientology, memory traces in which the vicissitudes of prenatal life are still retained. A borrowing of the neurophysiological term for memory traces, permanent and heritable physical change in the tissue of the brain, posited as the reason for human memory.

enhanced radiation weapon (milit) a neutron bomb, which concentrates on killing humans, especially with extra-heavy fallout, while leaving more buildings standing than would a 'normal' nuclear weapon.

en plein (espionage) messages that are broadcast or written in plain, uncoded speech. (cf: *plain text*)

en plein (gambling) when a single number in roulette, or in another banking game, is backed with one's whole bet.

enrichment (educ) the offering to a child of above-average opportunities to learn at a level not generally available to his/her less advanced peers; extra knowledge and stimulation for bright children who learn the basic curriculum fast.

entertainment values (TV) the pre-eminence, even in programmes otherwise devoted to 'education' or 'facts', of an air of 'enjoyment', of amusement for its own sake, so that no-one used to the banalities of TV might possibly find themselves forced to exercise a modicum of intelligence.

entrepreneurtia (business) a pun on entrepreneur/inertia: the problem inherent in large organisations where the powers that be have exerted their own limits of inventiveness on getting to the top and are now determined to squash any similar efforts that might unseat them.

entropy (science) the mathematical measure of the amount of organisation taking place when one form of energy is converting into another. *Low entropy*: order; *high entropy*: chaos.

entry (sport) in hunting, the basic training of young hounds when they are first put into the pack during the cubbing season.

entryism (pols) the infiltration of democratic institutions by those who use such democracy to gain admission but once in control ensure that such democracy is not available to their opponents.

envelope (espionage) the limitations of speed, altitude and other technical assets which bound an aircraft's performance.

envelope (psychology) the processes by which an individual selects from the environment those aspects with which he/she can deal and rejects the rest.

envelope (archit) the shell of the building which gives it its basic shape and support.

environment (pavlov) basically meaning place or atmosphere, *environment* has become a vogue word applied indiscriminately to work, restaurants, education, real estate and any subject in which the writer/speaker feels the mundane *place* is insufficiently weighty.

environment (sociol) 1. the whole world outside of a human being's physical/psychic being. 2. the physical surrounds, which are deemed to have a major effect on one's growing up and subsequent behaviour. 3. the 'other people', the rest of the world that influence one's own life.

environmental art (art) structures that totally enclose the spectator, inside which he can move around. A reflection of the desire felt by many artists to escape the limitations of the single (and often small) 'art object', competing for attention with all its peers and rivals.

ephemeralisation (econ) a term coined by R. Buckminster Fuller (1895–1983) for increasing the obsolescence rate of all goods in order to accelerate the recycling of elements.

epsilon (computers) from the standard mathematical term for a small quantity. 1. a small quan-

E

tity of anything. 2. adj. very small, barely marginal. 3. 'within epsilon of. . .' close enough to be indistinguishable for all normal purposes.

equity (futures trading) the residual dollar value of a futures trading account, assuming its liquidation at the going market price.

equity (finance) the net worth of a firm or corporation (its total assets less its total debts); this equity belongs to the partners or shareholders.

equity capital (finance) aka: *net worth*: the total funds invested in a business by its owners.

equivalent operational capability (milit) a euph. to cover a situation where previously ordered/designed materiel/technology failed to reach its specifications and thus, rather than surpassing that equipment it would replace, could only duplicate, at far greater (because more recent) cost, the earlier capabilities.

ER (milit) (abbrev) enhanced radiation, a euphemism for the weapon that possesses such ER, the neutron bomb which substitutes the large-scale destruction of human beings for that of objects.

ERCS (milit) (acro) Emergency Rocket Communications System: in the event of all land and air based communications being destroyed, a number of Minuteman ICBMs (qv) are fitted with radio transmitters instead of warheads; once launched, these rockets are programmed to broadcast from many miles high those orders that will command submarines to fire their weapons.

eroduction (movies) aka: *sexploiters*: *ero*tic pro*ductions*, cheap sex-based films made for Japanese consumers.

erosion (pols/US) the decline of a political lead over the opposition as registered in the regular opinion polls.

error box (science) in astronomy, the box-shaped representation of an area in the sky inside which it can be assumed that a particular celestial object can be found or celestial event took place. The aim of astronomers is to shrink these 'boxes' to obtain the greatest possible accuracy in placing the event or object.

ersatz architecture (archit) architecture based on borrowings from many sources, either as exact copies or in pastiche. Such secondhand creativity is regarded by some as the authentic culture of the masses and it is suggested that a new principle of mediocrity is required to evaluate it properly.

escalation (milit) first used as early as 1938, but popularised by nuclear futurologist Herman Kahn in the 1950s, the concept of a build-up of military forces and conflict that leads to nuclear war. Kahn has listed a 16-step 'escalation ladder' that takes opponents from 'disagreement' to 'all-out war'.

escalation control (milit) a concept central to the current idea of 'winnable' and 'limited'

nuclear warfare: that the escalation of such wars, even when missiles have been fired, can still be held in check. (cf: *austere wars*)

escalation dominance (milit) the theory that one side (the US) must have the capability (qv) to mount the escalation ladder one step ahead of the other (USSR) and thus be ready at the top in a position of strength.

escalator (econ, business) a clause, contract or agreement that provides for an increase (and, though rarely, a decrease) in payments, taxes, wages, etc. to meet changing circumstances.

ESI (milit) (acro) Extremely Sensitive Information, super-secret classification code that covers only the SIOP war plan (qv).

est (new therapy) from Erhard Seminars Training, the creation of Werner Erhard (formerly John Rosenberg): an eclectic package of 'self-realisation' which is on offer to those who so desire over three weekends of abuse, sensory deprivation and psychological processing towards an improved state of mind.

est-hole (new therapy) a graduate of est (qv).

establishing shot (movies, TV) 1. the opening shot of a scene that shows the location and those characters who will be performing the story. 2. the first appearance of a character and the obvious delineation of that character within the plot.

ethicals (medic) medicines that are only available through a doctor's prescription and which are only advertised through the professional medical press.

ethnics (pols/US) any American who is neither WASP (White Anglo-Saxon Protestant) nor black; such groups tend to hyphenate their nationality: Irish-American, Mexican-American and so on; referred to as *ethnics* by politicians who have to make sure when campaigning not to insult such groups and to pander to their internal nationalism.

ethology and art (art) ethological theory (the science of function and evolution of animal behaviour patterns) when applied to art, suggests that people have built species reactions to certain visual combinations of form/colour in the way that animals respond to specific danger signals. Thus it might be possible to create such combinations with the intention of triggering such responses in humans.

ETS *v* (milit) (abbrev) *e*stimated *t*ime of separation: to be discharged from duty, esp. at the completion of one hitch (qv) or cruise (qv).

eunuch rule (pols/US) a clause in state constitutions that prohibits governors from succeeding themselves until they have allowed one further term of office to pass by. The rule was enacted to stop governors from building self-perpetuating, graft-ridden 'machines'.

eurobond (econ) a bond, esp. those of US corporations, sold outside the US but which is denominated and paid for in dollars and which yields interest in dollars. (cf: *eurocurrency*, *eurodollar*)

eurocommunism (pols) the various forms of communism espoused by the parties of Western Europe (esp. France and Italy) which pay lip service to Russia, but in fact maintain policies of their own, fitted around the realities of their own nation rather than along the inflexible lines of some future international revolution.

eurocrat (govt) those bureaucrats, culled from the member states of the Common Market (EEC) who staff the myriad agencies of the EEC headquarters in Brussels. The term carries much of the same disdain that is attached to its root: bureaucrat.

eurocurrency (econ) money, particularly US$ and Japanese¥, that is held outside the country of origin and used in the money markets of Europe.

eurodollar (econ) deposits of US$ with banks outside the USA; these overseas banks need not necessarily be in Europe. Such currency is barred from being taken back into America.

eurogroup (milit) in NATO (the North Atlantic Treaty Organisation) a group formed by defence ministers of member countries for the formulation of European defence policy.

evaluated information (espionage) the gathering of intelligence proper, as opposed to clandestine 'black' methods of destabilising nations or sanctifying (qqv) individuals. The collecting of available information of the desired sort and its analysis in the light of one's own needs and queries.

evaluation of intelligence (espionage) Western military intelligence agencies use two tables for the evaluation and appraisal of any information they receive: 1. the *reliability of source* and 2. the *accuracy of the information*. These two channels are divided as follows: 1a. completely reliable; b. usually reliable; c. fairly reliable; d. not usually reliable; e. unreliable; f. cannot be judged. 2i. confirmed by other sources; ii. probably true; iii. possibly true; iv. doubtful; v. improbable; vi. impossible to judge.

evening up (futures market) aka: *offset*: buying or selling to offset an existing market position.

event (milit) 1.euphemism for the site of a nuclear test. 2. an accidental failure or breakdown of any nuclear device, including reactors and power plants.

event tree (science) a diagram with 'branches' labelled to show any possible consequence of the event under consideration, with especial concentration on possible failure or breakdown.

eventuate (sociol) to happen, to result, to turn out.

everest syndrome (academia) the tendency of researchers to study something 'because (like Sir Edmund Hillary's alleged reason for scaling Mt. Everest) it is there', rather than devoting time and talent to something with a useful outcome.

evoked set (marketing) a small group of brands which are considered as possible purchases by a buyer.

EW (milit) (abbrev) electronic warfare. (cf: *elint*)

exacta (horse-racing) a bet in which one must choose the first two horses – in order of their finishing – in any race. (cf: *perfecta*, *trifecta*)

exceptional (educ) a pupil who is well above the average learner. (In theory a dull child is exceptional as well, but the word is only used in a positive sense). (cf: *less able*)

excess *v* (educ, govt) to cancel the assignment of a teacher or civil servant to a job when that particular job has been eliminated through over-staffing or re-organisation. The individual concerned remains on the payroll until they are actually dismissed.

EXCL (computers) (abbrev) exclamation point.

exclusive *n* (press) an article, of news or feature material, published in one newspaper or journal only, precluding any similar coverage by a rival.

exdis (espionage) (abbrev) *exclusive distribution*: US Cabinet restriction of information to select group, no more than 12 people; stamped on special green covers for such documents.

ex dividend (stock market) used in sales of stocks to indicate that the next forthcoming dividend is not to be included in that sale.

execute time (computers) the time required for a machine to carry out an instruction or series of instructions.

executive (computers) a program that helps manage the actual operating of the machine.

executive action (espionage) the assassination of a head of state.

executive fallout (business) the redundancies of executives whose jobs have been duplicated after their firm has been taken over.

executive privilege (pols/US) the right claimed by a US President to withhold certain information from the judiciary and the Congress. Once an alternative phrase for 'presidential privacy', Richard Nixon's brandishing of the concept in order to save himself from impeachment over Watergate has degraded it for the foreseeable future.

exex (movies) popular written abbrev. for executives.

exfiltrate (milit) to move out from behind enemy lines; to extract oneself stealthily from a dangerous position.

exhibs (movies) (abbrev) *exhibitors*: the owners of the cinemas where the films are actually shown.

exit (computers) to abandon one program or mode of operation and to move into another.

exit (sport) in bridge, to deliberately relinquish the lead.

E

expansion club (sport) in US sport, a club that has bought a franchise from a professional league and which can now start to buy players from other, established, teams. Expansion in a sports context means essentially *new*.

expediters (pols) aka: *pushers*: middlemen essential to a bureaucratic socialist state who actually pull the strings that get things done; experts in the shortcuts and back alleys of Soviet bureaucracy. (cf: *tolkach*)

expendable art (art) artworks made of cheap, easily decaying materials and all art that incorporates expendability as its essential aesthetic and thus reflects the artist's indifference to permanence in his work.

experience (advert) a redundant amplification used by copywriters who wish to improve the sound of their product: 'The XYZ Experience. . .' simply means driving the car, eating the food, drinking the drink, etc. Similarly the exhortation *'Experience. . .'* is merely a 'weightier' way of suggesting that one 'try. . .'

experience curriculum (educ) using the practical experience of those concepts that are being taught instead of simply teaching them as abstracts which have to be absorbed.

experience effect (business) the fact that the longer one works at a job, the less each item should cost; industrial costs decline with accumulated experience in performing them.

experiential (new therapy) a key word in all New Therapies (qv). Only through experience (which differs as to the discipline involved) can the individual grow (a state equally various as to the therapy concerned).

experiential referent (sociol) for those who have no knowledge or experience outside the confines of their own experience, the way of using that personal experience as a basis for all one's judgements.

experimental aesthetics (art) a branch of psychology which attempts to evaluate empirical 'truths' about art, its appeal and its elements and generally investigate its cultural values.

expiries (advert) customers who have once subscribed to a magazine but no longer do so.

explication (govt) a word very popular among EEC bureaucrats to mean a highly detailed explanation, probably from Fr. 'explication de texte', a detailed examination of a literary work.

exploitation (movies) 1. all phases of publicity, advertising, promotion to market the finished product. 2. the making of films that depend on a specific topic which is worked hard for a number of decreasingly successful attempts and then abandoned: *blaxploitation, sexploitation* (qqv). Such films lack any intrinsic value other than the possibility of spectacularly vulgar promotion techniques.

exploitation pictures (movies) see *exploitation* (2).

explore *v* (medic) to perform an exploratory operation.

explosion shot (sport) in golf, a shot that 'explodes' the ball from where it has been lodged in a sand bunker.

explosion wipe (TV) a wipe (qv) that bursts out from the centre of the screen, exploding over the picture it removes.

exponential smoothing (business) aka: *adaptive forecasting*: a forecasting technique which aims for added accuracy by weighting the results with regard to significant trends within the area under consideration; popularly used for inventory and production control, forecasts of margins and other financial data.

exposure (rock business) the promotion of the product (qv), an equivalent to exploitation (qv).

exposure weights (marketing) the measure of the value of the exposure of one advertisement in several different media.

extend (milit) USMC: to re-enlist for one or two years beyond one's original period of service.

extended problem solving (marketing) aka: *new task*: a buying situation in which the buyer has no knowledge or experience of the product category.

extension (gambling) the maximum sum of money a bookmaker will take on at his own risk for each event; any sums over this he will 'lay off' on fellow bookies.

externalisation (stock market/US) the transaction of deals in shares by transmitting orders to buy and sell on the floor of the Exchange, rather than through a broker's office.

externality (govt) anything that occurs for which plans have not been prepared in advance; a surprise, usually an unpleasant one. The usual method of dealing with externality is to *internalise* it, by creating a plan that will deal with it now and in the case of it occurring again. This does not, however, preclude the appearance of *other* externals.

extra (movies) a crowd actor who has no dialogue other, possibly, than 'rhubarb' (qv).

externalise labour costs (econ) the persuading of a customer to perform part of a required job himself, usually in the form of 'do-it-yourself'; in retail trade, the encouraging of self-service supermarkets, petrol stations, etc.

exteropsychic functioning (new therapy) in TA (transactional analysis, qv): the concept of the parent (qv), the judgemental part of one's being.

eyeballs (aerospace) the various positions of the eyeballs when travelling in space have created a variety of astronaut shorthand, ie: *eyeballs down*: suffering severe positive acceleration; *eyeballs up*: under a negative g-force, downward acceleration; *eyeballs in*: acceleration from behind when upright, from below when prone; *eyeballs out*: deceleration when upright.

eyes only (espionage, govt) a notation on secret or sensitive documents that precedes the name of the person for whose eyes and none other it is destined. (cf: *need-to-know*)

E

F

fabulous invalid, the (theatre/US) the stage itself which survives endless setbacks, prophecies of its demise, yet keeps coming back like an ailing invalid, still a trouper to the last.

faces (police/UK) 1. general reference to known criminals (cf: *bodies*). 2. those taxi-drivers who refuse any but high-paying fares described as 'airport faces', 'nightclub faces', 'abortion faces' etc.

facilitator (new therapies) a member of Rogerian group who quickly suppresses anyone who attempts to offer a less than completely enthusiastic statement by smothering them with calming embraces and general repetition of the ideology and 'facilitates' their acceptance of the therapeutic 'party line'.

facility trip (govt, pols) trips made by bureaucrats, national or local politicians, usually at the expense of tax- or rate-payers in order to 'explore local conditions' etc. Those who criticise such trips tend to brand them as *junkets* with its implication of non-stop amusement and very little 'research'.

facility visit (public relations) a press visit for interviews or picture-taking which is arranged, along with plenty of food and drink, to benefit those individuals, companies or products that a PR wishes to push.

fact-finding *n* (US family court) euphemism for the *trial* in this equivalent of UK juvenile court.

faction (publishing) a work of fiction that is taken with only minimal alterations from events that actually happened. The literary equivalent of TV's docudrama (qv).

factography (art) the method whereby a photographer/artist operates more as a journalist who presents as 'art' a selection of pictures and information (always with a political import) which is reminiscent of the 'dialectical documentary' style of the Novy Lef group of the 1920s.

factoid (publishing, media) a published statement that takes on the 'reality' of a fact by virtue of its having been published and absorbed by the public. Often referring to unsubstantiated events that have developed into modern myth. Coined in 1973 by Norman Mailer as a defence of such factoids in his 'biography' of the late Marilyn Monroe.

factory (police/UK) the police station, especially the gloomier, Victorian relics with the implications of dark, satanic imprisonment.

factory (drugs) a wholesale distribution point for narcotics.

fade (sport) in golf, a controlled curve from left to right by a right-hander and right to left by a left-hander.

fade *v* (gambling) to cover all or part of the shooter's (qv) main bet on his own achieving a point (qv).

fade (media) 1. (radio) the gradual reduction of the volume. 2. (movies, TV) the gradual reduction of the brightness of the picture, or the volume of sound.

faded giant (milit) US Dept. of Defense Nuclear Accident Code: an accident within a nuclear reactor.

fade in (TV, movies) the slow emergence of a scene out of blackness (cf: *fade-out* 2)

fade-out (media) 1. (radio) intermittent, temporary loss of sound through atmospheric disturbance. 2. (TV, movies) the gradual fading out of a picture into blackness.

fade out (milit) US Dept. of Defense Level 1 war readiness: every commander is to act for himself in the ultimate state of nuclear combat.

fail *v* (stock market) the failure of a broker or his firm to deliver promised stocks at a given time.

fail-safe (milit, aerospace) an in-built mechanism that in theory will take over in the case of mechanical breakdown and restore the system to a safe situation; in international relations, the concept of establishing procedures that will not permit a nuclear war to be triggered 'by mistake' or by a lone psychotic. US bombers have a *fail safe point* to which they fly in the case of an emergency but which they must not pass unless so ordered; this permits the checking of whether or not the emergency must finally lead to war; if not, the bombers are ordered back.

failsoft (computers) aka: *graceful degradation*: the ensuring that while one part of the computer's mechanism may be faulty, this fault does not destroy the overall capacity to work. Full efficiency will obviously be impaired but it will still be possible to run programs, no data will be lost, etc.

fair *v* (movies) in animation, the making sure that all movements blend together smoothly and that there are no jumps or jerks in the film.

From the traditional use of fair (qv) in the aircraft industry.

fair *v* (aerospace) the smoothing of the exposed parts of the aeroplane to reduce air resistance to a minimum.

fairbank *v* (gambling) aka: *throw a cop*: 1. for the dealer or bank to make a cheating move on behalf of a player in order to encourage him to bet more heavily and stay in the game longer – at which point such moves will be directed *against* him. 2. to let the player win a prize or a bet.

fair list *n* (indust relats) aka: *union label* (US): the opposite of a black list: those individuals and companies with whom union agreements have been made and which therefore are acceptable for trading.

fairness doctrine (media/US) aka: *equal time*: the principle in radio and TV which permits rival points of view to make themselves heard or seen when dealing with controversial issues. (cf: *balance*)

fairy money (advert) from 'money-off' coupons that were attached to such household products as 'Fairy Liquid': the money that manufacturers reimburse the retailer who accepts these coupons from his customers.

fake *v* (music) in jazz, for musicians to improvise a passage.

fake *v* (sex) for a homosexual hustler to *fake X out* is to con him into paying extra to enjoy apparently exceptional sexual 'equipment'.

fake book (music) an illegal publication of otherwise copyrighted musical melodies from popular music, plagiarised and sold to musicians.

fake the marks (stock market) for shares to change hands at fictitious prices which are announced in order to trick a broker's rivals.

Falklands factor (pols/UK) the phenomenon following the Falklands War in 1982 whereby an otherwise unpopular Conservative government, and in particular the Prime Minister Mrs. Thatcher, could for a while do no wrong (despite no apparent alleviation of the catastrophic economy) since it was under their leadership that the war had been won.

fallback (milit) the material – earth, remains of buildings, etc. – that is blown into the air by a nuclear explosion and ultimately, and radioactively, falls back to the ground.

fallback *n* (indust relats) something available in an emergency; something that can be relied upon if all else fails; esp. of a minimum wage that is still paid even if work is (temporarily) unavailable.

fallback position (pols/US) a tacitly accepted position to which a politician accepts from the start of a new policy or negotiation that he will be willing to retreat.

fallibilism (science) coined by the mathematician Charles Pierce (1839–1914): the concept that in science (or in everyday life) there are no beliefs so absolute that they might not in fact be fallible.

falling leaf (aerospace) an aerobatic manoeuvre in which an aeroplane is deliberately stalled, then let sideslip while losing height until the power is regained.

fall line (sport) in ski-ing, the logical, natural route from the top of a slope to its bottom, the course a rolling ball would follow.

fallout (milit) radioactive debris following a nuclear explosion; the deaths and genetic damage caused by fallout may equal or surpass those caused by the initial explosion of a weapon. (cf: *enhanced radiation*)

fallout *n* (pols) by an extension of the military use (qv): the unpleasant or unexpected side-effects of a political decision, statement or other action. (cf: *externality*)

false image (photography) the result of using a defective lens: a secondary image appears on the plate or photographic paper in addition to the desired picture. (cf: *ghost*)

false move (movies) an unplanned or erroneous action by an actor during a shot; such a move may well confuse a technician into thinking the move was a cue and he will compound the error by making his own false move.

false positives (criminology) predictions of future criminal activities that turn out to be wrong.

false positives (medic/US) a diagnosis that states incorrectly that a patient has a particular disease. Thus *false negative*: the diagnosis that states incorrectly that a patient is free from disease.

false sponsors (espionage) false leads, covers (qqv) or similar blind alleys designed to confuse the opposition.

family (crime/US) in the US Mafia, a division of the overall organisation, containing 450/600 members who on the whole have no legal or blood ties, but are linked by an intense sense of inter-personal loyalty; a criminal grouping with its own territory and internal hierarchy.

family brands (marketing) the use of the same brand name across several product categories.

family ganging (medic/US) the unethical practice of persuading or requiring a patient who is genuinely in need of care to bring along other members of his family so that the programme under which he is being treated can charge the public funds or insurance company for each of them. (cf: *pingponging*)

family house (TV/US) a TV viewing daypart (qv) in which it is supposed children will be watching and thus sex and violence are banned from all programmes then screened. (cf: *prime time, early fringe, late fringe*)

family jewels (espionage) from sl. 'family jewels' to mean male genitals: used by the CIA to denote such internal and potentially embarras-

F

F

sing secrets that the agency would prefer were never disclosed in public; skeletons in the espionage closet; eg: CIA assassinations and similar illegal destabilisation (qv).

family violence (social wk) a general term that covers 'baby battering' and 'wife battering' and is being extended to cover a newly accepted phenomenon 'granny bashing' – the ill-treatment, often physical, of those aged relatives who live with or are looked after by their family.

famished (milit) US Dept. of Defense radio code: have you any instructions for me.

fan (sport) in baseball, to dismiss or strike out a batter, who 'fans' his bat ineffectually at the passing ball.

fan (police/UK) a fast, superficial body search in which the searcher's hands move quickly over the subject's clothes, 'fanning' them for any suspicious items.

fanac (TV) the activity for or by the fans of the scifi series 'Star Trek'.

fancy *n* (sport) a term coined in the 18th century for those rich and poor who followed prizefighting, horse-racing, gambling and kindred excitements, still popular with sports writers who wish to evoke a period flavour in their references to such fans.

fanning (police/UK) stealing performed by a pickpocket.

fanny (milit) RN: the mess kettle; kettle, here, meaning any small, round, general duty utensil.

Fanny Adams (milit) RN: either tinned meat or the stew that has been made from it; a derogatory reference to its being butchered from a murder victim of 1867.

fanny-dipper (sport) in surfing, an ordinary swimmer – who merely wets his behind – rather than a surfer.

fantasy fit (sex) the dressing up by a homosexual hustler (qv) to satisfy those clients who enjoy 'costume' games – usually as a Hell's Angel, construction worker, Nazi or similar 'macho' figure.

fanzine (media) any magazine produced nonprofessionally by the fans of a specific celebrity, film, book, fictional character, TV series, etc. (cf: *crudzine*)

fargo (espionage) a listening device concealed on an agent's body for the relaying of his conversation with a target back to a remote tape recorder or witness.

fari 'n ponciu (Mafia) Sicilian dialect lit. 'to mix a drink': to knife.

farm *n* (milit) the launch sites of anti-ballistic missiles; possibly from their being 'planted' in underground silos.

farm *v* (sport) in cricket, the playing of a batsman in such a way that he manages to receive the majority of balls bowled.

farmers (milit) RN: a derogatory nickname for helicopter pilots used by those who fly fighters.

farm team (sport) aka: *farm club*: in baseball, a minor league club affiliated to a major league organisation in which new players can be groomed and from whose ranks the future major leaguers are recruited.

fartlek (sport) from Sw. trans 'speed play': in running, a training method for middle- and long-distance races in which bursts of fast running are mixed with slower periods.

fascinoma (medic/US) a pun on fascinate and -oma (as in carcinoma) meaning illness: any particularly interesting disease.

fashion goods (commerce) any goods – not necessarily clothing – that depend for their appeal on shifting tastes and their ability, with fast-altering design or style, to take advantage of those shifts.

fast *a* (science) in nuclear physics, those processes that involve fast neutrons (those neutrons that have not been slowed down by any moderator after being produced by the fission of a nucleus) such as fast breeder reactors or fast fission.

fast pace (milit) US Dept. of Defense War Readiness Code: level four (out of five) of readiness.

fast side (sport) in soccer, the shortest distance from a goalkeeper's point of view, for the ball to travel from a player into/towards the net; thus *slow side* the longest distance.

fast track *n, v* (business) upwardly mobile, 'whizkid', go-getting executives are said to travel in 'the fast track': the quick way to the top, with all the excitement and risk that such speedy travel can involve. Thus *fast-tracking* describes such activities.

fast-track procedure (govt/US) to cut through bureaucratic red tape.

fast track/slow track (sex) aka: *hard track/soft track*: used by black pimps to describe the difference between the East Coast cities (esp. New York) (hard/fast) and the West Coast (soft/slow); also used to denote the main centre of street-walking in any given city.

fat (gambling) aka: *loaded*: anyone who has plenty of money.

fat (theatre) a meaty, important role which is defined less by its size, which may not be great, but by its dramatic effectiveness.

fat (press) the printer's description of type-setting which is easy, fast and simple.

fat (sport) in golf, a ball that has been hit too low – well beneath the ideal distance and accuracy-producing centre.

father file (computers) when a file is updated, the original file becomes the *father file*, the file prior to that the *grandfather file* and the latest file the *son file*.

fat man (milit) the detonator of a fission bomb which uses plutonium as a charge.

fattening up (milit) officially known as 'rehabilitation': a system whereby troops just returned from a tough operation are given special treatment, extra supplies and similar luxuries calculated to keep them happy, psychologically sound and ready for the next turn of duty.

fat work (indust relats) any work in which it is reasonably easy to obtain productivity bonuses; those who achieve this are *grabbers*. The opposite is *lean work*.

fault-tree analysis (business, science) a system that starts by positing a failure and then attempting to trace it step by step back to its source. Fault-trees are feasible in theory, but when used to deal with an infinitely complex machine, rather than the popular model of a car that won't start, they can vanish into the thousands of possible causes, each of which must be traced and eliminated before looking at the next.

faulty internal dialogue (new therapies) in assertiveness training, a means of developing an individual's psychological self-reliance (something on the lines of a 1980s Dale Carnegie course), the idea that one's self-perception and inner feelings are not adjusted to the correct 'positive' attitude.

favourite son (pols/US) a candidate for the Presidency who is backed mainly by the party and political leadership of his own state. Every convention sees the nomination of a number of favourite sons who stand less as serious candidates than in order to promote the interest of their own state, so achieved by bartering its support for promises from the actual candidate.

fax (press) (abbrev) facsimile: the transmission by wire or radio of graphic material from one newspaper to another, or from a remote source to a paper.

FBS (milit) (abbrev) *forward based systems*: a term coined by Soviet negotiators to describe those US forces other than ICBMs (qv) such as missiles based in NATO or other allied countries or on aircraft carriers or submarines, all capable of delivering a strike against the USSR.

fearnought suit (milit) RN: a protective suit made of specially treated strong woollen cloth worn for fighting on-board fires.

feather *v* (sport) in snooker or billiards, to run the cue backwards and forwards across the bridge between finger and thumb prior to making a shot.

feather-bedding (indust relats) essentially the obtaining of pay without having to do the work; a situation where a lax employer permits the unions to impose such rules as they wish on the production, such as creating extra jobs where none are needed.

feathering (press) when the ink smears on the paper, causing the words to be blurred and hard to read.

feature (computers) any surprising property of a program which may or may not have been appreciated by the original creator of the program. If the feature is not documented, it can be termed a *bug* (qv) but likewise the apparent error that is classed as a bug may become a feature once it is documented and can therefore, for all its oddness, be expected.

feature (movies) a fictional entertainment film of more than 3000' or running longer than appx. 34 minutes. *Second feature* on a double bill is a film of less importance than the main feature, or one that initially gained poor reviews and has thus been relegated.

feature (press) a non-fiction article, usually longer than a news story and usually illustrated, or an interview published in a newspaper or magazine.

featured players (movies, TV) leading actors who are ranked below the actual stars but above the *supporting players*; often ranked as *guest stars*, a title that currently applies almost without exception to anyone who is given a role in a TV series.

FEBA (milit) (abbrev) the *forward edge of the battle area*: the line on a battlefield where the opposing forces are actually facing and fighting each other in reasonably close contact.

federal revenue enhancement (govt/US) a bureaucratic euphemism for the raising of national taxes.

feed *n, v* (TV) a transmission, or the act of transmitting. (cf: *bird*)

feed (theatre) the 'straight man' who works alongside the comedian and provides him with the 'feed lines', the cues for his jokes.

feed *v* (sport) in soccer, to pass the ball to another player.

feedback (rock business) any reviews, comments, opinions from the media, retailers or consumers concerning a new product.

feedback (new therapies) one person's reaction to another's action or speech by analysing, criticising, agreeing but always in some way modifying the original statement by the response.

feedback (pols) the response from one's peers, supporters, potential voters or opponents that comes in reply to a politician's action or statement. Such response is available both during a campaign and after election to office although the candidate's *own* feedback may well differ as to his altering status.

feeding (radio) the transmitting of live or recorded material to one other station or to an entire network along specially reserved post office lines. Thus *refeed* the repeat transmission of material already sent; *clean feed*: the sending of a live event with no commentary or a programme intended for the network but which will have added to it the relevant voice-overs, advertisements etc. from each separate station; *line feed*: any feed that is booked on the post office line.

F

feel a collar (police/UK) to arrest a suspected person. (cf: *get/give a tug*)

feeling talk (new therapies) in assertiveness training, the voicing of 'meaningful dialogue' rather than idle chatter.

feep (computers) 1. *n* the softly ringing bell of a display terminal. 2. *v* to cause the display to make a 'feep'.

feet dry (milit) air intercept code: I am over land; the designated contact is over land.

feet wet (milit) air intercept code: I am over water; my designated contact is over water.

feevee (TV) pay cable TV in US including various specialist subscriber channels for 24 hour news, first run movies, sport, porno, etc.; scheduled for UK in the near future.

felix (milit) British Army nickname for bomb disposal units.

fellow traveller (pols) one who sympathises with communism but has not actually joined the Party; by extension anyone who agrees with a specific philosophy, but is unwilling to make a firm and public commitment.

fen (TV) the recognised plural of fan, rather than usual fans, when referring to dedicated watchers of the scifi series 'Star Trek'.

fence mending (pols) for a politician, whatever his national activities, to make sure that those within his constituency are properly looked after – they, after all, will be responsible for maintaining him in power.

fertile (science) in nuclear physics, a material – usually uranium[238] or thorium – capable of being changed into a fissile isotope by the capture of a neutron.

fetichism of output (pols) the obsession within socialist countries of reaching the pre-set norms of output designated in advance in a specific economic plan, irrespective of the quality or the quantity that is actually required under the current circumstances.

feu de joie (milit) Fr. lit 'fire of joy': a ceremonial firing of blanks for which a line of troops fire off their rifles one after another, each immediately following his predecessor; the whole line fires three blanks per man.

few (milit) any total of men or objects less than eight. (cf: *many*)

FGA (marketing) aka: *FMI* (abbrev) *free give away*; *free mention*: premiums (qv) given away to purchasers of whatever product is being promoted.

FIDE (aerospace) (acro) *flight dynamics engineer*: an engineer who deals with the dynamics of a space flight, such as velocity, elevation, changes in height or direction. (cf: *GUIDO, RETRO*)

fidelity bond (commerce) aka: *fidelity insurance*: a policy taken out by an employer to protect him against the possible dishonesty or non-performance of an employee.

FIDO (aerospace) (acro) *fog investigation*

dispersal operation: a method of dispersing fog above airports by using the heat from petrol burners.

field (medic) that area of a patient's body that is actually being operated on.

field (TV) 50% of the whole TV picture of (in UK) 625 lines. Each 'frame' that one sees is composed of two interlaced fields of 312.5 lines each.

field (govt) the 'real world' of want, poverty, violence, deprivation, social inequality, greed and similar variables which define everyday life for the majority and onto which a government or bureaucracy attempts to impose its solutions or plans.

field (computers) a subdivision of a record, a single item of information that relates to the rest of the record; if the record were a quotation, there might be fields for the name, the source, the words themselves, the date, etc.

field music (milit) USMC: 1. a drummer or a trumpeter. 2. a small drum and bugle corps created by amalgamating all the various single field musics on a post into one group.

field painting (art) field painters treat a picture's surface as one continuous and extended plane with the whole picture regarded as a single unit with the result that neither the ground nor the figures are given greater value.

FIFO (computers) (acro) *first in first out*: a method of storing data so that the first piece to have been filed can be the first one available for retrieval.

fifteen and two (advert/US) a discount system offered by newspapers to agency space buyers: 15 per cent commission plus 2 per cent discount for prompt payment.

fifteen minutes (theatre/US) a call to remind actors that the performance starts in fifteen minutes. (cf: *the quarter*)

fifth column (pols) a clandestine group of one's own supporters operating in an enemy country, or within one's own borders, if under occupation; or a similar enemy group in your country or one which you occupy. From the siege of Madrid (1936) when the loyalist General Mola claimed that in addition to the four columns of his army laying the siege there was a fifth column of secret supporters within the city.

fifth pathway (medic) a means for an individual who has obtained all or most of his/her medical training outside the US to enter post-graduate training in the US by fulfilling certain set criteria.

fighter alley (milit) civil pilots' nickname for the airspace over the Ruhr in Germany where the air is thick with NATO fighters intermingling with the commercial jets.

fighting for one's corner (pols) 'which, freely translated, amounts to ensuring that whoever else faces the consequences of expenditure cuts, it is not their department' (L. Chapman, *Waste*

Away, 1982). A concept that expands to cover the Minister's efforts to escape the blame for any unpopular measure. (cf: *CYA*)

file (press, radio) to send in, write, or tape a story for a newspaper or radio news programme.

filibuster (pols) a technique, originated in America and based on Rule 22 of the Senate which allows for unlimited debate on any measure before it need be brought to the vote, used by politicians who wish to defeat a specific measure (usually when they are in a minority and the measure is otherwise popular) in which they arrange non-stop speeches, one after another, to defeat or at least amend the measure. Filibustering is banned in the House of Commons where too lengthy a speech can be deemed irrelevant by the Speaker and the MP ordered to sit down. In Japan a similar style of delaying tactics is translated as the *cow waddle*: whereby members of the Diet take infinitely long to progress from their seats to the ballot box.

fill or kill (stock market) an order to offer a trade to the pit (qv) three times and to be cancelled if not executed immediately.

fills (press) extra material inserted in a story or in a page of news.

fills (music) in jazz, extra, possibly improvised material inserted into a piece to lengthen it, add new interest and generally appeal to the listener.

fill your card (sport) in big game hunting, the promise to kill off a pre-selected number or type of animals that the hunter has chosen before starting the hunt.

film (movies) the use of *film* with neither definite nor indefinite article is ever popular amongst the cognoscenti and the cineastes. The implication is of some great and limitless concept that has little relation to the actual wheeler-dealer commercial world of popular film production and exploitation.

film horse (TV, movies) a device used in editing rooms which separates the various picture and sound tracks as and when they are required.

film noir (movies) a Fr. coinage for the genre of US gangster thrillers, particularly those made by Warner Brothers, in the 1930s and early 1940s.

film tree (TV, movies) a wooden stand used in editing rooms on which are clipped various lengths of film that will be needed for cutting and splicing.

filth *n* (crime/UK) general term for the CID, the detective branch of the British police.

final cut (movies) the final stage of editing: the film that the audiences will see. The power to determine the final cut is often the subject of jealous infighting between the front office (qv) which takes a business perspective and the director, who prefers an artistic one.

final order (milit) the last command to military leaders, instructing them to fire at will and let every man act for himself, issued if the world was locked in the death throes of a spasm war (qv).

finding *n* (US law) in the Family (juvenile) Court: the conviction of a defendant.

finding the balance (stock market) when referring to accounts, the process of making sure that all entries in those accounts have been properly completed; ie: balancing the books.

fine cut (TV) the last stage of editing a TV film or programme when all cutting is over and the material is ready for public exhibition.

fine grain print (movies) a print which uses high quality stock (qv) which has no silver salt deposits (which deteriorate in time) and which is used for making duplicate negatives.

fine-tuning (pols) the art of excising any embarrassing or politically redundant material from a candidate's speech or broadcast and thus both putting the candidate in the best light and depriving his detractors of an opportunity to attack a weak point.

finger *n* (aerospace) in airport architecture, a long, narrow pier which stretches out from the main building to enable a number of planes to park around it and embark or disembark their passengers.

finger *v* (police) to betray or inform a person or plan to the police.

finger man (gambling) 1. one who points out a gambler, who is presumably well-off, to a hold-up mob. 2. one who tells police of an illegal gambling game.

finish fetish (art) an obsessive concern on behalf of several US artists to give their art works the sort of high-gloss super-smooth surface most often found on new cars.

finite deterrence (milit) war plan considered by Eisenhower and Kennedy administrations in which US nuclear forces were stripped down to a fleet of (nearly) invulnerable submarines. Political and milit. pressures ended this theory, though it was briefly disinterred by ex-submariner Jimmy Carter in late 1970s.

fink (indust relats) a company spy or a worker who refuses to join a strike. (cf: *scab*)

finsburies (movies) rhyming slang: Finsbury Park – arc (light).

fire and forget *n* (milit) any missile that has a self-guiding smart (qv) internal computer that steers it towards its target with no help from its launcher and which can thus be 'forgotten' once it has been fired.

firebreak *n* (milit) from the term in forestry for a bare strip of land between woods, intended to suppress spreading fires; the theoretical gap between conventional (qv) weapons and their use and the starting of a fullscale nuclear war.

fire brigade (milit) from the normal use: a highly trained, extra-mobile military unit designed to deal speedily with any outbreaks of trouble

F

wherever its commander feels it should be employed. Originated in Vietnam, and now epitomised by the US Rapid Deployment Force.

firefight (milit) a short-range ground engagement between opposing forces and using mainly light, short-range weapons.

firing step (theatre/UK) a platform in the flies (qv) where slack ropes are coiled out of sight.

firm (commerce) 1. a market in which prices are steady. 2. a *firm* offer or bid is one that carries no conditions as opposed to a 'subject' bid, which is subject to such conditions. 3. *in firm hands*: holders of securities with a respectable pedigree and not short-term operators.

firm (police) an ironic use of the normal business term to describe of gang of organised criminals – a group of robbers, car thieves, forgers, etc.

firmware (computers) 1. software and hardware (qqv) so integrated as to make individual items indistinguishable. 2. a handwired logic circuit that can perform the functions of a program.

first Australians (govt, sociol) a euphemism for Aboriginals. (cf: *native Americans, New Commonwealth*)

first call (TV) a TV company exchanges the right for first call on an actor's services at any time they need him for guarantee to continue giving him work.

first column (espionage) on the analogy of fifth column (qv) as a hostile force: the revival or protection of friendly regimes or the arming and financing of guerillas whom one wishes to see take power. Given its coinage by the CIA, it can be assumed that such regimes and guerillas will always be anti-communist or rightwing.

first generation (tech) used in all areas of technology – aerospace design, hifi equipment, computers, etc. – to describe the earliest, and thus relatively simple or crude models of a specific machine or piece of equipment.

first line managers (indust relats) the lowest level of management – foremen, supervisors etc. – who actually deal regularly and closely with the workforce.

first man through the door (movies) the leading villain. (cf: *heavy. dog heavy*)

first notice day (finance) the first date, varying by contracts and exchanges, on which notices of intention to deliver actual financial instruments against futures are authorised.

first olive out of the bottle (business) the first olive in the bottle tends to get in the way of the free flow of those beneath it: thus any hindrance or impediment to the free flow of ideas, trading, action or progress. This can be a person, a legal tangle or any similar nuisance that must be dealt with.

first run (movies) the first time a new film is exhibited.

first strike (milit) the first attack in a nuclear war; thus *first strike capability*: the ability to launch a first strike with the intention of destroying an enemy's capacity to retaliate. (cf: *second strike*)

first team (movies) those actors – the stars and the support – who are actually filmed, rather than their stand-ins who take their places for the arrangement of the lights, the camera angles and similar aspects of the take.

first use (milit) the first use of a specific intensity or type of military measure; thus, if a first strike (qv) were conventional (qv), then a nuclear second strike (qv) would still be the *first use* of such weapons.

fiscal drag (econ) the time that elapses between the government's originating and legislating for an economic policy and its theoretically or even practically taking effect.

fish (milit) RN: 1. a submarine. 2. a torpedo.

fishhead (milit) RN: any naval officer on a carrier who does not fly. (cf: *black shoe*)

fishing expedition (pols/US) an early fact- and theme-finding probe undertaken by a party committee in order to assess good issues and tactics for a forthcoming campaign. Usually based on looking in depth at the plans of the opposition party. Such an expedition has no pre-set aims, but will use whatever useful material is 'hooked'.

fishplates (sport) aka: *hangers*: in mountaineering, an expansion bolt that will take a small bracket which helps overcome long expanses of rock with no possible foothold.

fishpole (TV) a hand-held microphone boom, appx. 2 metres long.

fitter (movies) a musical director or conductor who was given the task of fitting appropriate music to silent films.

fit-up (theatre) a temporary stage that can be taken down and moved from venue to venue according to need; by extension the theatrical company who tours with a fit-up.

fit up *v* (police) to frame a villain for a crime that he may well not have committed, by 'planting' evidence, bringing in perjured witnesses, etc. Staunchly denied by the police, endlessly claimed by the criminals. From the idea of making the crime 'fit' the villain.

five and nine (theatre) the basic theatrical makeup, based on the numbers of makeup sticks given by their makers, Leichners.

five biggies (new therapies) coined by Leonard Orr for his Theta rebirthing therapy: the five major areas of personal problems which must be dealt with and overcome if an ideal life is to be achieved: 1. birth trauma, 2. parental disapproval syndrome, 3. specific negatives, 4. unconscious death urge, 5. other life times. Confront and come to terms with all these and all must be well.

five by five (aerospace) excellent radio reception, based on a 1–5 scale for both volume (loud) and audibility (clear). Thus reception can be 4+5, 5+3, etc.

five duties (pols) as prescribed by the Communist Party of Vietnam: 1. devotion to communism, 2. the striving for political, ethical and occupational self-improvement through study and training, 3. close co-operation and rapport with the masses, 4. the maintenance of party discipline, 5. the support of the policy of proletarian internationalism.

five good drive (pols) in the People's Republic of China, a campaign launched in 1963 for raising productivity. A 'five good' team excels in 1. implementing party policy, 2. promoting political education, 3. fulfilling the collective production targets, 4. fulfilling these targets in an economical way, 5. doing all tasks in the way ordered and established by the state.

five mile high club (airline) a 'club' whose membership is open to anyone, crew or passengers, who have made love in an aircraft, supposedly cruising 5 miles up in the sky.

five percenter (pols/US) on the analogy of 'Mr. Ten Per Cent', the show business agent: a self-appointed fixer who claims to know 'the right people' and can negotiate a lucrative contract with the government for a 5% kickback.

five pure classes (pols) in the People's Republic of China: 1. the workers, 2. the poor and lower-middle peasants, 3. soldiers, 4. good party officials, 5. revolutionary martyrs.

five recommendations (pols) in People's Republic of China: 1. civility, 2. politeness, 3. public hygiene, 4. discipline, 5. morality.

five Ws (press) the traditional questions a reporter should ask and should then include in the perfect lead paragraph of his story: who, what, why, where, when?????

fix (espionage) a complex of pressures specially engineered by a sanctifying (qv) team to control the target they are blackmailing. Fixes can be *low intensity*: only marginally compromising, if such mildness will achieve the right effects on an easily scared person, or it may have to be upgraded if the target is found to be brazening things out. The perfect situation is an *okay fix*.

fix *n* (aerospace) a reliable indication of the position of an aircraft by taking a bearing – either visually or by radio – of that airplane with reference to fixed objects.

fix (drugs) one injection of a narcotic drug; the smallest amount of the drug that can be purchased.

fixer (gambling) a person who has the right political connections to ensure that an illegal gambling enterprise will be – for the right price – fully 'protected'.

fixing (finance) the twice daily determining of the price of gold on the London Gold Market, carried out in the offices of bankers N. M. Rothschild by representatives of the four firms of bullion dealers.

fix money (gambling) payoffs to local police, politicians etc. that permit gamblers or casino owners/operators to purchase 'protection'. (cf: *ice*)

fizzer (milit) British Army: a charge sheet; thus *on a fizzer*: on a charge for some breach of discipline.

fizzer (sport) in cricket, a ball that keeps fast and low and possibly changes direction radically after it has pitched.

flack (entertain) a press or publicity agent.

flack (pols/US) analogous to the entertainment use (qv), a government official who propounds the official line, an apologist; such officials may be high or low in rank.

flag (press) see: *banner*.

flag *n, v* (computers) any type of indicator that marks a part of the data or program for special attention; to mark the data or program with a flag.

flag (aerospace) a warning plate that flicks up on an aircraft's control panel either to point out a current malfunction or the possibility of a problem that will occur if no immediate action is taken to deal with it.

flag (sex) aka: *fladge*: (abbrev) flagellation: magazines or films portraying flagellation for sexual/pornographic purposes.

flag (press) a statement of the name, ownership, address, etc. of a publication which is printed on an editorial page or the front page.

flag *v* (milit) to attach some special indication to a file that announces to any other user that it must not be altered in any way.

flag (TV, movies) a square board or stand that is used to mask a light or to shade the camera lens.

flag day (computers) a software (qv) change which is not compatible with current or future models and which will therefore cost the user a great deal of money.

flag-flying (gambling) in bridge, to make an overbid that would almost inevitably fail, just to liven up the game.

flagging (TV) vertical breakup at the top of a TV picture on second rate video recordings.

flag list (milit) RN: all active officers of flag rank (equivalent to that of admiral): admiral of the fleet, admiral, vice-admiral, rear-admiral on the General List, plus officers of equivalent status on the lists of instructor, medical and dental officers.

flags (milit) RN: a flag-lieutenant, the admiral's aide-de-camp.

flagship sites (commerce) the leading, showplace stores, hotels, garages, etc. on which a retailer concentrates his energies, advertising, promotion and probably greatest pride.

flagwaver (TV) an intermittent fault, due to some mechanical malfunction, which is hard to trace and may not be conveniently occurring

F

when the engineer is actually attempting to track it down.

flak (pols) 'negative feedback': adverse comment and criticism from the public, opposition or even fellow party members after the making of an unpopular policy or decision. Thus *flak-catcher*: a (usually junior) bureaucrat set up as a buffer between the complaining public and his superiors.

flak (milit) orig. from World War II *Flieger-abwehrkanone*: anti-aircraft gun and currently used as sl. for any anti-aircraft defences, incl. missiles. *Flak jacket*: bullet proof jackets not necessarily worn by airmen but by anyone who wishes protection from wounds.

flake *n* (police/US) an arrest that has as its main justification the officer's need to meet a specific quota or the satisfying of a public demand for increased police efficiency. (cf: *accommodation collar*)

flaking (police/US) planting incriminating evidence on or around the suspect to facilitate the arrest.

flam (music) a particular beat played on the side-drum.

flame *v* (computers) to speak incessantly and obsessively on a particular topic of little interest but to oneself; or to talk arrant and apparent nonsense about an otherwise interesting subject. (cf: *rave*)

flap (milit) any mild state of emergency.

flapping (horse-racing) any racing that is not subject to National Hunt Committee or Jockey Club rules or, in greyhound racing, those of the National Greyhound Racing Club. Thus *flappings*: small race meetings of this type; *flapping track*: a small, unlicensed greyhound racing track.

flap potential (espionage) from the military use (qv) any subject which, if brought to public light, would guarantee embarrassment to both the CIA in particular and the US government in general. (cf: *family jewels*)

flaps and seals (espionage) CIA: the standard course given to agents in the interception of mail.

flap shot (sex) aka: *wide open beaver*: in film or still pictures, a close-up of the labia and the vagina.

flaps well down (business) from the espionage term to describe an agent who – possibly through fears for his current efficiency or the likelihood of future career problems – is attempting to 'fly low', and is trying to keep well out of his superiors' way: in business, a more positive use that implies someone who knows just what he's doing and would rather get on with his job with minimum interference from above.

flare *n* (air crew) the pulling up of the plane's nose immediately before landing so that the plane sinks down slowly onto the runway rather than flying onto it.

flare (sport) in US football (abbrev) *flare pass*: a quick pass out to a back who is heading towards the sidelines.

flare (TV) dazzle off reflecting surfaces that is shown up in the camera's shot.

flare *v* (theatre/UK) to place and regulate the light and sound equipment.

flare out (aerospace) see: *flare*.

flaring (tech) the burning off of the natural gas found in conjunction with oil in oilfields; the current uses of natural gas for its own energy has led to a great diminution in flaring.

flash (TV) 1. a very brief shot. 2. a performer infinitely too pleased with himself and far too keen to show it.

flash (press) a brief news report sent over the wire, usually preceding a more detailed and longer story. Thus the *news flash* of TV, radio.

flash (drugs) the brief, pleasurable sensation that comes after the injection of narcotic drugs; by extension the immediate sensation that follows a deep puff of a strong marijuana cigarette.

flashback (movies) a break in the narrative that permits the insertion of a scene, episode, or sometimes the rest of the film which is told as a chronological back track; to childhood, another country, and so on.

FLASH NUDET (milit) US code: nuclear detonation recorded.

flashpack (commerce) a package which displays a 'special reduction' price, '50p off' etc.

flash roll (police) a wad of money which is never actually used, but is 'flashed' ostentatiously around to convince a criminal, eg. a drug dealer, that one wishes to make a purchase, at which point an arrest will be made.

flat *a* (sport) in US football, a team that is stale, lacking in energy or 'go'; the opposite of flat is either *crisp* or *up*.

flat *n* (horse-racing) those races along a course that involves only distance and no jumping; the racing that takes place in spring, summer and autumn. (cf: *flapping, sticks*)

flat *n* (TV, movies, theatre) a large moveable section of scenery made of wooden battens and stretched canvas or reinforced hardboard which is painted to represent a 'wall' or similar large piece of the background.

flat *a* (audio) a properly designed system which amplifies all frequencies equally with no 'discrimination' over a wide waveband.

flat (photography) a picture lacking in contrast between black and white.

flat (stock market) stock that carries no interest.

flat (commerce) unvarying, fixed, uniform, unmoved by changing external conditions. Eg: a flat fare, which works for all distances, irrespective of length, such as found on New York subways, etc.

flatbacker (sex) black pimp usage for a prostitute

who offers quantity to her pimp rather than quality to the clients.

flatfoot (milit) USMC: a sailor.

flat joint (gambling) aka: *flat store*: any crooked gambling environment.

flatline *v* (medic/US) from the flattening of the oscillating line on the monitor screens when the patient's heart is no longer beating: to die.

flat passers (gambling) crooked dice which have had the 6–1 sides shaved on one die and the 3–4 sides on the other, producing an excess of 4, 5, 9, 10 throws.

flats (publishing) small, thin, glossy, over-priced children's books produced to exploit the indulgent Christmas market.

flatties (police) from *flatfoot*: policemen; uniformed officers.

flat top (milit) USN: an aircraft carrier; *baby flat top* a smaller aircraft carrier, usually a cargo vessel which has been converted into a carrier for the duration.

flavour (science) a specific type or variety of quark (qv); there are approx. five flavours so far discovered.

flavour (computers) variety, type, kind, style. The addition of new varieties makes something *flavourful*. (cf: *vanilla*)

flea (medic/US) a medical intern, so called because they hover about the patient's bed.

flex form (press) a style of newspaper design that is based around the advertisements, allowing for them to be centred on a page or otherwise placed so that copy must flow around them rather than setting its own design.

flexibility (indust relats) the willingness of a union 'shop' to overlook strict demarcation lines and/or to accept movement of personnel to other parts of the plant or company.

flexible response (milit) the concept of meeting aggression with a suitable level of counter-aggression and in the relevant environment; always, unless that aggression is a nuclear first strike, leaving the option of escalation (qv) available if required or feasible.

flexitime (indust relats) aka: *flextime, flexible time*: the staggering of working hours in an attempt to improve an employee's working standards by offering a more relaxed 'day' than the usual 'nine to five'; research has shown that this choice (within some limits) of working hours has improved standards/productivity, since workers are using those hours at which they are themselves most alert and efficient.

flies (theatre) that area above the stage where lights, scenery, etc. are suspended and can be raised/lowered as required. Such scenery is *flown*.

flight attendant (air crew) an antonym for the traditional *stewardess*, part of the contemporary urge to alter facts by 'softening' language, esp. job descriptions.

flight capital (econ) funds that are transferred from one country to another, often in the direction of the anonymity of a Swiss numbered account, in order to avoid taxes, hide illicit profits, hedge against inflation, etc., etc.

flight envelope (aerospace) a set of limits – speed, altitude, range, payload, manoeuvrability, etc. – that exist in the design and capabilities of any model of aircraft.

flimsy (milit) RN: an officer's certificate of service.

flip (milit) in gunnery, the jumping around of the barrel of a gun at the moment of discharge.

flip (finance) a flexible loan insurance plan in which a down payment is made into a savings account from which payments can be taken to supplement the interest when the loan falls due.

flip chart (advert) a campaign presentation prepared on a number of pages linked by a ring binder and which can be 'flipped through' from page to page.

flip-flop (computers) the basic memory device of a computer: an electronic circuit with only two stable states. By placing a pulse on its input it can be made to alternate between these states. One flip flop stores one bit (qv) of information.

flipflop *v* (pols/US) from the uses both as 'somersault' and in a computer context: the ability of a politician to hold two opposing views simultaneously, an essential tool for the aspirant leader by which he can baffle first a constituency and later the whole electorate.

flipper (theatre/US) a short, narrow flat (qv) which is nailed to another larger flat in order to support it.

flipping (finance) the practice of unscrupulous private finance companies ('loansharks') who not only charge above average interest on a loan, but then charge interest on that interest if payments are not made swiftly enough. (cf: *vigorish*)

float *v* (finance) of a national currency: to fluctuate in respect of the general international currency market as regards its exchange rate.

float *n* (advert, press) a headline placed inside a large surrounding area of white space, in which it 'floats'.

floater (police) a dead body found floating or drowned in water.

floaters (prison/UK) paperback books which have been sent in to one inmate and which then circulate throughout the prison population.

floating point (computers) aka: *scientific notation*: the handling of very large numbers in the machine's limited space by moving the decimal point and performing the calculations with each number expressed as a factor of 10.

flog *v* (theatre) to remove the dust from canvas by beating it with a number of canvas strips secured on a wooden handle: the *flogger*.

flog the clock (milit) RN: the practice of illicitly

advancing the clock so as to shorten one's time on watch.

flong (press) a sheet of papier maché used to make a mould from a forme from which is cast a plate for printing a page of the newspaper.

flood (TV, movies) any unfocussed light source.

flooding (psychology) a method of treating a sufferer from a particular phobia by the gradual and controlled exposure of the patient to the cause of the phobia.

floor *n* (stock market) the trading area of the London Stock Exchange.

floor (TV) the ground area of a studio; thus *on the floor*: a programme in studio protection.

floor art (art) aka: *distributional art, ground art, litter sculpture*: modern style of sculpture that eschews traditional styles in favour of spreading out over the gallery or artist's studio floor. This use of the floor is parallel to the painter's use of a background against which the subjects of a painting are set.

floor broker (futures market) a member of the futures exchange who is paid a fee for executing orders for clearing members or their customers.

floorman (horse-racing) the assistant to a tic-tac man (who communicates the shifting odds from the larger bookmakers to the smaller ones by a series of established hand signals); a book-maker's runner.

floor trader (futures market) aka: *local*: a member who generally only trades for himself, for an account he controls, or who has such a trade made especially for him.

flop (police/UK) any house where a criminal can dump his weapons, burlary tools, loot, etc. so as to be 'clean' by the time the police come to search his person and property.

flop *v* (advert) to reverse a picture (for printing purposes), left to right or vice versa.

flopper (crime) one who specialises in defrauding insurance firms by 'falling down' on apparently 'dangerous' supermarket floors or staircases, collapsing in front of slow moving cars, etc. always making sure that it is worth the victim's while to pay up rather than make a fuss.

floppy (stock market) a *floppy market*: an unsteady market.

floppy disc (computers) a flexible storage medium, similar visually to a 45 rpm record, on which data is memorised and retrieved by the read/write head (qv).

flopsweat (entertain) the beads of sweat that break out on a performer's face when a performance goes wrong; especially used by stand-up comedians when they 'die' on stage.

flower bond (econ/US) US Treasury bond that was purchasable at below face value but redeemable at full face value if the money was to be used in payment of federal estate taxes (death duties). In this capacity they were known as 'flowers at the funeral'. Since 1976 such bonds

have incurred some capital gains tax and thus lost much of their appeal.

flub *v* (movies) for an actor to make a mistake in a speech.

flub (sport) in golf, a mishit, or to mishit the ball.

fluff *v* (drugs) a method of cutting (qv) such powdered drugs as heroin or cocaine by pulverising them extremely finely and then adding an adulterant, such as talcum, that is of similar consistency.

fluff *n* (commerce) in the motor trade, spare parts.

fluff *v* (theatre) to make a mistake on stage, to forget one's lines. (cf: *flub*)

fluff *n, v* (sport) in golf either a mishit or the act of mishitting the ball. (cf: *flub*)

fluffy (sport) in golf, for a ball to sit high and easily hittable on top of the grass.

flugie (pols/US) a rule that only benefits the creator of the rule and one that can always be altered by that maker to stop anyone else from using it to their own advantage.

fluids and electrolytes (medic/US) a code for alcohol that has been put aside for the doctors and nurses to relax with after work.

flush (computers) 1. to scratch out superficially. 2. to end work for the day. 3. to exclude someone from an activity.

flush on warning (milit) in the case of receiving a warning of in-coming hostile ICBMs (qv), an order for all aircraft threatened to take off at once so as not to be caught and destroyed on the ground or within range of the explosions.

flutter (audio) a rapid fluctuation in the pitch or volume of a sound; a variation in speed of a recording medium occurring above 15/second.

fluttering (espionage) to give lie-detector tests to one's own operatives to double-check their loyalty on a specific mission.

fly (sport) in US football a specific pass pattern in which the receiver runs straight down the field.

fly *v* (theatre) to hand scenery. (cf: *flies*)

flyby (aerospace) a space mission that does not land on a planet, but flies close enough to it for special cameras and other monitoring equipment to send vital information back to Earth.

flying eavesdropper (milit) USN spy plane, the EC-121.

fly pitchers (police) unlicensed street traders who keep up a running battle to attract custom without the attention of the police.

FOBS (milit) (abbrev) *f*ractional *o*rbit *b*ombardment *s*ystem: a strategy of attack in which rockets are fired in a low earth orbit (100 metres appx.) and on approaching their target are forced out of the orbit and down to the earth by the firing of retrorockets. This should help keep the missiles beneath radar spotting and defensive retaliation until the last moment.

focus *n* (theatre) a spotlight for the star.

focus groups (advert, pols) a small sample group is selected – c. 20 people on a psychodemographic basis (all types from all areas) – and they are then put together in one room for a period and asked to air their views on the subject on which you require information. This session is taped and filmed and is then analysed in depth for the planning of a campaign, questions for mass polls, etc.

focus puller (movies, TV) an assistant to the cameraman who adjusts the lens to fine tolerances during the filming; also doubles as a film loader. (cf: *clapper-loader*)

foggy bottom (pols/US) shorthand for the US State Department, now used with the implication of the fogginess of some of those who work there and the decisions they impose on the nation, but stemming from a real place, a local name for the town of Hamburgh, a town long since swallowed up into Washington DC and then noted for its swamps and the mists that they often produced.

FOH (theatre) (abbrev) *front of house*: 1. the lobby and the business and box offices. 2. anything in front of the proscenium arch. 3. the audience. 4. the staff who work in (2), business and administration rather than actors and technicians.

folding money (TV) aka: *direct costs*: money paid to any organisations that are not already part of the TV company itself. Thus *indirect costs*: all those production costs that are spent on items or people already owned or employed by the company.

fold up *v* (drugs) for a dealer to abandon his trade and stop selling drugs.

folio *n* (press) 1. a side of copy. 2. the running headline of a page. 3. a tabloid sheet (qv).

foner (press) in US, a story covered simply by making phonecalls.

fonfen (crime/UK) from Yiddish for 'telling tales': the 'spiel' that a con-man uses to entrance and ensnare his victims.

font *v* (TV/US) to display letters or figures over a television picture to add extra information to the commentary that goes with that picture. From press use of a *type font* (an alphabet of letters in a particular face) and from the production of these inserts by a *vidifont machine*.

foolish old man who removed the mountain (pols) a dictum of Mao Tse Tung's originated in 1945 as a means of explaining the Maoist approach to the theory of knowledge: ideas must be turned by workers into a material force that will in turn change the world.

footage (movies) the length of a film calculated in feet and inches. Videotape is measured in minutes and seconds, but no convenient temporal equivalent has yet emerged for this recording medium.

football (pols, milit) an attaché case which contains the day's nuclear war go codes (qv) and which is carried by a special officer who accompanies the US President at all times.

footprint (aerospace) the area in which it is predicted that debris from the collapsing satellite or other space vehicle will land as it returns to the earth.

footprint (milit) the pattern into which it is calculated that the various warheads from a MARV (qv) bus (qv) should land when hitting their targets.

footprints (communications) the area covered by the broadcasts from any one TV satellite in the DBS (direct broadcasting by satellite) system.

foozle (sport) in golf, to make a mishit.

force *v* (sport) in cricket, to bat aggressively.

forced coverage (movies) despite an error having been made in a scene, the director might choose to finish the take, then to reshoot the extra material and insert it at the editing stage.

force deficiency (milit) failings in either planning or the amassing or efficiency of men or materiel.

fore *n* (TV/US) the start of a piece of tape that contains one news item. (cf: *aft*)

fore-end (milit) RN: the forward space in a submarine used for storing the torpedoes and as living quarters for some of the crew.

foreground (computers) that program which has priority over any other *background* or *secondary* programs that the machine may be running simultaneously.

foreigner (indust relats) a 'moonlighting' job undertaken by a worker who is ostensibly unemployed and thus collecting unemployment payments.

foreign print (press) newspapers produced outside London for distribution inside the metropolis; such printing is disliked by London print unions.

forgiving systems (computers) a computer or other system which allows the novice user to make some mistakes without disastrous consequences. Confused users may have the option of a 'help' button which will print out on the VDU screen some helpful suggestions whereby they can find their way out of the mess.

form (police) the previous convictions or record of a criminal, from the use of form, with similar meaning, to refer to race-horses.

formalism (art) the assignment of priority in art to the work's form at the expense of any other characteristics, esp. its content.

formalism (theatre) a movement that started c1890 in Russia and began as a reaction to the excessive naturalism of Russian theatre then spilled over into its own excesses of symbolism and stylisation.

formalism (pols) for a communist to accept criticism or acknowledge a duty but not in any real way to alter his conduct; often expressed as

F

'formalist perversion', an attack that extended to literary, theatrical and artistic formalists.

format v (pavlov) a word that means to design in a specific manner, according to the task, item or personality under consideration which has gained enormous popularity in business, media, educational and sociological fields.

form 700 (air crew) a form that must be signed every time a captain takes over an aircraft preparatory to making a flight; in it he confirms that he is personally satisfied with all pre-flight checks, maintenance and inspection.

formula investing (stock market) investing according to a plan under which more funds are invested into equity securities when the market is low, and more are put into fixed income securities when the market advances.

FORTRAN (computers) (acron) *for*mula *tran*slator: the most widely used and generally popular scientific programming language.

forty-eight (milit) USMC: a two-day or weekend leave pass.

forty-eight sheet (advert) a billboard poster size: 20′ wide by 10′ deep.

forward integration (commerce) the taking over by a manufacturer of his wholesalers or retailers with the intention of controlling the whole market and thus consolidating his position. (cf: *backward integration*)

forward market (futures market) the making of deals concerning commodities which are not currently available for trading but which will be at a given future date.

foul (theatre) when ropes, flats, lights have all become entangled in the flies (qv).

found objects (art) fr. Fr. *objets trouvés*: in Surrealist theory, the taking of any random object and presenting it as art, worthy of standing with more 'respectable' art.

four beauties (pols) in people's Republic of China: 1. of the spirit, 2. of the language, 3. of behaviour, 4. of the environment.

four bigs (pols) in People's Republic of China: four freedoms of expression 1. speaking out freely, 2. airing one's personal views fully, 3. holding great debates, 4. writing big character posters (qv).

four firsts (pols) in People's Republic of China, a series of priorities: 1. the human factor over weapons, 2. political work over other work, 3. ideological study over political work, 4. living ideology over book learning.

four flush (gambling) aka: *bob tail flush*: a flush (all cards of the same suit) containing four and not five cards and thus useless; the root of the non-gambling, derogatory use for this term.

four modernisations (pols) a scheme launched in 1975 in the People's Republic of China: 1. agriculture, 2. industry, 3. defence, 4. science and technology.

four olds (pols) in People's Republic of China: 1. ideas, 2. customs, 3. cultures, 4. habits.

four plus a (medic/US) to the utmost degree, completely, exceptionally, absolutely, utterly. From the method of reporting results of laboratory tests as *negative, one plus*, up to *four plus*.

four sheet (advert) a poster size: 40″ wide by 60″ deep.

fourth cover (advert) the back cover (of a magazine or newspaper); thus *first cover* = front cover, *second cover* = inside front cover, *third cover* = inside back cover.

fourth market (commerce) the trading of unlisted (in the stock market) securities directly between investors, bypassing the conventional trading methods. (cf: *third market*)

fourth wall (theatre) a concept in traditional theatre that the stage has three actual walls and a fourth one, across the proscenium arch, that cuts off the action from the audience.

fourth world (pols) the world's poorest and most backward/underdeveloped countries. (cf: *Third World*)

four wall (movies, theatre) rental on a *four-wall basis* of either a cinema or a theatre is the rental of the site to a producer (theatre) or exhibitor (movie) under which agreement the renter will pay all operating expenses but instead of the usual percentage of the take, pay only an agreed fixed sum, irrespective of how many tickets are sold.

four waller (TV, movies) a fully enclosed set with four actual, but adjustable walls, inside which a camera can move, facilitating the construction of more complex sets.

foxhole (milit) a small hole in the ground in which a soldier sleeps and fights (cf: *basher*). Thus *foxhole circuit* appearances by USO/ENSA or other forces entertainments teams who went to visit the troops in situ.

fox message (computers) a standard message used to test computers as well as teletypes and similar electronic communicators: the basic 'the quick brown fox jumped over the lazy dog 1234567890' which contains all the letters of the alphabet and every number.

fraction (pols) in communist use, originally all the Party members inside a larger unit of nonparty members, such as a Trades Union membership. Since 1940s this has become a derogatory use, akin to deviationist (qv) and refers to those Party members *within* the overall party who repudiate the party line. Thus *fractionalism*: the organising of small groups to influence or alter party policy; a forbidden practice.

frag v (milit) (abbrev) *frag*mentation grenade: originated (as a word, though probably not as a practice) during the Vietnam War: the assassination of one's own (either unpopular, or, more important, incompetent and thus personally dangerous) officer by tossing a grenade at him during a battle.

frame *n* (gambling) from bowling use: a hand or deal of cards.

frame *n* (sex) as a comment on her physique: an exceptionally thin prostitute.

frame *n* (movies) a single picture on a strip of film, projected for exhibition at a usual speed of 24 frames/second. 'Film is truth 24 times a second' (Jean-Luc Godard).

frank discussions (pols) a euphemism that emerges regularly from meetings between world leaders or their lesser surrogates and implies that there was little agreement and possibly some strong arguing.

frankenstein (gambling) the bolting together of four slot machines to which is attached only one handle; players must insert money in all four machines to stand a chance of a multiple coup, otherwise the handle only spins the machine into which cash has been dropped.

frap *v* (sport) in sailing, the adding of strength by tying together cables or lines.

frappé (sex) 1. beating (fr. Fr. *frapper*: to beat). 2. fellatio with ice-cubes in the girl's mouth (on the lines of 'creme de menthe frappé', etc.).

fraternity (social wk) an idealised goal of all welfare services which should, in a broad sense, have a linking fellowship of the same values and aims; also the concept of 'human fellowship' which claims that 'all men are brothers' and in itself is a reason for the establishment of social welfare agencies.

fratricide (milit) the theoretical result of a number of MIRV/MARV warheads detonated out of absolutely simultaneous synchronicity (which given the distance travelled would be more than likely): the various massive explosion would tend to destroy other warheads or at least cause serious changes in the accuracy of their guidance systems. (cf: *dense pack*)

FRD (govt/US) (abbrev) Formerly Restricted Data: material that has been removed from the status of RD (Restricted Data, qv) and is being transclassified to that of NSI (National Security Information, qv). FRD, despite appearances, does *not* mean that the data involved has been declassified.

freak off *v* (sex) in black pimp usage: the enjoyment of sex without money changing hands.

Freddie (milit) in air intercept code: a controlling unit.

Freddie Mac (econ/US) the Federal Home Loan Mortgage Company. (cf: *Ginnie Mae*)

freebie (gambling, prostitution, drugs, etc.) anything for nothing in these areas where such transactions are rare.

free-fire zone (milit) an area in which any moving creature, human or animal, is deemed a target for bombs, rockets, artillery or small arms.

free forms (art) organic biomorphic shapes – kidney/boomerang/eggshapes – produced by

hand drawing that epitomised many popular design motifs in 1950s.

freefreighting (air crew) the use of one's own aircraft for the transport home of whatever commodities/items one might wish to have brought back. Some pilots escalated this into large-scale import businesses of fresh out of season fruits and similar exotica, bringing in far more than the permitted 100 kilos/person allowance. As popular in the military as in civil flying.

freelance (milit) air intercept code: I am in manual control of the aircraft.

free ride (stock market) a method whereby a broker can make a deal and turn a profit without actually investing any money: a purchaser buys and sells within the shortest permitted settlement period – five days – and never has to produce cash, merely move the shares.

free ride (gambling) playing part of a poker hand without betting.

free ride (pols) a campaign undertaken by an officeholder who will be able to continue in/ return to that office in the event that he fails to win election, thus risking little more than his personal prestige.

free-rider (indust relats) an individual who refuses to join a union but (where there is no closed shop agreement) is able to benefit from whatever wage agreements are negotiated by that union.

free rocket (milit) a missile that is not controlled by a launch computer or wire while in flight. (cf: *fire and forget*)

freeze (movies) an instruction to actors to hold their positions; used for 'trick shots' in which things or people suddenly 'pop up' in the film.

freezebank (medic/US) a fridge which stores blood, bone grafts, organs etc. for use in emergencies and other operations.

freeze frame (movies) a device whereby the action on film appears to freeze into a still; accomplished by printing one frame a number of times.

freeze-out (gambling) a variety of poker in which players continue until they lose their entire bankroll at which point they drop out and the winner ends up with all the original stake money.

freeze-out proposition (gambling) a lengthy series of bets between two gamblers which are based on a pre-arranged set of rules and betting conditions, all leading towards the result in which the winner takes all.

french *n*, *v* (sex) fellatio.

French drive (sport) in cricket, a snick through the slips. (cf: *Chinese drive*)

French's edition (theatre/UK) the authorised performance edition of a play, used by amateur companies, provincial theatres, etc. which includes prop lists, lighting and sound cues,

F

stage directions, special effects, etc., all as used in the original West End production. Published by Samuel French Ltd of 26 Southampton Street WC2.

frequency (advert) the number of times an individual is exposed to a given advertisement. (cf: *reach*)

Freudian aesthetics (art) the application of Freud's theories to art has touched on areas including: dream symbolism, the role of the unconscious in the production/appreciation of art, the origins and motivations of creativity, the relation between art and neurosis, art as a possible therapy, the relevance of psycho-analysis to an artist's personality and creativity, etc.

fried (computers) 1. burnt out, non-working due to hardware failure. 2. of people, to be exhausted, esp. of those who continue to work notwithstanding their tiredness.

fried egg (sport) in golf, a ball that is half buried in the sand.

friendly fire (milit) firing by one's own side aimed, unwittingly, at one's own troops.

friendly ice (milit) RN/USN: the polar ice canopy is *friendly* when it offers good 'skylights' for the submarine to surface occasionally, or *hostile* when it is so thick as to seal the ice cap completely.

a friend of ours (crime) in the US Mafia, a member of one of the US families (qv); the use of *mine* instead of *ours* refers only to a personal friend, who may or may not be a member of another family, but who has none of the ties 'ours' implies.

fringe *n* (TV/US) those dayparts (qv) that fringe prime time (qv). (cf: *early fringe, late fringe*)

frobnicate *v* (computers) to manipulate, to adjust, to tweak, usu. abbrev. to *frob* and derived from *frobnitz* (qv). Unlike tweat and twiddle (qqv) frobbing implies aimless manipulation.

frobnitz (computers) a widget, a thingummybob, a whatdyoucallit, any unspecified and usually small and fiddly object. Originally used with the same meaning by model railway enthusiasts. (cf: *frobnicate*)

frock (TV, theatre) a costume – male or female.

frock *v* (milit) USMC: to allow an officer who has been selected for promotion (and so notified) but not yet made his number (qv) to assume the style, title, uniform and authority of the rank he has now attained.

frog (computers) akin to crock (qv) as a statement of distaste or, as *froggy*, as a derogatory adjective.

frog hair (pols/US) money for use in political campaigns.

frog hair (sport) in golf, that well cut grass that divides the fairway from the green itself and is of a length and smoothness somewhere between the two.

from each according to his ability, to each according to his needs (pols) Marx's policy of work/personal income relations in the ideal state of achieved communism. Under the previous, intermediary stage of *socialism* Marx allowed a remaining trace of inequality, by replacing *needs* by *work*.

front (music) the first part of the song, prior to the 'bridge'.

front *v* (drugs) for a purchaser to give the dealer the required price of the drugs before seeing the merchandise; the dealer then vanishes and returns, if he is honest, with the promised drugs, which, for safety's sake, if he works on the street, he will not keep on his person, but in a convenient and nearby hiding place.

front end (advert) the initial response to a promotion.

front-end *n, v* (computers) simply an amplification of 'the front' or 'to place at the front'; *front end processor*: a secondary unit that backs up the functioning of the main processor by taking on a variety of basic tasks and performing them ready for the main unit to take advantage of such spade work and get on with major operations.

front-end load (stock market) sales commissions and other expenses to a broker that make up part of the early payments of an investor under a long term contract for the buying of mutual funds shares. From the 'load' – the commission etc. – being paid at the 'front'.

front-end money (commerce) aka: *seed money*: money paid in advance to set up a project.

front five (sport) in rugby union, the first row (three men) and second row (two men) of the scrum who are considered as a single tactical unit who act as the powerhouse of the scrum and the tactical focal point of the play.

frontlash (pols) the reverse of a backlash, a word coined by President Lyndon Johnson in 1964 to explain how the threatened racist backlash against his civil rights legislation was submerged in the frontlash of its many supporters.

frontline *n* (sociol, pols) from the military use of a line of confrontation: certain streets in the UK's West Indian areas, notably Railton Road, Brixton SE24, where the black community feel their rights and freedoms are most heavily under assault, and where such rights and freedoms are paraded most provocatively (in white/police eyes).

frontline states (pols) those black African nations who border on South Africa and formerly on Rhodesia before it became Zimbabwe.

front office (movies) the business departments of film companies, quite possibly in New York rather than in Hollywood where the films are actually made.

front porch campaign (pols/US) originally a

supposedly dignified style of campaigning whereby the candidate 'held court' on his own front porch, or at least in his own house, and dealt with such delegations, power-brokers, individuals, interest groups and so on who came to visit. Now as an epithet for a lazy candidate who refuses to go out to meet and court the voters.

frost (TV) a lighting filter that diffuses light.

frost-call (milit) USMC: a procedure established within a command whereby under certain emergency conditions all officers and other key personnel may be alerted by special notification.

frozen (econ) credits, assets etc. that can neither be liquidated nor realised in any other way.

frozen playlist (rock business, radio) a playlist (qv) that has no changes, no new entries or other additions in a given week at a radio station.

frugalise v (commerce) in motor manufacturing, the drive to retire the old 'gas-guzzlers' and find a popular series of cars that would consume less petrol and show proper respect for the energy crisis.

fruiting (aerospace) the refusal of friendly aircraft to respond to radio interrogation by potentially hostile communicators.

fruit salad (milit) a chestful of international medal ribbons displayed by a senior officer. (cf: *scrambled egg*)

frustrated cargo (commerce) any shipment of supplies en route from one port to another which is stopped prior to arrival and for which further instructions as to its disposition must be obtained.

FTA (indust relats) (abbrev) *failure to agree*: shorthand for the breakdown of union/management pay negotiations.

fuck off n (new therapies) in primal therapy, an expletive used toward the patient in an attempt to curtail any attempts by the patient to raise topics that are not directly orientated towards the object of the therapy: the primal (qv).

fudge (press) 1. the attachment to a rotary press that can insert stop press news. Thus: 2. a piece of stop press news which is inserted in the *fudge box*: a small piece of white space left available for such news.

fuff (TV) fake snow for wintertime effects.

fulfilment (business) the achievement of any set goal, selling one's quota, serving a client, etc.

fulfilment (advert) 1. filling orders for a product. 2. inserting the parts of a mail-out promotion into the envelopes prior to addressing and sending them off.

full and plenty (milit) RN: food in excess of the official helpings.

full-court press (pols/US) originally (and still) a basketball term to describe an intensive harassing defensive move; absorbed into the Nixon White House of early 1970s where it shed the defensive vestiges and survives today only as a sports metaphor for an all-out effort.

full generation n (milit) total war footing, with a potential of 10,000 nuclear weapons.

full-line forcing (business) persuading a buyer to contract for a number of less popular goods in order to obtain enough of the lines that are in high demand and he really wants. Thus he obtains 'the full line' of goods to get the few that are really sought after.

full-out (press, advert) to start a new paragraph of typesetting without the usual indentation.

full service agency (advert) a large agency who can supply not only the creative talent – copywriting, art direction – but all the ancillary services such as market research, space buying, campaign strategy and anything else the client might require. (cf: *boutique agency, hot shop*)

fully functioning (new therapies) in Rogerian therapy, a body and mind that are working at peak efficiency, a combined physical and mental excellence that will provide an ideally adjusted individual.

fulminate (medic) of a disease, sudden and severe developments.

functionalism (sociol) the method of studying the functional interactions and adaptations of particular phenomena within a given structure.

functionalism (archit) the concept that the function and purpose of a building should be the main sources of its shape and style; embodied in Louis Sullivan's (1850–1924) dictum 'form follows function'.

fundamental painting (art) art theory and practice which concentrates on the process of painting, stressing the literal physical character of the materials, searching for an essential definition of painting. Its critics attack such a search for being simply 'paintings about paintings'.

funds (stock market) 1. cash. 2. a common term for Government securities. 3. investment portfolios.

fungible (business) orig. a legal term: 'to take the place, to fulfil the office of': in business terms, the idea of one person's being moved around as and when he is needed. Often used in the phrase 'the fungibility of technical people', whose skills are used for specific tasks and then called up again elsewhere.

funk art (art) from blues/jazz use of funk to mean 'rough', 'down to earth': a type of pop art (qv) produced from bizarre objects put together in eccentric combinations and often with sexual or scatological connotations.

funkspiel (espionage) from Ger. 'radio game': originally a World War II term used by the US OSS (forerunner of the CIA) and still referring to the feeding of false information over the radio, using double agents (ostensibly those more one's own men than the enemy's) to support its veracity.

F

funny *n* (espionage) a misleading dossier of false information assembled for the building up of a cover (qv) story.

furlough *n* (milit) USMC: a period of authorised leave for an enlisted man.

furniture (commerce) in the book trade, those bound matching sets that are often purchased but rarely read, acting instead as expensive shelf-fillers in private libraries.

futures (finance) all contracts that cover the sale or purchase of financial instruments or physical commodities for future delivery on a commodity exchange; promises to trade in securities/commodities at a specific future date and handled at the *forward market* rather than the spot market (qv) which deals only in actuals (qv).

future shock (sociol) from a book title, *Future Shock* by Alvin Toffler (1970); a state of stress and disorientation occasioned by an excess of dramatic and continuing changes in society – especially technological advance that alters the entire basis and assumptions of that society. 'Future shock arises from the superimposition of a new culture on an old one. It is culture shock (qv) in one's own society' (Toffler, op. cit.).

futurism (art) founded by the Ital. poet Marinetti, an early 20th century movement – based in painting but touching literature and drama – that concentrated on its violent renunciation of tradition in favour of some imagined law of machine-like perfection.

futuristics (sociol) the study of the future, appearing under a variety of titles, ie: *stoxology* 'the science of conjecture', *mellology* 'the science of the future', *futurology* 'the study of the future' and *alleotics* 'the study of change'.

FX (TV, movies) (abbrev/acro) a notation of scripts to indicate *effects*; *SFX*: special effects.

F

gabriel *n* (computers) an unnecessary stalling technique. 'X is pulling a gabriel. . .'

gaff (dancing) a dancer's belt, the protection under his tights for his genitals.

gaff (theatre/UK) 1. a portable, improvised theatre (cf: *fit-up*). 2. any cheap, second-rate theatre.

gaff *n, v* (gambling) aka: *G, gimmick*: any secret device to aid or achieve cheating. Thus *gaffed dice*: crooked dice. *To gaff a wheel*: to fix a roulette wheel in the house's favour.

gaffer (TV, movies) the chief electrician; thus *gaffer grip*: a spring-loaded claw that holds a small lamp; *gaffer tape*: general adhesive tape used for fixing the electrics.

gag (theatre) orig. an ad-lib, currently meaning a joke.

gag order (media) a court order (US) that restricts the media from reporting the proceedings at a given lawsuit. Known in UK as *reporting restrictions*.

gag rule (pols) any actions or regulations in Parliament or Congress which can limit their debates. Started in the sedition acts of 18th century which were known as 'gags'.

gallery (milit) USMC: a land or sea mess; a mobile field kitchen (all with the traditional Marine naval rather than army use).

gallery (TV) the production control room overlooking a TV studio. (cf: *box*)

gallery hit (sport) in cricket, a shot that the crowd enjoy; the implication of the theatrical 'playing to the gallery'.

game (police, sex) *on the game*: working as a prostitute.

game art (art) essentially those toys, games, playthings made by artists; also those art works which encourage the involvement of the spectator, produced by artists who believe that adults as well as children need the vital cultural functions served by play.

game plan *n, v* (pols, business) orig. the strategy prepared for a particular game of US football: taken by politicians (esp. the Nixon White House where the President once actually sent in a play to the Washington Redskins – which play resulted in their opponents scoring) and businessmen to mean a planned strategy to achieve given goals within defined rules.

games (sex) the embellishment of straight homosexual sex by the addition of *toys* (qv) such as vibrators, whips, etc. (cf: *party*)

game theory (business, milit) a mathematical theory developed for describing and analysing competitive situations: used by the military and by businessmen to assess a range of possibilities and their concomitant variables both in a hypothetical battlefield or its commercial cousin, the marketplace.

ganging (tech) a single knob that is capable of a number of different controls on a piece of equipment.

Gang of Four (pols) 1. (China) the former leaders of Cultural Revolution (qv) who were immediately pilloried after the death of Mao Tse Tung in October 1976: 1. Wang Hung-Wen (vice-chairman of the cultural committee of the Party), 2. Chang Ch'un Chiao (politburo member), 3. Chiang Ch'ing – Jiang Qing – Mao's widow and cultural supremo), 4. Yao Wen-Yuan. All were accused of counter-revolutionary revisionism, and after their trial (Feb. 1980–Dec. 1981) were all found guilty. Sentences: (1) life imprisonment, (2) and (3) death, commuted to life imprisonment, (4) 20 years jail. 2. (UK) four leading members of the Labour Party who broke away in 1981 to found the Social Democratic Party (SDP): Roy Jenkins, Shirley Williams, David Owen and William Rodgers. Their nickname was modelled facetiously on their Chinese counterparts.

gap sheet (business) a personal file prepared on a candidate for promotion and filled not only with a list of his past achievements but with those skills yet to be attained or improved (the 'gaps'). Assessment is based on both parts of the file.

garage (milit) US intelligence term for the Soviet's hardened (qv) defences which protect the launch sites of the SS-20 missile (supposedly the equivalent of the US cruise missile).

garbage (computers) inaccurate or useless data.

garbage (sports) used in a variety of sports (ice-hockey, basketball, tennis) to imply an easy shot or scoring opportunity. Thus *garbage collector*: an ice hockey player who specialises in taking advantage of garbage shots.

garbage (aerospace) miscellaneous objects and debris which are orbiting the earth – pieces ejected or possibly broken off a variety of space craft.

garbage collection (computers) the rewriting of routines in order to eliminate any items in the memory that were only referred to once and will never be needed in any subsequent program.

garbage housing (archit) buildings made from rubbish and other detritus, but unlike the makeshift dwellings of slums and shanty-towns, this waste has been designed with such secondary use in mind, ie. the WoBo bottle brick, etc.

gas! (computers) an explanation of intense annoy-ance, implying that whoever caused such anger ought to be sent swiftly into the nearest gas chamber. Allegedly orig. 1978 when the killer of San Francisco's Mayor George Moscone was scheduled to be executed that way.

gas (medic/US) anaesthesiology; thus *gas passer*: an anaesthesiologist.

gash (milit) RN: waste, possibly from the galley; anything that is no longer wanted.

gash print (press) a useless piece of paper; a bad print that should be thrown away.

gas meter bandit (police/UK) ironic reference to a petty thief.

gate (TV, movies) the part of a camera or a projector through which the film travels; each frame is held momentarily and that image is projected onto a screen at 24 frames/sec. (cf: *hair in the gate*)

gate *v* (gambling) to stop the dice moving before they have actually come to rest. Usually when a roll or the dice look suspicious.

gate (sport) in cricket, *through the gate* a ball that passes between the bat and the pads and often proceeds onto the stumps.

gate fever (prison) the unsettled, apprehensive and excited feeling that a prisoner naturally feels as his sentence draws to a close. By exten-sion, any show of impatience when waiting for something to happen.

gate guardian (milit) the stationary and often vintage aircraft that stands at the entrance gate of many military airfields.

gate happy (prison/UK) a disease prevalent among any prisoners whose sentence has only a short time to run. (cf: *gate fever*)

gatekeeper (sociol) 1. a useful middleperson who can help connect individuals with social welfare agencies. 2. those who control access to useful/important figures within organisations: receptionists/secretaries who always claim their employer is 'in conference' etc.

la gauche de salon (pols) Fr. description of a 'professional' socialist possibly equivalent to US limousine liberal (qv), and similar adher-ents of 'radical chic'. (cf: *academic socialism*)

gazlon (police) from Yiddish: a sneak thief, a derogatory description from police or amongst villains.

gazump *v* (commerce) aka: gazoomph: orig. use in the motor trade for the fraudulent closing of a sale to one buyer and then, seeing that prices are rising, offering the same vehicle to another buyer before the first one (who was asked less money) has managed to collect his purchase. In 1970s when the property market was booming, the use was concentrated on UK real estate deals, although gazumping, like the legit-imate market, is less active in 1980s.

gearing (stock market) the relationship between fixed interest capital and equity (qv). *Highly-geared* ordinary shares are those where the fixed capital is high compared with the equity capital. *Low geared* implies the opposite.

geedunk (milit) USMC: the resturant or bar on board ship. (cf: *slop chute*)

generalisability (pavlov) the ability or suitability of a concept for fitting neatly into any general therapy.

general service (milit) the regulation issue of equipment; by extension, a person who is conscientious, strict, well turned out and thor-oughly versed in the regulations. (cf: *GI*)

generation (art) an art critic generalisation for groups of artists who are of roughly similar age and who emerge into the public eye at about the same time. The devout hope that genera-tion will follow generation, each new, bright and more innovative than the last, is a modern fantasy beloved of all those who batten onto culture – businessmen as well as critics – and is hardly restricted to art.

generation (TV) the successive reproductions of a videotaped programme: the original is the *master*, the first copy is *second generation*, a copy of that is *third generation* and so on. Quality of picture/sound diminish as the generations succeed each other.

generation (tech) successive developments of a piece of equipment – a computer, a hifi, a robot, etc. – in which each new generation can be assumed to be more sophisticated, efficient, capable, etc. (cf: *state of the art*)

genny (TV, movies) aka: *gen*: (abbrev) generator: a portable generator, usually mounted on a large truck, which provides electricity for the lights during location filming.

gentrification (commerce) in real estate, the taking over of former slums or similarly run down 'inner city' housing (which may in its earlier days have in fact been smart, bourgeois housing) and renovating it back towards its former status. Usually the pre-occupation of young, upwardly mobile professional middle-class couples. (cf: *block-busting*)

geometric abstraction (art) a broad category, encompassing both sculpture and painting. which finds in geometric forms the universal symbols for rational, idealist concepts.

geometry of fear (art) a phrase used to charac-terise UK sculpture of 1950s, influenced by

Giacometti and Richier: figurative, often using tortured surface textures and enclosed in cage-like structures. An angst-ridden style supposedly reflecting the post-war emotions of the era.

George (aerospace) an automatic pilot in an aircraft; poss. from the colloquialism 'let George do it'.

George (theatre/UK) a traditional name for any stage-door keeper. In the US, the equivalent is *pop*.

George Spelvin (theatre/US) the regular pseudonym of any performer who plays two parts in the same production, used on the programme in addition to his own. The original Spelvin might have been a member of New York's theatrical Lamb's Club. An early 1970s star of porno movies took the name Georgina Spelvin, a joke noted by the 'profession'. (cf: *Walter Plinge*)

gerrymander (pols) the division of voting districts or constituencies in such a way that one party will gain unfairly at the expense of its rivals. From one Elbridge Gerry (1744–1814) one time Vice-President of the US and a leading practitioner (although not the originator) of the redrawing of political maps in one's own favour.

get *n* (sport) in tennis, the action of returning the ball.

get *n* (horse-racing) the progeny of a sire, those 'children' which he has 'begotten'.

getaway man *n* (milit) in a military formation used for patrols: if the squad is moving in a shallow V shape, the man at the centre of the V is, logically, 'the point man', those at either extremity are 'getaway men', so called from the theory that in the event of an ambush, point may be captured/killed, but they can disappear.

get behind (new therapies) to understand, to appreciate: both with the over-riding implication of offering approval and support. The image of standing behind a leader and standing up to any criticism.

get centred (new therapies) to be true to oneself, to appreciate one's inner being and individuality and to work towards making this the basis of a new and improved life.

get down (new therapies) orig. an exhortation shouted to rock groups, urging more intense playing: currently seen as abbrev. of *get down to* (a job or task is assumed) and thus used with implications of dedicating oneself either to some job, or to an emotional framework or commitment.

get-in *n* (theatre/UK) the moving of the flats (qv) and other equipment carried by a touring company into the theatre prior to setting up the stage. Thus a *good get-in* implies a large scene dock (qv), easily negotiated entrances, etc.; the opposite is a *bad get-in*.

get in touch with yourself (new therapies) a popular incantation for those searching for a

better life through the various new therapies (qv): the concept of coming to terms with oneself as an individual by way of concentrating on one's true inner being.

get it on with (new therapies) to have sex with; an equivalent to UK 'have it off' and as such, possibly more sl. than therapeutic.

get it together (new therapies) a popular generality describing the process of trying to realign or integrate one's self in the overall bid for self-awareness, self-improvement or whatever the particular therapy offers as its goal. From the 1960s/1970s hippie sl. for doing something reasonably efficiently, often as in 'Get it together, man!'

get mud on your boots (archit) for an architect to leave his office and actually visit the site of the building which is being constructed as dictated by his plans.

get-off *n* (music) an improvisation or break (qv) during a performance of jazz.

get off it (new therapies) in est (qv) the result of a successful est training: 'the est equivalent of confession' (A. Clare and S. Thompson, op. cit.) in which the subject comes to appreciate the established patterns within his/her life and starts being able to discard them.

get off on (new therapies) from the 1960s drug use for enjoying the effects of a drug: to enjoy, to reach a new and more satisfying emotional state as a result of something; *get off on* can also mean the physical/emotional attraction that comes with pleasurable sex.

get-out *n* (theatre) the total weekly cost of a production; from the touring company's reference to the taking of enough money at the box office to permit them to pay their bills, rent, etc. and move on to the next town. (cf: *nut*)

get-out *n* (TV) the clearing and cleaning of a studio after a production has finished.

Get Out of My Emergency Room (medic/US) see: *GOMER*.

get stories (TV) amongst the fen (qv) of 'Star Trek', the stories written by over-identifying fans, who contribute to the various fanzines (qv) and whose subject matter is invariably the capture, torture, possibly murder or execution of one of the main characters (esp. Mr. Spock) who appear unscathed and super-heroic in the properly written TV episodes. (cf: *Mary Sue stories*)

get wet (milit) to get blood on one's hands, spec. after cutting an enemy's throat. (cf. *wet work*)

get your act together (new therapies) aka: *get your head together*: both implying the pulling oneself back from a potential problem, breakdown or similar emotional disability; getting one's *head* together stems from the idea of coming back to reality after one's 'mind has been blown' by a drug (probably LSD).

ghost *n* (TV) a spectral secondary image on the

G

screen; a *leading ghost* appears to the left of the true image, a *following ghost* to its right.

ghost (movies) an extra image above or below the main image on the screen, caused by faulty synchronisation between the shutter and the intermittent mechanisms of the projector.

ghost (milit) 1. a spurious signal on a radar screen that does not correspond to any target at the location indicated. 2. the deliberate electronic projection of fake targets by one fighter to confuse the radar scanning of an enemy or of his home base.

ghost *n, v* (educ, indust relats/US) an absentee either in school or at work who is counted as present none the less; such cheating at school occurred since funds were allocated according to the total register and an absent pupil meant less cash; at work the 'ghost' was clocked in so as to ensure his being paid full wages, whether or not he was actually entitled to them.

ghost (milit) RN: the splash that signifies a shell has missed its target and landed in the sea.

ghost *v* (movies) for a professional singer to dub (qv) the songs that are allegedly sung in the film by the star who, in fact, will only be lip-synching (qv) the lyrics.

ghost *n* (theatre) the manager in his capacity as paymaster to the company. Thus a stock question on payday (Friday) 'has the ghost walked?' (intensified by the punning reference to *Hamlet*). (cf: *treasury call*)

ghosted (press, publishing) material, supposedly of the autobiographical type (and often with the accent on true and lurid confessions), that has actually been written by a professional writer/journalist on the basis of interviews with the celebrity under whose name the work is published. (cf: *as-told-to*)

ghoster (sport) in sailing, 1. any boat that makes comparatively good way despite the lack of wind. 2. a special sail, similar to a Genoa rig (a large jib that overlaps the mainsail) but made of especially light material.

ghoster (TV) a film production that goes on past 1 a.m. and thus incurs all the expensive union-negotiated financial penalties that such late-night filming creates.

ghosting (prison) the removal from one prison to another of an inmate who, for whatever reason, is spirited out of one cell and into the new one while the other prisoners in both prisons are either asleep or otherwise unaware of the departure/arrival.

ghosts and fairies (commerce) in hairdressing, euphemisms used by the stylists for fake appointments put into the diary when they want an extra-long lunchbreak or plan to sleep late on the next morning. The management, as in many such fiddles, is tacitly aware, but considers that the expertise so indulged is worth a few hours freedom.

ghost-word (press) a spurious word that has orig-

inated not in any real etymology but through a long-dead printer's error; usually developed from such mistakes in dictionaries, eg: the 'verb' *foupe* was found included in Dr. Johnson's Dictionary when he assumed that the long *s* used in a work of William Camden's (1605) was in fact an *f*.

GI (milit) (abbrev) government or general issue: for the equipment so issued to the military and by extension as an adj. to describe anyone whose bearing, attitude, opinions and so on are thus inclined. (cf: *general service*)

giant *n* (science) in astronomy, one of the class of large, diffuse stars. (cf: *dwarf*)

gibson girl (milit) USN: a portable emergency radio carried amongst stores on navy life rafts.

gifted *a* (educ) a child who is appreciably above the educational average of his peers, and as such, like the child in need of remedial care for his backwardness, may well need special treatment far removed from merely praising his achievements.

gig *n, v* (rock business) a performance played by a rock band or singer; to give such a performance or concert.

gigabit (computers) one billion bits (qv). Similar multiples are *kilobit*: 1000 bits, *megabit*: 1 million bits, *terabit*: 1 million million bits.

gigantomania (sociol) the obsession, prevalent among all ranks and nationalities of leader with the achievement of huge undertakings simply because of their size, without any thought as to cost, effectiveness, usefulness or similar consideration.

GIGO (computers) (acro) garbage *in* garbage *out*: a dictum that states if one puts worthless data into a computer, then the machine can only give worthless data back.

gilt-edged (commerce) any stocks of high quality and reliability; spec. British Government stocks, certain highly ranked corporation stocks and certain public authority issues.

ginger (sex) a dishonest male prostitute.

Ginnie Mae (econ/US) (acro) Government National Mortgage Association; thus *ginnie maes*: stock certificates issued by this agency. (cf: *Freddie Mac*)

gin out *v* (business) from the cotton gin, an appliance for separating the useful and waste parts of cotton: in business terms, to analyse a situation or problem and obtain the required and relevant results and information.

gin pendant (milit) RN: a pendant flown by a ship's officers to inform officers aboard other ships that drinks are on offer in their wardroom. (Usually this is a pendant signifying 'starboard').

girl (milit) any nuclear device that fails to explode. (cf: *boy*)

girl (drugs) cocaine; see *drug names*.

give a tug (police) to make an arrest; thus the villain talks of *getting a tug*.

giveback (indust relats) 1. the surrender by a union of previously won fringe benefits in return for wage increases or new concessions from the management.
2. the acceptance during a recession by trades unions of (temporary) reduction in pay in return for guarantees of continuing employment.

give quickies (sex) for a gay hustler (qv) to fellate a client, probably in some public place, thus necessitating speed.

giver (stock market) someone who has purchased shares and wishes to delay delivery until the following account, thus effecting a contango (qv). The giver must *give* interest to the deliverer of the securities to make up for delaying the payment.

giver aircraft (aerospace) the tanker which brings fuel to another aircraft in a mid-air refuelling operation. (cf: *receiver aircraft*)

give up (stock market) 1. a deal which one broker executes for the client of a second broker and the commission for which must be shared between the two brokers. 2. that part of a commission earnt by a broker from a major client which he is directed to turn over to a fellow broker who has provided certain specialised services to that client during the same deal.

giz (milit) USMC: (abbrev) gizmo, any miscellaneous, unidentified object, thingamajig, etc.

gizzit n (milit) British Army: from corruption of 'give us it!': any looted item.

glamour issue (stock market) shares of companies that are considered at a given time to be fashionable; as of now these include electronics, robots, micro-processors, chips, etc.

glass n (milit) RN/USN: a telescope; *glasses*: binoculars.

glass v (sport) in surfing, the becoming smooth and glassy of the sea.

glass shot (movies) the shot achieved by the painting on glass of a part of the background; this is held carefully in front of the camera so that live action and real background can be properly blended together with the glass. This enables extremely elaborate sets to be created at a fraction of the cost of building them or attempting to find a suitable location.

glide path (aerospace) the 'path' down which a landing aircraft flies onto the ground.

gliding shift (indust relats) aka: *gliding time*: any work shift that functions on flexitime (qv).

glitch n (computers) from Yiddish *glitchen*: slide: any form of unexplained electronic interference that involves the computer, either in the electricity supply or the program function. Possibly first used by German scientists working for US space programme at NASA.

glitch (astronomy) a sudden change in the rotation of any heavenly body, planet or star. From the computer use.

glitch (tech) *glitch* meaning a slight and unex-

plained error is used throughout technology, incl. TV, radio, radar, motor racing (where the Yiddish 'to slide' is most literally interpreted), space flight and more.

glitch (pols) when an unexplained but crucial electronic breakdown or burst of interference can result in major problems for a candidate (esp) or an incumbent of office. Eg: faulty transmissions of speeches, especially those in translation can ruin otherwise satisfactory communications/conferences; likewise badly printed campaign literature, malfunctioning microphones, etc.

globe and anchor (milit) the US Marine Corps emblem, adopted in 1868.

GLOCKEM (milit) (acron) ground launched cruise missile.

glork (computers) 1. a term of mild surprise, usually tinged with outrage. 2. used as a convenience description when the correct name has slipped one's memory. 3. an antonym for glitch (qv) but esp. reflexively as in 'the system just glorked itself'.

glossy (media) 1. a magazine printed on glossy paper (usually a fashion or social publication). (cf. *slick*). 2. a photograph with a glossy surface, often used for publicity purposes, as in '8 by 10 glossies'. 3. a film depicting supposedly sophisticated, fashionable life – as lived, in naive eyes, within the pages of glossy magazines and portrayed in glossy photos.

gnat's (TV) (abbrev) *gnat's ass*, *gnat's prick*: the tiniest, barely significant morsel. Used to describe a movement, an amount, a piece to be cut during editing.

gob (milit) USN: any enlisted man.

gobble down (computers) to obtain data.

gobo (theatre, movies, TV) 1. a portable 'wall' covered in sound-absorbing material. 2. a small black screen used next to a light to diffuse the light or otherwise create a desired effect.

go codes (milit) the US codes that are transmitted in the event of launching a nuclear war. These codes, which change daily, are carried in a briefcase called the *football* (qv) by an officer who must never leave the President's side. Only on receiving these codes, which must match with counter codes and similar security devices, can the military begin a nuclear attack.

go-devil (tech) the name for various devices used in farming, mining, oil-drilling, logging etc. and differing in application accordingly. Ie: in farming it can be a form of rake, in oil-drilling a cleaner for pipes, in logging a special tool for splitting stubborn logs, etc.

go down in flames (TV/US) the failure of a news team to put together, however hard they try, some item that should have met that night's programme deadline. (cf: *crash*)

gods (theatre/UK) the highest tier of seats in a traditional auditorium and by extension, those

G

who sit there and who, while their seats may only be cheap and far from the stage, like their mythical namesakes, may have the greatest critical influence on the success or otherwise of a production.

God slot (TV/UK) a period on Sunday evening approx 6pm–7pm that is set aside by statute or constitution (for commercial or state television) for the broadcasting of ostensibly religious programmes. In effect, although there is usually some form of hymn-singing (as there is on Sunday mornings) such programmes usually bend the rules as far as they can without actually declaring themselves atheist. (cf: *closed period*)

God's medicine (drugs) a name for morphine (see *drug names*) attrib. to Sir William Osler, who observed, 'yes, it is God's medicine, for if it were any better, it would be kept in heaven for the angels to use.'

God squad (medic/US) aka: *God committee*: special advisors to a hospital's staff who deal with such ethical problems as terminal cancer, patients who demand to be allowed to die, parents of terribly damaged new born babies who might not wish them to be helped live, the switching off of life support systems for human 'vegetables' etc. In other words, officials who, in medical terms, are 'playing God'.

gofer (entertain) a corruption of 'go for. . .' and thus anyone used around a TV or movie studio, record company or studio, and any similar place to run errands for the stars and serve as a general dogsbody. Some gofers, like newspaper copy boys of old, can rise high, but usually a derogatory description, esp. when referring to executives who would not like to see themselves thus lowly.

goffer (milit) RN: any non-alcoholic drink; perhaps from shandy*gaff*.

go for broke (milit) for an airplane to fire all its aimable weapons simultaneously on one part of the target.

go-go fund (stock market) risky, short-term, volatile and above all speculative investment dealing; the implication is of the style of a discotheque where go-go dancing was originated.

go green *v* (milit) to transfer a phonecall from an open line to a secure one; from the use of green telephones for secure lines. (cf: *scrambler*)

gold (record business) one million units; *go gold* is to sell a million records, either of a 45rpm single or an album. (cf: *platinum*)

Gold Codes (milit) the special war codes carried in the football (qv) and available at all times to the US President.

golden hours (TV, movies) union term for those lucrative hours worked at weekends, on public holidays, at night, etc. (cf: *bubble*)

golden shower (sex) prostitute's (male or female) term for urinating on a client.

goldfish (theatre/opera) a singer, usually one of the choir, who appears to sing, but is actually resting his/her voice by mouthing the lyrics and thus, opening and shutting a silent mouth, appears like a fish.

goldie (milit) US Dept. of Defense code: the aircraft's automatic flight control system and electronic bomb guidance system are engaged and awaiting commands from the ground control computer. *Goldie lock*: the ground controller has full control of the aircraft.

gold-plating (milit) the habit indulged by the US Pentagon of attaching every conceivable piece of arms or avionics gadgetry to aerospace equipment that has already been commissioned; such embellishments are always supposedly in the name of combat efficiency, but they rarely bear in mind any form of economic efficiency.

go matrix *v* (business) the changing of a corporation's structure from the traditional 'pyramid' to a matrix form in which various axes are created, each containing a department – research in one, sales another, project planning another, etc.

GOMER (medic/US) (acron) *get out of my emergency room*: 1. a notation on the file of a patient (very often an elderly one) whose less than vital problems are withholding the possibility of real medical aid to someone near death. 2. patients, apparently too sick to stay at home but not so sick as to die, requiring long term care and keen to take every advantage of the hospital and its staff. Female GOMERs are *GOMER*es.

gondola (commerce) island counters used in self service stores for the displaying of merchandise; the typical unit of the typical supermarket.

go negative (pols/US) for a candidate and his staff to launch a campaign geared to exposing the opponent's weaknesses rather than to promoting his own strengths.

gong *n, v* (milit) British Army: a medal or the awarding of a medal.

gonk (sex) prostitutes' derisory description of the client; from a particularly stupid, stuffed doll briefly popular in the early 1960s.

gonnophta (police) a skilled woman pickpocket; from Yiddish *gonnif* 'a thief'.

go/no-go (aerospace) the step by step method of check and countercheck by which space missions are carried out; all decisions are jointly taken by the crew and mission control whenever a new step has to be taken and only if all concerned say 'go' is that step taken.

good (media) aka: *real television, good television, good radio*, etc: not an assessment of quality in the traditional sense – artistic values, cultural standards, etc. – but an opinion of what, in the critic's view, television or radio ought to be doing and the extent to which a particular event fulfils this ideal criterion. Thus, for its drama, immediacy and the fact that print could never have achieved such 'live' coverage, the televising of the SAS shootout at the end of the 1981 Iranian Embassy siege was *good television*, irrespective of the violence involved and the subsequent, *pace* the Falklands, near deification of the SAS. (cf: *sexy*)

good ball (sport) in rugby union football, the possession of the ball which sets up a move upon which a potential try-scoring combination or run can be built.

good box office (theatre) a play that is attracting many paying customers. Thus *good house*: full houses for each performance, much like 'good box office'; *good theatre* an effective, dramatic play that pleases the audience and acts well (qv).

good numbers (movies) successful grosses (qv) at the cinema box offices.

good samaritan law (medic/US) a statute that protects all medical personnel from any legal problems that might arise from their using their skills in an emergency – ie: a car crash in the street – to help injured people who are not their patients and thus do not fall under the general insurance carried by a hospital.

good shop (theatre) a part for which the pay may not be especially good, but one in which 'people notice you' and is therefore excellent professional exposure.

goof-ball (drugs) barbiturates (see: *drug names*).

goofy (sport) in surfing, one who stands with his *right* foot forward, the equivalent of boxing's *southpaw*.

googly (sport) in cricket, an off-break bowled to a right handed batsman with what appears to be a leg-break action. (cf: *bosie*)

googol (science) sl. for 10 to the hundredth power.

googol (commerce) by extension from the scientific use (qv), the description of a salesman of a deal or commission that has netted him an exceptional sum of money.

goon squad (indust relats) company thugs hired to break strikes.

goon squad (sport) in ice hockey, specially recruited players whose job is to beat up and generally intimidate their opposition rather than worry about playing the game itself.

goon stand (movies) a large stand to hold equipment for lighting or modifying lights on a set.

goon suit (milit) RAF: one-piece coverall rubber suit for protection when flying in low temperatures.

goose *v* (business) by extension from the usual, sexual meaning: to gee up one's business or its personnel by giving them a sudden shock.

GOP (pols/US) (abbrev) the *Grand Old Party*: the Republicans, coined c1880s, influenced by the naming of PM William Gladstone as Britain's GOM, grand old man.

gopher (crime) a real sucker for a con-man's pitch.

gorilla (business) a very important person with power and influence, a true 'heavy weight'; thus the *gorilla scale*: a system of grading a firm's major personnel, rating as 800 pounders and 400 pounders or simply '*the* gorilla'.

gorilla pimp (sex) black pimp description of a pimp who controls his stable (qv) of women through threats, fear and violence.

gork (medic/US) 1. a person suffering the after-effects of an anaesthetic; 'spaced out' and disorientated. 2. a patient whose brain has ceased functioning, through accident or disease and has thus been rendered a 'human vegetable'.

go round (theatre/UK) for a friend, relative, business associate, or any non-actor to visit a performer in his/her dressing room after a show. One 'goes round' to the back of the stage. In US: *go behind, go back*.

go-see *n* (entertain) 'It's like an audition: you go-see if they like you. . .' (Andy Warhol, 1982).

go South with it (gambling) . to put money in one's pocket, either legitimately, or otherwise. 2. to remove a card or cards from the deck surreptitiously.

go-team (sport) in US football, an antonym for the offensive team.

Gotham (entertain) sl. for New York City; hometown, inter alia, of superheroes Batman and Superman.

got his feet muddy (police/UK) someone who has already been in trouble with the law. (cf: *form*)

go to Cain's (theatre/US) to close a show; from Cain's Transfer Co. of New York City, which flourished 1886–1933 and was the main renter of costumes, props and sets to touring companies. Thus a visit to Cain's warehouse implied taking back what one had out on loan.

go toes up (commerce) to go bankrupt, with implication of a corpse with its toes pointing into the air.

go to the mattresses (crime/US) in US Mafia, to go to war with another gang; while the war continues, the soldiers (qv) do not live at home, but in special hideouts where they sleep on mattresses and rarely stay for two consecutive nights at the same address.

gouge (business/US) from USN and (obs.) student use for a cribsheet: information, which may be 'good gouge' or 'bad gouge'.

goulash (gambling) a redeal of cards which are not shuffled but simply pushed together after a round has been dealt and no player (in bridge or whist or similar games) has chosen to bid. Formerly known as *mayonnaise*.

goulash communism (pols) coined 1961 by N. S. Khrushchev to denounce the 'local' mixtures of communism advanced in the name of the

Party by various Western European Communist Parties. (cf: *tutti-frutti communism, eurocommunism*)

go under the rule (stock market/US) when a member fails to complete a deal, the Chairman of the Stock Exchange must buy or sell those shares and thus complete that deal.

go up *v* (educ) at Oxford and Cambridge Universities, undergraduates (rather than students) *go up* rather than attend and *come down* rather than leave.

go up in the air (theatre/US) aka: *make an ascension* (UK): to miss a cue, to forget one's lines (cf: *dry, fluff*)

government relations (public relations) a variation of government lobbying – the forwarding of the interests of a specific group by professional lobbyists who work hard and continually on Congressmen and bureaucrats to further their ends: the forwarding of the interests of a specific company in its dealings with the Administration by the use of a public relations corporation. Obviously restricted to the larger, more influential corporations, the PR executive's task is to encourage a feeling of mutual usefulness between the Administration and his client on the lines of the famous 'what's good for General Motors is good for the USA'.

go with the flow (new therapies) a perfect example of the development of a marginally more demanding concept which has turned, through popularity into a therapeutic, 'pop philosophical' cliché: the original phrase, which exhorts those concerned to let themselves move in tune with all the different experiences that make up life, instead of fighting against that powerful current, was 'floating with a complex streaming of experience' (Carl Rogers, *On Becoming A Person*, 1961).

grab *n* (indust relats/US) the company store.

grace days (commerce) three days allowed for the payment of any commercial transaction over and above the time actually stated in a commercial bill.

grade creep (business) a method of regrading one's employees during a period when the government is demanding a wage freeze (qv) which makes it possible to boost their pay without actually breaking that freeze. However, in the long run, such *ad hoc* increases lead to *earnings drift* (qv) which can prove harmful to a company.

gradualism (pols) coined with reference to the abolition of slavery c 1835, the concept of slow and steady change rather than violent overturn or the instant adoption of a totally new political direction.

gradualism (milit) escalation towards war that is directly linked to the progress, or more likely the lack of progress in gradually disintegrating negotiations.

grafilm (art, movies) defined by J. Byrne-Daniel

in 1970 as 'a graphic/poetic approach to film-making rather than a photographic/prosaic one'. Involves the careful consideration of the elements in every shot so that each individual frame is a considered composition.

graft (pols/US) the making of money by a politician through the use of dishonest or underhand means: accepting bribes (though such blatant methods died to a great extent with the 19th century); the kickbacks when a major public works programme is contracted in the 'right' direction; the many gifts for exercising political patronage or similar favours.

grainy (photography) a style of photograph that concentrated on the coarse, rough indistinctly defined style of image. Particularly favoured during the 1960s.

Grammy (rock business) the pop music business's equivalent annual award to Hollywood's Oscar (qv) and television's Emmy (qv): from the abbrev. of gramophone, with a diminutive -y suffix, and awarded by America's National Academy of Recording Arts and Sciences.

grand-daddy (medic/US) an oversized sanitary pad.

grandfather (govt/US) 1. *a*: relating to or based upon rights or privileges that date from before the passage of a new law or regulation. 2. the exemption of a person, persons or a company from the restrictions of some new law or regulation. Both (1) and (2) stem from *grandfather clause*: an obs. provision in the Constitutions of some Southern states exempting from suffrage restrictions the descendants of men who voted before the Civil War.

grandfather rights (civil aircraft/US) certificates granted in perpetuity to certain US civil airlines to fly internal routes; signed by the US Civil Aeronatics Board in July 1940. Thus *grandfather routes* the routes flown by those carriers ever since 1940. This use originates in the administrative use of grandfather (qv).

grand slam (milit) US Dept. of Defense code: all hostile planes have been shot down.

grapes (milit) USN: aircraft refuelers on US aircraft carriers who wear distinctive purple jackets.

graphics (computers) anything in representational or pictorial rather than in written form that appears on screen of a VDU.

grass (aerospace) a fuzzy pattern on a radar cathode ray tube which indicates the presence of electrical noise.

grass *v* (sports) in contact sports, to knock to the ground.

grass (police/UK) an informer, from rhyming slang grasshopper=shopper=one who 'shops' his fellows to the police.

grasseater (police/US) a corrupt policeman who accepts such bribes and similar favours that are offered, but does not actually solicit them himself. (cf: *meateater*)

grass hand (press) a temporary printer who fills in while a regular employee is absent.

grass roots (pols) a political concept usually advanced by the left that cites the great mass of the voters, unsullied by cynicism or sophistication and swayed only by their instinctively populist aspirations; less idealistically, the rank and file of any party who may want to make themselves felt, but in the event need to be driven to the polls and will probably vote for personalities rather than policies.

graveyard shift (gambling) the early morning shift of any casino or other gambling establishment.

graveyard shift (business) the shift running from 12 midnight until the early hours of the morning, c 4 a.m. Orig. from ship (naval or merchant) use, implying that in the dark, rough hours, there were more disasters than at other times.

gravy (theatre/UK) 1. easy laughs from a friendly audience. 2. good lines or business, that get plenty of audience response in a farce or comedy.

gray (sociol, pols) (UK sp. *grey*) an adj. used since 1960s to denote pensioners or 'senior citizens', usually those formed into pressure groups or some form of activism (qv) on the analogy with the Black Panthers who fought and demonstrated for the black cause. Thus *Gray Panthers* (founded c 1972) who demand attention to the elderly in areas of health, crime, housing, finance and utilities; and a 1982 study of elderly homosexuality: *Gay and Gray*.

graze *v* (milit) artillery shells that burst on impact; the opposite of air burst (qv).

grazing (commerce, crime) a method of low-intensity shop-lifting whereby the subject picks up some small edible object, eg: a chocolate bar, unwraps it, eats it and tosses away the paper before he arrives at the checkouts. A very restrained version of the murderess who killed her husband with a blow from a frozen leg of lamb and destroyed the evidence by serving *gigot aux flageolets* to the investigating officers.

grazing fire (milit) a steady burst of fire that sweeps parallel to the ground and never rises above the height of an average upright man.

grease *v* (milit) to kill.

Great Alliance (pols) in the People's Republic of China, the concept – flourishing only for the duration of the Cultural Revolution (qv) – that all revolutionary mass organisations had the right to representation on revolutionary committees.

Great Leap Forward (pols) in the People's Republic of China, Mao Tse Tung's effort between 1958 and 1961 to make major steps forward in the Chinese economy and consolidate the communist revolution in China. A lack of adequate planning, the dearth of modern equipment due to China's deliberate isolation from capitalist societies and a series of natural disasters destroyed any chance of success the GLF might have had.

Great Patriotic War (pols) the official Soviet term for World War II which for Russia lasted from Hitler's overturning of the Nazi-Soviet Pact in 1941 until 1945.

greedy pigs (police/UK) derisory description of the punters (qv), the simple public who want something for nothing and come whining to the police when they find not only have they had nothing but they've sacrificed quite a good deal for good measure.

Greek (sex) an indication, on an advertisement or in a contact magazine, that the prostitute so advertised will indulge clients with sodomy, 'the Greek art'.

Greek (advert) garbled letters used to indicate the size but not the actual words of an advertisement, especially where there is a large amount of body copy. In UK use: *Latin*.

green (theatre/UK) the stage: both from rhyming sl. 'the greengage' and from the green carpet that was regularly placed on the stage for the performance of tragedies in the 18th and early 19th centuries.

green (sport) in horse-racing and greyhound racing, for a horse or dog to be a novice; *running green*: to be scared of the crowds, the noise and the general atmosphere and thus to race below true form.

green ban (indust relats) in Australia, the refusal of some trades unions to have their members work on environmentally or socially unacceptable projects.

green currency (pols, econ) any of the artificial Eurocurrencies (qv) created in 1969 for transactions by farmers with the express intention of ensuring that whatever may be the fluctuations of the member nations' *real* economies, the green currency would remain stable, and with it the livelihoods of Europe's peasants.

green department (movies) studio department for the supply of all 'garden' equipment, produce, lawns, flowers, trees, etc. for filming.

green eyeshade (educ, press) a student term for any professor of journalism/communications whose teaching and/or research concentrates on the 'practical' arts of editing and reporting.

greenfield *a* (commerce) rural and undeveloped sites, often near towns/cities but not designated as actual protected green belts – the strips of land that surround an urban centre, and prevent one large town simply sliding into the outskirts of another through builders' greed for new land.

green film (TV) a positive film that has just returned from the laboratory – it may not yet even be completely dry.

greenhouse (medic/US) a special structure that is placed over an operating table and the patient

G

and the surgeon(s) and nurses who are conducting the operation as an extra precaution against bacteria.

greenhouse (aerospace) a long plastic/glass canopy that covers both the front and rear cockpit in an aircraft.

greenhouse effect (science) in meteorology, the phenomenon that permits the heat of the sun to pass through the atmosphere and warm the Earth, but prevents it from escaping again.

greenie (sport) in surfing, an abbrev. of *greenback*, a large wave just before it breaks. (cf: *grinder, dumper*)

greenlight *v* (movies) to agree to a deal, an analogy of traffic lights.

greenlining (govt, sociol) an increasing series of attacks on the socially divisive practice of redlining (qv) specifically by attempting to revive the inner cities and to make investments there viable and appealing once again. (cf: *gentrification, blockbusting*)

green paper (govt/UK) a Government publication that offers 'not a policy already determined, but . . . propositions put before the whole nation for discussion' (Michael Stewart, 1969). (cf: *orange paper, white paper, blue books*)

green pound (econ) the British version of the green currency (qv) by which agricultural transactions are made throughout the EEC. Sterling is the 'green pound', and there are green lire, francs, deutschmarks, etc.

green revolution (sociol, econ) the increase in the production of cereal crops in developing countries after the introduction of high-yield varieties and the application of scientific and planned methods to their agriculture.

green room (theatre) an offstage sitting room in which actors can rest or entertain friends; thus, *to talk green room*: to indulge in theatrical gossip.

greens (milit) USMC: the green service uniform. (cf: *blues, whites*)

green time (traffic) the length of time traffic can move through a green light.

gremlin (sport) aka: *gremmie*: 1. a young surfer. 2. someone who frequents surfing beaches but only to make trouble, not to surf.

grey (sociol, pols) see *gray*.

grey hair *v* (business) the concept of using an older person's skills and experience to further one's own ideas; used by consultants and marketing specialists to indicate the use of such senior figures as short-term aides for specific problems.

grey-out (aerospace) a less severe form of blackout, caused by the blood's actions in the head during steep climbs or dives and the subsequent loss of consciousness, total in a *blackout*, only partial in a *greyout* that can result from such manoeuvres.

greys (prison/UK) a pair of 'smart' grey trousers required, in some prisons for wear either to visits or to Church.

grid (theatre, TV) the openwork 'ceiling' above a state or a TV studio from which lights and scenery can be suspended and which contains a cat walk for technicians to move around.

grids (art) those painters who opted during the 1960s for art that was completely abstract/nonrelational still needed some form of neutral structure to work with/against and chose the grid that painters have always used to square off their canvases.

grief therapy (sociol) supportive therapy for the recently bereaved, often carried out between an 'encounter' group of four or five similarly bereaved individuals under the direction of a highly trained counsellor.

grift (crime, police/US) replaced graft as a description of various con-games when the politicians started to use graft (literally and linguistically) as their own. Grift implies non-violent crime, as opposed to *heavy rackets*.

grimeson (crime) in US Mafia, a commission made up of the bosses of all the families (qqv).

grim-gram (govt) from a '*grim* tele*gram*', a term coined in 1980s to deal with the weekly lists of the murdered and the missing that are assembled by embassy personnel in El Salvador and sent back to Washington for analysis.

grind (gambling) low limit banking game which requires a good number of players to make the house a decent profit. Thus a *grind joint* or *grind store* denotes the sort of place where such a game is being held.

grind *v* (movies) to project films or TV shows.

grinder (milit) USMC: a parade ground or drill field.

grinder (audio) a reasonably lengthy burst of atmospheric disturbance, probably caused by lightning. (cf: *click*)

grindhouse (movies) second rate movie theatre for running the sort of films that studio 'grind out'; possible implication of couples 'grinding' in the back row?

grip (movies) in general, a studio employee used for moving heavy equipment around, for any job that requires a 'tight grip'; spec. the man who lays the tracks for the camera dolly (qv) to move along.

groaner (sailors) whistling buoys which actually sound more as if they were in pain, thus the name.

gronk *v* (computers) 1. to clear a wedged (qv) machine of its jammed-up state and to re-start it. 2. to break down. 3. of a person, *gronked*: to feel totally exhausted or otherwise ill. 4. of machines, to cease functioning; of people, to collapse or give in to exhaustion set off for home and sleep.

groomers (air crew) the team of cleaners who set to work on a commercial aircraft as soon as the passengers have deplaned (qv).

gross *n* (movies) the money a film earns in the cinemas before any deductions as to tax, expenses, salaries etc. are made. Thus a *big grosser*: a successful film; *percentage of the gross*: those involved with the filmstars, director, writer – are often offered points (qv) rather than a fee, which are calculated as a percentage of the gross takings.

gross height examination (aerospace) a nose dive.

grot (milit) British Army: a cabin on a troop ship.

grounding (new therapies) in bioenergetics (qv) the concept of one's being as an entity attached to the ground through the feet and therefore the creation by such of a 'oneness' with the earth of personal strength, stability and confidence.

ground zero (milit) the part of the ground that is situated directly under the exploding nuclear weapon. (cf: *hypocentre*)

group form (archit) a term that refers to the sum of relationships between a number of buildings: in other words, the form of individual buildings being subordinated to the form of the group as a whole.

group 10 (civil airlines) a discount fare initially created for the use of tour operators. Now widely used by airlines to mask from IATA and similar authorities special discounts to individuals. The passengers are consolidated into a group simply by paperwork – although none of them ever realise it – and the letter, if not the spirit of the IATA rules is still respected.

grovel (computers) to work interminably and without apparent progress. Often used as 'X is *grovelling over* such and such'. (cf: *crunch*)

grow *v* (milit) RN: to stop shaving in order to grow a full beard and moustache.

growl *n* (music) in jazz, a deep, throaty, rasping sound coming from a wind instrument.

growler (aerospace) test equipment for checking short circuits in electrical machines.

growler (milit) satellite communications link which is used to provide secure (qv) communications that cannot be monitored by hostile land-based equipment.

grubber (sport) 1. (rugby) a forward kick of the ball along the ground. 2. (cricket) a ball that is bowled and runs flat along the ground.

grunt (milit) US army: the lowest rank of infantryman; a description first used in Vietnam in 1960s and allegedly stemming from the soldiers' (justified) complaining as they marched through hostile, frightening terrain.

G-spool (advert) aka: *dub* (qv): a video-taped duplicate copy of a TV commercial which is sent out to network TV stations for their use.

G-suit (aerospace) fr. G: gravity: a specially designed suit which is intended to help jet pilots, astronauts and anyone else who has to encounter g-forces during acceleration to deal better with the physical effects of those forces.

guard (gambling) in bridge, a card which accompanies a higher card of the same suit.

guard books (advert) a file kept in an agency of all the advertisements prepared and published for a specific client over a number of campaigns; such a file doubles as a collection of useful and relevant information on a client's advertising preferences, products, etc.

GUIDO (aerospace) (acron) *gui*dance *o*fficer: an engineer in charge of a space flight; the chief navigation officer at Mission Control. (cf: *FIDO, RETRO*)

guinea (horse-racing/US) a groom; undoubtedly racist, but guinea usually means Italian, and 90% of US grooms are black.

gulliver (aerospace) from Lemuel Gulliver, hero of Swift's *Gulliver's Travels* (1726) who stood out as a monster among the tiny Lilliputians: a device made of adhesive cords which would be fired out along the surface of a planet and then rewound, on the principle that some micro-organisms, were they to exist, would have stuck to the ropes and might be analysed on the spacecraft's return to earth.

gulp *n* (computers) a unit which consists of a number of bytes (qv), considered as a word.

gumbah (crime) from Ital. 'compare', lit. 'godfather', corrupted by US pronunciation: a friend, an ally in battle.

gun (sport) in surfing, a heavy surfboard.

gun *v* (commerce) *to gun a stock*: to force a rival into letting go a quantity of shares which one wishes to purchase.

gunfire (milit) British Army: a hot drink served at reveille; from the custom of firing a cannon at the start of each day at which point those officers awakened would doubtless have been offered a morning cup of tea.

gunge (science) a soft, sticky mass from various gaseous mixtures of chemically abundant compounds. Officially termed *tholin* (Gk: muddy) by its discoverers Carl Sagan and B. N. Khare, but most of their peers preferred gunge.

gung ho (milit) slogan adopted during World War II by USMC: enthusiastic, keen on a fight, aggressive. From the Chinese *kung* 'work' *ho* 'together'.

gung ho (pols/US) the same sense of enthusiasm and aggressiveness that applies to the military in a political context; often the attribute of young campaign volunteers, or junior members of an in-coming White House team who are raring to go, spoiling for a fight and keen to show the world what fine stuff they're made of. Eg: John Dean, H. R. 'Bob' Haldeman, John Ehrlichman et al.

gunny (milit) USMC (abbrev) Gunnery Sergeant.

gunship (milit) a helicopter with door-mounted heavy machine guns and air-to-ground missiles.

gunslinger (finance) 1. a high risk, high performance investment fund that takes a capital role.

G

2. the manager of such a fund, with, it is assumed, characteristics to match.

gusanos (espionage) from Sp. 'worms'. Intelligence sl. for volatile but often useful anti-Castro Cubans, many of whom live in Florida, waiting to go home.

gut course (educ) from the idea of a 'soft underbelly' or a flabby 'beer gut': the courses in further education that are considered to be soft options.

gut feeling (new therapies) instinctive spontaneity that comes right from the viscera and as such beloved of all new therapies; the opposite of mind-tripping (qv), ie: thinking something out and employing a degree of intellectual analysis, the result of which might not be the 'gut' belief in the therapy on which such groups depend.

gutter (press) the white space that surrounds any printed page.

guttersnipe (advert) a small poster that is affixed down at the street level, almost in the gutter, rather than high up on a building or billboard.

Guzz (milit) RN: the home base of Devonport.

gypsies (theatre/US) a chorus line in a Broadway musical.

G

H (drugs) (abbrev) heroin (see: *drug names*).

habit hierarchy (sociol) one's personal system of conducting any particular idiosyncratic rituals: scratching parts of the body in a special way or other and similar regular repetitions.

hacienda *n* (aerospace) nickname for the Office of Aerospace Research. (cf: *legoland*)

hack *n* (milit) USMC: to be *under hack*: to be arrested by an officer for breach of discipline.

hack (press) once a derogatory description of a penny-a-line hack of all trades journalist who wrote anything as long as there was a cheque at the end of it; such timeservers naturally still exist, but hack is used more and more as a slightly ironic, somewhat affectionate term for one's fellow journalists, esp. in a context such as war reporting, where all are suffering together in temporary cameraderie.

hack *n* (pols) a derogatory description of a time-serving, graft-ridden politician whose interests lie with himself and those whose influence had him selected rather than one who has his constituency, let alone his country at heart.

hack (computers) 1. a quick job that produces what is required but with little sign of standards or quality. 2. the result of a *hack job*. 3. *neat hack*: a clever technique; also, a stylish practical joke if such a joke features neatness, harmlessness, cleverness and real surprise value. 4. *real hack*: a crock (qv). 5. *hack together*: improvise a system quickly but sufficiently smartly to ensure its working. 6. to suffer something emotionally or physically. 7. to work on something, with the added sense of that something as being central to one's professional life and relevant to the whole essence of why one pursues that profession in the first place. 8. to pull a prank on, see (3). 9. to waste time. 10. *to hack up (on)* see (1) and (2). 11. *hack value*: the reason for expending effort on what appears otherwise to be a pointless goal, were that goal not simply the pleasure gained from hacking. 12. *happy hacking* a farewell, *how's hacking?* a greeting among hackers (qv) and *hack hack* a temporary farewell.

hack *n* (aerospace, milit) an aeroplane, probably captured in hostilities or too old to be used for potential active service, working out its life as a general utility or transport vehicle.

hack and slay (D&D) a style of play which emphasises brute force over subtlety.

hacker (computers) 1. someone who enjoys learning the details of programming systems and how to stretch and develop their potentials, as opposed to most users (qv) who are satisfied with a minimum understanding and daunted by the threat of anything more complex. 2. one who programs enthusiastically and will spend hours so doing just for the pleasure of the discipline.

hack it *v* (milit) the ability to keep going no matter what the conditions, the weight of one's pack, the intensity of the hostile fire and any other negative factors.

hack it (pols) pretty much an equivalent use to that found in the military, other than that hostile fire may be verbal or printed rather than coming from ordnance, and that the forced marches are those through a lengthy campaign or against a powerful opposition rather than across treacherous terrain.

hair (computers) the complications which render a problem hairy (qv). Often seen as the phrase *infinite hair*, denoting very great complexity.

hair in the gate (TV, movies) fine shavings of emulsion that accumulate as film runs through the camera gate (qv) and, like tiny fibres, will ruin the filming unless they are removed at regular intervals.

hairy (computers) 1. exceptionally and unnecessarily complicated. 2. completely incomprehensible. 3. of people: high-powered, dictatorial, exceptionally skilful and/or incomprehensible (all of which depend on one's overall feellings pro/con the person described). Does not have to be a programmer, but merely someone whom one encounters and who might be so categorised.

HAL (computers) (acron) *h*igh-order *a*ssembly *l*anguage: a language in which computers can communicate data amongst themselves without human interference.

Haldane principle (pols/UK) a concept named for Prof. J. B. S. Haldane (1892–1964) who stated that ideally government research agencies should be completely isolated from and external to the influence of those government departments which might eventually benefit from such research.

half *n* (theatre/UK) a call to the company reminding them that there are 30 minutes (actually, by tradition nearer 35, in the same way that the quarter (qv) is nearer 20 min. than 15) before curtain up. (cf: *thirty minutes*)

half and half (sex) fellatio followed by conventional intercourse, a variation offered by a prostitute to her client for more money than the basic charge/sex.

half a piece (drugs) half an ounce of a narcotic, usually so expensive as to be restricted to wholesale transactions. Thus *quarter piece*: a quarter of an ounce. (cf: *piece*)

half seats (theatre) seats that are half obscured by their being placed behind a pillar in the auditorium – a problem especially common in New York's old Metropolitan Opera House; such seats were not, however, available at half price.

half stick (press) a small portrait block half the column measure. (cf: *porkchop*, *thumbnail*)

half-word (computers) a group of consecutive bits (qv) which can be dealt with as a single unit, that occupy the storage of half a word unit in a computer memory.

hall test (marketing) a selection of passing consumers are pulled off a street, then brought to a question and answer control centre – a large hall – where they are subjected to an interview on whatever product or topic the researcher wishes to study.

halo *n* (advert) the knock-on effect that uses the popularity of a bestselling product to enhance the sales of another item produced by the same manufacturers.

halo effect (psychol) the improved results that will be obtained from the subject of an intelligence test, interview or similar examination if the atmosphere in the test is one of approbation and the subject is made to feel 'good'.

haloing (press) an error in printing when each letter is surrounded by a border produced by the ink reproducing the shape of the metal on which that letter is set in relief.

ham (theatre) (abbrev) *hamfat*, *hamfatter*: actors who give inexpert or more usually over melodramatic performances; from those second rate, and thus poor actors who in earlier days were forced to rub hamrind over their faces as the base for powder rather than being able to afford the more sweet-smelling and sophisticated oils.

ham and egg shift (indust relats) in mining, the shift between 10 am and 6 pm, harking back to an era when a man would eat his ham before work began and his eggs upon its termination.

hammered (stock exchange) 1. when a member or firm on the Exchange cannot meet his liabilities, he is declared a defaulter, which announcement is made by the striking of a wooden mallet on a desk in order to attract the attention of his erstwhile colleagues. Then the head waiter (qv) of the Exchange hits three strokes and announces the defaulter's name. 2. to force down a price.

hammer price (stock exchange) the price realised for the remaining shares of a member who has just been hammered (qv).

handbasher (TV, movies) a hand-held sungun (qv) of approx. 800W.

handbook (gambling) a street bookmaker who accepts bets 'in his hand'.

handcuffed (theatre) an actor's description of an audience who will not applaud. They are similarly pilloried as *sitting on their hands*.

handful (prison/UK) a sentence of five years. (cf: *stretch*, *lagging*)

handful (police) £5.

hand-holding (public relations) the first task a PR must get done: the convincing of a client that come what may he, the PR, is doing a wonderful job, despite any fears or even accusations to the contrary; *then* he can devote himself to his client's business.

H&I (milit) (abbrev) *harassment and interdiction*: a method of deterring a possible surprise Vietcong attack during the US involvement in Vietnam, by random firing, usually at night, which might or might not hit the enemy, but should keep him at bay.

handicapper (horse-racing) any horse that is running in a handicap race.

handle (gambling) the total amount of money that changes hands over a day's betting at a racecourse before bookmakers can assess the final profit/loss figure.

handle (sport) in cricket, *to give (it) the long handle*: for a batsman to take control of all the bowlers and score freely and continually.

handler (computers) that part of a program which controls the functioning of one of the peripherals (qv).

handler (espionage) a member of the security services who deals personally with a given agent.

hand-mucker (gambling) aka: *holdout man*: a cheat whose speciality is palming the cards.

handshake (computers) the communication between any two parts of the system.

hands-on (educ, business) practical involvement in either learning – where students can obtain real experience of possible future jobs – or in business where there is a similar implication of rolling up one's sleeves and getting involved, rather than simply reading or talking.

hands-on session (pols) really coming to grips with a political problem, 'getting one's hands dirty' in the same way as the business use (qv) of hands-on.

handwriting (design) the style that indicates to any peer that a particular designer has created the object in question, whether it be in fashion, graphics, illustration or any other visually identifiable medium. The handwriting being, in all cases, that of a 'signature'.

handwriting (espionage) the different styles – speed, pressure, etc – that identify to the expert the various users of morse or cypher keys in communications.

handyman special (commerce) in US real estate: a house that requires a good deal of repairs, possibly appealing to do-it-yourself enthusiasts.

hang (sport) in cricket or baseball, for a ball to slow down and appear to 'hang' in the air.

hang (horse-racing) for a horse consistently to veer to one side.

hangar queen (aerospace) an aircraft that is continually laid up in the hangar awaiting repairs. A facetious implication of effeminate homosexuality is given to the inanimate plane.

hangar rat (aerospace) any non-flying personnel who have a variety of unspecified ground or maintenance jobs on an airbase.

hang five (sport) in surfing, to ride with the toes of one foot hooked over the front of the board; *hang ten* is to protrude both feet. Either method of riding right at the front of the board is aka: *nose riding*.

hanging paper (police/US) the pursuit of passing dud cheques, carried out by a *paperhanger*.

hanging up (police) used to describe a cabbie who lingers around theatres and similar places intending to drive up and snatch a fare without waiting in the regular rank.

hang in there (new therapies) to sustain an emotional position whatever the odds; to take a stand and not relinquish it, whatever the pressure. Those who tell another to 'hang in there' tend to imply their backing, if not their actual participation in the problem.

hang loose *v* (new therapies) the opposite of being uptight (qv): to coast through life taking the good and the bad as one finds them and letting neither disturb one's equilibrium. (cf: *go with the flow*)

hangtime (sport) in US football, the amount of time a punted ball stays in the air; the longer it hangs, the more time the defensive team have to tackle the receiver.

hang tough (pols) a variation on 'toughing it out' first coined to encourage heroin addicts who were attempting to withdraw from drugs at the Synanon Foundation in California: used by politicians to stress that once they have adopted a position or stance, they intend to stick by it. Politicians will also refer to *hanging in there* (qv) in much the same way.

happening (press) a story.

happenings (art) art's action events of the 1960s, happenings were a cross between an art exhbition and a theatrical performance with great emphasis on shock value and the involvement of the spectator rather than permitting passive viewing. With artists as their inspiration, such 'performances' stressed the visual and tactile over the literary and verbal.

happy hour (milit) USMC: a period set aside each evening for serving half-price drinks in the NCOs' and officers' mess, as in many civilian bars.

happy talk (TV/US) a style of news broadcasting in which all topics, no matter how grave or disturbing, are given a jokey, light-hearted veneer and whenever possible, a serious topic is replaced by a humorous one; the over-riding effect of such broadcasting is to give its consumers a totally false view of the world.

hard (milit) bases, silos and similar missile installations which have extra protection, often in the form of reinforced concrete and underground bunkers, against hostile nuclear warheads. Thus *hard sites* are those so protected. (cf: *soft*)

hard architecture (archit) the growth of a sterile and inhuman style of architecture, particularly for constructing prisons, mental hospitals and similar dumping grounds for 'second-class citizens'; with their windowless, impersonal rough textured style, such architecture merely underlines the feelings of alienation and isolation that such buildings already contain.

hardball *v* (pols/US) from professional baseball's use of a correct hard ball, rather than the amateur, if popular, game of softball: used in politics to imply a tough, no-nonsense attitude to problems in particular and government in general. Also popular in *business* use, often referring to a refusal to give way easily on a contract or similar deal.

hard coal (tech) any grade of coal that contains more than 60% carbon by weight.

hard copy (computers) copy that has been printed out from the records in a data bank (qv) or other retrieval system. The opposite of the 'magnetic' records held on tape or disc (qv).

hard currency (econ) a term without precise meaning but when used in context of UK, the currency of any country with which the UK has an adverse balance of payments in currency transactions which has to be settled in dollars or gold; a relative rather than a specific term, reflecting the relations between one currency and another varying as to their strengths and weaknesses around the world.

hard-edge painting (art) a type of painting that views the entire picture surface as one unit and thus has no division between the 'ground' and the 'figures' upon it. Paintings that are geometric, crisp and with no apparent interest in personal, emotional statements.

harden *v* (milit) to defend one's weapons systems, particularly ABMs and ICBMs (qqv) by reinforcing the sites and silos at which they are stored with the intention of making them impervious to hostile missile strikes (although most defences accept that even the 'hardest' silo cannot, if it is to be a useful part of its weapons system and not simply a static concrete shroud, expect to withstand a direct hit).

hard money (govt) a programme which manages

H

to attract a regular supply of funds from its inception onwards, whether or not the circumstances or progress of that programme actually merit this continuing government investment. Such programmes may well deserve their money, but may get away with incompetence if, for instance, they are bolstering the image or power base of an individual who cannot afford to have them be seen to fail. (cf: *soft funding*)

hard money (educ, pols) that money appropriated for academic use that comes from government (federal or state) and can thus be considered guaranteed when colleges are preparing future budgets. (cf: *soft money*, *hard/soft funding*)

hard news (media) factual, theoretically important information that leads the TV and radio news programmes and would appear on the front page of a serious newspaper. (cf: *soft news*, *happy talk*)

hard rock (music) simplistic, noisy, 'macho' music that appeals to 'headbanging' denim-clad northerners (UK) or beer-swilling Midwesterners (US); the musical equivalent of fantasy's 'sword and sorcery' and games playing's 'dungeons and dragons'.

hard rock *n* (gambling) 1. a tight player who risks little, bets cautiously and rarely bluffs. 2. a gambler who refuses to lend anyone money. 3. a player who is hard to beat.

hard science (science) any of the natural or physical sciences: chemistry, physics, biology, geology, astronomy. (cf: *soft science*)

hard-sectoring (computers) a slow means of informing a machine's drive system where a sector (qv) starts on a floppy disc (qv). A hole is punched in the disc to show the machine where each sector beings. (cf: *soft-sectoring*)

hardship categories (govt, soc wk) euphemism for the poor.

hardship post *n* (milit) anywhere that troops must suffer less than the usually comfortable conditions prepared for US forces overseas.

hard target kill potential (milit) the extent to which an ICBM (qv) can be guaranteed to destroy targets protected against nuclear attack.

hard tasks (business) jobs that involve direct assembly in the manufacture of a product or the participation in providing an actual service.

hard ticket (movies) films exhibited in separate performances (as opposed to continuous programmes), booked for long runs in one cinema, offering reservable seats with possibly high prices: generally a cinema version of a successful legitimate play. (cf: *roadshow*)

hard time (prison) finding one's incarceration in prison hard to bear; often such problems are intensified by the prisoner rebelling against the system and thus getting even 'harder' time by losing remission, spending time in solitary confinement, etc.

hardtops (movies) cinemas with roofs, ie: the usual buildings designed for projecting and viewing films, rather than open-air drive-ins.

hardware (medic/US) surgical equipment.

hardware (aerospace) a completed rocket, as opposed to the software (qv) that comprises its engineering, guidance system, etc.

hardware (milit) a general term for military materiel (qv), weapons and equipment. In these terms, software (qv) tends to mean the human beings involved in wars.

hardware (computers) the actual machinery – electrical, mechanical, structural – that comprises the working parts of a computer as opposed to the software (qv) with which it is programmed and otherwise made to work.

hardwarily (computers) an adjectival use of hardware (qv): 'Hardwarily, the machine is excellent. . .' There is no use for *hardwary*.

hard way *n* (gambling) to make one's point (qv) 'the hard way' is to score even numbers, 4, 6, 8, 10 with pairs of 2s, 3s, 4s, or 5s instead of combinations of odd numbers – of which there are more on the dice and thus should be easier to throw.

hardwire *v* (computers) a circuit that is wired directly to a computer; by extension *hard-wired* implies anything that is directly and firmly attached to something else: ie specific expressions that are part of every human face.

harmonisation (indust relats) aka: *staff status*: an arrangement whereby *all* members of a company are seen as having equal status; there are still salary differentials, but socially everyone is equal and all groups are expected to have their say in determining company policy.

harmonogram (art) a machine-engraved linear design which features an extremely high level of precision as to mathematical/geometric patterns; eg: the complexities of a British bank note.

Harriet Lane (merchant navy) the cargo ships' equivalent of RN Fanny Adams (qv): canned meat and the stews made from it.

has a sign on his back (gambling) a phrase describing a cheat so well known that he . . .

hash-mark (milit) service stripes in the US forces, each one represents four years' service.

hassling (milit) USAF: engaging in mock aerial dogfights for training purposes.

hasty breaching (milit) the creation of instant pathways through enemy minefields by crude methods such as tossing grenades and thus exploding them or pushing heavy rollers or broken down vehicles ahead in order to trigger the mines.

hat (police/US) a bribe of $5, as in 'go buy yourself a hat'. (cf: *drink*)

hat *n* (govt, police, etc) any corrupt financial dealing: bribery, payoffs, kickbacks, black marketeering. All stem from the phrase 'go and buy yourself a hat' which accompanies the passing over of the money.

hatched (US govt) dismissed from one's post in any federally funded agency for violating the Hatch Act, which specifically forbids any political activity by federal employees.

hat-trick (sport) in cricket, the taking of three wickets in three consecutive balls, so-called from an earlier tradition of awarding a hat to a bowler who achieved this feat; now used also in any sport where a player scores three goals, ie: football, hockey, etc.

Havana riders (air crew) any hijackers, although the phrase originated in the popular destination of many early 1960s hijackers who wanted to fly to Havana in Cuba.

have numbers (milit) radio code: I have received and understood the information on wind speed and direction and my designated runway for my landing.

Have Quick (milit) the code name for a current US development of air-to-air, air-to-ground jamming-resistant UHF communications for the USAF.

have the weight (crime/US) said of a buttonman (qv) who possesses a particularly large amount of money: 'he has the weight'.

hawk (pols, milit) to advocate an aggressive posture and policy in foreign relations. Coined as *war hawks* in 1798 by Thomas Jefferson to describe those who wanted a war with France and later for those who actually achieved the war of 1812 with England. Hawk enjoyed a popular revival as the opposite of dove (qv) during the Vietnam war, and has been maintained in general use ever since.

head (press) (abbrev): headline (in a newspaper).

head crash (computers) the breaking down of a computer when the read/write head (which 'reads' or 'writes' the information that is stored on a disc, qv) actually touches the surface of the disc it is processing and thus at worst completely destroys the data and in any case, seriously harms its storage.

header (TV) a short, teasing, pre-credits sequence of a film or programme which highlights the action to come.

headhunt (business) to search out and recruit top executives, often with the implication of stealing them from their current employer in order to take advantage of their special abilities, rather than waiting for them to make the first approach; *headhunters* who perform such recruitment may be employed by the firm who is looking for talent or may operate as a consultancy hiring themselves out to such interested parties.

headhunter (sport) in US contact sports, esp. ice-hockey, those players whose task is to ensure that any of the opposition's stars are speedily removed from the game, or at least intimidated out of their usual prowess, rather than actually to involve themselves with any skilful aspects of the team on which they play.

head out (radio) a tape so wound that the loose end is at the beginning of the interview, programme or whatever has been recorded and thus available for immediate use without any rewinding. (cf: *tail out, top and tail, turn around*). A head-out tape should show a green leader (qv).

headphones (medic/US) a stethoscope.

heads (milit) orig. in RN, but currently mainly USN: the ship's latrine, from its position in early sailing vessels in the head, or bows of the ship. In USN and USMC use, extended to lavatories on a shore base.

heads (radio) (abbrev) news headlines or highlights.

headset (new therapies) one's overall attitudes to life: the way in which one's head is set.

heads up (milit) radio code: 1. hostile planes have broken through our defences. 2. I am not in a position to engage hostile attackers.

head-tripping (new therapies) used at the Esalen Institute (California) to mean 'thinking', but a general word for thought that derives from the 1960s LSD 'trip' and which was converted in hippie sl. to mean any form of activity, good, bad, active or passive whether or not LSD was actually involved at the time.

head up display (aerospace, computers, etc.) a projection of instrument readings – in a car, a cockpit or any vehicle – that is taken from the actual dials and put onto the windscreen so that drivers, pilots, etc. can read off the information without taking their eyes from the way ahead.

hear *v* (new therapies) to understand and appreciate; 'I hear you' implies a deeper level of listening than purely understanding the superficial statement that is being made; like many such concepts, stemming from the slightly mystical responses coming from a couple of people enjoying some form of mind-expanding drug and thus claiming a greater comprehension than they might otherwise be able to attain.

heart (theatre) the padding out of their tights by actors, acrobats and anyone who might have to take an otherwise painful fall.

heat (TV/US) tension within the script/action of a show.

heater *n* (sport) in baseball, a fast ball.

heat island (science) a geographical area from which a measurably greater output of heat is radiated than from those areas surrounding it; often a concentration of industrial plant.

heavies (press) a description used by those journalists on the 'popular' tabloids (qv) for the 'quality' papers such as *The Times, Guardian* and *Daily Telegraph*, and their Sunday equivalents.

H

heavies (aerospace) wide-bodied commercial jets: Boeing 747, Douglas DC-10, etc.

heavies (police/UK) aka; *heavy mob*: the Special Patrol group or the Flying Squad. (cf: *Sweeney*)

heavy (movies) 1. a villain, the antagonist (cf: *dog heavy, first man through the door*). 2. adj. use, from the hippie sl. of 1960s, an influential or important person, a 'heavy producer' etc.

heavy *n* (crime/US) a safecracker. (cf: *peterman*)

heavy *a* (sport) in golf, describes a ball lying embedded in sand.

heavy (theatre) cf: movie use (1); thus 'second heavy', 'third heavy' etc.

heavy *a* (stock market) a *heavy market*: one in which share prices are falling.

heavy (new therapies) from hippie sl. of 1960s: meaningful, portentous, intense; aggressive and antagonistic; important, vital.

heavy metal (rock music) cf: *hard rock*.

heavy roller (aerospace) any extremely important and influential executive, client or contract. From a mix of gambling's 'high roller' (big bettor) and a massive engine or aircraft being 'rolled out' of the hangar.

heavy textiles (prison/UK) official euphemism for mailbags which are hand-sewn in British prisons as 'employment' for those imprisoned.

heavy water (science) deuterium oxide (D_2O): used in 'heavy water' nuclear reactors.

hedge *n* (crime) the crowd that forms around the periphery of a three-card-monte game.

hedge (commerce) to insure against any losses by setting up whatever fail-safe (qv) devices are considered necessary for a given situation. Thus *hedge-selling* deals with an in-built hedge, whereby each purchase is matched with a sale or vice versa, ie: a purchase or sale for future delivery is made at the same time to offset and protect an actual merchandising deal.

hedge-fund (commerce) 1. an investment group concentrating on capital gains. 2. an investment fund established to speculate on the capital given over by private investors.

hedgehog (milit) 1. the all-round defence of an area, employing anti-tank, anti-aircraft and anti-personnel defences. 2. (RN) a salvo of depth charges fired from a ship with the intention of saturating a hostile submarine with simultaneous explosions.

hedgehop *v* (milit) RAF: to fly very low, skimming the ground and 'hopping over the hedges'.

heel and toe watch (milit) USMC: men standing watch who take alternate duties with one succeeding the other for an indefinite period and only taking a rest while the opposite number is on watch.

hegemony (pols) from Gk. *hegemon*: leader or ruler. 1. superpower policies; similar to imperialism (qv). 2. (China) used by Mao Tse Tung spec. to attack the Soviet Union's neo-colonialism, esp. as regarded China. 3. *bourgeois hege-*

mony: the aspirations, in Marxist terms, of one class (esp. the bourgeoisie) to rule the others, particularly by conditioning the masses to accept such rule as 'natural' and 'common sense'.

helm *v* (movies) to 'take the helm', thus to direct; a *helmer* is a director.

helping (soc wk) cf: *caring* (professions).

helping the police with their enquiries (police/UK) a vintage euphemism stemming from any British police station to inform the media or the public that an individual or individuals ('a man', 'three women') are under arrest or have at the least been picked up for questioning. Such 'help' is not usually voluntary.

here (new therapies) aware, understanding, appreciative of someone else's problems; another therapeutic usage that originated in 1960s hippie sl., perhaps from the attempts of one LSD 'tripper' to comfort the fears of another, lost in the loneliness that LSD can bring out.

herring bone *v* (sport) in skiing, a method of climbing without kick turns which leaves herring-bone shaped tracks in the snow.

hesiflation (econ) a condition of spasmodic, stop-go economic growth accompanied by high inflation. (cf: *inflation, stagflation*)

hesitation marks (medic, police) small scars on the wrist of a suicide who has slashed his/her wrist, that indicate initial half-hearted scratchings, the hesitation before making the actual, fatal cut.

heterogeneous grouping (educ) the opposite of ability grouping (qv): taking pupils and arranging them into classes based only on age irrespective of any variations in ability.

heterosis (business) in biology, the fact that when two species with different characteristics are mated, the resulting offspring may well be stronger and larger than the parents: in business the idea that the combination of two projects of different types may yield exceptional and better-than-expected results.

heuristic (computers) in essence, trial and error: a computer faced with a set problem will analyse all the possible solutions before coming up with the ideal one and then, if necessary, moving onto the next stage of its activity.

heuristic (educ) used especially of science teaching: the emphasis that such teaching must centre on practical methods of experimentation and investigation.

heuristic (sociol) the creation of models to facilitate the working out of a solution or hypothesis.

hiccup (stock market) a short-lived decline in the market.

hickey (press) 1. any ornament in the type. 2. a blemish in the printing or in the engraving of an illustration.

hierarchy of effects (marketing) a marketing model that suggests that buyers move through set sequences as they progress from awareness of a product to actually purchasing it. Used frequently in the study of advertising and its effects.

high abstraction (sociol, business) those able to conceive of and use abstract ideas: description of elite individuals in an organisation: the technocrats, the decision makers, the powerful and influential figures. (cf: *low abstraction*)

high belly strippers (gambling) a deck of cards so doctored that the cheat knows when the high cards are appearing. (cf: *low belly strippers*)

high burn rate (business) in aerospace terminology, a rocket that burns the bulk of its fuel early to ensure a fast takeoff; extended to business use, it implies a person or project that puts out a great deal of early effort or production in order to ensure a successful launch.

high end of the conflict spectrum (milit) used by US National Security Advisor William Clark in 1982, a Pentagon euphemism for war.

high fliers (stock market) fashionable issues that provide an above-average return on an investment. (cf: *glamour issues*)

high fliers (govt/UK) the top ranks of the civil service, often selected early in their career, on the instinct of their superiors as well as some indications of their potential, for grooming from the early 20s onward as potential mandarins (qv).

high hat (TV, movies) the smallest of those supports available for raising a camera from ground level.

high image (business) cf: *high profile.*

high-level language (computers) a group of programming languages which are designed for general use, independent of any one machine. Thus *low level language*: a language designed for the operation of and use by only one specific machine.

high net worth individuals (govt) bureaucratese for the rich.

high popular (sociol) a variation on very popular, as *low popular* is on unpopular: these uses of high/low (similarly found in many areas of social science) rather than more usual modifiers, stem from the 'scientific' desire to imply a statistical/measurable basis to such an evaluation, thus in this context, one should assume some unspoken table on which popularity is assessed.

high profile (espionage) 1. to act in an obvious manner, making no effort to hide oneself or one's occupation – although this openness may only be a way of protecting one's cover (qv). 2. *v*: to draw attention to an impostor, a member of the opposition whose cover one has managed to blow.

high profile (entertain) aka: *high image*: well known, famous, ostentatious, in the public eye. Used as a verb, the seeking out of such qualities or styles. (cf: *low profile*)

high-Q (movies) a pun on IQ (intelligence quot-

ient) for film executives to assess the bankability (qv) of the talent (qv) or a property (qv) as to drawing the crowds or providing an appealing story.

high roller (gambling) orig. those gamblers who rolled dice for high stakes, but long since expanded to include any heavy bettors.

high-sidin' (sex) black pimp usage to imply strutting around, showing off, bragging and generally lording it over one's acquaintances.

high stream (business) *high stream industries* are sophisticated, science-based, often incorporating ecological/sociological standards that their predecessors never considered except, possibly, as a hindrance to the pursuit of profit. (cf: *low stream*)

high tech (archit) a design fashion popularised in mid/late 1970s in which the styles most usually found on and around the factory floor – exposed pipes, steel staircases, heavy duty materials for floor and wallcoverings, etc., etc., – were transmuted into the home or office where one would now start finding various technical artefacts – dentist's trolleys, hospital taps, etc. – in place of the traditional domestic supplies. This factory/workshop style originally depended on actual materials used in 'tech' environments, but soon degenerated into *slick tech* in which the look was mass produced for easy purchase.

highway (computers) a major path along which signals travel from one of several sources to one of several destinations. (cf: *bus*)

hilites (radio) a short news item representing a succinct summary of the top line of a news story; hilites are broadcast in regular intervals between the full-length news bulletins – possibly every 15 minutes, using 4 hilites each time.

Hill *n* (pols/US) Capitol Hill: the legislative branch of the US government; as opposed to the *White House*: the executive branch. It is a geographical description too: Capitol Hill stands 88′ above sea level.

hill and dale (record business) the grooves of a record with their ups and downs which are traced by the stylus when the record is played.

hip pocket client (entertain) a phrase used by an agent to refer to any client he represents who is not currently under contract and is metaphorically sitting right there in his hip pocket, waiting to pop out and grab some work.

historical materialism (pols) the essence of the Marxist historical view: 'The mode of production in material life determines the general character of the social, political and spiritual processes of life. It is not the consciousness of men that determines their existence, but . . . it is their social existence which determines their consciousness. . .' (Marx, *A Contribution to the Critique of Political Economy*, 1859). In other words, the 'relations of production' (the way in which material production of goods and

H

the relations between the classes are organised) forms the base (qv) of society and this in turn creates the superstructure (qv) – the whole of society's political, spiritual, intellectual, etc. life.

historicism (archit) an excessive regard for the institutions and values of the past; a retreat in the eyes of many critics, to exactly those views that the 19th century 'modern movement' was determined to replace.

historicism (sociol) 1. a philosophical belief that historical development is the most important and fundamental aspect of human existence, and that historical thinking is therefore the most important type of thought. 2. the belief that historical change occurs in accordance with laws and that the course of history may be predicted but cannot be altered.

hit (drugs) cf: *fix*.

n (business) for a project, concept or meeting *to have a hit* means that it has some impact, some validity. If there is no impact there are no 'hits'.

hit (computers) the successful comparison of two items of data.

hit *v* (movies, TV) *to hit* something (usually a light or the mechanism for a special effect) is to turn it on. (cf: *kill*)

hit *n* (sex) in homosexual hustling (qv) terms, a rich client who is interested in establishing a regular (sexual and economic) relationship. From US hobo (tramp) sl: hit = a charitable person (someone you can 'hit on' for cash).

hit a century (sport) in big game hunting, to kill one hundred of the same species; taken from the cricketing phrase for the scoring of 100 runs in an innings.

hitch (milit) US Army: a period of service, usually 4 yrs. (cf: *cruise*)

hitchhike *v* (radio/US) for a radio programme sponsor to advertise one of his products in addition to the one that is being featured on the show. (cf: *cowcatcher*)

hit list (pols, govt) a list of tasks or projects on which action must be taken.

hit on *v* (sex) black pimp usage for approaching a woman in order to persuade her to join a stable (qv) of prostitutes.

hits (gambling) a pair of crooked mis-spotted dice which will never throw a 7 and will continually produce certain numbers on or against which a cheat can bet.

hit the bricks (indust relats/US) to go on strike; from the sl. for walking the street (rather than being at work).

hive-offs (business/UK) aka: spin-offs (US): the formation of a new or subsidiary company by distributing extra stocks.

hiway culture (art) the icons and allied hardware generated by the world of US road transport, epitomised by the motifs of traffic signs, petrol

stations, commerce, truck stops etc. found in the work of many pop (qv) artists.

hobby-bobby (police/UK) part time special constables.

hobson's (theatre/UK) from rhyming sl.: Hobson's choice = the voice.

hod *n* (horse-racing) a bookmaker's satchel.

hodad (sport) in surfing, a show-off who hangs around the surfing beaches, boasting of his exploits and trying to pick up girls but who has rarely, if ever, tried to surf.

hog (drugs) see: *drug names*.

hoist (crime, police/UK) to shop lift, thus *hoister*: shop lifter. (cf: *boost, booster*)

hold (drugs) for a dealer to possess some drugs for sale. Thus the 'coded' question: 'Are you holding?'

hold *n* (aerospace) an area of airspace over a commercial airport's control zone where incoming aircraft can be kept safely flying around a radio beacon at regulation distances from each other, until they can be cleared for landing. (cf: *holding pattern*)

hold *n* (aerospace) any delay in the countdown of the launch of a rocket.

hold harmless provision (govt) that part of a government aid programme that spares those who receive it from further harm or deterioration by allotting them sufficient money to make up any shortfall in local funding. From the *insurance* use in which such a provision prevents the insured party from suffering any extra costs or expenses.

holding company (commerce) a trading company which possesses the whole of or a majority control of the share capital of one or more other companies.

holding pattern (aerospace) aka: *stacking*: the group of aeroplanes circling a beacon and awaiting clearance to land at an airport; the concept of stacking comes from the arrangement of the planes in ascending ranks, each circling above the other.

holding pattern (stock market, commerce) from the airport use: a situation in which nothing is happening, the market is neither up nor down, trade is static.

hold-out artist (gambling) a gambler or cheat who lies to his partners or confederates when asked how much money he has made out of a game or evening's gambling.

hold-out man (gambling) a card cheat whose speciality is palming cards, then holding them until such time as it is propitious to reintroduce them into the play.

hold the book (theatre) aka: *on the book*: to act as the prompter, reading from the prompt book.

hold the rag (crime/UK) for a con-man or long firm (qv) proprietor to be left with a quantity of worthless stock.

hold-up (sport) in bridge, the tactical refusal to play an otherwise winning card.

hold-up (milit) the total amount of material tied up in a separation plant used for manufacturing nuclear warheads.

holeout *v* (sport) in golf, to sink the ball into the hole and thus finish that particular part of the course.

holiday *n* (milit) RN: any gap in a row; a part missed when painting the ship.

holism (new therapies) coined in 1926 by General J. C. Smuts (1870–1950) to define 'the one synthesis which makes the elements or parts act as one or holistically': now favoured by a variety of new therapies (qv) all of which like to emphasise the relationship between biological and psychological well-being which, together, make up the 'whole' person.

hollow tooth (police/UK) ironic reference to Scotland Yard.

Hollywood numbers (sex) homosexual hustler (qv) term for any sex acts – ie 69 – that derive their names from numbers.

home and colonial (police/UK) from a defunct chain of grocery stores: the London-based Regional Crime Squad which is composed of officers from the Metropolitan (home) and provincial (colonial) forces.

homebrew *n* (sport) in Canada, a player, esp. in football teams, who is a native of the town for which his team is named.

home key (music) the basic key in which a work is composed.

homeport *v* (milit) to establish a base in a port that is near a fleet's area of operations.

homer (milit) a base that locates aircraft and then guides them in via bearings taken from radio transmissions.

home show (TV) any documentary made within the UK.

honcho (pols/US) from Jap. *han cho* 'squad leader': the boss, the senior person. thus *to honcho* something is to take care of something personally and ensure it is carried out.

honey barge (milit) USN: a garbage scow.

honey cart (air crew) a sanitary servicing vehicle that drains aircraft lavatories, flushes them out and refills them.

honey wagons (movies) portable lavatories used on location by film crew.

hoofer (theatre/US) a dancer, especially a tap dancer.

hook (sport) aka: *crest, shoulder*: in surfing, the top portion of a wave.

hook *n* (music) a catchy 'jingle' or phrase in a song that keeps the listener humming it and sticks in the brain.

hook *n* (TV/US) any aspect of a script that deliberately sustains the audience's fascination: an accident, a surprise, 'who shot JR?' etc.

hook *n* (crime) 1. (UK) pickpocket. 2. (US) (abbrev) hooker = prostitute.

hook (gambling) 1. to be on a losing streak. 2. to lose money.

hooker (TV) the first part of a programme, designed to attract the viewers into the material/ storyline and keep them interested in what follows. (cf. *hook*)

hooking (crime) 1. (UK) picking pockets. 2. (US) engaging in prostitution. 3. (UK) a dishonest informer who tries to fob the police off with some story that is being told strictly for his own benefit.

hoop (horse-racing) 1. the horizontal stripes of colour that are used in many trainers' 'silks' which jockeys wear when racing. 2. (Aus.) by extension from (1): a jockey.

hoot owl (indust relats) the midnight shift in factories.

hoover *v* (prison/UK) in Borstal, to steal a fellow prisoner's food.

hop *n* (gambling) aka: *shift*: a secret move made after the cut which puts the cards back in the original position and negates that cut for the cheat's benefit.

hopped up (horse-racing) a horse that has been given some kind of drug.

horizontal divestiture (business) the disposal of a company's holdings in companies or organisations that produce similar products to its own.

horizontal escalation (milit) a situation in which the response to one crisis is to initiate another one elsewhere.

horizontal escape (espionage) when an agent breaks the vertical need-to-know (qv) chain of information by seeking protection for himself by sharing certain facts with a third party whose knowledge of these facts is intended to form his 'insurance' against betrayal.

horizontal integration (business) the expansion of one's business by taking over competitors who are engaged in approximately the same type of enterprise.

horizontal music (music) the successive sounds which form the melodies, as opposed to the verticals, the simultaneous sounds forming harmonies.

horizontal proliferation (milit) the increase in the number of nations who claim to possess nuclear armaments.

horizontal publication (publishing) the publishing of books for a general interest market.

horizontal unions (indust relats) craft unions. *Vertical unions*: industrial unions.

horse (drugs) heroin: see *drug names*.

horse (prison/US) a guard who is bribed to smuggle extra supplies – drugs, tobacco, etc. – in and take letters out of jail.

horse cock (milit) USMC: either salami or baloney.

horse opera (TV) from soap opera (qv): a Western series. (cf. *carbolic soap opera*)

horse-trading (pols) hard political bargaining.

horsey (advert) used among art directors and designers to dismiss an ugly or badly propor-

H

tioned layout, especially that which is too large for the space allotted.

hosepiping (movies) badly (shakily) hand-held 8mm camera-work. The shots produced end up resembling a hosepipe spraying out water at random.

hospitality room (TV) aka: *hospitality suite*: a reception room at a TV studio set aside for giving guests a drink before and after they are appearing on a programme. Such suites and rooms are often found when a company wishes to impress favoured customers – at a conference, a big exhibition such as the Motor Show, etc., etc. Big sporting events – test matches, major horse races, etc. – are also popular venues for such company entertaining, esp. when a company is sponsoring the sport.

hosting (TV) 1. the presentation of a show by a front man or woman. 2. (US) the engaging of an 'expert' to appear at the start of a film and explain it to the American audience; thus Alistair Cooke, a token upper-class Mid Atlantic Man, was used to explain the TV version of Evelyn Waugh's *Brideshead Revisited* when it appeared on 'Masterpiece Theatre'.

hot (science) radio-active.

hot (radio) a notice placed on a tape machine to indicate that the tape wound on to it is being edited and that it should be left there, however much the next person wishes to use a machine for their own work.

hot (movies) 1. see *bankable* (qv). 2. an idea or property (qv) not yet exposed either to a producer or to the public.

hot (media) in the definition of Marshall McLuhan (1911–1980), a *hot* medium is one that is full of detail and information and which requires little or no involvement from the listener or the viewer; radio is a hot medium, TV is a cool one.

hot (indust relats) associated with or affected by a labour dispute; thus *hot cargo clause*: an agreement whereby a lorry owner promises not to handle the goods of a firm with whom his union is in dispute.

hot (commerce) *hot bills* are newly issued Treasury bills, those bills of exchange that are issued by the government in large amounts every week and which are redeemable in three months.

hotbunk *v* (milit) RN ratings term for crowded accommodation in cramped submarines: those off duty sleep in the bunks just vacated by the active watch.

hot buttons (TV) those buttons by which a home viewer can 'vote' or otherwise participate in interactive (qv) television.

hot dog (sport) 1. (surf) a particular type of board, somewhere between the usual size and the larger gun (qv). Thus used for one who rides a hot dog, aka *hot dogger*; a stylish surfer who can perform intricate manoeuvres on the

waves. 2. (skiing) an exceptional skier who likes to impress with his/her abilities; thus a showoff as well as a star.

hot engines (aerospace) spec. piston engines; any engine that tends to overheat and break down.

hot issue (stock market) so popular a new issue of stock – usually common (qv) stock – that it goes to an immediate premium price of several points above par.

hot lot (police/UK) the Flying Squad or Special Patrol group. (cf: *heavy mob*, *Sweeney*)

hot money (finance) 1. the money owned by investors who jump from one investment to another at the slightest shift in the rate of return. 2. money that is kept moving from currency to currency in a bid to avoid losing out if any one currency starts to depreciate noticeably against the others. 3. any illicitly obtained money, through fraud, theft or other swindling.

hotpot (horse-racing) a horse that has been heavily backed.

hot pursuit (milit) an internationally accepted manoeuvre whereby a military force can cross a border in 'hot pursuit' of enemy (usually terrorist) troops who have made an incursion into that force's home country and which pursuit is neither hindered nor is it seen as an invasion or a military threat.

hot rock (aerospace) an inexperienced pilot, eager to show off.

hot set (movies, TV) a set that has been lit, dressed (qv) and generally made ready for shooting. (cf: *dead set*)

hot sheet (police) a list of stolen cars, outstanding traffic fines, etc., circulated to all policemen concerned – traffic dept., beat policemen, etc. – for their use on a given day.

hot shoe (photography) a socket on a camera to which a flashgun may be connected and which serves as an automatic electrical connection for the lighting of that flashgun.

hot shop (advert) small, informal, creative agencies that flourished particularly in the late 1960s and which were successful in pulling away accounts from the larger agencies. (cf: *boutique agencies*)

hotshot (drugs) a means of disposing of a customer who is no longer discreet or who is trying to cause trouble for the dealer: instead of the (relatively) pure heroin that is usually sold, the customer receives some poison (usually strychnine) – or the powdered battery acid that accumulates on a car battery – and when he injects this, he will die.

hotspotter (milit) those theorists of the results of a nuclear explosion who believe that the resultant radiation will accumulate in 'hot spots' – areas of concentrated radiation – rather than simply spreading evenly throughout the whole area that would be affected. The hotspots so created would also be the site of the maximum biological damage. (cf: *averager*)

hot stoves (music business) open bribes to persuade disc jockeys to plug certain records.

hot switch (TV) the change of coverage from one event to another without any transitional voice over to smooth out the cut (qv) from an announcer.

hot-turn (milit) for an aircraft to return to base, refuel, rearm and take off on a new sortie without ever turning off its engines which thus remain 'hot' during the 'turn'.

house *v* (police/UK) to trail someone to their home address and to make sure they are regularly there for such time as it might be desirable to interview or arrest them.

the house (stock market) either the premises of the Stock Exchange or its trading floor. (cf: *Floor*)

house (theatre) 1. the auditorium. 2. the permanent management of a theatre, as opposed to the touring company which is only there temporarily. 3. the patrons who have bought tickets for a given performance. Thus a 'good house' or a 'poor house'.

house job (press) a piece in which one member of a newspaper's staff will write in praise of the work of another, or less venally, give that work some publicity, good or bad. (cf: *market letter*, *log-rolling*)

housekeeping (computers) aka: *book-keeping*: those operations of a computer that make its work possible, but having nothing to do with its actual performance, running of programs, calculating of figures, etc.

housekeeping bill (pols/US) ostensibly a minor bill that deals with the alteration or modification of some legal or legislative technicality; but as such these bills can be used to slip by something infinitely more important that is hidden amongst the sub-clauses and must therefore be checked for carefully by an alert opposition.

house style (business) the corporate handwriting (qv) or group identity which finds visual form in a company's logo, letterheads, house magazine, advertising and similar productions. All such designs contribute to establishing the company in the public eye.

housewife (TV) the broadcasting daypart (qv) that is assumed for advertising purposes to capitalise on a housewife audience – from 10 am to 3 pm.

housewife (milit) pron, 'huzzif': a small fabric case that rolls up and which contains a sailor's all purpose sewing and mending kit for use at sea.

howgozit (aerospace) a dial that shows how much fuel is remaining in the aircraft's tanks to enable it to make a safe journey home.

huck out (milit) aka: *hog out*: to give a thorough scrubbing out, a 'spring cleaning'.

huddle *n* (sport) in bridge, a period of thought in which a player considers his/her next call or play.

human factors engineering (indust relats) the design of factories, offices, plants etc. with an emphasis on the position and needs of the humans employed and working in them.

humanist art (art) humanist art attempts to struggle against the increasing domination by technology of all areas of life. It is divided into four categories: political, absurdist, existential and metaphysical.

human potential movement (new therapies) an amalgam of various mental therapies, including the many cults that seem invariably to start life in California and a number of simplified theories that have trimmed classical psychoanalysis of any real dedication by the patient and replaced it with a simple 'cure' apparently available to anyone who is able to pay the fees and somewhat removed from Freud's original conceptions.

human resource administration (business) an amplified title of the corporation's personnel department: dealing with hiring, firing, pensions and other aspects of employee life.

humbug *n* (sex) black pimp term for a trumped up, phoney charge levelled by the police.

humint (espionage) (abbrev) *human int*elligence: the gathering of material by means of human beings – spies, sanctification (qv) – rather than by electronic surveillance. (cf: *comint*, *sigint*, *telint elint*)

hummer (police/US) a fake arrest on the slightest of pretexts, usually in order to allow the police to search their suspect.

hump speed (aerospace) the speed of a hovercraft at which the drag of the water is at its maximum.

humpty dumpty (pols/US) from the Lewis Carroll and nursery rhyme character: a loser, someone who is riding for a fall.

hung *a* (sex) (abbrev) well-hung, having a larger than usual penis.

hung-up (new therapies) depending on the personality of the speaker, to be *hung-up* can denote a degree of worry anywhere on a nervous spectrum from mildly depressed to a fullscale obsession trembling on the edge of break-down and/or hospitalisation.

hungus (computers) large, unwieldy, barely if at all manageable.

hunter-killer (milit) naval vessel designed to trace, pursue and then destroy enemy vessels; target is often a submarine, but there are also hunter-killer submarines.

hunting (TV) 1. a film camera that will not maintain a constant speed. 2. a video-tape machine that cannot maintain a constant speed.

hustler (sex) male prostitute who deals only with homosexuals but who will never admit to being homosexual himself and who will take only an

H

active, never a passive role in his various sexual encounters. Aka: *ass pro, bird taker, buff boy, bunny, business boy, career boy, cocktail, coin collector, commercial queer, crack salesman, dick peddler, fag boy, flesh (peddler), foot soldier, gigolo, he-whore, Hollywood hustler* (one who is a little too smooth), *party boy, puto* (Sp.), *rent, rent-boy, sport, sporting goods, trabajado* (Sp: 'worked over'), *working girl*, etc.

hybrid (computers) a machine that uses both analog (qv) and digital methods.

hybridise *v* (business) in gardening, to make a new species by combining two others; thus in business to take two companies and combine them to produce a third, entirely different one. It is also assumed that the hybrid company should be stronger and livelier than its progenitors.

hymnbook (TV) what a director calls the camera script.

hype *n, v* (entertain) to build up an act, a record, a film, etc., by exaggerating its appeals, promoting and advertising it to the greatest extent possible. The implication of hype is always one of slightly fraudulent huckstering, but a hype that works is a merchandising success, even if one that fails is only a hype.

hype (crime) aka: *laying the note*; *the sting*; *on the hype*: the short-change racket, a swindle involving the persuading of a sales clerk to give change for £10 instead of £5.

hyperspace (soc sci) used to denote a full and exhaustive range of possibilities (a usage far removed from the more popular concept of hyperspace as the farthest boundaries of space, for which scifi writers have invented the hyper-drive and similar arcane aerospatial properties).

hyphenates (sociol) the various racial groups in the US: Mexican-American, Irish-American, Italian-American and all others who 'hyphenate' their nationality. (cf: *ethnics*)

hyphenates *n* (TV, movies) writer-director, writer-producer, director-cameraman, etc. – the various double-job permutations in TV and films all of which are denoted by the linking hyphen.

hypocentre (milit) the ground directly beneath a nuclear explosion. (cf: *ground zero*)

hypothetical point (airline) a means of extending cheap fares by creating a fictional destination which one never actually visits but which must be included on an itinerary – either before, during or after one's journey; once this point is included, one's maximum permitted mileage, on which bargain fares are estimated, is increased and thus a fare can be legitimately reduced without breaking any rules.

hysterical historicals (publishing) a genre of best-selling fiction which involves the traditional historical romance, but with greater amounts of violence and particularly sex, usually in the form of rape, sanitised only slightly in its 18th century or Regency frills and furbelows. (cf: *bodice-rippers*, *sweet savagery*)

H

ICBM (milit) (acron) *i*ntercontinental *b*allistic *m*issile: a missile that is capable of penetrating targets within either US or USSR territory when fired from ground or sea launches.

ice (gambling) bribes paid to police and/or politicians to ensure that a casino or other gambling establishment is not raided or otherwise disrupted.

ice (theatre/US) 1. a tip or premium paid by a ticket agent to the Box Office treasurer or the producer for a supply of tickets in addition to those he is usually allotted. 2. the premium charged by an agency on ticket sales.

iceberg company (business) a company where two-thirds of its trading is carried on at a lower than break-even point.

iceberg theory (pols) the thesis that under normal conditions only appx 3% of the population are ideologically or idealistically inclined; Marxists believe that such a figure can be increased if the political environment is altered through agitation, propaganda etc.

icebox (medic/US) the hospital morgue. (cf: *the cooler*)

icebreaker (theatre) a fast, snappy song and dance routine for the chorus girls that comes early on in a musical.

iconics (art) a proposed science that would stand for pictures as linguistics stands for language. Iconics would be concerned with that body of knowledge common to art and aesthetics, cognitive and perceptual psychology education, learning linguistics, semantic and computer graphics.

ID *v* (police) to *id*entify.

ID *n* (radio) a station's name, theme tune, and 'logo' – a jingle that goes with the name.

ideal point (marketing) consumers' perceptions of the ideal attributes of a product, used in attitude models and perceptual mapping.

ideational 1. (sociol) coined by P. A. Sorokin in 1937 to describe the sort of culture that placed the spiritual above the materialistic. 2. (educ) a misreading of the word by 'progressive' teachers to mean simply those children who use ideas and imaginations and can grasp some form of theories.

idiosyncrasy (medic) an individual's hypersensitivity to a particular drug or any other substance which can be swallowed or sniffed and which has an adverse effect on that person.

idiot board (TV) the boards that are held up next to the camera to provide cues and prompts for the announcer, comedian, etc., when there is no autocue machine. Thus aka: *idiot card*, *idiot sheet*, all of which aids are held up by the *idiot girl*.

idiot light (tech) a warning light, usually red, that goes on to indicate a mechanical malfunction on an appliance.

idiot tape (computers) an input tape for computer setting which has been perforated but does not include directions for justifying or corrections.

idle money (econ) money that is lodged in bank balances and is not being used either for investment or speculation.

idle time (computers) the machine is on and ready, but is yet to perform the allotted job.

iffy (police/UK) suspect, doubtful, dishonest.

igloo (air crew) 1. the security cover over cargo consignments awaiting transportation. 2. a specially protected area on an air base where nuclear weapons are stored. Thus *igloo space*: an underground storage space, reinforced with concrete and steel, for the storage of weapons and ammunition.

ill (espionage) arrested on suspicion for questioning; imprisoned.

illegal operation (computers) any operation which the computer is unable to perform.

illegals (espionage) used by KGB for their spy systems operating outside USSR and under control of officers who are not based – as are many alleged KGB operatives – at their embassy.

illegitimate (horse-racing) formerly used to describe steeple-chases and jumping races as opposed to flat racing. (cf: *the flat*, *the sticks*)

illegitimate (theatre) popular productions with the emphasis on spectacle, not on literary quality. (cf: *legitimate*)

illusion (philosophy) *the argument from illusion*: a philosophical concept claiming that material objects cannot be seen directly but must be somehow perceived from 'sense-data', or impressions and that they alone are directly perceived.

image (radio) interference that occurs in the form of a high pitched whistle of constantly changing pitch plus unwanted morse signals.

image (computers) data from one medium, ie a punched card, recorded on another, ie tape.

image *v* (sociol) to accept or project a given image; often used rather than simpler 'imagine'.

imagism (poetry) a movement in poetry launched c1912 by Ezra Pound, Amy Lowell and others; the main point of English poetry's transition into modernism.

imp (science) (abbrev) *i*ndeterminate *m*ass *p*article: a hypothetical nuclear particle that has no defined mass.

impact *n, v* (pols) the effect, result; used verbally: ie: 'the cutbacks impacted the grass roots negatively'.

impacted (soc sci) an urban area suffering an excessive and unusual strain on public resources, caused by a sudden influx of new residents. Thus *impact aid*: federal economic aid to those schools where government employees are educated; *impact area*: a community, ie: a military base town, where a lower than average number of taxable properties limit public finances.

imperialism (pols) a synonym in communist terminology for capitalism: 'the highest form of capitalism' (Lenin). Its essential features are the concentration of capital, the division of the world into international and financial monopolies. The imperialism of the USSR is cited by the West as the involvement of Russia with countries – Afghanistan, Angola – which she wishes to draw into the Communist bloc.

impossibilism (pols) the belief in ideas, particularly the more Utopian areas of social reform, that can never actually or realistically be put into positive effect.

impractical (theatre) aka: *impracticable*: a piece of stage furniture or any prop that appears real or usable but in fact is not. (cf: *practical*)

impressionism (arts) 1. (music) a style of music epitomised by the work of Debussy in the 1880s which substituted the harmonic system for the themes and structures of the Romantic composers (eg: Beethoven). 2. (art) the work of a group of French artists – Monet, Degas, Renoir, Cézanne, etc. – which stands as the source of most of 20th century art, launched at their major exhibition in 1874. The movement concentrated on the movements of light, disregarded sombre colours and outlines, and generally stood for lightness and gaiety.

imputation (econ) an economic theory of value whereby value is attributed to productive resources in accordance with their contribution to the value of their products.

in and out trading (stock market) the buying and selling of the same shares within a short period.

in-basket situation (business) refers to the 'in' and 'out' trays of the traditional office desk: thus, a problem that has arrived for consideration but upon which no action has yet been taken.

in benefit (indust relats) a member of a trade union who has subscribed his/her dues.

in-cap (milit) (abbrev) incapacitant: any substance that will render an enemy temporarily out of action but will not permanently damage him.

incendijel (milit) aka: *incenderjell*: an inflammable jelly weapon, an alternative to napalm with similar effects, composed of polystyrene, petrol and benzene.

incident (police/US) any event worthy of investigation, from bomb hoaxes to dog bites.

incitative planning (pols) in socialist countries, those incentives created to augment the efficiency of an overall economic plan.

income elastic (econ) the stretching of any income to take up any possible increases by new expenditure. Often on previously unaffordable luxuries.

incoming *n* (milit) shells fired from hostile artillery.

incontinent ordnance (milit/US) bombs that fall in areas where they should not have been dropped, usu. on friendly villages, troops, etc.

indeterminate architecture (archit) a theory evolved in the early 1960s which felt that buildings should be designed to incorporate any future changes/expansion that might occur in the organisation that occupied them; thus such design was always 'indeterminate' from the start.

index (computers) 1. a sequence or array of items, each of which refers to a record on file. 2. one of a continuous sequence of numbers each of which specifies one of an ordered sequence of items.

index fund (stock market) an investment fund composed of stocks chosen to match in their values the performance of the whole market over a period of time.

Indian system (business) refers to the low cost of wages in India: such a system automates all unskilled jobs other than those where it is still cheaper to employ humans rather than install machines.

indicative planning (econ) economic plans in which targets and tasks are defined in general rather than specific terms or directives; common in capitalist countries in dealing with nationalised industries.

indie (movies) (abbrev) independent: any film made by an independent company (other than one of the majors (qv) or that company. Also a cinema, distributor or anyone concerned with movies who is not affiliated to a large chain.

indifferentism (pols) in socialist countries, a lack of commitment to social problems and developments.

indirects (TV) (abbrev) indirect costs: the running costs of a company – the staff, the equipment – that will always need paying for, whether or not they are actually involved in a production.

indispensable labour (pols) aka: *necessary labour*: in Marxist terms, that proportion of labour that goes to earn the subsistence, maintenance and reproduction of a worker and his family.

individualisation (soc wk) the recognition and understanding that every client has a particular personal problem and personality and must be treated as such rather than as one of a mass of similar cases.

individual learning department (educ) a euphemism for the remedial classes for teaching backward pupils.

indulgency pattern (indust relats) a lenient style of management.

industrial (movies) any film about or for business and industry which is not intended for commercial exhibition.

industrial action (indust relats) euphemism for a strike, an event epitomised, in the eyes of critics, by its industrial *in*action.

industrial property (commerce) a collective description of the commercial rights that stem from trade marks, patents etc.

industry (movies) the film business. (cf: *the profession*)

industry leadership programmes (public relats) a campaign designed to place one's client – either corporate or individual – at the head of his profession, industry, brand, etc.

inertia selling (commerce) a sales technique whereby the merchandise is sent, unsolicited, and is then followed up with a bill.

inflation (econ) an increase in the supply of money over the quantity of goods available for purchase. This pushes up the cost of those goods that do exist. Thus *hyperinflation*: a situation where the monetary demand increases too rapidly; people attempt to beat inflation by spending heavily before prices increase even further and thus merely intensify the process. *stagflation*: a situation in which both money prices and unemployment are rising to increasingly high levels; *reflation*: an attempt to manage currencies and thus restore a previous, less inflationary price level, aka: *disinflation*. (cf: *demand pull inflation, cost-push inflation*)

influentials (public relats) aka: *opinion leaders*: those figures whom a PR feels must be influenced before all others, given their own ability to influence large numbers of other people.

informational entertainment (TV) aka: *soft news*: a type of news broadcasting which minimises factual information and places everything within a context more akin to a purely entertainment programme. Low on 'importance' but easily assimilable by those who want few demands on their intelligence. (cf: *happy talk*)

information technology (media, computers) a popular generality that covers many innovations in the techniques of computing, microelectronics and telecommunications to produce, store and transmit a wide spectrum of information.

infotainment (TV) see: informational entertainment.

infrastructure (econ) the vital services and essential fabric of a nation's life: roads, housing, medical care, educational facilities. Such entities have no direct effect on economic growth but are indispensable to its continuation.

in front of the gun (drugs) a dealer who carries on his trade knowing that he will be offered no protection from his wholesalers if he is arrested. Such dealers, often fresh from hospital or jail, are happy to accept such terms just to maintain their own supply of drugs.

ingenue (theatre) a juvenile lead, esp. a naive, sweet young girl; known in 19th century melodrama as 'the singing chambermaid'.

inherited audience (TV) an audience who have been watching one programme, possibly one with high ratings, and will not bother to change channels but will simply settle into whatever programme appears next.

initialise (computers) aka: *preset*: to reset a system to its starting position in order to make sure that every time the program starts running everything works in the same way.

initial margin (futures market) the margin (qv) required to cover a specific new position.

injection (aerospace) aka: *injection*: the process of sending a satellite or manned capsule into orbit.

ink *v* (entertainment) to sign a contract or similar deal.

innocent murmurs (medic/US) palpitations of the heart which need not arouse fears of illness.

innovators (marketing) the first buyers of a new product who start off the adoption process (qv).

in one (theatre/US) aka: *in a front cloth* (UK): a scene played in an imaginary area bounded by a 'line' extending from the farthest downstage left wing to the farthest downstage right wing. Thus: *in two*: the 'line' is from the second left to right wings; *in three* the 'line' is from left to right threequarters of the way upstage; *in four*: the lines run from the left to right upstage.

inoperative (pols) no longer true, a lie: originated in White House Press Secretary Ronald Ziegler's statement to the press corps in 1973 that various categorical statements made by President Nixon and generally known to be untrue were, as of that date 'inoperative'.

in place (espionage) the subject or target of an investigation or surveillance has arrived at a destination where observation has already been set up.

in-put (computers) any data or program instruc-

I

tions that are fed into the machine; the physical medium on which these are represented.

insert *n* (movies) a shot inserted into a dramatic scene which will allow the audience to get a better look from the screen character's point of view at whatever – a headline, corpse, etc – is causing the drama.

in-service *v, n* (govt) 1. to train non-bureaucrats to improve their performance. 2. *to hold an in-service*: the setting up of a training process.

in-service education (educ) a teacher still taking new courses to add to his/her basic qualifications which have started off their teaching career.

insider (stock market) members of the stock exchange who can use their special knowledge to make profits on deals that the general public would not have been able to appreciate at the right moment.

installation (art) an *installation show* is one in which the positioning of the art works depends crucially on their relations to the layout and environment within the gallery, ie: how they are installed.

institutional advertising (advertising) advertising that refers to the firm or business itself rather than promoting the product it creates.

instruction (computers) a single step in a program – each program thus is made up of a series of instructions.

instrumentalities (pols) in post-Revolutionary Iran, those essential forces – Revolutionary Guards, mullahs (preachers) and hezbollah (militia) – who provide the leadership with its basic support and continue to suppress any opposition. They are the 'instruments of Allah'.

insults (medic) the process of creating monsters by injecting the growing foetus with a harmful substance to produce deliberate malformation – used by teratologists in their studies of congenital malformations.

insurance (sport) the process whereby a winning team consolidates its lead and ensures that the opposition cannot even attain a tie.

insurance poor (business) to hold so much insurance that simply paying the premiums against any possible eventuality leaves insufficient funds to continue a normal or enjoyable life.

intake team (soc wk) those social workers who deal with the immediate casework – usually referral, decision-making and assessment – that comes with a new client.

integralism (pols) a philosophy that stresses the amalgamating of every individual difference into one, far more useful whole in which all society is to be linked effectively together for the benefit of all.

integrated (milit) in the *integrated battlefield* any combinations of conventional, nuclear and biological/chemical weapons are used.

intelligence probe (espionage) breaking and entering a target's premises for the collecting

of useful information, or the planting of bugs (qv).

intelligent terminal (computers) a terminal which has some computing ability built into its machinery.

intentions model (marketing) a model of consumer attitudes that intends to predict intentions to buy.

interaction (soc wk) the detailed study of behaviour, its biological base and its cultural setting.

interaction matrix (business) a chart to help solve those problems – such as the layout of a factory – where physical positioning is particularly vital.

interactive video (TV) those televisions, almost wholly in the US, which are linked by a special handset to the broadcasting studios and which can therefore involve the viewer with the programme, ie: by giving instant question and answer verdicts on a given program by pressing the right buttons at the programme host's prompting.

intercept (espionage) any information picked up by the use of a clandestine microphone, telephone tap or similar bug (qv).

interdict *v* (milit) to make an area unsafe for enemy action or movement.

interdiction bombing (milit) bombing such targets as will interrupt or even destroy enemy communications and/or transport. (cf. *corridor bashing*)

interest inventory (educ) a checklist of a pupil's interests to reveal their relative strengths. Used for helping with career choices and elicited through various standardised multiple choice tests.

interface (computers) anything that serves to connect two separate systems in a machine.

interface *v, n* (new therapies) from the computer use (qv), any form of relationship between individuals; thus A can interface with B at an interface, ie: they can talk at a given location.

interleaving (computers) the simultaneous performance of two programs by a computer which can fit the secondary or background (qv) program in the microspaces between the performing of the primary or foreground (qv) program.

interliners (air crew) those passengers that are transferring from one airline to another at an airport.

inter-media (art) aka: *mixed media*: the use of a large variety of devices and techniques from many artistic areas to produce a complete show or entertainment.

internal colonialism (pols) the exploitation by the nation as a whole of its minority races, religions and cultures.

internalisation (stock market) a method of transferring stocks between brokerage offices rather than transmitting orders through the floor of an Exchange.

internal orientation (business) a job that is centred in the main office or company headquarters with little travel or fieldwork.

international travel and talk (business) internal corporate slang for ITT, the telecommunications conglomerate.

internationalism (pols) anyone, in socialist terms, who is prepared to defend the USSR without reservation or conditions because the USSR is the base of the international revolutionary movement and to defend this movement without defending the USSR is impossible. Often used with the adj *proletarian* and the opposite of *bourgeois nationalism*.

interpreter (computers) software (qv) that translates a high level language (qv) into a machine code (qv) which responds directly to the computer's operation and which it can 'understand'.

interrabang (press) aka: *interrobang*: a punctuation mark that simultaneously expresses astonishment and surprise.

interrupt *n* (computers) the automatic breaking off of the operation of one program in order to run another one, after which the original program is completed.

interrupter (police/UK) a court interpreter.

intervention (pols) in the EEC Parliament, any contribution to a debate.

intervention (soc wk) antonym for the taking of any action by a social worker as regards a particular case. Intervention can be strong – as between a married couple – or weak – any purposeful action taken by a social worker.

interventionalist (pols) in EEC terminology, the interfering in people's lives with the object of achieving a policy objective.

intervention area (milit) the defined limit of operations in a small war, ie: Suez, the Falklands, etc. (cf: *austere war*)

intervention currency (finance) the action of the International Monetary Fund in sustaining the currencies of the 118 member nations by buying their own currencies with dollars when they seemed likely to dip below a set level of control or selling them in exchange for dollars if they appeared to be rising too high.

in the dark (milit) air intercept code: 'not visible on my scope'.

in the money (horse-racing) of both horses and bettors: to be 1st, 2nd or 3rd in a race or to have betted on the horse that has run in one of those places. Thus *out of the money* refers to any other runner in a race.

in the round (theatre) a performance given in the theatre where the auditorium surrounds the stage, as opposed to forming the 'fourth wall' of a proscenium stage.

in the sack (drugs) when a dealer has erroneously

sold drugs to a policeman or Federal agent and cannot hope to avoid arrest.

intimism (art) a form of Impressionism (qv) applied to domestic interiors rather than to landscapes; usually referring to the work of Bonnard and Vuillard.

into (new therapies) strongly involved with, interested in, concerned with, fascinated by, etc.

intraspecific aggression (soc sci) conflict between people of the same race, culture, religion, etc: a civil war.

intra-war period aka: *trans-SIOP period*: the period during which the actual nuclear exchanges are in progress.

in-tray exercise (business) aka: *in-basket exercise*: a training scheme within a fully simulated office environment with letters, memos, decisions to be made, etc; the trainee must deal with everything that arrives within a set time.

introduction (stock market) the issuing of new shares by a company, not directly to the public but only through the medium of the Stock Exchange.

intrusions (press) the Australian press's equivalent to doorstepping (qv).

inuit art (art) Eskimo art; *inuit* is the Eskimo word for the Eskimo people.

inverted market (futures market) a market in which the nearer months are selling at premiums to the further off months.

investigative phase (medic) experimental surgery, used to reassure patients who would prefer not to feel that the surgeon was not wholly expert in his work.

investment dressing (commerce) in the fashion trade, the purchase of high-priced clothes and accessories on the principle that such purchases will last longer than cheaper ones would.

invisible exports (econ) non-commodity exports; financial and personal services rendered by a country's natives to foreigners – banking, insurance, tourism, etc.

invisible hand (econ) coined by Adam Smith in *The Wealth of Nations* (1776): the inevitable regulation of any economic system by anonymous market forces.

invisible painting (art) any paintings that have colour values so closely attuned that they exist only on the threshold of human perception. At first glance these works appear to have no differences in tone or colour but the eye will accommodate in due course.

invisible supply (commerce) 1. uncounted stocks of a commodity that are in the hands of wholesalers and manufacturers and cannot thus be counted properly into statistics. 2. stocks outside commercial channels but still theoretically available to the market.

invitation (gambling) in bridge, a bid which encourages the bidder's partner to continue to game or slam.

IP (prison/UK) (acro) *in possession*: whatever a

I

prisoner has in his possession at a given time and which is checked and noted, ie: on his leaving and returning to his cell when receiving a visit.

iris *n* (movies) a moveable diaphragm on a camera – like the expanding and contracting iris of the eye – which permits the camera to create a shrinking or increasing circle on the screen.

Irish hurricane (milit) aka: *Irishman's hurricane*: RN: a flat calm.

Irish pennants (milit) RN: loose ends of rope fluttering in a breeze.

iron (milit) aka: *dumb bombs*: USAF: any bomb that has no guidance system and is simply dropped vertically on to the target. (cf: *smart bombs*)

iron *n* (theatre) the safety or fireproof curtain.

iron *n* (aerospace) all magnetic parts of an aircraft's construction, irrespective of the actual metal involved.

ironmongery (sport) in mountaineering: picks, crampons, other metal equipment used for climbing the mountain.

iron rice bowl (pols) in Chinese communist terminology, guaranteed material security, usually a steady job; an iron rice bowl, unlike a porcelain one, will not break.

irredentist (pols) a national yearning to regain such territory as was once part of that nation but has long since been taken away by treaty or conquest.

ish (media) (abbrev) issue of any magazine, especially fanzines (qv).

island *n* (milit) RN: the superstructure of a ship, especially that of an aircraft carrier.

island *n* (police/UK) HM Prison Parkhurst, on the Isle of Wight.

island of stability (science) a group of superheavy chemical elements with extremely stable nuclei.

island site (advertising) a space for a newspaper advertisement which is surrounded by at least three sides of editorial matter.

issue management (public relats) the preparing through PR of the public for the reception of an 'issue' in the way that those who have created that issue wish it to be received, usually when in fact its every aspect would otherwise be totally unpalatable to the public.

I statement (new therapies) a therapeutic technique that forces the patient to reconsider his words by turning every statement that starts off 'You . . .' into one that starts 'I . . .'.

iswas (milit) USN: a rough and ready calculating device; orig. a mechanical aid used on World War 2 submarines.

it (new therapies) the essence of est (qv): 'what is, is, and what ain't, ain't'. 'It is you experiencing you without any symbology or any concept' (Werner Erhard).

it (new therapies) coined by Georg Groddeck (1866–1934): 'a force which lives in us while we believe we are living'.

Italian rehearsal (TV) the reading through of a script at top speed with no 'acting' by the cast; this is supposed to help in learning lines.

item (computer) any quantity of data that is treated as one unit – a record or a group of records.

I've been moved (business) corporate slang for IBM, used by employees with reference to the constant reposting of executives.

I

jack dusty (milit) aka: *jack of the dust* (US): naval description of a rating or enlisted man in charge of a ship's dry provisions.

jacks (police/UK) detectives.

jacks (drugs) (abbrev) jacks and jills: rhyming slang = pills. Capsules of heroin, often obtained by a registered addict on a prescription and then sold.

jack shalloo (milit) RN: a naval officer whose main aim is to become popular with the men.

jack strop (milit) RN: a new recruit who tries to pass himself off as an old hand.

jack-up (commerce) in the oil business, a type of offshore drilling rig which is towed to an appointed spot and then lowers its legs onto the sea bed.

jam roll *n* (prison/UK) fr. rhyming sl.: parole.

jank (milit) to change altitude and direction simultaneously in attempting to avoid anti-aircraft fire.

jankers (milit) British Army: fatigue duty or confinement to the punishment cells.

jargoon (police/UK) a fake or otherwise worthless 'diamond ring'; from the original word for a zircon.

jaunty (milit) RN: the master-at-arms.

jawbone (pols) a policy of urging management and union leaders to accept wage restraint, first associated with President Lyndon B. Johnson c 1964. From jawbone: sl. for talking one's way into something one wants, often credit at a store or bank.

JEEP (milit) (acro) Joint Emergency Evacuation Plan: US contingency measures for instant evacuation of selected milit. and civilian specialists picked to run the USA during and after a nuclear war.

jeopardy assessment (econ) the power of the government in the US to make an immediate assessment of an individual's tax liability and to seize any money or possessions if the IRS feels that the subject is about to leave the country to avoid payment.

jerk in (commerce) in the second-hand car trade, to turn back the mileometer in order to make a car seem 'younger'. (cf: *chop the clock*)

jerk off *n* (movies) a stunt in which a character is suddenly hauled vertically out of his seat in a car or on a horse; they hang suspended while their erstwhile conveyance continues to move on.

jet jockey (aerospace) a pilot or astronaut with exceptional skill in manoeuvring his craft.

jet shoes (aerospace) special boots to enable astronauts to walk in the weightless conditions of the moon.

jet upsets (air crew) high speed dives, often at a high banking angle.

jew *n* (milit) a ship's tailor.

jigger (sport) in golf, a short iron club used for approach shots.

jigglers (police/UK) skeleton keys for opening tumbler locks.

jim crow laws (pols/US) any custom or law that is designed to humiliate blacks; from a song popular in Kentucky c 1840 which soon had the Negroes identified with the equally black crow.

jimmying (police/UK) from the instrument used to break open doors, safes, etc: to get into movies, dog-tracks or any other entertainment without buying a ticket.

jimmy the one (milit) RN: the first lieutenant.

jims (sex) inoffensive men who get their satisfaction from hanging around street prostitutes as they go about their business.

jink (milit) USAF: to take evasive action. (cf: *jank*)

jitter (audio) a video image that flutters during projection.

job *n* (police/UK) the profession of policing; also the name of the Metropolitan Police magazine.

job action (indust relats) a variation of industrial action (qv) in which workers stage a go-slow or work-to-rule rather than an all-out strike.

job and finish (indust relats) an agreement whereby the worker agrees to perform a set number of tasks in a day and then to consider his work finished, whether or not it has taken him the usual eight hours.

job backwards (stock market) to remake one's calculations using hindsight and working out what should have happened if one had only known what was about to occur.

jobber (theatre/US) orig: an actor employed for a specific part in a particular production; currently a small role in a touring company. From *job actor*: one who was out of regular work and glad of the one job.

jobbers (stock market) members and member firms who maintain the shares market, buying and selling amongst themselves but never dealing with the general public who buy from *brokers*.

job one (commerce) in the motor trade, the first production car of a new line; the saleable product of years of planning and development.

jobsworth (rock business) a time server, a petty official, anyone who refuses a request with the intonation 'It's more than my job's worth . . .'

jockey (finance) *to be the jockey* in venture capitalism is to take control of an investment situation by running the management side of the venture.

jockey *v* (sport) in soccer, to move backwards, forwards or sideways in order to cover any directional changes by the opposition players.

Joe I (milit) the first Soviet testing of atomic weapons in August 1949, named for then leader Joseph Stalin, 'Uncle Joe'.

joey *n* (prison/UK) an illicit parcel or any other unofficial consignment from the outer world.

joey (milit) a Royal Marine; the Marines collectively are *jollies*.

jog (theatre/US) aka: *return piece* (UK): a narrow flat (qv) placed at right angles to another flat either to form a corner or break up a flat wall. Thus *jogging the set*: to vary the wall surfaces.

jogging (finance) banking terminology for a method of storing information.

john (sex) from John Doe (qv): a prostitute's client (male or female).

John (milit) at Royal Military College, Sandhurst: a cadet in his first two years at the college. (cf: *Reg*)

John Doe (law/US) a general term to cover any un-named citizen. fem: *Jane Doe*.

Johnny Armstrong (milit) RN: any hard work that involves pulling or hauling.

joint (drugs) 1. marijuana cigarette 2. the hypodermic syringe used to inject narcotics.

joint *n* (horse-racing/US) a small battery operated device that will give a horse an electric shock to stimulate it during a race.

joint mouse (medic) a small fragment of bone or cartilege floating in the cavity of a joint.

joker (govt/US) a clause or amendment inserted in a piece of legislation which does not make its real effect known at first; thus any part of a contract that frustrates one of the parties to that contract.

jonah (gambling) 1. a superstitious player. 2. a person whose presence is assumed to bring bad luck to other players.

JR (prison/UK) (acro) *j*udgement *r*espited; usually and incorrectly interpreted as 'judge's remand'; in either case, the imprisonment under full prison regulations, although without the benefit of a job, of a former remand or bail prisoner who has pleaded guilty but must wait out the trial of those confederates similarly charged who have pleaded not guilty.

Judd's dictum (art) a remark of the US sculptor/writer Don Judd who answered the perennial question 'But is it art' by replying 'If someone calls it art, it's art'.

judge's rules (law/UK) a set of rules that are supposed to govern the interrogation of suspects in police custody.

judy (milit) air intercept code: 'I have contact and am taking over the intercept'.

juice (pols) from the sl. for electrical current: political power.

juice joint (gambling) a crooked gambling game in which dice or a roulette wheel are controlled by 'juice' – hidden electrical magnets – in or under the table or wheel.

juicer (movies) an electrician.

juke *v* (sport) aka: *sell a dummy* (UK soccer). US football: to 'fake' an opponent by pretending to make one move but actually making another.

jumbo-cut (movies) an abrupt cut from one scene to another with no gradual transition.

jumboise (commerce) to enlarge a ship, esp. an oil tanker, by inserting extra sections of deck between the bow and stern.

jump *v* (theatre) 1. to forget some of the lines and to jump forward in a script. 2. a one-night stand, or the distance between them.

jump-cut (movies) the removal of portions of the narrative to tighten up the action or plot.

jumper (police/US) an actual or potential suicide victim; not necessarily one who is about to leap from a tall building.

jumper (TV) a length of cable that provides a variety of different connections for attaching the lights.

jump-up (police/UK) aka: *van-dragging*: robbing lorries by jumping onto the back and dragging off the goods.

Jungian aesthetics (art) Jungian art theories stress the conscious or unconscious use by an artist of various archetypes in his work and the semi-conscious awareness of the 'collective unconscious'.

junior *n* (law/UK) the barrister who assists the leader (qv) in a legal case; in general a barrister who is not yet a Queen's Counsel.

junk bond (stock exchange) a high-risk, non-corporate bond that is bought at less than its face value.

junkets (pols) those expenses-paid trips offered to politicians by interested parties, or trips funded from public money that politicians take allegedly for fact-finding (qv) purposes. Used in a derogatory sense by the critics of such expenditure.

junk sculpture (art) sculptures that employ miscellaneous street debris either as collages or assemblies. Sometimes as found objects, sometimes transformed as the artist desired.

junksport (TV) such artificial sporting competitions – Superstars etc – which have been created for TV and in which the stars of one sport take on those of others, none of whom are allowed to compete in the one area in which they are actually expert.

jury (theatre/US) the first night audience who 'judge' a play.

jus (milit) French Foreign Legion: coffee.

justify (press) to even up the lines in a column of print so that both sides of that column run down the page in a straight line.

juve (sex) (abbrev) juvenile: child pornography; films, pictures, etc.

juve (theatre) (abbrev) juvenile (qv).

juvenile (horse-racing/US) a two-year-old horse.

juvenile (theatre) a youthful role or the star youth role. Thus *juvenile powder*: makeup that approximates a youthful complexion.

J

K (govt/UK) a knighthood.

kaffir circus (stock market) those brokers who deal in South African gold mining shares.

Kahn energy (science) the quantity of fission energy for the radio-active destruction of one major nation's total population, assuming there to be no civil defense nor shelters. For the US or USSR this has been estimated at 10,000,000,000 tons.

kahuna (sport) in surfing: a fictitious 'god' of surfing, from the Hawaiian word for priest, expert or wise man.

kamikaze (sport) in surfing: a planned wipe-out (qv) when the surfer has to leave the board and start swimming for shore.

kangaroo ticket (pols/US) a ticket in which the nominee for vice-president has greater electoral appeal than does the one for president.

Kapitalistate (pols) from Marx's *Das Kapital*: a concept of the American Marxist James O'Connor, that modern capitalism is dominated or at least supplemented by direct or indirect state intervention.

kata (medic) (abbrev) katathermometer: used for measuring the cooling power of ambient air.

kazik (commerce) in the rug trade: a bad rug lacking quality and probably overpriced.

KB (crime/UK) (abbrev) knockback: a disappointment or rejection, particularly of an appeal against sentence or for parole.

keeper (sport) US football: a play in which the quarterback keeps the ball and runs with it instead of attempting a pass to his receiver.

keeper (medic/US) the appendix: 'you go in there with a steel blade, you find 'er and you keep'er' (S. Shem, *The House of God*, 1978).

keeper (press/US) any story that is held over for use at a more propitious time.

keeping your belt on (sex) a hustler who rigorously preserves his cherished self-image of absolute masculinity by refusing ever to take a passive role in a paid homosexual encounter.

kegler (sport) in bowling: anyone who plays ten pin bowling, skittles or allied sports.

keister (crime/US) 1. a burglar's tool box or satchel. 2. a safe.

kelly (commerce) in oil business, a square joint on top of the drill stem that passes through a square hole in the rotary table.

kensington gore (movies, TV) a pun on the street that runs south of Hyde Park: fake blood used for deaths and disasters on the screen.

kerb weight (commerce) motor trade: the weight of a car without occupants or luggage but with oil, water and some petrol.

key *v* (advertising) to distinguish an advertisement by including some special feature that will immediately appeal to the consumer.

key (drugs) (abbrev) a kilogram.

key book (public relats) any publication in which a PR's client is very keen to appear.

keyer (TV) a vision mixer effect which cuts holes in the main picture and enables captions or other material to be inserted.

key grip (movies) the chief grip (qv).

keyhole (aerospace) that area through which a spacecraft must pass in order to reach its objective.

keyhole wound (police, medic) the wound sustained after being shot with a worn gun: since the barrel is no longer perfectly smooth, the bullet tumbles rather than rotates and thus tears a ragged entry wound and causes bad internal damage in the victim. Harder to treat than a wound from a new gun.

key light (TV, movies) the main light used to illuminate a particular person or object; esp. that light used for the star.

keynoter (pols/US) aka: *keynote speech*: the opening address at a political convention or other meeting that sets the tone, outlines the topics to come and attempts to promote a feeling of unity.

keystroke *v* (computers) to type a single letter or number into a computer.

khaltura (pols) in Russia, those black market operations deemed necessary for the functioning of the economy and thus unofficially connived at by the authorities. Factories that produce consumer goods will siphon off a percentage for the black market where their producers can sell them and thus augment their pay.

ki (milit) aka: *ky*: RN cocoa.

kibitzer (gambling) a non-player who nonetheless likes to comment and advise the players on the progress of the game.

kickback *n* (commerce) in oil business, the sight of mud bubbling up through a bore-hole that can be a warning of a possible blow-out.

kicker (gambling) a high third card retained in

the hand as well as a pair that have been made in draw poker.

kicker (press) 1. a metal arm used to divide the flow of newly printed newspapers by pushing every 25th, 50th or 100th out of line to help the making up of bundles. 2. a story that runs down the left hand column of the page, thus kicking it off.

kicker (TV/US) aka: end-pieces: light, possibly humorous stories that can be put at the end of a news programme.

kick-out (sport) in surfing, pressing down the rear of a surfboard to turn it and thus mount a wave.

kicksorter (technology) in electronics, a device to classify electrical pulses according to their amplitude.

kid shows (entertain) in carnivals, the freak show: because freaks are seen as another variety of children and thus these are shows *by* children, although not especially *for* them.

kidvid (TV) television shows designed for children.

kif (drugs) see: *drug names*.

kilburn (police/UK) (abbrev) rhyming sl: kilburn priory = diary, the official police notebook that is produced in court.

kill (press) to stop a story before it is set or printed.

kill (radio, TV) to stop a story before broadcasting, because of libel, inaccuracy or simply because it is out of date.

kill (theatre, movies, TV) aka: *save*: to turn off a specified light.

kill fee (press) the money paid to a freelance writer who has submitted a commissioned story which is then not printed; often 75% of the original fee.

killick (milit) RN: a leading seaman, from his badge which bears the symbol of an anchor (sl: killick).

kill line (milit) that point or distance in space where an anti-ballistic missile can destroy an incoming missile.

kill ratio (milit) the difference between the number of hostile troops and those of one's own side who have been killed in action. (cf: *body count*)

kilter (gambling) a hand that consists of card of little or no use.

kinetic architecture (archit) a school of architects who claim that traditional architecture is too static to respond to modern social pressures and posit a 'kinetic' style that incorporates adaptable building that can so respond, with moving walls, foundations on rafts, etc.

kinetic art (art) aka: *The Movement Movement*: any art work that requires and incorporates a degree of movement: of the work itself, of the spectator in front of it, of a part of the work by the spectator. Thus *kinetic sculpture*: a form

of sculpture which requires the same movement/involvement as kinetic art.

king pair (sport) in cricket, for an opening batsman to be dismissed with the first ball of both his innings in a match.

kinker (entertainment) in the circus, an acrobat or contortionist.

kip *n* (sport) in gymnastics: a vigorous and rapid extension of the hip joint in order to raise the centre of gravity of the body.

kipper (milit) RN: a torpedo: aka: *tinfish*. (cf: *fish*)

kiss the mistress (sport) in bowls, to barely graze the jack (orig: the mistress).

kitchen (gambling) a part of the casino at Monte Carlo where gamblers can place smaller bets than in the more prestigious *salle privée*.

kitchen junk school (art) the realist paintings of four UK artists – Bratby, Greaves, Smith, Middleditch – working in the mid 1950s. They specialised in squalid scenes, often actual kitchens, and anticipated much of the content of pop art (qv) even if their style remained basically academic.

kite (law/UK) a junior (qv) barrister who is allotted a case at an assize court when the plaintiff can find no other defender.

kite (stock market) an accommodation bill.

kiting (medic) the illegal alteration of a prescription to increase the number of pills or other drugs written down by the doctor.

kiting (police/UK) the passing of dud cheques.

Kitty Hawk (police/customs) Heathrow airport code for HM the Queen; *Kitty Rainbow* the Duke of Edinburgh.

kiwi (aerospace) 1. a ground test reactor which is never intended (like the kiwi bird) to fly. 2. RAF crew members who do not fly but remain on the ground to service the aircraft.

klinefelter (medic) named for Harry Klinefelter jr. (1912–): a syndrome that causes hermaphroditism, and is found in those people with an extra X sex chromosome (XXY, XXXY and XXYY). (cf: *Turners*)

klong (pols) coined 1972 by Frank Mankiewicz (working for Sen. George McGovern's campaign) as 'a sudden rush of shit to the heart': a reaction of horror when one realises that one's own mistake will lead/has led to a far greater problem.

kludge (computers) 1. an improvised do-it-yourself lashup which may well work. 2. a factory made computer which still has some (endearingly) odd characteristics.

kneecap (milit) (acron) National Emergency Airborne Command Post: a Boeing 747 fitted out with accommodation and equipment for ensuring that the US President plus his civil and military advisers could still fight a major nuclear war – assuming he could reach the plane – even were Washington destroyed. The

K

plane has fuel for three days and carries the President, 15 staff officers and 27 crew.

knife-fighting (milit) short-range aerial dogfights that resembles the close contact of fighting with knives.

knife-rest (milit) a barrier or obstruction composed of barbed wire and timber.

knitting (milit) RN: girls in general or a specific girlfriend.

knock v (commerce) in second hand car trade: to sell a car at a loss, to 'take the knock'.

knockback (police, criminal) a rejection or dismissal, esp. of an application for bail or parole.

knockdown n (movies, TV) a temporary, portable, collapsible dressing room for use on location.

knock-down path (aerospace) the route taken by airport firefighters when approaching a crashed and burning plane, when flames have to be 'knocked down', ie: blown aside.

knocker (commerce) a door-to-door salesmen who knocks (or rings) at every potential client's home.

knocker, on the (police/UK) from the legitimate knocker (qv): a conman who tours houses to sell or buy goods and specialises in persuading or bullying the old to sell off their treasures cheaply.

knock-for-knock (business) an agreement between two insurers that each will pay his own policy holder in a dispute, regardless of actual liability.

knocking on the grass (press) when a reporter is sent on a difficult story and cannot face actually approaching the bereaved parent, raped girl, etc, he tells the office that they weren't at home and instead of knocking at the door, knocks on the metaphorical front lawn.

knockoffs (commerce) in the fashion trade, cheap copies of best-selling lines and models (eg: a royal wedding dress) aimed at the mass production market.

knockoffs (publishing) quick hack productions that echo a best-seller – usually non-fiction and tied into a major event, eg: the Falklands War – to cash in on the public appetite for such material.

knock-out (commerce) aka: *knock*: an illegal private auction held by a 'ring' of mutually supportive dealers who have deliberately kept the prices low at the genuine auction and will not bid in earnest against each other until it is over.

knots (sport) surfing: a surfer's status mark – the bruises and cuts gained from battling the waves and his board.

knowledge n (police/UK) the compulsory learning of London's streets, specifically a number of basic routes, that any aspirant taxi-driver must undergo and without the passing of which he will not receive the Metropolitan Police licence. (cf: *white coats, brown coats*)

knowledge base (soc wk) theories, of psychology and sociology, which provide the background for practical social work.

kop (sport) soccer: a bank of terracing for the supporters of the home team, spec. the one at Liverpool FC. From the battle of Spion Kop during the Boer War (1899–1902) which took place on a hill near Ladysmith.

Kremlin (police/UK) ironic description of New Scotland Yard.

Kunstkompass (art) a listing of the supposed 100 best Western artists, devised in 1969. Like all such lists, the criteria which make it up are subject to many criticisms and the subjective opinions of those who are asked to help compile it.

Kunstlerroman (lit crit) a novel that takes as its theme the making of a novelist.

kurumaku (business) in Japan, a business fixer, lit. 'a wire puller'; fr. Kabuki theatre where the word means 'Black curtain', thus implying the off-stage activities of a such a figure.

kye (milit) RN: 1. dirty. 2. see *ky, ki*.

K

laager (milit) a close defensive formation adopted at night by tanks which form a circle inside which unarmoured vehicles may be parked.

label *n* (record business) a record company, whose label is affixed to its products.

label (computers) a character or set of characters chosen to identify a statement in a program so that it may be identified for use elsewhere in that program.

laboratory experience (educ) any situation at which pupils are present for the purpose of instruction or observation. In the context of teacher training, the student teacher is the researcher and the pupils become his/her raw material or guinea pigs.

laboratory techniques (marketing) orig. restricted to the use of psychological models for market research; now includes such general studies as simulated shopping for pricing research.

labour shed (econ) the area from which the labour supply is drawn.

lace up *v* (TV) to thread a film into a projector for viewing or transmission.

lackey (pols) a popular leftwing term of abuse denoting a lick-spittle follower of the ruling class, invariably the bourgeoisie. From the orig. meaning of 'footman'. (cf: *running dog, capitalist roader*)

ladder *n* (milit) USMC: stairway.

ladder *v* (milit) RN: a method of finding an accurate firing range by increasing and decreasing successive salvos until the enemy is pinpointed.

ladder man (gambling) a casino employee who sits on a high chair and watches for any errors or cheating by players or croupiers.

ladder of participation (govt) in urban planning this ladder ranks the various degrees of public participation: (from the least influential) manipulation; therapy; informing; consultation; placation; partnership; delegated power; citizen control.

ladies (espionage) aka: *sisters*: ironic reference to amateur or professional women who are involved in blackmail operations. Ladies will start the process of seduction, but the sisters actually sleep with the target (and may well be thus photographed/taped).

ladies (sex) black pimp reference to prostitutes.

laggard (stock market) a share that has for no apparent reason lagged behind the average price of its peers or of the market in general.

lagger (econ) an economic indicator that maintains an existent trend for some time after the state of the general economy has moved on in a different direction.

lagging *n* (prison/UK) a sentence of three years or more.

lambs (stock market) ignorant or inexperienced speculators on an Exchange.

lame duck (pols/US) any office holder who cannot be re-elected; spec. *lame duck President*: the President who has been defeated in November's election but must serve on until the following January when his successor takes office under the constitution.

lame duck (business) any business, industry or other enterprise that cannot survive without government intervention.

lame duck (stock market) any member of the Exchange who has been hammered (qv); the Court of the London Stock Exchange that considered such defaulters was formerly known as the *Duckery*.

lammy (milit) RN: a duffel coat.

lampshade (milit) (abbrev) *radiation lampshade*: a device for determining the height of an atomic airburst; it is about 1′ wide and shaped like a lampshade.

lance-jack (milit) British Army: lance corporal or lance bombardier.

land *n* (technology) an area between adjacent grooves, ie: those on a gramophone record.

land art (art) the use of the land to create art, eg: controlled seeding of a field, etc. Such projects required aerial documentation to make them accessible to the public. (cf: *earth art*)

Land Crabs (police/UK) London River Police nickname for all earth-bound members of the Metropolitan Police. (cf: *Matelots*)

landscape *v* (business) to create an open-plan office where all employees, regardless of status, are contained in the same area, divided only by low partitions.

landscape (advertising) any booklet or picture in which the horizontal dimensions are greater than the vertical ones.

l and w (medic/US) (abbrev) *living and well* a file notation to describe a patient in ideal health.

language (computer) any of the many systems and rules that have been created for the operation of a computer (cf: *BASIC, FORTRAN, COBOL, high-level language, machine code*).

language (art, advertising) the overall style and visual tone of a design or layout; thus *to break the language*: to alter that style by including an incongruous or unlikely typeface, visual, etc.

language arts (educ) reading, writing, speaking and listening.

lantern (theatre/UK) 1. a light or a lighting unit. 2. the skylight over the stage that acts as an extra protection against fire.

lap (milit) in naval mine warfare, the area assigned to a sweeper or section of sweepers for clearing. Thus *lap track*: the track to be followed by a sweeper; *lap turn*: a turn made by a sweeper between two runs through a designated lap; *lap width*: the path taken by one sweeper as it clears mines.

lapping (commerce) an accounting fraud in which shortages are concealed by a series of entries that keep postponing the receipt of money or of an asset from one accounting period into the next.

laser art (art) the use of lasers (light amplification by stimulated emission of radiation) either as tools for artists or in the production of holograms or forms of light art (qv).

lashup (science, computers) any form of make-shift or home-made machine or gadget. (cf: *kludge*)

last trading day (futures market) the final day under an exchange's rules during which trading may take place in a particular delivery month.

la sunnambula (Mafia) fr. Ital: 'the sleepwalker': the law.

latch (computers) a circuit which, when triggered, stores whatever appears on its inputs and saves it for subsequent use.

late blooming (psychology) the concept that an individual who has shown no apparent benefit over a period of therapy may well show it in their life some months after concluding that therapy.

late fringe (TV/US) a statistical TV daypart (qv) that follows prime time (qv) and lasts from 11.00 – closedown. (cf: *early fringe, housewife, late night*)

late night (TV/US) a statistical TV daypart (qv) that is reckoned from 10.30 pm to 12.00 midnight. (cf: *early fringe, late fringe, housewife, prime time*)

latency (computers) the time that elapses between the instruction to perform an action and the actual performance of that action.

latent (police) used of fingerprints which are invisible to the naked eye.

latent period (milit) the time that elapses between an individual's exposure to radioactive fallout and the onset of the effects of that fallout.

laugh-track (TV) a tape of pre-recorded laughter

which is dubbed (qv) onto a comedy show to create the effect of a studio audience.

launch on warning (milit) the firing of one's own missiles after hearing that enemy missiles are approaching but before they have arrived.

launch window (aerospace) that period when the Earth and a target planet are in a mutually favourable position for the launching of a rocket and/or capsule.

launder *v* (pols) the transfer of any funds that have been obtained illegally into a bank, usually in a foreign country, and the subsequent redemption of those funds via a legitimate source.

laundry list (pols/US) a detailed and often lengthy list of plans, priorities or other political intentions, often part of a speech.

lavender (movies) positive film stock used for producing duplicate negatives; a print made from such stock.

lawing (crime) see: *corner*.

law 29 (sport) in Rugby Union, a non-existent law that is otherwise referred to as a 'common-sense law'.

lay *v* (pols) for a minister or MP to place certain documents before the House of Commons for the information of fellow members.

lay down (gambling) for a player to lay down a hand of cards before all the betting is finished in order to show that his hand cannot be bettered by any other player.

lay member (new therapies) used at the Synanon drug addiction centre for those individuals who had not actually been addicts but who wished to undergo the centre's style of encounter therapy that is essentially designed to keep addicts off drugs.

lay off (gambling) for a book-maker to place a bet with a fellow book-maker in order to insure himself against a heavy loss on a particular horse or horses.

lay off a course (milit) RN, RAF: to work out a given course on a chart.

lay official (indust relats) a union member who is the unpaid holder of some office in that union, eg: a shop steward.

lay on *v* (drugs) to give a small sample of drugs to a potential customer without asking for payment. (cf: *taste*)

lay pipe *v* (US/TV) to make sure that the audience gets to learn the life history and background of all the regular characters in a series.

lay tracks (TV) to arrange a number of film sound tracks in exact relation to each other and to the film pictures.

lazarus layers (pols) in Marxist terms, the poorest sections of a capitalist society.

lazy (milit) air intercept code: 'equipment indicated at standby'.

lead *v* (milit) to shoot, to shoot at; using leaden bullets. Also, *to lead down*.

lead (press) the main news story in the paper, or the opening paragraph of any story. (cf: *lede*)

lead *n* (commerce) in real estate, any customer looking for a property.

leader (econ) any economic indicator that sets off in a new direction before the bulk of the market follows this new trend, eg: the level of a particular company's stock prices.

leader (commerce) goods advertised and sold below actual cost. (cf: *loss leaders*)

leader (law/UK) a senior barrister, often a Queen's Counsel, who leads a prosecution or defense in court. (cf: *junior*)

leader (radio, TV, movies) a length of blank film or tape, possibly in a particular identifying colour, that is attached to a film or tape for threading it into a projector or tape recorder. Thus *academy leader* (movies) has a numbered countdown for synchronisation purposes.

lead out *v* (press) to add blank spaces by inserting slugs of lead into a story and thus lengthen it to fit the required design of a newspaper page.

leads and lags (finance) in international finance, the hastening or delaying of paying different currencies in the hope of gaining from any possible alterations in their relative exchange rates.

lead through (sport) in mountaineering, when two climbers take it in turns to act as the leader of a team.

lead time (commerce) the time taken to manufacture a specific item.

lead time (business) the time taken between the origination of a new concept and its final creation and/or delivery.

leaf *n* (advertising) two pages.

leak *n*, *v* (pols) the discovery by the press and thus the public of facts that politicians may not wish revealed; many leaks, however, are deliberate and can be planted on eager journalists with the intention of confusing, rather than informing; the leak is also a weapon used by one politician against another or for the furtherance of his/her own interest.

leakage (milit) referring to any missile that penetrates all lines of defence and strikes its target.

leaky (milit) a submarine's nuclear reactor that is inadequately sealed against leaks of radioactivity.

lean *a* (technology) used of a variety of products to indicate a sub-standard performance, quality or content.

leaning to all sides (pols) the diversification of Chinese trade since 1960; prior to 1960 China traded almost exclusively with socialist countries, a process known as *leaning to one side*.

leaper (police, press) anyone who is threatening to jump, is actually jumping or who has completed jumping from a building in order to commit suicide. (cf: *floater*)

leap-frog *v* (indust relats) a method of gaining higher wages: the use by one group of workers

of the fact that a similar group has already gained a desired increase to influence their own claim, or to point out that a lesser group has so profited and that their own differential status must be maintained.

leatherneck (milit) USMC: a marine.

leave *n* (sport) in billiards, the position of the balls at the end of one player's stroke or break.

leaving here (TV/US) it looked good leaving here (NBC) or it left here all right (CBS/ABC): US TV's stock rejoinder to public complaints about bad reception or similar interference with their transmissions.

lede (press/US) a spelling differential to describe the lead story in a paper or the lead paragraph of a story and avoid confusion with lead: the space between the lines of that story. (cf: *lead*, *lead out*)

left footer (sociol) used in N. Ireland to denote a Roman Catholic; orig. in the different styles (Protestant/Catholic) of turf-cutting in Ulster. Catholics used spades with the lug on the left side, Protestants those with the lug on the right.

leftism (pols) in socialist terms: the refusal to make necessary compromises (esp. in W. European communist parties) with the right as are sensible and necessary.

leg *n* (milit) US paratrooper term for those troops who have not yet gained their certificates of jumping proficiency.

leg *n* (press) the length of a story as it appears on a page: thus one that runs over three columns is 3 legs, and so on.

leg art (press) aka: *cheesecake*: any pictures, eg: *Sun* page 3 girls, of pretty, scantily clad girls used in newspapers or magazines. Male versions, when they are found, are *beefcake*.

legend (aerospace) any fixed, printed notice in an aircraft cockpit.

legend (milit) RN: the estimated or planned dimensions and performance of a ship before construction or testing.

legend (espionage) an operational plan used for cover; a false biography used by a spy.

legend (advertising, press) a caption to a photograph or illustration.

legislative advocacy leadership (govt) lobbying for specific interest groups.

legitimate (arts) 1. (music) serious music as opposed to jazz, rock, pop etc. 2. (theatre) (often abbrev *legit*) literary plays rather than musicals, farce, melodrama, etc.

Legoland (milit) RN: the British Fleet Headquarters at Northwood, Middx.; from a make of plastic building bricks for children, referring thus to the architecture of the building and possibly to the fantasies created inside.

legs (movies) aka: *leggy*: any film that shows staying power at the box office: 'this one will run and run'. Thus *legless*: a flop.

legs (TV) see: legs (movies)

L

legs (publishing) aka: *page-turners*: best-selling books whose staying power has the same connotation as the movie use (qv).

leg theory (sport) aka: *bodyline* (bowling): in cricket, a form of aggressive bowling whereby one pitched the ball short on the leg stump in the hope of forcing the batsman to offer a catch to a ring of specially positioned fieldsman. Such bowling, in the England tour of Australia in 1932/33 very nearly brought the two countries to diplomatic blows.

leisure development (commerce) a specially designed retirement ghetto for old age pensioners.

lemonade (drugs) a weak sample of heroin.

lemon juice (milit) US Dept. of Defense: code for the second lowest state of war readiness. (cf: *defcon*)

lemon socialism (pols) the sort of half-hearted socialism epitomised by the UK Welfare State where state intervention under capitalism takes the place of real socialism; likewise the propping up by the state of declining industries rather than imposing on them a proper economic plan for a socialist future but opting instead for an illusory, capitalist 'sound' economy.

length (theatre) 1. a unit of 42 lines by which parts can be measured and compared. 2. a row of lights suspended from the same unit.

lens louse (press) members of the public who cannot resist posing for any camera despite the fact that the cameraman is rarely pointing it at them; aka: *anglers*: anyone who always tries to present their 'best angle' to the lens.

lenser (movies) the director of photography.

lensing (movies) the shooting of the film.

lepper (horse-racing) a good jumper, often used in hunting terminology.

less developed countries (pols) the current variant on *under-developed* countries or the Third World (qv).

lethality (milit) the ability of a weapon and its launch platform to hit and destroy targets.

letterbox (sport) in mountaineering, a rectangular hole in a narrow rock ridge.

letterbox (espionage) a place or a person that acts as a drop (qv) for information that must be channelled between members of an espionage team.

letterbox (TV) an electronically projected oblong in the bottom third of the TV screen into which extra information – subtitles, election or sports results, etc – can be projected.

letterhack (TV) amongst fans of the scifi programme 'Star Trek' one who corresponds prolifically with other fen (qv).

letter stock (stock market) unregistered stock which a company will not offer on the open market for fear of driving down the price of its officially registered stock; instead it is sold well below market value but with the advantage of

avoiding time-consuming and expensive bureaucracy.

letting it all hang out (new therapies) the concept that the absolute declaration of one's emotions, irrespective of potential offence, intimacy, etc., will have a beneficial effect on one's personality and the conduct of one's life. In the event, such 'open-ness' is little more than an insensitive flailing around of the subject's ego. (cf: *authenticity, go with the flow*)

lettrism (art) an international avant garde movement, est. c 1950, who wish to replace both figuration and abstraction in painting and sculpture with a new formal structure based on letters or signs.

lettuce (finance) paper money.

level money (commerce) in second hand car trade: the most appropriate exact multiple of £100.

levels on the splonk (bookmakers) evens, in betting odds.

leverage (finance) the ratio of debt to the proprietor's capital. On the basis of the mechanical lever which will use a little energy to move great weights. Thus *to leverage up*: to invest a small sum and borrow a much larger one.

leverage (pols) the indirect pressure that can be brought to bear on a politician by his influential supporters or other interested parties.

L.F. gear (police/UK) (abbrev) *long firm gear* often quite legitimate goods offered as the proceeds of a long firm fraud (qv) in order to attract a particular sort of customer who enjoys such flirtation with crime.

LGM (science) (abbrev) *little green men*: originally applied to pulsars by their discoverer, Anthony Hewish (1924–) with reference to scifi fantasies of extraterrestrials.

liberty (milit) a short leave in the navy, 24 hrs (RN), 48 hrs (USN).

library (theatre) a ticket agency.

library (computers) an organised collection of routines, esp. such a collection designed for one specific machine; such routines are often referred to to enable the machine to function but are not part of its actual memory.

library shot (movies) any hired film of useful material that would otherwise cost time and money to shoot and does not need to be originated for a specific film: a plane taking off, a train departing, etc. (cf: *stock shot*)

lick (rock music) a short musical phrase, particularly runs of notes on the lead or bass guitar.

lick-a-take (crime) in West Indian terminology, to pull off a successful robbery of a bank, shop, etc.

lid (pols/US) the suspension of activity on a particular topic during which time politicians and political reporters can deal with other things.

lid (drugs) approx. 1 oz marijuana.

life *n* (crime) the world of pimps, drug dealers,

or any other fantasy existence of successful and lucrative criminality.

life-actor (business) one whose position as an executive is underlined by complete and total identification and commitment to the job.

lifeboat ethics (govt) a style of foreign or domestic policy in which decisions are made strictly as to expediency/political priority and not on humanitarian grounds; thus the weakest are usually deserted to their own inadequate devices.

life-cycle analysis (marketing) a method of forecasting a new product's sales by analysing its life cycle: ie: the growth of acceptance by the various levels of purchaser from the early adapters, the early majority, the late majority and the laggards.

lifed a (aerospace) maintenance programmes for older aircraft which check all items with a specific 'life' and replace them when necessary.

lifer (milit) a career soldier, sailor, airman or marine in the US armed forces.

lifestyle (sociol, media) the way individuals or groups choose to live and the items and attitudes that epitomise the many varieties that may be chosen.

lifestyle concept (advertising) the marketing philosophy that notes the extent to which individual or family lifestyles influence consumption.

lifestyle merchandising (commerce) any sales outlet, esp. in the fashion trade, that attempts to arrange its departments or areas according to the consumers' lifestyles rather than the usual divisions by product group.

lifestyle segmentation (marketing) the subdivisions of a market based on lifestyle – interests, activities, opinions and values.

LIFO (indust relats) (acron) last in first out: the most recently employed worker is the first to lose his/her job when a firm has to issue redundancy notices.

lift (police) to arrest.

lift v (press) to raise lines of type from a composing stick onto a galley, or to prepare them for the distribution of type.

lift v (sport) in foxhunting, to remove the hounds from a lost scent in the hope of their finding it again elsewhere.

lift engrams (new therapies) in Scientology, the bringing out of prenatal memories for the purposes of therapy and the destruction of the 'aberrative content' in the patient's life.

lift-off (aerospace) 1. the launching of a rocket. 2. (parachuting) to open the parachute while standing on a wing and thus be lifted off the plane by the moving air.

liggers (rock business) hangers on, freeloaders, general term for good-for-nothings who besiege rock concerts, stars and journalists.

light and shade (theatre) the variations and gradations of delivery, dramatics, plot, etc in a given play or performance.

light art (art) the use of light in art; colour organs, fireworks, projected light, lasers, neon tube sculpture.

light bucket (science) in astronomy, a telescope which collects and focuses a large quantity of low-intensity radiation in its lens (the bucket).

lights (theatre) an electrician. (cf: *sparks*)

light water (science) water that contains less than the normal proportion (approx 0.02%) of deuterium oxide. (cf: *heavy water*)

light work (gambling) cards that are marked with very fine lines for the use of cheats; thus *strong work*: marking with heavy lines.

limb n (aerospace) the edge of a star or planet, esp. the sun, which is visible to a spacecraft.

limbo (movies, TV) any area or set that has no specific identification and thus useful as background for close-ups and inserts (qv).

limdis (espionage) (abbrev) *limited distribution*: a notation on a secret file that limits its readers to a maximum of 50 people. (cf: *exdis*)

lime (theatre/UK) any light, esp. a spotlight.

limited enquiries (police/UK) a euphemism for there being little to be done that will help an enquiry or complaint.

limited problem solving (marketing) aka: *modified re-buy*: a buying situation in which the buyer has some knowledge and experience of the product category.

limit order (futures market) an order given by a customer to a broker which has certain restrictions upon its execution such as price and time.

limousine liberal (pols) the type of wealthy liberal whose affection for the masses and concern for their plight is modified by his never having to meet them except, probably, as employees.

linage (press) 1. the charge made by a newspaper for each line in a classified advertisement. 2. the rate per line paid to freelance writers.

line n 1. (ballet) the total effect of the way a dancer's limbs and body are placed either in movement or repose. 2. (music) an instrumental or vocal melody; any structured sequence of notes or tones.

line n (advertising) a unit of space in buying print advertisements: one fourteenth of an inch high by 1 column wide.

line (business) (abbrev) *bottom line* (qv).

line (stock exchange) a large amount, spec. a line of shares.

line n (drugs) a measure of any inhalable drug – heroin, cocaine, amphetamine sulphate, etc – put on a mirror and scraped into a thin line ready for putting up the user's nose.

line (business) *above the line* and *below the line*: alternative descriptions of whether or not an account is in credit. *To pay on the line*: to pay promptly.

line work (gambling) the embellishment of

playing cards that have patterns of lines on their backs for the use of cheats.

link (radio) see: *cue*.

linkage (pols) a philosophy particularly allied to President Carter's administration (1976–1980) whereby Congress was only willing to ratify SALT II (arms limitations talks) if Russia would also take steps to improve her domestic policy on human rights, set up a grain deal, moderate 'imperialism' in Africa, etc. (cf: *detente*)

linkman (media) anyone who acts as the 'host' of a programme that contains several items and provides the verbal links between them.

lion tamer (espionage) in a blackmail operation, a strong arm man who makes sure that the target, once told that he is being blackmailed, does not make an embarrassing and potentially destructive fuss which could thus ruin the operation.

lippy (TV) in the make-up department, lipstick.

lip-sync (TV, movies) (abbrev) lip-synchronisation: sound that is recorded at the same time as pictures and which can be exactly synchronised to the lip movements of the relevant speaking character.

liquid cosh (prison/UK) any heavy tranquilliser – largactyl, etc – used to control otherwise unruly prisoners.

liquidisation (futures market) any transaction that offsets or closes out a long or short position. (cf: *offset, even up*)

liquidity (economics) the interchangeability of assets and money.

liquidity crisis (econ) a lack of ready cash available in the banks for lending to companies.

list-broker (commerce) anyone who trades in mailing lists, useful for companies, charities, inertia salesmen (qv), etc.

listening post (press) cities or places in them which are used by journalists to catch up on local or national gossip, to get stories and to cultivate sources.

listing *n* (commerce) in real estate, a property offered by its owner for sale, lease or rent.

literal *n* (computer) aka: *constant*: an instruction in a program which tells the machine how to operate that program rather than acting as an address or label (qqv); any symbol that means nothing more than itself.

literal *n* (press, advertising) aka: *typo*: a spelling error in printed matter.

little Jimmy (gambling) bingo use: the number 4.

little Joe (from Kokomo) (gambling) the point of 4 in craps.

little old ladies (media) eccentric, complaining letter writers of either sex who constantly bedevil anyone who offers opinions in the press or on TV.

little science (sci) such research or technology that requires few or inexpensive resources.

little steel (busi/US) the group of smaller steel producers.

livarisi la petra di la scarpa (Mafia) lit. 'to take the stone from one's shoe': to revenge oneself.

live *a* (theatre) any set that will be required again during the performance.

live *a* (audio) any room or enclosed area that has a relatively long reverberation time.

live card (gambling) a card that has not yet been played; either hidden in the pack or in an opponent's hand.

live food (commerce) in the health food trade, food that is 'still growing', thus fresh rather than packaged products.

live labour (pols) the Marxist description of an indispensable element in the mode of production: the purposeful expenditure of physical or mental energy during production; as this expenditure attaches itself to the product as one of its actual values, it becomes *materialised labour*.

liveware (computers) the human beings – programmers, analysts, etc – who are involved with computers. (cf: *hardware, software*)

living dead (stock market) such financial situations that neither prosper nor fail to any special extent, but merely exist interminably without any positive or negative resolution.

living in place (new therapies) the idea of one's being continually aware of the effect that everything has upon one – breathing, walking, drinking coffee and so on.

living room group (new therapies) a small encounter group; the opposite of the larger *growth centre*.

living sculpture (art) the use by an artist of his/her own body, its processes and products as the actual artwork, often as a *tableau vivant*. This concept can be extended to include animals and living plants. (cf: *performance art*)

loadability (commerce) in transport, either private or commercial, the facility with which a vehicle can be loaded.

loading (psychol) the extent to which any one factor influences an overall situation, often expressed in statistical form; such factors can be increased or decreased in the final analysis in accordance with the importance of that influence.

lob (gambling) aka *jerk*: a hanger-on at a gambling establishment who runs errands for the players. (cf: *gofer*)

lobby *n, v* (pols) the use of special pleading by various interest groups to ensure that their particular requirements and aims are looked after by the legislature. Thus the *farm lobby*, the *small business lobby*, the *environmental lobby* etc. From the 18th century use of an antechamber to the British House of Commons as a public room in which interested parties might meet and entreat their MP.

lobby-fodder (pols/UK) members of the House

of Commons who have little influence on its affairs but who still count when it is time to register a vote by walking into the 'yes' or 'no' lobby.

lobby-shopper (sex) any prostitute who solicits in hotel lobbies.

lobsterscope (theatre/US) aka: *flickerwheel* (UK): a slotted disc that can be rotated in front of a light to simulate slow motion effects.

local (computers) equipment that is installed in your own office or home and can function fully and independently, not merely a terminal.

local *n* (futures market) one who has bought a futures contract to establish a market position and who has not yet closed out the position through an offsetting sale; the opposite of short (qv).

localitis (milit) a military quirk whereby each commander sees his own position or area as central to the overall situation and urges such actions which simply do not bear on that situation; especially found in those whose actual positions are remote and marginal. By extension, a problem amongst diplomats in minor postings who attempt excessively to forward such a nation's causes.

location *n, a* (movies) any shooting of a film that is done away from the studio, 'on location'.

lock away *n* (stock market) a long term security that can be 'locked away' as an investment for the distant future.

locked in (stock market) an investor who resists taking the profits on his shares in order to avoid paying the capital gains tax that would involve.

lock on *v* (aerospace) for radar or any guidance system to trace a target and then automatically to 'follow' it as long as necessary.

lock-up *n* (printing) a device for the securing in place of a page of type.

loft *n* (theatre) that part of the stage area above the grid (qv).

loft bombing (milit) the use of an airplane's speed to project its bombs as if they were artillery shells; used to save the plane from being vaporised by the fireball that explodes under it.

lofting (aerospace) the reproduction of the original plans for an airplane in full size and the ironing out of any possible errors. Those who perform this task are *loftsmen*, their workplace is the *mould loft*.

log (sport) surfing: a large, cumbersome surfboard, resembling an unwieldy treetrunk.

logger *v* (milit/US) from Afrikaans *laager* 'camp': the hasty building of a makeshift circular defensive camp.

logic (computers) 1. the operations performed by a computer for the purposes of sorting, collecting, comparing, etc. 2. the system and principles that are the basis of the operation of a computer, of representing operations and variables (cf: *flip-flop*) by electronic and other signals.

logical *a* (computers) (abbrev) logical device: the use of an arbitrary name to refer to a physical device; thus *logical* implies a meaning that does not necessarily correspond to reality.

logical atom (philos) one of the essential and indivisible elements into which some philosophers maintain that statements can be analysed.

log in *v* (computers) aka: *log on*: to gain access to a computer by using a password (qv). Thus *log off/out*: to shut down that access by the use of a further password, either a word or number.

logoptics (art) a trademark registered in 1974 of a pictorial sign system designed to replace verbal language (ie: the instructions on medicine bottles) by a simpler, universal system.

log-rolling (pols, media, etc) from US frontier practice of everyone helping everyone else when it came to shifting heavy logs: the mutual aid between politicians whereby each would ensure their own interests were backed up when necessary by their friends and would in time return the favour; similarly found amongst critics who are also creators and thus write each other congratulatory reviews.

loid (crime/UK) from rhyming sl: Harold Lloyd = celluloid: a picklock made from a celluloid strip that works on spring (Yale) locks.

loiter *v* (milit) for a fighter plane to stay near the battle area, awaiting instructions from ground or base commanders for making swift strikes into that area. Thus *loiter time*: the length of time a plane can 'loiter', included in its specifications with its range, eg: '300 miles plus 2 hrs. loiter time'.

LOL in NAD (medic/US) (acro) *l*ittle *o*ld *l*ady in *n*o *a*pparent *d*istress: any patients (of either sex) who enjoy the comforts of a hospital but have no immediate or critical physical problems. (cf: *Gomer*)

lollipop flights (air crew) the flights at the start and end of school terms with a larger than usual proportion of children on board.

Lombard Street (finance/UK) shorthand for the financial centre of London, 'the City'; the British equivalent of Wall Street (qv).

long *a* (stock market) 1. a jobber (qv) who has bought more stock than he has sold and is in a bull (qv) position. 2. of Government stocks: having a life of more than appx. 15 yrs.

long bomb *n, v* (public relations) from the US football scoring move in which a quarterback throws to his receiver standing near or in the end-zone for a 6 pt. touch down: a supreme piece of PR work, exposing the client as required or better. (cf: *key book*)

long firm fraud (police/UK) a fraud in which a large amount of goods are purchased on credit then sold quickly and cheaply; the 'firm' established for the deal then vanishes without paying off the wholesalers.

L

longform (radio/US) programmes which concentrate on lengthy, in-depth news features and analysis, rather than collections of brief headlines and newsflashes.

long hedge (futures market) a hedge (qv) against a fall in interest rates; thus *short hedge*: a hedge against a rise in interest rates.

long legged (sport) sailing: any vessel that draws a lot of water.

longs (stock market) long term stocks.

long term team (social work) a group of social workers who deal with cases that are assessed as being likely to continue for some time, esp. over a minimum of 3 mths.

long Tom (photog) especially high-power lenses for still or TV/movie cameras, often used for long-distance work or in espionage for surveillance and 'candid' shots.

look-down, shoot-down capability (milit) the combination of airborne radar (look-down) and air-to-air missiles (shoot-down) for mutually useful destructive action.

looker (commerce) one who expresses interest in looking over various properties, but who obviously has no real interest in buying one.

look-in (sport) US football: a quick pass thrown to a receiver who is running diagonally across the centre of the field.

Looking Glass (milit) the flying command post which preceded Cover All (qv). So called because it reflected (like a mirror) in the air those same control and command capabilities of land-based posts.

look-out book (govt) a list of prohibited or suspect aliens used by HM Customs for checking immigrants to the UK; twenty different codes list some 20,000 suspects – political subversives, immorality, criminal offences, lack of work permit, etc; not everyone is barred, but the 'book' aims to ensure that all are known.

look-see (commerce) in fashion: the audition taken by a model who is looking for work from photographers, magazines, etc.

loop *n* (computers) a sequence of instructions that are repeated over and over by the computer until such time as a given criterion has been fulfilled.

loop *n* (govt/US) in the Reagan Administration, that inner circle of advisers who receive top level restricted information.

Lord Whelks (press) in *Private Eye*: Lord Matthews, proprietor of Express Newspapers, Trafalgar House, Cunard Lines, etc; so called after his proletarian origins.

loose change (govt) minor concessions/demands that determine the course of diplomatic negotiations. (cf: *bargaining chips*)

loss leader (commerce) a product which is offered at an exceptionally low price in order to tempt buyers towards other, more expensive products.

loss-pricing (commerce) the holding down of prices despite the possible losses this may entail, in the hope of luring customers away from one's (temporarily) more expensive rivals.

lost (milit) any shell or mortar round that has not been seen to explode by a spotter.

lost sculptures (sculpture) 'lost' stands as the opposite of 'found' as in 'found objects' (qv): sculptures with so sparse a visual appeal that they may be seen simply as nondescript objects of the everyday world. Thus *invisible sculpture* where the spectator must take the structure of such a work purely on trust.

lot (movies) the land around a film studio, and owned by that studio, which can be used for exterior filming.

Lot's wife (milit) RN: the salt cellar in the mess.

lounge *n* (entertainment) the auditorium, usually a night club, in which a singer or comedian performs. (cf: *room*)

love-bombing (sociol) the softening up process aimed at a potential convert to a 'cult' religion (Moonies, Hare Krishna, etc) whereby its members saturate the neophyte with affection, optimism, Utopian theories, etc, and thus seduce him/her into the cult, at which point the realities may seem less appealing but escape from conditioning has become less simple.

loving (new therapies) usually as 'loving relationship': the emphasis is on emotional rather than physical love, although the inference is on a fully integrated relationship (hetero- or homosexual) in which the needs, feelings and all other desires of each individual are accepted and nurtured by the other. (cf: *caring*)

low (commerce) in the antique rug trade: a rug with insufficiently long pile; a worn rug.

low abstraction (sociol, business) those incapable of conceiving of or manipulating abstract concepts: essentially white collar proletariat; the lower echelons of a corporation, employed in routine and spiritually unrewarding occupations such as filing or copy-typing.

lowball *v* (commerce) for a salesman to lure customers by offering an estimate so low that there is no possibility that, once contracts are signed, it will be honoured.

lowballer (stock market) an investment manager who deliberately underestimates any future predictions of expected financial results.

low belly strippers (gambling) a pack of cards prepared for cheating in which the edges of the high cards are concave – after being 'stripped' with a scalpel – and can thus easily be identified. (cf: *high belly strippers*)

low key (movies, photog) any image in which the majority of tones are dark or grey.

low loader (TV) a low, wheeled, flatbed platform towed behind a moving vehicle for the cameraman to shoot interiors of that vehicle, chase sequences, etc.

low profile (milit, business, govt) in a military

L

sense, the keeping of a low profile by vehicle, weapon or human will offer the least target to enemy troops; thus in government or business use low profile implies anonymity, the resistance to publicity, the reluctance to extract oneself from a grey mass. (cf: *high profile*)

low-stream industries (business) small industry with the accent on the individual or local aspects rather than the multinational corporation; almost a cottage industry.

lox (aerospace) (acron) *l*iquid *ox*ygen: the main propellant for rockets.

LPC (milit) British Army: (acro) *l*eather *p*ersonnel *c*arrier: a boot.

LPT (computers) (abbrev) line printer.

L-systems (milit) early versions of early-warning command and control systems developed in the period immediately following the US's perceived humiliation after the launch (1957) of Sputnik I. These various systems were amalgamated into the National Military Command System.

LTP (TV/US) (abbrev) living telops: pictures on a screen that show the story for which the commentary is provided not by an on-the-spot reporter, but by the newscaster reading over those pictures.

lucky dip (air crew) the practice of aircraft loaders who snatch suitcases, bags or packages at random, on the off-chance that they might contain something worth stealing.

lucrative target (milit) any target worth considering for destruction.

lucy (advertising) aka: *grant*: the proprietary names of two photographic processors most generally used by graphic designers.

lucy (theatre) a light with a 24″ diameter lens.

lugger (gambling) anyone who transports players to a game of cards, dice, roulette, etc.

lulu (govt/US) from 'in lieu of': a flat payment made to legislators to cover expenses and replacing their need to itemise such expenses for greater scrutiny by the Treasury.

lumber (gambling) 1. the spectators at a casino. 2. players who have run out of money, 'dead wood'.

luminal art (art) aka: *luminist art*: any art form which is based on lights or lighting effects.

lunar armour (aerospace) a special hardened aluminium spacesuit used for missions on the moon.

lunar window (aerospace) the launch window (qv) through which a spacecraft must pass to achieve a successful moon landing.

lunchtime abortion (medic) any quick abortion – and thus possible during a lunch-break – which is carried out by the use of vacuum aspiration.

lurk *v* (milit) RN: ordered to perform a distasteful job without any chance of escaping the duty.

L

M (govt) (abbrev) MBE.

M1, M2, M3, M4 (econ) (abbrev) Money 1. 2. 3. 4. M1: the basic money supply, consisting of currency in circulation plus demand deposits held in current (cheque) accounts. M2: the money supply of a country, including M1, also commercial bank time deposits but not certificates of deposit. M3: the overall money supply of a country, including M2, plus deposits in savings and loan associations, etc, and certificates of deposit. M4: (not generally used by economists) savings bonds and credit union shares.

ma (theatre/UK) a theatrical landlady.

Macbeth trap (theatre/US) a trap door covering a lift on which such surprise entrances as that of Hamlet's father, sundry ghosts, etc can be made.

macer (police/UK) a thief or cheat; a practitioner of the three card trick.

Macguffin (movies) a plot device created by Alfred Hitchcock (1899–1981) as a 'demented red herring' after which the characters in his films chased but which in the end had absolutely no relevance to the plot or its solution.

machine art (art) any artwork created from mechanical or electronic devices. Thus *machine sculpture*.

machine code (computers) aka: *machine language*: the binary notation 'translation' of any other language (BASIC, COBOL, etc) which can as such be 'understood' by the machine and is necessary for the machine to perform the required tasks. (cf: *high-level language*)

machine time (computers) the time a machine takes to perform a given task. (cf: *user time*)

machtpolitik (pols) from Ger. 'power politics': power politics; the use of strength rather than mere diplomacy to achieve a required result. (cf: *realpolitik*)

mack man (sex) probably from Fr. 'maquereau': pimp. Thus *hard mack* a tough, sadistic, mean pimp; *sweet mack* or *sugar pimp*: a generous, tolerant pimp.

macky (theatre, TV) from Fr. 'maquillage': make-up.

Macready pauses (theatre) a marked pause or noticeable catching of the breath before delivering certain lines. From William Charles Macready (1793–1873) whose delivery epitomised such melodramatics.

macromarketing (commerce) the investigation of marketing behaviour by analysing an entire marketing system. (cf: *micromarketing*)

MAD (milit) (acro) *m*utually *a*ssured *d*estruction: the basis of the nuclear standoff between USA and USSR – any nuclear war must inevitably lead to the total destruction of the world of today. Under the Reagan Administration a new concept, of a *winnable* nuclear war, has been emerging.

made bills (econ) bills of exchange that are drawn abroad and payable abroad, but negotiable in the UK.

made up/made down (stock market) the process of settling those deals left unresolved by a member of the Exchange who has been hammered (qv).

madman theory (milit) developed by President Richard Nixon on the principle that were he to act crazy enough, his opponents would deem him capable of the worst excesses and thus negotiate, if only to stop the world vanishing in a nuclear holocaust.

magazine (TV) in the Teletext information system, a group of 100 visual 'pages' indexed together for coding purposes.

magic *a* (computers) 1. as yet unexplained, or too complicated to explain. 2. a feature of the machine's operation which is not generally publicised, but which allows for operations that would otherwise be considered impossible.

magic acid (science) in chemistry, fluorosulphonic acid (FSO_3H) into which antimony pentafluoride is dissolved and which thus possesses exceptional qualities as a reagent.

magic bullet (medic) a drug or other medicinal agent that can destroy disease carrying bacteria, viruses, cancers, etc, without harming the host.

magic moment (TV, movies) a time, just after sunset, when there is still sufficient light for shooting, especially useful for 'romantic' scenes.

magic numbers (science) those numbers that indicate particular stability in a proton or neutron count: 2, 8, 20, 28, 50, 82, 126 (and possibly 184).

magic numbers (gambling) a number that represents a combination of wins for a leader (as in a football league) and losses for the rivals which automatically guarantee the leader's ultimate victory.

magic shop (new therapies) in psychodramatic therapy, the concept of creating for the patient a 'magic shop' in which he can ask for anything he wants and must 'pay' with something he himself values. The therapist is the 'shop-keeper' and the intent is for the patient to thus appreciate the conflicts within himself.

magic spot (medic) guanosine tetraphosphate (ppGpp), the appearance of which in cells is supposed to inhibit the synthesis of ribosomal RNA. Thus named from the unexpected spots that show up in cells so affected.

magnetic bottle (science) a magnetic field that confines a plasma in a thermo-nuclear reaction.

magnetic mirror (science) 1. a magnetised surface that reflects light. 2. a magnetically charged field that causes advancing particles to be repelled.

magnolia (pols/US) shorthand for anything referring to or coming out of the American South.

maiden (horse-racing) a horse that has yet to win its first race; thus *to break one's maiden* is to achieve a first victory; both terms are equally applicable to jockeys.

mail art (art) any art in which the use of the postal system plays a major part; by its nature this art is often collaborative, as in a 'chain-letter' collage.

mail box (computers) a set of locations within the machine's RAM (qv) storage area which are reserved specifically for those instructions addressed either to a peripheral (qv) or to another microprocessor.

mail cover (espionage) the illegal opening of selected mail by the CIA; when practised by the FBI, the operation is called the *mail run.*

mailing shot (advertising) the sending out of material to potential customers as part of a campaign.

mainframe (computers) the largest type of computer installations with great capacity, large and static equipment, requiring installation in air conditioned rooms and other special criteria for use. Orig. used to describe the main framework of the central processing unit within a large computer but now, with the development of mini- and micro-computers, to mean that large, central machine.

main plane (aerospace) the principal supporting surface of an aircraft.

mainstream *v* (social wk) for a social worker to gain government recognition, funds and action for a pet project by taking it off the sidelines and forcing the relevant authorities to take notice.

mainstream (rock business) to adapt one's music to a more generally popular if less demanding style. (cf: *MOR, AOR*)

mainstream economics (econ) in Marxist terms, the type of Western capitalist economics that is based upon market forces and analysis at the expense of any social or political factors.

mainstreaming (educ) to place the exceptional child – whether more or less intelligent than his/her peers – back into the normal classroom world of the 'average' children.

maintenance margin (futures market) a sum, usually smaller than the initial margin, but a part of it, that must be held on deposit at all times against the possibility of a customer's equity (qv) dropping down to or below the level of this deposit, at which point it can be used to bolster that equity.

major (commerce) any major company, implying usually the multinational conglomerates on a general level, and the various field leaders when taking more specific industries.

majors (movies) the large film companies – MGM, Columbia, Paramount, etc – as opposed to the indies (qv).

make an ascension (theatre/UK) to forget one's lines or one's business; they simply 'fly into the air'.

make a number (milit) USMC: 1. to gain a promotion when a vacancy occurs. 2. to pay one's respects to a senior officer.

make good (gambling) for everyone in a round of betting to place a stake in the pot equal to that bet by the first player in a round.

make off (theatre/UK) 1. *n* one of the two flats (qv) furthest downstage to the left and right of the set. 2. *v* to tie up a rope.

make-up (finance) the balancing of accounts at a set date.

make-up editor (press) aka: *stone sub, stone editor, production editor*: the editor who supervises the setting up of the individual typeset pages of a newspaper.

malhini (sport) in surfing: from Hawaiian 'stranger', a novice or beginner.

mallet *v* (milit) British Army: to shell.

man *n* (drugs) 1. the dealer or connection. 2. the police.

managed bond (econ) a special bond fund into which an investor buys and whose managers then invest on the basis of their own expertise in whatever areas will produce the ideal returns.

managed currency (finance) a currency system that is managed by the government of the nation which uses it.

managed news (pols) that information supplied by government sources and press officers which sets government interests over public ones, particularly when it comes to hiding 'sensitive' and controversial facts. (cf: *word-engineering*)

management by exception (business) the reduction of extraneous material in management decision-taking by eliminating all information from reports other than that which details a significant deviation from a plan, budget or other established procedure.

M

management buy-out (indust relats) a situation whereby the management of a liquidated company use their own cash to buy up their firm and start it working again.

manchesterise *v* (indust relats) in the cotton industry, the unrestricted importation of low-cost textiles from abroad which tends to undermine home industry. Originally used by European rivals of 19th century Manchester, but latterly used by a declining Manchester itself.

mandarin (govt) a senior British civil servant, supposedly possessor of the intellect, deviousness and subtle powers of his Chinese predecessor. (cf: *brahmin*)

mandated programme (TV) a programme that the IBA (the British independent television authority) compels all its affiliated stations to broadcast.

m and e track (movies) (abbrev) music and effects track: a tape of the music and any special effects in a film which is used at the editing and dubbing (qv) stage of assembling a film.

mandies (drugs) mandrax (methaqualone); see *drug names.*

M and M (medic/US) (abbrev) *m*orbidity and *m*ortality: who is still sick and who has died, the basic statistics for discussion at the regular scheduled conference of a hospital's medical hierarchy.

manfredi (movies) a film stunt in which cars are spun at high speeds to simulate dramatic crashes.

manifold (commerce) aka: *bible*: in the meat trade, a hard, round portion of a cow's stomach which is generally consigned to the pet food market.

manipulated democracy (pols) the Marxist concept that the alleged 'choices' between left and right in a capitalist state are in fact no choices at all and that all such elections are simply cypher votes for handpicked and non-representative candidates.

manipulative (sociol) a popular feminist buzzword for the condemnation of whatever particular male excess is deemed worthy of attack within the relevant context.

manor (police/UK) aka: *patch*: any police district or unit of police administration.

man-rate *v* (aerospace) to certify a rocket or other space vehicle as safe for manned flight and operation.

many (milit) eight or more; planes, troops, tanks, guns, etc. (cf: *few*)

MAP (milit) (acro) *m*ultiple *a*im *p*oint *s*ystem: the concept of reducing the vulnerability of static missiles which stand in silos by shuttling them about between a variety of underground silos and thus, ideally, confusing hostile forces. MAP was one of the systems designed to protect the proposed MX system. (cf: *dense pack*)

map (computers) a diagram which explains where the programs and other data are stored within a computer system.

map of Ireland (commerce) in the hotel trade, the chambermaid's description of semen stains on bedsheets.

marage (aerospace) (acro) martensite ageing: a superhard steel with minimal carbon content and high in nickel, which is used in constructing rockets. It can be rolled to a very thin gauge and will withstand extremes of heat distortion.

marathon (new therapies) an extra-lengthy session of group therapy.

marbling (commerce) in the meat trade, the thin layers of fat which streak the best varieties of lean meat and when cooked will help keep it moist.

margin (stock market) an amount payable on a speculative order by a client, the balance of which is financed by the broker. If the price of a share bought 'on the margin' falls so far as to require the use of that margin payment, the broker may close the transaction rather than place his own capital at risk.

margin (futures market) a cash amount of funds which must be deposited with a broker or a leading member of the exchange as a guarantee of fulfilment of a futures contract.

marginal *n* (pols) a constituency of the House of Commons in which the vote may go unpredictably to either of the main contenders in an election.

marginal *a* (computers) 1. extremely small. 2. of minimal worth or merit. 3. with an extremely low probability of succeeding.

marginalism (econ) an economic system which lays stress on any marginal factors in the economy.

marginal weather (aerospace) weather conditions that are barely acceptable for either safe or legal flying.

margin call (stock/futures markets) a demand for extra funds after a fall in prices or problems with delivery to guarantee the margin (qv) or the overall investment.

margin men (drugs) drug runners or smugglers who act as middlemen between the bulk importers and the wholesalers; margin men often manage to resist the lure of their wares and work simply for profit.

mark (espionage) any victim of blackmail or an allied confidence trick who can be conveniently used on the basis of this weakness, even though there was no pre-arranged plan to trap him. (cf: *target*)

mark (milit) a code word indicating an order to fire a weapon.

mark *n* (stock market) the price at which a bargain has been executed and which is thus recorded in the press and in the Official List.

M

mark *n* (computer) a punched hole in the paper tape used by older and larger computers.

market (stock market) the actual dealing floor of the London Stock Exchange.

market aggregation (marketing) aka: *undifferentiated marketing*: the concept that assumes all consumers in the market to have similar requirements and as such can be reached and persuaded in the same way.

market communism (pols) aka: *80% communism*: a rare concept that postulates a Communism which places 20% of its economy within free markets, notably those dealing in luxury consumer items.

market letter (press/US) a directive from the proprietor or editor indicating that a specific story is to be covered and that it is to be written in a specific way (possibly to praise or condemn the proprietor's special interest or bugbear). (cf: *house job*)

market order (futures market) an order to a broker telling him to buy or sell at once at the best possible price.

market penetration (marketing) a strategy for obtaining extra sales with the same product and the same target market and concentrating on gaining a greater share of that market.

market potential (marketing) the maximum amount of a product that can be bought from suppliers in a given period, given an intense promotional effort throughout the market.

market research (marketing) the study of a market for a product.

market segmentation (marketing) the subdivision of a market into relatively homogeneous parts, so that plans can be made to cover each of the segments thus created; a popular way of defining the various target markets.

market Socialism (pols) orig. in 1930s by Otto Lange: a strong market economy with only a minimum of discreet planning and state interference but with a predominantly social ownership of the means of production.

marketing concept (marketing) the concept that an organisation must attempt to understand and anticipate consumer needs as a basis for all decisions affecting its own market.

marketing mix (marketing) the composite of plans created by an organisation to cover promotion, pricing, research, distribution and so on; and the finding of a correct balance between the various areas so developed.

marketing research (marketing) the study of the marketing of a product.

mark it! (TV, movies) an instruction for the clapper loader (qv) to operate his clapperboard prior to the start of a new take (qv).

mark mark (milit) a command from a ground controller to a pilot instructing him to release his bombs. (cf: *mark*)

mark of the beast (milit) RN: the colourful flashes worn on the lapels of a midshipman's jacket.

mark to mark (stock market) the process whereby all the profits and losses of a day's trading are paid in and out of the Clearing House (qv).

markup *n* (govt/US) the process of putting a legislative bill into its final form.

mark-up *n* (commerce) the amount a retailer adds on to the wholesale price of goods to pay his overheads and provide a profit.

mark-up (crime/UK) *at the mark-up* implies a villain (or corrupt policeman) who takes more than his fair share of a bribe, a blackmail payment or the proceeds of a robbery.

married failure (milit) in naval warfare, a mine that has failed to detach itself from its seabed mooring despite being electronically triggered.

married print (TV, movies, advert) a film which is correctly synchronised as to sound and picture.

marry *v* (stock market) the setting of one transaction against another, such as a buying order against a selling one.

marry Mistress Roper *v* (milit) to enlist in the Royal Marines; from the RN nickname for the Marines, whose naval skills were considered to be those of a woman, in particular the mythical and cack-handed Mistress Roper.

marry up *v* (commerce) for an auctioneer to put two lots together when one is obviously less likely to sell on its own due to damage, worthlessness or some other defect.

Martini norm (business) the concept that one supplier in an industry is, as far as consumers are concerned, much the same as another. This assumption, disastrous for marketing such rival products, is ostensibly overcome by the provision of drunken lunches and similar inducements to salesmen and retailers.

MARV (milit) (acron) *m*anoeuvrable *r*e-entry *v*ehicle: any missile that can be steered electronically onto the target. (cf: *MIRV*, *smart bomb*)

Mary Ann (milit) USN: a floating salvage crane used to pick up aircraft that have fallen off or overshot carriers.

Mary Sue stories (TV) amateur storylines written by fans of US TV's scifi series 'Star Trek'; such stories invariably centre on the author's self-projection as 'Mary Sue', a hitherto unknown who saves the TV heroes, seduces her favourite star and generally takes over.

marzipan (commerce) in the second-hand car trade, the filler used to make good the bodywork of a crashed or ageing car.

mashie (sport) in golf, the traditional name for the Number 5 iron.

mashie-niblick (sport) in golf, the traditional name for the Number 6 or Number 7 iron.

mask (movies) a technical device for blocking out part of the filmed image.

M

mask *v* (advertising) the blocking out of unwanted parts of picture required in an advertisement by covering them with card or paper.

massive retaliation (milit) a nuclear policy originated c1960 with the intention of launching a savage, nuclear counter-attack against any aggression, no matter how restrained, and irrespective of whether or not that aggression involved nuclear weapons.

MAST (aerospace) (acro) *m*ilitary *a*nti-shock *t*rousers: special pressurised trousers worn by astronauts.

master (record business) 1. *n* the tape of a record after the mixing process (qv) is completed. 2. *n* a vinyl record which is used as the basis for the mass production of a particular record. 3. *v* to complete the final stages of making a record, ie. producing (2).

master shot (movies) 1. a shot in which the camera is so placed as to encompass all the action that takes place. 2. a single shot of an entire piece of dramatic action into which detail – close-ups, reaction shots, effects, etc – can be interlaced at the editing stage.

masthead (press) the title of the newspaper plus a list of its personnel printed in a box and placed in a conspicuous position somewhere in the paper.

masthead (TV) by extension from press use (qv), the symbol of a station or production company that precedes a programme or broadcast.

masthead (advertising) the specific style of the name or title of a paper or magazine.

mat (press) (abbrev) matrix: 1. the stereotypers' flong (qv) after a mould has been made. 2. the individual brass letter moulds on a linotype composing machine.

match dissolve (movies) a (clichéd) dissolve from one scene to another whereby an object in one scene – say a church clock – turns into a similar object – a watch face – in the next one.

matched orders (stock market) 1. the illegal manipulation of a price by the simultaneous ordering of different brokers to sell and buy the same stock. 2. a legitimate matching of buy and sell orders by a specialist in a stock who aims to arrange an opening price that matches as nearly as possible the previous closing price (qqv).

Matelots (police/UK) Metropolitan Police nickname for the London River Police. (cf: *Land Crabs*)

materialism (pols) the philosophy that the universe consists only of matter and that any concept of a spiritual basis to the universe or to human minds is irrelevant. (cf: *historical materialism, dialectical materialism*)

materiel (milit) from Fr. for 'material': all the non-human resources of an army – guns, ammunition, planes, missiles, electronic surveillance equipment, explosives, etc.

mateys (milit) RN: dockyard workers.

matrix (govt) originally meaning a place of origin or growth, or the mould from which copies might be taken, matrix (like parameter, qv) has taken on many and flexible meanings for bureaucrats. Used in government, it can mean 1. context; 2. one variety of many; 3. the totality of an event or concept.

matt (movies) aka: *matte*: a device that blends actors who have been filmed in a studio with backgrounds either shot on location or created by special effects. The actor is shot against a non-reflective background, eg. black velvet; a high contrast negative is then combined with the desired background and thus 'monsters' or 'ghosts' can appear in the same scene as humans, all equally 'alive'.

matt down (music) to perfect one's playing or singing. From the painter's putting a smooth, matt surface on his work.

matter (press) any manuscript or copy that has to be printed; type that has been composed. Thus *live matter* is awaiting printing, *dead matter* has been used.

matter art (art) a genre of the 1950s in which the artist used such 'unworthy' materials as sand, cinders, sacking etc in place of or as well as traditional oil paint. The intention was to add extra 'reality' to the work.

mature *a* (TV) a euphemism for violence or sex in programmes or films.

mayday (milit, radio) from Fr. 'm'aidez!' = help me!: an international radio callsign for emergency assistance; usually broadcast over 121.5 mHz.

maximax (business) a strategy that concentrates on making decisions which will maximise potential profits, however much such decisions may also intensify potential risks. (cf: *maximin, minimax*)

maximin (business) aka: *pessimism criterion*: a business strategy in which all decisions are designed to maximise the chances of incurring the minimal potential loss, however much that may simultaneously minimise potential profit.

maximum price fluctuation (futures market) aka: *limit price* the maximum amount the contract price can fluctuate up or down during one trading session.

maximum security dormitory (prison/US) cellblock.

mazut (commerce) in the oil trade, a viscous liquid residue left from the distillation of Russian petrol, used as fuel oil or low-grade lubricant.

MBFR (milit) (acro) *m*utual and *b*alanced *f*orce *r*eductions: one of the negotiating demands involved in US/USSR arms limitation talks.

MBO (management) (acro) *m*anagement *b*y *o*bjective: the manager and his assistants decide on the firm's objectives and the workers agree to work towards them. This style of consultative management is intended to alleviate stress in industrial relations as well as boost wages and productivity, since the workforce should now feel it has a personal interest in the firm's prosperity.

ME (new therapies) (acro) *marriage* e*ncounter*: a style of therapy for married couples who meet in small encounter groups for discussion and theoretically the improvement of their own relationships. Despite ME's current non-denominationality, it was founded in the 1950s by Fr. Gabriel Calvo, a Spanish priest and brought to the US by Chuck Gallagher, SJ, in 1968.

meaningful (sociol) usually seen as a prefix to 'relationship' or 'experience' and implying something exceptional and out of ordinary, with a deeper spiritual appreciation of the relationship/experience involved than might otherwise be expected. (cf: *caring*, *loving*)

measles (espionage) CIA use for a death achieved without any apparent cause other than natural ones.

meatball (milit) USN: the arrangement of coloured lights on the deck of a carrier by which a pilot can correct the speed and direction of his approach at night and land accordingly; in the daytime the lights are replaced by a mirror into which a light is shone at 3° and similar course corrections can be made against this reflected light.

meateater (police/US) a corrupt policeman who is not satisfied with those bribes he is offered, but demands such payments of his own volition. (cf: *grasseater*)

meat rack (sex) a gathering place, found in most cities, for young homosexual prostitutes; that in London is found at Piccadilly Circus, next to the County Fire Office.

meat shot (sex) in pornographic films or pictures, a close-up of an erect penis, the 'open' vagina, or actual penetration during intercourse. (cf: *flap shot*)

meat wagon (prison/UK) a police van which contains separate compartments for the transport of prisoners either to and from the courts or between various prisons.

meat wagon (medic/US) aka: *trauma truck*: ambulance.

meat wagon (police) aka: *Black Maria* (UK): any police van for transporting officers, taking away those arrested, ferrying prisoners from jail to court, etc.

meaty *a* (theatre) aka: *fat*: a good, showy role with plenty of lines, business and emotion.

mec (milit) French Foreign Legion: a well dressed legionnaire; probably a corruption of Fr. 'maquereau' = a pimp.

mec art (art) (abbrev) mechanical art, those 'paintings' produced entirely by the creative manipulation of photo-mechanical reproduction processes, epitomised in the work of Robert Rauschenburg and Andy Warhol.

mechanic (gambling) a skillful cardsharp who uses sleight of hand to gain his successes.

mechanical *n* (press, advertising) the artwork and its accompanying copy assembled and ready for printing.

mechanical games (gambling) any games of chance that lack the element of skill (ie: in poker): craps, roulette, etc.

mechanic's grip (gambling) a method of holding a deck of cards which facilitates dealing from the bottom of the pack and similar tricks: three fingers are curled around the long edge of the deck while the index finger is at the narrow upper edge away from the body.

media behaviour (sociol) an assessment of an individual's attention to the various forms of media as sources of news and information.

media buzz (rock business) the growing interest in a new record from the press, TV, radio and specialist publications, all of which aids promotion and sales.

media event (pols, PR, etc) any supposed event of importance that is staged less for its actual effect than for its impact on the TV, radio and print journalists who have been mustered to take note of it.

media fragmentation (marketing) the concept that there are too many outlets for the concentration of a successful campaign; the customers are assailed by too many appeals to their pockets for one to make the desired impact.

media vehicle (marketing) any specific communications medium: TV, radio, print.

media weight (marketing) 1. the measure of various qualitative factors when planning where to advertise. 2. the quantity of advertising used in a promotion.

Medicaid mill (medic/US) a private clinic where the doctors indulge in malpractice by charging the Medicaid health insurance scheme for services that are either unnecessary or were never even performed for a patient.

medium dated (stock market) a gilt-edged (qv) security which has more than five but less than ten years to run before its final redemption date.

MEECN (milit) (acro) Minimum Essential Emergency Communications Network: US last-ditch radio network carried on aircraft or satellites; all use very low frequency transmitters and would be activated if other, more sophisticated communications were destroyed.

meet *n* (police/UK) an appointment, 'one to meet', usually with the implication that a policeman is meeting a contact, an informer, or a villain.

meet 'em and street 'em (medic/US) the process of evaluating admissions to a hospital Emergency Room whereby those insufficiently hurt to be considered real emergencies are sent smartly back onto the street.

meg *v* (movies) from the abbrev. for *megaphone*

M

which was used by directors in the silent movies era: to direct a picture; thus *megger* is the director.

meg (finance) $1,000,000.

megadeath (milit) 1,000,000 deaths, a basic unit for the assessment of possible casualty rates in a nuclear war. Thus *megacorpse* the detritus of one megadeath; *megadestruction* the destruction of several megadeaths.

megastructures (archit) aka: *omnibuildings*: the concept of erecting vast new structures which would replace existing cities, submerge individual styles in a 'total environment' and facilitate the demand for 'total mobility'.

MEGO (press/US) (acro) *my eyes glaze over*: anything that combines undeniable importance with massive tedium in considering it.

meller (movies, theatre) (abbrev) melodrama.

melon-cutting (stock market) the dividing up and sharing of large and generous profits.

melon-cutting (gambling) the dividing up of heavy winnings, often by a syndicate of horse-race bettors.

meltdown (energy) the collapse of the core of a reactor at a nuclear power-station, possibly through the malfunction of its cooling system, when it has become heated above its melting point. Such a meltdown may well cause a major disaster if it develops a critical mass of fissile fuel which can sustain a chain reaction and thus a nuclear explosion.

memorial release (movies, records) the cashing in on the death of major stars by the speedy re-release of their greatest films or records.

memory (computers) that part of a computer in which data and programs can be stored and from which they can be retrieved when required.

memory bank (computers) the memory unit of a computer plus the data it contains.

mental handicap (soc wk) a euphemism for 'sub-average intellectual functioning and impaired adaptive behaviour'.

menu (computers) a list of instructions and service options which appears at the start of a program and which shows the user what particular tasks he may expect to accomplish.

menu (TV) the 'trailer' which list the items that will be featured in a news review programme, ie: 'Nationwide', BBC-TV.

merge and purge (advertising) aka: *purge and merge*: the blending of two mailing lists by purging those names and addresses that appear in both and merging the remains for a definitive list.

message unit (advert) the preferred description of advertising slots on TV or radio.

mess traps (milit) RN: kitchen equipment and utensils.

metal Mike (sport) in yachting, the automatic helmsman. (cf: *George*)

metamatics (art) a series of combination sculp-

tures and painting machines created and built by Fr. artist Jean Tinguely from 1955 to 1959.

metapolicymaking (business) the making of policy on how to make policy; it involves three main elements: identifying problems, values and resources and allotting them to various policymaking units; designing, evaluating and redesigning the policy-making system; determining major policy making strategies.

meteor bumper (aerospace) a protective structure built onto the exterior of a spacecraft to make it secure from being damaged by a shower of meteors.

method *n* (theatre) a system for training actors which emphasises inner emotional experience, discovered through improvisation, over technical expertise; based on the theories and practice of Konstantin Stanislavsky (1863–1938) and elaborated and continued at the Actors' Studio in New York, founded in 1947 by Lee Strasberg, Cheryl Crawford and Elia Kazan.

Mexican stand-off (gambling) the quitting of a gambling game when one has lost or won only a small amount; from the sl. meaning of a confrontation in which neither party has an edge and both are most likely to give up and walk away.

mezzanine financing (finance) on the principle of 'getting in on the ground floor', those investors who offer finance not at the very start of a project but just before it is opened up to the public at large.

Michigan bankroll (gambling) a large and ostentatious bankroll which consists of many low denomination bills wrapped around with one large one.

Mickey Mouse *n, a* (milit) anything petty, unnecessary, outdated, obstructive; regulations that exist for nothing but the sake of having regulations.

Mickey Mouse *n* (movies) a sound track style in which the music that accompanies a film relates directly and even mimics the action on the screen; initially a cartoon technique but extended into general use.

micromarketing (commerce) the analysis of a marketing situation by looking only at an individual firm or consumer. (cf: *macromarketing*)

MICU (medic/US) (acro) *medical intensive care unit*. Thus *SICU*: surgical intensive care unit.

midder (medic/UK) (abbrev) midwife, midwifery.

middle eight (music) the eight bars in the middle of a conventionally structured tune, often structured separately from the rest of that tune.

middle novel (lit crit) the second or third novel of a writer whose original work showed potential but who has yet to achieve a massive paperback advance or film sale. In the current literary marketplace, such novelists find fewer and fewer buyers for their worthy but, alas, uncommercial efforts.

middleware (computers) computer software (qv) designed to perform tasks that stand midway between control programs and applications programs.

midrash (milit) USN: (abbrev) *midnight rations*: the late night meal on a nuclear submarine.

mike *v* (audio, TV, movies) to place a microphone near someone, or to attach one to clothes or the throat for the purposes of recording.

mike (drugs) (abbrev) microgram: the basic measure of LSD (qv).

mileage (TV) the potential long run of a TV series format for a situation comedy or soap opera (qqv). (cf: *legs*)

milieu therapy (psychol) a form of group psychotherapy that relies mainly on the environment created by the patients involved and the staff and unit who deal with them.

military advisors (milit) unofficial troops sent by the superpowers into those countries where they wish to advance their causes or bolster up their supporters. The theory is that such advisors have no real involvement, the practice is that they at least train local troops and often fight alongside them as well.

military medium (sport) in cricket, straight, regular up and down bowling that makes up in accuracy what it lacks in speed but on neither count worries a reasonable batsman.

milk *v* (theatre) to obtain the maximum audience reaction, whether for a joke, a dramatic incident or whatever.

milk run (air crew) orig. RAF/USAF use for bombing missions that encountered little anti-aircraft fire, now used by commercial airlines to describe the routine flights to and from the major European capitals.

Millerandism (pols) a derogatory left-wing term to describe those socialist MPs in any country who are elected on a radical platform but drift inexorably to the right. From the career of A. Millerand (1859–1943), elected to the French parliament as a radical in 1885 and who moved so far to the right that from 1920 to 1924 he was the President of the Republic.

minder (police/UK) a strong-arm man who takes care of a criminal, collecting protection money and similar payments, working as a bodyguard and generally stands in as 'muscle'.

minder (press) Ministry of Defence press censors who were in charge of the war correspondents in the Falklands from April to June 1982; much resented for their interfering and inconsistencies.

mind fucking (new therapies) in est (qv) terminology: thinking.

mind-set (new therapies) one's mental attitudes and opinions, by inference those which are firmly set and which one is unwilling to alter without a struggle.

minimal art (art) aka: *ABC art, anti-illusionism, barebones art, cool art, know nothing nihilism, literalist art, idiot art, object art, reductive art, rejective art, primary structures*. Almost always in the form of sculpture, such art rejects any elements of illusion or expressiveness in favour of clarity and simplicity, eg: Carl André's controversial pile of bricks at the Tate Gallery.

minimax (business) aka: *regret criterion* a business strategy which concentrates on minimising the possibility of a maximum loss. (cf: *maximax, maximin*)

minimum price fluctuation (futures market) the smallest amount of price movement possible in the trading of a given contract.

mini-page (advertising) a press space appx. 75% of the width of the page and 75% of its depth, completely surrounded by editorial matter.

mini-series (TV) the television version of a best-selling novel, or possibly the remake of a once major film, which is divided up for maximum audience ratings and advertising revenue over three or four nights.

minus advantage (espionage) an operation that failed and resulted in those involved being left in a worse position than they were before it was launched.

minus advantage (business) by extension from the espionage use (qv), a new venture that has failed and has left the company who launched it in a worse off commercial position than previously.

Miranda (law/US) from the case of Ernesto A. Miranda vs the State of Arizona (1966): a set of rules established by the US Supreme Court whereby US police must inform a suspect of his due rights and privileges before they begin his interrogation. Thus *Miranda card, Miranda rights, Miranda warning, Miranda rule*.

MIRV (milit) (acro) *m*ultiple *i*ndependently targeted *r*e-entry *v*ehicle: a missile that carries a number of warheads all of which can be programmed to destroy a different and disparate enemy target.

misfeature (computers) a feature in a computer that is not adequate to deal with new situations that arise in the operation of that machine.

misses (gambling) crooked dice that have been fixed to come up more 7s than point numbers.

missile gap (milit, pols) a plank in John F. Kennedy's campaign in 1960 was that the USSR had created a 'missile gap' by investing heavily in nuclear weaponry while the US under President Eisenhower had not bothered. Statistics proved that this was a fake issue created to drum up scared votes, but as a means of forcing through military expenditure, the concept has proved popular ever since.

Mister Prospect (commerce) a salesman's term for the person in a company who might actually make a deal and have some responsibility for useful decisions.

M

Mister Wood (police/UK) a truncheon.

MIT (futures market) (acro) *market if touched*: a price order that automatically becomes a market order if the price is reached.

Mivtzam Elohim (espionage) fr. Hebrew 'the wrath of God': covert Israeli international assassination squads.

mix *n*, *v* (movies, audio, TV) the mixing of a number of pictures or tapes to create a finished programme, film or record. Thus *mixer* (broadcasting) the person who actually operates the machine that mixes and balances the sound transmission. (cf: *master*)

mixed manning (milit) a military unit composed of troops from a variety of nations.

mixologist (music) a disc jockey, especially one who specialises in scratching (qv).

M'Naghten Rules (law/UK) those criteria which must be answered by any defendant who is intending to plead insanity as a defence from criminal actions; from the trial in 1843 of Daniel M'Naghten, murderer of Sir Robert Peel's secretary Edward Drummond, who was acquitted on the grounds of insanity.

mob (milit) a battalion, a regiment, any military unit.

Mob *n* (crime/US) one of the various euphemisms for the American families of the Mafia; others include 'The Syndicate' and 'organised crime'.

mobicentric manager (management) a flexible manager, possibly the blueprint for the future of business executives, who has no particular loyalty and no long-term company position but shifts quickly and efficiently from task to task and company to company; as well as the gains that he can make, the mere fact of continual movement is reward in itself.

moby *a* (computers) probably from H. Melville, *Moby Dick* (1851): large, immense, complex.

modality (pols) a popular diplomatic word that implies the method for attaining the end one desires.

mode (computers) the general state of being, used most commonly, despite its technological background, to refer to humans.

model (sex) a euphemism for a prostitute of either sex, particularly those who work by the telephone – call-girls and call-boys – and who advertise themselves as 'models' in shop windows and contact magazines.

moderate *v* (science) in nuclear physics, to slow down a neutron; to provide a reactor with a *moderator*, a device to slow down neutrons in order that they may cause fissions more readily.

modernism (art) an international movement throughout the arts that developed towards the end of the 19th century and, in its turning away from and progressing beyond the previous values and styles, paved the way for the many developments of 20th century art.

modoc (milit) USAF: anyone who joins the Air Force for the glamour, the society or the

fulfilment of some other fantasy unrelated to the realities of military life.

modular art (art) any painting or sculpture that is based on a unit of size and measurement that is repeated throughout the work.

modulo prep (computers) except for.

mogul (sport) in skiing, a bump in a ski run.

moko (theatre/UK) paint distempered with oil so as to give a glossy surface to scenic pieces and flats.

mole (espionage) a deep cover agent, put in place many years before he/she can be of use, but on the assumption that such an agent will gradually gain greater access to the centres of power, increasingly useful and damaging as time passes. *Mole* is a perfect example of the blurring of fact and fiction: while Francis Bacon uses the word in his *History of the Reign of King Henry VII* (1622), it was otherwise to be found in the works of John Le Carré, notably *Tinker Tailor Soldier Spy* (1974). In a BBC-TV interview in 1976 Le Carré claimed that *mole* was a genuine KGB term, but it was the televising of *Tinker Tailor* . . . plus the revelations of 'The Fourth Man' (Anthony Blunt) in October 1979 that took *mole* out of fiction and into the headlines for good.

Monday morning model (indust relats) damaged or defective goods from a production line: the workers involved being off sick, tired or hungover after the weekend, or simply depressed by the prospect of another week on the line.

Monday morning quarterback (sport) specifically in US football, in which the big games are played on Sunday afternoons: armchair critics who offer their own erroneous opinions on the results of the previous day's games, written up in Monday's newspapers.

Monday's newcomers (TV) a closed circuit showing of the latest commercials to be used by the independent TV networks and put on every Monday.

money illusion (econ) the illusion that an increase in the amount of one's wages automatically means an increase in their value; in a badly inflationary period, one might be lucky to remain even as well off as before and quite likely one might be markedly poorer.

mongolian (TV) when the flaps that shade a TV light are set in a slanting position.

monk (press) a smudge or blot of ink on the printed page.

monkey *a* (milit) RN: small.

monkey bridge (milit) RN: the after end or stern of a vessel.

monkey forecastle (milit) RN: a short low forecastle, used for anchor gear.

monkey fist (movies) aka: *monkey paw*: a piece of rope work dangled from a sound or camera boom in order to stop people walking into the boom and thus ruining a shot.

M

monkey jacket (medic/US) a hospital gown.

monkey pole (theatre/UK) a special pole with a hole in it through which lines can be threaded and then guided when lashing flats (qv) together.

monochromatic painting (art) aka: *monotone painting*: paintings produced in a single colour or a single tone.

monolithic *a* (pols) that condition of communist perfection sought in both ideology and organisation. The Communist Party is monolithic when it is 'carved from a single block, having one single will, and uniting all shades of thought in one stream of political activity' (Moscow Radio, April 1953).

monopsony (commerce) a market situation in which there is only a single buyer for any commodity.

montage (movies, TV) 1. the whole art of editing and assembling the various takes, shots, close-ups, effects etc into the final programme or film. 2. spec: an impressionistic sequence of short dissolves used to bridge a time gap, set a situation or establish background for the main story.

Monte (police/UK) (abbrev) Three Card Monte (qv).

Monte Carlo method (computers) a trial and error method of calculation in order to discover the best solution to a problem; ideally suited to a machine which is able to perform the infinity of calculations required with speed and accuracy. From the random numbers of the roulette tables of Monte Carlo.

monty hall (D&D) a type of dungeon or campaign where the rewards are disproportionately large when compared to the dangers involved in getting them; from Monty Hall, host of US TV's 'Let's Make A Deal', a game show of similar characteristics.

moody *n* (police/UK) lies, deceit, anything that goes wrong and prevents one achieving an expected and desired result.

moondoggle (aerospace) useless exploration of the moon that is wasteful of time, money and energy. (cf: *boondoggle*)

moonlight *v* (indust relats) to take a second job in addition to one's main employment; usually a nighttime job.

moose (milit) from Jap. 'musume' = girl: US forces in Japan or Korea usage for local girls.

MOOSE (aerospace) (acro) *m*anual *o*rbital *o*perations *s*afety *e*quipment: a device to protect an astronaut who is working in outer space; a space life raft.

MOR (rock business) (acro) *m*iddle *o*f the *r*oad: simple popular music of little lyrical or musical merit but adequate and saleable fodder for the pop charts and radio stations.

morgue *n* (press) newspaper cuttings libraries, where 'dead' stories from yesterday's papers are laid to rest.

morkrumbo (press/US) journalese; from the Morkrum machine that brings wire service reports to US newspaper offices.

morning drive (radio/US) a time segment created for advertising and statistical purposes: the period from early morning until 10 am.

morning line (gambling) the list of probable betting odds on the day's horse races which appears in the morning papers; such odds may well change as the races concerned approach. These are also the odds printed on the daily racecard available at the course.

morning prayers (milit/UK) daily briefing of the staff officers during a war or battle.

M (drugs) Morphine; see *drug names*.

MOS (movies) (acro) allegedly from a German director's instruction *M*it *o*ut *s*ound: a script direction indicating that a scene should be shot without its dialogue.

mossback (pols/US) a dedicated reactionary, one who resists all change at any time. From the idea of a creature that moves so slowly that it permits mosses to grow on its back.

mothball *v* (milit) to take out of service and store disused, obsolete or excess equipment and material (qv). Thus *demothball*: to take out of storage, refit and send back into service.

mother (recording) a grooved disc that is made from the plating of an electrotyped master matrix and is used as the stamper in the mass production of records.

motherboard (computers) a circuitboard with space for all the printed circuits required by a system – the various interfaces, the memory, etc.

mother-bombs (milit) canisters that are dropped and disintegrate, showering shrapnel grenades below.

mother-in-law research (business) research that draws its conclusions from the sampling of a small group, usually of relatives, friends and neighbours. Often used both to underline a decision that is already desired, or alternatively to kill off a plan that wider research might still support.

motion discomfort (air crew) euphemism for air sickness.

motivate *v* (sex) in black pimp terminology, to force onself to do something, ie: for a girl to start her night's work.

mouse (computers) a small, wheeled box, attached to a computer, first developed in 1960 by Xerox; when teamed with suitable software (qv) and graphics a mouse can improve on the performance of keyboard-only computers in the field of high resolution graphics.

mousetrap (milit) USN: an anti-submarine warfare device that throws depth charges ahead of small ships as they move through the sea.

Movement *n* (lit crit) a genre of English poets in the 1950s, including such men as Philip Larkin, Kingsley Amis and John Wain.

M

moves (record business) the various positions that a record may take as it moves up and down the charts; the movements a record makes within a US radio Top Forty station playlist.

mow *n* (sport) in cricket, a sweeping shot that resembles someone cutting grass with a scythe.

muck and bullets (TV) in make-ups departments, the 'dirtying down' of extras for scenes that require a grubby feel.

muckey muck (pols/US) usu. *high mucky muck* probably from Chinook 'hiu' (plenty) 'mucka-muck' (food) denoting a powerful man in the tribe: any political bigwig; often used by lower echelons to attack the party leaders.

mud (commerce) in the oil business, a liquid – often clay and other substances suspended in water – that is pumped down the inside of a drill pipe and up the outside and acts as lubricant, coolant, cleanser of the drill cuttings and a seal against the leakage into the bore of water or gas.

mudder (horse-racing) aka: *mud-runner, mudlark*: a horse that runs at its best on a muddy course.

MUF (technology) in nuclear energy and weapons development: (acro) *material unaccounted for*, those amounts of nuclear material – plutonium or enriched uranium – which have vanished without trace from the government stockpiles and are marked thus on the annual inventory.

MUFTI (prison/UK) (acro) *minimum of force tactical intervention squad*: a specially trained prison riot squad, composed of prison officers who are supposed to use tactics rather than brute force in dealing with disturbances in the prison.

mug *v* (theatre) to make exaggerated facial expressions.

mugshot (police) head and shoulders, front and profile shots of criminals placed on file with their fingerprints for identification purposes.

mugs (crime) to a confidence trickster of any persuasion, the foolish, gullible public at large.

mule *n* (drugs) a smuggler or courier of contraband drugs.

mule (sport) in yachting, a large triangular sail, sometimes used on a ketch.

mullahed (prison/UK) to be beaten up severely.

mulligan (sport) in golf, a free shot awarded to a player who has made a bad one, not counted on his score-card.

multicam (movies) (abbrev) *multicamera*: the making of a film in which the director has more than one camera shooting a scene simultaneously. Often used for action sequences or chases when the various angles can be intercut for maximum effect.

multilateral (pols) any agreement, treaty, trade negotiation, arms talks, etc that concerns three or more countries.

multiplane (movies) an animation technique pioneered by Walt Disney in *Fantasia* (1940): instead of building up drawings by laying the 'cells' directly over each other, the illusion of depth could be created by leaving a slight space between the celluloid images of the foreground, the main figure, the background, secondary figures, etc.

multiple kill capability (milit) any weapons platform (a plane, ship, tank) which holds more than a single type of weapon: guns and bombs, bombs and missiles, several types of missile, etc, etc.

multiples (science) the principle that all scientific 'discoveries' are in fact progressive developments and that the 'star' who arrives at the important conclusion is only bringing to a close the work of many unsung predecessors.

multiples (art) an extension of the traditional 'limited edition' concept, whereby multiples are artworks that can be repeated in production, theoretically without limit, from a basic matrix.

multiple track plan (educ) a method of dividing up children for classes. (cf: *ability grouping*).

multiplex *v* (movies) the conversion of one large old cinema which is no longer paying its way into three or four smaller auditoria which can show a selection of films at the same time.

multiprogramming (computers) the maximising of a machine's output by doubling the load in the operating system and having it switch between programmes at high speed and thus working on both of them nearly simultaneously.

multistable deterrence (milit) a three-way theory of nuclear stability: 1. a devastating capability for retaliation after a first strike; 2. the holding by both sides of so credible a first strike capability that neither would be advised to start a war; 3. the balance of terror epitomised by (2) should lead to the reduction of potential tension flashpoints across the world.

mum (sociol) a specific use of the word to mean the working-class mother who remains an influence on her children, even after they have left home and married.

mumblage (computers) the topic of one's mumble (qv).

mumble (computers) said when a correct response is either too complicated to provide or when the speaker has not yet properly thought it out. A general sign that the 'mumbler' is unwilling to start a long conversation.

mummerset (theatre/UK) fake peasant accents adopted by actors to denote a supposed rural origin. From a mix of Somerset and 'mummer'.

munchers (milit) RAF: Nimrod submarine reconnaissance aircraft, so nicknamed for the allegedly lavish meals that their crews take with them for their 10 hr. missions.

mung *v* (computers) 1. to make major alterations in the computer file, usually irrevocable ones. 2. to destroy data accidentally.

M

murder one (law, police/US) a charge of first degree (pre-meditated) murder.

Murphy game *n* (police, crime) a prostitute's fraud, whereby a client is lured into an alley or a bedroom at which point, bereft of trousers and dignity, he is faced by a supposedly 'outraged brother' or 'husband' who takes his money, and possibly his trousers, and departs with the girl.

museum restoration (arts) a standard of restoration that lets the cracks show up more obviously than in *perfect restoration*.

mush (sport) in surfing, the foam produced when a wave breaks.

mushroom (archit) a reinforced concrete pillar that broadens out towards the top and with its reinforcing rods passing up through the pillar into a concrete slab that forms part of the floor above.

music (milit) electronic jamming.

musical graphics (art) aka: *implicit notation*: drawings and designs with the purpose of stimulating a musician to produce sounds that in some way can be heard as related to those designs.

Music Row (music) the centre of the country music business, in Nashville, Tennessee.

musique concrete (music) trans 'concrete music': developed by Pierre Schaeffer in 1948, a style of music that involves sounds of all sorts – human, mechanical, animal, natural – which are combined on tape for its performance.

mustang (milit) an officer in the US forces who has been promoted from the ranks.

mute *n* (movies) any film print – positive or negative – which has no synchronous sound track.

mutton (print) aka: *em quad*: a space the square of the type body.

mutual interdependent fixation (new therapies) obscurantism for marriage.

mutuality (indust relats) the agreement between employers and workers on the going rates for each part of the production process made prior to any introduction of major changes in company policy or practice.

muzzler (police/US) a minor criminal; spec: a frotteur.

MVP (sport) in US professional sport (abbrev): Most Valuable Player.

mystery shopper (advertising) a manufacturer's representative who tours shops asking for a specific product. If the retailer offers or demonstrates the manufacturer's version of this product, he will be rewarded. Such 'shoppers' are also used to motivate normal shoppers who are in the store at the same time.

M

N (computers) 1. a large and indeterminate number. 2. an arbitrarily large and perhaps infinite number. 3. a variable whose value is specified by the current context.

N *a* (computers) 1. Some large and indeterminate number of objects, *There were N bugs in that crock*; also used in its original sense of a variable name. 2. An arbitrarily large and perhaps infinite, number. 3. A variable whose value is specified by the current context. *We would like to order N wonton soups and a family dinner for N-1.* 4. Nth: *adj*. The ordinal counterpart of N. *Now for the Nth and last time* . . .

nabes (movies) (abbrev) neighbourhoods: local cinemas rather than the major first-run houses.

nadgers (TV) any small technical problem in equipment.

naff (TV) useless, unpleasant, vulgar; originally a TV word but spilt into and recently out of popular usage.

naive (art) any painter who has not been trained in a formal manner.

naives (pols) recruits to the British Social Democratic Party (SDP); previously apolitical, at least insofar as they had joined no party; usually leftish, educated, middle class.

naive user (computers) someone who wishes to use a machine but knows little about its operation and is not particularly keen to learn properly.

naked call (stock market) an option to buy a stock or other security not actually owned by the seller.

name *n* (stock market) a ticket labelled with the name of the purchaser, handed over to the selling broker on 'ticket day' or 'name day'.

name *n* (commerce) an underwriter at Lloyds of London.

name day (stock market) the day on which the seller of registered securities receives from their buyer a ticket with the name and details of the person to whom the securities are to be transferred. (cf: *name*)

name ID (pols) (abbrev) name identification: the recognition of a candidate's name by those who are supposed to be voting for him.

nano-second (computers) one thousand millionth of a second.

nape *v* (milit) to bomb with napalm.

narrative figuration (art) narrative art that represents events in time (with or without a storyline) on a single canvas. Frequently its imagery is distorted and its subject matter fragmented, and several sequences may be compressed into one painting.

narrow (stock market) a *narrow market* can offer quotations on only a very small number of stocks; a dull market.

narrowcasting (radio, TV) the transmission of programmes that are aimed specifically at a small, tightly defined audience.

nart (art) a coinage combining 'nothing' and 'art' created by critic Mario Amaya in 1966 and meaning essentially that in the world of art, less equals more. Nart is characterised by impersonality and boredom of repetition.

nasties (video) videotapes featuring ultra-horrific, sadistic films of mutilation, cannibalism and similar painful excess; cheaply produced abroad and highly popular in the video rental market.

nationalism (pols) 1. when describing a non-aligned country, an admirable example of standing as a bulwark against US imperialism. 2. referring to those countries struggling against USSR domination, then 'bourgeois nationalism (is) a dangerous enemy, and a criminal associate of international reaction'.

National Military Establishment (milit) the US military machine.

nationals (TV/US) a weekly breakdown by the Nielsen TV Index company of the programme ratings throughout the US.

native Americans (sociol) a belated recognition, at least in bureaucratic and liberal vocabularies, of the American Indians. (cf: *first Australians, New Commonwealth*)

NATO phonetics (milit) the internationally agreed phonetic code for use in military and civil radio communications: A Alpha, B Bravo, C Charlie, D Delta, E Echo, F Foxtrot, G Golf, H Hotel, I India, J Juliet, K Kilo, L Lima, M Mike, N November, O Oscar, P Papa, Q Quebec, R Romeo, S Sierra, T Tango, U Uncle, V Victor, W Whiskey, X X-ray, Y Yankee, Z Zulu.

naturalism (art) aka: *socialist realism*: a socialist creative method that is obligatory for artists and writers. In essence all artists should be committed to extolling and strengthening the Communist status quo in every vestige of their work and in accordance with the party line.

Realism in this context equals the reflection of 'reality' within its revolutionary development.

navaglide (air traffic) an airport instrument approach system with the ability to indicate distance by utilising a single frequency.

navaglobe (air traffic) a long distance navigation system that automatically indicates bearing by using low-frequency broadcasts.

navar (air traffic) (acro) navigation and ranging: a navigation and traffic control system for aircraft.

Nav. House (milit) RN: (abbrev) Navigation School at H.M. Dockyard, Portsmouth.

NBC (milit) nuclear, biological and chemical warfare. (cf: *ABC*)

'ncarugnutu (Mafia) trans: 'carrion': any Mafioso who breaks *omerta*, the oath of silence.

nearbys (futures market) the nearest active trading month of a financial futures market.

near cash (stock market) aka: *near money* short term investments that can easily be transferred back into cash.

neatlines (milit) aka: *sheetlines*: those lines on a military map that immediately border the main body of that map.

neck/head/nose (horse-racing) distances under a length by which horses are deemed to have been separated: 4 noses = 1 head; 2 heads = 1 neck; 2 necks = half a length.

neck lock *n* (law/UK) the vertical curl at the base of a barrister's wig.

needle time (radio) that proportion of broadcasting time that is devoted to recorded music.

needs sensing (govt) the finding out by bureaucracies and social agencies of what exactly the people want. Those who check and discover such wants are variously *needs sensors* and *needs assessors*.

need-to-know (govt) the concept that no information need be passed on to anyone who does not have the 'need to know', a classification that is both arbitrary and which rarely includes either the media or the public at large.

negative cost (movies) the sum of the costs both above the line and below the line (qqv): the cost of producing the finished version of the film, of paying all the bills other than those for advertising, publicity and printing copies of the film.

negative deficits (govt,business) an obscurantism to mask the simple concept of *profits*.

negative feedback (govt) feedback (qv) that maintains stability by monitoring change and suppressing it when it threatens to alter the status quo.

negative interest (econ) money deducted from or paid on interest.

negative option (business) aka: *inertia selling* (UK): the choice one has of accepting or rejecting unsolicited products that are sent through the mails.

negatively privileged (sociol) a euphemism for *poor*.

negative sum game (business, econ) a 'game' played by managers and economists in which the amount that the losers lose exceeds that which the winners win.

negative targeting (pols) the concept of aiming one's political campaign not to boost one's own image, but to undermine that of one's opponent, harping on his past errors, using leaflets, 'black' propaganda etc.

negotiated (milit) used by the SAS (Special Air Service) commandos as meaning the execution of their given targets during a mission.

nelson (sport) in cricket, the score of 111.

NEMO (media) (acron) *not emanating from main office*: any remote radio or TV broadcast.

neoconservatives (pols) a style of conservatism that rejects the extremes of liberal/socialist utopianism and continues to feel that democratic capitalism is the ideal method of government, but does allow for a degree of welfare state interference – payments to the needy, health insurance, etc.

neocorporatism (econ) the close co-operation in public policy between the state and organised economic interests.

neopsychic functioning (new therapies) in transactional analysis (qv), the concept of the *adult*, the grown-up life that we have to lead in order to survive in society.

nesting (computers) the inclusion of a small routine or block of data within a larger routine or block of data.

network *v* (govt) the linking of a bureaucratic department to the area it is supposed to be serving by forming miniature bureaucracies that link the people in the field (qv) with those in the office.

network *v* (radio, TV) to broadcast the same programme simultaneously over all the stations or affiliates (qv) that make up one company's network.

network *v* (computers) the linking together of a number of machines to pool data, speed operations and to enable many users to enjoy greater access than they could by using only one machine.

never *n* (milit) RN: *to do a never*: to shirk.

never enough (new therapies) in primal therapy (qv), a stock phrase to explain how as a child in a 'non-giving' world one could never get what it was one really wanted.

New (milit) RN: a naval cadet in his first term on a training ship; the equivalent of a public school fag.

New Age (sociol) the new spirituality that emerged from the 'counter-culture' and the 'alternative society' of the 1960s and developed into a number of cult religions, variations on traditional Oriental themes and a general move into the mystic. (cf: *new therapies*)

N

New Brutalism (archit) an 'ethical' movement in 1950s British architecture which sought to replace the diluted styles of the period with a specific dedication towards the original strength and integrity of modern architecture, using structures and materials 'honestly' and 'truthfully' in the style of Le Corbusier.

new class *n* (pols) coined in 1957 in Milovan Djilas's *The New Class*: the emergent elite of the various Communist bloc states, officials and bureaucrats who were strengthening their own position and, just like the bourgeoisie, enjoying privilege, corruption, bribery and consumer luxuries far beyond the dreams of their alleged peers, the masses.

new Commonwealth (govt) the identifying description of those immigrants who come from states other than Canada, Australia and New Zealand, ie: coloured immigrants. It is noticeable that real chronology has no bearing on this 'new' category, since India, on racial rather than any other grounds, is thus included. (cf: *first Australians*, *native Americans*)

new Communist man (pols) aka: *Soviet Man*: Marx's model citizen, a character based on 10 criteria: 1. ideologically pure; 2. honest and brave; 3. law-abiding; 4. no acquisitive instincts; 5. he subordinates his individual needs and desires to those of the common good; 6. he respects and protects social property; 7. he is socially co-operative; 8. he enjoys all round occupations and recreational activities; 9. he is wholeheartedly Marxist; 10. he is a committed internationalist.

new criticism (lit crit) a school of criticism which centres on the analysis of texts with special reference to the ironies, ambiguities, paradoxes and other linguistic styles; founded by US critic John Crowe Ransom in 1941.

new frontier (pols/US) a slogan and a concept coined in the 1930s but brought to prominence by President John F. Kennedy when he accepted the democratic nomination in 1960: 'We stand together on the edge of a new frontier – the frontier of the 1960s, a frontier of unknown opportunities and paths, a frontier of unfulfilled hopes and threats . . . (it) is not a set of promises, it is a set of challenges.'

new informalists (art) aka: *new colourists*, *lyrical colourism*, *beautiful painting*: the general description of a number of contemporary US painters who produce large scale abstract pictures of a highly decorative nature and pursue the 'natural way of forming matter' in opposition to the 'formalism' of US painting in the 1960s.

new journalism (press) a genre of involved, concerned (although not especially campaigning or 'investigative') journalism that emerged in the mid-1960s from such writers as Tom Wolfe, Gay Talese, Jimmy Breslin, Hunter S. Thompson et al. Aiming to resurrect the 'social realism' of the 19th century, the new journalists rejected the traditional objective style of reporting in favour of a trumpeted personal viewpoint, unrestrained speculation on almost any aspect of the story, a lack of worry as to absolute facts, chronology and other 'straight' aspects of writing.

New Left (pols) coined as a description by US sociologist C. Wright Mills (1916–1962) the New Left were youthful radicals who rejected the traditions of the 'Old Left' (qv) and attempted to inject novelty and energy into what was, in the wake of McCarthy, Hungary and similar attacks and disillusions, more a name than an active radical movement. At its height during the protests against the Vietnam War, the new left barely survived the end of US involvement and thus its main rallying point.

new look (pols) the alteration in US defence policy that emerged during the Korean War and started the trend to de-emphasise conventional forces in favour of nuclear strategic planning.

new materialism (art) a broad category that embraces anyone who works in 'unworthy' materials to produce an amalgam of painting, sculpture and stage props.

new Puritanism (sociol) a derogatory description by US nuclear power supporters to attack those who are attempting to control the further spread of nuclear power in the US energy programme.

news (espionage) the conveying to a blackmail target that he/she has been suitably entrapped and that it might be wise to start paying off in information, etc unless embarrassing exposure is preferable – which targets rarely feel to be the case.

news advisory (public relats) a brief announcement of a forthcoming event which is intended to alert the media to this event without actually informing them of any detail as to its content.

news break (media) 1. any newsworthy item of information. 2. spec. in the *New Yorker*: small, amusing items from various US magazines that are printed at the bottom of columns in the magazine.

new sensualism (archit) a movement in modern architectural design whereby buildings are sculptural and possess a sensuous plasticity of form in contrast to the hard-edged rectilinearity that is usually equated with 'modern architecture'.

newsies (pols/US) shorthand for the media: divided further into *wires* (the wire services), *reels* (TV) and *stills* (print journalism).

newspaper (prison) a thirty-day jail sentence; supposedly the time it would take an illiterate to read one.

news peg (media) a news story that forms the basis of an editorial, a feature, a cartoon, etc.

new therapies (sociol) a variety of modern quasi-psychiatric therapies, including est, transactional analysis, rebirthing, co-counselling, primal therapy, etc (qqv), which have become popular in the last decade, most of which can be traced back to easy simplifications of Freudian concepts and which, unlike Freud himself, aim to eliminate the learning processes of analysis and provide all who pay their fees with a near miraculous 'cure'.

new thing (arts) in jazz and in black writing, a development in the 1970s which emphasised aggressive and original playing and writing and reflected the developments in black consciousness at the time.

new time (stock market) 1. of dealings: having the settlement postponed to the next settling day. 2. of prices: to have prices quoted for the next settling day before the previous settlement is completed.

new wave (rock music) the 'punk' music of 1976/77, epitomised in such bands as the Sex Pistols, the Damned, the Clash and the Jam.

new wave (movies) from the Fr. 'nouvelle vague': a trend in film-making that developed in France in 1950s and included the work of such directors as Truffaut and Godard.

newszine (TV) any fan magazine that contains only facts and information and rejects any amateur fiction.

niblick (sport) in golf, the traditional name for the Number 9 iron.

nickelling (milit) the fouling of a gun's bore by small pieces of the cupro-nickel casing of the bullet.

NIE (milit) (acro) National Intelligence Estimate: the CIA assessment of the USSR current nuclear capability and its future nuclear force structure.

nigger (movies) large black cloth screen used to shield the camera or to create lighting effects.

nigger-stick (prison/US) four foot long truncheons used by warders and police.

night cap (milit) from acronym NCAP: night combat air patrol.

nightingale wards (medic) a type of hospital ward in which several patients can be accommodated together.

Nightwatch (milit) US code: National Emergency Airborne Command Post, a converted Boeing 707 in which a 'reserve' Commander-in-Chief (often the Vice-President) will fly during a war and from which he can take over military control if the President is killed.

nightwatchman (sport) in cricket, a batsman from the lower order of the team sent in to defend when a wicket has fallen within a few minutes of the close of a day's play.

nineteenth hole (sport) in golf, the clubhouse and in particular, its bar.

ninety (TV) a 'made-for-TV' film that lasts ninety minutes.

ninety days (gambling) in craps, the point of 9.

ninety day wonder (milit) a graduate of a ninety day officer's training course, thus an inexperienced, possibly incompetent soldier.

Noah's syndrome (business) the management situation in which a scheme is prepared to cope with possibly adverse circumstances and the proponent of that scheme refuses to relinquish any vestige of it, even though reality has no bearing on the pessimistic theories there embodied.

no-city strategy (milit) the theory that in a nuclear war missiles would be targeted on enemy forces rather than on his population. (cf: *counterforce, countervalue*)

no-cut contract (sport/US) a contract for a professional sportsman that guarantees that he will not be cut (qv) from the team at any time during the pre-season practice or during the subsequent season.

nod *v* (theatre) to take a bow at the end of a performance.

nodders (TV) the interviewer's reaction shots, often no more than nodding at the answers his questions receive, which are usually filmed after the actual interview and edited into the tape prior to transmission.

nodding donkey (commerce) in the oil business, the device that continues pumping out oil from a well when the oil stocks cannot rise naturally at the required production rates; the device looks something like a perpetually nodding donkey's head.

noddle *v* (music) to improvise on a music instrument, or to play a particularly decorative series of notes.

noddy cap (milit) RAF: a protective cap that covers the sensitive nose of a missile; from the pointed cap worn by a popular children's comic character.

nodis (govt) notation on classified documents: (abbrev) no distribution. Such documents are meant only for the one person to whom they are sent on an eyes only (qv) basis. (cf: *limdis, exdis*)

noforn (govt) (abbrev) no foreigners: notation on classified documents which forbids anyone but accredited US citizens to read them.

no go *v* (movies) to turn down a potential deal.

no heroics (medic/US) a notation on a terminally ill patient's chart to stop medical staff from taking any remedial action if the patient suffers a heart attack since both the patient and his/her family would prefer not to put off the inevitable death any longer.

noise (computers) any changes in the electronic signal that ought not to be there; interference. (cf: *glitch*)

noise level *n* (govt, business, science) the general levels of activity in any organisation – the existence of which may well defeat even the most scrupulous researcher who will lose a specific

N

objective amongst the mass of comings and goings.

noise word (computers) a word included in a program to improve its readability but not actually employed in running that program and as such it is ignored by the machine.

no joy (milit) radio code: I have been unsuccessful, I have no information.

no-knock (police/US) a raid by police on a private home which comes without permission or warning; the provisions of a search warrant specifically provide for the entering officers to identify themselves and ask permission to enter.

nolle pross (law) (abbrev) nolle prosequi 'I am unwilling to pursue': the abandonment by the prosecution of its case against the defendant.

no-load fund (stock market) a mutual fund which charges little or no commission to buyers and involves no sales organisation.

no-loads (stock market) shares that are sold at their net asset value without any commission being added.

nolo contendere (law) from Latin 'I do not wish to contend': a plea by a defendant that does not actually admit guilt per se, but does lay him open to a judgement and sentence without a defence, although he can still contest the truth of any charges in a collateral proceeding.

no Mayday (medic/US) code issued to relevant staff advising them that they should not attempt further resuscitation of a given patient should that patient's situation decline severely.

nomadic furniture (design) on the principle that the average American moves home every 3/4 years, this furniture is designed for easy shipment, stacking, assembly, etc.

nominal price (futures market) price quotations on futures for a period in which no actual trading took place.

nominal yield weapons (milit) a nuclear bomb with an explosive yield of approx. 20,000 tons.

nommus! (crime/UK) a warning cry at the approach of police used by costers, pitch and toss players, illegal street traders, etc.

nonce n (prison/UK) any sex offender.

nondescripts (police) unmarked police cars for surveillance purposes.

non judgemental attitude (social wk) the belief, fundamental to effective casework, that concepts of guilt or innocence are irrelevant to the assessment of a situation, although some evaluation must be made as to the client's attitudes, standards and actions.

non-relational art (art) while 'relational' paintings depend for their effect on the idea of 'figures in a field', non-relational paintings have a single uniform space, avoid depth effects, and stretch from edge to edge across the canvas, thus giving greater importance to the shape of that canvas.

non-theatrical (movies) an exhibitor's term which embraces any show for which there is no paid admission: charities, schools, etc. Also covers all showings of 16mm films.

non-volatile memory (computers) a memory system that will retain its content even if the machine's power supply is switched off; ie: discs, tapes and the internal ROM (qv) memory.

noon balloon (air traffic) the 'rush hour' in air traffic control at Miami Airport when from 11.30 am to 2.00 pm a plane lands or takes off every 45 seconds.

NORAD (milit) (acro) *North* American Air *Defense* Command.

normalisation (pols) the return of a socialist country to the status quo after a period of liberalisation, ie Czechoslovakia after the 'Prague Spring' of 1968 and Poland after the imposition of martial law in 1981.

normative (educ) a pupil who achieves the normal standards, ie an average child.

normative forecasting (business) a system of forecasting that posits a future demand, mission or goal and then attempts to plot backwards in time from the achievement of that goal through the steps that would have to be made to take a company from today up to that achievement. Rather than predicting some idealised future, normative forecasting takes account of possible problems and obstacles and focuses not on what might, but on what should happen.

North (econ) the industrially advanced and technologically sophisticated countries of the world, the bulk of which happen to lie north of the Equator. (cf: *South*)

northpaw (sport) in baseball: a right handed player.

nose (horse-racing) see: *neck*.

nose n (radio/UK) the 'top' of a story, the one line that sums up everything that follows; the equivalent of print journalism's lead (qv).

nose-in (air crew) the position of a commercial aircraft waiting on its stand for passengers to complete boarding.

nose picker (commerce) a salesman's derogatory description of a potential client who cannot make up his/her mind and has no power of decision-making within the firm.

no-show (air crew) any passenger who fails to take the seat booked in his/her name.

no-show (indust relats/US) any worker, especially one on a government payroll, who collects a salary but fails to turn up to do the job; by extension, a fake 'worker' who does not exist but whose name is put on the payroll and whose salary is thus collected by a corrupt official.

no side (sport) in rugby football, the signal for the end of the game; the final whistle. Possibly from the idealised sporting concept of there being no hard feelings – 'side' – once the rough and tumble of the match was over.

no sky line (archit) a line in a room from behind which no sky is visible to those looking out of a window from table height.

notams (air crew) regular notices issued to all aircrew detailing information on a route.

not doing well (medic) a euphemism for dying.

note verbale (diplomacy) an unsigned diplomatic note, written in the third person, which acts as a type of memorandum.

not for attribution (pols, press) aka: *deep background* the release of information to a journalist on the understanding that its source will not be mentioned or even hinted at in the story. In the case of any difficulties arising with the publication of such a story, the journalist is honour bound to take whatever problems arise without in any way incriminating his source.

notice (theatre) a review in the newspapers.

notice day (futures market) a day on which notices of intent to deliver pertaining to a specified delivery month may be issued.

notice paper (govt) a paper supplied to members of the British House of Commons which gives the current day's proceedings.

notice up (theatre) the show is due to close.

notionals (espionage) fake businesses which exist only on their headed notepaper and serve as the cover employer of CIA or other intelligence service personnel or as the sponsor of various activities which are fronts for subversive, 'black' operations.

notional weekend (TV) days other than Saturday and Sunday which are counted as the weekend for the purpose of fulfilling union agreements that state that members must have two days off in a week, even if they work over the real weekend.

no-touch (medic) a method of dressing wounds in which no-one may touch either the wound or its dressings.

nouveau roman (lit crit) a term coined by Alain Robbe-Grillet c1955 and further expanded in a book of essays, *Pour un nouveau roman* (1963). In essence Robbe-Grillet rejected such traditional trappings of the novel as plot, narrative, character delineation and analysis; instead the novel should be about *things*, a systematised, analytical and highly detailed record of objects – in rooms, adorning people, etc. etc. It was through such infinite details that the reader was to appreciate the mental state of those who were experiencing or seeing these objects.

nouvelle vague (movies) see: *new wave*.

novelist (USSR prisons) a prisoner who makes a confession, voluntary or otherwise.

novelty (commerce) in fashion, the sort of fabric that is made from more than one basic fibre and which may be in an unusual or exotic weave.

no-win (pols) often found in 'no-win situation' or 'no-win contest': any conflict or position from which the protagonist(s) is/are unable to extract

him- or themselves without suffering some form of defeat or loss.

NPC speciality (medic/US) (abbrev) *no patient care* speciality: after an initial year as an intern, all junior doctors must opt for a speciality in which they will make their career; NPC specialities include X-Rays, anaesthesiology, pathology, dermatology, ophthalmology and psychiatry. (cf: *Rays, Gas, Derm, Path*)

NSI (govt/US) (abbrev) National Security Information: any information the disclosure of which could be expected to cause at least identifiable damage to the national security; including military, scientific, technological, diplomatic intelligence, nuclear and many other restricted subjects.

'ntasciatu (Mafia) trans: 'dried out': a victim who has been killed with a blast from a sawn-off shotgun.

NTP (stock market) (acro) *not to press*: when a security has only a limited market, a jobber may well sell shares that he does not actually own on the understanding that the buying broker will not immediately press for delivery.

nuance *v* (govt) to approach a problem or topic with an infinity of subtlety, emphasising the 'grey shades' in all one's dealings. The adjective *nuanced* is also in use.

nucflash (milit) US Dept. of Defense Nuclear Accident Code: 1. an accident which has the potential of sparking off an actual war with the USSR. 2. warning of a (still) unidentified object on missile early warning radar.

nuclear art (art) a short-lived movement in Italy c1957 which opposed all fixed forms of art, particularly any type of geometric, abstract creations, and instead proposed experimentation with a variety of automatic techniques.

nuclear thimbles (science) special containers to hold radioactive waste, designed by the American Atomic Energy Commission to hold some 103 million galls. of waste.

nuke *n, v* (milit) (abbrev) nuclear: 1. *n* a nuclear weapon. 2. *v* to attack with nuclear weapons.

number (sex) a client for a homosexual prostitute.

number cruncher (computers) a computer that is specially designed to perform lengthy and complex calculations at speeds of several million operations per second, thus dealing with problems that would take humans whole lifetimes to attempt.

number facts (educ) the basic mathematical abilities: add, subtract, multiply and divide.

number one (milit) RN: a first lieutenant, esp. when he is second in command to the captain.

numbers *n* (TV) the weekly Nielsen Television Index statistics that tell the industry how programmes are being rated throughout the US.

number two (theatre/UK) a provincial town that is not especially famed for its theatre or its appreciative audiences, rather than the large,

N

popular touring theatres and the cities in which they are.

nuplex (industry) a complex of manufacturers all of whom use nuclear power within their factories or plants.

nursery (sport) 1. (cricket) any club or part of a club that is set aside for the training and promotion of talented young players. 2. (skiing) the *nursery slopes* are reserved for novice or inexperienced skiers.

nursery finance (finance) the loaning of funds by stockjobbers or large institutions to such successful private companies who are due to become public companies within a maximum of 36 months.

nurse's goals (medic) specific indications of illness and the treatments therefore required for bringing the patient back to good health.

nut *n* (theatre, movies) the total of all overheads in a theatre, cinema or any public auditorium, which total must be paid before the owner can start making a profit. Thus *off the nut*: in profit; *on the nut*: in deficit.

nut (gambling) from the entertainment use (qv), the living expenses and other overheads that a gambler must meet from his winnings.

nut (police/US) a bribe given to a corrupt policeman. (cf: *bung, grasseater, meateater*)

nut-cutting (pols/US) from sl. for 'castration': generally referring to dirty work in politics, especially in the area of giving and withholding patronage and favours in return for loyalty, betrayal and the gradations between.

nybble (computers) half a byte (qv) or four bits (qv).

O (drugs) (abbrev) opium, see *drug names*.

O (movies) a rating for pictures established by the US Catholic Conference; O = 'morally offensive'.

O (govt) (abbrev) OBE, Order of the British Empire.

O & M (indust relats) (abbrev) organisation and methods studies: special studies to research and improve the running and efficiency of a company's management or a local or national government department.

O & O (TV) (abbrev) owned and operated: those five VHF stations that a major TV network can actually own under Federal law, rather than those affiliates (qv) which are merely allied to the network; O & O stations are invariably in the major cities.

oater (movies) aka: *horse opera*: a Western film; cowboys and Indians, ranchers and farmers, etc.

obbo (police/UK) (abbrev) observation. (cf: *obs*)

OBE (econ) (acro) *one big explanation*: coined by Prof. Jim Ball of the London Business School, the idea that there is one all-embracing explanation for the economic malaise that the UK (and the world) is suffering, and concomitantly, that there is one simple solution.

obie (movies) a small lamp on a camera mounting, which is used to enhance an actor's appearance; c250W power.

obie (theatre/US) an award for Off Broadway (OB) productions. (cf: *Emmy, Oscar*)

object art (art) orig. used to describe the paintings and constructions of the Futurist, Dadaist and Surrealist schools which incorporated previously 'non-art' objects; later used in the 1960s as an alternative to minimal art (qv) in that minimalists emphasise the 'real' materials from which 'art' is made.

object code (computers) aka: *object program*: that 'language' which is so coded that the machine can 'understand' it and thus perform its required operations. (cf: *machine code*)

objecthood (art) a term of Formalist criticism that contends that there is a conflict between our reading of physical works of art as art, and as objects; thus, when we view a painting as an object we are no longer regarding it as art. The task of modernist painting is to defeat or suspend this objecthood without resorting to the illusionist pictorial devices of the past.

objectification (pols) in Marxist terms, the process of transmitting labour – ie. value – into the objects of that labour; by extension, the struggle by man for mastery of nature and of his social destiny.

objectivism (pols) in Marxist terms what the West might call 'impartiality', and as such a pejorative: a rightist disease which sees problems where the Party says there are none, by attaching too much importance to 'facts' and 'reality' when the Party line quite clearly negates such facts, however accurate they may be.

obs (police/UK) (abbrev) observation. (cf: *obbo*)

obscurate (govt) the preservation of bureaucratic obscurity in the face of all investigation and enquiries.

observer (milit) the second crew member in a two-seater military plane; the job title is traditional, originating in the First World War, and the observer's tasks now cover electronic warfare, command and guidance of weapons, navigation, anything except the actual flying of the plane.

OC (business) (acro) organisational climate: the overall atmosphere of an office or factory; *positive OC* is required for maximum productivity and ideal industrial relations.

occasion dressing (commerce) in fashion terms, the purchasing of 'Sunday best' or 'party' clothes.

occurrences (police/UK) a variety of events that include sudden death, suicide, injury to policemen, etc.

odd-even (science) in nuclear physics, 1. of or pertaining to nuclei of an odd mass number and those of an even mass number. 2. nuclei which contain an odd number of protons and an even number of neutrons.

odd-lot (stock market/US) any transaction involving a smaller number of shares than it is usual to deal in. Thus *odd-lotter*: a small investor, a speculator who habitually buys stock in less than round lots.

odd-odd (science) in nuclear physics, 1. of or pertaining to nuclei of an odd mass number only. 2. nuclei with an odd number of protons and an odd number of neutrons.

off (theatre) (abbrev) off stage; either of people or of effects and music.

off (stock market) shares that are lower in value,

by a stated number of points or a specific value, than at a previous quotation.

off *v* (milit, pol) used both by radicals and soldiers to mean kill.

off Broadway (theatre/US) that part of the New York professional theatre that works outside the mainstream of musicals and 'straight' plays and is geographically and ideologically outside the Broadway style, especially in its espousal of experimental works.

offer (futures market) the indication of a willingness to sell a futures contract at a given price. (cf: *bid*)

office (sex) the area, usually some part of a street, where a homosexual hustler establishes his pitch and meets his clients.

office (stock market) 1. *general office*: those departments of a stockbrokers' which deal with accounts and the transfer of securities. 2. *in the office* indicates that an initiating order has been given by a broker's own clients, rather than coming from the market.

office (aircrew) the cockpit or flight deck of a commercial airliner.

office hours (milit) USMC: a regular daily occasion on which the Commanding Officer can see marines for discipline, commendation, the answering of requests and similar business.

office manager (sport) in motor rallying, the co-driver who takes care of navigation, checkpoints, documents and similar tasks outside that of driving the car.

officer (espionage) a staff member of the CIA, as opposed to an agent (qv).

off-line (computers) any computer that is neither part of nor under the control of a central machine.

off-off Broadway (theatre/US) the most radical and experimental of New York theatre which exists outside the 'real' theatre and concentrates on the impromptu, the improvised and the extreme, often only marginally definable as 'theatre'.

offset (econ) a purchase whereby the revenue spent is balanced by that earned.

off-shore funds (finance) investments that are registered outside an individual or company's home country and which are therefore liable to advantageous tax situations due to the choice of the country of registration.

off the board (gambling) a bookmaker's refusal to accept a bet on a given sporting event.

off the reservation (pols/US) a politician who remains within his party, but refuses to support that party's candidate.

off the shelf (aerospace) a plane that has been fully developed to military requirements and standards and is available for manufacture and procurement without the need for any further modifications.

off year (pols/US) those years in which there are

Congressional elections but no Presidential election.

oggin (milit) RN: the sea; from 'hog-wash'.

oh-one (milit) USMC: a clerk, from the number 0100, the four digit number that is appended to Marine service numbers and shows his MOS (military occupational speciality).

oilberg (commerce) massive oil tankers with a capacity of 300,000 tons plus; so called since the bulk of the ship when full is hidden beneath the surface of the sea.

oil burner routes (milit) published routes across the US along which the armed forces are permitted to carry out low level, high speed training missions.

oilcan operation (govt) any variety of cosmetic changes that are supposed to be tackling a problem in the bureaucracy: but rusty parts are only being oiled when they need to be replaced.

oil spot (milit) in a war of occupation, the first village or population centre to be captured and used as a base for spreading one's influence further; the first part of the 'troubled waters' to receive the pacifying oil.

oily *n* (prison/UK) any legal visitor, often a solicitor's clerk or his assistant; the main solicitor himself becomes an 'oily' since he, in fact, is an assistant to the barrister.

oilywad (milit) RN: a seaman with no particular skills and/or no particular ambitions.

old (social wk) a man aged between 65 and 75; a woman between 60 and 75.

old bill (gambling) a word or a hand signal (an open palm) which asks the initiated 'is there another card cheat in this game?'

Old Left (pols) the traditional liberal socialist Left which preceded the more melodramatic and radical New Left of the 1960s (qv); on the whole its members accepted traditional Marxism and the Party's directives but rarely considered the urban guerilla tactics of their youthful successors.

old man (milit) the commanding officer.

old-old (social wk) a member of either sex who is aged 75 or older.

old salt (milit) USMC: any veteran, long-serving member of the Marines.

olive branch routes (milit) low level training routes established over the US for the use of B-52 bombers. fr. the motto of the SAC (qv) 'Peace Is Our Profession'.

Oliver (horse-racing) *to put the Oliver Twist on*: the clandestine placing of an incorrect entry in the betting ledger.

omee (theatre/UK) a man, especially a landlord or an itinerant actor. From Ital. 'uomo' = man, also from Parlyaree, a theatrical jargon.

omerta (Mafia) from Ital 'umilita': the Mafia code that asks for submission to the leader and the group as well as silence as regards their activities.

on a bell (movies) the warning bell that rings on

a film set prior to a shot to ensure that all concerned are silent.

on call target (milit) a specific nuclear target which will be attacked on a direct command, rather than simply at a certain time.

one big one (gambling) $1000.

one for the shelf (stock market) any share that is expected to stand as a secure, long-term investment.

one glass of water doctrine (pols) originated by Lenin, then abandoned by him, but still maintained as 'pei-shui-chu-i' by Chinese Communists: the concept that sexual desire should be no more vital to a revolutionary than a glass of water.

one house bill (pols/US) legislation that is never intended to pass into law – or through either Congressional House – but is used for publicity purposes only by a specific politician.

one house veto (pols/US) aka: *legislative veto*: the power under the US Constitution that enables either the Senate or the House of Representatives to veto any Presidential initiative.

one legged (TV) a poor sound quality in the transmission.

one-lunger (sport) in yachting, any boat driven by a single cylinder engine.

one on/one off (prison/UK) when a prisoner is moved around the prison, from the control of one set of officers to another, the officer bringing the prisoner announces 'One off' as he hands over the prisoner to a new escort who similarly announces 'One on'.

one per cent out look (commerce) in fashion, the idea of wearing various traditional costumes – dinner jacket, etc – with the addition or substitution of a single discordant item.

one-pipper (milit) a second lieutenant.

one plus one (TV) a specially small camera crew – one cameraman, one soundman, one reporter and one electrician – used for reporting war zones or for clandestine surveillance for investigative programmes.

one plus one (rock business) a merchandising concept for tape cassettes: one side contains the pre-recorded music of the purchaser's taste, the other is left blank for later home recording.

ones *n* (prison/UK) the first floor of cells in a prison wing; thus *twos, threes, fours.*

one sheet *v* (theatre, movies) to give a show or film the lowest possible billing; referring to the smallest available size of poster which would be used to advertise it.

one-shot (publishing) a publishing idea – often a small magazine linked to publicising a specific event or fad – that is produced once only and with no hope or intention of any sequel.

one-stop (rock business) the music industry wholesalers who are only 'one stop' away from the manufacturers; these middlemen sell records to retailers, juke boxes, etc.

one-time pad (espionage) in cryptography, a

secret message which is encoded in a cypher devised for that one occasion and subsequently destroyed or abandoned.

one-twenties (TV) a 'made-for-TV' film that lasts 120 minutes. (cf: *nineties*)

one-two-three bank (finance) a bank that is superior to a mere moneylender, and which while offering concomitant services and prestige, is not a fully established clearing, commercial or merchant bank; a fringe bank.

on-going (pavlov) happening now, continuing, in action: a redundant and over-popular phrase, usually found in combination with 'situation'.

onion (milit) RN: in calculating a ship's speed, a fraction of a knot.

onion skin concept (govt) multilayered: when used with reference to the gradual development of aid throughout the world, the idea that one proceeds through the layers of the onion, starting with, perhaps, the advanced countries and moving gradually through successive layers or nations.

on-line (computers) any system in which a central processing unit controls the operation and the peripherals (qv). (cf: *off-line*)

on-line (air crew) in commercial airlines, on or pertaining to the regular routes allotted to and flown by those airlines.

on lobby terms (pols/UK) the British equivalent of the US 'not for attribution' (qv) relationship between politicians and the press, whereby a politician can say what he likes, in the confidence that he will never be cited as a source.

on one's card (theatre) the free admission to various entertainments available to an actor who produces an Equity (actors' union) card at the box office.

on space (press) payments to freelance writers which are based on the copy printed, rather than on a retainer that is paid irrespective of actual work published.

on spike (theatre/US) aka: *on its dead* (UK): scenery, furniture or props that are arranged correctly on their various marks ready for a performance or a scene to begin.

on the beat (sex) aka: *on the game, on the turf, in the racket*: the practice of prostitution by either sex who solicit for customers in the street.

on the blanket (pols) the practice by IRA prisoners in the Maze Prison, N.I. to protest against their not being allowed the status of political prisoners, by refusing to wear regulation clothing and instead living wrapped in a prison blanket.

on the deck (aerospace) flying at a minimally safe altitude, as low as possible.

on the line (air crew) the flying of regular commercial flights.

on the plate (theatre) on the switchboard; refers back to the 'plate': the control panel which operated the gas-powered illuminations of the 19th century theatre.

on the slit (police/UK) airport thieves who slit open mailbags and luggage in the hope of finding a lucrative reward.

on the tin (police/US) using one's 'tin' – the official badge – to gain free admissions, meals and other favours.

on the trot (police/UK) on the run.

on top (horse-racing) any bet announced to a bookmaker with the phrase 'on top' is a spurious bet, made by an accomplice to egg on the other punters who have yet to make up their minds; it will not be recorded in the ledger and no money will change hands whatever the result. (cf: *rick*)

oojiboo (milit) British Army: thingummyjig, whatdycallit, whatsis.

op art (art) an art movement of the 1960s which specialised in producing dramatic effects on the viewer's optical system by creating sharply painted abstract patterns whose colour and contrasts forced the eyes to deal with fluctuating images, a 'shimmer' and other visual illusions.

op-ed (press) (abbrev) *op*posite the *editorial*: a page of opinionated or feature material, usually related to the current news, that appears in US papers opposite the editorial page; often the home of the paper's regular columnists.

open (new therapies) the opposite of uptight (qv): vulnerable, willing to accept new ideas and concepts, offering accessible emotion, parading one's feelings.

open admissions (educ) aka: *open enrolment*: the policy of enrolling all and every student in the college of their choice, irrespective of their being able or not to fulfil the admissions standards of that college but with the intent of thus eradicating the advantages that the more privileged (white, middle-class) child possesses in such competitions, even if such a policy would sacrifice the educational standards of the colleges so affected.

open broad *v* (movies) to launch a new film simultaneously at a number of leading cinemas right across a given market or country. (cf: *roll out*)

open cold (theatre/US) to open a new play in New York, without benefit of the usual round of out-of-town try-outs.

open classroom (educ) aka: *open corridor*: a style of education, especially at primary level, where children are not forced to stay in a classroom or at their desks but enjoy unstructured education, centred on investigation and discussion rather than traditional and formal instruction.

open contracts (futures market) contracts which have been bought or sold without the transaction having been completed by subsequent sale or purchase, or making or taking actual delivery of a financial instrument.

open convention (pols/US) a political convention which starts off when no one candidate can claim a safe majority; this majority, it is assumed, will emerge as the convention proceeds.

open door (TV) access television (qv) for minority groups: they put together the content and the presentation and a studio expert helps out with the necessary technical details.

open-door policy (indust relats) the policy whereby trade union officials and/or shop stewards have the right of access to senior managers.

open housing (govt/US) the official prohibition of any racial or religious conditions being attached to the sale of a house; thus, by extension, a policy aimed to end the creation of ghettos, inner city slums and general divisiveness within urban populations.

opening *n* (futures market) the period at the start of a trading session officially designated by the Exchange during which all transactions are considered to have been made 'at the opening'. (cf: *close*)

opening price (futures market) aka: *opening range*: the price or range recorded during that period officially designated the Opening (qv).

open interest (futures market) a number of open futures contracts; refers to unliquidated purchases or sales.

open-jaw ticket (air crew) an airline booking that takes one route out and another one back; or a trip that comes back along the out route, but terminates at a different destination.

open-list *v* (commerce) for a retailer to set prices between two limits, neither of which is especially higher or lower than the full price.

open order (stock market) an order to a broker that remains good until it is either cancelled or fulfilled.

open sky (pols) the proposal of Pres. Eisenhower at the 1954 Geneva Convention that the US and USSR should permit each other unlimited aerial photography of their territories. The Soviets rejected such an idea but the US commenced a programme of secret U2 surveillance flights, the existence of which was discovered when the U2 piloted by Gary Powers crashed in 1960, wrecking a summit conference.

open the kimono (business) a means of countering possible opposition by taking potential buyers into one's confidence and revealing details of future products or similar otherwise secret information – which disclosures should sufficiently impress the client as to ensure his signing a lucrative contract.

open up (theatre) 1. in acting, to turn the body fully towards the front of the stage to increase the required emphasis of a line or gesture. 2. any form of on-stage emphasis, such as picking up a prop, or similar business.

operant conditioning (business) the persuading of one's workforce to do what you wish them to do – often by providing incentive schemes, productivity bonuses, etc.

operating system (computers) aka: *supervisor, monitor, executive*: the software that is required to manage a system's hardware and logical resources (qqv), including scheduling and file management.

operational analysis (indust relats) a branch of applied psychology that is designed to achieve ideal relations between a machine and its human operator; the main intention being to eliminate the inevitable human errors that can mar effective joint productivity.

operationalise (govt) to put into operation.

operator (computers) any symbol within a program that indicates that an operation is to be performed: +, −, *, #, etc.

opinionaire (sociol) a questionnaire that is designed to obtain the opinions of a respondent. 'A word of doubtful usefulness' (R. W. Burchfield, *OED Supp.* Vol. III).

OPM (finance) (acro) *other people's money*: the ideal financing for a speculator: you obtain someone else's money and use it as you see fit; if you profit then everyone benefits and if you lose, only the other person has to suffer the loss.

opportunism (pols) in Marxist terms, those proletarian leaders who use their own positions to subordinate the class struggle and the demands of ideological purity to their own selfish ends, most notably in collaborating with the bourgeoisie and enjoying the trappings of such a lifestyle.

opportunity class (educ) aka: *opportunity room*: a euphemism for those special classes in which backward pupils are given 'an opportunity to learn'; such pupils are 'not quite bright enough to be classed as slow' (J. LeSure) (see Bibliog.).

opportunity servicing (aerospace) servicing on an aircraft that can be carried out at any convenient time, although such times must fall within the broad limits set down for the checking of the components so involved.

Oprep (milit) (abbrev) US code: operations report; these cover a multitude of worldwide events in which US forces are involved.

opticals (movies, TV) all visual tricks, special effects, and other techniques that involve laboratory work on the print.

optical wand (computers) an electronic device that is used in supermarkets to 'read' the pricing bar-codes that are printed on many packages.

optimise the objective function *v* (business) to find a plan that best allocates the available resources towards the achieving of the desired goal.

optimum mix (milit) the US nuclear strategy of the 1960s that preceded MAD (qv): the concept

of sending one devastating first strike that would destroy all Soviet weapons, factories and population centres at a stroke. (cf: *massive deterrence*)

option (stock market) the right to deal in a security at a fixed price over a specified period. Thus *call option*: the right to purchase a share at the 'striking price' (the exercise price at which a holder can call for stock) over a period of up to 90 days; *put option*: a similar right over selling the shares; *double option* the rights of either buying or selling over the 90 day period.

option art (art) works which allow the artist and the spectators a number of choices in the arrangement of those elements which make them up.

opt out (radio) aka: *pot out*: that moment during a networked transmission – a news broadcast, a live feed (qv), etc – when a local station has the chance to discontinue its receiving of that material and return to their own programmes. The opt out point would be fore-warned by a time check or similar notification.

opt-out *n* (radio, TV) a programme broadcast by a regional or local TV or radio station for local consumption only and from which the other network stations can choose to opt out.

oral note (diplomacy) a written but unsigned communication which is given the status of the spoken word and is thus useful but not binding on those parties using it during a negotiation.

orange book (govt) reports published in yellow covers that deal with marketing of foodstuffs and other commodities.

orange force (milit) the 'hostile' force during NATO simulated wargames and other exercises; since 'blue force' (qv) represent the NATO forces, it must be assumed that 'orange' has replaced 'red' out of some sense of tact towards the Soviet bloc.

orange goods (commerce) those products rated at a medium level of consumption, servicing and markup: ie clothes.

oranges sour (milit) US Dept. of Defense air code: weather unsuitable for flying; thus *oranges sweet*: weather suitable for flying.

orchestra (espionage) a term coined by Lenin and subsequently adopted by major intelligence services to refer to those tame 'targets', suitably primed by threats and/or blackmail, who can be used when necessary but are generally left to await such a summons until a suitable occasion arises.

orchestra stall (theatre) the very front rows of the stalls, adjacent to the orchestra pit. (cf: *bald-headed row*)

orderly *a* (milit) any officer or NCO who attends to the domestic side of the troops; known individually as *orderly dog*: an officer; *orderly buff*: sergeant; *orderly pig*: corporal.

orderly market (stock market) a steady market

O

with a good supply of buyers and sellers as required. (cf: *disorderly market*)

ordinary *n, a* (commerce) common stock without any preference; those shareholders who possess such stock.

oreo (milit) US armed forces: a derogatory description by black troops of their fellows who appear to be toadying to the white authorities; from Oreo Cookies which are made of two chocolate wafers surrounding a white sugar cream filling; *oreo* has replaced the earlier 'Uncle Tom', with much the same meaning.

org (entertainment) (abbrev) organisation: any show business corporation, agency, chain, etc.

organicity (business) the degree of participation by subordinates in the establishment of goal-setting and in decision-making within an organisation; also the maintenance of open lines of communication between all levels of an organisation.

organise (milit) British Army: to scrounge, to obtain unofficially, to steal.

organismic sensing (new therapies) a concept developed by Carl Rogers, pioneer of encounter therapy, to infer the use of one's entire being, its mental and physical attributes, in experiencing a given situation or person.

original *n* (commerce) in fashion, a garment especially designed as part of a designer's new collection of clothes and first revealed when that collection is officially displayed to clients and journalists.

original classification authorities (govt) the power to classify information which has not been classified previously.

originals (TV) the standard costumes worn by the regular characters in a long running serial or soap opera (qv).

ornamentation (music) the use of grace notes to embellish melodies.

orphan (commerce) in the second-hand motor trade, any discontinued model of a car.

ortho (medic) (abbrev) orthopedics: a surgical speciality that concentrates on dealing with bones.

orthopad (medic) an orthopedic surgeon.

oscar (TV) a light diffuser, split into adjustable quarters, which varies the power and/or direction of that light. Thus *female oscar*: 75% of the illumination is blacked out; *male oscar*: 25% of the illumination is blacked out.

Oscar (movies) annual awards for excellence in various branches of film-making, given by the Hollywood Academy of Motion Picture Arts & Sciences; the award was allegedly named for one Oscar Pierce, a US wheat and fruit grower, whose niece worked in pictures and who remarked on seeing one of the statuettes in 1931 how greatly it resembled her uncle.

OTH (advertising) (acro) opportunities to hear: a statistical reference to the number of times a member of a target audience is exposed to a station that is running a specific advertisement. The 'weight' (or impact) of a campaign can be judged by the average OTH for all members of that target audience.

OTH-B radar (milit) (acro) over the horizon backscatter radar: radar that can transmit signals from objects that are out of the line of sight by following the earth's curvature; 'backscatter' means that the signals come back along the same track; potential range appx. 1800 metres.

other body (pols/US) members of the Senate or House of Representatives refer to one another as 'the other body'. (cf: *another place*)

other ranks (milit) members of the armed forces other than commissioned officers.

other shoe syndrome (business) in the case of a number of executives in a firm being made redundant, those survivors, rather than feeling relieved, find their own morale sabotaged as they wait for 'the other shoe' to come down on them; thus the cost-cutting plans that caused the first firings can backfire to such an extent that the survival of the company may be threatened for all its new economic neatness.

other than honourable discharge (milit/US) the equivalent of the enlisted man's 'dishonourable discharge', sanitised for the supposedly more sensitive (since middle/upper class) officer.

OTH radar (milit) (acro) over the horizon radar: radar signals that follow the earth's curvature and thus capture objects far out of the line of sight; these signals hit the target then bounce up to the ionosphere before returning to the monitor. (cf: *OTH-B radar*)

OTS (advertising) (acro) opportunities to see: the television version of radio advertising's 'opportunities to hear' (OTH). The total exposure of an advertisement to a potential target viewer.

OTSOG (sociol) (acro) on the shoulders of giants: a concept of the development of learning through the continual transfer of one innovator's discoveries to his successors and so on.

OTT (movies, TV) (acro) over the top: an expression of disgust, amusement, shock, delight beloved of TV and movie film crews.

out *n* (radio) the last few words of a given tape, written on the cue sheet (qv), on the label and the box which contains the tape: using the out and a timed length, the engineer, producer or presenter can plan accurate programmes which incorporate tapes and live material.

out (radio, CB) a signal in radio communications (military and civilian) that the speaker has finished his conversation and wishes to cease talking.

outcue (radio/TV) a cue that indicates that a given broadcast or transmission is about to end.

outfit (drugs) aka: *works*: the syringe and other implements that a drug addict requires to administer injections.

outfit (milit) any group of servicemen, large or small.

outfit (commerce) in the terminology of Canada's Hudson Bay Company: one fiscal year, dating from June 1 to May 31; at the end of the outfit a full inventory was taken of the Company's stocks.

outlaw n (sex) to a black pimp, any prostitute who does not work for a pimp. Similarly, a freelance homosexual hustler.

out of (horse-racing) Horse X 'out of' Horse Y: the dam of a horse. (cf: *by*)

outseg (pols/US) (abbrev) *outseg*regate: to offer policies that are more racist and segregationist than those of one's opponents.

outsert (advertising) the opposite of insert (qv): any advertisement or other promotional material attached to the outside of a product or its package.

on the outside (espionage) an agent who works in the field; thus *on the inside*: the case officer who runs that agent from his office.

outlay creep (govt, business) the gradual increase in government or corporation expenditure that occurs aside from any actual plans involving specifically increased budgets.

out of rack (TV) a film that has slipped in the projector so that the individual frames no longer register with the gate (qv) and the frame borders appear across the screen.

output (computers) 1. *n* the results one receives from operating the machine. 2. *v* to transfer information from the machine to an external peripheral, ie: a cathode ray tube or a printer.

outreach n (govt, soc wk) the extending of government or social services beyond their current or conventional limits; especially in a situation where the people at whom these services are aimed are seen to be uninterested in using them and it is deemed necessary to take the services out to them, whether they desire such aid or not.

outside (sport) in surfing, 1. that part of the sea beyond the breakers. 2. a call of 'outside!' means that a set of large surfable breakers is starting to roll in.

outside (milit) USMC: the civilian world outside Marine camps.

outside man (police) an individual who may take on one of several specialist roles in the carrying out of elaborate confidence tricks.

outsider art (art) that art produced by artists who stand outside 'normal' society and its social conditioning. Their highly original works are designed to satisfy their own psychic needs rather than that of the public. Many of these artists are hermits or schizophrenics, but their ranks exclude naive, folk, prison, tribal or children's artists.

outside work (gambling) any tampering with dice that concerns their external surfaces.

outside world (pols/US) those voters or parties that exist beyond the horizons and allegiances of the party which is using that phrase; non-aligned voters who have yet to be accounted for on the pollsters' lists.

outstanding (milit/US) top of the six army ratings, ie: 1. outstanding, 2. superior, 3. excellent, 4. effective, 5. marginal, 6. inadequate. These ratings apply only to officers and are used on their 'efficiency reports'.

out-take (TV, movies) those sequences or scenes that are rejected by the editor/director at the cutting stage and are not incorporated in the final film; out-takes often include unscheduled moments of humour, actors forgetting their lines, special effects failing to work, etc.

out-takes (business) by extension from the film/TV use (qv), those parts of a commercial presentation that are deliberately dropped prior to making that presentation to the client.

out-turn (econ) actual, practical results, predictions that did turn out as planned, as opposed to random, if detailed, estimates.

over (press) those copies in excess of the print run which are deliberately printed up so as to allow for wastage.

over-achiever (educ) those pupils who attain higher standards in school than IQ and other tests would indicate might be expected; rather than praise such efforts, many teachers see such achievements as the result of fears, excessive parental pressure, etc. (cf: *under-achievers*)

overalls (milit) British Army: close fitting trousers worn as part of the uniform; esp. by cavalrymen.

over and under (sport) in shooting, a shotgun with its barrels positioned one above the other, rather than in parallel.

overcrank (TV, movies) to operate a camera or projector at a faster speed than is correct and thus create 'slow motion' on the screen. Thus *undercrank*: to operate the camera or projector more slowly than is correct and therefore achieve 'fast motion' on the screen. Both varieties of 'cranking' come from the early cameras which had to be handcranked and were more susceptible to such fluctuations in operating speed.

overdub *v* (rock business) to add extra sound tracks to a basic recording – either more instruments, vocals, special effects, or whatever necessary.

overflow (computers) the generation through its calculations of a number that is too great for the computer to display or to use for further calculations.

overhead (press/US) a wire service bulletin that carries local news only and thus goes on 'over' the major newspapers to its various local destinations.

overhead *n* (computers) that time a computer uses purely for the maintenance of its own systems, rather than that used for running programs for the user. Such an overhead can detract marginally from the efficient and speedy running of those programs.

overhead (milit) USMC: the ceiling.

overkill (milit) the concept of being able to destroy a target more than once, a requirement that justifies the firing of many missiles but has no useful military application. (cf: *underkill*)

overmatter (press) matter (qv) that has been typeset but is superfluous to the needs of a given issue or edition.

overnight money (finance) ultra-short term loans that are offered for the duration of one night only.

overnight multiple (finance) the dramatic results of a public offering of shares otherwise held only by insiders (qv). Usually such an offering increases the value of insider holdings 'overnight'.

overnights (TV) expenses paid to employees who have to stay away from their homes when working on programmes that are remote from the company's headquarters.

overnights (TV) the instant ratings provided by A. C. Nielsen for each day's US TV viewing and which are available on the following morning.

overpressure (milit) nuclear blasts that are strong enough to destroy hardened (qv) missile silos.

overs *n* (police/UK) that surplus of property or money that has been taken in a robbery and might now itself be stolen by other thieves, unless it can be hidden safely.

overstretch *n* (milit) an overextension of military forces.

over the counter (stock market) the buying and selling of stocks between firms or individuals rather than involving the Stock Exchange in the deal; legitimate, private, 'unlisted' dealing.

over the fence (aerospace) that moment in a landing just before the actual touchdown; the 'fence' is the boundary of the airfield.

overture and beginners! (theatre) the call to those actors who are to be 'discovered' on stage at the start of a play's first act, warning them that it is time to take their positions.

overview (govt, media) a general, wide-ranging view; from the concept of flying up and making an 'aerial surveillance' of an abstract problem.

own *v* (sport) in foxhunting, the moment when the hounds show that they have found a scent.

own goal (milit) in IRA terminology, the self-destruction of a terrorist who mistakenly triggers his own bomb before he has been able to plant it.

o.z. (drugs/US) pron. 'oh zee': one ounce, a common measure of marijuana or hashish.

ozoners (movies) drive in cinemas, where one can theoretically enjoy the fresh air and 'ozone'.

P

PA (movies) (abbrev) *personal appearances*: the promotional tours by film stars to accompany the release of a new movie.

pacers (indust relats) aka: *speeders, bell-horses*: fast workers who are used by the management to accelerate production or to establish a high rate for the setting of piecework norms.

pacification (milit) the removal of hostile guerilla opposition from an area, often by such measures as destroying potentially friendly towns and villages – rather than let them act as bases for insurgents – and crops, cattle, etc which might help them with supplies. Such efforts, rather than secure the loyalty of the local population – whose houses, crops, etc are being destroyed – tend largely to send more of them into guerilla ranks.

pack *n* (theatre) aka: *scene pack*: a group of flats, all used in the same scene, which are placed together in the scene dock.

pack *v* (computers) the saving of space within a computer memory by using electronic 'shorthand' to represent various data, which shorthand can be 'unpacked' when the data is actually needed for calculations.

package (radio) aka: *wrap*: a newsreader's script which sums up one or a number of stories; made up of his/her comments, interviews, pieces of 'actuality' (qv) and any other useful ingredients.

package (crime/US) 1. the victim of a kidnapping. 2. the victim of a gangland assassination team.

packaging (art) originated by the Surrealist Man Ray with a one-off mysteriously wrapped package, the wrapping and bagging of objects large and small has been developed greatly in recent years. Most notable packager is Christo, who wraps sections of Australian cliffs and similar massive natural structures.

packet (computers) a segment of data which is processed as a single unit in a communications system. Thus *to packet*: to sort out and segment suitable pieces of data for processing as a unit; *packet-switching*: the transfer of packets over a communications system, each one restricted in size and bearing a specific address (qv).

pack shot *n* (advertising) a close-up shot of the product for which the advertisement is being made, usually the final and climactic shot of the film.

pact *v* (movies) to sign a contract. (cf: *ink*)

pad (police/US) *on the pad*: to share in the corrupt payments received by members of a police force from local citizens, both law-abiding and criminal.

paddlefoot (milit) USAF: an infantryman; a member of the ground crew who maintain the airplanes but do not fly.

Paddy (milit) RN: *doing Paddy Doyle*: serving a period of detention in punishment cells.

paganini (movies) in Italian film crews, a system of graded blocks to raise or lower a camera's height with great speed and accuracy. (cf: *two-four-six*)

page (computers) a block of information that fills the VDU screen on a computer and which can be read as one might a page of a book or file.

page traffic (advertising) an estimate of the numbers of readers per page of a publication.

page-turner (publishing) a best-selling book that keeps its readers turning from page to page. (cf: *legs*)

paid off in gold (drugs) when a dealer makes an arrangement to sell drugs to an undercover policeman who shows his golden badge instead of a wad of money when the drugs have been produced.

paint *v* (medic) to appear on the screen of a cathode ray tube.

paint *n* (gambling) any picture cards.

paint (milit) for an object to create a blip on a radar screen, esp. one that reveals itself as the position of an aircraft.

painterly painting (art) used to translate the Ger. 'malerisch', an attempt to represent in the artist's technique the vague and shifting essence of a subject. This style of painting is characterised by colour, texture and stroke rather than contours or line.

painting down (movies, TV) to create fake 'Negroes' by making up white actors in blackface.

painting the bus (business) the cosmetic, artificial alteration of a plan, proposal or request which still leaves the essence of that plan or proposal unchanged; expedient window-dressing with no really substantial modification.

paintpot (TV) a lever on a telecine machine by which a producer can make electronic alterations in the colour ranges of a transmission.

pair *v* (pols) for members of rival parties to agree

to abstain together from voting at such times as one of the two is unable to attend the legislative assembly; a popular practice in the House of Commons, the US Congress and other parliamentary bodies.

pair of spectacles (sport) in cricket, the score by a batsman of 0 runs in both of his two innings, which double 00 supposedly resembles a pair of glasses.

PAL (milit) USMC: (abbrev) *prisoner at large*: an individual who is being punished by being confined to camp limits.

palimony (law/US) a blend of 'pal' and 'alimony' that refers to the payments that a growing number of former lovers of no especial abilities themselves, are managing to extract from the celebrities with whom they once happened to have lived.

pallet bombing (milit) a means of bombing targets by placing bombs on flat pallets and then throwing both bomb and pallet from the doors of the plane.

pam (theatre) (abbrev) panorama.

pan (music) in West Indian steel bands, a drum made from the top of a 44 gallon steel barrel; by extension *pan* represents the whole lifestyle that surrounds steel-band music.

pan (milit) US Dept of Defense code: the calling station has an urgent message concerning the safety of a ship, aircraft or other vehicle or person either on board or in sight of the aircraft.

pan (movies) (abbrev) panoramic shot: the action of rotating the camera in a horizontal mode to create a long, flat shot.

pan, down the (sport) in motor-racing, too far behind the other cars to be in real contention.

pancake (TV, movies) a small chunk of wood, hidden from the camera, on which short actors can stand to bring them up to the correct height for their role.

pancake (milit) US Dept of Defense code: I wish to land.

pancake *n* (air crew) a specially designed bullet for use by airline security guards who have to fire pistols inside a pressurised cabin: the bullet is in fact a canvas bag filled with lead shot which will make a killing wound at close range but will have slowed down so much by the time it reaches the far end of the plane that it will not penetrate the hull.

P & S (futures market) (abbrev) *purchase and sale* statement: a statement provided by a broker showing changes in the customer's net balance after the offset of a previously established position (qv).

panel (press) a short item indented at either side, usually in bold face or italic type, with a rule or border top and bottom.

panhandle (aerospace) the firing handle of an ejector seat.

Panhonlib (commerce) (abbrev) Panama,

Honduras, Liberia: a merchant ship registered in one of these countries and flying a flag of convenience. (cf: *Panlibhonco*)

Panlibhonco (commerce) (abbrev) Panama, Liberia, Honduras, Costa Rica: a merchant ship registered in one of these countries which is flying a flag of convenience. (cf: *Panhonlib*)

panopolis (govt) aka: *cloud city, open field*: in urban planning the gradual movement of population away from dependence on one centre towards the establishment of a number of separate centres and hierarchies as that population increases and becomes more dispersed.

panpot (audio) (abbrev) *pan*oramic *pot*entiometer: an instrument which can vary the apparent position of a sound by altering the strengths of the signals to a number of speakers without altering the overall signal strength.

pantouflage (govt) the tradition in the French civil service for its senior members to move smoothly and automatically into equally senior and influential positions within the nation's industries.

pantry check (marketing) a check into what is on the subject's kitchen or larder shelves; when combined with a dustbin check (qv) the market researcher can provide his client with a *home audit*.

pants *n* (prison/UK) a scrounger – 'he's always on the bum'.

pants (aerospace) aka: *spats, trouser*: the fixed fairing that covers a plane's wheels and landing gear.

papavero (Mafia) lit 'a real Daddy': a big shot, a senior Mafioso.

paper *n* (finance) any form of money that is not in currency or specie: stocks, bonds, loan certificates, etc.

paper (theatre) 1. advertising material put up outside the theatre. 2. v. to give out free tickets (*paper*) in order to fill a poor house. Thus a *paper house*: an audience composed almost entirely of free admissions.

paper gold (econ) aka: *Special Drawing Rights*: a means of international exchange created by the International Monetary Fund (IMF) whereby indebted governments can obtain extra funds to alleviate their debts.

paper tiger (pols) in Chinese Communist terminology: any country, person or weapon that looks outwardly terrifying but is in fact no more dangerous than a tiger made from paper. Coined by Mao Tse Tung in 1946, when he told correspondent Anna Louise Strong 'All reactionaries are paper tigers'.

par (sport) in golf, the standard score in strokes assigned to each hole and as such the score expected, in fair conditions and barring disasters, of a first class player going round a given course. Thus a given hole is known as *par-three*, *par-four*, etc.

par (press) (abbrev) a *par*agraph.

para (medic) (abbrev) paraplegic; thus *quadra*: (abbrev) quadraplegic.

paraffin budgie (commerce) on an oil rig: a helicopter.

parajournalism (press) a type of unconventional journalism which brought in the writer's personality, urged a greater involvement than was traditional for newspaper reporters and took many liberties with once sacred facts. (cf: *new journalism*)

parallelism (computers) the simultaneous handling by a computer of a large number of calculations.

parameter *n, v* (pavlov) a boundary, a limit, a basic factor, a framework. Parameter has a number of highly specific, technical and abstruse meanings in mathematics, none of which seem to have been appreciated by those who have elevated it into one of the most widely used (and abused) vogue words.

parameter driven software (computers) a scheme whereby a user can specify a number (perhaps 50%) of the attributes he requires in a program; such programs are created with a number of in-built variables which can be used or discarded according to the individual's whims; a compromise on having a full program constructed to one's individual needs.

parametric design (archit) an architectural school of the mid-1960s which emphasised the analysis, measurement and reconciliation of all those elements which they termed 'parameters' in a building.

parasite (aerospace) any aeroplane which relies on another for propulsion and lift. Such a vehicle can either ride on the back of its *parent* or be towed behind it.

parasite (pols) in Marxist terms those people without any legitimate occupation of their own who batten onto the efforts of those who do; first used to attack absentee landlords but currently extended to define all those who rebel (in the way of Western youth) against the constraints of socialist states.

parcel *n* (prison/UK) rather than remain all night with a plastic bucket full of excrement, prisoners prefer to wrap it in newspaper and toss the resulting 'parcel' out of the window.

parchment (milit) RN: a rating's service certificate on which his abilities and personality are noted by the commanding officer of each ship on which he serves.

parent (science) in nuclear physics, a nuclide that becomes transformed into another nuclide (known as the *daughter*) by nuclear disintegration.

parish pump (pols) parochial local or national politicians who are unable or unwilling to extend their knowledge or interests outside their own small social or geographical limits.

parity (milit) a situation whereby two hostile nations can offer equal military capability in the case of a conflict between them; esp. the struggle between US and USSR.

park (sport) in soccer, the actual pitch; thus *keep it on the park*: keep the ball in play, rather than kicking it over the sidelines into touch.

parking orbit (aerospace) an orbit in which a spacecraft waits prior to moving on, either to land, to proceed to another planet, etc.

parlay *v* (gambling) to exploit something with great success, spec. to take a small stake and make it into substantial winnings.

parrot (milit) aka: *IFF* (identification of friend or foe): transponder equipment in military aircraft used to tell hostile and friendly aircraft apart. Thus *strangle the parrot*: switch off the IFF transponder.

parse *v* (computers) to understand a program or an instruction properly.

participatory art (art) art works that are created specifically to encourage the participation of the spectators. Such genres as Kinetic Art, Cybernetic Art, Happenings, Environmental Sculpture (qqv) all demand a degree of this participation.

party *n, v* (sex) the actual intercourse between client and prostitute; 'what kind of party did you fancy . . .?' various styles of party come at various different prices.

party line (espionage) the official point of view of an intelligence agency.

partyness (pols) trans. from Rus. 'partinost': the use of the Party and its ideology as a guide and inspiration in every part of one's daily life, professional, social and recreational.

party plan (advertising) a scheme for selling products by setting up parties ie: Tupperware parties – whereby a hostess volunteers to provide a few refreshments, the salesman brings along his wares and afterwards the hostess receives some gifts or discounted goods as her reward.

pasadena (movies) aka: *el paso*: two punning references to the idea of *passing* a deal, ie: turning it down but remaining open to further suggestions; from the poker call of 'pass' in which one skips a round of betting but still remains in the game.

PASCAL (computers) an algorithmic language for programming computers; now surpassed and mainly replaced by COBOL and FORTRAN (qqv).

pass *v* (rock business) to turn down a deal or a new singer or musician. (cf: *pasadena*)

pass a dividend (finance) the voting of a company's directors against the issuing of a dividend that year.

pass-along (econ) the way in which the increased costs to a producer or a creator of a service are passed along to the consumer or purchaser in the form of higher prices, rents, etc.

pass-along readership (advertising) aka: *pass-on readership*: those readers who do not actually buy a magazine or newspaper but still read someone else's copy and as such are potential targets for its advertising.

passenger (gambling/UK) aka: *goat* (US): a poor player at cards.

passengers (milit) the multiple warheads that are fired from a MIRV (qv) bus (qv) on a signal from its computer; each missile should have an accuracy of between 600' and 100', either of which should be adequate to destroy its chosen target.

passive defence (milit) any non-aggressive (unarmed) modes of defence: cover, concealment, subterfuge, dispersal, mobility.

pass-over *n* (aerospace) that time when a spacecraft crosses over a given point.

password hacker (computers) a meddler in a computer room who is merely trying to pick up any random information by fiddling aimlessly around the machines. (cf: *hacker*)

pasteboard *n* (theatre/US) a ticket.

pasteup (advertising, printing) elements of an advertisement, booklet, newspaper page, etc., are assembled and pasted onto a white board (suitably ruled as to col. width, etc, when necessary) to show correct positions.

patacca (police/UK) fr. Ital 'worthless rubbish': fake jewellery in general; spec: a fake 'Swiss watch', aka: *mug's ticker, ramped watch* and peddled by fake 'jewellery salesmen' and airline stewards.

patch *n* (police) an area within the jurisdiction of a particular police station; an individual policeman's beat. (cf: *manor*)

patch *v* (technology) to connect up temporarily one electronic device to another, esp. one radio or telephone system into another.

patch *v* (advertising) to alter one small element of a layout or a plate.

patch *v* (computers) to make a minute alteration in a program or in the workings of the machine.

patch system (social wk) a method of organising local authority social work whereby each geographical area is designated to one or two social workers and all referrals that arise in those areas are taken by them.

path (medic) (abbrev) pathology.

patrial (govt) those who have the right of abode in the UK; thus *non-patrial*: the opposite; in many cases the two words seem to stand for 'white' and 'coloured' as far as immigration practice is seen to work.

patrimonial (diplomacy) that area immediately subtending a nation's coastal waters which belongs to that nation, although the shipping and airplanes of other nations may pass through or above them with impunity; measured at approx. 200 miles beyond the edge of the territorial waters, themselves 12 miles from the coastline.

pattern bargaining (indust relats) negotiations that bring in examples of settlements by similar groups of workers and their employers as a means of using such precedents to further their own claims.

pattern variable (sociol) a phrase coined by Talcott Parsons in his theory that all social action could be found within a range of five main dichotomous patterns of behaviour.

pavement princess (CB) Citizen's Band radio terminology: a prostitute.

pave paws (milit) a proposed development of phased array radar which is to be installed on the east and west coasts of the US and is intended to offer an early warning of a sea-launched nuclear first strike.

pawn *v* (stock market) to use one's stocks as security for a bank loan.

pax (air crew) from 'passengers': the fare paying travellers.

paybob (milit) RN: the senior accountant officer.

payoff *n* (crime) a confidence trick whereby the victim is lured into making a large bet or investment by his initial success with a smaller bet or investment; once he is persuaded to put forward a larger sum, he is sure to lose it all.

payload (aerospace) bombs, warheads, etc carried by a military plane; the capsule, instruments, astronauts, etc carried by a rocket.

payload (air crew) that part of an airliner's load from which the company makes its money: the passengers and the cargo and possibly airmail.

payola (record business) the payment of bribes, in cash and commodities, to disc jockeys to play specific records more than others and thus ensure their increased sales. Allegedly wiped out after the 'payola scandals' of the 1950s, but few insiders would really believe that. Thus *plugola*: the purchased plugging of specific records on the radio; *royola*: extra royalties available for corrupt disc jockeys from the records they plug.

pay or play (movies) a contract which forces the studio to pay a star or a director for their services, whether or not the movie in which they are concerned is ever made.

PC (gambling) (abbrev) percentage: an advantage gained either by offering less than true odds or by using crooked dice. Thus *percentage dice*: crooked dice which work in the cheater's favour; *PC game*: a percentage game in which the bank always keeps the advantage by offering less than honest odds; *percentage tops and bottoms*: a pair of crooked dice, one of which is mis-spotted, usually by having two 2s or 5s on the same dice.

PDL (computers) (acro) *p*ush *d*own *l*ist: any priority queue, the set of whatever things the operator must do next.

pea (horse-racing) in Australia, the favourite; refers to the pea that is used in a three-shell-game and which signifies the winning shell.

peaceful nuclear technology (pols) the description of any nuclear research or development that ostensibly concentrates on energy and ignores the military possibilities of enriched uranium; the results of such researches and projects are termed *peaceful nuclear devices*.

peacock alley (commerce) the main lobby or promenade of fashionable hotels; orig. describing that of the Waldorf-Astoria in New York.

peak experience (new therapies) coined by Abraham Maslow, breakthrough moments of supreme emotional significance that transcend any other levels of perception that may hitherto have been achieved; the sensing of life's every nuance with one's entire being.

peak hour (TV) aka; *peak time*: a daypart (qv) at which time TV viewing figures are most concentrated; from approx 6.30 pm to 10.30 pm, allowing for seasonal and daily (the weekends are different) alterations.

peaking (pols/US) a method of campaigning that seeks to bring every effort to a triumphal crescendo in the day or so prior to the actual election.

peak shaving (technology) the storing of energy when demand is low so that it can be used to bolster supplies when demand becomes more intense.

peanut gallery (theatre/US) the highest gallery with the cheapest seats and most vociferous theatre-goers. (cf: *the Gods*)

pearling (sport) in surfing: when the nose of the surfboard goes under the waves during a ride.

peasant painting (art) the spare-time paintings of Chinese peasants in the years following the Cultural Revolution of 1966. Characterised by technical proficiency and stylistic uniformity.

pec (sport) in body-building, a *pec*toral muscle; thus *lats*: lateral muscles, *trips*: triceps.

peck horn (music) in jazz, a mellophone or saxophone.

PED (prison/UK) (acro) *parole eligibility date*.

peddler (drugs) a retail dealer in narcotics, as opposed to a *connection* who is a wholesaler.

pedestal (TV) the voltage level in a TV transmission that equates with the black tones.

pedestal (aerospace) a raised box between the two pilots which houses many of the controls and the interfaces (qv) between various systems.

peekaboo (business) from the computer terminology for the checking of punched cards by placing one on top of the other and seeing whether or not the holes were all punched correctly: the taking of a number of elements in a business situation and seeing if they match up or not.

peep *n* (espionage) a specialist in clandestine photography.

peg (sport) in cricket, a stump.

peg *n* (milit) British Army: a charge; usually as *on a peg*: on a charge, under arrest.

peg *v* (gambling) 1. to place a marker that indicates the dealer in a card game or the point in craps. 2. to mark cards by pricking them with a drawing pin concealed in a bandage on a finger or thumb.

peg back (horse-racing) to overtake or gain on another horse.

peg house (sex) a brothel for male homosexual prostitutes; thus *peg-boy*: one who frequents a peg-house.

peggy (milit) RN: a ship's mess steward.

peg prices (finance) prices that are held at artificial levels, usually determined by government interference.

penaid (milit) (abbrev) *penetration aid*: any device, destructive or non-destructive that is used to guide missiles onto a target.

pencil *n* (gambling) the privilege of signing cheques in a casino and having them picked up by the casino: 'the power of the pencil'.

pencil whip *v* (business) the practice of overworked and harried executives who pass reports, sign letters, accept expenses, sanction defective work, etc rather than examine them in detail; it is simpler to initial the document and pass it on elsewhere.

penetrate (espionage) to infiltrate an enemy organisation – its government, its intelligence service, etc – as a spy. Thus *deep penetration*: long-term penetration by spies whose usefulness may take years to materialise and who are put in place with the knowledge that years will pass before they need be called upon. (cf: *mole*)

penetration (advertising) the number of homes that are actually watching a particular advertisement.

penetration aids (milit) decoy objects that are released from a missile in order to divert anti-ballistic missiles – ranging from dummy warheads to plastic 'missile' shapes.

penetration pricing (commerce) the setting of a low price to encourage widespread purchasing of a new product.

penetration rate (marketing) the proportion of a target market that buys a new brand at least once.

penguin (milit) RAF: 1. a training machine, with all the details of an airplane but without its flying power, used for novice airmen. 2. a non-flying member of the Air Force: ground crew, clerks, etc.

penguin suit (aerospace) an astronaut's space suit, basically tight-fitting overalls.

penman (police/UK) a forger.

penny stock (stock market) a common stock which has a value of less than one dollar – thus highly speculative.

pensioneer *v* (pols) to campaign in an election on the basis of a promised rise in the old age pension rate.

people (air crew) the passengers, but not the crew, on an airliner. (cf: *souls*)

people journalism (media) that style of journalism dedicated to the celebration of the famous;

from the social section of *Time* magazine, entitled 'People' and, latterly, from *People* magazine, which exists solely on celebrities.

people-related problems (indust relats) any errors that stem from human failings – forgetfulness, hangovers, drinking at work, drugs, worry, instability, temper, etc, etc – rather than the breakdown of the machinery.

people's democracy (pols) a political system in which power is regarded as being invested in the masses; spec, in Marxist terms: the intermediate stage between bourgeois democracy and Soviet democracy; 'a dictatorship of the proletariat without Soviet form' which will develop into full socialism under the auspices of the Soviets and the implementation of the class struggle.

people's detailing (archit) a style of housebuilding popular in Britain in the 1950s; devoid of taste, it indulged every petty bourgeois obsession with scaled down grandeur, all imprisoned in super-suburban environments.

people sniffer (milit) a chemically based machine that can 'sniff out' enemy troops in densely overgrown or jungle areas. By analysing the air, it checks for the ammonia odours of human sweat and also notes the tiny seismic reverberations of human walking.

pepper fogging (police/US) the spraying of rioters with tear gas, brandnamed Pepper Gas.

pepper's ghost (theatre) a trick used to create a 'ghost' on stage by using an inclined sheet of plate glass onto which an actor can be projected as if 'walking through air'; first developed by Prof. John Henry Pepper (1821–1900).

perch *n* (theatre) a platform on which lights are sited and directed onto the stage.

percher (police/UK) an easy arrest.

perceptual realism (art) the work of Jack Chambers since 1969 in the form of realistic paintings (based on colour photographs, accompanied by abstruse verbal statements). The aim of this work is to create a type of 'pure' visual experience that exists before culture intervenes and clamps pre-ordained assumptions on the spectator's vision.

percy (milit) British armed forces: an officer or an educated other rank.

per diem (business, movies) expenses and allowances paid either by the day or on the basis of each day's expenditure.

perennial candidate (pols/US) any politician who stands continually for office but equally continually fails to gain his objective.

perfecta (gambling) a combined bet in horse-racing that involves both the first and second horses in a race. (cf: *exacta*, *quinella*)

perfect competition (econ) market competition in which all elements of monopoly are removed and the market price of a commodity is beyond the control of individual buyers and sellers – neither of whom have any preference as to the

various units of the commodity that is for sale, nor as to the individuals involved.

perfect market (econ) a market situation, either real or theoretical, from which all adverse factors have been removed.

perfects (gambling) dice that are true cubes, measured to the nearest 1/10,000 of an inch.

performance art (art) any form of 'artwork' which comprises a variety of forms: dancing, acting, music, films, video, etc, all of which have the intention of executing a prescribed course of action before an audience.

performance contract (educ/US) the contracting with a private educational organisation to accept an agreed fee to improve the educational standards of a given group of public school pupils.

performer (milit) RN: a sailor who makes a habit of causing trouble.

peril point (econ) the point beneath which the lowering of import tariffs can begin to have seriously harmful effects on native industrial production.

period of grace (business) the time allowed to a party in a contract to fulfill those obligations that have been incurred within that contract.

peripherals (computers) equipment linked to the central processing unit of a computer which enhance and increase its basic functions: printers, magnetic discs, tapes, terminals that connect with other machines, etc; peripherals may be 'smart', containing some processing ability of their own, or, if bereft of such ability, 'dumb'.

peripherals (public relations) secondary, provincial, low circulation or low audience media; of only marginal use in a PR campaign.

perisher (milit) RN: the periscope course for officers selected for service in submarines; from a corruption of 'periscope' and that idea of the course being 'perishing hard'.

permanent arms economy (pols) in International Socialist terminology: the United States of America.

permanent revolution (pols) a theory developed by Lev Trotsky (1879–1940) whereby the security and continuance of the Soviet Revolution depended on there being a series of European revolutions to stand beside it.

permissible dose (science) the amount of radiation that, in the light of present knowledge, can be absorbed by a human being without appreciable bodily injury. Given the advances of knowledge, this dose seems to be shrinking as that knowledge increases.

person (sociol) in the decade and a half since the burgeoning of the women's liberation movement, the attack on 'male' vocabulary – spokes*man*, chair*man* – has led to the use of *person* in a variety of neologisms: chairperson, spokesperson, etc; despite the ostensible androgeneity of this use, it can usually be assumed that in such awkward contexts, 'person' equals 'woman'.

personal construct theory (social wk) 'A person's processes are psychologically channelised by the way in which he anticipates events' (George Kelly, in L. Sechrest, *The Psychology of Personal Constructs: George Kelly*, 1964).

personal explanation (pols) a statement made by a member of the House of Commons to his fellow members in an attempt to mitigate such conduct as was being considered as unacceptable on moral, social or criminal grounds.

personalisation (advertising) the making of a form letter that accompanies unsolicited advertising material sent through the post into a more personal communication by adding 'Dear Mr. X . . .' at the start; a process much aided by the speed and accuracy of word processors.

personality promotion (advertising) a version of the mystery shopper (qv) but aimed not at retailers but at housewives: a representative calls at a house, asks the housewife whether she has certain of his firm's products; if she can produce some and answer a simple product-related question, she will receive some form of reward.

personal social services (social wk) 1. those social services that are concerned with the needs and problems that inhibit an individual's ideal social functioning, his freedom to develop his personality and to gain his goals through relations with others. 2. a list of local authority welfare departments and other particular services available.

personalzine (TV) a magazine produced by a single fan as a showcase for his own writings, drawings, ideas, etc; especially popular among the followers of the TV scifi series 'Star Trek'.

personnel reaction time (milit) the time that elapses between a warning of a nuclear attack and the implementation of full defensive measures on an airbase, ship, command post, etc.

persuader (media) 1. (TV) an electrode in the TV tube that deflects the returning beam of scanning electrons in to the electron multiplier. 2. (press) a tool used to force the type into the forme and to ensure that it is properly spaced and tightened up.

PERT (business) (acro) *p*rogramme *e*valuation and *r*eview *t*echnique: a method of controlling the progress of long-term projects by analysing each successive step as it is taken both on the basis of the step in isolation and as it exists in relation to the rest of the project.

pessimal (computers) maximally bad.

peter (police, crime) a safe, thus *peterman* an expert in opening safes, by extension *peter*: the nitroglycerine used in breaking into safes.

peter *n* (prison/UK) a cell.

peter *n* (sport) aka: *echo, come-on* (US) in bridge, a high-low defence which is used as a sign of encouragement to one's partner.

Peter principle (business) coined by Dr. Lawrence Peter in 1969: the concept that in a large organisation, every individual is promoted to one level above his/her actual competence.

petro-dollar (econ) surplus dollars that are accumulated by oil-exporting nations and which are used for investments in and loans to oil-importing countries. Also, when based on UK currency, *petro-sterling*.

P.G. (drugs) (abbrev) paregoric; tincture of opium.

phase (computers) 1. *n* the phase of an individual's waking/sleeping cycle as regards the normal 24 hour cycle, especially relevant to those who choose to work at night and thus 'breakfast' at 7 pm. 2. *change phase the hard way*: to stay awake for a long time in order to enter a different phase of (1).

phased withdrawal (milit) 'A rout with insufficient means of transportation' and thus one that is forced to proceed slowly, or, in euphemistic terms, in phases.

phase zero (govt) the inception of a new government or bureaucratic program; nothing has yet happened: it is possible that if the right funds, personnel, and go-ahead are not available, nothing ever will.

Philadelphia lawyer (law/US) a lawyer of great ability and an expert in exploiting the tiniest legal loophole to the advantage of his client.

Philistines (gambling) loan sharks who lend money at extra-high interest while offering less time than usual for repayments.

phone it in *v* (movies) a writer who is considered by his studio to have put less than his best efforts into a screenplay and seems to have dictated it off the top of his head without bothering to make revisions is said to have 'phoned it in'.

phone quality (radio) an interview or report that has been recorded from a phone line and is thus of less than perfect quality, but will have to be transmitted nevertheless. (cf: *studio quality*)

phones (record business) phone-out research by a record company who have their staff phone random individuals to canvass their opinions of certain records that are currently being played on the radio. Thus *good phones* and *bad phones* depending on the response thus elicited.

phono *n* (radio) aka: *phone out*: an interview conducted over the phone which can either be broadcast live or transferred first onto tape. (Not to be confused with the audience participatory 'phone-in programmes'.)

photomontage (art) a technique of cutting up and re-assembling photographs in order to create a new composite image with a meaning other than that of the individual pictures. First used to effect by John Heartfield and other Dadaists in Berlin in the 1920s.

P

photo-realism (art) art works that depend for their effect on super-detailed portraits which might be colour photographs but for the materials used.

phrase *v* (dance) the linking of various movements into a single choreographic sequence.

pianola hand (sport) in bridge, any hand that is easy to play; from the pianola, an instrument which incorporated machinery and thus allowed it to play by itself.

piccolo (commerce) in the hotel trade, a junior page or waiter who is just embarking on his career.

pick *n* (sport) in basketball, a permissible block whereby an offensive player can obstruct a defensive opponent so long as his positioning does not interfere with that player's normal movement.

picking bids off the wall (commerce) in auction sales, 1. the creation by the auctioneer of an imaginary bidding contest in order to stimulate some real bids from the public. 2. the creation by the auctioneer of a fake bidder who will force the one actual bidder up to and ideally beyond the reserve price.

pick it up (movies) an instruction to an actor from the director, asking him/her to speed up the delivery of lines and the performance of business.

pickle (theatre) a small, elongated spotlight.

pickle (milit) US Dept of Defense code: bombs or missiles have been triggered manually and are aimed at a surface target.

pick up *v* (milit) USMC: to promote an officer who has been previously passed over.

pickup *n* (press) typeset material that is used repeatedly in successive editions of a paper and is thus kept set up permanently.

pick-up (public relations) aka: *placement*: the using by TV, radio or the newspapers of a PR handout.

pick up *n* (sport) in shooting, the collection of retrieved game by a hunting party; the quantity of game that has been shot.

pick up man (police/UK) aka: *at the pick up*: a small-time thief who specialises in stealing from unlocked motorcars, or simply grabbing whatever packages or luggage that is left momentarily unattended.

pictology (art) an analytical method of attributing and evaluating paintings; it involves the checking of artworks for a variety of constant factors: spontaneity of line, organisation of surface, contrasts of light and dark and of warm and cold colours, etc, etc.

pictorial rhetoric (art) an identifiable mass-media 'language' developed through certain devices which are used in advertising picture and graphic layouts; based in the clichés of such layouts, this language is used increasingly by 'fine' artists in an attempt to communicate with a wider audience.

picture black (TV) the light level of the darkest element of a TV picture or the picture signal voltage that corresponds to it.

piece (press) an article for a newspaper or magazine.

piece (milit) USMC: a gun or artillery piece.

piece (crime) any kind of weapon used for robberies, hold-ups, murders.

piece (drugs) a measure of a powdered narcotic (heroin, morphine) approx. equalling 1 ounce.

piece of manpower (TV/US) a description, faintly derogatory, of the major network stars: newscasters, anchormen, etc.

pie-chart (business) a graphic device of showing proportions/shares/etc of a given whole by drawing a circle with segments dividing it; like a cake cut into slices, viewed from above.

pied d'éléphant (sport) in mountaineering, an 'elephant's foot': a padded sack that is used to keep the lower parts of the body warm when the climber is resting or sleeping.

piffing (milit) gunnery training with rounds of sub-calibre firing; the word echoes the 'pff' noises such rounds make.

pig (technology) a spherical, cylindrical or 'dumb-bell' shaped object that is propelled down a gas or oil pipeline by gas, air or liquid pressure for the purposes of clearing and cleaning it; an *intelligent pig* can carry instruments for recording details of the internal state of the pipe.

pig (commerce) *to draw pig upon pork*: when the drawers and drawees of a bill are the same – a foreign branch of a firm drawing on its London head office, etc – and there are no documents for goods attached to the bill. (aka: *pig upon bacon*)

pig (pols) a popular description for police in particular and the power structure in general by radicals from the 1960s onward.

pig (technology) a container that holds radioactive materials.

pig-board (sport) in surfing: a board that has a wide tail and a narrow nose.

pigeon (TV) a member of the public who is used to transport urgent film back to headquarters when a film crew are working abroad and conditions make it impossible for them to send such film openly.

pigeon (crime) 1. *pigeon drop* a confidence trick that is launched by the dropping of a wallet at the feet of a victim; the con-man tells his mark that they can share the cash if he, the victim, puts up some more money as an act of good faith. 2. (abbrev) *stool pigeon*: one who informs to the police.

pigeon (milit) air intercept code: your base bears X° and is Y miles away.

piggy back *v* (medic) to add a second fluid 'intravenous drip' bag to the first one.

piggybacking (movies) the unofficial showing of an extra feature film on a weekly programme which should only be showing that film which the distributor wishes seen.

piggy back legislation (pols) to use one piece of legislation as a means of passing another, by quietly attaching it and hoping that both bills will pass together without comment.

pigtail (theatre/US) aka: *tail* (UK): a short piece of cable used for stage electrics.

piker (gambling) a poor sport, a timid gambler.

piker (stock market) a cautious investor, one who will only speculate on a small scale.

pill palace (medic/US) the hospital pharmacy.

pill pusher (medic/US) any general practitioner or specialist in internal medicine rather than a specialist in a variety of surgical work.

pill rolling (medic/US) any symptoms of nervous anxiety, esp. the twitching of fingers as if rolling something between them.

pilot (TV) the test programme of a potential series; often somewhat longer than an episode of the intended series and used to check whether the format will stand up to exposure.

pilot launch (marketing) a method of test marketing by launching a product on a limited basis in order to iron out the possible problems that will accompany a national scale launch.

pimp-crazy (sex) any prostitute who suffers at the hands of her pimp yet keeps returning to the same man.

pimped down (sex) amongst black pimps, being dressed for the part in *pimp shades* (dark glasses), *pimp socks* and a whole wardrobe of flashy, ostentatious garments.

pimp's arrest (sex) the revenge of a pimp on a girl who decides to leave his employment: he turns her over to the police; this involves no risk to himself and in addition lets him regain the bail money that he has had to have posted continually against the likelihood of her being arrested for soliciting. Once a new girl is found that bail money must be posted again.

pin *n* (espionage) a camera with a lens so tiny that it can be hidden in a variety of everyday objects around a room and used for perfect surveillance pictures.

pinard (milit) French Foreign Legion: any type of wine.

pinch hitter (sport) in baseball, a specially hard hitting batter who is brought in to pull the team out of a crisis.

pin-down (milit) the concept of saturating enemy missile bases with so many warheads that the resultant electro-magnetic confusion will render their out-going guidance systems useless.

ping *v* (theatre) to speak one's lines softly, with no special emphasis.

pinger (milit) an acoustic array carried in an aircraft's cockpit to help in anti-submarine warfare. Thus extended to the crewman who operates the ASW equipment.

ping pong (milit) a missile that carries a camera and after taking its pictures at various pre-determined heights, releases a parachute and lets the camera float back to a pick-up point.

ping-pong (medic/US) the sending of a patient, with no real need for such treatment, to a variety of specialists and clinics, all of whom can then claim Medicaid insurance payments for their (pointless) labours. (cf: *family ganging*)

ping-pong (music) in West Indian steel bands, a drum cut about seven inches from the top of the barrel which carries from 26 to 32 marked notes.

ping-pong diplomacy (govt) those tentative attempts to re-establish international relations between China and the US, which were initiated in 1971 with the sending of a US table-tennis (ping-pong) team to the People's Republic.

pink (sex) aka: *beaver*: close up shots of the open vagina used in hard-core pornography, either on film or in magazines. (cf: *flap shots*)

pink *n* (horse-racing/US) (abbrev) *Pink*erton: a race track security man, usually recruited from the Pinkerton Detective Agency.

pink (milit) RN: secret, confidential; from the colour of the signal pads used for writing such messages.

pink button (stock market) a jobber's clerk, who looks after a firm's communications, both within the exchange and outside it.

pink collar (indust relats) 1. jobs held by women in cosmetics factories. 2. any jobs held by women. (cf: *white collar*, *blue collar*)

pink lady (medic/US) phenobarbital elixir: an anti-nausea drink which is coloured pink.

pink noise (science) random noise that differs from white noise (qv) by having a greater proportion of low frequency components.

pink paper (pols) a parliamentary notice, printed on pink paper, which gives each day or week the details of all papers either presented to Parliament or printed by orders of the Government; the first pink papers were issued as an experiment in 1889 and ratified for continual use in 1894.

pink puffer (medic/US) a thin patient who is suffering from emphysema.

pinkslip *v* (entertainment) to dismiss from a job.

pink slip (indust relats/US) to dismiss an employee; from the practice in US colleges to signify a failure in examinations by printing this information on pink paper.

pink-tea picketing (indust relats) a small group of pickets who are being unobtrusive; refers both to the restrained level of the picket (pink rather than radical 'red') and the 'tea-party' atmosphere so created.

pinky-cheater (medic/US) aka: *finger cot*: a sterile

finger-stall or glove used by doctors when making vaginal or anal inspections.

Pinnacle (milit) US code: a message thus flagged must by-pass local commanders and be sent direct to Joint Chiefs of Staff and thus the President.

pin-party (milit) RN: the working party on a carrier that prepares aircraft for takeoff and deals with them after they have returned to the flight deck. (cf: *grapes*)

pin-splitter (sport) in golf: any shot that lands dead on the pin.

pintail (sport) in surfing: a surfboard which has a back end tapering to a point.

pip (milit) British Army: the stars worn on an officer's epaulettes to distinguish his rank: one for a second lieutenant, two for a first lieutenant, three for a captain. (cf: *one-pipper*)

pipe *v* (milit) USMC: to notice, to look at.

pipe *n* (press/US) a story which has a basis of facts but which has been embellished by the reporter to gain it greater prominence and interest.

pipe-line *n* (sport) a large wave or the hollow of such a wave; also that part of the shore where such waves can be found and ridden.

pipe-lining (computers) the regulation of computer processes whereby one must be concluded before another can be initiated; using special modules which can operate concurrently, these processes can be speeded up and thus vastly increase the machine's operations efficiency.

pipe the side *v* (milit) RN: to escort a person (usually an officer) on board a ship to the accompaniment of the correct tribute from the ship's pipes.

pirate *n* (espionage) electronic surveillance which uses electricity that is 'pirated' from a telephone wire, with the permission of the telephone company.

pisscutter (milit) USMC: aka *fore-and-aft cap*: a regulation garrison cap.

pissing post (pols/US) a politician's home territory or power base.

pistol (milit) in bomb disposal units: the fuse that sets off a bomb.

pit *n* (sport) in US football, the centre of the line, where opposing heavyweight players battle to attack/defend the quarterback; the implication is of the pure animal viciousness of the brute contact.

pit (milit) British Army: a bed; spec: a cabin on a troopship. (cf: *grot*)

pit (stock market) that area in the market, usu. slightly lower than the surrounding area, where the actual dealing and trading takes place.

pit boss (gambling) aka: *pit inspector*: a casino official who supervises a gaming table, watching players and croupiers alike for cheating or mere mistakes. (cf: *ladder man*)

pitch (sport) in mountaineering: a section of the climb.

pitch *v* (drugs) to sell narcotics in small amounts; thus the dealer who conducts such a business.

pitch (crime) that part of a street worked by a prostitute, three card monte team, illegal street trader, etc.

pitch fly (commerce) amongst street traders, a seller who takes over someone else's pitch (qv) without permission.

pitchpole *v* (sport) in yachting, to be upended completely by heavy seas and to somersault forward, stern over bow.

pit lizard (sport) in motor-racing: a woman who devotes herself to pursuing racing drivers.

place-money (horse-racing) 1. money that is bet on the chance of a horse coming second or third, but not first. 2. the money paid out on horses that come second or third (in US second only) in a race.

placer (police/UK) the middleman between the thief and the receiver of stolen goods (the *fence*); he negotiates the 'placing' of stolen goods with the best receiver for that particular variety of goods.

placing (stock market) the finding of specific buyers for large quantities of stocks, especially a new issue.

plain-sewing (sex) the restricting of the services of a homosexual prostitute to mutual masturbation only.

plain text (espionage) in cryptography: uncoded language. (cf: *en plein*)

plane *v* (sport) in surfing: to ride a wave with the hands protecting the face by forming a spear-shape which thus cuts through the oncoming water.

plank (pols) one of the positions upon which a campaign is based; a number of planks form the entire platform (qv).

planning continuum (milit) an alternative phrase for military strategy.

planning horizon (econ) in socialist countries, the years that have been included in the current economic plan.

plant *n* (sport) in snooker, a shot that uses one red ball to tap another one into the hole without hitting the second ball directly with the cue ball.

plant *v* (pols, press) the placing of information by a politician with a journalist who will publish it as a scoop; such information can be genuine, in which case it is planted to benefit the politician; it may be false, in which case the reporter is being used as a pawn in a larger political scheme. (cf: *leak*)

planting (public relats) the placing of a promotional piece with the desired newspaper or magazine, or the putting of one's client onto a TV or radio show that will offer maximum publicity.

plasma (aerospace) rocket fuel.

plasma display (computers) any peripheral (qv)

that has a screen on which information may be displayed.

plastic (police, crime) credit cards, bank cards, etc; thus *on the plastic*: carrying out a variety of frauds with 'plastic money'.

plastic *a* (theatre) any scenery which is three dimensional, as opposed to flats (qv).

plastic memory (science) the phenomenon in physics that when certain kinds of plastic are first moulded into a distinct form, then melted so that the form is lost, if they are then allowed to cool, that original form is to a great extent resumed.

plat (commerce) in real estate, a surveyor's proposal for the sub-division of a plot of land, submitted to a local government official in the *plat book*.

plate *n* (horse-racing) a horseshoe; thus *racing plate* those special horseshoes that are used for races.

plate *v* (sport) in baseball, to cross the plate, ie: to score a run.

plater (horse-racing) (abbrev) *selling plater*: a race, and the horses in it, of poor quality; all horses in a selling plate are available for purchase once the race has been run.

platform (pols) the whole group of principles and promises that make up a political campaign. (cf: *plank*)

platinum (record business) a record that has sold 1,000,000 copies and thus becomes a 'platinum disc'; thus *double platinum*: 2,000,000 copies. (cf: *gold*)

platoon *v* (sports) for a sportsman to specialise in playing one play or in one position.

platoon grouping (educ) the teaching of a specially selected small class of pupils.

plausible denial (espionage) a cover story which should serve to convince any investigator that they are mistaken in their suspicions of an individual or an organisation.

play book (business) from the US football use of a book to contain the many varieties of plays to be used in a game: the corporation files that contain plans, manuals, charts and all the other details of the institutional programme.

player *n* (medic/US) a patient.

player (sex) a pimp; by extension, anyone who uses wit and brains rather than sweat and strain to make money, obtain women, etc.

playing the man (sport) the use of deliberate violence in contact sports; a reverse of the old 'sporting' credo whereby one 'played the ball, not the man'.

play pussy *v* (milit) RAF: to fly into cloud cover in order to avoid being discovered by hostile aircraft.

play them in (theatre/UK) aka: *play the first spot* (US): the first actor or actors to appear on stage in Act I, scene i.

plea-bargain (law) the process whereby a defendant can bargain with the court to have

his sentence reduced if he is willing to plead guilty to some charges, while others will be dropped, and thus help to speed up the legal calendar, albeit depriving himself of the possible advantages of pleading a general 'Not Guilty' in front of a jury.

pleasure bar (air crew) the first-class drinking area in large international jets – 747s, DC10s, etc.

plebe (milit) at the US military academy at West Point, NY, any new cadet in his first year; intended to cover the entrants to all US military or naval academies.

plot (theatre) a plan that shows the positions of furniture and props on the stage as needed for the various scenes; thus *lighting plot*: a plan of the lighting as it varies from scene to scene.

plot *n* (milit) RAF: a group of hostile aircraft as they come up on a radar screen.

PLU (sociol) (acro) *people like us*: a shorthand description for the peers of the British upper or upper-middle classes; often found as 'not PLU'; a descendant of the 'U' and 'non-U' classifications of the 1950s.

pluck *n* (sport) in yachting, a pull or a tow from another boat.

pluck *v* (press) a printing fault that occurs when the ink is not spreading properly and detaches itself in places from the surface of the paper.

pluck *v* (milit) US armed forces: to cashier or retire an officer compulsorily.

plug *n* (sport) in fishing, a lure that can be made to dart and dive, popularly chosen for catching pike.

plug (media) any form of advertisement, publicity, promotion.

plug *n* (publishing) a book that will not sell well.

plugola (radio/US) money that is paid to broadcasters to mention, in passing, those products whose manufacturers are giving out the bribes. (cf: *payola*)

plug-in architecture (archit) a style of design that incorporates one basic structure and a number of secondary units that can be attached to it as and when the client desires.

plugs (aerospace) mass produced uniform sections of fuselage airframe which can be added to or subtracted from commercial airliners as and when the airlines and their bookings require.

plumber (milit) RAF: an armourer or engineering officer.

plumber (medic/US) a urologist whose medical speciality is 'the water works'.

plumbing (espionage) lit: the stopping of leaks (in the government and security services); plumbing and the *plumbers* – those who did the dirty work – came to prominence during the Watergate Scandal of 1972/1974 when it was found that the 'zeal' of President Nixon's 'plumbers' had led them into massive instances of breaking the law, all for the sake of their President.

plum book (govt/US) an official US government publication that lists all those available government posts that a President may fill by his personal appointment. (cf: *rainbow book*)

pluralism (pols) a political philosophy that opposes the idea of a single state authority and which desires to give equal powers to all those bodies that represent the various segments of a society.

pluralism (indust relats) the die-hard attitude of some trade unionists who declare that the basis of all industrial relations must be 'us vs. them' and that the two sides can never really reach agreement, but merely wish to crush the desires or aspirations of the other.

plural relations (pols) aka: *separate development*: two euphemisms used by South African politicians to disguise the essential racism of the apartheid policy.

plush family *n* (theatre) empty seats in the auditorium, ie: the plush covered seats that can be seen from the stage.

PM (commerce) (abbrev) *push money*: a form of payola (qv) paid to salesmen and retailers if they push a given product harder than its rivals; PM is often paid for each item or product thus sold.

PO (prison/UK) (acro): principal officer.

pocher (archit) from Fr. 'to fill in, to stencil': a type of design where the external walls and the internal rooms do not correspond; ie: octagonal rooms built within a square exterior. The 'dead space' between the inner and outer walls is *poché space* and such rooms and buildings are drawn on a *poché plan*.

pocket (sport) in US football: a small area in the backfield where the quarterback is heavily protected by his linemen as he prepares to throw the ball.

pocket (milit) an area held by friendly troops who are surrounded by hostile forces; thus *pocket of resistance*: an area of resistance, often in the face of overwhelming odds and as such destined in the end to be over-run.

pocketbook issue (pols/US) aka: *bread and butter issue*: those political issues that are most genuinely interesting to the voters, usually concerning how much money they have in their pockets and how much it will purchase for them; more pertinent than the more abstract issues of foreign policy etc.

pocket codes (sex) the homosexual community uses brightly coloured bandanna handkerchieves to signify to each other a variety of sexual preferences; these handkerchieves are kept hanging out of the back trouser pocket and those who prefer a passive role have them in the right hand pocket while those who prefer the active one use the left.

pocket universe (D&D) a small experimental

area created by the Dungeon Master to test possible innovations within the larger world of the game.

POCO (govt) in the Common Market (EEC): (acro) *political co-operation*.

pogey bait marine (milit) USMC; a sissy, a weakling; from *pogey bait*: sweets.

pogo (milit) air intercept code: switch to the preceding channel or, if unable to establish communications on that channel, switch to the next channel after it.

pogo *v* (aerospace) severe longitudinal vibrations in a rocket.

point (business) from the military use of *point* to describe that man who leads a patrol through enemy territory: the head of a negotiating or bargaining team.

Point *n* (milit) (abbrev) the US Military Academy at West Point, NY.

point *n* (pols) from the military use of *point* as patrol leader, that candidate in a Presidential election who is front-runner and is thus most vulnerable to attack both from his opponents and from disenchanted members of his own party.

point (econ) a fractional number used when quoting shifts in interest rates (one point = one per cent) or in international currency exchange (one point = one hundredth of the lowest denomination of a country's currency).

point defence (milit) the close-quarters defence of one's own position at a late stage of a battle when enemy advances have made it impossible for such fighting to be kept at a distance.

point of no return (aerospace) a geographical position or a particular time during a flight when an aircraft's fuel supply becomes too low to enable the aircraft to return safely to its own or another friendly base.

points (movies) (abbrev) percentage points: that percentage of the gross takings of a film which may be allotted to a star actor, a director, even occasionally a writer; thus 'X has points in this movie . . .'; 'what they give writers instead of money' (Fran Lebowitz, *Social Studies*, 1981).

points (theatre) those gestures, vocal tricks and similar variations on technique that are used to underline the climax of a single speech or of a whole role; on the whole the 'making of points' is not considered to be within the best standards of acting, but rather the sacrifice of the larger effect for some easy applause.

point target (milit) a target so small that it requires only a single co-ordinate on a map, eg: missile silos.

poison *v* (technology) materials used in the control rods of nuclear reactors – boron, cadmium, etc – to *poison* or inhibit the fission reaction and thus make a chain reaction and nuclear explosion impossible.

poison (science) in chemistry, any substance

which destroys or reduces the activity of a catalyst.

poison *n* (police, crime) the criminal 'antecedents' that are read out in court prior to the sentencing of a defendant who has been found guilty of a new crime.

poison at the box office (theatre) a play or other entertainment that repels rather than attracts paying audiences.

poisonous weeds (pols) in Chinese communist terminology, any writings or other propaganda that attacks Mao Tse Tung; thus those individuals who propagate such attacks.

poke *n* (sport) in cricket, an aimless, tentative shot by a batsman, such shots often lead to the batsman's being caught behind the stumps.

pole *v* (sport) in baseball, to hit the ball hard.

polecat (TV) a length of alloy tubing which is braced between two walls or between the floor and the ceiling in order to support a number of lights.

police *v* (milit) aka: *crum up* USMC: 1. to tidy or straighten up either a place or a person. 2. *n* a condition of great neatness and cleanliness, either of a place or of a person.

police action (govt, milit) a military intervention by one nation into the territory of another ostensibly when that nation is deemed to be breaking international law; or, more honestly, when either of the superpowers feels that political or military developments within a nation are such that they are threatening the superpower's interest and that nothing short of sending in troops will preserve that interest.

policeman (science) in chemistry, a short glass rod with a rubber tip attached to one end, used for separating solids from liquids in microchemistry.

policeman (sport) in ice hockey, a heavyweight player whose task is to protect his own goal-scorers, supposedly by fair means alone, but usually by violence, fouls and other illegal tactics.

police positive (police/US) aka: *police special*: a type of pistol used by policemen and manufactured by the Colt company.

police power (sociol) a concept in US law that implies the extension of government authority in repression of individual habits and tastes simply because the so-called 'public interest lobby' demands such suppression.

policy keyboard (business) a range of policy options open to executives on a decision-making level; the skilled executive should be able to 'play' such a keyboard with the fluency of a concert pianist.

political thinking (pols) in Marxist terms, a mixture of ideological purity and civic responsibility, each of which should breed the other; on a general level, the involvement of the individual or group in the social and political life of the Party and the State.

polling (computers) the scanning by a central processing unit of all peripheral terminals and the 'asking' of them whether or not they have any data to offer.

poll the room *v* (aerospace) to demand a consensus opinion from all those involved in monitoring and directing a space flight before launching the vehicle and its astronauts on the next stage of their mission or when attempting to sort out any technical problem; in business terms, the request to anyone concerned for some help or advice in the solving of a problem.

polycentrism (pols) coined by P. Togliatti (1892–1964) in 1956, the concept that each national communist party should have the right to establish its own autonomous style and that none need pay any more than formal respect to the Soviet model. Thus, by extension, the concept that there should be more than one centre of power in any political/ideological group, not simply Washington and Moscow.

POM (computers) (acro) *p*hase *o*f the *m*oon: used facetiously when attempting to explain why a particular event turned out the way it did, especially if it went wrong.

Pompey (milit) RN: Portsmouth. (cf: *Guzz*)

pong *v* (theatre) 1. to ad-lib when one has forgotten the actual line. 2. (the opposite of ping, qv): to overemphasise one's lines, to speak more loudly than a line warrants.

pongo *n* (milit) 1. (RN) a marine, a soldier. 2. (British Army) an officer.

ponsonby rule (govt) named after Arthur Ponsonby, 1st Lord Ponsonby (1871–1946) who signed a minute in 1924 that permits the Government to authorise an agreement without Parliamentary approval if the document has been available and Parliament has failed to act upon it within 21 days.

pontoon (prison/UK) 21 month jail sentence, from the card-game in which a score of 21 is the optimum hand.

pony (press/US) a brief bulletin from a news agency which details only the highlights of the day's news.

pony (police, crime) £25.00.

pony (theatre) a small chorus girl who dances and sings in musicals.

pony (educ/US) a revision notebook used for help in college examinations.

POO (business) from an aerospace acronym: 'Program Zero-Zero'; to 'go to POO' meant that astronauts were to clear their on-board computer so that it could receive fresh data; in business terms *going to POO* means that executives should clear out all old assumptions and information and prepare to absorb such new material as will be necessary to make fresh decisions in a new situation.

pooh-bah (pols/US) from W. S. Gilbert and Arthur Sullivan's comic opera *The Mikado*

(1885): an official of great self-importance and pomposity. (cf: *muckey-muck*)

pool *n, v* (press) the putting together of resources and information by a number of otherwise rival journalists; either because communications home are so limited that such co-operation is the only way anyone can get a story home or because the local authorities, often military commanders, will not deal with individuals but give out only a regular general statement.

pop *n* (sport) in baseball, a ball hit high into the air but which goes straight up and down and thus provides an easy catch.

pop *v* (drugs) to inject a narcotic drug. Thus *skinpop*: to inject a drug under the skin rather than directly into a vein, the practice in general of the novice user. Those who inject into a vein are *mainlining*.

pop (theatre/US) traditional name for the stage-door keeper. (cf: *George*)

P.O.P. (advertising) (acro) *p*ost *o*ffice *p*referred: a reference to the regulation sizes of envelopes used by post office sorters and which should be returned when asking for mail order goods.

pop art (art) an art movement that developed in the 1960s and drew its inspiration from every variety of mass, popular culture, drawing heavily on its 'visual vocabulary' and its invariably commercial techniques. The subjects were treated impersonally, with no political or moral statements attached and the art often echoed the mass production techniques of industry.

popeye (milit) air intercept code: I am in cloud; I have reduced visibility.

poplarism (pols) the policy of excessively generous social welfare on behalf of a local council; often flying deliberately in the face of a national government which is committed to cutting back on such hand-outs; originated in 1919 when the Labour controlled Poplar (East London) council pushed up local rates to unprecedented heights in order to fund a massive programme of council welfare to the needy.

popular art (art) those best-selling but anonymously produced art-works with no pretensions to 'fine art' or in any way 'modern' or experimental, but which appeal massively to the bulk of the non-discerning British public.

population (marketing) a group of people, selected in some systematic manner, who are used as a sample for market research.

popout (sport) in surfing: a poorly made surfboard.

Popperian (philos) from Sir Karl Popper (1902–) whose most widely known theory states that scientific laws are only justified by the extent of their resistance to falsification and who has constantly attacked those parts of Marxism that curtail individual freedom.

poppers (drugs) amyl nitrate, see *drug names*.

pop up (aerospace) see *cold launch*.

porch (aerospace) a small platform that is attached to the outside of a spacecraft's hatch.

pork (pols/US) federal government funds that are obtained for a particular person or area on the basis of manipulating political patronage.

porkbarrel (pols/US) 1. the state or Federal treasury into which local politicians can 'dip' for funds that they require for their local areas and to indulge the spread of their political patronage. 2. *porkbarrelling*: the use of state or federal funds to provide public works that would otherwise be beyond the budgets of those areas that require them.

pork chop (indust relats) a full time union official who works not for ideological reasons but because he has gained the job through patronage, family ties or as a payoff for services rendered.

pork chop (sociol) a black in the US who is willing to accept a position that is inferior to that of his white peers.

porkchop (press/US) a portrait that measures one half of the column's width in a given publication.

pork-knockers (commerce) freelance gold and diamond prospectors in Guyana whose name derives from the staple content of their rations.

porpoise *v* (aerospace) for a plane to show it is in trouble by deliberately flying an exaggerated up and down course through the air.

porpoise (milit) RN: a submarine that is moving through the water like a porpoise: first rising to the surface and then submerging.

porridge (prison/UK) one's time in jail, traditionally referring to the daily ration of porridge served up for breakfast.

port (computers) any socket on a machine into which a variety of terminals and other peripherals (qv) can be plugged.

portable (indust relats) the concept that rights, privileges, pension plans and the like should be transferred with an employee when he/she moves to another firm rather than their being dropped wholesale and thus needing a whole new process of building them up. Thus *portability*: a condition whereby workers may effect such transfers without problems or conditions.

portable (computers) a program that will adapt simply for use on a variety of computers.

portfolio (stock market) a collection or list of securities held by one individual or corporation. Thus *portfolio investment*: the purchasing of securities in a number of companies.

portrait (advertising) a page or illustration size in which the dimensions of the height exceed those of the width.

portrait page (advertising) see: *mini-page*.

posigrade (aerospace) referring to a small rocket that can be fired briefly to give a forward thrust to a rocket.

position *v* (business) to market a particular product by targeting one segment of the market and emphasising the extent to which that product is required by that segment; the choosing of the right market for the promotion of a new product.

position n (stock market) the state of any broker's or jobber's book (qqv), revealing where he stands in the market.

position (futures market) an interest in the market, either long or short (qqv) in the form of open contracts (qv).

position paper (pols) a document prepared to illustrate the position of any national group – government, unions, etc – on a currently vital issue; a written statement of attitude or intentions.

positive action (law/US) any aggressive action in the committing of a crime: assault, rape, hold-ups, etc.

positive control n (milit) the sending of nuclear bombers to a holding position, prior to recalling them to base or sending them on to their targets in USSR.

positive discrimination (govt) the hiring of minority group members, even though their actual abilities might not earn them the job in a normal competition; such hiring is intended to make up for the inherent problems, especially in education, that such minorities suffer. (cf: *affirmative action*)

positive labour relations (indust relats) aka: *positive personnel practices*: euphemisms for a growing movement to outlaw unions, break up their presence in the workforce and to make it harder for them to recruit new members; currently a US phenomenon, but spreading towards Europe.

positive neutrality (diplomacy) the adopting by smaller nations of a posture whereby they establish good, and therefore lucrative relations with all the great and superpowers, but studiously refuse to become involved in their political rivalries.

positive policing (police/UK) the concept of active policing in an urban riot – charging the rioters, using tear gas, etc – rather than simply holding the 'thin blue line'.

positive sum game (business) a variety of 'game' played by economists, bureaucrats, planners, etc in which the result gives a greater number of winners than losers; such games embrace the workings of multinational corporations, the nuclear energy programme, etc. (cf: *negative sum game, zero sum game*)

possibilism (pols) a political philosophy which concentrates on the inception of social and economic reforms and changes which are actually possible, rather than merely utopian. (cf: *impossibilism*)

POSSLQ (sociol) (acro used by the US Bureau of the Census): *p*ersons of the *o*pposite *s*ex *s*haring *l*iving *q*uarters. (cf: de facto couple)

post n (medic/US) (abbrev) post-mortem: an autopsy. Thus *do a post*: perform an autopsy.

post-attack blackmail (milit) a tactic for waging nuclear war which is designed to minimise defensive damage while maximising first strike offensive damage; one's first strike should destroy hostile defences but spare, as yet, any population; the next stage should be to threaten that population with annihilation if surrender is not immediate.

posted price (commerce) a price for crude petroleum which is used as a reference for calculating those taxes and royalties paid by oil companies to oil-producing countries.

poster session (science) a meeting of scientists where their work is exhibited in visual displays and the study of these displays is used as a basis for subsequent conversations and consultations between them.

post-formalist art (art) a contrast to the Formalists who emphasised the formal properties of an art object; post-Formalists emphasise systems instead of objects, procedures over results; their aim is to establish an interactive relationship with the world.

post-impressionist art (art) a school of early 20th century artists who sought to reveal the structural form of a subject without paying absolute attention to its actual appearance.

post-launch survivability (milit) the ability of a given weapons system to deliver its bombs on target after having penetrated the enemy's defences. (cf: *pre-launch survivability*)

postman (govt) a principal officer in the Civil Service; a word culled from John Le Carré's *Smiley's People* (1979) and taken into general use.

post-modern design (archit) a movement in architectural design that represents a reaction against the tenets of modernism (qv); in essence a return to the metaphor of the body rather than that of the machine; the return of a belief in and tolerance of the irrationality and emotionality of human beings.

post-modernism (art) a movement across the art world that rejected many of the advances and experiments of the 20th century and substituted a return to certain classical or historical styles and techniques.

post-production (movies) all work on a film that follows the completion of the principle photography (qv): the mixing, editing, dubbing, special effects, printing, etc.

post-synchronisation (movies) the adding of sound, by dubbing (qv) it onto visuals that have already been shot; such work may be necessary when it has been impossible to shoot – probably while on location – on a completely silent set and thus background noises have to be eliminated.

post-traumatic neurosis (milit) the current euphemism for the problems that engulf a soldier whose mind has, in the long or short run, been overwhelmed by the stresses of battle, the 1980s (and post-Vietnam) successor to *shell shock* (World War I) and *battle fatigue* (World War II, Korea).

posture (milit) a nation's military strength and readiness as far as such factors effect its capability to fight a war.

pot (radio) (abbrev) potentiometer: a machine that preceded the invention of faders and which engineers formerly used to dim sound on a broadcast. Thus *to pot*: to fade out.

pot (radio) (acro) *pot*ential *out take*: the cutting short of a programme. Thus *pot a tape*, *finding a pot*: the choosing of a suitable moment in a programme for cutting it off; *pot point* that moment on the tape which is marked ready for the cut-off; *tight pot*: a programme so constructed that the pot point must be taken very quickly and accurately so as to maintain the sense of what is transmitted without cutting off in mid-sentence or turning sense into nonsense.

POT *v* (police) (acro) Prevention of Terrorism: thus, to arrest a suspect under the Prevention of Terrorism Act.

pot *v* (sport) in rugby football: to score a dropped goal.

potato-masher (milit) a type of grenade the shape of which vaguely resembles a potato-masher.

Potomac fever (pols/US) from the River Potomac which flows through Washington DC: a lust for power.

poultry dealer (sex) a homosexual pimp who specialises in young boys – 'chickens'.

pounce (milit) Department of Defence code: I am in position to intercept the target.

poverty trap (sociol, econ) the situation of poor families who receive means-tested benefits: when the main provider finds a job, these benefits must be relinquished, but in many cases without these benefits, the family's real income is actually less due to the provider being unable to qualify for a well-paid job.

power excursion (tech) in nuclear energy, an accidental runaway condition in a nuclear reactor.

powerhouse *n* (gambling) a particularly strong hand in a card game.

power politics (pols) any national or international policymaking that rests on the assumption that sabre-rattling has a better chance of gaining an objective than does peaceful negotiation; the concept that 'might is right'.

practical *a* (TV, movies, theatre) anything used on a set that actually 'works' – edible food, smokable cigarettes, slammable doors, etc.

practical politics (pols) a euphemism for expedient politics: cutting corners both legal and moral to 'get things done'; a style that exceeds mere cynicism but stands marginally short of outright dishonesty.

practicum (educ) an alternative for practical: field work, laboratory research, any learning that is not simply by rote.

pragmatic (politics) looking at what can be done in politics rather than dreaming of what might be done; down to earth rather than utopian.

praiser *n* (entertain) a public relations person or a press agent.

prayer card (pols) a card used by a member of the House of Commons to reserve a seat during morning prayers.

precleared fire zone (milit/US) an area in which anything living, human or animal, is deemed a legitimate target for US forces; the euphemistic version of *free fire zone*.

preem *n*, *v* (entertain) the premiere of a film, play, show or TV programme or series; to launch a new film, play, etc.

pre-emptive strike (milit) to attack the enemy before he has had a chance to realise that the attack is coming. (cf: *splendid first strike*)

pre-fade (radio) material that is performed before a programme is actually faded up for transmission – often in a studio discussion or a live concert.

preferential defence (milit) a defence plan that concentrates defences on certain key areas – military, government, industry – at the expense of those considered less valuable – population centres with no 'valuable' personnel, etc.

preferential shop (indust relats/US) a business that gives its hiring preference to members of unions.

pre-flight *v* (milit) to run a full check on an aircraft and its weapons systems prior to take-off.

pre-launch survivability (milit) the ability of a given weapons system to ride out a pre-emptive, surprise first strike and then to retaliate successfully against enemy targets. (cf: *post-launch survivability*)

pre-med *n* (medic) (abbrev) pre-medication: any medication given prior to an operation or any other major treatment.

premia (indust relats) overtime, bonuses, incentive payments – any payments over and above basic pay.

premium (futures market) the excess of one futures contract price over another, either within the same financial instrument or not; the opposite of discount (qv).

premium (advert)
1. any item of goods offered by a company to its consumers, retailers, wholesalers and salesmen.
2. spec: any product offered either with another product or after the purchase of the first product.

premium (stock market)
1. in the case of a new issue, the excess of the market price over the sale price.

2. the excess of a price over the nominal value of quoted stocks.

3. *dollar premium*: the excess over the official rate of exchange which must be paid for investment dollars required to purchase securities outside the Sterling Area.

premise *v* (pavlov) to take as a basic assumption.

pre-owned (commerce) in the second hand car trade, a euphemism for a second hand car.

prep *v* (movies) (abbrev) to *pre*pare: the promotion of a new film prior to its release.

pre-production (movies) all the work performed on a film prior to the principle photography (qv) – writing the script, developing the story, casting, costumes, hiring the cameraman, director and crew, etc.

prequal (publishing) the idea of capitalising on a best-seller whose pessimistic author has foolishly killed off his hero or heroine by having him write a story of their adventures *before* the action that has been narrated in the current popular book. A concept that has been used in films and TV also.

presenting problem (social wk) the problem that a client may well put forward to a social worker as a mask for the real or basic problem, with which the client finds it much more difficult to deal; a symptom rather than a real case for treatment.

press (sport) in gold, 1. to put too much effort into a shot.

2. a side-bet that is proposed and/or taken during a game.

press *n* (psychol) anything in the environment to which a need in the organism responds – either positive or negative.

press availability (pols) a variety of press conference in which the speaker makes no statement of his own but opens himself at once to press questioning.

press flesh *v* (pols) aka: *glad-handing*: the endless handshaking, shoulder-tapping, baby-kissing etc.to which campaigning politicians seem to have to submit in order to endear themselves to the masses.

pressie (radio) aka: *presser*: a press conference.

press roll (music) a drum roll produced by pressing the sticks against the drum head.

pressure cooker (medic/US) the intensive care unit. (cf: *MICU*, *SICU*)

prêt (milit) French Foreign Legion: pay day.

prêt-à-porter (commerce) off the peg clothes, made up in a range of standard sizes and colours.

pre-to-post (advert) the concept that a consumer's attitude to the possibility of purchasing a product alters after he/she has seen it being advertised; a basic test to determine whether or not advertising actually works.

pretzel (music) a French horn; thus *pretzel bender*: a French horn player.

prevail *v* (milit) the current concept of fighting

a nuclear war: that it is actually possibly to fight and win one – as if one were still using conventional weapons – and thus, however appalling the interim casualties and destruction, the US believes that it can, in the event, prevail, ie: win.

preventive action (espionage) the concept that prevention is better than cure when fighting enemies (or supposed enemies) of the state and used to justify a variety of illegal activities (mail cover (qv), electronic surveillance, telephone tapping, etc) by the FBI and CIA.

preventive detention (govt) the imprisonment of one's (political) enemies in order to nullify what, if free, might have been their effective opposition to one's rule. It is unnecessary for them to have committed any actual crime.

preventive war (milit) the concept that war is inevitable and that given this fact, one may as well get on with it as soon as possible and do one's best to win it, whatever the horrors and costs involved; the *prevention* here is of defeat, not of conflict.

previous (police) (abbrev) previous convictions. (cf: *form*)

prexy (business) aka: *prez*: (abbrev/corruption) president (of a company).

price-lining (business) the practice of offering a class of goods in a limited number of price categories so that one can optimise total sales throughout the related group.

price-point *v* (business) to set a bargain price on a particular item.

price scissors (econ) the relationship between the price of agricultural and industrial goods; ideally agricultural prices should be held down while industrial ones rise in order to provide plenty of cheap food for the workers.

pricked (sport) in hunting or shooting, the disabling of game by shooting.

prick farrier (milit) RAF: a medical officer.

primal *v* (new therapies) the central purpose of primal therapy: to relive one's birth: such a 're-birth' is generally accompanied by shouts, screams, yells of 'Mummy!' etc.

primal pains (new therapies) 'the central and universal pains which reside in all neurotics', the evocation through pain and shouting of one's earliest infantile traumas, the source of all one's subsequent pain and thus central to the inner delvings that make up primal therapy.

primary health care (soc wk) the role of the general practitioner, and those nurses, health visitors and similar ancillaries who work with him/her, in containing and treating the illnesses which are encountered in the surgery; as the 'primary health worker' who is nearest to the community, the GP has taken on the responsibility of dealing with all the immediate manifestations of illness in his/her area.

P

primary market (future market) the principal underlying market for a financial instrument.

primary poverty (sociol) such extreme poverty that denies one the chance of buying the bare necessities of life.

primary structure (aerospace) those parts of an aircraft the failure of which would seriously endanger the safety of those flying in it.

primate aesthetics (art) the study of creativity amongst apes and chimpanzees and the analysis of their discernible visual preferences.

prime beef (milit) USAF: (acro) world wide *b*ase *e*ngineer *e*mergency *f*orce created either for direct combat support or to assist local forces who are attempting to tackle major natural disasters.

prime crew (aerospace) the original person or persons who have been trained and briefed to fly a particular space mission; as opposed to the *backup crew* one or more of whom stand ready to take over in the case of illness, accident etc.

prime mover (milit) an extra large and strong truck designed to haul weapons, tanks and other military equipment plus crews and ammunition.

prime time (TV) the chief day part (qv) which covers early to mid-evening viewing and as such is considered the main viewing time in most households; programmes transmitted in prime time are usually low in taste or intellectual demands but highly successful; the advertising rates that accompany them are the most expensive.

primitive art (art)
1. artists who were working in pre-Renaissance Europe and the art-works they produced.
2. any artist who has not been trained formally or those who choose to imitate such naive styles.

Princeton First Year (sex) an allusion to the alleged homosexual practices among freshmen at Princeton University: the achievement of orgasm by rubbing the penis between the partner's thighs.

principle photography (movies) the filming of the main body of the film, rather than the pre- and post-production or special effects processes; this main phase of shooting denotes that period when a film is 'in production'.

print-out (computers) the printing on a long strip of paper of the results and processes of a computer's calculations on a particular program.

prioritise *v* (govt) to make a subject into a priority.

prisoner's friend (milit) an officer appointed in a court martial to act as the defendant's counsel.

private *n* (medic/US) a private doctor; thus *double O private*; a derogatory joke (based on the James Bond books) for a supposedly incompe-

tent but expensive private doctor who is 'licensed to kill'.

Private Case (educ) in the British Museum Reading Room (the British Library) a collection of books that are considered to be pornographic.

private notice question (pols) aka: *PNQ*s: questions that may be asked by member of the House of Commons after the statutory period of daily 'question time' and which refer either to matters of urgent public importance or to the arrangement of parliamentary business.

private treaty (commerce) in real estate, the placing by an owner of a reserve price on his property and the subsequent asking of interested parties to make written bids and to submit them for consideration; on a pre-set date, all communications are opened and the property goes to the highest bidder; such deals are fully binding in law.

privatisation (govt, indust relats) the hiving off by a government of portions of hitherto nationalised industries and the returning of such organisations to private hands.

privileged sanctuary (milit) any military base from which attacks can be made but for whatever reason remains inviolate itself.

privileges (stock market) a contract whereby one party secures the right, but not the obligation, to buy from or sell to another party a specified amount of a commodity or a security at a predetermined price. (cf: *puts and calls*)

proactive (govt) to plan in advance; to react pre-emptively.

probabilism (philos) the theory that laws, in whatever fields, are not invariant, but state only probabilities and tendencies.

procedure (computer)
1. the writing of a program which is designed specifically to solve one special problem.
2. aka: *subroutine*: a small program that covers a task that needs to be repeated over and over again; such a subroutine is built into a main program.

process *v* (movies, TV) to develop and to print reels of film.

process art (art) painting or sculpture where the actual process of creation becomes the subject of the work and the final object is primarily a record of that evolving process.

procession (sport)
1. (cricket) the rapid collapse of a number of wickets so that the in-coming and dismissed batsmen form something of a procession across the pitch.
2. a race in which the winner leaves all rivals to trail in a long line behind him.

produce (horse-racing) the offspring of a dam.

producer's goods (econ) goods such as raw materials and tools which satisfy need only indirectly – in the creation of actual consumer goods.

producer's profits (movies) a fictional sum of money from which a notional percentage is offered to a neophyte in the movie business; no such profits exist – the only area from which money can be taken is the gross (qv).

product (record business) what an artist creates: the music or the songs.

product initiation (marketing) the familiarisation with a product undergone either by its salesman or by the consumers. Thus *product initiation training*: a course set up to teach salesmen to market their product most successfully.

production *a* (commerce) in motor manufacturing, a model that is made for normal production and subsequent public sale, rather than a special test model which never runs on public roads.

production brigade (econ) in socialist countries, a picked team of workers from within a commune or collective who are required to meet a given agricultural production norm. Also *production team*: a smaller version of the brigade.

productive (medic) a cough that brings up mucus or sputum into the throat.

product life cycle (marketing) a cycle of stages in the market's acceptance of a new product; these stages can be analysed as the level of the product class, the product form or that of the individual brand.

Profession *n* (theatre) the craft, calling, and personnel involved in the theatre; as opposed to the Business or the Industry, both reflecting the commercial basis of the film world.

professional foul (sport) in soccer, a deliberate foul committed by a defender when there seems no other way of stopping an opponent from scoring a goal. (cf: *profit foul*)

profile *n* (computers) in computer dating firms, the person with whom an applicant for a partner is matched.

profit foul (sport) in professional basketball, a deliberate foul that stops the opposition scoring an otherwise certain two points. (cf: *professional foul*)

pro forma invoice (commerce) an invoice sent to a purchaser in advance of the ordered goods so that all necessary paperwork can be completed.

programmed art (art) the post 1945 work of Bruno Munari which takes the form of small viewing screens each of which displays changing colour and shape combinations produced by small electric motors which turn moveable parts; the programming consists of the artist's choosing the length of a cycle of transformations on an individual screen.

programmed management (business) a systematic process whereby a manager is given a developing set of actions and steps by which he may successfully accomplish a series of specified objectives.

programme mix (TV) a complete portfolio of a TV company's forthcoming productions.

programme music (music) descriptive music, the opposite of absolute music (qv), which is intended to convey the impression of specific subjects, topics, objects, etc.

programme pictures (movies) aka: *programmer*, *B pictures*: exotic, action-packed melodramas with little plot, less intellectual content but with lurid titles – *The Virgin of Stamboul, Under Two Flags* – and a high turnover at the box-office; rendered obsolete by the advance of TV and no longer made, although their contemporary equivalent is the 'made-for-TV' picture.

programme year (TV) a breakdown of a company's complete schedules for an entire TV 'year', stretching from one autumn to the end of the following summer.

project Blue Book (milit) USAF: the official dossier that the US Air Force maintains on unidentified flying objects.

projected art (art) any art works which require projection equipment for them to be seen; such techniques mean that films and slides make available far more of an artist's work than could normally be encompassed within a single gallery.

proletarian internationalism (pols) the direct corollary of cosmopolitanism (qv): the desperate desire by satellite nations and individuals within them to become more Russian than the Russians; such enthusiasm acts as a useful cloak for Soviet imperialism.

proletarianisation (pols) the gradual loss of the control of the means of production by small producers who are swallowed up by big business; instead of inching their way into the bourgeoisie, they are forced downwards into the ranks of the proletariat.

proletarian redemption (pols) in Marxist terms, the historic mission of the downtrodden workers: the emancipation of themselves and their peers from servitude to capitalism.

proletarian revolutionary line (pols) in Chinese Communist terminology, up to 1978: the ideology and the policies of Chairman Mao Tse Tung.

proletkult (pols) in the world of art the complete negation of the past and its potential influence in favour of concentrating on *now*, particularly as far as 'now' reflects the basic facts of a worker's life; a factual description and celebration of proletarian life is art enough for a revolution.

proliferation (milit) the mass production of nuclear weapons and other armaments. Thus *non-proliferation treaties*: attempts to cut back on the growth of this accelerating arms production.

PROM (computers) (acro) *p*rogrammable *r*ead

only *me*mory: a memory that can be programmed by electrical pulses; such PROM chips can be purchased blank and then programmed for specific needs; *erasable PROMs* can be erased and re-used. PROMs are a good way for users to implement their own tailor-made personal programs.

promise (police/UK) *on a promise*: awaiting information, tip-offs, gifts, favours, possibly bribes; if one is meeting a woman, then awaiting sex.

promo (media) (abbrev) promotion: any kind of advertising or marketing to sell a new product; giveaways, free gifts, foreign tours, press lunches, a vast spectrum of persuasion from the most costly and unique to the cheapest and most obvious.

proofing (milit) British Army: the stealing of any unattended pieces of equipment, personal possessions, etc.

property *n* (advert) anyone who is regarded as a draw at the box office; usually a *hot property*.

proposition cheat (gambling) a cheat who never once gives his opponents/victims even the thought of a win; a cheat with a 100% advantage in every round or game.

proprietories (espionage) fully functioning commercial firms which combine their daily business activities with providing fronts for a variety of agents to carry out missions, surveillance and allied intelligence work; the staff of these firms, including those who keep to the business side, are all CIA members.

props (theatre) nickname for the Property Manager.

prop the prick (sex) the proffering by a homosexual hustler of his anus for his client to enjoy anal intercourse.

prospect *n* (crime) the selected victim or dupe of a pickpocket or conman.

prospects (radio) a list prepared twice a day by the *intake editor* (who supervises the various news stories that continue to arrive over wires and from reporters) which puts forward those possible news stories that a station's reporters should be covering as well as any continuing stories that might crop up in a new guise during the day.

prosumer (sociol) those people who perform for themselves such services hitherto performed by specialists and experts; e.g. do-it-yourself fanatics.

protection (crime) the extortion of money by gangs or individuals who threaten to break up a shop, pub, club etc, unless the owner starts paying regular weekly bribes; the only protection involved is that from the gang themselves.

protective reaction (milit) bombing raids targeted on anti-aircraft installations, on the principle of 'get them before they get you'.

protest vote (pols) the casting of one's vote for a candidate who has no chance whatsoever of winning, purely for the purpose of registering

one's disgust with policies, personalities or just general efforts of the 'legitimate' candidates.

protocol (computers) a set of inbuilt rules that govern the flow of information within the machine and between the various components, thus maximising the efficiency of each operation.

prove *v* (medic) in homoeopathic practice, to give a sample of a drug to a healthy person in order to check the symptoms it produces.

prowl *v* (crime/US) to rob; spec: to look over the site of possible break-in to check over the exits, ease of access, visibility from the street, etc.

prowl rat *n* (crime/US) a mugger who specialises in beating up and stealing from women.

prozine (TV) a professionally produced science fiction fan magazine.

pseudo-event (media) an event created with no more justification than the desire of those concerned to have their names and pictures in the papers and, better still, on television; often arranged by an advertising agency or public relations firm. (cf: *media event*)

PSI (science) any psychic phenomenon that cannot be simply dismissed out of hand or explained away through some variety of legitimate science.

psychiatric deluge (soc wk) the domination of psychoanalytic rather than psychiatric ideas in social work; this began to be noticed in the US shortly after World War II and has latterly spread to the UK.

psychiatric imperialism (soc wk) the psychiatric establishment in the US and UK who are opposed to such revisionist thinkers on mental ill-health as R. D. Laing, Thomas Szasz, David Cooper et al.

psychic income (econ)
1. aka: *psychic compensation*: the non-monetary and non-material satisfactions that ideally accompany an economic or work activity.
2. the non-measurable mental and emotional satisfaction a consumer gleans from an item or a service that he/she purchases.

psychobabble (new therapies) coined in 1976 by US writer R. D. Rosen in *New Times* magazine and subsequently in his book: *Psychobabble*: *Fast Talk and Quick Cure in the Era of Feeling* (1977). 'Institutionalised garrulousness', 'psychological patter', 'this need to catalogue the ego's condition' – all by-products of the mass of new therapies that offer easy cures to the various maladies that afflict the affluent American young of the late 20th century.

psychodrama (new therapies) created by J. L. Moreno c1937, a type of psycho-therapy in which a patient, helped by other patients, a therapist and his assistants, acts out his/her traumas and by thus dramatising these problems and fears, hopes to seek a way of coming to better terms with them or eliminating them completely.

psychographics (advert) a technique of working out the values, attitudes and life styles of all sections of the consuming public.

psychological pricing (business) the pricing of a product to enhance its sales appeal or increase its value to the consumer; in another form, the trick of taking a 25 ¢ item, marking it up to 29 ¢ and thus convincing the customer that far from being conned, they have gained a useful 1 ¢ off the supposedly normal price of 30¢.

psy-ops (milit) aka: *psy-war* (abbrev): psychological operations, psychological war: active propaganda that uses actions – some friendly, others frightening – rather than words to persuade those at whom it is aimed that you are better supported than opposed; further characterised in the Vietnam War as 'winning the hearts and minds' of the Vietnamese people.

PTP (TV) (acro) *pre-transmission pee*: especially needed by anchormen on election marathons, royal weddings, etc.

pubcaster (TV/US) any broadcaster from Public Broadcasting Services (PBS), the subscription funded station that has no advertisements and attempts to offer a slight improvement on the networks' prime time pap.

public art (art) artworks, usually sculptures, that are designed specifically for large public open spaces; such sculptures, unlike their classic and monumental predecessors, tend to be sited at ground level and are easily accessible to pedestrians and spectators to enjoy at close quarters.

publics (public relations) specific target groups for PR campaigns: large or small homogeneous groups, eg: blacks, students, teenagers, the stockholders of a single corporation, the users of a certain brand of video cassette, etc.

pudding (espionage) a derogatory reference to the United Nations Organisation, its membership and its efforts.

puddle *n* (sport) in rowing, the circular, rippled disturbance that remains on the surface of the water every time an oar is pulled out at the end of a stroke.

puff pipe (milit) on vertical take-off aircraft, a pipe through which compressed air is blown to help stabilise the aircraft.

puggled (milit) British Army: very drunk.

pull *v* (aerospace) to operate anything on an aircraft.

pull *n* (advert, print) a proof or a print taken from a page of type or a block for an illustration.

pull *v* (sex) to persuade a prostitute to leave another pimp's stable (qv) and start working for a new master.

pull *n, v* (police/UK) an arrest, the act of arresting a suspect.

pull-back *n* (movies) a shot in which the pulling away of the camera gives the illusion that the background is moving gradually further away.

pull-out (sport) in surfing: the steering of a surfboard over or through the back of a wave in order to bring the ride to an end.

pull the breakers (TV/UK) to go on strike; literally, the action of pulling out the breakers, the main circuit switches which would deprive the studio of lights and power.

pull the plug *v* (stock market) to withdraw one's support from a share, which has maintained it at an artificial level for the purpose of making a deal, and thus let the natural price reassert itself.

pull-through (gambling) a sleight-of-hand trick that gives the illusion of cutting a pack of cards fairly, but in fact the two halves are replaced exactly as they were.

pulpit (sport)
1. (yachting) a tubular metal guard rail around the bow and/or stern of a boat.
2. (game fishing) a small platform built for a harpooner to stand when fishing for swordfish and similar game.

pulpit (milit) RAF: an aircraft's cockpit.

pulsing *n* (milit) a method of sending large convoys across the Atlantic from the US: infrequent surges of large numbers of ships (300–500) are sent across, with as heavy as possible anti-submarine defences to guard them.

pump-priming (business) the use of judicious investments to stimulate a flagging market or overall economy.

pump-priming (pols) the using of Federal funds to stimulate the economy, particularly during a depression or as a hedge against accelerating inflation.

punched paper (theatre/US) a free admission pass.

punching it (sex) homosexual hustler's reference to the tedium of his professional encounters; from the concept of punching a time clock in a factory or office.

punch up (TV) to switch any source – telecine, VTR, slides, captions, etc – into the main transmission.

punch up (TV, movies) to manipulate the colours in a film or on a TV picture to improve contrast, shade, brightness and general effect. *Punch-up* can also be used for actors when they attempt to put more life and 'sparkle' into a performance.

punk (prison/US) a passive, youthful homosexual; the 'girl' who is used by other prisoners, or who attaches himself to an old prisoner for a 'marriage' that may last the duration of their sentences.

punt *n* (stock market) an investment in shares that really have only a minimal chance of proving profitable; from the gambling use, meaning a foolish long shot.

punter (gambling) anyone who bets on horses, dogs, casino games, football pools; the inference is invariably of an outsider and therefore a potential loser; thus *mug punter*: a particularly gullible bettor.

punter (crime)
1. the gullible public; anyone outside one's own coterie.
2. spec: (prostitute) the client.
3. (Glasgow gangs) a non-gang member who supplied weapons, bought up the proceeds of robberies, etc.
4. (Australia) a pickpocket's assistant, who catches the victim's attention while he is being robbed.

pup *n* (commerce) anything worthless; thus *to sell a pup*: to palm off something of no value (now absorbed into S.E.).

pup (TV, movies) a small keylight; *baby pup*: a smaller version. (cf: *babykicker*, *inky dinky*)

puppyfoot *n* (gambling) the ace of clubs (from its apparent visual resemblance).

pups (press/US) those sections of the large Sunday newspapers which are printed in advance of the main section and are delivered separately to suburban wholesalers. (cf: *bulldog*)

purple (milit) air intercept code: this unit is suspected of carrying nuclear weapons.

purple airway (air traffic) aka: *purple zone*: any route reserved for aircraft carrying members of a royal family.

push *n*, *v* (sport) in cricket, a batsman's stroke that merely eases the ball away, with no great force or direction.

push and pull (art) a theory of dynamic pictorial tensions: the 'in and out' forces that can been seen in abstract paintings composed of many patches of colour; the pictorial depth is created not by perspective but by the control of the colour relationships.

push-back clearance (air crew) permission to move an aircraft onto the runway in readiness for taxiing and then take-off.

pusher (theatre) a stagehand.

pusher (drugs) a seller of drugs; spec: a low level seller who is never involved in bulk purchase or sales.

pusher (aerospace) an aircraft which carries a propeller behind the main wings.

push-money (commerce) see: *PM*.

push-up *n* (crime, police) *at the pushup*: picking pockets in a crowd, rather than on the street.

pusser's crab (milit) RN: a regulation issue boot: (pusser = purser).

pussy (crime) furs: thus *pussy mob*: a gang of fur thieves.

pussy posse (police/US) members of a Vice Squad who specialise in arresting street prostitutes; the Vice Squad in general.

put (stock market) the right to deliver a specific commodity at a certain time for a designated price. (cf: *call*, *straddle*)

put a bid on the book (commerce) at an auction, to give the auctioneer a limit of bidding for a specific lot and to let him do that bidding in one's absence.

put and call (stock market) see *put*, *call*.

put on the farm (crime/US) in the US Mafia, to suspend a member temporarily from his activities; either as a punishment for some error or to hide him away from the authorities; such suspensions usually involve 'internal exile' somewhere in the US.

put the horns on (gambling) any attempt to improve one's luck – changing seats at the table, carrying a 'lucky piece' or some other superstitious device.

put the mouth on (sport) used by sports commentators who find that they need only mention a player's talent, good form or luck and some disaster invariably overtakes him; from the West Indian voodoo practice of 'talking' someone into trouble.

put-through (stock market) a transaction in which a broker arranges the simultaneous purchase and sale of shares. (cf: *marry*)

putty (milit) RN: a ship's painter.

put up *v* (press) to print in capitals.

put your hand up (police) to confess; from the image of answering a question at school.

pylon (medic) a temporary artificial leg without a knee joint.

pylons (lit crit) those poets of the 1930s – Auden, Isherwood, Spender, et al. – who concentrated on industrial scenes and imagery in their work.

pyramid *v* (stock market) to use the profits of a series of transactions gained from either a continuous rise or fall in prices to buy or sell additional stock on a margin (qv).

pyramid *n* (press/US) a headline of several lines in which those lines gradually lengthen, one beneath the other. (cf: *deck*)

pyramid *v* (stock market) to build up one's stock from the proceeds of previous successful deals.

pyramid selling (commerce) the extension of a franchise by the selling not of one's product but of further franchises and these new franchise holders then sell further franchises in their turn, thus creating a hollow pyramid in which there is little real merchandising but a great many outlets with nothing to offer.

Q & A (radio) (abbrev) *q*uestion and *a*nswer: any programme item that uses an expert or pundit and a reporter; the use of this expert means that the discussion is not simply a random interview, but a supposedly informative conversation.

Q boat (police/UK) a 'plain clothes' police car with a plain clothes crew, used for surveillance of suspects; from the Q boats – disguised merchantmen with concealed guns – used in World War 2. (cf: *nondescripts*)

QC (air crew) (acro) quickchange: aircraft that are constructed for simple and speedy alteration from passenger to cargo use and back again.

Q clearance (govt/US) the highest US government security clearance which includes access to nuclear weapons secrets.

QR (medic/US) (acro) quiet room: a euphemism for a locked, padded room which is used for otherwise uncontrollable patients who require maximum restraint.

quad *n* (tech) a unit of energy equivalent to 10^{15} British Thermal Units or 10^{18} joules.

quadriad (govt/US) a special group of top Presidential economic advisers: Chairman of the Council of Economic Advisers, Secretary of the Treasury, Director of the Office of Management, Chairman of the Federal Reserve Board. (cf: *troika*)

qualified (sex) an experienced, efficient and profitable prostitute.

quality of life commercial (advert) an advertisement that stresses the potential of a given product to enhance the purchaser's quality of life.

quantification (govt) the reduction of complex problems to simple yes/no solutions by concentrating on statistics and replacing nuances by numbers.

quango (govt) (acro) *q*uasi-*a*utonomous *n*on-governmental *o*rganisation: a government body which acts outside the usual civil service departments as an ostensibly public organisation but which is funded by the Exchequer; quangos can be created and staffed as quickly and as sweepingly as there are topics on which there might need to be discussion and subsequent administration.

quantify *v* (milit) to calculate on a general rather than specific level, thus intending to prove a point which, when considered in detail, might not prove valid.

quantophrenia (sociol) an obsession beyond sense and reason with results that are gleaned from statistics, especially when such results fail to reflect the more subtle facts of a situation.

quap *n* (science) a hypothetical nuclear particle, consisting of an anti-proton and a quark (qv).

quark (science) coined in 1961 by US physicist Murray Gell-Mann: the proposition that all subatomic particles are composed of combinations of three fundamental particles, the *quarks*; from 'Three quarks for Muster Mark' in James Joyce's *Finnegans Wake* (1939). The three types were called *flavours*, notably the *down quark*, *up quark* and *strange quark*. Subsequent research has revealed three more quarks: the *charmed quark*, or *charm*, the *bottom quark*, or *beauty* and the *top quark*, or *truth*. Other theories claim that there may be as many as 18 quarks in all.

quarter *n* (theatre/UK) a warning call to actors reminding them that the performance starts in 15 minutes.

quartering (indust relats) the practice in factories or offices whereby any employee who clocks in to work even two minutes late is automatically deprived of a whole quarter hour's wages.

quarter up price (stock market) aka: *probate price*: the price of a security accepted by the Estate Duty Office in the estimation of death duties: normally the bid quotation from the Official List plus one quarter of the difference between that and the offered quotation.

quasimodo (sport) in surfing, riding a surfboard in a crouched position; from the posture of the fictional 'Hunchback of Notre Dame' in Victor Hugo's *Notre Dame de Paris* (1831).

queen bee (milit)
1. WAAF: the director of the Women's Auxiliary Air Force.
2. a remote-controlled aircraft which is used for target practice.

queen's hard bargain (milit) RN: a lazy or incompetent seaman who is felt not to be earning his pay.

Queen's Pipe/Queen's Sewer (govt) the furnace and the drain used by H. M. Customs for the destruction of contraband tobacco and alcohol.

query languages (computers) a variety of experimental languages constructed to eliminate the problems that non-experts have in communicating with computers and the learning of high-level languages (qv) such as BASIC or COBOL (qqv); the intention is to allow operators to use standard English in instructing the machine and have the machine understand such commands.

queue (computer) a sequence of tasks or messages held in auxiliary storage memory until a machine can begin processing them.

quick *n* (sport) aka: *quickie*: in cricket, a fast bowler.

quick and dirty (govt) cheap, easy and generally second-rate methods of getting things done – constructing equipment, setting up committees, etc.

quinella (gambling) a bet in which a gambler is required to select the first two horses in a given race.

quota *n* (TV/UK) that amount of material that is not made in the UK (or Australia and Canada) that is permitted for transmission on British TV; currently 14% of the total programming.

quota quickie (movies) a cheap, speedily produced film made by US companies in countries outside the US; these films were peddled in the countries of manufacture so that 'real' Hollywood films could be imported and shown.

quota sample (marketing) the selection of a market research sample based upon collecting individuals with certain required and observable characteristics.

quotation (stock market) the current published price (in the Official List or the press) of any commodity or share.

rabbi (pols/US) a political patron; no religious meaning is involved.

rabbit (milit) RN: any smuggled or stolen item.

rabbit (tech)
1. see *pig*.
2. a container that takes material into a nuclear reactor or any other place where it is to be irradiated; powered by hydraulics or air pressure.

rabbit (gambling)
1. a timid or cautious gambler.
2. a sucker or inexperienced player.

rabbit (sport)
1. in US track sports: a pacemaker, or particularly fast member of a running squad.
2. in UK sport, a weakling, a coward, anyone who fails to pull their weight on a team.

rabbit (sport) in golf: a useless player, an amateur.

rack *v* (commerce) in the oil trade, to pile up sections of drilling pipe.

rack (milit) USMC: a bed or cot. (cf. *sack*).

rack *n* (medic/US) a cardiac board (a hard, rigid piece of wood) which is placed beneath a patient who is undergoing pulmonary resuscitation.

rack jobber (record business) a wholesaler who specialises in buying records from the manufacturer and selling to those large stores who display records on racks.

radiating elements (aerospace) the electronic 'eyes' that have replaced antennae on multi-function array radar.

radio pill (audio) an electronic circuit that generates a radio frequency circuit, developed in 1950s by RCA, and used for internal examinations of the human system that could not otherwise be performed without surgery.

radish communism (pols) that profession of communism whose ideological purity is suspect; like a radish which is red on the outside only, a description originally coined by Stalin to attack the Chinese Party.

raffredori (Mafia) lit. 'a chill': the increase of police pressure that leads to a temporary cutting back in visible Mafia activity.

Rag (milit) British services: the Army and Navy Club; coined c1858 by Capt. William Duff, 23rd Fusiliers, who called it the 'Rag and Famish'.

rag *n* (theatre/UK) the act curtain or a tableau curtain: any curtain that divides into two rather than rises as a whole sheet.

raggie (milit) RN: a mess jacket (obs.); a friend so close one could share one's polishing rags with him.

rag order (milit) British Army: a state of appalling messiness.

rag top (commerce) in the motor trade: a convertible or soft topped car.

raid the market (stock market) an attempt to destabilise the market and bring down prices.

rail *n* (sport) in surfing: the edge of the surfboard; thus *rail turn* a trick turn during which one edge of the board is submerged.

rails (horse-racing) the fence that forms the boundary of a race-course; thus *on the rails*: a horse or horses that run nearest to that fence.

rainbow book (govt) in UK local government, a book in which the salaries of councillors and other officials are listed; its pages are variously coloured as to the grade or occupation of those included.

rainbows (drugs) see: *drug names*.

rainbow shot (sport) in basketball, a shot that arches neatly from the player's hand down into the basket.

rainmaker (business/US) any businessman, especially a lawyer, who uses his political connections to bring business to the firm.

rainmaker (public relats) a public relations man who brings in the promotion, coverage and publicity just as he promised.

rally (futures market) the upward movement of prices following a decline.

rally *v* (theatre/UK) to increase the dramatic effects of a performance by speeding up dialogue and business.

RAM (computers) aka: *read/write memory*: (acro) random *access* memory: that memory within a machine that allows information to be stored or retrieved in a random fashion in a short time, that part of the machine into which one loads/unloads programs. (cf: *ROM*)

rambler (commerce) in real estate, a single storey house, often the suburban imitation of a ranch-house. (cf: *rancher*)

ramp *n* (business, crime) any financial swindle, spec. the fraudulent increasing of a commodity price in order to gain profits. Thus *banker's ramp*: a Labour Party bugbear which claimed that the banks would engineer a fake economic crisis whenever Parliament was attempting to increase welfare provisions for the needy.

rancher (commerce) in real estate: a ranch-style suburban property; *ranchette*: the same, in a smaller version. (cf: *rambler*)

random *n* (press) a special frame used to contain type when making up a page.

random art (art) art based on the laws of chance, involving the statistical techniques derived from probability or information theory.

range *n* (futures market) the extreme high or low price recorded over a specific time.

rap *n* (police/UK) a charge against a suspect; *rap sheet* the charge sheet in a police station.

rap *v* (new therapies) conversations, often within encounter groups, in which one's feelings are laid out, supported, analysed or criticised. Thus *rap session*, *rap group*; from black sl. through hippie use.

rapping (music) aka: *jive-talking* a style of music and entertainment in which the disc jockey talks in rhyming sentences, often with a witty or pointed lyric, to the background of a variety of records, thus, *rapper*: one who performs in this way. (cf: *scratching*, *toasting*)

rapture of the deep (sport) aka: *nitrogen narcosis*: in diving, a dazed or light-headed sensation that comes with breathing in heavily nitrogenised compressed air.

rassing (milit) British forces: the acquiring of any item illegally; from the RN acronym *RAS*: replenishment *at* sea.

raster (TV, video) an unmodulated TV picture that comprises the horizontal lines one sees on the screen.

ratchet jaw (audio) in Citizen's Band radio: anyone who talks excessively when other breakers (qv) are waiting to use the frequency.

rat-fucking (pols/US) the clandestine disruption of an opponent's campaign by a variety of tricks, both legitimate and actually illegal; from S. California campus politics, where such trickery was developed and in which universities many of the 'ratfuckers' employed by President Nixon in the 1972 campaign were educated.

rathole *v* (commerce) in the oil industry, the drilling of a hole of smaller diameter at the bottom of one that has already been pushed to its limit.

ratio *n* (movies) the ratio of the width of the screen to its height: prior to 1953 this was 4:3 or 1.33:1; current standard screens are betw. 1.66:1 and 1.85:1; Cinemascope is 2.35:1; VistaVision is shot at 1.33:1 but screened at 2:1.

rationalisation (business) the cutting back on staff, supplies, etc to improve an economic position; supposedly a means of cutting down on inefficiency, poor methods, etc but in the event, usually a euphemism for redundancies.

rationalisation (TV) the adapting of films made for cinema projection down to the dimensions of the TV screen.

rat pack *n* (milit) British forces: dehydrated Arctic rations.

rats (milit) low flying enemy raids.

ratten *v* (indust relats/US) to compel workers to go on strike by removing their tools and materials.

rattle *n* (milit) RN: *in the rattle*: in confinement, or on the commander's list of defaulters.

rattle *n* (police/UK) *on the rattle*: a policeman who has been reported to a senior officer and is facing punishment.

rattler (police/UK) the London Underground railway.

rattle the cage (pols/US) any attempt by a politician to break out of the restraints imposed by his staff.

rave *v* (computers)
1. to persist in discussing a specific topic.
2. to speak with alleged authority on a subject about which the speaker knows very little.
3. to complain to someone who has no authority to remedy the problem.
4. to irritate someone by one's conversation.
5. to preach at someone.

rave *n* (entertain) a superlatively laudatory review.

ravio (milit) French Foreign Legion: anything obtained illegally.

raw *a* (computers) data that has not yet been analysed, sorted, assessed.

raw *a* (espionage) information that has only recently been collected and has yet to be analysed or otherwise put to use.

raw feels (psychol) the immediate 'gut' reaction to a stimulus without any subsequent refining by one's emotions.

raw jaws (sex) aka: *cowboy*, *choirboy*: any hustler who has yet to establish himself in the profession.

rays (medic/US) (abbrev) X-Rays; a medical speciality for hospital doctors.

RD (govt/US) (abbrev) Restricted Data: any information about the design, manufacture or use of nuclear weapons. Such information is classified under the US Atomic Energy Act 1946. Such material is never actively classified: the very fact that it falls in this area renders it secret from the moment of its inception.

RDT & E (milit) (acro) research, development, test and evaluation: the stages of creating a new weapon for military use.

reach *v* (police, crime) to approach, probably successfully, a policeman or other authority, with a proposal of bribery. (cf: *can I speak to you?*)

reach *n* (marketing) aka: *coverage*: the proportion of a target audience that is exposed to an advertisement at least once.

reach and frequency (advert) the measuring of the penetration of a specific advertisement into its target market. The sum of the *reach*: the measure of those viewers who see an advertisment, with the *frequency*: the average number of exposures per individual over a given time.

react *v* (milit) for one unit to come to the aid of another which is suffering hostile attacks.

react *v* (stock market) of share prices, to fall after they have risen; the opposite of rally (qv); thus *reaction*: a downward movement of share prices.

reactionary *n* (pols) a politician who wishes to reverse the progress of politics and society and return to an earlier era; generally used to condemn conservatives and the right.

read *v* (sex) to realise that a transvestite is in fact a man and not the woman he is made up to resemble.

read *v* (computers) to put coded data into a machine or to take it out; thus, *read-in* or *read-out*.

readability formula (educ) the writing of (text) books in such a way that the language and concepts involved are suited to the academic abilities of those who will be using them.

read-around ratio (computers) the number of times a particular piece of information can be extracted from the memory and read without having an adverse effect on those pieces stored next to it.

reader *n* (press, advert) an advertisement that is designed to appear as normal newspaper copy and thus set in the style and typeface of the paper in which it will appear.

readers *n* (gambling) any sort of marked cards that can be 'read' by the initiated.

read in *v* (espionage) the reading of documents, reports, and allied information in a case in order to familiarise oneself with a mission involving the subject of such information.

reading *n* (theatre)
1. an audition.
2. a performance in which an actor offers his/her particular rendering of the role.

reading notice (press) any advertisement that resembles the editorial copy in a newspaper. (cf: *reader*)

read off *v* (milit) USMC: to reprimand severely; to publish the findings of a court-martial.

ready cap *n* (milit) a military aircraft that is in a situation of readiness for instant take-off.

ready-made *n* (art) coined by Marcel Duchamp, (1888–1967) to describe the Dadaist innovation of taking everyday objects and exhibiting them as bona fide works of art.

ready room (milit)
1. a room or a hangar where hardware (especially missiles and other unmanned vehicles) are prepared for use, launching, etc; particularly common on warships.
2. the briefing room on an aircraft carrier where pilots receive details of their missions.

realia (educ) three-dimensional teaching aids,

models, etc – which are used in the classroom to relate verbal teaching to actual events.

realism *n* (law) the theory that the law is best discovered by studying actual legal decisions and precedents, rather than statutes and similar legislative acts.

realism (pols) the philosophy that power is the subject of politics, and not ideology, civil rights, doctrine or any other side-tracked issue.

reality programming (TV) aka: *actuality programming*: non-fiction TV shows which are based on the exploits of actual persons (or even animals) and which use these to justify a mass of entertainment with a thin coating of information.

real money (econ) the actual value of the money one possesses, rather than the face value; influenced by inflation, recession, international currency fluctuations, etc.

realpolitik (pols) politics that depend on practical realities and day to day expediency for their direction; such ideology as there is will always be subordinated to actual needs; on an international level, the taking of such steps that benefit oneself or one's plans and not one's moral image before the rest of the world.

real time (computer) the actual time in which something takes place; thus the analysing and calculating by a computer of such information as it actually comes in to the machine rather than dealing with a tape or similar recording of that information.

real user (computers)
1. anyone who uses the machine for a specific purpose, rather than a *hacker* who is working on the machine for the joy of seeing what it can offer.
2. anyone who pays for time on the computer; a commercial user.

real wages (econ) the value of wages in the face of inflation; the drop in value that stands against the ostensible increase in cash paid per week.

real world (computers)
1. those people who are not involved professionally or academically with programming or engineering of computers.
2. anywhere outside a university.
3. the world of the commuter, the 9–5 office, rather than the informal hothouse world of programming.

rear admiral (milit) USN:
1. an enema.
2. a specialist in the treatment of haemorrhoids.

reasoned amendment (pols) an amendment to a bill already before Parliament which tries to stop any further reading of that bill by proposing a number of alterations which would so change its character as to render it useless to those who first introduced it.

rebirthing (new therapies) based on Otto Rank's theory of the birth trauma, a therapy devised by Leonard Orr with the aim of '(unravelling) the birth/death cycle and (getting) your prosperity trip together and (getting) you to realise that truth is your guru'; the organisation that propagates rebirthing is named Theta, representing the non-physical and immortal part of the human being.

recall capability (milit) the ability to recall one's weapons or forces after initially setting them in motion.

receivables (business) the money currently owing to a company either for products or services to customers and which is categorised between actual assets and bad debts; the steady collection of receivables forms the basis of good cash flow.

received pronunciation (educ) aka: *standard English, BBC English, Oxford English*: the neutral 'correct' pronunciation of English still taught in many schools; the English spoken by the middle classes of south-east England.

receiver aircraft (aerospace) that aircraft in a mid-air refuelling operation that is taking on fuel supplies. (cf: *giver aircraft*).

reconceptualisation (sociol) the looking at a problem in a new way.

reconciliation (econ) the practice in accountancy of ironing out apparent discrepancies in two statements to produce balanced accounts.

recovery (futures market) a rise in prices that follows a decline.

rectification (pols) in Chinese Communist terminology: the periodic checking of the ideological standing of Party members; censures emerging from this range from mere criticism to absolute expulsion from the Party.

red (finance) *in the red*: in debt; from the red ink once used in ledgers to denote indebtedness.

red alert (milit) an attack by hostile aircraft or missiles is imminent or in progress.

red band *n* (prison/UK) a trusty, who wears a red band on his arm to denote his status.

red book (govt) the weekly digest of intelligence prepared for UK government officials.

recess *n* (prison/UK) the toilets, sluices.

red book (advert/US)
1. the *Standard Directory of Advertising Agencies*.
2. the *Standard Directory of Advertisers*. Both of these volumes are regularly bound in red.

red bourgeoisie (pols) see: *new class*.

red box (milit) the safe, on submarines and bombers, and in missile launch bases, where the launch codes are kept ready for an actual war.

red button (stock market) Settlement Room clerks who check their firm's bargains and who wear red buttons in their lapels. (cf: *pink button*)

redcap (milit) British Army: military policeman.

red cat theory (pols) in Chinese Communist terminology, the concept that there are no ideological boundaries to set against the acquisition of technical knowledge; capitalist computer science, etc. is as useful as its communist equivalent: 'It is irrelevant if the cat is red or not, as long as it catches the mouse' (Deng Xiaoping (1904–)).

redcoats *n* (entertain) the British.

red dog (sport) in US football, a play in which one of the defensive team rushes the passer of the ball.

red dwarf (science) in astronomy, an old, relatively cool star. (cf: *red giant*)

red-eye (air crew) a flight that takes off late at night and arrives very early in the morning, its passengers emerged with eyes red from lack of sleep.

red giant (science) in astronomy, a large, relatively cool star.

red goods (advert, commerce) products that are frequently purchased, speedily consumed, soon replaced and then purchased over again: e.g. fresh foods; red goods rarely offer very high profits.

red hat (milit) British Army: a staff officer, from the red band around his regulation officer's cap.

redhead (TV, movies) a variable beam light, c800W, constructed from glass fibre.

red herring (finance) an advance copy of a prospectus for an issue of securities that must be filed with the Securities Exchange Commission (SEC); on it is written in red; 'not a solicitation, for information only'.

red line value (aerospace) in aircraft specification, those values on the dials that must *never* be exceeded if safety procedures are to be maintained.

red-lining (commerce) the practice amongst loan firms and building societies of drawing a real or imaginary red line around certain areas of cities, usually the impoverished 'inner city', to signify that no credit will be allowed to any individual living in those areas, irrespective of actual credit worthiness, personal records, etc. The result of such red lining is to accelerate the decline of these areas, thus preparing them for lucrative development plans that may well enrich the redliners.

red noise (audio) sound that shows a higher variance in the lower frequencies; coined by Prof. E. N. Lorenz in 1961.

red-out (aerospace) the loss of vision that can assail an individual who is secured to a seat only by a shoulder harness during the time his aircraft enters a period of power and sustained deceleration.

red pipe (medic/US) an artery.

reds (drugs) see: *drug names*.

redshirt *v* (sport) in US college football, the extension of a star player's usual four-year eligibility by taking him out of competitive teams for one of those years, during which times he can practise and develop and then re-enter the team to render it even greater services, and still play for four years altogether.

re-educate (pols) the conditioning of an errant individual into the following of an ideologically pure line; this can involve political classes and the staying some time in the countryside with 'workers and peasants' who should eradicate one's bourgeois backsliding.

reef v (crime) to steal; spec. to pull up the lining of a victim's pocket in order to remove its contents.

reel n (movies) a set length of 35mm film: orign. 1000 feet, but now either 2000 or 3000 feet.

reel (advert) a composite reel of film carried by the directors of commercials so as to display their past achievements to potential new clients. (cf: book)

re-entry (sport) in surfing: a trick involving 'skating' along the top curl of a wave.

refer back v (indust relats) a motion that the matter under discussion be taken off the agenda to be reconsidered and brought forward again at a later date.

reference v (archit) to state the overall theme, design or style of a building.

reflation (econ) see: inflation.

reformism (pols) in Marxist terms, minor and gradual changes in the labour movement and towards a limited socialism, but genuine destruction of exploitative capitalism.

refresher (law/UK) an extra fee paid to barristers for each day a trial over-runs its initially allotted period before the Court.

refugees (pols) recruits to the British Social Democratic Party (SDP) who were formerly members of the Labour Party. (cf: naives)

Reg (milit) at the Royal Military College, Sandhurst: a senior cadet. (cf: John)

regie-book (theatre) from Ger. 'Regiebuch' = director's book: a notebook kept by a director in which the current production is detailed along with ideas, experiments, etc. for its improvement.

regime n (crime/US) in US Mafia: a division of 40–60 members, led by a caporegime (qv).

regime (aerospace) one specific mode of operation, clearly defined and distinguished from any other type of operation by the same device.

regimental a (milit) maintaining or following strict discipline.

regular a (science) in astronomy, a satellite that maintains as near as possible a circular orbit around its planet.

regulator (econ) a means of manipulating the economy between Budgets whereby the Chancellor of the Exchequer may alter the going rate of taxation.

rehabilitation medicine (medic) a special branch of health care that concentrates on the severely disabled and the effort to restore them to an independent, dignified place in society.

re-heat (aerospace) to augment the speed of an aircraft by adding afterburners which burn up additional fuel with the oxygen that remains in the combustion gases after they have once passed through the turbine.

reification (pols, sociol) in Marxist terms, the degeneration of a worker from a human individual into a mere unit of labour.

rejectionist (pols) any Arab who refuses to recognise the existence of the state of Israel; thus Rejectionist Front: those Arab states that ascribe to this view.

rejoneo (sport) in bull-fighting, the art of fighting the bull from horse-back; thus rejoneador: a mounted bull fighter who places the rejon: a metal tipped, wooden handled spear.

relativism (pols) in Marxist terms, the belief that orders from above may be adapted to one's own view of local conditions; thus historical relativism: the concept that there can be no objective standard of historical truth since every historian will impose their own 'truth' on the available data; ethical relativism: that everyone creates their own ideas of moral standards and no general guideline can be determined; cultural relativism: no absolutes exist by which a culture can be judged, one must study too many and too complex varieties of factors for the easy making of such a decision.

release (music) in jazz, a passage of music that serves as a bridge between repetitions of the main melody.

release n (record business) a new record, which has just been 'released' by the company for retail sales.

relief tube (aerospace) a crew member's personal urine tube, which usually discharges directly into the air.

religious punishment (pols) in post-Revolutionary Iran, a variety of tortures applied to the ideologically impure in the name of religion: whipping with chains or rubber hoses, being suspended from the ceiling by one's arms which are handcuffed behind one's back, electric shock modified by the 'Apollo machine', an iron 'space helmet' which amplifies the victim's screams.

reload v (crime) the ensnaring of a sucker in a confidence game: the operator lets his victim win a few small bets prior to persuading him to wager, and automatically lose, his whole bankroll.

relocate v (business) the moving of one's business to new premises.

remainder v (publishing) to sell off books that will not sell at their full price at bargain rates, either through normal bookshops or through a 'remainder shop' which specialises in such bargains.

Rembrandt n (TV) a film that is particularly excellent; Rembrandt lighting: the angling of the keylight at 45° to the subject which is being illuminated.

Remington raiders (milit) USMC: clerk typists.

remit *v* (indust relats) a method at Trade Union conferences of burying a resolution without even bothering to vote on it: such resolutions are remitted, ie: referred to the Conference Executive for future (that is, never) consideration.

remote *n* (TV, radio) any programme that is shot on location and broadcast direct to the network without passing through studio facilities; an outside broadcast.

removables (aerospace) all items that the flight crew must remove from the outside of an aircraft prior to take-off.

rencontre (science) an organised, but informal meeting of scientists.

rendezvous (aerospace) the planned meeting and possibly docking together of two space capsules during a mission in space.

renewal (govt) usually as *urban renewal*: the development of urban areas, implying that the old and/or slum areas have first been demolished.

rent (sex) to obtain money from someone in exchange for homosexual favours.

rent boy (sex) aka: *renter* a young, male homosexual prostitute, who can be rented for one's enjoyment. (cf: *meat rack*)

renter (movies) one who organises the distribution of films to the exhibitors who show them in cinemas.

renversement (aerospace) any aerobatic manoeuvre in which the aircraft has to reverse direction.

rep (milit) British Army: (abbrev) report, always modified by a specific description of the subject of that report, thus: *ammo*: exchange of fire; *arrest*: insurgents arrested; *bang*: an explosion; *baton*: rubber bullets used; *car*: suspected vehicle; *cas*: casualties; *crowd*: rioting mob; *explo*: explosions; *find*: the discovery of a cache of arms, ammo, etc; *inc*: incident; *int*: intelligence; *shell*: shelling; *shot*: insurgents are firing at the Army; *tug*: vehicle breakdown.

rep (theatre/UK) (abbrev) repertory:
1. the system of playing through a season of regularly alternating plays, all using the same company.
2. a provincial theatre company; stock company (US).
3. all the parts an actor has learnt during a career.

repeat buying (marketing) the continual buying of familiar brands by an individual.

repeaters (commerce) regular visitors to the same hotel.

repeat rate (marketing) those purchasers who have tried a new product once and then return to buy it a second and possibly further times.

repêchage (sport) fr. Fr. 'to rescue, to give a second chance': in track sports, an additional qualifying heat in which the fastest losers in previous heats have the chance to reach the finals.

repertoire (computers) those instructions that have been specifically prepared for the operation of one computer or one 'family' of computers.

reply *n* (law) the final speech of a Counsel in a trial.

reply device (marketing) in mail order merchandising, the coupon that is attached to the offer that allows the customer to make a purchase.

reply vehicle (marketing) in mail order merchandising, the postcard or stamped addressed envelope that accompanies an offer and allows the customer to make an order.

repo (commerce) (abbrev) repossession: the confiscation of goods purchased on hire purchase and for which the monthly payments are no longer being made; thus *repo man*: one who collects from defaulting customers.

repple depple (milit) a corruption of *replacement depot*: a staging point where US troops who have been serving overseas are assembled prior to flying or sailing back home.

representational art (art) the opposite of abstract art, the painting or sculpturing of figures as far as possible as they appear to the artist's eye.

reprise (marketing) in mail order merchandising, the restatement of the basic offer in a letter that accompanies that offer; often placed as a postscript to that letter.

repro (art) in antiques, the expert imitation of an antique piece, especially an item of furniture.

repro *n* (press) in offset-litho printing, the strips of typeset copy that are pasted onto boards and then photographed to make a negative from which the material is printed.

reproduction (econ) in Marxist terms, the continuation of the capitalist economy by the regular turning of part of that economy's product into more capital; thus *simple reproduction*: that reproduction in which the amount of capital remains constant and any surplus is simply used up in other consumption; *enlarged/expanded reproduction*: the conversion of any surplus into extra means of production.

rep-tile (maths) aka: *reptile*: two dimensional figures of which two or more can be grouped together to make larger scale models of themselves.

request man (milit) RN: a sailor who makes a written request to an officer.

res cogitans (philos) the concept of man as a thinking being, esp. from Descartes, 'Cogito ergo sum' (*Meditationes*, 1641).

res communis (law) common property.

rescue bid (gambling) in bridge, any bid that attempts to save one's partner from a difficult position.

reservation (pols/US) a particular political party; thus *on the reservation*: maintaining one's loyalty to one's party. (cf: *off the reservation*)

reserve *v* (art) in ceramics, to leave a pot or similar artefact in its original colour without additional painting or decoration.

reserve *n* (commerce) in auction sales, (abbrev) reserve price: that price put on a given lot to which the bidding must rise, if not exceed; otherwise the lot is withdrawn from the sale. (cf: *upset price*)

res extensa (philos) a material thing considered as an extended substance, the material cosmos in which humanity exists.

res gestae (law) the facts of a case, the 'things done', especially that evidence that includes spoken words.

residence (espionage) an intelligence agent (of the KGB) who works in a foreign country and is attached to his embassy, invariably under some anodyne title; thus *residentura* the intelligence establishment maintained by the Soviets in a foreign country.

residual family (sociol, govt) a family who refuses to leave an area, usually one scheduled for slum clearance, despite their standing in the way of an edifice of bureaucratic intentions.

residuals (entertain) any payments made to performers, writers, directors, etc for the repeat of a play, TV programme, etc.

residuate (govt) to maintain a residual profile, ie: to appear as rarely and as insignificantly as possible.

res integra (law) a point in law that is neither covered by a previous decision nor a current rule of law and must therefore be decided on principle.

res ipsa loquitur (law) Lat: 'the thing speaks for itself': the principle that the proven occurrence of an accident implies the negligence of a defendant, unless he can provide another, exonerating cause.

resistance area (stock market) aka: *resistance level*: the price level that a share reaches in a rising market and at which it stops because of the increased attractiveness of that price to potential sellers.

res judicata (law) any point that has been decided by a competent legal authority.

res non verba (philos) material, solid things rather than insubstantial talk.

res nullius (law) property that cannot and does not belong to anyone.

resource aggregation (commerce) the calculation of the requirements of each resource for each time period, worked out on a common basis of rules.

resource profile (commerce) those resources required to perform a certain job.

resource time (commerce) the length of time a specific resource is required for the performance of a given task.

responaut (medic) a patient who depends on any form of artificial breathing aid.

responsibles (theatre/UK) small but important roles in touring or rep (qv) companies; thus the actors who take such roles.

resting (theatre/UK) out of work. (cf: *at liberty*)

restricted (govt) documents that may not be revealed to the general public for alleged reasons of national security. (cf *classification*, *RD, FRD, NSI*)

restructuring *n* (business) the shutting down of companies to save money.

restructuring (indust relats) aka: *productivity bargaining*: the alteration of wage, job or salary structure.

result (sport) in soccer, a victory.

result *n* (police, crime)
1. (police) an arrest, a successful conviction.
2. (crime) an acquittal.

result player (gambling) a gambler who specialises in hindsight: telling the other players what they should have done after a hand has been played or a throw rolled.

ret (press) the second side of a sheet of paper.

retail audit (marketing) aka: *shop audit*: a continuing research programme that uses a panel of retailers to check the progress or lack of it in a specific line or product.

retain *v* (sport) in soccer, a system whereby a player might be kept on by a club although his actual contract of employment has expired; no other club could offer to buy him and his current club had no obligation to use or sell him.

retained *v* (educ) euph: backward; a child who is not clever enough to rise a form with his peers and has to be 'retained' at his current level for a further year.

retinal art (art) paintings designed to appeal primarily to the eye and emphasise basic sensuality over any attempts to introduce an intellectual tone into art.

retread *n* (milit) from the idea of repairing and re-using otherwise useless automobile tyres: an officer who was retired and is brought back into the forces for further employment.

retreatism (sociol) the philosophy of dropping out of life and its various responsibilities, trials and tribulations.

retro (entertain, art) (abbrev) retrospective: a show or exhibition that gathers together the great creations of a major figure in entertainment or the arts.

retro (commerce) in fashion, (abbrev) retro-gressive: clothing styles that look at the past rather than developing towards the future; harking back to the 'looks' of earlier eras.

Retro (aerospace) an engineer who specialises in the operation of the retro-rockets in a spacecraft. (cf: *FIDO, GUIDO*)

retroactive classification (govt) the concept that previously unclassified material, esp. arti-

R

cles already published and circulated publicly, were in fact secret and should henceforth be withdrawn from files and never republished.

retrograde manoeuvre (milit) aka: *strategic withdrawal*: euphemism for retreat.

return (theatre)
1. ticket stubs.
2. a critical review.

re-up *n*, *v* (milit) US forces: to enlist for a further period of service, one who has so re-upped.

revanchism (pols) the philosophy of desiring revenge for past defeats, betrayals; esp. the regaining of territory that was taken through a disadvantageous treaty that followed a military defeat.

revenge barter (commerce, pols) aka: *revenge counter-sales*: a deal in which Western traders import goods from Socialist countries and force those countries to accept payment in kind rather than the cash that they actually want.

reverse (advert, press) the printing of a picture back to front, left becomes right, right becomes left.

reverse angle (TV, movies) a shot that represents the opposite point of view from that seen in the preceding shot.

reverse bigotry (pols) the use of 'positive racism' to emphasise that a party or politician is absolutely devoid of any bigotry and thus to garner the votes of the minority to whom it or he is so ostentatiously favourable.

reverse discrimination (govt, pols) the discrimination against members of a dominant group, ie: White Anglo-Saxon Protestants, in order to make up for previous discrimination against minorities, esp. in giving jobs or college places to such minorities over the claims of (sometimes better-qualified) WASPs.

reverse out (press, advert) a printing process that makes black appear white and vice versa.

reverse western position (sex) the opposite of the traditional missionary position: the woman straddles the man.

revisionism (pols) the attempt, in Communist countries, to 'debase, emasculate (and) destroy Marxism by (the) . . . reconsideration, distortion and denial of its fundamental tenets' (*Russian Political Dictionary*, 1958); originated as a policy by Edward Bernstein (1850–1932) who suggested c. 1895 that evolution was a better way of creating socialism than revolution. (cf: *hegemony*)

revolve (theatre) a circular section of the stage that can be revolved to reveal new sets, characters, etc.

rewrite (press/US) to edit a reporter's copy for publication; thus *rewrite man*: a subeditor.

rhubarb! (theatre, TV, movies) the muttering of a crowd of extras who are traditionally told to say 'Rhubarb, rhubarb!' over and over again.

rhubarb *n* (sport) in baseball, an argument or slanging match between players and possibly the umpire and managers on the field of play.

rhubarb *n* (milit) a low level flight intended to shoot up whatever targets happen to present themselves.

ribbon *n* (press/US) a headline, in smaller type than the main headline, that runs across the page above that main headline.

rick (gambling) a phoney bet that is made by a book-maker's accomplice in order to encourage other punters (qv) to get their money down; such a bet is never entered in the book-maker's ledger, nor is any money paid in or out. (cf: *on top*)

ride *v* (music) in jazz, to play with an easy, flowing style.

ride *v* (TV) to monitor the levels of the sound and vision signals.

rideman (music) in jazz, the leading soloist, who establishes the rhythm.

riders (milit) RN use for non-military personnel carried on submarines.

ride shotgun (business) to be ready for any eventuality; from the 'Wild West' practice of stagecoaches being manned by a shotgun carrying guard who rode alongside the driver and kept a lookout for Indians or bandits.

ride the clock (indust relats/US) 'to leave the plant during working hours without punching your time-card out, so that you will be paid for the whole day. It is usually only shop stewards who have the opportunity to do this: their absence will not be noticed immediately since they are away from their machines much of the time on union activities' (letter from T. S. Holman, 6.10.81).

ride the gain (radio, TV) to regulate the volume of a programme in order to transmit it properly over the equipment one is using.

riding the boards (advert/US) driving around an area to check the billboard advertising that one has had erected.

RIF (business) acro) reduction *in force*: the elimination of low priority jobs for the sake of economy; this may not imply the dismissal of the job-less individual since he may, through seniority, be allowed to bump (qv) a junior employee out of *his* job, even though such a bump would mean a reduction in authority.

riff *v* (music) in jazz, playing improvised phrases.

riff money (movies, TV) money earned in part-time jobs outside one's regular employment; 'pin-money'.

rifle *n* (theatre) a 2.4KW spotlight with an adjustable beam.

rig *n* (audio)
1. the two-way radio set used by Citizen's Band radio broadcasters.
2. any 'pirate' radio transmitter that is not authorised by the authorities.

rigged for red (milit) USN use for the 'nighttime' of a strategic submarine, when red lights replace 'daytime' white ones.

rigging (indust relats/US) any pro-union propaganda material.

rigging *n* (theatre, TV, movies)
1. all ropes, blocks, pulleys, wires, weights and anything else used for hanging scenery or lights.
2. the catwalk around the top of a studio or stage used by electricians.

right *n* (sport) in surfing: using the right foot; thus *left*: using the left foot.

right finger *n* (police) a skilful thief.

rightism (pols) in Communist countries, the failure of a Party member to realise that while certain compromises must be made, they are always temporary, tactical, and undertaken for a specific objective only; they are not meant to alter or undermine the basis of Communist doctrine. (cf: *revisionism, leftism*)

rights (stock market) anything to which a shareholder is entitled; *rights issue*: the issue of extra shares (usually as a proportion of those already held) to those who already own shares in a company.

right to know (pols, press) a journalistic concept whereby nothing – information, secrecy, evidence in a trial – is permitted to resist the enquiries of the press, no matter that such probing may run contrary to individual rights.

rim (press/US) a semi-circular copy desk in US newspaper offices where the sub-editors sit; thus *rim man*: a sub-editor. (cf: *slot*)

ring *n* (commerce) in auction sales, a group of two or more persons – usually but not always dealers – who agree before the sale not to outbid each other and thus eliminate the competition and keep the price down. After the lot or lots have been secured, the members of the ring hold a private auction, the knock-out (qv) or *settlement*. The difference between the price achieved in the sale room and the knock-out is called the *dividend* and it is shared between all members of the ring.

ringer (milit) RN, RAF: wings on an officer's sleeve denote his rank, thus *one-ringer*: sub-lieutenant, flying officer; *two-ringer*: lieutenant, flight lieutenant; *half ringer*: warrant officers, pilot officers, both of whom have half rings; *two and a half ringer* (two 'fat' and one 'thin' rings): lieutenant commander, squadron leader. (cf: *pip, one-pipper*)

ringer (police/crime)
1. a phony car with fake documents, made of a variety of parts, etc.
2. a horse or dog, substituted for another in a race; either to lose a race by removing a favourite or to win one by supplying a far better animal.
3. by extension from (1) & (2), any genuine looking fake.

ring-fence *v* (finance) a method of dealing with

tax demands by setting aside a certain item from the rest of a company's accounts for consideration on its own.

ring-fence *v* (econ, govt) to erect barriers around certain industries or occupations in order to maintain the work-force within that occupation, e.g. making miners stay working as miners; such control is only imposed during wartime and would not otherwise be tolerated.

ringing (police/UK)
1. taking two cars, usually half-serviceable wrecks, and creating a 'new' car from parts of each.
2. altering the documentation of a car to improve the chances of selling it.

ringing out (futures market) the practice of periodically settling any outstanding futures contracts before they mature; often performed by a third party to those involved in the original deal.

ring in one's nose (gambling) *to have a ring in one's nose* (like a bull): to be losing heavily and betting heavily and impetuously in an attempt to get even.

ring the bell *v* (sport) in US football, to smack someone so hard on his helmeted head that the resultant shock waves through his skull can cause disorientation, slight concussion and short-term impairment of motor and speech mechanisms.

rint (govt) (abbrev) radiation *int*elligence: any information concerning radiation, either in nuclear reactors or military use. (cf: *humint, comint, elint*)

rip *n* (police/US) the fine of one day's pay.

rip *n* (entertain) the musical punctuation of a violent or melodramatic action or line on stage by the playing by the orchestra of a fast glissando up to a heavily accented note.

rip and reader (TV/US) a newsreader; from the tearing off of sheets from the wire service machines and Telexes.

ripper (crime/US) an implement used to 'rip open' safes.

ripper bill (pols/US) bills brought it by one legislative body to destroy their opponents' power base.

ripple *v* (milit) to fire a large batch of rockets in a timed sequence; a typical gap might be 0.01 secs. between each firing.

rippled attack (milit) a strategy whereby one fires off missiles in timed salvos, thus hoping to trick the enemy into using all his defences on the first few salvos and leaving him defenceless against subsequent attacks.

rise *n* (theatre) the raising of the curtain at the start of a play or act.

riser *n* (aerospace) a vertical take-off and landing aircraft.

risk-benefit judgement (govt) the assessment of whether in a particular project, the inherent risks of its performance outweigh or otherwise the benefits from its being achieved. Popularly used in such controversial plans as the proliferation of nuclear power stations when the public are urged to make the 'right' risk-benefit judgement.

risk-capital (finance) any funds that are offered for financial or business speculation.

Risley (entertain) in the circus, the juggling of one acrobat by another one who is lying on his back and pedalling his feet in the air; from Richard Risley Carlisle, US acrobat, d.1874.

river dog (tech) a device that holds a gas pipeline on the bottom of a river.

road *n* (commerce, entertain) the circuit of visits, shops, auditoria, clubs and so on that anyone who travels or tours – salesmen, rock bands, etc – must follow.

road apple (theatre/US) a touring actor; originally horse droppings found on the roads.

road company (theatre/US) a touring theatrical company.

road crew (rock business) aka: (abbrev) *roadies*: the technicians and stagehands who accompany a rock band and prepare the stage, the special effects, the equipment, the sound system, etc; thus *road manager*: the touring manager who takes care of the band's on-tour requirements, checks the venues, supervises the road crew, etc.

road rash (sport) in skateboarding, the bumps, bruises and general wounds accumulated by falling off the skateboard.

roadshow *n* (movies) a prolonged exhibition of a new film at selected major cinemas, prior to the general release of the film at smaller, local theatres; roadshows offer bookable seats, higher prices, superior locations.

robot art (art)
1. a form of kinetic art that makes use of the natural forces and movements of the earth and elements to activate mobiles and to structure light and shadow.
2. sculpture that combines robotic and human forms.

rock *n* (sport) in baseball, a mistake, thus *pull a rock*: make an error.

rock and roll (TV) the backwards and forwards movement of the various prints and soundtracks during audio dubbing (qv).

rocker (milit) USMC: one of the curving stripes under the three chevrons that indicate the rank of sergeant; these indicate the actual grade of sergeant.

rocker *n* (sport) in surfing, the upward curve on a surfboard.

rock happy (milit) USMC: a soldier whose mind is suffering from serving too long a tour on a remote Pacific Island.

rocking cockpit (aerospace) a flying simulator that has all the features of a working aircraft and which is used for the training of pilots before they start actual flying.

rocks and shoals (milit) USMC: the punitive articles of the Uniform Code of Military Justice.

rocky (milit) RN: officers of the Naval reserves; from their 'wavy' stripes of rank and their (alleged) poor sea-legs.

roger (aerospace) code: I have received and understood your message.

rogue (computers)
1. an aberrant result.
2. a misplaced item, or an item that is inserted into the machine out of its usual order.

role (sociol) the behaviour that an individual chooses to take on in response to a given situation.

rolfing (new therapies) aka: *structural integration*: from Ida P. Rolf (1897–1979) who developed a therapy based on 'deep massage' and intended to relax mental tensions through dealing with muscular, physical ones.

roll *v* (movies) to start filming, to shoot a scene.

roll-back (econ) the return of prices to a lower level through action from government or business.

roller (sex) blue films.

roller *n* (TV) the end of programme credits, printed on a roll of paper which is fed around a cylinder placed in front of the camera.

rolling break-even (movies) a method of cutting down profits and thus avoiding the payment of 'points' (qv) to those who are owed them by continually increasing a film's advertising budget; a process that works only so long as those who are expecting extra percentages fail to realise what is going on.

rolling plan (business) a long-term plan that is subject to regular revisions in the light of its development; each revision re-projects the plan forward the same amount of time as was comprised in the original projection.

rolling strikes (indust relats) a series of strikes that follow one upon another in various factories and in various towns.

rolling up (press) preparing a lithographic plate for printing.

roll-out *n* (sport) in US football, a play in which the quarterback runs out of the space made by his blockers before passing.

roll out *v* (movies) the opposite of open broad (qv): to launch a new movie in a series of steady, successive waves, each one taking in more cinemas.

roll out *v* (aerospace) to reveal a new model of an aircraft and to fly it in public for the first time.

roll out *v* (marketing) to launch a new product.

roll-over *n* (econ)
1. the extension or transfer of a debt or any other financial transaction.
2. the reinvestment of money gained on the maturing of bonds or stocks.

3. a new issue of bonds or stocks to replace one that has just matured.

ROM (computers) (acro) *read only memory*: a permanent store of information within the computer which the machine cannot read but which users cannot alter, ie: the system that actually makes the computer work.

Roman culture (sex) orgies, group sex.

rookie *n* (police, milit, sport/US) a novice, a new recruit.

room *n* (entertain) the hall, club, auditorium, etc in which a singer or comedian performs.

room tone (movies) background noises.

roorback (pols/US) a lying smear aimed at the wrecking of a rival candidate's campaign; from the fictitious *Travels of Baron Roorback* published in the US in 1844.

rooster tail (sport) in surfing, the curved plume of water thrown up by a surfboard.

ROP (advert) (acro) *run of press*: to order space for an advertisement, specifying no special provisions as to its place in the publication or within the TV schedules; thus *ROM*: run of month, *ROW*: run of week, *ROY*: run of year.

rope *n* (milit) a type of anti-radar chaff (qv) that consists of long strings of metallic foil or wire and which is designed to confuse the guidance systems of missiles and radar on planes, ships or land.

ropeyarn Sunday (milit) USMC: a weekday afternoon, usually a Wednesday, when drill, instruction, training and work are abandoned in favour of organised or individual recreation.

ro-ro ship (commerce) (acro) roll-on roll-off ship: a merchant ship designed so that tourist or commercial traffic can drive on at embarkation and drive off again at the ship's destination.

rort *v* (horse-racing) for a book-maker to shout the odds at a race.

rosalia (music) the identical repetition of a melody in a key one tone higher, keeping the exact interval between the notes.

rose *n* (medic/US) a comatose, extremely weak patient who is expected to die; from the excessively pink colour of the skin and the frailty of the person so described.

rose box (sport) aka: *strum box*; in yachting, the strainer at the end of a suction pump on a bilge pipe.

rose garden rubbish (pols/US) apparently ad-libbed, but in fact carefully prepared, Presidential comments for delivery on official occasions, many of which take place in the Rose Garden of the White House.

rosinbackfl8 (entertain) in the circus, a bareback rider, who uses rosin rubbed into the horse's back to help keep his/her footing.

ROT (radio) (acro) *record of transmission*: the recording of a live transmission as it is broadcast; for archive use, etc.

rotate *v* (sociol) the concept, after a supposedly amicable divorce, of swapping various mutually cherished possessions rather than let one former partner have everything.

rotate *v* (air crew) to pull up the nose of an aircraft moving along the runway and take off.

rotate *v* (milit) US forces: to take an individual or unit out of front line duty and give them a period of less arduous duty as a respite.

rouf (prison) backslang: four: a four year sentence.

rough *n* (advert) the basic layout of an advertisement that precedes the finished product and may well be altered several times.

rough-cut (movies) the first basic assembly of a film with the narrative in order and the soundtrack synchronised. (cf: *rough mix*)

rough it up *v* (gambling) to bet heavily and thus intensify the atmosphere of a game.

rough mix (record business) the first, basic mixing together of the various recorded tracks of a song or piece of music. (cf: *rough-cut*)

roughneck (commerce) on oil rigs, the men who work on the floor of the rig; unskilled labourers. (cf: *roustabout*)

round house (milit) US Dept. of Defense code: level three war readiness.

round lot (stock market/US) the basic unit of trading on the New York Stock Exchange: excepting some special instances, this means 100 shares of stock or $1000 worth of bonds.

round robin (gambling) a race or sports bet which involves the playing of all two- or three-race or sports combinations on three or more horses or teams.

rounds (commerce) articles that are naturally or artificially produced in spherical shapes.

round trip (commerce) on oil rigs, the pulling out of one set of drill pipe, rods, bit, etc from the hole and the replacement of the whole assembly with fresh equipment.

round tripping (sport) in baseball, scoring a home run, and thus running round every base.

round tripping (econ) the practice of earning profits by borrowing on one's overdraft and using the money to lend out for interest in the money markets.

round turn (futures market) the procedure by which an individual's long or short position (qqv) is offset by making an opposite transaction or by accepting or making delivery to the actual financial instrument.

roustabout (commerce) on oil rigs, a general or manual labourer. (cf: *roughneck*)

route *n* (horse-racing/US) a long race: anything in excess of 1 mile.

route, go the (sport) in baseball, to pitch throughout an entire game.

routine *n* (computers) a short program.

routine (theatre) any rehearsed and prepared act, sequence of actions or lines, or any other short performance.

routine response behaviour (marketing) aka: *straight re-buy*: a buyer's behaviour in routine situations where the brand is known, the choices understood and the buyer has purchased the product before.

rover n (video, TV) nickname for a Sony Portapack video camera.

roverback (sport) in US football, a combination cornerback and line-backer who takes on either role according to a given situation or a specific play.

royal (govt/US) government security classification, estab. Sept. 1980, that supersedes 'top secret'.

RPG (computers) aka: *Dungeons & Dragons*: (acro) *role playing games*: a variety of fantasy adventure games which are popular among computer users – although a computer is not vital – and which let the players work out their own sophisticated fates in a Tolkienesque world of 'sword and sorcery'; all such games stem from the original 'Dungeons & Dragons', the creation of Gary Gygax in 1974.

rub n (milit) RN: a loan.

rubber (sport) in baseball, orig. the home plate, now the pitcher's mound.

rubber aircraft (aerospace) an aircraft at a very early stage of its design and sufficiently flexible for major alterations to any aspect of that design to be made.

rubber chicken circuit (pols/US) the round of official dinners, fund-raising banquets, campaign meetings and every other meal that a politician must attend for his own career and at which, almost invariably, his hosts provide one or another version of the same indigestible chicken.

rubber heels (police) those policemen whose job it is to investigate possible breaches of discipline – accepting bribes, helping robberies, etc – amongst their colleagues on the force.

rubbish v (sport) in surfing, to tip a surfer off his board into a wave.

rubby-dubby (sport) in game fishing the minced fish – mackerel, pilchards, etc – which is used as a bait for larger fish esp. sharks.

rub down v (police) to search a suspect by passing your hands over his/her body.

rub queen (sex) a male masseur who supplements his income by doubling as a homosexual prostitute.

ruff (music) a drum beat used in military drumming.

ruf mord (espionage) fr. Ger. 'character assassination': the blackmailing of diplomats, especially those who work at the United Nations Organisation.

rug n (entertain) a hairpiece, a toupee.

ruggsy (milit) British Army, esp. paratroops: aka: *warry*: a super-tough image involving a skinhead haircut, large boots and a tattered T-shirt for the maximum display of muscles.

rug-ranking (govt) in Canadian bureaucracies, the establishing of a secretary's pay by linking it to the status of the official for whom she works; from the idea of seniority in an organisation being determined by the size of the carpet (if any) that is placed in one's office.

Rule 43 (prison/UK) solitary confinement for a prisoner's own protection; many sex offenders, informers, and other prisoners who would be at risk within the general prison population either choose or are assigned solitary confinement under this rule.

rule off v (commerce) to close the books for that day.

rules n (horse-racing)
1. the Jockey Club Rules of Racing.
2. National Hunt Rules.

rumble v (air crew) to steal food and drink from the airliner's in-flight stores.

rummage squad (govt) an elite squad of H. M. Customs officers who make random checks on commercial airlines, especially in regard to potential smugglers amongst the cabin crew; they board the aircraft before the crew have disembarked and search both their persons and the aircraft with extreme thoroughness.

run v (TV) to transmit.

run n (commerce) on oil rigs, the distance drilled during a period of drilling with the same bit.

run n (computers) a particular execution of a task or program by a computer.

run a flat (theatre) to carry scenery about the stage.

runaround n (press) type that is set in a shorter measure so that it will fit down the side of an illustration.

run a team v (espionage) to direct and organise a team of agents who are working in the field.

runaway shop n (indust relats/US) a plant that is transferred from one location to another in order to avoid safety or similar trade regulations or to prevent trade union activity by recruiting a whole labour force of new employees.

rundown (sport) in baseball, a play whereby two players attempt to tag a batter who is caught between them.

rundown sheet n (gambling) a list of entries and betting odds for the horses in a day's racing.

run down the game v (sex) amongst black pimps, for one experienced pimp to explain the nuances of his profession to a new recruit.

run gang n (air crew) maintenance engineers who make regular checkups on commercial aircraft.

run-in n (crime) a place to which stolen goods are driven after a robbery and at which they may be hidden for a while.

run it by (new therapies) to consider a topic: with the image of items being brought out for consideration at an auction sale or for selection for a gallery exhibition.

runner (police/UK) a suspect who is likely to abscond if let out of jail or allowed bail by the Court; thus *do a runner*: to abscond.

runner *n* (prison/UK) an escape.

runner (prison/US) a trusty, a prisoner given special privileges and who is allowed greater freedom to move around the jail.

runner *n* (commerce) a freelance antique dealer.

runner *n* (press) letters or figures set in the margin of a page – especially of long poems – to aid reference.

running dog (pols) in Chinese Communist terminology, 'zougou' = running dog: a lackey, a subservient figure, one who serves imperialist/ capitalist masters.

running for the exercise (pols/US) a candidate whose campaign cannot succeed and is merely going through the motions out of a sense of pride, foolhardiness, etc.

running like a dry creek (pols/US) a candidate who is failing to work as hard or make the level of impact his advisers and managers want to see.

running speed *n* (movies) the speed at which a film moves through the projector: currently 24 frames per second; silent films were shot at 16 fps and it is that difference, not the incompetence of their makers, that makes them look jerky on today's technology.

run-off (pols/US) if no candidate in an electoral primary contest has gained a proper majority, then a run-off election is held between those two candidates who polled highest and with the other runners-up eliminated.

run-out *n* (crime) a mock auction in which worthless material is sold at apparently super-bargain prices with a great deal of patter and noise, thus, *run out mob*: those who carry on mock auctions.

run over the hill *v* (milit) USMC: to force someone to resign or to seek a transfer.

run scared (pols) for a politician to avoid dangerous complacency by campaigning as if his opponents were continually presenting major threats to his chances of winning, even if the polls might advise him otherwise; to keep alert, sharp, ahead of the game.

run strong (gambling) to operate a casino crookedly.

run the rule over (police) to investigate a suspect both face to face and by checking his record.

run up *v* (milit) to have an individual brought up before the Commanding Officer charged with an alleged breach of service regulations.

run-up *n* (stock market/US) the rapid increase in the value of a share or of a commodity.

ruptured duck (milit) USAF:
1. a damaged aircraft.
2. a discharge medal awarded to ex-servicemen, which bears the motif of the US eagle.

rurp *n* (sport) in mountaineering: (acro) *r*ealised *u*ltimate *r*eality *p*iton: a very small piton.

rushes (movies) the day's takes, developed that afternoon or evening, and available for immediate consideration by all those concerned. (cf: *dailies*)

rush roller (medic/US) an emergency patient who is taken immediately to the operating room without the usual preparation of a shave, a scrub and an enema.

S

SAC (milit) (acro) US Strategic Air Command, based in Omaha, Nebr. and responsible for missile and bomber warfare.

sachem (pols/US) a political leader; from the Algonquin Indian name for a supreme chief; first used in US politics c1876.

sack *v* (sport)
1. (US football) to tackle the quarterback while he is retreating behind the line of scrimmage and preparing to pass the ball.
2. (baseball) one of the bases.

sacker (sport) in baseball, a man who plays on a given base, the number of which usually precedes, as in 'second sacker'.

sack time (milit) aka: *sack drill*: USMC: sleep.

sacred (computers) reserved for the exclusive use of something.

sacred cow (press)
1. a figure who is exempt from criticism; usually the family or friends of the proprietor.
2. copy that must not be cut or altered.

sacrifice *n, v* (sport) in baseball, a *sacrifice hit*: a hit that inevitably dismisses the batter, but which advances one of his team from one base to another.

Sadler's Wells make-up (theatre) makeup for an impoverished company: plaster from the walls, dirt from beneath the benches.

safe house (espionage) a building used for housing defectors or other sensitive individuals, or for meetings during clandestine operations to give instructions or debrief an agent, etc.; also used by secret police forces for the imprisonment and/or torture of their prisoners.

safety (sports)
1. (baseball) a safe hit.
2. (US football) safety man: a player who plays in the deepest back position on the field.
3. (US football) the act of carrying the ball into one's own end-zone and the concomitant sacrifice of two points.

safing (milit) the reducing of (nuclear) weapons from a state of readiness to fire back to a safe condition once the emergency which caused their arming has passed.

sail (milit) RN, USN: the conning tower of a submarine.

sailer (sport) in baseball, a pitched fast ball that takes off, ie: sails.

salami tactics (pols) coined in 1952 by Matyas Rakosi, communist premier of Hungary, to explain how the Communist Party cuts out its opponents in slices, by forcing its nominal allies to purge themselves to such an extent that they are soon too weak to stand against the Communists when they make their bid for power.

SALT (milit, pols) (acro) *strategic arms limitation talks*: a series of negotiations between the US and the USSR which aim to limit the nuclear arms race; coined 1968 by US bureaucrat Robert Martin; the talks began in November 1969 and have continued ever since with little real advances being made. Under President Reagan, they have been renamed START: strategic arms reduction talks.

salt a memo *v* (govt/US) a technique of checking for possible leaks by altering the same memo that goes to various individuals by just one word: thus, if a leak does occur and the memo is reproduced, it will be possible to trace the specific version to the individual to whom it was originally sent.

salt an account (commerce) aka: *salt the books*: to make fictitious entries in a firm's books with the intention of persuading a potential buyer of that firm that it is worth far more than is actually true, from the practice of 'salting a mine': the dumping of a few real diamonds, gold or whatever the mine was supposed to yield, so that a prospective investor would think he was putting his money into something other than the actual dud that was being peddled.

salted weapon (milit) a nuclear weapon whose explosion will yield more than the average levels of radiation.

salting out (medic) a method of abortion in which a saline solution is injected into the uterus in place of the amniotic fluid; this should kill off the foetus within one hour.

salvage operations (espionage) the destruction of incriminating evidence.

salvos (milit) air intercept code: I am about to open fire.

SAM (milit) (acro) *surface to air missile*.

samizdat (pols) fr. Rus. 'self-publishing': the dissident 'underground press' that works to copy and disseminate otherwise forbidden literature, criticisms and other works that are banned in the USSR.

sanctify (espionage) to blackmail a target for the

sake of using such blackmail to obtain information.

sanctuary radar (milit) long-range air defence radar that does not reveal its presence to approaching aircraft and thus can be neither jammed nor attacked.

sand *v* (gambling) to mark the edge of cards with sandpaper.

sand and spinach (milit) brown and green 'jungle' camouflage.

S & B boys (sex) (abbrev) sex and breakfast boys: cheap hustlers (qv) who will happily barter their services for a meal.

S & D (theatre) (abbrev) *s*ong and *d*ance.

sandbag *v* (gambling) a betting situation in poker where two players are locked in raising each other and continue to do this with no consideration for any third player who may be unwilling to drop out but equally loath to bet so heavily.

sandbagging (sport) in motorcycle racing, a stratagem whereby the favourite lets the rest of the field go on ahead, confident that when necessary he can regain the lead and win the race as expected.

sandpit *n* (TV/UK) a large-scale map used by TV news/current affairs programmes to illustrate the progress of wars, sites of disasters, etc.

sanitise *v* (espionage) to remove any embarrassing, incriminating or classified material from documents that are revealed to the public, or within government departments where 'insecure' people might read them; by extension, used in general political/government context for the keeping of the 'dirt' out of the public or press arena.

sanitised violence (TV/movies) screened violence that is so stylised and so far removed from reality that its effects can be claimed to be minimal.

sans (press) type that has no serifs – the flourishes and adornments on individual letters.

sarbut (police/UK) used in Birmingham only: a police informer.

satellite *v* (TV) to transmit foreign news and other programmes by one of the various communications satellites. (cf: *bird, feed*)

satisfaction note (commerce) in insurance, an acknowledgement by an individual claiming repayment from an insurance company that the repairs made to his car after a crash are satisfactory.

satisfaction piece (commerce) in real estate, a notice issued to confirm that a mortgage has been fully paid up.

satisficing (business) the aiming for a specific, pre-determined level of profits/sales/other success; the inference is that this level is specific, and one is not merely trying for any degree of improvement; also used in business as a more complicated way of saying 'satisfy'.

saturation attack (milit) an attack intended to overstretch any enemy defences and to knock out as many as possible suspected targets.

Saturday night special (police/US) aka: *junk gun*: a small handgun, often purchased through a mail order firm, carried and often used to satisfy the mindless passions of a Saturday night.

Saturday night special (finance) a take-over tactic in which the buyer offers to purchase a company's stocks without hitherto warning the company and thus attempting to pre-empt its efforts to challenge the bid. (cf: *dawn raid*)

saunter (milit) air intercept code: fly for the best endurance your aircraft can offer.

sausage board (sport) in surfing, a surfboard that is rounded at both ends.

save the food (movies) an instruction to actors and technicians to refrain from eating prop food since a take may have to be shot again.

sawdust joint (gambling) an inferior or unpretentious casino. (cf: *carpet joint*)

saw the baby in half (business) a management decision à la Solomon which will satisfy neither of two opposing parties and which in the long-run may well mean the cancellation of a project.

sbirri (Mafia) lit. 'the traditional enemy': the police.

scab (indust relats) a worker who refuses to join his/her peers when a strike has been called.

scab unions (indust relats) aka: *company union*: unions who are more inclined to satisfy the demands of the company at which their members are employed than those of the workers themselves.

scag (drugs) see: *drug names*.

scale *n* (entertain) the regular rate for the job, act, performance, thus *to pay scale*: to pay the basic rate, as negotiated by the union, without any special rates for celebrities or VIPs.

scaler (indust relats) the union-negotiated and determined rate of pay for a job.

scalp *v* (futures market) to trade for small gains; usually involving the establishing and liquidating of a position within short time, often on the same day.

scalper (theatre/US) a ticket tout who buys bulk tickets and sells them to desperate customers at several times their face value.

scalpers (gambling) gamblers who make bets on two opposing teams in such a way that they manage to gain an edge over the book-maker.

scalp-hunters (espionage) members of the intelligence services who are on the look out for potential defectors and will help them achieve this intention.

scam *n, v* (drugs, crime) any form of trick, swindle, racket, confidence game; spec: a large-scale scheme for the importation and selling of illegal drugs.

scamp (advert) the rough sketch of a design for an advertisement.

Scans (sex) (abbrev) Scandinavians: imported,

possibly smuggled magazines, books and films of Danish and Swedish pornography, supposedly 'harder' than the UK variety and concomitantly more expensive.

scatback (sport) US football: a fast-running backfield player.

scatter *v* (sport) in baseball, of a pitcher who keeps the score down and yields only a few hits.

scattersite housing (govt/US) aka: *scattered site housing* (UK): government-sponsored housing that is intended to break up the concentration of the poor in inner-city areas by spreading such projects all over a city.

scavenger sale (commerce) in real estate, a property that has been put up for sale because the previous tenants failed to keep up their rental payments.

scenario (movies) aka: *shooting script*: the script from which the movie will actually be shot, with the dialogue, the camera angles and other technical directions included.

scenario (new therapies) a corruption of the movie use (qv) which extends its meaning to include any possible course of action, the description of an event, any circumstance, situation, happening, etc.

scheduled territory (econ) between 1947 and 1972, any group of countries, usually within the British Commonwealth whose currencies were linked to sterling; after 1972, the UK, Channel Islands and the Isle of Man.

schleppers (entertain) fr. Yiddish 'schlep' = to haul, to drag, to carry: the entourage of hangers-on that surround a show business star. (cf: *gofer*).

schmatte (commerce) aka: *schmutter*: fr. Yiddish 'schmatte' = a rag: in fashion, clothing, the rag trade.

schoolie (milit) RN: a classroom instructor.

schooner on the rocks (milit) RN: a joint of meat baked with batter and potatoes.

schuss-boom (sport) in skiing: to ski at high speed.

scientism (sociol) 1. the concept that in the name of science anything can be promoted and accepted: goods, values, services, decisions; 2. the concept that scientific methods are the only methods for the study of humanity in any of its forms.

scissorbill (indust relats/US) a non-union worker; a worker who has some source of income other than his wages.

scissor cross (theatre) the simultaneous crossing of a stage by two actors, each going in the opposite direction.

scissor up *v* (business) corporate plagiarism; the cutting up and reassembling of a variety of concepts, theories and ideas that have not originated in one's own head but which it is hoped will fool or please those to whom they are presented.

scoop *n* (TV) aka: *sky pan*: a 500W light suspended from the ceiling.

scoop *n* (sport) in surfing, the upturned nose of the surfboard.

scoop *v* (medic) to perform a mastectomy.

scoop *v, n* (press) to gain an exclusive story ahead of one's rival newspapers; the story thus gained.

scope *v* (medic) a general medical abbreviation which refers, in a given context, to a variety of medical and surgical instruments and their use on a patient.

scope and sequence (educ) the amount of material covered in a syllabus and the order in which it is presented to the pupils.

score (gambling)
1. the money won in a game or at a casino.
2. to win money at gambling.
3. to win money by cheating.

score *v* (drugs) to buy drugs.

score *v* (public relats) aka: *hit*: to find a media outlet for a given piece of promotion and thus please the client for whom the piece was written.

scorp (milit) (abbrev) scorpion: nickname for inhabitants of Gibraltar.

scout *n* (commerce) in oil drilling, an employee hired specifically to keep an eye on what rival companies are doing.

scramble (milit) RAF: to take off rapidly.

scramble (milit, espionage) to make a telephone call unintelligible to potential eavesdroppers by using a scrambler to distort the spoken words; only by using equipment to unscramble the resulting electronic noise can the call be understood.

scramble (sport) in golf, to play erratically but still with the chance of making an occasional fine stroke and even winning the odd match; thus, *scrambler* a golfer who plays in this way.

scrambled egg (milit) the gold braid worn on an officer's cap.

scrambling (sport) in US football, the weaving and dodging of a quarterback who runs to and fro behind his blockers attempting to find the best way to pass or to run himself.

scran (milit) British forces: food.

scrap *n* (advertising) a photograph or other illustration cut from a magazine or newspaper and used as a guide for a drawing, or for getting a rough idea of how a photo-session should be arranged to obtain the required pictures for a proposed advertisement.

scrape *n* (milit) a hideout dug 18" deep and covered first with chicken wire and then hessian netting threaded with grass and plants.

scratch *v* (sport) in snooker, to make a stroke that incurs a penalty, spec: hitting the cue ball into a pocket.

scratch *v* (horse-racing) to withdraw a horse from a given race after the period allowed for so doing has expired.

scratcher n (commerce) on oil rigs, a device put down the well in order to clear the bore.

scratch hit (sport) in baseball, a hit that is neither an error nor a clean base hit but one which allows a batter to reach first base safely.

scratching (music) the use by a disc jockey of two or three turntables, each with a different record, to create a composite musical collage; the 'scratching' refers to his moving the stylus of each turntable to a pre-selected spot on the records.

scratchpad (computers) aka: *workspace*: an area of a machine's memory reserved for short-term working with, or storage of, a material that can then be erased; a small, fast and re-usable memory.

scratch wig (theatre) a rough wig used by comic actors.

screamer (press)
1. an exclamation mark.
2. a large headline.

screamer n (commerce) in second hand motor trade: a persistently complaining customer.

screamer (sport) in golf, a particularly powerful shot.

screen n (sport) in US football, a manoeuvre that cuts off an opponent from the play.

screenplay (movies) the plot and dialogue of a film, but no technical instructions. (cf: *scenario*)

screw v (crime) to break and enter; thus *screwer*: a skilful housebreaker.

screw n (prison/UK) aka: *twirl*: a warder. (cf: *white shirt, bully beef*)

screwdriver operation (industry) any semi-skilled task that requires the dexterity to operate a screwdriver but little else.

scrieve v (milit) RN: the drawing up of a ship's lines and plan by a naval architect.

scrip n (stock market) any form of security, especially those in bearer (qv) form.

scrip issue (stock market) an issue of shares to existing share-holders made possible by the capitalisation (qv) of reserves.

scroll v (computers) the moving up or down of a 'page' of information on the computer's screen.

scrub n (sport) a player belonging to a weaker team in a given sport; a team composed of such second rate players.

scrub n (aerospace) a mission that has been cancelled either before or during countdown and prior to the launch.

scrubber n (milit) USN: a mechanism for disposing of the carbon monoxide created by the continual breathing of the c150 strong crew of a nuclear submarine.

scrubbing (tech) the removal of certain impurities from either manufactured or natural gas by passing it through an oil spray or bubbling it through an oilbath.

scullion gullies (milit) USN: the moulded plastic trays used in naval messes to facilitate serving portions of food.

scuttlebutt (milit) USN, USMC: gossip; from the orign. meaning of scuttlebutt: a ship's water cask or drinking fountain and thus the idle chatter amongst those men who gathered there for a drink.

scut work (medic) all the trivial and/or unpleasant chores – either dirty, tedious or both – that have to be performed in a hospital.

sea dust (milit) USMC: salt.

sea gull (milit) USMC: chicken.

sea of instability (science) in chemistry, a group of superheavy chemical elements with highly unstable nuclei. (cf: *island of stability*)

seatwork (educ) whatever work will keep the children sitting at their desks, working and quiet, while the teacher is free to correct other work, prepare the next lesson, etc.

secondary action (indust relats) various actions by workers who are not actually party to a dispute: blacking, secondary picketing, sympathy strikes.

second level carrier (air traffic) local or regional air line services. (cf: *third level carrier*)

second order threat (milit) some theoretical military struggle perhaps 20 years in the future which continually justifies vast government spending on building an ever larger military machine.

second strike (milit) the retaliatory attack by whichever of the superpowers has already been hit by a first (and possibly pre-emptive, qv) first strike (qv).

second strike counterforce capability (milit) the possession of missiles that, having survived the full force of the hostile attack, could be used to 'win' a war, by firing them any time – days, even months – after the first encounters had ceased. (cf: *deep-basing*)

second unit (movies) a subsidiary film crew – director, camerman, technicians, etc – who deal with location works, stunts, special effects, etc.

sectarianism (pols)
1. the activities of evangelical Christian sects in the USSR in defiance of state-approved atheism.
2. in China, those who wish to opt out of the worker-peasant state and set themselves up as a new class (qv) of elitist bourgeoisie.

section eight n (milit) in US armed forces, a soldier who qualifies as mentally broken down and may thus be discharged on health grounds.

sector v (computers) to divide up a floppy disc (qv) in order to facilitate and speed up the retrieval of data.

secure v (milit) USMC: to stop an activity.

security (stock market) a general term that includes all stock market investments.

seek igloo n (milit) long-range early warning radar sites to pick up approaching trans-polar ICBMs; currently being developed by the US.

seek talk (milit) UHF communicators for the

USAF which will be impervious to any enemy attempts at electronic jamming; currently being developed by the US.

seek time (computers) the time in which the random access memory (RAM) can retrieve a given piece of data from a floppy disc.

seg n (TV) (abbrev) segment: one programme of a series.

segue n (TV) (pron: *segwee*) a bridging transition in sound, an aural mix (qv).

selective ordnance (milit/US) napalm; the precise selectivity this modern version of 'Greek fire' offers the bombing pilot has never been explained.

selectivity n (soc wk) the concept that irrespective of status or income, those who most require services are those who should most definitely receive them. (cf: *universalism*)

select out v (govt) a bureaucratic euphemism for dismissal from a job.

self-actualisation (new therapies) aka: *self-fulfilment*, *self-realisation*: the appreciation by an individual of his/her own potential and the full, creative development of that potential; the intention, in many cases, of the various new therapies available to those who feel they have 'lost' themselves.

self-dealing (finance) 1. the borrowing from or lending to a company by an individual who owns that company.
2. the use of a charitable foundation as a form of unofficial bank which can make its funds available for loans to some of its more influential contributors.

self-generating (business) aka: *self-motivating*: an executive who is able to spur him/herself on to tackling the tasks that must be faced and who generates new ideas for the firm in which they work; a live-wire. (cf: *self-starter*)

self-liquidator (advertising) an offer which, although very attractively priced, still covers the cost to the advertiser.

self-noise (milit) naval: the noise produced by a ship as it passes through the water, as opposed to the noise of the ocean itself.

self-starter (business) an executive who provides his/her own motivation and ideas for the job in hand. (cf: *self-generating*, *self-motivating*)

selling against the box (stock market) when a large shareholder wants to shield the selling of some shares from the rest of the market he sells short (qv) and delivers borrowed certificates rather than the shares that he actually holds in his (theoretical) strong box.

sell on close v (futures market) to sell at the end of a trading session at a price within the closing range (qv); thus *to sell on opening*: to sell at the start of a trading session and within the opening range (qv).

sell out v (futures market) to cover, offset, or close out a long position (qqv). (cf: *buy in*)

sell up v (commerce) to persuade a customer to take a more expensive item than had been the object of his/her initial interest on entering the shop.

semantics (pols, milit) euphemism for *words* as in 'I am not going to debate semantics' meaning 1. I am not going to argue; 2. I am not going to reveal the unpleasant/inadmissible facts behind my hypocritical and inaccurate statement.

seminar n (govt/UK) a Cabinet level committee for economic policy talks, instituted by James Callaghan in 1979 and consisting of the Prime Minister, the Governor of the Bank of England and a few extremely senior economic advisers.

send v (radio) see: *feed*.

send down (police) for a judge to sentence a guilty man to a term of imprisonment; refers to the steps that lead down from the dock to the cells at the Central Criminal Court in London. (cf: *up the steps*)

senior n (TV, movies) a 5K incandescent, focussing spotlight.

sensitive (govt, espionage) files so utterly secret (and potentially damaging either to a government or to its intelligence service) that they can never be released from the premises of that intelligence service itself; such files often contain material that is less interesting to foreign governments, but, with a mass of scandals and errors in high places, more fascinating to the public from whom they are deliberately withheld.

sensitivity training (new therapies) a form of group therapy in which participants are working towards the gaining of a deeper understanding of themselves.

serial art (art) the production of a series of pictures as variations on a theme, rather than attempting in each painting to create a definitive masterpiece.

service delivery (soc wk) the concept of social work as a group of discrete but interconnected services which must be delivered to those requiring them by competent people in an efficient and useful manner.

services (milit) technical experts – medical, ordnance, communications, etc – who advise staff officers on their particular area of expertise.

servicing (public relats) to make material available to the media in the hope that they will pick it up for publication.

set of books n (business) a new company started from an idea and based on venture capital (qv).

settlement price (futures market) the daily price at which the Clearing House clears all received trades. The settlement price of each day's trading is based upon the closing range (qv) of that day's trading. Settlement prices are used to determine both margin calls (qv) and invoice prices for deliveries.

S

set up n (drugs) the arrest of a dealer, often on information received by the police.

set-up (espionage) the trap into which a potential blackmail victim will be drawn by a team of sanctifiers (qv): a bedroom with a surveillance camera or tape, etc.

set-up (TV/US) a shot of the reporter who is about to deliver a news report – usually in the form of a voice-over – retailing his report while the viewer sees only the pictures that accompany it.

782 gear (milit) USMC: basic field kit including rifle, bayonet, canvas shelter, first aid kit, eating utensils, field pack, cartridge belt, leggings, bedding, poncho, etc; from the number of the form that specifies this equipment.

seven guarantees (pols) in Chinese Communist terms: guarantees of a minimum standard of living in the better communes: 1. food, 2. clothes, 3. medical care, 4. housing, 5. maternity pay, 6. marriage allowance, 7. burial allowance.

seven sisters (commerce) the seven largest international oil companies: British Petroleum, Exxon, Gulf, Mobil, Royal Dutch Shell, Standard Oil of California, Texaco (as in 1979).

severe damage (milit) an SAC (qv) category of bombing effect: the reduction of targets to dust. Thus *light damage*: rubble; *moderate damage*: gravel.

sexism (sociol) discrimination and prejudice based on sex, usually biased against women; the stereotyping of women into 'mother', 'mistress', 'typist' etc.

sexy (TV) newsworthy events, notably those involving war, disaster, death – anything suitably violent or shocking.

shading (gambling) a method of marking cards by delicately shading in given areas of the backs of cards.

shadow a (pols/UK) those members of the Opposition who are appointed to the 'shadow Cabinet': non-executive parallel roles to those Ministers who are actually in government.

shadow gazer (medic/US) a radiologist.

shakedown n (drugs) a con-game whereby an addict attempts to convince a dealer that he has hidden some drugs in the dealer's home and that unless he is given a large quantity of free drugs immediately, the police will be tipped off to the dealer's address.

shamateurism (sport) the accepting of money by a player who is ostensibly an amateur and thus supposedly above such payments; in the event those athletes who are sufficiently popular for promoters to attract large crowds when they are appearing, often find their 'expenses' are somewhat higher than might genuinely be needed. (cf: *appearance money, boot money*).

shanghai (milit) USMC: to get rid of an unpopular and/or incompetent individual by effecting his impromptu or involuntary transfer to another posting.

shank v (sport) in golf, to hit the ball with the neck of the club.

shapes (stock market) where one purchase is satisfied by a number of sales, or vice versa, the part deliveries are known as shapes.

shapes (gambling) dice that have been altered in such a way to make them less than perfect cubes.

share v (new therapies) in est (qv), the confessing in public of one's innermost angsts and agonies, a concept and a word taken directly from the traditional evangelistic 'holy roller' churches.

share n (TV) the rating of a TV audience that assesses the percentage of sets actually in use and watching a specific show; a 30% share is considered the minimum feasible for a show to survive on the air.

sharps (medic/US) discarded blades and needles that have been used during an operation.

shash n (TV) the flickering 'snowstorm' that can appear on a TV screen – caused by a lack of proper vision signal.

shave (drugs) the equivalent of cut (qv) for other drugs: the paring down of a cube of morphine prior to splitting it up for sale.

sheep dipping (espionage) 1. the use in clandestine operations of a military instrument – either equipment or personnel – usually under civilian cover.

2. the placing of individuals within (subversive) groups for the purposes of surveillance of those groups.

sheet n (advertising) the basic size of a poster: 28″ x 42″.

sheftsvo (pols, govt) the Soviet equivalent of 'empire-building': the use of patronage and influence for one's personal advantage by party bosses and other senior officials.

shelf life (commerce) the time that any perishable item will remain fresh; the maximum shelf-life is now marked on many such items by a 'sell-by date'.

shelf-talker (commerce) a small point-of-sale device with promotional copy printed on it which is fixed to the shelf in a supermarket next to the product which is to be boosted.

shell company (business) 1. a company which exists on paper but not in fact and is used for illegal reasons – tax avoidance, etc – rather than actual trading.

2. a company that is registered for the purpose of its name and then made available for sale to anyone who requires a ready-made company.

Sherman statement (pols/US) a final and absolutely irrevocable statement that a politician is not about to run as a candidate in an election; from the statement of General William Tecumseh Sherman in 1884: 'I will not accept if nominated, and will not serve if elected'.

sherpa (diplomacy) from the Himalayan guides

who take climbers up to the highest mountains: those members of the various diplomatic corps who arrange the details of international 'summit' meetings between major leaders.

Sherwood forest (milit) RN: the rows of Polaris missile tubes on a nuclear submarine.

shift the cut (gambling) to return in secret the two halves of a cut pack of cards to their original positions.

shift units *v* (record business) to sell records through retail outlets.

shill *n* (gambling) a house player who is employed to encourage the public players to join in the betting.

shill (crime) a decoy player, allied to the promoters of the game, who pretends to bet, and is allowed to 'win' in street games of three-card monte; his successes are intended to lure the public into laying down their money.

shiner *n* (gambling) a small, concealed mirror which is used to reflect the face of the cards as they are dealt face down around the table; usually hidden in a ring, on a coin, etc.

shinplaster (stock market/US) worthless promissory notes.

ship *n* (aerospace) any aircraft.

ship over (milit) USMC: to re-enlist. (cf: *re-up*)

shipped gold (record business) a record that has already amassed 500,000 plus orders from retailers before it has even been released.

shirt fronts (commerce) in real estate, the false facade attached to a house in which the bulk of materials are cheap and the building standards are second rate but which can be sold to the unsuspecting as a superior property.

shirtsleeve environment (aerospace) the ideal environment of a high-flying aircraft or a space capsule: special clothing can be dispensed with and human efficiency maximised by the wearing of normal garments which do not impair movement and bodily flexibility.

shit on a shingle (milit) USMC: corned beef hash on toast.

shocky (medic/US) sudden drops in blood pressure during an operation.

shoes *n* (espionage) false documents.

shoo-in *n* (pols/US) a certain winner in an election; from the horse-racing term which derives from the jockeys in a race getting together beforehand to decide which horse is going to win and for everyone else to shoo it in past the post.

shoot *n* (advertising) a photographic session, esp. on location rather than in a studio.

shoot *n* (commerce) in oil prospecting, the seismic mapping of an area by sending waves of energy through the earth's crust and using special microphones – 'geophones' – to measure reflection and thus depth.

shoot around *v* (TV, movies) to shoot a scene, even though one of the actors involved is

missing; their lines and shots will be added later and edited in as necessary.

shoot 'em up *n* (TV) a particularly violent TV programme.

shooter (gambling) the player who is currently throwing the dice in a game of craps.

shooters (new therapies) miniature orgone boxes, designed by Wilhelm Reich.

shooting a letdown (air crew) the approach and landing procedure of a commercial aircraft.

shooting ratio (movies) the ratio of all the film shot to that amount used to make up the finished film.

shoot off *v* (TV) the siting of a camera so that a part of the studio is visible in shot.

shop *n* (theatre/UK) a theatrical engagement; thus *seasonal shop*: working summer season only, etc.

shop *n* (espionage) any intelligence agency.

shop (advertising) an advertising agency. (cf: *hot shop*)

shop *n* (stock market) the South African gold market.

shopper (sex) a man who enjoys checking over the available hustlers (qv) but only looks, rarely 'buys' since no-one is ever 'Mr. Right'.

shopper *n* (press) a publication that resembles a newspaper (on a local level) but which consists of 90% advertising and which, on the basis of that revenue, can be distributed free to all the households in a given area.

shopping (sport) in billiards, to pot one's opponent's ball; from the sense of betraying an accomplice to the police: 'shopping'.

short *n* (movies) a film, usually non-fiction, that runs under 3000' or under 34 minutes.

short (stock market) 1. holding a bear (qv) position; a jobber who has sold more stock than he has bought. (cf: *long*)
2. of Government stocks, having a life of less than five years.

short (futures market) one who has sold a futures contract to establish a market position and who has not yet closed out this short position through an offsetting purchase. (cf: *long*)

short *a* (drugs) a portion of drugs that is less than the dealer claimed it would be.

shortcake *v* (gambling) to give someone short change.

short doors (TV, movies) the small adjustable flaps attached to the sides of a light.

shortenings (finance) the inexplicable but common shortfall in large cash deposits: ie the loss of one £5 note in a bundle of £20,000.

short eyes (prison/US) a child molester.

short finals (aerospace) the last point of approach to a landing; usually defined as commencing at an airport's inner ground marker.

short selling (futures market) selling something that is probably not owned with the idea of buying it back quickly at a lower price.

short squeeze (futures market) a situation in

which a lack of supply tends to force prices upwards.

shortstops (gambling) bettors who have little money available for risking.

shotgun (sport) in US football, an offensive formation in which the quarterback lines up directly behind the center in order to receive a direct snap from the line.

should cost technique n (milit) a method whereby the Pentagon attempts to impose economic structures on the costing of defense projects by establishing a figure that such projects 'should cost'; if this figure, assessed within the Pentagon, contradicts the estimates put forward by manufacturers, those estimates have to be altered to fit the Pentagon wishes.

shoulder n (air traffic) 1. that time of the year when travel is marginal and bookings slump. 2. that time of the day when the rush of landings/takeoffs slows down for a while. (cf: *noon balloon*)

shoulder (sport) in surfing, the calm portion of a wave breaking on the beach.

shouts (police/UK) radio alerts broadcast to patrolling police vehicles, usually in response to 999 emergency calls.

show v (gambling) to throw in one's hand during a card game.

show n (horse-racing/US) the third place in a race, after 'win' and 'place'.

showcase v (movies) to release a film in many cinemas across the country; this level of release follows first-run (qv).

show-out n (police/UK) the nod or other sign of acknowledgement that is made by a police informer when he is meeting his police contact in a public place – a pub, etc.

show print (TV) the final print of a programme that is selected for transmission.

shrimp boat (air traffic) one of the small plastic chips that air traffic controllers place next to an electronic radar blip and thus help keep track of the aircraft for which they are responsible.

shrinkage (commerce) a retail trade euphemism for shop-lifting; many stores assume an annual level of shrinkage and if this drops it may as well reflect an overall decline in customers as an improvement in their security operation.

shroud n (commerce) in the rug trade: (abbrev) funeral shroud: implying that a rug costs so much and is probably worth so little that rather than sell it the dealer will end up, financially and literally, using it as his shroud.

shtick (entertainment) aka: *schtick*: the basic elements of an entertainer's act, esp. the style adopted by a comedian; the implication is of tried and tested material on various topics that can be trotted out to please given audiences.

Shubert alley (theatre/US) a popular gathering place for New York actors: a short, narrow private street that runs between West 44th and West 45th Streets, off Times Square; named for the family of theatrical producers and managers whose office is in the Sam Shubert Theatre, the stage door of which opens into the alley.

shunt n, v (sport) in motor racing, a crash; to have a crash.

shunter n (stock market) a broker who transacts business with provincial exchanges and attempts to make his profits on the differences in prices between the markets.

shutter v (entertainment) to close up, to 'put up the shutters'.

SI (milit) Special Intelligence: collected by sigint (qv) and kept apart fr. other milit. intelligence.

sick (milit) air intercept code: equipment indicated in operating at less than 100% efficiency.

sick-out (indust relats) in order to avoid legal penalties that may accompany an actual strike, the organised absence, through 'illness' of employees.

side n (theatre/US) a script prepared for an individual actor in which only his/her speeches, entrances, exits and cues are listed.

sidebar n (press) a piece designed to accompany a larger feature, giving extra information or pointing up one particular aspect of that feature, which is printed alongside it.

sidehead (press) a sub-heading in the text set flush left.

sieve n (medic/US) an intern in the emergency room who allows too many non-emergency patients in for treatment and thus increases an already excessive workload. (cf: *wall*)

sifting (computers) 1. the translation by a computer of one high level language (qv) to another.
2. a method of internal sorting within a machine, where one set of records are moved around to allow the insertion of a further set.

sightseers (crime) see: *hedge*.

sigint (security) (abbrev) signals intelligence: the intelligence derived from the processing of electronic intelligence and communications intelligence (surveillance and satellites). (cf: *elint, comint, humint, telint*)

signature (milit) 1. the 'blip' that appears on a radar screen and signifies the presence of some object.
2. the sound made by a submarine propeller that can be picked up by undersea electronic scanners.

significant quantity (nuclear physics) the amount of enriched Uranium-235 required to make an atomic bomb.

silk n (law/UK) a Queen's Counsel.

silly season n (press) that period, essentially the summer holiday season, when hard news (qv) seems to vanish and the front pages are filled with trivia and absurdities. (cf: *closed period*)

silo operator (theatre/US) the owner of a summer theatre, so called because such seasonally open

S

theatres tend to be in the corn belt states of the Midwest.

silver tux (aerospace) a special variety of astronaut suit. (cf: *Apollo suit*)

simolivac (aerospace) (acr) *s*ilicon, *mol*ten *i*n a *vacuum*: a synthetic 'moon rock' with some of the same properties as the real thing, produced by Earth scientists.

simple labour (econ) in Marxist terms, the basic unskilled labour of the lowest level of productivity.

simple pimp (sex) in the world of black pimps, a pimp who has reached his limits; one who will never fulfil the pimp's main aim – to progress on to higher things.

simplex (computers) communication down a data line in one direction only. (cf: *duplex*)

simulcast *v* (TV radio) (abbrev) simultaneous broadcast: the broadcasting of an event – usually of a concert (both classical and rock music) – in which TV supplies live pictures and FM radio supplies stereophonic sound to accompany it.

sin bin (educ) any remedial class or institution designed to deal with persistent school troublemakers.

single *n* (movie, TV) a shot of one character only.

single (theatre) a flat (qv) one foot (1′) wide.

single clad (TV, movies) scenery that is designed and built to be viewed from one side only.

single-o (sex) a freelance homosexual prostitute; from the carnival sl. for an act that is good enough to stand by itself in the promotional billing.

single-stroking (press) the concept that a print union (the National Graphical Assoc. in the UK) who were formerly responsible for all newspaper typesetting on linotype machines, will permit journalists and the advertising department to set copy directly onto computerised terminals after the installation of such modern equipment.

singularity (science) a hypothetical point in space so distorted by gravity that nothing can escape being crushed into infinite density and microscopic volume; a black hole.

SIOP (milit) (acro) the Single Integrated Operational Plan: US title for the full-range of interlocking contingency plans for the fighting of a nuclear war; first compiled in 1960 and modified continually since.

Sir Jams (press) *Private Eye*'s nickname for grocery magnate Sir James Goldsmith.

sitcom (TV) (abbrev) situation comedy: a programme, usually screened as a series, which takes a specific group of characters in a particular background and uses their (mis)adventures and mutual interaction as the source of a continuing comedy; ie: 'Dad's Army', 'Hi-De-Hi', 'All in the Family', 'Sgt. Bilko', etc.

sit down *v* (sport) in golf, to land on the green and stop dead without rolling any further.

sit flat *v* (aerospace) for a spacecraft to be in the correct orbit with all equipment functioning as it should be.

sit position *v* (milit) to collect strategic information in one of the many US bases for electronic surveillance. (cf: *comint, elint, humint. sigint*)

sitting (new age) meditating.

situation (pavlov) a redundant, descriptive word, often found in combination with 'ongoing' (qv) to mean anything that is continuing to happen, or with some noun as qualifier, ie: war situation, riot situation, etc.

situations *n* (movies) the cinemas where films are exhibited.

six-ace flats (gambling) crooked dice for use by a cheat.

six in the gate (TV, movies) when the number '6' shows in the camera's gate (qv) the film is ready to be used for shooting.

six-sheet *v* (theatre, movies) 1. to exaggerate, boast, lie.
2. to promote a show or film with extremes of ballyhoo and excessive advertising; from the largest size of poster: six-sheet.

SIX teams (espionage) (acro): *s*abotage, *i*ntelligence and e*x*periment: small groups of agents who are sent on special missions for the purposes of SIX.

skag (drugs) see: *drug names*.

skeds (movies) (corruption of) schedules.

skein *n* (TV) a series that is made by one of the webs (qv): ABC, CBS, NBC, rather than an independent production company.

skew (TV, video) a vertical breakup of the top of the picture on poor video recordings caused by maladjusted tape tension.

skid artist (police/UK) a skilful getaway driver.

skim *n* (gambling) the retention of a portion of the profits of a casino from being declared to the tax authorities; this money is sent out of the country to foreign banks which will launder (qv) it before it is returned to the country of origin: thus *to skim, skimming*.

skimmers (milit) USN: surface shipping.

skimming (crime) the use of profits from an illegal operation, eg: drug trafficking, to establish a legitimate business for the channelling of such profits and the provision of a front for future operations.

skimming (business) a pricing policy designed to maximise profit margins by launching a product at an artificially high price, then, as it grows in appeal, gradually dropping that price so as to saturate the market.

skimming (medic/US) 1. the practice in health programmes that are based on prepayment or a capitation basis of seeking to enrol only the healthiest/minimal risk people in order to control costs.
2. the practice in such health programmes of denying members the services they have paid for as a way of holding down costs.

skinning (milit) the disarming of a person or of a weapon.

skins (theatre) tights.

skip *v* (commerce) in the hotel trade, to leave without paying one's bill.

skish (sport) an angling competition which uses a standard bait which is cast twice at each of ten targets.

skit *n* (espionage) a faked event that makes the entrapment of a blackmail victim even more plausible: a 'police raid' or the entry of 'an irate husband' – all of which characters are purely created for the occasion – in order to convince the victim that his problems are absolutely genuine and that going along with the sanctifiers' (qv) demands is his only escape.

skull *v* (sport) in golf, to hit the ball too far above its centre.

skull *v* (movies) aka: *take*: to make an exaggerated physical reaction to a line, gesture or event.

skull *n* (theatre/US) an admission pass.

skunk works (milit) a small team of highly trained experts who are given a project by the Pentagon and told to get on with it; they suffer minimal interference and like the animal in question, are left alone by the curious; this freedom allows them a greater latitude than most defence contractors, with little government supervision.

skyhook (sport) aka: *bathook*: in mountaineering, a hook which can be attached to the smallest of projections and to which an etrier – small portable steps – can be attached.

slack *n* (new therapies) aka: *free attention*: in co-counselling (qv) the period (c 60 mins) during which the counsellor listens to the client; they then swop roles and finally exchange notes.

slack capacity (air traffic) too many available aircraft with too few passengers using them.

slack fill (marketing) the filling of containers or packets in such a way that despite the splendour of the packaging, they actually contain more air than they do the advertised product.

slamming (gambling) 1. a fast game with plenty of heavy betting.
2. cheating.

slap *n* (theatre, TV) make-up.

slashers (movies) a genre of film in which victims, almost invariably women, are slashed with razors, knives, hatchets and similar weapons; possibly a sub-conscious backlash against the allegedly 'castrating' advances of feminism.

slash print (TV) a black and white print of a colour programme which is used for dubbing (qv).

slat *n* (sport) in skiing, the ski itself.

slate *n* (pols/US) a list of political candidates; the implication is that like a schoolchild's slate, the names written on it can be easily erased and replaced.

slate *n* (TV) a brief marking shot of the clapperboard (qv) that is placed at the start of a take.

slaughter *n* (police) a place where villains might hide recently stolen goods.

slave *n* (TV, video) any machine that is controlled by another machine.

Sleaford Tech. (milit) RAF: a derogatory reference to RAF Cranwell, the service's main training centre in Lincolnshire.

sledging (sport) in cricket (abbrev: sledgehammering: the practice (esp. in Australia) of aiming continuous and aggressive insults at the opposing players during the match.

sleeper *n* (business) an apathetic, lazy and unambitious executive who has no interest either in his own progress or that of his firm.

sleeper *n* (espionage) see: *mole*.

sleeper *n* (media, entertainment) a book, play, film, TV programme or any other form of entertainment that creates no major stir on its launch but slowly builds up until after a while, perhaps as long as a year, it becomes immensely popular and lucrative.

sleeper *n* (horse-racing) an apparently lackadaisical horse that suddenly 'wakes up' and runs a winning race.

sleeper *n* (gambling) money or a bet on a gambling table or roulette layout by a player who has forgotten about it.

sleeper (pols/US) an amendment placed secretly on a bill which will pass with it, but whose effect is separate to that of the main bill; a bill whose full effects are not appreciated at the time it was passed and which will only become apparent once it starts to operate.

slice of life spot (advertising) any advertisement that bases its appeal on creating an atmosphere of 'real life' rather than unattainable glamour.

slickem (milit) (acr) sea launched cruise missile. (cf: *glockem*, *alchem*)

slimwear (sex) a euphemism in fetichist magazines for latex and rubber garments.

slingshot (aerospace) the use of a planet's gravitation pull to alter the course and increase the speed of a passing spacecraft.

slip *v* (air crew) to change crew; thus *slipstops*: those places where an aircraft stops to change its crew.

slippage *n* (pols/US) the gradual collapse of a lead that had been assessed by opinion pollsters; a problem that tends to occur as an election nears.

slipper (medic/UK) a urine bottle given to bedridden male patients.

slipstream *v* (sport) in motor-racing, to take advantage of the low-pressure area created behind a fast-moving car by driving within that area and thus avoiding wind-resistance.

slop (press/US) typeset material that is left over after all the pages have been filled.

slop *v* (milit) USMC: to consume fast and plentifully; thus *slop up*: to eat to excess; *slop down*: to drink to excess.

slop chute (milit) USMC: any local tavern, civilian or military.

slop out *v* (prison/UK) to empty one's latrine bucket in the morning, also collect fresh water, etc.

slot *n* (press/US) the inside of the semi-circular copy desk; thus *in the slot*: the seat where the copy chief sits, supervising the sub-editors who sit around the rim (qv).

slot *n* (TV) a transmission segment.

slot *n* (aerospace) a specific orbit in outer space.

slot *n* (sport) in US football, a gap in the defence line, usually between the end and the tackle.

slot time (air traffic) a specific time within which the aircraft must become airborne; if this slot is missed, a new one must be arranged and this will mean further delay.

slough *v* (gambling) aka: *slough up* to close up (a game).

slug *n* (radio) the name of a story; this slug is used to identify any story that runs through a day's broadcasting or even longer; all material pertaining to that story will be labelled in accordance with the slug and the name of the reporter who 'voiced' (qv) the tape is added on.

slug *n* (press) a line of type or a blank line set on a Linotype machine: thus, *slug machine*: a Linotype machine.

sluice-gate price *n* (econ) under Common Market (EEC) regulations, the quarterly imposition of minimum prices for agricultural products which are imported into the EEC from non-member states; if goods are imported below these prices, the importer must pay an additional levy.

slum *n* (milit) USMC: beef stew.

slush (publishing) unsolicited manuscripts which very rarely make their way into becoming actual books.

slush fund (pols) any illicit political financing; the collection of money that is not declared as part of one's permitted level of campaign funding, which money may be used for paying off members of one's campaign staff whose activities (as in the Watergate scandal) one would prefer kept from public knowledge.

SMA (milit) (acro) *s*tandard *m*etropolitan *a*rea: a figure used for the calculations of the numbers of deaths in a variety of levels of nuclear attack; the US, for instance, has 53 SMAs.

smalls (press) the small advertisements run in the 'classified' section; usually printed in 6pt. type or possibly smaller.

smart *a* (technology) any form of technological advance that involves the use of computers.

smarten *v* (computers) the introduction of computers into any hitherto non-technological area of life: banking, supermarket checkouts, etc.

smartlet (milit) a small fragmentation bomb with its own guidance system.

smart weapons (milit) any form of precision guided munitions, esp. those with built-in computers, variable radar frequencies, anti-jamming devices and similar means of homing in accurately on a target despite all the defences, electronic and conventional, that may be encountered.

smear *n* (aerospace) bad radio reception due to the transmission of another message on top of the one which one wishes to hear.

Smersh (espionage) fr. Rus. 'death to spies': but only used (*pace* 'James Bond') from 1942 to 1946; in this period its responsibilities included: 1. military counter espionage, 2. political supervision of the armed forces at home and 3. those Russian troops operating abroad, 4. the elimination of any dissidence within Russia, 5. the 're-education' (qv) of those who had been 'tainted' by their spell out of Russia.

smoke-filled room (pols/US) the concept of a group of influential political patrons meeting together in the early hours, wreathed in smoke and alcohol fumes, to decide on a party's presidential candidate and to scheme towards his being nominated; from the statement by Ohio Republican Harry Daugherty who backed Warren G. Harding for the Presidency in 1920: 'the convention will be deadlocked, and after the other candidates have gone their limit, some twelve or fifteen men worn out and bleary eyed from lack of sleep, will sit down about two o'clock in the morning, around a table in a smoke-filled room in some hotel and decide the nomination'.

smudge *n* (sex) still pornographic photographs, or magazines including them.

smuggler's eye (govt) the ability among H.M. Customs officers to spot the smugglers among the rest of the innocent passengers who file past them at airports and other entries to the UK.

snake *n* (econ) a system of jointly floated currencies established in 1972 by the then member states of the EEC, and whose exchange rates are allowed to fluctuate against each other, but within a wider margin against other currencies.

snakecheck (pols) the checking of any public speech or statement to ensure that nothing gets through that might rebound adversely on the speaker; from the idea of checking a sleeping bag for unwelcome snakes before using it.

snake-eyes (gambling) when the 1 spot appears on both dice.

snap *n* (radio) flash news on a teleprinter or an agency wire.

snapper *n* (entertain) a comedian's punch-line.

snapshot *n* (computers) a printout of the state of a program during the running of the program; snapshots are helpful when attempting to isolate bugs (qv) in the program.

snap-up missile (milit) an air-to-air missile that is capable of hitting a target far higher in the sky than is the plane that served as its launch platform.

snare pictures (art) the name given to his own work by Daniel Spoerri: accumulations of objects (like those remaining on a table after a meal) which are 'snared', ie: affixed to boards, hung off walls and variously presented as 'art'.

snarf *v* (computers) to grab; spec: to take a large document or file for the purpose of using it with/without its creator's permission.

sneak *v* (gambling) to run a game without the knowledge or protection of either the police or the local villains.

sneakie *n* (espionage) any small, easily concealed means of visual or aural surveillance.

snipe *n* (pols/US) political posters that are put up on any 'free space' – walls, telegraph poles, etc – for which, unlike billboards and TV/radio time, the candidate need not pay.

snippet journalism (media) the broadcasting or writing of serious information, ie: the news, in small, easily assimilable chunks that act as a series of headlines but convey few useful facts.

SNOBOL (computers) (acro) string orientated symbolic language: a programming language created especially for dealing with complex strings of symbols.

snobs (milit) British Army: the regimental boot maker.

snoot *n* (TV) a conical attachment that can be fitted to a light and thus concentrate the beam.

snottie (milit) RN: a midshipman, allegedly from the habit of such junior seamen of wiping their noses on their sleeves; thus *snottie nurse*: the lieutenant who is assigned to supervise the midshipmen.

snow *n* (TV, video) random interference that causes 'blizzard' effects on a screen.

snow (theatre) a free pass; thus anyone who uses one.

snow man (milit) US Dept of Defense code: level seven war readiness.

soaksite (commerce) an arcade site used by the distributors of coin-operated games to test out the appeal of a new electronic game.

soap (espionage) a corruption of so-pe, (abbrev) sodium pentathol: a mix of sodium pentathol (a truth serum but simultaneously a depressant) with a form of amphetamine to induce articulate confessions from a subject so dosed up.

soap (medic/US) (acro) subject, objective, assessment, plan: the basic guidelines for working out the best methods of care for the treatment of a particular patient.

soaper (drugs) aka: *sopor*: soporific drugs, barbiturates and methaqualones.

soap opera (TV, radio) afternoon and morning long-running domestic series set in a variety of supposedly 'average' homes; the 'soaps' were started in the 1920s on US radio and the sponsor for the first one, 'The Goldbergs', was Procter & Gamble, who used it to sell their soap; thus *horse opera*: Western series, *carbolic soaps*: soaps set in hospitals.

soarboard (aerospace) a board on which were recorded the various achievements of the US space programme.

sob snatch (crime) a particular type of crime found in airports, railway stations and similar places associated with travel: as the weeping passenger puts down his/her luggage to embrace loved ones, the thief grabs the luggage and vanishes with it into the crowds.

SOC (radio) (acro) standard *o*ut *c*ue: the stating by a reporter of his/her name and dateline to sign off a report.

social atom (new therapies) in psychodrama (qv): the significant human influences upon one's early life: parents, siblings, perhaps a special teacher.

social Darwinism (pols) a society arranged on Darwinian lines; the survival of the fittest (individual, nation, social class) and the subservience or death of the weaklings.

social imperialism (pols) orig. coined by Lenin to attack those Social Democrats and others who refused to join the Russian Revolution during World War I; latterly used by the Chinese to attack all aspects of Soviet Communism.

socialisation *n* (soc wk) the learning of the processes of living within a society or social group, the adopting of appropriate roles within accepted norms.

socialism with a human face (pols) the journalistic shorthand for the ill-fated 'Prague spring' of liberalisation in Czechoslovakia under Alexander Dubcek in 1968.

societal marketing concept (marketing) a view of marketing's role that concentrates not merely on short-term desires but on the long-run welfare of the consumer.

sock (entertain) aka: *socko, sokko*: extremely successful.

socked in (aerospace) an airfield shut to flying because of poor visibility.

soffia vento (Mafia) lit. 'the wind is blowing': the heat's on, the police are becoming over-active.

soft *a* (milit) undefended targets; missile silos and other targets, esp. cities, that have not been given adequate defences to withstand a nuclear explosion. (cf: *hard*)

soft dollars (econ) that portion of an investment that can be taken as an income tax deduction.

soft focus (movies) a diffused effect that is used for shooting 'romantic' scenes and other 'atmospheric' effects.

soft funding (govt) government schemes that cannot rely on an endless flow of funds: for a variety of reasons – the scheme is not working, it is no longer fashionable – the funds are cut off half way through the project. (cf: *hard funding*)

soft landing (aerospace) the landing of a spacecraft on a planet or back on the earth without causing any damage to itself.

soft landing (econ) the slowing down of the rate of economic growth without simultaneously causing a recession or high unemployment.

soft loan (econ) a no-interest loan granted by the US to a developing nation.

soft market (stock market) a market in which prices are falling or the volume of buyers is decreasing.

soft money (educ) college funds that come from uncertain sources: alumni gifts, foundation grants, government schemes, etc. (cf: *hard money*)

soft news (media) news stories that lack immediacy; the treatment of news as another, slightly less amusing, but still primarily entertaining medium and therefore the keeping of its informational content down to a minimum while playing up its personalities as another variety of TV celebrity.

soft ordnance (milit/US) napalm.

soft pedal (pols) the playing down of a particular issue, even if it is still dealt with on a minor level.

soft player (gambling) 1. an inexperienced gambler 2. a player who is overwhelmed by winning heavily.

soft science (science) any of the social or behavioural sciences: psychology, sociology, etc.

soft-sectoring (computers) a means of finding the start of sectors on a floppy disc (qqv) and thus to find required data more quickly by using a program instruction rather than the slower punched hole system of hard-sectoring (qv).

soft target (milit) see: *soft.*

software (computers) the programs which give the instructions to the hardware (qv); packages that have been worked out in advance and which will instruct the machine in the performing of a variety of tasks – word processing, mail sorting, accounting, etc.

software (milit, aerospace) the plans, designs and operating instructions of aircraft, weapons, rockets etc.

software rot (computers) aka: *bit decay*: the gradual decline in the efficiency of pre-packaged software which ceases to work if left unused for too long.

soldier (crime) a basic member of the US Mafia; all soldiers are allied to a family and will fight for that family in any inter-Mafia feuds.

soldiering (indust relats) time-wasting.

solidarism (econ) the economic concept that every individual has certain financial obligations to those members of society who are less well off.

sophomore (sports) in US horse-racing, a three-year-old horse.

souls (air crew) the entire human complement of an aircraft: crew and passengers. (cf: *people*)

sound (espionage) aural surveillance of a blackmail operation to ensure that not only are any verbal blunders fully recorded, but that if the target becomes obstreperous, suitable force can be brought in to calm him down.

sound-bite (TV/US) aka: *sound cut*: a piece of news reporting in which the reporter is seen delivering his story.

sound-orientated (govt) an official who prefers to hear a report than to read one.

soup (science) the waste products of a chemical process.

soup (sport) in surfing, the froth formed by a wave breaking on the beach.

soup *n* (movies) fluid used for developing film in laboratories.

soupe (milit) French Foreign Legion: any form of food.

source code (computers) aka: *source program*: a program which has been prepared in a high-level language and has to be translated into an object or machine code (qqv) for the machine.

source credibility (marketing) the degree of trust placed in a source of communications.

South *n* (econ) those nations of the world which are generally less wealthy and less developed and tend to be found in the Southern hemisphere. (cf: *North*)

SOW (milit) (acro) stand *off* *w*eapons: air to surface missiles that are fired at the air defences that surround the primary target; this allows planes to attack and destabilise a number of targets without having to endanger themselves by penetrating any of them.

space (new therapies) 'where one is at' (qv); the mental position that one has adopted; one's attitude toward the world one lives in and the way in which one deals with that world.

space gun (aerospace) a handheld instrument that propels the astronaut while he is working outside the capsule.

spade *n* (sport) in golf, an alternative name for no. 6 iron.

spaghetti (aerospace) 1. the complex masses of electrical, hydraulic and other cables within an aircraft. 2. the coloured piping that is slipped over wires and which serves to identify one from another.

Spaghetti Western (movies) a cowboy film made by Italians, esp. the director Sergio Leone, which is long on 'atmosphere' and minimal on 'dialogue'; often starring US actors, most notably Clint Eastwood and Lee Van Cleef.

spam in a can (aerospace) a derogatory self-description of the early astronauts; former test pilots, they were disgusted that the computerised non-orbital space flights would render them powerless passengers with no responsibility or manual control of the vehicle.

spanker (air crew) an aircraft in first class condition and excellent maintenance; esp. in the area of fuel economy.

sparaciu (Mafia) lit: 'asparagus': a prison warder.

spare parts dependency (pols) the selling of sophisticated weaponry by major powers to lesser ones with the knowledge that so complex is this weaponry that the buyers will be continually dependent on the expertise and the spare parts that the sellers can offer if they wish to capitalise on this high technology.

sparks (TV, theatre/UK) an electrician. (cf: *juicer*)

spasm war (milit) a conflict in which both sides abandon themselves to uncontrolled reflex attacks; goals, aims, plans and any other modifications are rendered irrelevant in the gut directed mania.

can I speak to you? (police/UK) the approach by a villain who wishes to suggest a bribe to a policeman.

spearing (sport) 1. (ice hockey) using one's stick as a spear to attack opponents. 2. (US football) butting an opponent with one's helmet.

special *n* (theatre) a spotlight that illuminates that part of the stage where something special happens: a door, window, etc.

special activities, special programmes, special update programmes (milit) euphemisms (for budget purposes) for SI (qv).

special class (educ) euphemism for backward pupils.

special drawing rights (econ) a special scheme for members of the International Monetary Fund to be able to draw on that fund according to their investment within it. (cf: *paper gold*).

special situation (business) an exceptional corporate position or prospect that offers unusual chances for capital gains.

specific (medic) a specific disease: usually used in front of a patient to imply an 'unmentionable' disease, possibly syphilis.

spectacular *n* (advert) aka: *pop-up*: in mail order merchandising, three-dimensional material that jumps up when its envelope is opened.

speed (drugs) see: *drug names*.

speed! (movies) a call to the director by his sound man to indicate that the sound equipment is operating correctly.

speranzari (Mafia) lit 'to get hope': to escape overseas to avoid arrest.

spider (TV, movies) a folding metal brace that holds a camera tripod firmly on shiny surfaces; thus *rolling spider*: a wheeled device fitted under the tripod, sometimes on tracks, to increase the flexibility of camera movements.

spider box (movies, TV) a junction box from which are connected a number of lights.

spider hole (milit) a camouflaged foxhole. (cf: *scrape*)

spieler (radio/US) a radio announcer.

spieler (police/UK) an illegal gambling house; a gambler.

spiff (commerce) a commission on articles sold; orig. paid only in drapers' shops to the assistants. (cf: *PM*)

spike *v* (milit) the programming of two warheads to explode as nearly as possible at the same moment over the same target: this simultaneous explosion will multiply the destructive effects by far more than merely one plus one.

spike *n* (futures market) a rapid, sharp price increase.

spike *n* (theatre) a mark on the stage that denotes the exact position of a piece of furniture or other prop.

spike *v* (sport) in US football, for a player who has scored a touch-down to express pleasure by hurling the ball, point-down, onto the pitch and thus bouncing it high into the air.

spike *v* (radio, press) to reject a story for publication or broadcasting.

spike a temp (medic/US) for a patient to show a sudden temperature; from the inverted sharp 'v' on the temperature chart.

spin *n* (prison/UK) an unexpected search either of one's person or cell.

spin a drum (police/UK) to search a suspected house.

spingularu (Mafia) lit: 'grubber up of cigarette ends': a petty thief, a category of villainy outlawed by the Mafia.

spin-timed (radio) the rough, speedy method of timing a piece of tape by running it through the tape recorder on 'spool' or 'fast forward'; this is a highly inaccurate means of timing a piece and the producer must be warned in case the tape runs out early.

spitball *v* (govt, business) to speculate, from the fact that the veteran baseball players who threw spitballs had little idea of how their pitches would turn out.

spitting (milit) Dept. of Defence Code: I am laying sonar buoys and will be out of contact for a while as I am flying at very low levels.

splash *v* (milit) 1. to shoot down a hostile plane with a sea-to-air missile. 2. target destruction verified by radar or visual source. 3. a code word sent to an observer 5 secs. before the supposed explosion.

splash (press) a major story with a larger than usual headline given exceptionally large prominence.

splat *n* (computers) name for the symbol '*'.

splatter movies (movies) a genre coined by director George Romero to cover such films as *Texas Chainsaw Massacre* and other exceptionally bloody films. (cf: *nasties*)

splendid first strike (milit) a pre-emptive first strike that destroys the enemy's forces before he can launch them.

split run (advert) the use of slightly different advertisements in different editions of the same

S

paper; often used for different areas of the same town, or alternatively such changes are run in alternative copies to ensure a good spread of the two varieties; thus *split test*: the slicing of a mailing list into two or more parts in order to compare different styles of mail order merchandising.

split ticket (pols/US) a vote cast by a voter who has no regard for party candidates.

sploshing in on (gambling) to bet heavily with a book-maker.

spoiler (pols/US) a candidate who knows he cannot win himself, but is determined to try since he may thus split his rival's ticket and ensure that he too fails to be elected. Thus, *spoiler party*: a third party which intends quite specifically to ruin the chances of one of the two major parties and help see it defeated at an election.

spoilers (aerospace) speed brakes: panels on top of the wings which block the airflow and speed up the rate of descent; the most powerful 'spoilers' are *lift dumpers*.

sponges (technology) temporary employees hired by a nuclear energy plant to perform certain tasks where there is a risk of radiation poisoning.

spontaneity (pols) in Marxist terms, the belief that both the emancipation of the proletariat and the collapse of capitalism will come through spontaneous demonstrations of worker solidarity.

spontaneity (new therapies) 'the response a person makes which contains some degree of adequacy to a new situation or novelty to an old one' (J. L. Moreno, *Who Shall Survive*, 1934).

spoof *v* (milit) British Army: misleading or planted information for the purposes of fooling the enemy.

spoof (milit) to copy a hostile IFF (qv) reply code; thus *spoofer* (Dept of Defence code) contact is employing electronic and/or tactical deception methods.

spook *n* (espionage) a member of an intelligence group, esp. the CIA; from the original recruits to the pre-CIA OSS (a World War 2 security group) who like their UK opposite numbers were recruited from the Establishment; in the case of many OSS men, from Yale University's 'Skull and Bones club', an exclusive, secret student club.

spook *n* (medic/US) a psychiatrist.

spoon *n* (sport) in golf, the traditional name for a number 3 wood.

spoon (drugs) a measure of drugs, appx. 2 grams.

spot *n* (radio) the length and position of an advertisement.

spot *v* (aerospace) to form up the aircraft on a carrier deck preparatory to launching them by catapult.

spot coverage (media) on the spot live broadcasting or reporting.

spot market (futures market) a commodities market in which the products in which one is dealing are actually available for immediate sales for cash. (cf: *forward market*)

spousal support (sociol) a euphemism for alimony.

spouse fares (air crew) the scheme whereby when one partner flies at full fare – probably on company expenses – the other can get a 50% reduction as 'husband' or 'wife'.

spray *n* (espionage) an invisible electronic substance which can be sprayed onto an object and which will then act as a directional transmitter to monitor a subject over limited distances.

spread (futures market) the simultaneous purchase and sale of futures contracts for the same instrument for delivery in different months or the simultaneous purchase and sale of futures in different, but related instruments for delivery in the same or different months.

spread *n* (TV) a programme that increases its running time during the production schedule.

spread-eaglism (pols) the US equivalent of British jingoism.

spreadover *n* (indust relats) staggered hours, or split shifts.

spread the broads (crime) to cheat at cards; spec: to perform the 'three card trick'; thus *broad tosser*: anyone who works the three card trick; *broad tossing mob*: a gang of confidence men specialising in this swindle.

sprint (horse-racing) a short race, under one mile.

spud (TV, movies) the pole that fits into a turtle (qv) in order to connect it to a light.

sputnik (TV) a 2KW focussing lamp.

squad (espionage) the team of musclemen and surveillance experts who provide backup for the ladies (qv) who are actually involved first hand in trapping the target of political blackmail. (cf: *sanctify*, *peeps*, *lion-tamers*)

squad bay *n* (milit) USMC: barracks for junior NCOs and privates.

square *n* (sex) the various urban centres where hustlers gather: Times Square (New York), Pershing Square (L.A.), Union Square (San Francisco) and so on.

square away *v* (milit) USMC: to arrange one's possessions, bedding and spare kit in the prescribed military manner; to make sure that those under one's command are correctly disciplined.

square wheeler (commerce) in second hand motor trade: aka: *bottler*, *palm tree*: a car that won't sell and stands out on the forecourt without any buyer being interested in it.

squawk *n* (air traffic) a four figure number that acts as an identification number for every plane that appears on the air traffic controller's radar screen.

squawk (milit) a transponder that identifies an aircraft on a radar screen.

squawk book (air crew) the book kept by commercial airlines maintenance engineers which lists all those faults that must be dealt with in the fleet of planes.

squawkbox (TV) a two-way communicator for connecting the control box and the studio floor.

squawker *n* (gambling) a poor loser.

squeegee agreement (stock market) an agreement whereby one guarantees to back a security within a stated time at a loss.

squeeze and freeze (econ) government measures to control wages (squeeze) and prices (freeze).

squeeze the shorts *v* (stock market) to force those who have sold short (qv) to pay high prices in order to cover their deliveries.

squelch *v* (audio) aka *quiet*: to reduce the volume of a radio signal in the absence of a sufficiently clear transmission.

squibs (movies) electronically controlled explosions that are used to simulate 'bullet hits'.

squid *n* (science) a super-sensitive device for measuring magnetic fields.

SRO (theatre/US) (acro) standing *room* only: a completely full theatre; thus verbal use, *to SRO* the house: to fill the theatre.

stab *a* (indust relats/US) anything established; thus *stab wages*: the negotiated daily rate for a given job.

stability of cadres (pols) in Communist countries, a scheme of avoiding any one official establishing himself a network of patronage. Party officials, once elected, were confirmed in office for life rather than finding themselves subject to the whims and favouritism of local or national bosses.

stable (sex) those prostitutes who work for the same pimp.

stable (espionage) from commercial sex use (qv): those women who work as 'Mata Haris' for intelligence services who use political blackmail as a means of extracting information. (cf: *ladies* and *sisters*)

stack *v* (aerospace) to assemble a multi-stage launch vehicle.

stack *n* (air traffic) a queue of aircraft, all ranged at 1000′ distances above each other, circling an airport and awaiting their various permissions to land.

stag *n* (stock market) an insider who applies for a new issue before it is generally available and still on a special offer, then sells his shares four or five days later when dealings commence and the price has risen considerably.

stage manager (sex) a pimp who runs a stable of homosexual male prostitutes.

stagflation (econ) aka: *slumpflation* stagnant economy allied to rising unemployment and growing inflation. (cf: *inflation*)

stagger *n* (TV) the first complete rehearsal of a TV drama.

stakhanovite (econ) in Communist countries, a 'storm-shock worker' who regularly exceeds any labour norms and is seen by the leadership as an outstanding figure; from one Alexei Stakhanov, a Ukrainian miner, who in 1935 began increasing his output by the skilled organisation of a group of subordinate workers; for this he was allowed incentive payments and as such alienated many of the rank and file workers; now canonised for ever as a Hero of Soviet Labour.

stale bull *n* (stock market) stock that is retained for a long period without making a profit.

Stalin's organs (milit) originally coined in World War 2 for a Soviet rapid firing missile launcher which sounded like an organ and looked like a bunch of phalluses; revived more recently to describe the Russian made 122-BM-21 rocket launcher, especially popular in Africa.

stand *n* (advert) a poster that fills a whole billboard: 24 sheets.

stand-alone *n* (computer) a piece of a computing system that can stand alone and perform its task without requiring the linking in to any other machine.

standards and practices (TV/US) the morals and ethics department of a major network; the checking of adherence to all Federal regulations.

standfirst (press) introductory matter that stands separately on the page from the actual story it introduces.

stand in the doorway (pols/US) to make a dramatic and possibly vote-winning stance on an issue about which one may well be able to do very little.

stand on velvet (stock market) to succeed in one's speculations.

stands *n* (stock market/UK) the raised seats in which stock exchange waiters (qv) sit and from which they maintain communications between the various firms that trade at the Exchange.

standpattism (pols/US) to maintain one's position come what may; with edges of reactionary theory.

stanza (TV, movies) 1. a segment (qv) of a TV series. 2. a week at a given cinema.

star *n* (prison/UK) (abbrev) star prisoner: a first time prisoner.

star rank (milit) officers whose official vehicles are awarded stars to denote their rank: field marshal (5 stars), general (4 stars), lieutenant general (3 stars), major general (2 stars) brigadier (1 star).

starter home (commerce) in real estate, a basic house with few amenities but a reasonably low price, the first house a young couple are likely to buy.

starvation (computers) see: *deadlock*.

stat (medic/US) fr. Lat: 'statim' = at once, immediately: to do something at once.

state capitalism (pols) in Marxist terms, a

S

country that combines some nationalisation with some free enterprise.

state chicken *n* (Dept of Defence code) my fuel state requires recovery, a tanker or my plane being diverted to an airfield closer by. Thus *state lamb*: I do not have enough fuel to make the required intercept and then to make my way back to the carrier.

stateless currency (finance) money and credit which have no specific government to administer them but simply fuel the random ups and downs in the financial market.

state monopoly capitalism (econ) in Marxist terms an alliance between monopoly capital and a substantial state presence in the operation of a nation's economy; seen generally as a capitalist smokescreen behind which profits can be raised and the struggling proletariat can be suppressed.

state of the art (technology) the level of scientific or technological advance in a given industry at the present moment; thus *state of the art contract*: a contract for construction, design, etc, that calls for the use of techniques currently in use.

state of the whole people (pols) the official designation of the Soviet Union since the 22nd Congress of the Communist Party in 1961; by extension it stands for an ideal state, without a vestige of class antagonism and for the socialism that can only truly exist when the 'exploiting classes' have been eliminated.

state tiger (milit) Dept of Defence code: I have sufficient fuel to return to the carrier; my mission is successfully accomplished.

static Marxists (pols) a derogatory term that accuses many communists of a dogmatic adherence to the letter of the law and of ignoring the more subtle spirit.

station (air crew) an airport.

station-keep *v* to fly in formation.

station march (TV) the opening identifying theme tune broadcast when a TV channel comes on the air at the start of a day's transmissions.

station time (TV) aka: *local time*: a period in the US TV day that is reserved for the affiliates to show their own programmes or syndicated shows; no network shows are aired.

statism (econ) a controlled, planned economy.

status deprivation (soc sci) a person whose unpopularity stems from the image he offers to others.

status inconsistency (sociol) an individual who is not quite sure where he stands either socially or emotionally; an adolescent in his emotions.

status offender (law/US) any child or adolescent who is put into state 'care' because he is too unruly or disobedient to continue to live at home; not an actual offender, but too wild for his parents or the social services to handle.

status passage (soc wk) the transitional periods

that bond one existence – ie bachelordom – with another – ie: marriage.

stay with the money (movie) director's comment to a cameraman, telling him to keep filming the biggest box office draw on the set.

stealth (milit) a development programme attempting to create planes that can defeat radar, using low level radar and infra red signature.

steamy (sport) in golf a short shot or a putt that passes over or through the green.

steel beach picnic *n* (milit) the taking of exercise on the deck of USS *Nimitz* at those times when the regular flights are suspended.

steerer (gambling) an individual who persuades the people to come to an illegal gambling game; thus *steer game*: a crooked game to which the punters (qv) are steered.

stemwinder (pols/US) an orator or speaker who can rouse a crowd to enthusiasm.

step deal (movies) a contract for a script which is paid in pieces: every time the writer and his ideas surmount a new hurdle, he is allotted more money.

step high (drugs) the result of certain drugs: the belief/pretence that you are a bigger star in whatever profession you follow than may actually be true.

step on *v* (drugs) to cut a drug with some form of adulterant.

step on the laughs (entertain) a fault of a nervous comedian: to tell a string of jokes so quickly that the audience have not had time to laugh at one for fear of missing the next.

sterile *a* (milit) any weapons that are foreign manufactured and untraceable to their country of origin; thus useful for clandestine sales to a favoured, but possibly non-allied, country.

sterilise *v* (milit) to destroy all human habitation, crops and other vegetation in order to make it impossible for the enemy to make use of the village.

sterilise *v* (espionage) to 'clean up' any document that might be seen in public and make sure it offers no classified information.

sterility money (milit) extra pay given to submariners who risk the dangers of leaky (qv) nuclear reactors.

stick (journalism) one line of typeset matter.

stick (sex) in black pimp terms: prostitute.

stick (gambling) see: *shill*.

stick (press) a column of newsprint.

stick *n* (sport) 1. skiing: a ski pole. 2. surfing: a surfboard. 3. golf: a club.

sticker (indust relats) a worker who shows no interest in promotion.

stick him on! (police/UK) draw up a charge against him; write his name down on the charge sheet.

stickies (pols) in N. Ireland, the official branch of the Irish Republican Army; from the sticky backs of the Easter seals they have as Catholics.

stickman (crime) a member of a pickpocket gang who takes the freshly stolen goods from the dipper (qv) so that in the case of problems, the dipper can be searched with impunity.

sticks *n* (horse-racing) jumps or hurdles; essentially the sort of racing that occurs in winter.

sticks and whistles (prison/UK) the parade before a new group of warders go on their shift: a check that they all have their truncheon, whistle, special information about any particular individual or any developments, etc.

stick time (aerospace) flying time for test and space pilots.

sticky prices (stock market) steady prices that change only rarely.

sticky wicket (sport) in cricket, a damp, soft wicket, that provides particular problems for a batsman; of late a 'sticky' has vanished from tests since the wicket is now covered overnight and any possible moisture thus gained is kept out.

stiff *n* (movies) a flop.

stiff *a* (spot) aka: *dead*: in golf, a shot that stops so close to the hole that it must be impossible to miss the putt.

stiff *n* (prison/UK) an illicit, probably smuggled communication.

stiff *n* (commerce) in the hotel trade, any customer that fails to leave a tip.

stiff *n* (record business) a record that will not sell.

stilyag (sociol) in Russia, a type of unpopular youth who enjoys US and Western music and clothes: a tearaway.

sting *n* (radio) a brief (c. 10 sec) station identification theme used for weather, news, a particular programme or presenter.

sting *n* (TV) any short burst of music used as part of the links between programmes, station identification etc.

sting (sex) from the idea of a successful confidence trick; for a hustler to feel that he has fooled his client, even though that client may still have obtained exactly what he paid for.

sting *n, v* (crime) the successful carrying out of a scheme by a confidence man or gang.

stinkpot (sport) in yachting, a motor-propelled boat.

stir up the animals (pols/US) to set in motion any sort of controversy which can only have a negative effect upon one's campaign or career.

stitch up *v* (police/UK) for the police, in criminal eyes, to fabricate evidence in the courtroom in order to ensure a conviction. (cf: *fit up*)

stobing (video, TV) a visually disturbing effect created on the screen when TV raster (qv) lines and the patterns or colours of scenery or clothing clash.

stochastic process (business) any process is stochastic if it includes random variables: in business terms this is used for such a process as the forming of a queue, where the variables are the demand – the formation of that queue by customers – and the supply – the speed or efficiency with which they can be served or otherwise attended to.

stochastic simulation (business) any variety of research that comes down to trial and error testing of a number of variables in order to assess the possible effects of a policy or plan.

stock *n* (TV, movies) raw, unexposed film.

stock company (theatre/US) see: *repertory*.

Stockholm syndrome (sociol) the phenomenon in a kidnapping, hijack or any situation where hostages are taken whereby after a time the hostage, rather than fearing or hating his/her captors, starts to ally with them and even feel affection towards them in the face of the police/army and other authorities who are waiting for them to give up; first noted during a bank robbery in Stockholm in 1973.

stockpile energy (milit) the sum of the total energy available for use in a major conflict: one stockpile equals 40,000,000,000,000 megatons or 1.3 Beach (qv).

stock shot (movies) a shot or sequence that is hired from a film library rather than going to the expense of setting up the required scene; usually used when a director needs anonymous trains departing, aircraft landing, old newsreels etc.

stone *n* (press) the smooth steel or iron table on which newspaper pages are composed; orig. made of marble.

stonewall *v* (pols) for a politician to present an obdurate front to critics and questioners, whether political, press or public; orig. a UK use c 1876, but brought to real prominence by President Nixon's adamant stance throughout the Watergate scandals of 1972–74.

stonking (milit) British Army: extremely heavy, accurate and unpleasant shelling.

stooper *n* (gambling) one who searches racetrack stands for the chance of finding a discarded winning ticket.

stop a stock *v* (stock market) to agree to postpone the sale or purchase of a stock while taking its price to be that at which the deal was originally made.

stop-go (econ) a British economic policy that alternates expansion and contraction; generally considered a bad one since the continuous changes never give the economy time to establish itself properly.

stoploss order (futures market) an order to buy or sell a commodity when a specific price has been reached.

stop motion (movies) the single frame exposure of a film to permit rearrangement of models, etc. for 'trick shots' of 'monsters' and other models that cannot move themselves.

stop squawk (milit) air intercept code: turn off the IFF (identification friend or foe) monitor.

S

stove *v* (aerospace) a method of baking on a primary coat of epoxy to harden parts of a fuselage.

straddle *n* (stock market) 1. an option which gives the holder the right of a put & call (qv). 2. the condition of being long in one market and short in another (qv).

straight (sex) anything heterosexual: a client (for a prostitute), pornographic pictures, films, or their buyer.

straight (sex) normal, no frills intercourse, probably in the traditional missionary position; part of a prostitute's 'menu' of services.

straighten *v* (police, crime) to bribe; thus a *straightener*: a bribe.

straight standup (TV/US) the delivery of a report by a news reporter facing directly into the camera.

straight ticket (pols/US) to vote all the way down the party's nominated slate.

strange quark (science) the third quark, so called because the particles within it were seen to act in a strange way; such quarks possess the property of *strangeness*. (cf. *quark*)

strangle *v* (horse-racing) to hold back a horse from winning by pulling hard on the reins.

strap *n* (press) a subsidiary headline placed above the main headline.

strategic *a* (milit) possessing the capability or intent to fight a nuclear war.

strategic balance (milit) the comparative strengths of the two superpowers and their allies and satellites. (cf: *balance of terror*).

strategic doctrines (milit) a variety of theories on the best way to maintain deterrence and, if that fails, to wage a nuclear war. (cf. *SIOP*)

strategic submarines (milit) submarines that act as weapons platforms for nuclear missile launches rather than fighting ships themselves. (cf: *hunter-killer*).

strategic nuclear weapons (milit) those ICBMs (qv) capable of reaching targets inside Soviet territory. (cf: *tactical weapons*)

strategic warning (milit) a prior warning of imminent nuclear warfare that can be appreciated months or weeks before the crisis becomes insupportable and one side launches a first strike.

strategic withdrawal (milit) any level of defeat, from an ordered withdrawal that does have some degree of plan, to a simple panic-stricken rout; the level of order depends on the degree of euphemism that the censors wish to use.

straw hat circuit (theatre/US) a circuit of summer theatres.

straw man (commerce) in real estate, someone under whose name a broker illegally purchases one of his own listed properties for himself.

straw poll (pols) orig. a quick poll of the nearest voters, often those just emerging from a polling station, to gain a broad view of an electoral trend; lately the definite professional poll that is based on a largescale, but still random sample.

stray *n* (radio) atmospheric interference.

streamer (press) a multi-column headline that stands at the top of a page, but is not necessarily spread the full width of that page. (cf: *banner*)

street book (futures market) a daily record kept by futures traders of all their transactions.

street credibility (rock music) a hypothetical concept, possibly manufactured by fanciful music writers, of the 'artist' being able to relate genuinely to the 'real people', ie: the working class youth of the streets and housing estates who make up the audiences and buy the records; punk rock's answer to a social conscience.

stretch (prison) a sentence of one year.

stretcher match (sport/UK) in wrestling: a bout with no rounds, no time outs, no stopping for injuries; such a bout stops only when one of the participants is removed from the ring on a stretcher.

stretch-out *n* (entertain) the extra-long multi-seat limousines beloved of show business celebrities.

stretch printing (movies) a technical process that aims to make silent movies – run at 16 or 20 frames per second – adaptable for use on modern equipment which works at 24 fps: to do this every second frame is printed twice, but in the end, the jerky quality still persists.

striker (milit) UMSC: 1. an apprentice or aspirant who is attempting to learn a particular military speciality. 2. on a ship, an individual Marine assigned to the operation and maintenance of a specific gun.

strike rate (commerce) the success rate of a salesman, measured in the percentage of the clients he approaches who are willing to order his product.

strike suit (business) the practice of a minor shareholder in a corporation of instigating a suit against that corporation; if the plan works this will result in the corporation buying his shares at a very high price merely to deprive him of the right to pursue such a suit.

strike the set *v* (theatre, TV, movies) to dismantle the scenery, thus *striker*: a stagehand.

striking a blow for freedom (pols/US) an ironic code-word amongst politicians for a pleasant chat over a few drinks in the privacy of one's office.

string (sex) see: *stable*.

stringer *n* (press) a freelance correspondent for a newspaper, based either abroad or certainly away from the paper's national headquarters and whose local expertise and contacts give him an on-the-spot usefulness that surpasses that gained from sending out a reporter from the head office; such stringers often work full-time for their local paper, TV or radio station.

strip n (TV/US) a show that is scheduled for transmission at the same time every day; from the similar regularity of newspaper comic strips.

stripes (prison/UK) the yellow stripes sewn onto a prisoner's uniform to denote one or more previous escape attempts.

striping the lot (commerce) the painting of the parking lot at a new shopping mall with extra-wide spaces for the positioning of cars: this gives the impression of the mall attracting more customers than it really does, and when business picks up, the spaces can be repainted somewhat narrower.

stroke n (new therapies) in TA (transactional analysis) (qv): the basic unit of social intercourse, the giving to another that emotional stimulus for which they are searching.

stroke books (sex) pornographic novels or magazines written and used simply for masturbation; thus *stroke house* a cinema that shows pornographic films.

strong a (sex) hard-core pornography. (cf: *adult*)

strong force (science) aka: *strong interaction*: the force that causes neutrons and protons to bind together in an atom; the strongest force known in nature.

structural adjustment loan (finance) a World Bank term for the bailing out of the economies of poor and bankrupt nations.

structural crisis n (govt) in the Common Market (EEC): a problem that occurs when too much money has been spent in one area to the detriment of other areas, equally needy of funds.

structural funds (govt) in the Common Market (EEC): money to alleviate unemployment in areas hit by the recession.

structural unemployment (econ) unemployment that results from changes in the structure of the economy: new technology, population shifts, foreign economic influences, etc.

struggle – criticism – transformation (pols) fr. Chinese 'Tou-p'I – Kai': the three steps that were to be carried out in all parts of Chinese society during the Cultural Revolution. 1. the identification of and struggle against the capitalist roaders (qv). 2. the criticism and self-criticism of all involved in the movement. 3. the transformation of all organisations, systems, plans and methods into revolutionary socialism.

stub party (theatre/music) a reception following a first night or a concert.

studio quality (radio) material that has been recorded under controlled conditions in a studio, rather than an outside broadcast. (cf: *audio quality*, *phone quality*)

stuff (drugs) see: *drug names*.

stuff and other stuff (science) a mixture of energy producing particles: pions, baryons, photons, etc.

stump n, v (pols/US) the campaign trail; to campaign in the open air; both uses imply the candidate's standing on a tree stump addressing an audience of local people out in the country.

style (commerce) when appended to the description of a lot in an auction catalogue, the buyer is being told politely that the auctioneers feel that the piece is not genuine but only a reproduction.

sub (press/UK) (abbrev) sub-editor; thus *chief sub*: chief sub-editor.

subbotnik (econ) in the USSR, a day's work performed voluntarily and outside normal working hours, usually on Subbota = Saturday; started in 1919 to help the building of the Moscow–Kazak railway, it is considered that all the proceeds of such work must be given to charity.

subdeck n (press) a subsidiary headline that runs beneath the main headline. (cf: *strap*)

subemployment (econ) any form of inadequate employment, including actual unemployment and part-time or full-time employment that does not provide the worker with a proper living wage.

subject (stock market) an offer or bid from the market which has been made to more than one broker is considered 'subject', rather than 'firm' and may thus not be available unless one of those brokers accepts it immediately.

subjective probabilities (business) educated guesswork.

suboptimisation (business) a compromise solution which means that neither of the contesting parties will have things all their own way.

subscription (publishing) the initial order for a book made by individual booksellers with a publisher's salesmen; by adding up the subscription, the publisher can make a reasonable estimate of the first print run that book will require.

subsidiarity (business) the concept that headquarters staff do not perform any tasks that cannot equally well be performed by the subsidiary branch who were requesting help in the first place; from the Roman Catholic precept that the Vatican should not interfere in those matters best dealt with on a local level; currently popular amongst Common Market (EEC) officials who wish to restrict their activities to those which can best be performed by the EEC rather than those which are best left to individual member states.

substitution (indust relats) the use by employers of job creation schemes and the government grants that go with them to hire cheap young labour and deprive senior, experienced but unemployed workers of the chance of getting a job.

subtopia (archit) a fantasy world projected by optimistic architects and which combines suburbia with utopia.

success stories (public relats) aka: *case histories*:

S

stories planted around the media to point out how a client's product has been used before most successfully by many other people.

SUDS (new therapies) in assertiveness training: subjective *u*nits of *d*isturbance *s*cale: the noticing by an individual of how upsetting it can be when someone else starts shouting at you.

sudser (TV) see: *soap opera*.

suede shoe operators (business) a high-flying entrepreneur or salesman who is flashy and smart, both verbally and visually, although the suede shoes of the 1950s have been replaced by Gucci loafers; the inference is of high-pressure operators for whom ethics take a distant second place to closing a big deal.

sugar and sweetening (espionage) the various alluring inducements offered to a target by a team of sanctifiers (qv) who aim to trap him into a compromising position.

sugarbagging (sport/UK) in wrestling, the tossing of an opponent onto the canvas as if he were a bag of sugar; the usual effect is the vicious jarring of the vertebrae.

suicide squad (sport) in US football, the team that defend the player who kicks off and thus incur extreme violence from their opponents.

suite (computers) a suite of programs: a collection of separate, but integrated programs which are run consecutively in the performance of one major task.

summer stock (theatre/US) a second rate company who take old favourites on tour through the summer season.

sundown *v* (medic) to experience night time hallucinations because of strange surroundings, a problem that afflicts old people taken into a hospital or geriatric home.

sundowners (commerce) in the TV trade, repairmen who take on extra jobs.

sun gun (TV) a small, battery operated portable lamp.

sunk up (TV) a corruption of *sync up*: properly synchronised sound and vision.

sunray (milit) British Army radio code: the commander of a unit or a formation. (cf: *actual*)

sunrise industry (industry) the new, successful style of manufacturing industry, upon which the economic sun is supposedly rising: the manufacture and use of high technology items, featuring the use of microchips, robots and sophisticated automation.

sunset industries (industry) the old staples of the 19th century Industrial Revolution upon which, in their accelerating decline, the economic sun is setting: steel, shipbuilding, textiles, and other traditional trades; the decline in such industries is creating massive unemployment and many Western governments are forced to invest in them despite all sensible economic advice, both to sustain jobs and maintain votes.

sunset law (govt/US) a law that requires all US government agencies, commissions and programmes to undergo a regular re-assessment to check on their actual usefulness and efficiency.

sunshine (drugs) see: *drug names*.

sunshine law (govt/US) a law that obliges all government bodies – state, city and federal – to conduct their regular proceedings in public.

super (theatre/US) (abbrev) supernumerary: an extra or a walk-on; sometimes not even a professional actor.

super *v* (TV/US) (abbrev) to superimpose, either a caption or some form of special camera effect.

superdynamism (movies) coined by monster creator Ray Harryhausen for his individually created method of animating his range of rubber monsters.

superfecta (gambling) a bet that forecasts in correct order the first four horses in a given race. (cf: *perfecta, trifecta, quinella*).

supermobile *n* (business) a high-flying young executive who moves from firm to firm, continually getting new jobs through his excellence; especially those favoured recruits who are seen by a firm as worthy of training and grooming for the most senior positions and who will enjoy all the favours on offer prior to spurning every entreaty, not to mention the rage of those who have invested a great deal of money in them, and moving on.

supernuke (technology) an adviser at a nuclear energy plant.

superset (sport) in weight-lifting: exercises for one set of muscles to be followed by exercises for an opposing set.

supp (advert) (abbrev) supplementary spot: an extra commercial booked on top of an agency's regular order and given discount rates.

surf *n* (theatre/UK) an actor or technician who works in the theatre at night and takes another job in the daytime.

surface burst (milit) a ground level or extremely low nuclear explosion: such a burst lessens the spread of damage but produces massive cratering.

surfer's knob (sport) aka: *surfer's knot*: in surfing: a bump on the knee or instep that is characteristic of continual surfing.

surge *n* (milit) the ability (of USN) to put all strategic submarines to sea at once; the supposed response to a crisis.

surgical strike (milit) an attack, often without any declaration of war or even a warning, that is made to deal with a specific target; eg: the Israeli destruction of the Iraqi nuclear plant in 1981.

surplus *v* (business, govt) to dismiss, to fire.

surreptitious entry (espionage) the normally illegal breaking and entering of a house or office when the CIA or FBI consider that it contains items or documents that they require for the purpose of foiling enemies of the USA.

surrogates (pols/US) VIPs who undertake to make personal appearances for the candidate of their choice, thus simultaneously garnering possible support and saving him the effort of several appearances.

survey *n, v* (milit) USMC: 1. the regular checking of military equipment to see if it needs to be repaired or even discarded. 2. by extension from (1): a medical discharge. 3. second helpings of food in the messhall.

survivability *n* (milit) the ability to survive a full-scale war, esp. a nuclear one.

survivable weapons (milit) weapons that can endure a nuclear first strike and then be launched for a retaliatory second strike (qqv).

suspended painting (art) canvases without stretchers which are hung from walls or ceilings, then draped, pleated or twisted to create sculptural forms.

swab jockey (milit) USMC: derogatory nickname for a USN sailor.

swallow the anchor (milit) RN: 1. to malinger. 2. to retire from the navy.

swearing contest (law/US) a routine legal contest with cut and dried evidence and solid witnesses for both sides: the winner will be that side who can 'swear' their evidence most convincingly.

sweat boxes (prison/UK) the individual compartments in the meat wagon (qv).

sweat equity (business) 1. the effort that goes into a project – planning, selling to the customer, etc – rather than the hard cash. 2. (spec) a share or interest in a building given to a tenant who has helped with the building's maintenance or renovation.

Sweeney *n* (police/UK) from rhyming sl: Sweeney Todd: Flying Squad.

sweeps (TV/US) special Nielsen TV audience ratings that are prepared for November, February and May: diaries are kept by chosen viewers and Nielsen subscribers can thus obtain detailed viewing patterns for every station in the US; the months chosen are those traditionally reserved for the launching of the networks' potential blockbusters.

sweet as a nut (police, crime/UK) simply, easy: an arrest of a robber, etc.

sweeten *v* (music) adding instrumentation, often strings, to build up the 'feel' of a record.

sweetener *n* (finance) any special bonuses that are added to a project in order to tempt investors or potential customers.

sweet gas (technology) natural gas that has only minor impurities and which can therefore be used without purification.

sweetheart contract (indust relats) any labour contract that heavily favours the employer.

sweetman (sex) a pimp who lives off the efforts of only a single girl.

sweet savagery (publishing) a genre of romantic fiction in which helpings of sex and violence are added to the usual menu of historical or contemporary amorous fantasy; from *Sweet Savage Love* by Rosemary Rogers, although the first attempt at the genre was *The Flame and the Flower* by Kathleen Woodiwiss in 1971. (cf: *creepy weepies, hysterical historicals*).

swifter *n* (theatre) a taut steel wire along which objects or people can slide or 'fly' across the stage.

swift 'un *n* (police) an arrest for 'loitering as a suspected person'.

swing *v* (sex) for couples to meet for wife and husband swapping parties; the euphemism is used in magazines that advertise such delights.

swing *v* (drugs) to sell drugs.

swing credits (commerce) the allowance by East and West trading partners of a credit (between 5% and 20%) to cover seasonal trade fluctuations and the possible excess of imports over exports; on the whole these credits tend to benefit the Eastern (socialist) countries.

swing shift (indust relats) variable shift hours that are worked to maintain a factory's production.

swing voter *n* (pols) a voter who has no particular party allegiance and is just as likely to prefer a personality to a policy; such voters often provide the real imponderable in an election and can thus turn it to one side or the other.

swing with *v* (new therapies) to accept; to tolerate.

switch *n* (police, crime/UK) *at the switch*: stealing property by shop-lifting and then taking it back and asking for a cash refund.

switch dealing (commerce) the agreement by a Western country that it will take Socialist products which it neither wants nor needs as part payment for goods it is selling to that country; such excess Eastern products are then sold to a variety of specialist agents, usually based in Switzerland, who buy them for up to 45% discount and then offload them as and where they can. (cf: *revenge barter*)

switcher (TV/US) a vision mixer.

switcher (pols) a voter who is nominally registered with one party but who may equally well vote for its rivals at an election.

switching (futures market) liquidating an existing position while simultaneously reinstating that position for another month on the same financial instrument.

switch trading (commerce) international commodity trading that is paid for in other commodities, services, benefits or some variety of barter instead of cash.

swoop *v* (prison/UK) to wander around the prison, picking up discarded cigarette-ends for rolling into 'new' cigarettes of one's own.

symbiotic marketing (marketing) the alliance of the resources of two or more independent firms with the intention of maximising the joint marketing potential so created.

symbolic (computers) programs which use

alphanumeric symbols to represent the locations and operations of the machine.

symmetricals (theatre) padded tights used by actors, dancers, acrobats, etc.

sympathetic action (indust relats) support from another union or unions for that union which is actually involved in a dispute.

sync (TV, movies) (abbrev) synchronised: film and sound, shot and recorded simultaneously.

synergetics (design) the culminating concept of R. Buckminster Fuller's design philosophy: 'the behaviour of whole systems unpredicted by the behaviour of their parts taken separately'.

syntax (computers) a set of rules common to all high level languages (qv) which explain how commands in those languages may be used and fitted together in such a way that the program will work.

synthetic incentive (econ) in socialist economies, an incentive that is offered to all workers in a factory and based on the overall production rate rather than the singling out of any individuals.

systems hackers (computers) engineers and programmers who work to develop new computer systems. (cf: *hacker*)

S

T *n* (sport) in basketball: (abbrev) technical foul; thus *to get the T*: to have a technical foul awarded against you.

TA (new therapies) (abbrev) transactional analysis: a form of psychotherapy created by Eric Berne and Thomas Harris which concentrates on analysing individual episodes of social interaction by breaking each individual into a tripartite entity containing 1. the Parent, 2. the Child, 3. the Adult (as in Freud's superego, id and ego).

tab (drugs) (abbrev) tablet.

tab *n* (theatre) (abbrev) tableau curtain: any curtain that rises in festoons or splits down the middle rather than working as one large sheet.

tab *v* (milit) British Army (paratroops): the carrying of a 130lb. pack plus weapons for long distances and over difficult terrain in atrocious conditions; after this hike it is assumed that the paratroops will be fit and ready to fight whatever battle comes their way. (cf: *yomping*)

tab *n* (press) (abbrev) tabloid: 1 a tabloid newspaper. 2. a tabloid insert inside a broadsheet (qv) newspaper.

tab *n* (entertain) the bill, or costs of a production.

table *n* (computers) a collection of data which is stored in a memory and is readily available for reference.

tableau *n* (art) a form of sculpture that employs life-size figures and real accessories/props all frozen together into a 'real-life' scene; on the whole the spectator stands outside the tableau, but some are created as actual rooms into which one may walk.

table top *n* (advert) a still life shot of the product or its ingredients featured in given print or TV advertisement; no people are included. (cf. *pack shot*)

TACAMO (milit) (acro) *take charge and move out*: NATO airborne radio net carried 24 hours a day by 14 modified C 130 (Hercules) transports. These cover the whole earth and trail radio transmitters at the end of 6 mi. wires. This system is considered to be that most likely to survive in the event of a nuclear war, which is likely to wipe out or distort land-based radio, etc.

tachisme (art) the European equivalent of US action painting (qv) developed and popularised in the 1950s; artists sought spontaneity and intuitive style by dripping or throwing paint onto canvases.

tack-up *n* (theatre) a poster on heavy card approx 20″ by 24″ which is used to advertise a current product.

tactical loading (milit) the loading of a transport vehicle whereby priority is given to the tactical (ie: actual combat) needs rather than to administrative ones; in practice, this may mean lighter loads, concentrating on weapons and ammo rather than more general supplies. (cf: *administrative loading*)

tactical nuclear weapons (milit) short-range missiles which, unless fired from European bases near the USSR, could not penetrate Soviet targets. (cf: *strategic weapons, theatre weapons*)

tactical warning (milit) an alert prior to a nuclear war that comes anywhere from days to minutes before that war breaks out. (cf: *strategic warning*)

tactile sculpture (art) 1. sculptures produced with the intention of being enjoyed by the blind. 2. sculptures that are intended for touching and handling.

tag *n* (TV) the closing line of dialogue in a TV programme.

tail *n* (press) the bottom of a page.

tail (theatre) the smaller parts, listed at the 'tail' of the cast-list in a programme; similar to the cricketing use (qv).

tail (sport) in cricket, the lower end of the batting order, usually composed of the wicket-keeper and an assortment of specialist bowlers; thus *the tail wagged*: the lesser batsmen did far better than they might have been expected to do.

tailor made *n* (advert) aka: *one chain*: any promotion that has been especially designed for use in a single shop or by a single chain of stores.

tail out (radio) when a tape has not been wound back and the start of an interview is at the wrong end.

take *n* (TV, movies) an attempt, often unsuccessful, to shoot and record an entire sequence.

take *n* (press) a single portion of a story given to a compositor at any one time and the type he sets from it.

take a geographical (new therapies) in Alcoholics Anonymous: the concept that a major geographical move – of town, country, job, house, husband or wife – will help considerably in cutting down one's drinking.

take a meeting (movies) to hold a meeting; Hollywood executives and their staff invariably 'take' meetings and never call them, hold them or merely 'meet'; the inference being that meetings like phone calls are something one only accepts when there is no other more pressing business.

take a walk (pols/US) to leave one's party after an irrevocable argument.

take camera *v* (movies) for an actor to turn towards the camera.

take felt *v* (milit) RN: to retire from active service, and thus the wearing of a uniform, and to be given a desk job at the Ministry of Defence; the current replacement for the earlier *bowler-hatted*.

taken to see the cups (police/UK) up before the superintendent; such cups – for sporting and similar prowess – as a station might have won are displayed in the superintendent's room.

take one *v* (police/UK) for a policeman to accept a bribe. (cf: *straighten, can I speak to you?*)

take-out *n* (TV/US) a longer than average news report, broadcast with the news, but with a great deal more research and effort than the usual short news item; a feature within the news format.

take out *v* (milit) to kill a person or to destroy a weapon, a building or other target.

take report (medic/US) the taking of all the necessary details that concern the patient on her ward by a nurse who is arriving to start her shift: admissions, deaths, specific treatments, etc; thus *to give report*: for the outgoing nurse to pass on these facts.

take the Fifth (pols/US) to plead the Fifth Amendment of the US Constitution: 'no person shall be compelled in any criminal case to be a witness against himself to avoid self-incrimination'; a procedure often used in the face of Senator McCarthy's anti-communist witch-hunting of the early 1950s, latterly the province of alleged US Mafia members facing embarrassing investigation.

take-up *n* (soc wk) the receiving by an individual of some welfare benefit to which he/she is due; by no means all of those who may claim such benefits do so, the *take-up rate* is the percentage of those that do claim against those that should.

talent *n* (movies, TV, advert) actors, models, any human performers who are employed in these occupations to display themselves.

talk game *v* (sex) for a group of black pimps to gossip about their profession.

talking heads *n* (TV) anyone seen talking, usually in a head-and-shoulders close-up shot, on TV; talking heads programmes tend to ignore the dynamic visual opportunities of the medium and remain static and often didactic.

tally-ho (milit) air intercept code: target sighted, contact will follow soon; from the RAF use during World War 2, taken in turn from fox-hunting, to announce that hostile aircraft had been seen and a fight was about to commence.

talon *n* (finance) that part of a bond that remains after the interest coupon (qv) has been clipped off and cashed in.

T and A theme (entertain) (acro) tits and ass (arse/UK) theme: any show that depends on scantily clad (chorus) girls for its over-riding appeal.

tank *n* (movies) a pool kept at a movie studio for use when filming action at sea or using models of ships.

TAP (advert) (acro) *t*otal *a*udience *p*ackage: a specification of buying space on networked radio.

tap *n* (stock market) a security in which sales come consistently from one source esp. a government issue where the departments are gradually liquidating their holdings to the public.

tape *n* (milit) aka: *stripe*: British Army: the chevrons won by non-commissioned officers to distinguish their rank.

target (espionage) a victim specially selected as the target of a blackmailing scheme in order to extract from him/her such information as is required.

target language (computers) the machine language into which source languages (qv) must be translated to make them accessible to the computer.

target of opportunity (espionage) any source of information that has not been set down as a specific target but which becomes open to access by intelligence agents and is thus employed for such uses as it offers them.

target pricing (econ) in socialist economies, the use of flexible pricing – up and down – to achieve desired social objectives and to further a current economic plan; people's purchasing power is deliberately channelled to consume surpluses and to ignore scarcity.

target response (milit) the effect on troops, materiel and civilians of the blast, heat, flash and fallout from a nuclear explosion.

target servicing (milit) 1. the provision by military planners of worthwhile targets with either weapons or troops in place. 2. attacking a target with either conventional or nuclear weapons.

task *v* (govt) a bureaucratic back-formation from task (n): to be charged with a specific job or mission.

task closure (business) the ability to carry through a job or assignment right on to its completion; the office equivalent of closing out a sale.

task people (espionage) active intelligence agents of the various national agencies.

taste *n* (theatre/US) a share or percentage of the profits in a show.

taste *n* (drugs) 1. a sample. 2. a small amount.

taste *n* (computers) the quality of a program; this tends to vary as to the simplicity of that program: the more fiddling the program becomes, the poorer its quality is likely to be; thus *tasty, tasteful, tastefulness.*

tasty *a* (police/UK) of a villain who has already amassed a large record of previous form (qv).

tat *n* (theatre, TV) 1. costumes, especially old ones; thus *tatbox*: the container for the tat. 2. by extension, a poor performance.

tatts (gambling) dice.

taxing (prison/UK) in Borstals, the collecting of 'protection money' by threatening weaker prisoners with violence.

taxi squad (sport) in US football, those players who train with the team but are not chosen for the matches; allegedly dating from one owner who employed his non-playing footballers to staff his fleet of cabs.

TC (advert) (acro) till cancelled: a space buying specification which informs the newspaper, radio or TV advertising department that an ad will run until orders to discontinue it are issued.

team-handed (police) a gang of thieves or a posse of police.

tear-up *n* (gambling) a means of convincing a suspicious victim that he has not been cheated out of his money; the cheat acts affronted and ostentatiously tears up the cheque he has just been paid in front of the victim who wrote it; in fact he has palmed the real one and torn up a fake, leaving quickly to cash the real one before his victim realises what has happened.

teaser *n* (theatre/US) aka: *proscenium border* (UK): a short, horizontal curtain or flat (qv) used to mark the flies (qv) and frame the top of the inner stage opening, just behind the proscenium arch and in front of the tormentors (qv).

teaser (radio, TV) a trailer that advertises a future attraction, either for the same day or in the near future.

teaser (movies) a poster that lures the public into a film without actually offering any but the barest details.

tea-wagon (movies) the sound-mixer's console.

TE bread (sex) (abbrev) *top eliminator money*: the homosexual hustler's dream of the one client who will enable him to give up selling himself; from a boxing term for the fight that eliminates all but the best challengers for a title.

technical market (stock market) a market in which unnatural price levels are being maintained only through speculation and/or manipulation.

technical surveillance (espionage) any form of information gathering that depends on wiretaps, hidden microphones, etc.

technical trespass (govt, espionage) a break-in to premises by a member of the US government, usu. an FBI agent; no warrant or proper permission is ever obtained for such incursions.

technostructure (sociol) those people in a society who control the technology.

TECO (computers) (acro) *t*ext *e*ditor and *co*rrector: a peripheral (qv) that was developed at the Massachusetts Institute of Technology (MIT) but is now used for onscreen editing in many computers.

teeth arms (milit) the arms of the military services who actually engage the enemy – armour, infantry, etc.

teeth-to-tail ratio (milit) the ratio of actual combat troops to those they require in support; the nearer one is to fighting on one's home territory, the smaller this ratio needs to be; thus Germany will need less support than the US, if fighting in Europe, since the US troops are 5000 miles from home.

tele (new therapies) coined by Jacob Moreno to describe an aspect of his psychodramas: 'a feeling of individuals into one another, the cement that holds groups together' (J.L. Moreno, *Group Psychotherapy*, 1945).

telecine (TV) a system of transferring filmed material onto videotape for transmission as part of a TV programme.

telegraph *v* (gambling) 1. to reveal unintentionally the fact that one is about to make a cheating move. 2. in poker, to reveal, by some involuntary but noticeable movement or gesture, that one is either bluffing, holding a vital card or has some other lucrative secret at one's disposal.

telepuppet *n* (aerospace) a machine under remote control which is intended to erect space platforms.

telescope (TV) a device that uses a series of retractable tubes to suspend studio lighting at different heights.

telint (milit) *tel*emetry *int*elligence: the tracking and listening in to USSR missile tests. (cf: *comint, elint, humint, sigint*)

telling (milit) the communicating of air surveillance and other tactical data between the commander and various subordinate facilities.

telop *n* (TV/US) the projection of the pictures that accompany a news story while the reporter reads his story off camera.

ten (sport) in rowing, *to give a ten*: for a crew to row flat out for ten strokes.

tender *v* (futures market) to deliver against futures.

tender loving care (medic/UK) the stopping of active medical care to terminally ill geriatrics and the permitting or (with an overdose of tranquillisers or barbiturates) hastening of death.

ten great relationships *n* (pols) a relatively right-wing speech that Mao Tse Tung wrote in 1956 but kept suppressed until his death in 1976: the speech emphasised the importance of economic common sense over ideological purity and the need for the efficient marshalling of

T

resources, rather than the imposition of plans that owed more to political than productive imperatives.

ten great years (pols) in China, the first decade – 1949–1959 – of the communist revolution.

tenner *n* (TV) a 10KW incandescent focussing lamp.

tensile architecture (archit) any structure that is held rigid by cables or rods.

tension relief (sex) masturbation: one of the extra services that can be obtained at a so-called 'massage parlour' for a payment somewhat greater than that for the basic massage.

tentacle *n* (milit) a detachment of signals with its own radio and transport.

ten/two (espionage) an intelligence code for a hired killer who has been contracted to work for a government agency.

terminate with extreme prejudice (espionage) to assassinate; usually with the suggestion that the target is a major political figure or even a head of state.

termination capablity (milit) the ability of a nation or nations to bring a war to an end.

terpers (entertain) a corruption of terpsichore: singers, as in 'Tokyo Terpers Triade Towards Topless Taboo' (*Variety*, 13.10.1982).

territorial justice (soc wk) the distribution of resources within an area in proportion to the needs of that area.

tertiary care (medic) medical services that are provided by specialist units: neurosurgery, heart transplants, etc.

TF (advert) (acro) 'til forbid: see *TC*.

T-group training (business) a system of human relations training for business executives which emphasises the interpersonal events and the relationships that evolve through establishing a formal training group and letting those involved begin to communicate; the hope is that the lessons learnt in this group will be extended to use in the office.

that play (theatre/UK) aka: *the Scottish play, Harry Lauder, the unmentionable, the Caledonian tragedy, the comedy of Glamis*: a variety of names that subscribe to the UK theatrical superstition that Shakespeare's *Macbeth* should not be mentioned by name within a theatre.

that's nominal (aerospace) there are no problems; ie: within the nominated guidelines for a flight or mission.

Theatre (theatre) the dropping of any article, definite or indefinite, as in 'Film', implies the whole topic of the theatre as an art form and the intellectual opinions, discussions and developments that stem from it, rather than the plays or personalities that otherwise form the staples of theatrical conversation.

theatre armaments (milit) short-range weapons that can be used by troops who are involved in a face-to-face battle; nuclear weapons and conventional ones.

theatre nuclear forces (milit) see: *theatre armaments*.

theatre of chance (theatre) a theatrical style that played with words, delivering them at random, out of sequence and with no discernible script or narrative.

theatre of cruelty (theatre) a form of theatre based on the theories of Antonin Artaud (1896–1948): the audience is deliberately provoked, the actors subordinate plot and narrative to harsh physical and sensual rituals and the overall intention is for all involved to undergo a savage and shocking experience.

theatre of fact (theatre) plays that are essentially contemporary documentaries, based on dramatic representations of current events and often using actual public statements, speeches and documents to provide their script.

theatre of involvement (theatre) any performance that blends audience and actors in creating an experience that, whatever else it does, defies the conceptions of the bourgeois theatre and, in theory, changes the way one lives.

theatre of panic (theatre) coined by Fernando Arrabal (1932–1983) to define a genre of theatre that combined bad taste, rustic energy, awful tragedy and great fun, all of which deliberate contrasts were intended to promote a feeling of overall instability amongst the audience.

theatre of protest (theatre) any performance, in or out of a traditional theatre, that intended to make a social statement and, it was hoped, to influence the spectators to positive political action.

theatre of the absurd (theatre) a form of theatre that concentrates on the absurdity of the human condition, epitomised by the work of Samuel Beckett, Eugene Ionesco et al.

theatre of the mind (theatre) a popular theatrical style of the 1960s in which performances drew heavily on light shows, slides and ˉother attempts to recreate the experience of taking LSD (qv).

theatre of the streets (theatre) a form of the theatre of protest (qv) which concentrated on giving its 'performances' in the street and in the form of a confrontation with the Establishment and its mores.

theatrical (movies) any film that is designed for commercial exhibition in mass market cinemas.

theology *n* (media) at the British Broadcasting Corporation (BBC), the nickname for the international organisation and politics as carried on at senior level.

theory (computers) idea, plan, set of rules.

theory X (business) developed by Douglas MacGregor in *The Human Side of Enterprise* (1960): a management concept based on the categorisation of people as basically lazy, inept and thus needing a firm, coercive hand to keep them working. (cf: *theory Y, theory Z*).

theory Y (business) developed by Douglas

MacGregor (op cit): a management concept based on the theory that people are naturally productive and merely require the right kind of guidance from a concerned, involved and participative manager. (cf: *theory X, theory Z*)

theory Z (business) a management concept developed beyond MacGregor's theory X and theory Y (qqv) which targets the future management styles that will be required to deal with and include people whose concerns are not merely with their own firm but with a wider range of social and ethical considerations which were ignored by managers of earlier corporations.

therapeutic segregation (prison/US) solitary confinement cell; the prisons that contain such cells are sometimes termed *therapeutic correctional communities*.

there's work down (gambling) the announcement by one player that someone, somehow is cheating.

thesp (theatre) (abbrev) thespian: an actor.

the speech (pols) the one basic campaign speech with all the necessary points included, rhetoric well-presented and every other vital ingredient; this speech, with basic changes as to town, state of the weather, localised references and possibly jokes, can be delivered at any stage or in any place on a campaign tour.

thetan (new therapies) in scientology: the human spirit, the creative potential of which is the subject of scientology.

theta pinch (technology) the rapid compression of a magnetic field that surrounds plasma (highly ionised gas) to produce a controlled fusion reaction in a nuclear reactor.

thing (new therapies) see: *bag*.

thin route (air traffic) an intercontinental air route that is only lightly used by traffic.

third force (pols) any political group that can be seen as setting up a buffer between the superstates of the US and USSR.

third level carrier (air traffic) feeder or commuter services which, like suburban commuter railways, operate out of one major city airport. (cf: *second level carrier*)

third market (commerce) the market in listed stocks which are not traded on a stock exchange. (cf: *fourth market, over the counter trading*).

third party credibility (public relats) a public relations method whereby the target audience is persuaded of the truth of a client's claim since an ostensibly independent third party – not the PR or his client – can be found to support the claim; a far more subtle means of convincing the sceptical than direct advertising.

third world (econ) 1. the non-aligned nations of Africa and Asia. 2. the under-developed, or developing nations, although 'third world' is generally being replaced by south (qv).

third world briefcase (commerce) in the audio retail trade, those combination radios and stere-ophonic cassette players which tend to be favoured by otherwise impoverished black youths.

thirty (press) written usually as 30: the end of a piece.

thirty day boy (sex) a homosexual hustler who enjoys sex every day of the month and thus turns his promiscuity into cash.

38 (sex) aka: *34½, 37½*: supposedly half of 69 (soixante-neuf): mutual oral-genital stimulation, but as practised by homosexual hustlers, only the client actually ejaculates.

thirty minutes (theatre/US) a call to indicate to actors that the performance starts in half an hour. (cf: *the half*)

30 Rock (TV/US) (abbrev) 30, Rockefeller Plaza, the New York headquarters of NBC-TV.

threat assessment conference (milit) a check, max. 3 mins. duration, in which US commanders assess incoming missile threats and determine immediate response; with current USSR missiles, this leaves 19 mins. to impact.

threat azimuth *n* (milit) a missile launch that appears to be fired on a threatening path.

threat fan *n* (milit) a missile launch fr. USSR that is computed as targeted on the US or an ally.

three-card monte (police, crime) 'find the lady', the 'three card trick'.

three-D problem (milit) the assessing of targets for missiles by considering: *d*etection, *d*iscrimination and *d*estruction.

three-decker (sex) a three way sexual 'party': one man sodomises another man who is engaged in intercourse with a woman.

three-eye league (pols/US) a hypothetical club in which membership is gained by any politician who has visited the homes of the US's major minorities: Israel, Italy and Ireland.

three greens (aerospace) radio code: the landing gear is down and locked into position; from the lights that signify this.

three heart rule (milit) US forces: anyone wounded three times, and thus gaining three Purple Hearts, during the same tour of duty is automatically taken out of the combat zone.

three honest and four stricts (govt) a Chinese Communist campaign for law and order in the late 1960s and early 1970s: 1. honest people, 2. honest words, 3. honest deeds plus 1. strict demands, 2. strict organisation, 3. strict behaviour, 4. strict discipline.

three ill winds (govt) the post-revolutionary attack on the 'Eight Legged Essay': the ultra-complex, and massively dogmatic regulations that governed the Chinese government before 1949: 1. subjectivism, 2. sectarianism, 3. excessive formalism; all these three were to be absent from the new style of government.

three-in-one alliance (pols) the triumvirate that were destined to rule China once the Cultural Revolution had run its course: 1. the old cadres,

2. activists who had risen from the people during the Cultural Revolution, 3. troops of the People's Liberation Army (PLA); a blend of all three would form revolutionary committees and take over all aspects of Chinese government.

three magic weapons (pols) the three stages of the seizure of power by the proletariat as set down by Mao Tse Tung: 1. the formation of a united workers' front, 2. the armed struggle of the Party's armed units, 3. the construction of the Party which would consolidate worker power beneath the aegis of Communist doctrine.

three-ply organisation (business) the concept that an organisation is made of three inter-related 'plies': 1. ideational, dealing with the long-range view from a philosophical and ideological standpoint; 2. synergistic, dealing with a variety of specialist areas such as planning, analysis, research etc; 3. process, involving the technology and operations of the organisation.

three-sheet (theatre) 1. to exaggerate, lie, boast; from the idea of a large advertising poster. 2. to stand around in the lobby after one's performance and chat to the departing audience, to show off. 3. to have the leading role in a play.

three-sheeting (theatre) keeping on one's make-up after the performance; from the carnival term for applying one poster on top of another.

three togethers (milit) the principles of the Chinese People's Liberation Army: 1. work together, 2. eat together, 3. live together.

three-way girl (sex) a prostitute who is willing to offer all her orifices separately or simultaneously to one or more clients.

three-worlds theory (pols) a pamphlet published in China in 1977: 'Chairman Mao's Theory of the Differentiation of the Three Worlds as a Major Contribution to Marxism-Leninism': 1. the superpowers: USA, USSR; 2. the economically developed nations: West and East Europe, Canada, Australia, New Zealand and Japan; 3. Africa, Asia and S. America. In Mao's ideal plan, (2) and (3) should ally to defeat both members of (1).

threshold (indust relats/UK) the concept of tying wage increases to the cost of living index and thus raising the former automatically when the latter reaches certain levels.

threshold worker (indust relats/US) an inexperienced worker who is only on the threshold of gaining any expertise in his job.

throat (TV) the gap left in one wall of a set to permit access to a camera.

Throttlebottom n (US pols) shorthand for an incompetent, laughable vice-president; from the George S. Kaufman/Morrie Ryskind political satire *Of Thee I Sing* (1931), in which the supremely ludicrous V-P was named Alexander Throttlebottom.

throughput n (computers) the total amount of work done by a computer in a given period of time.

throw n (movies) 1. the distance between a projector and the screen onto which it projects; 2. the distance between a light and the area it can most effectively illuminate.

throw-weight n (milit) the capacity of the explosive warhead carried by an ICBM (qv).

thruster n (business) an ambitious, go-getting, high-flying executive. (cf: *sleeper*)

thrust stage (theatre) a stage with an audience on three sides, the thrust being that runway that extends out from the usual front of the stage.

thud (milit) 1. an air crash, esp. when an aircraft is shot down by anti-aircraft fire. 2. by extension from (1), the F-105 Thunderchief fighter, which was so susceptible to North Vietnamese ground-to-air missiles.

thumbnail n (press/UK) a portrait measured at 50% of the given column width.

thumbsucker (press) an essay in a newspaper or magazine which ruminates in a leisurely manner on some topic or another; occasionally, the writer who specialises in such pieces.

thunder box (theatre) aka: *rabbit hutch, rumble box, thunder run, thunder roller*: a method of creating artificial 'thunder' during a play by rolling iron balls inside a box.

tick n (futures market) aka: *point*: the minimum alteration, either up or down, in a price.

ticket n (stock market) a slip prepared by the buying broker to identify his purchase and which is passed to the selling broker either via the Settlement Dept. or through the jobbers (qv); thus, *ticket day*: the second day of the settlement and the one on which tickets must be passed. (cf: *name day*)

ticket (pols/US) a list of candidates for one of the parties. (cf: *slate*)

ticket n (police/UK) a search warrant or an arrest warrant.

tickets n (entertainment) a play, musical, concert, rock band, film, etc which has box office potential, eg: 'ET has tickets'. (cf: *legs*)

tickle n (gambling) a reasonable win.

tickle n (police/UK) a successful crime or a worthwhile arrest.

tick-tock n (press/US) a piece that details the chronological background to any major announcement or event.

tiger country (sport) in golf, an area of particularly dense rough.

tiger team (govt/US) a team of specialists chosen for their expertise in tackling a particularly difficult problem in their field.

tilt n (movies) upwards or downwards movement of the camera.

time equals minus infinity (computers) a hacker's (qv) term for as long ago as anyone can remember.

time frame (business) a fake technicality borrowed by businessmen who actually mean the length of time.

time line *n* (aerospace) duration (of a flight).

time off the cuff (indust relats) the recording by piece workers of a greater time taken on one job than was actually worked in order to accumulate some extra time in which to tackle a harder job which they could not easily accomplish within the officially allotted hours.

time sensitive target (milit) a target that remains vulnerable only if it can be destroyed before it can leave the ground: an aircraft or a missile.

time sharing (computers) the simultaneous use of the same computer by two operators, each of whom works from his/her own remote terminal; the machine actually works by shuttling between the two jobs but its speed is so great that as far as the operators are concerned, they are effectively working at the same time.

time urgent nuclear targets (milit) see: *time sensitive target*.

tin beard (theatre) a badly adjusted and made up crepe hair beard.

tincan (milit) USN: a destroyer.

tin soldier (sex) a voyeuristic male, often from the professional middle classes, who has no interest in sex for himself but enjoys volunteering to act as a prostitute's 'slave' (if masochistic) or companion.

tip *n* (milit) the warhead, both nuclear and conventional, of a ballistic missile.

tissue *n* (horse-racing) a racing form used by book-makers and other racing professionals.

tissue committee (medic/US) a hospital committee that evaluates all surgical operations performed at the hospital on the basis of agreement between the preoperative, postoperative and pathological diagnoses and on the acceptability of the procedures used to reach such diagnoses, thus *tissue review*: the report of this committee.

tit *n* (TV) any button on any machine used in the studio or control box.

T man (drugs) 1. (abbrev) top man: a large scale smuggler and distributor of drugs. 2. (abbrev) Treasury Man: a Bureau of Narcotics agent.

toasting (music) the practice of West Indian disc jockeys who add their own rhyming lyrics, often witty and/or relevant to current affairs, to a background of the bass line of a reggae song that can also be found with its own lyrics; thus, *toaster*: the disc jockey who performs this style of music. (cf: *scratch*)

toboganning (milit) a manoeuvre to facilitate mid-air refuelling of military aircraft from tankers; to compensate for the difference between the two aircrafts' speeds, both must dive from 20,000 to 10,000 feet to increase their joint velocity.

toby *n* (police/UK) a police division. (cf: *manor*, *patch*)

together *a* (new therapies) a state of calmness, efficiency, self-awareness, mental and emotional stability.

toil and doil (TV) (acro) *time off in lieu and days off in lieu*: a system whereby instead of taking overtime payments for working extra hours, employees can choose to take off extra days or hours, depending on how much they are owed, instead.

tokenism (sociol) the use by governments, businesses, the media and many other areas of essentially white male society of a few blacks, women, members of minority or handicapped groups for cosmetic, 'token' purposes; such variations on the 'visible negro' (qv) pander to a growing agitation, but do little or nothing to alter the reality of the situation.

tole *n* (milit) French Foreign Legion: regimental prison.

tolkach (pols) the unofficial but fully acknowledged system of 'string-pulling' and short cuts that every Russian attempts to manipulate in order to accelerate or even bypass Soviet bureaucracy.

tom (sex) a prostitute: formerly, in the days of street prostitutes in London, the girls were divided into *toms*: high-class whores who kept to Mayfair, and *edies*: rougher girls who worked the East End, Piccadilly, railway stations and 'the Baze' (Bayswater Road).

tom (crime) (abbrev) rhyming sl: tomfoolery = jewellery.

tombstone (press/US) two boldface headlines (in large, black type) next to each other on the same page.

tombstone ads (business) an advertisement placed in a print medium for the purpose of fulfilling contractual obligations rather than attempting to sell a product; eg: many grocery manufacturers offer discounts to retailers who will run such an advertisement, usually no more than a list of product names and the retailer's name and address.

tom patrol (police/UK) a special patrol for arresting street prostitutes, officially banned since 1959 but gradually reappearing in the British recession. (cf: *pussy posse*)

ton (sport) in cricket, one hundred runs.

tone track (movies) a recording of random background noise to provide the right atmosphere for a film. (cf: *room tone*)

tools *n* (indust relats) normal work as an engineering craftsman as opposed to office work on the union or national executive; thus *go back to the tools*: to return to a job after leaving an official post or losing an election to obtain one.

toot (drugs) 1. a snort of cocaine, to inhale cocaine. 2. a special instrument designed to help inhale cocaine, rather than the simpler rolled up note or MacDonalds straw.

top and tail (sport) in rugby football, an illegal and dangerous tackle whereby one opponent grabs the knees from one angle and the other gets the chest from another angle and together they corkscrew their victim onto the ground. (cf. *crackback*)

top and tail *v* (radio) to prepare a tape for transmission by fixing green and red leaders respectively to the start and finish of the tape.

top hat *n* (police/UK) a policeman's uniform helmet.

top hat pensions (indust relats) special pension plans for retiring senior management which feature extremely large annual payments, usually linked to the cost of living, as well, possibly, as a lump sum 'golden handshake' payment at the time of the actual retirement. (cf: *cloth cap pensions*)

topic A (press/US) the major topic of current interest on a given day or over a given period; it is paramount that any politician acquaints himself with every available detail of such a topic.

topless radio (radio) radio programmes which ask listeners to call in and chat about their personal sexual proclivities to a studio host and one or two experts – sex therapists, doctors, newspaper advice columnists, etc.

topline *v* (entertainment) to star; from one's position on the bill.

top man (sex) the sadist; thus *bottom man*: the masochist.

top of the line *n* (commerce) the brand leader, either through cost, efficiency, sales appeal or any other outstanding characteristic.

topper *n* (business, esp. entertain) the senior executive of a company.

top quark (science) a quark that may have a mass 13 times that of the proton. (cf: *quark*)

topspin (TV/US) that aspect of a show that keeps the audience's interest from one scene to the next.

topspin *n* (movies) a film that has bite, meaning, effectiveness, edge; in tennis the topspin shot 'bites' into the surface of the court.

top up for Mum and Dad *v* (air crew) to take on extra fuel when flying to an airport that is known to present particular problems in landing and take-off; the ensuring of having sufficient reserve fuel for flying, if absolutely necessary, to a safer alternative destination.

tormentor *n* (theatre/US) one of a pair of narrow curtains or flats placed just behind the teaser (qv) and used to frame the sides of the inner proscenium opening and to mark off-stage space at the sides.

touch base with *v* (movies) to make a phone call to someone.

touch-up time *n* (TV) the final adjustments to an actor's makeup prior to an actual take (qv).

tourist guide *n* (new therapies) in a psychodrama

group (qv), the therapist/expert who leads the group.

tout *n* (milit) in the Irish Republican Army (IRA) an informer.

toutery (film) a public relations and publicity firm.

tow truck *n* (medic) a special lift which moves a non-ambulatory patient out of a bed.

toy-boy *n* (sex) a junior gigolo who is taken as a lover by an older woman; he is invariably attractive, she is, at least, rich.

toys (sex) the accoutrements of sado-masochistic fantasy games – whips, chains, leather and plastic clothes, gags, spurs, high boots, etc, etc.

TPR (medic/US) (acro) temperature, pulse, respiration: the three 'vital signs' (qv) exhibited by a patient and for which a nurse or doctor must always check. (cf: *vitals*)

track *n* (computer) the channel on a floppy disc on which data is stored.

track (sport) in cricket, the actual wicket along which the bowler bowls, 22 yards in length; thus one can have a *fast track* or *slow track*.

tracking shot *n* (movies) any shot in which the camera moves backwards or forwards, following the action; these shots can be hand-held but the camera is usually mounted on specially rigged tracks.

trade *n* (milit) RN term, somewhat derog. (like upper class disdain of tradesmen) for submariners; generally discarded since WW2.

trade-off *n* (business) a method of assessing the best alternative ways of achieving any given objective.

trade paperback (publishing) a large format paperback, often a facsimile of a hard-covered edition, but in soft covers and selling at a price between the usual hard- or paperback ranges.

trades *n* (movies, record industry) (abbrev) the trade papers: *Variety*, *The Stage*, *Billboard*, etc.

trafficability (milit) the extent to which a given terrain will bear military traffic, and the type of traffic which it will bear.

traffic builder (marketing) any in-store promotion – usually in a supermarket or other self-service shop – that is designed to stimulate traffic of customers through the store.

trail *v* (radio) to advertise the up-coming attractions of the station.

train bombing (milit) bombs dropped in a sequence punctuated by short, regular intervals.

train-in *v* (milit) USMC: to end a drill or exercise.

tramp's lagging (prison/UK) a sentence of two weeks.

transaction (new therapies) in TA (transactional analysis): an exchange of strokes (qv), ie: the fulfilment of 'stimulus hunger' as in applause for an actor, etc.

transaction *n* (computers) any event that

requires a record to be generated within the computer's system.

transformation *n* (new therapies) in est (qv): the experience of undergoing est therapy.

transparency (business) the inability to assess whether or not a given company is or is not being subsidised.

transparency of information (govt) a phrase used by Common Market (EEC) bureaucrats: the clear labelling of commodities.

transparent action (computers) any action that the machine performs and of which the user is unaware.

transportation car (commerce) in the motor trade, a car that simply takes one from point A to point B, with no special frills, gimmicks or any other sales allure.

trap *n* (computers) aka: *interrupt*: a method of detecting erors when 'illegal' (unworkable) instructions are entered into the machine: the program stops functioning and a message is printed out stating that 'illegal' instructions have been used and then the program is terminated.

travelled blood (police) blood that has spurted from a severed artery.

traveller *n* (TV, theatre) a curtain that runs along a sliding track.

travelling salesman (sex) a hustler who obtains his clients by posing as a hitch-hiker, albeit without luggage or a real destination.

treads (TV) any steps or stairs built into the set.

treasury call (theatre) pay day in the theatre, usually on a Friday afternoon. (cf: *ghost*)

treatment *n* (movies) the first expansion of a basic script idea into a narrative form with rough sequences, the outlines of dialogue, camera angles, etc.

tree and branch (TV) a proposed method of installing cable TV in the UK whereby a main coaxial cable would be laid under roads (the tree) and each subscribing household would take a subsidiary cable (branch) into their own TV.

treff *n* (espionage) fr. Ger. 'Treff' = meeting, date: a clandestine meeting.

triad *n* (milit) the three-part division of the US strategic nuclear forces: land-based missiles, submarine launched missiles and long-range bombers.

trick *n* (police/UK) a turn at an unpleasant, tedious job.

trick *n* (sex) a client for any prostitute, hetero- or homosexual; thus *to turn a trick*: to service one client, the implication being that the prostitute is conning the client, making them pay for what a 'real man' could have had for free.

trickle diversions (govt, business) the gradual growth of problems within a system that develop so slowly and in so limited, albeit continuous a way, that they are overlooked in the face of the general activity (cf: *noise level*) until too much damage has been done.

trickledown *n* (econ) the theory that the profits generated by giving government aid to major corporations will eventually permeate through to lesser businesses and even the consumer.

trifecta (gambling) aka: *triple*: a bet in which the first three horses in a race, in the order in which they finish, have to be selected in order to win.

trigger pricing (commerce) the keeping open of old and obsolete facilities, eg: steel plants that offer employment but are in fact economically useless, by holding the price of their products well above what would be charged were they produced in new, cost-efficient facilities.

trim *v* (TV, movies) to change the carbon rods in an arc lamp; from the traditional trimming of the wick of a candle.

trims (gambling) cards that have been doctored by trimming some along one edge and some along another.

triple A (milit) anti-aircraft artillery.

triple hat *v* (espionage) for the same agent to undertake a variety of covert assignments at the same time, for him to wear several hats.

triple threat (movies) an individual who is proficient in three capacities: writing, producing and directing, and thus threatens anyone who is talented in only one.

tripling (sex) the inviting in by a husband and wife of a third party, usually another woman, for group sex or swinging (qv).

tripwire force (milit) aka: *tripwire position*: those troops who are stationed on a hostile border as the first line of defence; such troops are deemed expendable and their role is not to stop an invasion, merely to hold it up long enough for the major part of the defences to be activated.

troika (govt/US) a special group of Presidential economic advisers: Chairman of the Council of Economic Advisers, Secretary of the Treasury, Director of the Office of Management. (cf: *quadriad*)

Trollope ploy (diplomacy) the deliberate misinterpreting of foreign situations in order to act on that one which appears most advantageous to one's own interests; from a scene in a novel by Anthony Trollope (1815–1882) in which the heroine consciously decides to interpret a mere squeeze of her hand as an ardent proposal of marriage.

trombone *n* (movies) an extendable support from which lights can be attached to the ceiling or wall of a set.

tromboning (TV) the excessive use of a zoom lens on a camera.

tromp and stomp *n* (milit) USMC: the morning inspection, which is followed by close-order drill.

troops (pols/US) the lower echelons of party workers who perform the mundane, menial tasks that never make any headlines but may well 'get out the vote'.

troops *n* (pols) in Catholic areas of N. Ireland, the British forces. (cf: *Army*)

Trotskyism (pols) 1. the concept advanced by Leon Trotsky (1879–1940) that his rival Stalin had turned the Revolution into a bureaucratic tyranny. 2. that phase of the Revolution in which Trotsky was still attempting to rival Stalin for supreme power and which Trotsky lost. 3. in modern Communist Party ideology, any form of anti-Party heresy that stands outside the Party line.

Trotslot (TV) any programme, usually of current affairs, that attacks the Establishment position and thus is deemed, perhaps ironically, to be breeding red revolution.

trotting (commerce) in auction sales, the tactic whereby a dealer's ring (qv) will force an outsider up to an unrealistically high bid, at which point they will drop out and leave their rival with a large bill.

trough *n* (theatre) a long metal container which holds stage lights.

trout fishing (sex) the searching by a young hustler for a rich older man who will keep him in (temporary) luxury.

truck acts (indust relats) a series of acts passed between 1831 and 1940 which protected all those workers to which they apply – all manual labourers other than domestic servants – from abuses in the payment of their wages.

truck system (indust relats) the system, now largely outlawed, of paying wages in kind rather than in cash.

true believer (pols/US) used on two levels: by an ally to describe a fellow enthusiast; by an enemy to attack a fanatic; both descriptions refer to political supporters.

trufan (TV) a dedicated fan of TV's science fiction series 'Star Trek'; for such fans the only 'trufan' is one whose allegiance is solely to 'Star Trek' and not to any other programme or science fiction characters.

trunk (computers) a set of linking components that join one part of a computer to another; the equivalent of a bus (qv), but as applied to a larger machine.

truth *n* (science) the property of a top quark (qv). (cf: *beauty, charm, strangeness*).

truth-in-lending (finance/US) the legal requirement that any bank must explain fully all the details of any loan scheme that they operate.

truth squad (govt) members of government agencies who defend controversial positions in public by appearing as a group in press conferences or protest meetings to push the government point of view, often while posing as disinterested, but 'concerned' citizens.

truth squad (pols/US) a special team of opposition experts who follow a candidate around his campaign tour and attempt to unsettle him by producing facts and figures that are aimed to refute his various statements and promises.

try it out on the dog *v* (theatre/US) to try out a new play by giving a variety of previews in towns and cities outside New York; thus *dog house*: a preview audience, *dog show, dog town*.

tube (sport) in surfing, the hollow space beneath the curl of a breaking wave.

tube *v* (medic/US) for a patient to die, ie: 'he's gone down the tubes'. (cf: *box out, flatline*)

tube *n* (new therapies) a derogatory term used by an est (qv) instructor for those undergoing the weekend of training; the implication is that, devoid of any real personality, they are capable only of eating and, at the other end of the tube, excreting.

tube artillery *n* (milit) any weapon that has a barrel rather than one that is delivered by rocket: howitzers, mortars, field guns.

tucked up (police/UK) 1. of a situation that is fully under control; 2. a target under successful surveillance; 3. a suspect safely arrested.

tucked up (sport) in cricket, a batsman who is forced to play back and make a cramped, awkward stroke.

tug *v* (police/UK) to arrest, usually as *give a tug*. (cf: *pull*)

tuner *n* (theatre) a musical.

tunnel (econ) the restricted area of currency fluctuation in which the EEC 'snake' (qv) is supposed to move.

turf *v* (medic/US) to get rid of or pass on an unwanted patient from one ward to another or to a special surgical unit; a turf is usually preceded by a buff (qv) which legitimises the turf, but if that is inadequate, the patient comes back as a bounce (qv).

turkey *n* (drugs) fake drugs, esp. a capsule in which there is only chalk or sugar but no actual narcotic.

turkey *n* (medic/US) 1. any patient whom hospital doctors do not feel is a genuine case, but in fact a malingerer. (cf: *bounce, meet 'em and street 'em, sieve*) 2. a patient who has been mishandled by a hospital.

turkey *n* (movies) a flop.

turn *v* (drugs) for a dealer to agree to sell drugs to an addict.

turn *n* (stock market) the difference between the bid (qv) and the price offered by the jobber (qv); the jobber's turn is the same as the gross profit he makes on a security when he buys and sells equal amounts at the bid and the offered prices.

turn around *v* (espionage) to persuade an enemy agent to start working for one's own side.

turnaround *n* (movies) a situation in which a studio abandons a project and gives its producer a set time – usually 12 months – to find another buyer who is interested in it.

turnaround *n* (aerospace) the readying of the launch pad and all the other vital facilities that are needed for the successful launching of a spacecraft.

Turners (medic) hermaphrodites who are essentially women with some male characteristics; individuals who are technically female but who are completely devoid of an X chromosome. (cf: *Klinefelters*)

turnkey reactors (technology) tailor made 'off the peg' nuclear energy systems made in one country, usually the US, and sold around the world to interested parties. (cf: *turnkey system*)

turnkey system (computers) a system which has been designed, assembled and checked by its manufacturer as well as double-checked by the retailer and which is then turned over to the user who needs only 'turn the key' in the front panel lock for the machine to be ready for use.

turn over *v* (police/UK) to search someone's home, usually by making a destructive mess.

turnover *n* (business) the hiring and firing of staff.

turn over the covers (business) to look into both sides of a given problem.

turn round (radio/UK) to have a tape ready for use: edited, timed and running forwards.

turntable hit *n* (record business) a record that is regularly played on the radio and in jukeboxes but which is not actually bought in the stores.

turtle *n* (TV) a three-legged floor stand into which a lamp, connected by a spud (qv) can be fitted.

turtles *n* (police, crime/UK) as in rhyming sl.: 'turtle doves' = gloves, thus the gloves used by a housebreaker to mask his fingerprints.

tutti frutti communism (pols) the Italian communist party's joking description of its homegrown variation on the Soviet party line; coined in 1956 after N.S. Khrushchev had advocated the taking of individual roads towards the generally desired socialist millennium by the various Western communist parties.

TV-Q (TV/US) a popularity measure for a performer on TV; two areas are measured: the familiarity rating (who knows the performer's face?) and the Q-rating (who likes that face?) – together they make up the TV-Q rating.

tweak *v* (computers, TV) to fine-tune the machine.

tweaker *n* (TV) a small screwdriver used by electricians or carpenters.

tweedler *n* (crime, police/UK) a dishonest vehicle – stolen, faulty, etc – which is offered for sale as the genuine article.

tweedling (crime/UK) the selling of stolen property, of property that does not exist but for which money can be obtained in advance, of shoddy or worthless goods.

twenty-five (milit) a communications man, from his military occupational speciality number 2500.

twewe *n* (TV) the brand-name of a viewfinder,

manufactured in Germany, with which a director can assess the same shot as will be seen in the camera lens.

twiddle *v* (computers) 1. a small and insignificant alteration in the program; such a change often serves to fix one major problem but simultaneously creates several lesser ones. 2. to change something in a small way.

twilight shift (indust relats) a three to four hour early evening shift, often worked by married women employed in light industrial plants, or by those who are moonlighting (qv) elsewhere.

twinset (sport) in diving, a two-bottle aqualung.

twisting 1. (insurance) persuading a policy holder to alter a current policy or take on a new one for no other reason than that the salesman wants to make himself an extra commission on the sale. 2. (banking) shifting a long-term debt to a short-term one, or vice versa, so that one can take advantage of the changing interest rates involved.

twitch (sport) in golf, to suffer from nerves when putting. (cf: *yips*)

twitch factor (air lines) a decrease in the efficiency of members of a commercial aircraft's crew, esp. that of the pilot, through fear or the mounting pressure of the workload.

two-block *v* (milit) USMC: 1. to hoist a flag or pennant to a ship's yardarm. 2. to straighten up a field scarf and position it neatly in the centre of one's uniform.

two-four-six (TV) small wooden blocks, glued like a small set of stairs, each 2″ high, used by grips (qv) to lay and strengthen the camera tracks. (cf. *paganini*)

two lines (pols) in Chinese communist terminology, the clash between the bourgeois line and the proletarian line; individuals may change but the basic issue never alters: the bourgeoisie wish to suppress the revolution, while the masses, epitomised in the Maoist poster 'Bombard the Headquarters', yearn to smash once and for all the bourgeoisie and capitalist roaders.

two man rule *n* (milit) the regulation that no one individual should ever be allowed sole access to or control of any nuclear weapons; thus two men with two keys and two codes, etc, are required for the launching of a nuclear strike.

201 file (security, espionage) a special biographical file on any individual in whom the CIA is interested, either as a potential ally or as a possible or certain enemy; such a file is particularly detailed as to social life, friendships, sexual predilections, weaknesses, etc.

two tier bargaining (indust relats) when national pay agreements with a given union are subsequently backed up by local branch agreements which give further wages concessions to those branches on top of the original deal.

two-way man (sex) a hustler who will take a

passive role in sex, possibly for pleasure rather than simple trade. (cf: *three-way girl*)

two weeks under, one week out (theatre/US) a clause in a contract which gives a theatre owner the right to have a show closed within one week if its gross box office take drops below a pre-set figure for two consecutive weeks.

type *n* (milit) French Foreign Legion: an eccentric legionnaire.

tyre kickers (business) anyone who is charged with inspecting a project and does so only in the most superficial of manners; such negligence can stem either from genuine incompetence, or the fact that it is more important for a particular person to be seen looking over the project than for him actually to know what he is looking at.

T

ufocal (science) the optimum location for the possible sighting of unidentified flying objects (UFOs).

ugly American (diplomacy) that type of American who uses foreign 'aid' programmes to exploit, alienate and destabilise the country to which it is given; from the novel *The Ugly American* by William J. Lederer and Eugene Burdick (1959), but a misinterpretation of that novel in which a physically ugly American belies his unattractiveness by helping the country to which he is posted.

ulcer *n* (TV) a light diffuser made of a board from which various portions have been cut out and which is placed in front of a light.

ultimate painting (art) a series of paintings – 'The Black Paintings' – produced by Ad Reinhardt between 1960 and 1967 and which he termed 'the ultimate abstract paintings'.

UMA (indust relats) (acro) *u*nion *m*embership *a*greement: the closed shop.

umbilical *n* (aerospace) a large multiple cable connection between ground control and a spacecraft which supplies all necessary supplies and signals right up until the moment of lift-off.

umbrella *n* (TV) a reflector placed behind a light.

umbrella brigade (police/UK) Metropolitan Police nickname for the Special Branch, which deals with internal security.

unacceptable damage (milit) the concept that the damage one's own nation would suffer in a projected second strike (qv) might be too great to make it worth launching a first strike (qv) against the enemy.

unbundle *v* (business) to separate the costs of various operations within one firm or one project into their separate entities.

uncle (theatre, movies) 1. film agent. 2. theatrical backer.

uncorrected cybernetic machinery (new therapies) in est (qv): the human mind in the random, unplanned state that it is in prior to undergoing the transformation of est therapy.

uncut (sex) uncircumcised.

under-achiever (educ) any pupil who appears less competent than he/she ought to be given age, development, etc. (cf: *over-achiever*)

under-boss (crime/US) in the US Mafia, the 'sotto capo': the man who is second in command of a family (qv).

underclass (sociol) the absolute lowest of all classes, usually seen as members of variously disadvantaged (qv) minority groups.

undergraduate (aerospace) any member of an air crew who has yet to qualify in his speciality, esp. a pilot who has not 'gained his wings'.

underkill *v* (milit) 1. the inability of one's forces and/or weapons to defeat a given enemy. 2. something that causes far less harm than it might actually be capable of inflicting if given full rein.

underneath (radio) a record that continues to play softly while a disc jockey makes an announcement over its musical background.

undertaker's job (gambling) in horse- or dog-racing, an animal which was never intended to win; by extension, any useless idea or suggestion.

under the gun (gambling) in draw or stud poker a situation where a player must make some form of decision as to his betting or leaving the game before that round of play can continue.

under the rule (stock market/US) the conclusion of a half-finished deal by an official of the New York stock exchange when the dealer who initiated it has failed to close it out.

under wraps (horse-racing) a horse who is restrained from running at his best; possibly with the intention of disguising his real form prior to a more important race and thus giving his owner and others in the know the opportunity to attempt a betting coup.

unfair house (indust relats) aka: *unfair shop*: an employer who offers pay and/or conditions of work that fall below the standards generally accepted in the same industry or the local area.

union hall *n* (sex) an answering service that is used by homosexual 'call-boys'.

unitary approach (soc work) aka: *unitary model*: the concept that social work for all its different areas of interest, is an all-embracing phenomenon and that it should be viewed as such, as an overall manifestation of the management of social learning.

unit pricing *n* (commerce) a method of pricing that shows both the price per pound, ounce or other standard measure and, on that scale, the price for the actual item being purchased.

universalism (soc wk) the principle of running social services in such a way that all contribute equally and all are thus entitled to draw equal benefit; the opposite of selectivity (qv).

universe *n* (marketing) the individuals who make up a sample for the purposes of market research. (cf: *population*)

unk-unks (aerospace) those phenomena which are doubly unknown: in the first place they are not even known to exist, and if they were discovered, no-one would have any idea what they were.

unofficial classification (govt) a method of countering journalistic enquiries whereby a government official claims that the requested piece of information has been classified as 'secret' when in fact it has not.

unpractical (theatre) any prop or item of stage furniture that cannot actually be used on stage but exists only for its visual effect. (cf: *impractical*, *practical*)

unrecovered *a* (movies) a film that fails to make back its initial cost.

unscheduled engine removal (aerospace) any unexpected engine failure or other repairs ouside the normal maintenance schedules.

unsocial hours (indust relats) any working hours that do not correspond to those of one's peers and thus destroy one's social life: split shifts, overtime, weekend or night work, etc.

up (computers) 1. *a* in good working order; the opposite of down (qv) 2. *v* to create a working version of an otherwise malfunctioning machine.

up (horse-racing) whichever jockey is riding a particular mount, ie: 'Horse X, Lester Piggott up'.

upcut *v* (advert) the practice of cutting material out of a radio or TV programme in order to fit in extra commercials.

update *n, v* (radio, TV) 1. *v* to bring up to date (of a news item); 2 *n* an additional item referring to an earlier news story which brings that story up to date.

up front (new therapies) honest, revealing, emotionally unguarded, confessing one's deepest feelings.

upgrade *v* (air crew) to put a passenger who has only paid the economy fare into an otherwise half-full or empty first-class compartment.

uppers (drugs) general term for any amphetamine; see: *drug names*.

up quark (science) a quark which supposedly possesses an 'upward spin'. (cf: *quark*)

UPS (espionage) (acro) *u*ncontested *p*hysical *s*earches: break-ins by members of intelligence services for the purpose of extracting otherwise inaccessible information. (cf: *black bag job*)

upset price (commerce) in an auction sale, the price which the bidding for a given lot must equal or surpass; if this price is not reached, the lot is withdrawn.

upstream loans (finance) the loans given by subsidiary companies to their parent company when that parent has an insufficiently strong credit rating to obtain money elsewhere.

up the pole (milit) USMC: absolutely no drinking; complete abstemiousness.

up the steps (police/UK) on trial; from the steps that lead up from the cells straight into the dock at the Central Criminal Court (the Old Bailey) in London.

upthreat *v* (milit) to increase the aggressiveness of one's military posture vis-à-vis the enemy.

uptick *n* (business) an upswing in the business world.

uptight (new therapies) 'a word used to describe an individual experiencing anything from mild uneasiness to a clinical depression' (R. D. Rosen) (see Bibliog).

up time *n* (computers) that time during which a computer is functioning. (cf: *down time*)

up to speed (pols/US) for a politician to have the current facts and information at his fingertips; on the ball.

upward compatible (computers) a machine that can do everything the previous model could do, *plus* some exciting extras; a phrase used by enthusiastic computer salesmen.

ur- (arts) fr. Ger. 'original, earliest' and prefixed to a variety of words, often referring to the more serious areas of the arts, to denote purity or originality. (cf: *echt*)

US country team (espionage) the senior US co-ordinating team which supervises all intelligence operations in a given foreign country and which consists of the ambassador (or his equivalent) plus the heads of any US department or agency that is represented in that country.

use immunity *n* (law/US) a method whereby prosecutors can circumscribe the immunities of the Fifth Amendment (cf: *take the Fifth*) by offering witnesses immunity from any subsequent prosecution based on such self-incriminating facts they may reveal but which still permits them to name other useful names.

user (computers) a gullible programmer who believes whatever he is told instead of finding things out for himself.

user friendly (computers) a machine which can be handled without long months of training but which is designed to make its operation as easy as possible.

user time (computers) the time the human user requires to perform a given task with a computer.

use the user (advert) a promotional scheme which offers a premium (qv) to those consumers who are able to persuade fellow consumers to purchase a particular product.

USP (advert) (acro) *u*nique *s*elling *p*roposition: coined in the 1950s by US ad executive Rosser Reeves to describe that advertising process whereby one accentuates whatever attributes your product has that its many rivals allegedly do not.

utility (design) plain, economical furniture, made in sturdy, practical materials; 'utility' design was created betw. 1941 and 1951 when the UK government, in order to make the best use of scarce labour and raw materials, imposed a degree of state control on the production of furniture, textiles, clothes and some household goods.

U

vagnari lu pizzu (Mafia) lit: 'to dip one's beak': to take a rake-off or commission, on laundering money, selling stolen goods, smuggling drugs, etc.

valentine (TV) a soft light, 1KW or 2KW.

validation codes (milit) codes that authenticate the previous nuclear control order and assure launch officers that there really is a war on.

value billing (public relats) the charging of the client for the actual successes achieved in planting favourable pieces and other PR work rather than using a set tariff charged by the month.

value neutrality (sociol) anyone who professes no views as to what is 'good' or 'bad'.

vamp *v* (theatre) to improvise; esp. the using of makeshift or homemade props and scenery either through an emergency or simple poverty.

vamping (entertain) the extension of a given series or programme until a required actor or actress has worked out a current contract and can then start work for the new company.

vampires (medic/US) aka: *vultures*: anyone who works in a hospital laboratory.

van *n* (aerospace) airconditioned, towed vehicles which are used for any major engineering operations that have to be performed away from a proper workshop; ie the stripping, checking and reassembly of a large engine.

van dragging (police/UK) see: *jump-up*.

vanguardism (pols) 1. in Marxist terms, the need for a highly disciplined communist party, led by professional revolutionaries who stand as the vanguard of working class aspirations. 2. in a negative use, the leftist adventurism (qv) of elitists who forget the masses and interest themselves only in glorifying a few 'revolutionary heroes'.

vanilla *a* (computers) standard, run of the mill, ordinary. (cf: *flavour*)

vanity surgery (medic) plastic surgery for merely cosmetic purposes, such as straightening or shortening a nose, removing unsightly warts or facial hair, etc.

veepee (business) from VP: vice president.

ventilator (theatre) a play so appallingly bad that the audience leaves well before the final curtain, and their seats are filled only with fresh air.

venture capital (finance) those funds used for the financing of venture capitalism (qv).

venture capitalism (finance) aka: *risk capital*: the investment of long-term capital in ventures that are particularly prone to risk; such ventures are usually new ones. More specifically, capital provided for a new business undertaking by persons other than the proprietors.

verbal (police, crime) 1. *n* talk, conversation, spec: a confession. 2. *v* for the police to fake up a confession which is then read out in court in all its incriminating detail.

verbiage *n* (educ) any written material; no derogatory implication is involved.

verist sculpture (art) a three-dimensional sculptured equivalent of photo-realism (qv); such sculptures are created by taking casts from the human body in fibreglass and polyester resin.

verkrampte (pols) fr. Afrikaans: 'cramped': the extreme right wing of the South African National Party, die-hard supporters of apartheid, they fight against any concessions or compromises in the white South African way of life. (cf: *verligte*)

verligte (pols) fr. Afrikaans 'enlightened': the liberal wing of the South African National Party, still staunchly white supremacist, but willing to accept some compromises and concessions towards a changed status for black and coloured South Africans.

verstehen *n* (sociol) a process of empathy, followed by introspection through which it is considered that one individual may come to appreciate the reasons for another individual's behaviour.

vertical integration (business) a process whereby a company extends by taking over other firms who are in the same type of business but which work at other levels of the production process: suppliers, distributors, etc. (cf: *horizontal integration*)

vertical linkage (espionage) the formation of secure intelligence cells in which each person involved knows only his/her own role and that of the two individuals who are directly linked 'above' and 'below' in the organisation.

vertical proliferation (milit) the upward spread of the numbers of nuclear weapons in the hands of an increasing fraternity of nations.

vertical publication (publishing) producing books for a specialist audience. (cf: *horizontal publication*)

VFR (air crew) (acro) *v*isiting *f*riends and *rela*-tions: families who are visiting their former friends and other members of their families who have since emigrated; VFRs get no special fare reductions, but aged grannies or aunts do tend to get some extra personal attention from the cabin crew.

vicar *n* (govt) in the British civil service, an assistant secretary; taken from John Le Carré, *Smiley's People* (1979, televised 1982) and another example of life imitating Le Carré's art. (cf: *mole*)

vicious cycle (econ) a cycle of events that lead gradually to the decline of a national currency.

vidkids (entertain) the youthful addicts of computerised arcade video games such as 'Space Invaders' or 'Pacman'.

vid lit (TV) (abbrev) video literature: such programmes as 'Edward and Mrs Simpson', 'Jennie', etc: lavish costume dramas, based on loosely interpreted historical events but interested more in their glamorous personalities than in the factual background.

vigilance men (indust relats) union investigators who visit factories to check up on any possible management abuses and/or worker grievances and then report back to their headquarters before considering what action may be necessary.

vignette (advert) 1. any illustration, photograph or camera shot with deliberately 'atmospheric' fuzzed edges. 2. a TV commercial made up of short scenes, each of them different and often humorous, which tell ultra-short stories featuring the product as the major character.

vignette *n* (TV) a mask that is placed in front of a camera and which allows only a selected portion of the view to be photographed.

vigorish (gambling/US) aka: *the vig*: 1. the percentage taken by any operator who stands as 'the bank' in a gambling game; either a straight fee taken as a percentage of all winnings or a hidden levy that is taken automatically through the mechanics of the game. 2. the interest charged on a loan.

villuta (Mafia) lit: 'velvet': a prostitute.

vinyl *n* (record business) a record or records: from the substance in which records are pressed.

violin piece (press/US) esp. in news magazines, the lead story for that week, the piece that 'sets the tone'.

virgin medium *n* (computers) anything related to the computer that is absolutely untouched, eg: a roll of paper tape that has yet to be punched prior to its being used on a machine.

visibility (business) see: *high profile, low profile*.

visible negro (business/US) any black employee who is placed in the forefront of a firm – rather than hidden away as a janitor, maintenance man or nightwatchman – in order to convince anyone who cares that the firm offers equal opportunities to all races. (cf: *tokenism*)

visual *n* (pols/US) any event that offers the potential for taking photographs of the candidate: visiting factories, kissing babies, welcoming war heroes, etc.

vitals (medic/US) the three 'vital signs' that can help determine the state of a patient's health: temperature, pulse and respiration. (cf: *TPR*)

VO (prison/UK) (acro) *v*isiting *o*rder: an official chit that must be sent out by a prisoner (other than those on remand) to request the admission of his family or friends for a visit.

voice *v* (radio) to make one's report or conduct an interview over the air; thus a reporter *voices* a story. (cf: *voicer*)

voicer *n* (radio) a taped programme item – either on a cartridge or on a reel-to-reel tape – on which only the reporter is heard speaking; such a piece has no actuality (qv); such as the regurgitating of a piece of wire service copy of which the reporter is personally ignorant; voicers also cover court reports, foreign reports or opinion pieces.

voice wrap (TV) the use of a newscaster's voice to introduce a given news item which is then narrated by a reporter. (cf: *telop*)

volatile *a* (computers) a computer memory in which the stored information is destroyed once the power supply to the machine is turned off.

voluntarism (indust relats) a mutually agreed policy by both the unions and the employers as regards the ideal way of conducting industrial relations: the law should not intervene directly in the process of collective bargaining; the main threats to voluntarism are the various incomes policies which emerge from a succession of UK governments.

voting system (milit) a security system designed to prevent 'accidental' nuclear war: bomber and missile silo crews must obtain coded correlation of launch plans from an outside source, without which they are unable to remove the locks on their weapons; this system has not been applied to submarines, whose captains alone possess the power to control their missiles.

voucher (advert) a free copy of any print medium which is sent to an advertising agency and/or an advertiser to show that a commissoned advertisement was actually published as and when required.

vox pop *n* (TV, radio) fr. Latin 'vox populi' = 'voice of the people': interviews conducted at random with men and women in the street in order to elicit their views on whatever topic the broadcaster may throw at them.

vulgar Marxism (pols) simplified or misinterpreted Marxism, a caricature of the whole ideology; often the production of the naive, the ultra-left or any other socialist fanatic.

V

W

W (police/UK) (abbrev) warrant: an authorisation for a policeman to search a house or arrest an individual.

wafer (computers) the thin slice of silicon from which a semiconductor chip is made.

wage drift (econ) a gradual, unplanned escalation of national wage levels through individual companies offering higher increases than a government's policy has recommended.

wage-push inflation (econ) the inflation that results from too many and too substantial increases in wages.

wage stop n (econ) a principle in the UK that unemployed persons ought not receive more in welfare benefits than they might were they properly employed.

wahine (sport) in surfing: from Hawaiian 'woman': a female surfer.

waiter (stock market/UK) the uniformed attendants at the London Stock Exchange; from the waiters at the original coffee house where the Stock Exchange first began its affairs.

wait list n (air crew) a standby ticket; indicated as *WL* on the ticket.

walk n (aerospace) the steady orbiting of a spacecraft around a star or planet.

walk a flat v (theatre) to carry a flat (qv) in an upright position; to *walk a flat up/down*: to raise or lower a flat by hand.

walk back the cat v (diplomacy) in international negotiations, the retreating from a hard-line position to one in which more compromise may have to be accepted.

walk-in defector (espionage) a defector who turns him/herself over to the chosen nation and brings along secrets or similar information as the 'price' of gaining political asylum.

walking (aerospace) to advance an aircraft's throttles in asymmetric steps, ie: left, right, left, etc.

walking around money n (pols/US) aka: *street money*: money paid to those precinct workers who knock on doors and ring at bells in order to help their candidate's campaign and who generally labour to 'get out the vote'; such payments are not wholly legal, but do not constitute a major breach of electoral ethics either.

walking gentleman, walking lady (theatre) an extra, a bit part, a walk-on.

walk-through n (theatre) 1. a rehearsal without costumes but with the business that accompanies the dialogue. 2. a very small part, a walk-on.

walk-up n (commerce) in real estate, any building that has more than two floors but does not offer a lift.

wall n (medic/US) an intern in an emergency room who keeps the workload down to genuine emergencies by refusing to admit any but the most important cases; the opposite of a sieve (qv).

wall! (computers) an interjection that implies an indication of confusion; a request for more information.

wallpaper n (TV/US) stock footage, eg: the Pentagon, the White House, which serves as a background picture to any story that concerns its subject.

wallpaper (music) piped music in lifts, hotel lobbies, etc; Muzak.

Wall Street (finance/US) a general term that embraces the financial district of New York. (cf: *Lombard Street, the City*)

Walter Plinge (theatre/UK) an imaginary pseudonym used by an actor who takes two roles in the same production; possibly orig. c1870 to honour the stagestruck landlord of a public house opposite the Theatre Royal, Drury Lane who was generous in his credit and was finally rewarded by being given a benefit performance in his honour; another theory, in a letter from Norman A. Punt, FRCS Ed., in 1981: 'invented in a pub off the Strand by H. O. Nicholson, brother of my old friend Nora Nicholson, who died in 1973 after 60 years on the stage'. (cf: *George Spelvin*)

warehousing (TV/US) the re-running of successful series by independent stations while the same shows are still proving successful on a network first run (qv) basis.

war-fighting (milit) usually as in *nuclear war-fighting capability*: actually launching an attack rather than merely rattling nuclear sabres.

wargame v (milit) to experiment with a variety of putative 'battles', 'attack', 'nuclear strikes', etc. with the intention of developing a strategy that might have to be tested in a real war.

wargasm n (milit) a crisis that could lead to the outbreak of a war; the war that followed such a crisis: in both cases the image is of an escalating compulsion towards conflict that takes over from sense and restraint and must reach its nuclear climax.

warm-up *n* (sex) for a prostitute of either sex to wash a client's penis prior to having sex.

warning red (milit) radio signal: a hostile attack is either imminent or actually in progress.

warrantless investigation (govt, espionage) see: *technical trespass*.

wash *n* (police/UK) *at the wash*: a pickpocket who specialises in working in washrooms or public lavatories in airports, stations, hotels, concert halls, etc.

wash sale (stock market/US) an illegal deal between two brokers who arrange a fake 'sale' and thus create an illusory market price for a share; used for purposes of tax evasion.

wash-up *n* (milit) RN: a post-operation conference for discussing that operation and assessing its success, failure, short- and long-term effects, etc.

wastage *n* (indust relats) the reduction of manpower by simply leaving vacant the jobs of those workers who resign or retire from the company.

waste *v* (milit) to kill; the implication is of savagery, of 'laying waste' to a people and their homes.

watch list (espionage) a list of special words programmed into a computer to help it sort out specific material from a mass of otherwise incomprehensible documents.

watchman *n* (press) a piece of cardboard inserted between lines of metal type in order to point out an error in the setting.

watchpot *n* (govt) a back-formation of 'a pot that needs watching', coined, like so many others, by Alexander Haig when he was US Secretary of State; thus 'Lebanon is a Mid-East watchpot'.

waterhole *n* (aerospace) a part of the electromagnetic spectrum that is reasonably free of interference and which, it is felt, would be that waveband most likely to pick up signals from extra-terrestrial beings who wished to contact Earth.

water landing (air crew) landing in the sea or ocean, 'ditching'.

wax his tail *v* (milit) USAF: to lock in on a hostile aircraft's rear during a dogfight, from which position one's heat-seeking air-to-air missile should guarantee his destruction.

waxworks (pols/US) the main guests at a political dinner, who have to sit on a raised platform and attempt to hide their boredom behind frozen expressions which seem to originate in Madame Tussaud's exhibition.

weaponeering *n* (milit) the process of working out exactly which type and calibre of weapons are needed to cause required damage to a range of specific targets.

weapons tight (milit) an order given to air defence units when friendly as well as hostile

forces are flying in the area; no weapons are to engage targets until they are identified with 100% accuracy as enemy aircraft.

weathercock *v* (milit) the tendency of an aircraft or a missile to turn slightly in the same direction as the wind.

weave problems (sociol) problems that cannot be solved in isolation but which are related, and dependent on several or many interlinked situations, each of which must be considered in its due turn.

webs *n* (radio, TV) the major US broadcasting networks: NBC, CBS, ABC.

wedge *n* (sport) in golf, the traditional name for a number 10 iron.

wedged *v* (theatre/US) to be stranded without money in a hotel far from New York and with one's baggage held as security against the unpaid bill.

wedged (computers) to be in a locked state, unable to proceed further with one's calculations or running of a program. (cf: *deadlocked*).

wedge up *v* (prison/UK) for the sake of a protest or as a (temporary) defence against a beating from the prison officers, to barricade the inside of one's cell door.

weed *n* (crime) in the fairground, the 'official' pilfering from the till by the person running a stall; the owner accepts this stealing as long as it stays at a realistic amount; if it exceeds that amount he puts a second man on the stall and thus cuts down the weed to only 50% each.

weeding (crime) 1. stealing from one's employer. 2. stealing from a place where a crime has already been committed recently.

weekly *n* (movies) a weekly wage.

weep *n* (public relats) a sob story told by a PR, usually a press agent, who claims to a columnist that were this story not placed, his client would certainly fire him and his family, or worse still, he himself would suffer untold miseries.

weigh off *v* (police/UK) to sentence a condemned prisoner.

weight *n* (drugs) one pound weight (1 lb.); usually applied to hashish or marijuana.

weighting (marketing) the adjustment of raw data (qv) by assigning definite proportionate values, according to the desired degree of importance, to the various aspects of the data being considered; *London weighting*: the payment of extra wages to those employed in London to compensate for the higher cost of living in the capital.

well-end (sex) (abbrev) well-endowed: a man with a large penis; used as part of the descriptions provided by those hustlers who use contact magazines (qv) to attract clients.

well-firmed (theatre) a part that has been thoroughly memorised.

wellhead cost (commerce) the cost of bringing oil or gas to the surface, before any extra costs

W

for transport, refining, taxes, etc have been added.

we'll let you know (theatre) aka: *don't call us, we'll call you*: stock rejections of auditioning actors and actresses by directors, agents, etc.

wellness *n* (new therapies) the state of positive physical and mental well-being that is more than simply not being ill.

Weltanschauung *n* (pols) fr. Ger. 'world view': an individual's conception of and relation to the world in which he/she lives.

wet affair (espionage) aka: *wet stuff*: the KGB equivalent of the CIA's wet work (qv).

wet down *v* (milit) USMC: to hold a (drunken) party to celebrate one's promotion.

wet finger perspective (industry) a superficial assessment of a situation: only the tip of one finger has been dipped in to try the 'temperature', instead of rolling up one's sleeves and plunging both hands in properly.

wets (pols/UK) those members of the Conservative Party who disagree with Prime Minister Margaret Thatcher's hard-line monetarist economic policies, the most obvious result of which has been massive unemployment and widespread social suffering; Mrs Thatcher categorised all such weaklings as 'wet', implying both a schoolchild's derogatory sneer and the 'dilution' by such rebels of her policies.

wet sell (business) a business deal which is helped along by the increasing drunkenness of both participants.

wetware (computers) any organic intelligence, notably the 'wet' human brain which is neither hard- nor soft-ware (qqv).

wet work *n* (espionage) a CIA term to describe the use of assassination for political purposes.

what-if games (business) aka: *whif games*: planning experimentation which uses 'games' in which those involved ask 'What if. . .?' and attempt to follow through their various ideas to their solutions; such games have been made more complex and sophisticated by the inclusion of a correctly programmed computer in their workings out.

where one is at (new therapies) see: *where you're at.*

where you're at (new therapies) one's state of being; emotional, psychological, and, given the context, as regards one's opinions on any given topic. Like many such phrases (cf: *bag, go with the flow*, etc), derived from the drug-soaked hippie era of the late 1960s.

whiff *n, v* (sport) in golf, a stroke that misses the ball; to play such a stroke.

whiparound *n* (TV/US) a shot that pans (qv) all the way round a desk of newsreaders while the anchorman (qv) introduces them all in one continuous breath.

whip pan (TV) the rotation of a TV camera in a complete 360° circle; often used to denote the

movement of the action to another location but at the same time.

whipsaw *v* (stock market) to manipulate the market so as to cause a rival to buy high and sell low.

whipsaw *v* (pols/US) an illegal and corrupt procedure whereby a susceptible politician will collect bribes from those representing both sides of a given issue and deliver only to one or quite possibly to neither.

whipsaw *v* (indust relats) a bargaining process in which unions start by 'picking off' those companies which can least afford to fight a wage claim; these deals made, the union takes them to the harder-line employers and presents them as *faits accomplis*, satisfactory figures against which the other companies should have no option but to accept.

whiskers *n* (drugs) nickname amongst dealers for any Federal agent, or the whole Federal narcotics agency.

whiskey seats (theatre) seats on the aisle, popular both with critics, who need to get out before the rush and phone in their reviews, and those who like to escape to the bar when the action palls.

whistle-blower (pols) a government employee who is so appalled by the evidence of corruption or mismanagement that he sees around him that he decides to inform the press and thus the public of what he has discovered.

whistlestop *v* (pols) to campaign by touring local communities in a special train.

white *n* (press) any part of a page that does not carry printing.

white coat *n* (police/UK) the senior examiner at the Police Public Carriage Office – responsible for examining taxi-drivers on their knowledge (qv) of London. (cf: *brown coat*)

white coat rule (advert) the prohibition of the use in advertising of any real doctors, or actors made up to resemble them, on the principle that the public's natural trust in medical professionals could be used to sell second-rate products.

white collar workers (indust relats) staff employees; non-manual labourers. (cf: *blue collar, pink collar*)

white goods *n* (commerce) fridges, freezers, washing machines, etc. (cf: *brown goods*)

white hole (science) a hypothetical source of matter of energy, posited as the 'other ends' of black holes (qv) and as such expelling all the matter and energy which has been sucked into a black hole.

Whitehouse factor *n* (govt) the belief in the UK civil service that some standards of 'morality' must be imposed on people's freedom of choice in their entertainments, esp. that of television; from Mrs. Mary Whitehouse, a self-appointed censor of the British media.

white label *n* (record industry) a pre-release copy

of a record, perfect in all aspects but that the company's coloured and printed label has yet to be affixed to it, that is sent for reviews to journalists, radio stations, etc.

white land (govt) land that has been left unshaded on those maps which delineate ownership, development, demolition, etc: thus land which has been left untouched and which is not covered by any forthcoming planning decisions.

white paper (pols) an official statement of government policy and the background information that helped create that policy. (cf: *green paper, blue book*)

white radio n (espionage) propaganda radio that makes no secret of its origins, its political line or its targets, eg: Radio Free Europe, which bombards the Warsaw Pact countries with pro-US material. (cf: *black radio*)

white room n (aerospace) 1. a special building for the storage of unused space capsules. 2. a room kept surgically clean and purged of all dust and other foreign bodies and used for the assembly of those delicate mechanisms which are used in space flight.

whites (milit) USMC: a Marine officer's uniform.

white shirts n (prison) senior warders who are allowed to wear white shirts instead of the usual blue ones.

whitewalls n (milit) USMC: the regulation super-short Marine haircut in which the hair is shaved high up the back and sides.

whitewash v (sport) in certain sports, to defeat an opponent so completely that one loses no points, games, rubbers or any other portion of the encounter.

whizzer n (crime, police/UK) a pickpocket; thus *the whiz*: the craft of picking pockets.

who is it really? (new therapies) in primal therapy (qv), a basic trigger for the patient's inner emotions and deep feeling (qv); the patient is making some statement of attack on the therapist, who replies 'Who is it really?'; the repetition of this question will eventually force the connections that lead to the primal experience.

whole child concept (educ) the concept that one must understand the child not merely in the classroom but at play as well as at work and in the home as well as at school if that child is to gain the full benefits of being taught.

wholism (new therapies) see: *holism*.

wickets (theatre, movies) turnstiles, ticket offices, box offices.

widow n (press) an example of poor typography in which a single word is left dangling on a line by itself at the end of a paragraph.

wiggle seat n (police/US) a special lie detector that can be fitted to a chair and which will measure the bodily reactions of a suspect to various crucial questions.

wild line (TV, movies) an extra line of dialogue

that is recorded out of context and which can be cut in later to replace one that was delivered badly or simply used as an extra part of the dialogue.

wild track (TV, movies) aka: *non sync*: a tape of random sounds, not synchronised with any of the pictures, that can be used as and where necessary for aural atmosphere.

Wilkie (horse-racing) fr. rhyming sl: Wilkie Bard: card; a race-card.

willie n (espionage) 'This is the jargon for a person, often a newspaperman, who is used by real agents to pass on secret information and perform other subversive services without knowing it' (letter from Chapman Pincher, *The Times*, April 1981).

WIMEX (milit) Worldwide Military Command and Control System: network of computers, warning sensors, command sensors and communications used by US commanders to run the worldwide US troops.

win n (computers) a program that runs smoothly and encounters no unexpected snags.

win v (horse-racing) for a horse to come first, followed, in the US, by *place*: second, and *show*: third.

winchester n (computers) aka: *hard disc*: a data storage unit with far greater capacity, speed of access and general sophistication than the floppy disc (qv).

wind v (movies) (abbrev) wind up: to bring filming to a close.

window n (milit) strips of foil and wire that are dropped from a plane or shot up from a boat to confuse radar or the guidance systems of smart (qv) missiles. (cf: *chaff*)

window n (aerospace) an interval of time and/or a specific area at the limit of the earth's atmosphere through which a spacecraft must pass, first if it is to continue with a successful mission and later, if it is to make a safe re-entry.

window of vulnerability (milit) the military theory that US land-based missiles are inadequately protected against a hostile first strike (qv); it is this theory that launched the plans for the MX missile, with its multiple silo basing, railway tracks, dense pack (qv) etc.

window's open (gambling) a comment to point out that an inept and obvious cheat is at work.

windup n (TV) a signal from a studio floor manager – a winding motion with one or both hands – which tells a performer to speed up his act and draw it to a close.

wing v (theatre) to fasten one's script to one of the wing flats or some other part of the scenery when one has failed to learn it properly and thus needs an occasional reference during the performance; thus *wing it*: to make one's way through a performance more by luck than judgement.

winter book n (horse-racing) a book-maker's

W

early appraisal of the odds for races in the forthcoming seasons.

wipe *n* (movies) an optical device used for quick changes of scene: a line appears at one edge of the screen and moves across the screen, obliterating the old picture and pulling the new one with it.

wipe out *v* (sport) in surfing, the dumping of a surfer from his board by a wave he cannot handle.

wire (gambling) 1. the finish line at a race course. 2. a signal used between two card cheats. 3. (spec) in poker, a hand that has a pair with one card hidden face down and one showing on the table: a *wired* hand.

wired for sound (movies) an extra who has a few lines to say.

wire man (espionage) an expert in electronic surveillance techniques.

wishbone (sport) in US football, a play in which the half-backs line up further from the line of scrimmage than does the full back.

Wisc (milit) (acro) Warning System Controller, in charge of tracking incoming hostile missiles.

withdrawal of enthusiasm campaign (govt/US) a bureaucratic euphemism: a boycott.

withdrawn from the schedule (broadcasting/UK) a euphemism used by the British Broadcasting Corporation (BBC): banned, through governmental or internal BBC pressure.

withhold target *n* (milit) reserve nuclear target, not to be attacked unless specially indicated.

wizard *n* (computers) 1. a person who understands the most complex machines and can debug (qv) any problems that may come up. 2. a person whose expertise gives him certain privileges as far as operating his firm's or college's computers is concerned.

wolf trap *n* (aerospace) a device that reports on the possibilities of microbial lifeforms on planets; it sucks in samples of soil and air and immerses them in nutrient solutions; named for Dr. Wolf Vishniac.

wolly *n* (police/UK) a uniformed policeman, esp. a young and inexperienced constable.

wooden bomb *n* (milit) the hypothetical concept of an ideal weapon: 100% reliable, carrying an infinite shelf life, requiring no special surveillance, storage or handling.

wood family (theatre) empty seats. (cf: *the plush family*)

woodie (sport) in surfing, an old wood-panelled station wagon used by surfers to carry themselves and their boards.

woodpecker *n* (milit) the development by Soviet scientists sometime since 1977 of a high powered radar beam that follows the earth's curvature and thus removes the attacking bombers' advantage of being able to penetrate defences by flying 'under the radar'. (cf: *OTH, OTH-B radar*)

woollybacks (indust relats) non-militant

workers who may be members of a union but still allow the employers to treat them like woolly-backed sheep.

Woolworth weapons (milit, espionage) small, simply manufactured, short-life arms and other killing weapons: cheap, expendable and ideal for close-in combat, assassination and other quiet but deadly tasks.

woppitzer *n* (gambling) a kibbitzer (qv) who has bad breath or body odour as well as a propensity to comment on a game in which he is not playing.

word *n* (computers) a fixed number of bits (qv), varying as to the overall capacity of the computer, but always representing the maximum number of bits that the machine can handle at any one time.

word-engineering (govt) the doctoring of information so that the public learn only such facts as those handing out that information – the government, military, scientific agencies, etc – wish to have revealed; such engineering involves suppression, alteration and outright falsification. (cf: *managed news*)

wordies (theatre) a script.

work *n* (sport) in cricket, the combination of finger and wrist action with which a bowler makes the ball swing or spin in the air.

work *n* (gambling) crooked cards or dice.

workaround *n* (aerospace) a back up, alternative method available to astronauts and to ground control if any mechanism fails or a particular mission cannot be carried out fully.

work for Jesus *v* (indust relats/US) to put in extra work without asking for extra pay.

work in a few rips (sex) for a homosexual hustler to sodomise his client.

working girl (sex) aka: *working broad, working chick*: a prostitute.

work over *v* (milit) USMC: 1. to reprimand severely. 2. to lay heavy fire onto a target.

work print (movies) the first print that an editor considers; it contains all those takes which are to be used, to one extent or another, for the final cut (qv); the effects have been prepared and the soundtrack is roughly synchronised.

work the hole *v* (crime/US) the mugging of drunks on the New York subway.

work through *v* (soc wk) the discussion of a controversial or difficult subject in the hope that gradually a solution can be found by talking about the problem and working out the best way to deal with it.

work up *v* (medic/US) to perform a series of routine diagnostic procedures: X-rays, blood tests, ECG, enema, bowel run, etc.

work with the cramps (sex) for a hustler to accept the pain of being sodomised if the money is sufficient.

work your bolt (milit) USMC: to resort to extraordinary measures – legal or otherwise – to achieve a desired end.

wormhole (science) a hypothetical passageway in space that connects a black hole and a white hole (qqv).

Worzel (media) *Private Eye*'s nickname for Rt. Hon. Michael Foot, MP, former leader of the Labour Party, whose sartorial carelessness has equated him with a fictional talking scarecrow, beloved of many children, Worzel Gummidge.

wow *n* (video, tape recorders) slow variations of speed that affect videotapes and sound recording tapes.

wrap *n, v* (movies, TV) the end of the day's shooting: 'It's a wrap!'; to end the day's shooting.

wraparound *n* (TV/US) a general term for a news item in which an anchor man introduces the piece, the reporter concerned, either live or on tape, reads the story, with or without visual accompaniment, and the anchorman rounds it off and moves onto the next piece.

wrap-up *n* (pols/US) the standard wind-up speech delivered regularly by a touring candidate; experienced campaign staff and media people soon learn to recognise the wrap-up and to start moving off to their bus, plane or train once it begins.

wring it out *v* (aerospace) ostentatious flying that deliberately pushes an aircraft to the limits of its performance specifications.

write *v* (computers) to put information into a computer memory, either in the form of a tape or a disc/diskette. (cf: *read*)

write down/write up *v* (business) to reduce or increase the value of certain assets for the purpose of their inclusion in the company accounts.

write-in candidate (pols/US) a candidate whose name is not included on the printed ballot paper and who has to be written into the blank space provided by those voters who wish to support him; thus *write-in vote*: those who wrote in their favoured candidate and eschewed those proposed by the main parties.

wrong set (movies) a comment from the director to state that the set on which they have been filming is now finished with and that the actors and crew should move on to start work on a new one.

X *n* (gambling) *to have the X*: to control the gambling in a given city or state.

X (milit) USAF: the regular prefix to designate experimental aircraft.

X-movie *a* (espionage) a potential lady (qv) or sister (qv) who lacks the necessary subtlety and other attributes that would make her the perfect member of a sanctifying (qv) team.

Y

Y (milit) USAF: the regular prefix to denote a prototype aircraft.

yankee white (milit) the alleged super-WASP characteristics that are sought out for very high-risk workers in US national security areas.

yashmak (TV) a type of diffuser that covers only the lower half of the lamp; from the mask that covers all but the eyes of a devout Muslim woman.

YAVIS (psychol) (acro) *y*oung, *a*ttractive, *v*erbal, *i*ntelligent, *s*uccessful: those patients who are allegedly preferred by analysts above the less appealing and less articulate but possibly more genuinely needy cases.

yell *n* (theatre) a tremendous joke; from the response such a joke ought to obtain.

yellow-backs (sex) hard core picture books with a token story-line.

yellow books (govt) official government documents issued in bound volumes by the French government; the equivalent of the UK blue books (qv).

yellowcake (milit) uranium oxide, used in the manufacture of nuclear weapons.

yellow card *v* (theatre/US) for a touring theatrical company to request the local labour unions to supply stagehands as and when they are needed.

yellow-dog contract (indust relats) a contract in which the employer offers a job only on condition that current union membership will be terminated and that none of the workers will attempt to join a union or bring one into the plant (almost universally illegal).

yellow dog democrat (pols/US) a die-hard loyalist of the party, used only to imply praise.

yellow-dog fund (indust relats) a fund set aside for bribery and corruption or the paying for any distasteful tasks; illegal.

yellow goods (commerce) products that are bought only rarely and which offer high profits to the retailer: cars, stereophonic equipment, TVs, etc. (cf: *brown goods, red goods*)

yellow jacket (drugs) see: *drug names*.

yellow unions (indust relats) company unions who have no real interest in the workers but merely pander to the employers; from a strike in 1887 by miners at Montceau-les-mines in France: the company scabs (qv), themselves union members, met preparatory to breaking the strike in a hall where they covered the windows with yellow paper to keep out interested onlookers.

yield (milit) the force of a nuclear explosion, expressed in terms of the number of tons of TNT that would have been required to create the same explosion.

yield to weight ratio (milit) the assessment of the force of a nuclear explosion by comparing the force of the explosion to the size of the bomb.

yips *n* (sport) in golf, nervous fumbling and twitches that ruin one's concentration and one's swing.

yoga art (art) a type of Indian art which uses 'nuclear' or 'power' diagrams as an aid to yoga meditation.

yomping (milit) British Army (Royal Marines): the marching with weapons and a 120lb. pack across appalling terrain in very hostile conditions upon the premise that once this ultimate in route marches is concluded, the troops will be fighting a battle at the other end; possibly from a Norwegian word used by skiers to speak of the crossing of obstacles.

yo-yo *v* (business) for a company to alternate large and minuscule orders from a supplier with the intention of keeping him off balance; relations are similarly up and down with the client appearing satisfied or unhappy for no logical reasons; the net result of such tactics is to win negotiating points in highly competitive businesses by putting a supplier into emotional and economic dependence on his client.

yoyo (TV) (acro) *y*ou're *o*n *y*our *o*wn: a genre of investigative programme in which one public and/or controversial figure is placed alone beneath the lights and is questioned in detail and at length by a panel of knowledgeable experts and journalists who sit in the cool and quiet just beyond those lights.

yoyo mode (computers) a state in which the system alternates rapidly between being up (qv) and then down (qv) and back again.

YP (prison/UK) (acro) *y*oung *p*risoner.

yumpsville *n* (movies) the unsophisticated rural and smalltown audience whose favourite films mix sex and violence and keep the dialogue and intellectual stimulus down to a minimum.

zap *v* (computers) to erase the PROM (the programmable read only memory) by using special equipment.

zap *v* (medic/US) to administer electric shock treatment to a patient.

zap *v* (milit) to attack, to kill.

zebra *n* (medic/US) any obscure diagnosis.

zebra *n* (sport) in US football, an umpire; from the black and white striped shirts that umpires wear.

zero *v* (computers) 1. to set to zero. 2. to erase, to discard all data from a memory.

zero-base budgeting (business) aka: *zero line budgeting*: the starting every economic year with a budget which calls on all programmes, projects and similar terms that need funding to justify their continuing use of those funds; nothing is sacred and anything may be discarded if it is unable to prove its worthiness and efficiency.

zero delay *n* (TV/US) the showing by affiliates of taped network shows one week after their taping, thus as soon as they are distributed to the affiliates.

zero life *v* (aerospace) to restore a formerly worn-out aircraft to so excellent a condition it can be rated as brand new, with zero previous wear and tear.

zero option (milit) a theory developed by President Reagan in 1981; if the USSR will agree to scrap their SS-20 missiles, then the US will not deploy cruise missiles in Europe, thus creating a nuclear-free zone in Europe; the scheme has yet to find takers.

zero-sum game (business) a game theory conflict whereby the advantage that accrues to one party is exactly equal to the disadvantage suffered by the other party: such a 'game' works as a model for rivalries in a trade market, although it is naturally modified when that market is expanding.

zero-sum game (pols) a political or diplomatic confrontation in which there is no compromise: if one side wins, then the other has to lose; face cannot be saved.

zero-zero (milit) shorthand for a weapon moratorium in which neither superpower would increase their nuclear stockpiles. (cf: *zero option*)

zero-zero seat (aerospace) an ejector seat that works safely at ground level (zero height) and when the aircraft is stationary (zero speed).

zest (new therapies) in co-counselling (qv): the natural positive and optimistic feelings of a human being.

zinger (pols) a punchline at the end of a speech, or a line with particular force or emotional effect anywhere in a speech.

zipper *n* (milit) a combat air patrol that flies either at dawn or dusk.

zippers (sport) the permanent scars that disfigure the bodies of many US professional footballers through years of tough contact play.

zombie (gambling) 1. a gambler who betrays no emotions either when winning or losing. 2. a horse that seems to have no appetite for racing.

zoom bags (milit) flying suits worn by fighter pilots.

zoo *n* (milit) USMC: any jungle or jungle area.

zoo plane (pols/US) the second of the two planes that convey the candidate, his staff and the media during a campaign: the zoo plane is so called for its being used by the TV technicians, aka *animals*, but also for its generally offering a more relaxed and enjoyable atmosphere in which to travel than the reverential, earnest world of the plane in which the candidate himself travels.

zulu (aerospace) the aeronautical name for Greenwich Mean Time, so called since Greenwich is sited on 0° (zero degrees) longitude.

Z

BIBLIOGRAPHY

Arlen Michael, *The Camera Age*, Farrar, Straus & Giroux, New York, 1981.

Armstrong, Brian, *The Glossary of TV Terms*, Barrie & Jenkins, London, 1976.

Atyeo, Donald L., *Blood and Guts: Violence in Sports*, Paddington Press, London, 1979.

Baker, Sidney, *The Australian Language*, 2nd edn, Currawong Publishing, Sydney, Australia, 1966.

Bannock, Graham, Baxter, R. E., and Rees, Raj, *The Penguin Dictionary of Economics*, 2nd edn, Penguin Books, Harmondsworth, 1980.

Barnhart, Clarence L., Steinmetz, Sol, and Barnhart, Robert K., *A Dictionary of New English*, Longman, London, 1973.

Barnhart, Clarence L., Steinmetz, Sol, and Barnhart, Robert K., *The Second Barnhart Dictionary of New English*, Barnhart/Harper & Row, New York, 1980.

Berrey, Lester V., and Van Den Bark, Melvin, *American Thesaurus of Slang*, 2nd edn, Harrap, London, 1954.

Bonavia, David, *The Chinese*, Penguin Books, Harmondsworth, 1982.

Bowman, W. P., and Ball, R. H., *Theatre Language*, Theatre Arts Books, New York, 1961.

Boycott, Rosie, *Batty, Bloomers and Boycott*, Hutchinson, London, 1982.

Bullock, Alan, and Stallybrass, Oliver (eds), *The Fontana Dictionary of Modern Thought*, Fontana/Collins, London, 1977.

Butterfield, John, Parker, Philip and Honigmann, David, *What Is Dungeons and Dragons?*, Penguin Books, Harmondsworth, 1982.

Campbell, C., *War Facts Now*, Fontana Paperbacks, London, 1982.

Caputo, Philip, *A Rumour of War*, Arrow Books, London, 1978.

Clare, Anthony W., and Thompson, Sally, *Let's Talk About Me*, BBC Publications, London, 1981.

Cohen, Dr. Sidney, *The Drug Dilemma*, McGraw-Hill, New York, 1976.

Collinson, W. E., *Contemporary English*, B. G. Teubner, Leipzig and Berlin, 1927.

Complete CB Slang Dictionary, 9th edn, Merit Publications, N. Miami, Fla., 1980.

Counihan, Martin, *A Dictionary of Energy*, Routledge & Kegan Paul, London, 1981.

Cox, Barry, Shirley, John, Short, Martin, *The Fall of Scotland Yard*, Penguin Books, Harmondsworth, 1977.

Crouse, Timothy, *The Boys on the Bus*, Ballantine Books, New York, 1973.

Davies, Peter, *Davies' Dictionary of Golfing Terms*, Simon & Schuster, New York, 1980.

Evans, Ivor H. (ed.), *Brewer's Dictionary of Phrase and Fable*, 2nd rev. edn, Cassell, London, 1981.

Faust, Bernice, *Women, Sex and Pornography*, Penguin Books, Harmondsworth, 1980.

Federal Writers Project (New York), 'Lexicon of Trade Jargon', unpub. MS, in Library of Congress, 1939.

The Flier's Handbook, Pan Books, London, 1978.

Franklyn, Julian, *Rhyming Slang*, 2nd edn, Routledge & Kegan Paul, London, 1981.

Fraser, Edward, and Gibbons, John, *Soldier and Sailor Words and Phrases*, George Routledge & Sons, London, 1925.

Freed, David, and Lane, Mark, *Executive Action*, Charisma Books, London, 1973.

Goldman, Albert, *Elvis*, Allen Lane, London, 1981.

Gowers, Sir Ernest, *The Complete Plain Words*, 2nd edn, Penguin Books, Harmondsworth, 1973.

Granada Television, *Some Technical Terms and Slang*, Granada Television, Manchester, n.d.

Granville, Wilfrid, *A Dictionary of Theatrical Terms*, André Deutsch, London, 1952.

Green, Jonathon, *The IT Book of Drugs*, Knullar Publications, London, 1971.

Greener, Michael, *The Penguin Dictionary of Commerce*, Penguin Books, Harmondsworth, 1979.

Gunston, Bill (ed.), *Jane's Dictionary of Aerospace Terms*, Macdonald & Jane's, London, 1980.

Halliwell, Leslie, *Halliwell's Filmgoer's Companion*, 5th edn, Granada Publishing, London, 1976.

Hamilton, J. Dundas, *Stockbroking Today*, Macmillan, London, 1968.

Hayward, Brigadier P. C. H. (ed.), *Jane's Dictionary of Military Terms*, Macdonald & Jane's, London, 1975.

Heinl, Captain Robert D., *The Marine Officer's*

Guide, Naval Institute Press, Annapolis, Md., 1977.

Herr, Michael, *Dispatches*, Pan Books, London, 1977.

Hilgartner, Stephen, Bell, Richard C., and O'Connor, Rory, *Nukespeak: The Selling of Nuclear Technology in America*, Sierra Club Books, San Francisco, 1982.

Hodgkinson, H., *Doubletalk: The Language of Communism*, George Allen & Unwin, London, 1955.

Howard, Philip, *New Words for Old*, Hamish Hamilton, London, 1977.

Howard, Philip, *Weasel Words*, Hamish Hamilton, London, 1979.

Howard, Philip, *Words Fail Me*, Hamish Hamilton, London, 1980.

Howe, R. W., *Weapons*, Sphere Books, London, 1980.

Hudson, Kenneth, *Dictionary of Diseased English*, Macmillan, London, 1977.

Hudson, Kenneth, *The Language of Modern Politics*, Macmillan, London, 1978.

Hudson, Kenneth, *The Jargon of the Professions*, Macmillan, London, 1978.

Hutt, Allen, *The Changing Newspaper*, Gordon Fraser, London, 1973.

International Confederation of Free Trade Unions, *Glossary of Trade Union Terms*, ICFTU, Brussels, 1972.

Jarrett, Dennis, *Good Computing Book for Beginners*, ECC Publications, London, 1980.

Jenkins, Dan, *Semi Tough*, Star Books, London, 1972.

Johannsen, Hanno, and Page, G. Terry, *International Dictionary of Management*, Kogan Page, London, 1975.

Jones, Jack, and Morris, Max, *A–Z of Trades Unionism and Industrial Relations*, Heinemann, London, 1982.

Kaplan, Donald M., and Schwerner, Armand, *The Domesday Dictionary*, Jonathan Cape, London, 1964.

Kempner, Thomas (ed.), *A Handbook of Management*, 3rd edn, Penguin Books, Harmondsworth, 1980.

Laffin, John, *The French Foreign Legion*, Dent, London, 1974.

Lasch, Christopher, *The Culture of Narcissism*, Sphere Books, London, 1979.

Lee, William (William Burroughs), *Junkie*, Ace Books, New York, 1953.

LeSure, James, *Guide to Pedaguese*, Harper & Row, New York, 1965.

Maas, Peter, *The Valachi Papers*, G. P. Putnam's Sons, New York, 1968.

MacArthur, P., *Industrial Relations Terms*, Ashridge Management College, Berkhamsted, 1976.

McFadden, Cyra, *The Serial*, Pan Books, London, 1978.

Machlin, Milt, *The Gossip Wars*, Star Books, London, 1981.

McShane, Frank (ed.), *The Selected Letters of Raymond Chandler*, Jonathan Cape, London, 1981.

Magazines: *American Speech* (US); *Army* (US); *Collier's* (US); *Esquire* (US); *Futurist; HiFi Choice; International Video Yearbook* (1981); *Marine Corps Gazette* (US); *Melody Maker; New Musical Express; New Statesman; Newsweek* (US); *New Times* (US); *New York* (US); *New York Review of Books* (US); *Omni* (US); *Practical Computer; Practical Computing; Personal Computer World; Private Eye; Psychology Today* (US); *Quill* (US); *Rolling Stone* (US); *Spectator; Streetlife; Time* (US).

Mager, N. H. and S. K., *The Morrow Book of New Words*, William Morrow, New York, 1982.

Maurer, David W., *The Language of the Underworld*, collected and edited by Allan W. Futrell and Charles B. Wordell, University Press of Kentucky, Lexington, Ky, 1981.

Maurer, David W., and Vogel, Victor H., *Narcotics and Narcotic Addiction*, 4th edn, Charles C. Thomas, Springfield, Ill., 1973.

Mencken, H. L., *The American Language*, Alfred Knopf, New York, 1936, Supplements 1945, 1948.

Michaels, Leonard, and Ricks, Christopher, *The State of the Language*, University of California Press, Berkeley, Calif., 1980.

Miller, Don Ethan, *The Book of Jargon*, Macmillan, New York, 1981.

Miller, Tony, and George, Patricia, *Cut! Print!*, O'Hara Publications, Los Angeles, Calif., 1972.

Milner, Christina and Richard, *Black Players*, Michael Joseph, London, 1973.

Milton, David, Milton, Nancy and Schurman, Franz (eds), *People's China 1966–72*, Penguin Books, Harmondsworth, 1977.

Moynahan, Brian, *Airport International*, Pan Books, London, 1978.

Mueller, Robert K., *Buzzwords: A Guide to the Language of Leadership*, Van Nostrand Reinhold, New York, 1974.

Nemmers, E. E., *Dictionary of Economics and Business*, Littlefield, Adams, Totowa, N.J., 1978.

Newman, G. F., *Sir, You Bastard*, Sphere Books, London, 1970.

Newman, G. F., *You Nice Bastard*, Sphere Books, London, 1972.

Newman, G. F., *You Flash Bastard*, Sphere Books, London, 1974.

Newspapers: *Daily Express; Daily Telegraph; Evening Standard; Guardian; New York Times* (US); *Observer; Sunday Times; The Times; Variety* (US); *Yorkshire Post.*

Oliver, Gordon, *Marketing Today*, Prentice-Hall, Englewood, Cliffs, N.J., 1980.

The Oxford English Dictionary, 12 vols and Supplement, 1933; Supplements A–G (1972), H–N (1976), O–Scz (1982). Oxford University Press, Oxford.

Palmer, Joseph (ed.), *Jane's Dictionary of Naval Terms*, Macdonald & Jane's, London, 1975.

Partridge, Eric, *A Dictionary of the Underworld*, 3rd edn, Routledge & Kegan Paul, London, 1968.

Partridge, Eric, *Slang, Yesterday and Today*, 4th edn, Routledge & Kegan Paul, London, 1970.

Partridge, Eric, *A Dictionary of Slang and Unconventional English*, 7th edn (two vols), Routledge & Kegan Paul, London, 1970.

Pei, M., *Words in Sheep's Clothing*, George Allen & Unwin, London, 1970.

Plate, Thomas, and Darvi, Andrea, *Secret Police: The Inside Story of a Terror Network*, Robert Hale, London, 1982.

Powis, David, *The Signs of Crime*, McGraw-Hill (UK), London, 1977.

Prenis, John, *The Language of Computers*, Star Books, London, 1981.

Pringle, Peter, and Arkin, William, *SIOP*, Sphere Books, London, 1983.

Public Affairs Bureau, Washington, D.C., *A Dictionary of US Military Terms*, 1963.

Rawson, Hugh, *A Dictionary of Euphemisms and Other Doubletalk*, Macdonald, London, 1983.

Rodgers, Bruce, *The Queens' Vernacular*, Blond & Briggs, London, 1972.

Rosen, R. D., *Psychobabble*, Wildwood House, London, 1977.

Roth, Philip, *The Great American Novel*, Jonathan Cape, London, 1973.

Safire, William, *Safire's Dictionary of Politics*, rev. edn, Ballantine Books, New York, 1978.

Safire, William, *On Language*, Avon Books, New York, 1980.

Sampson, Anthony, *The Changing Anatomy of Britain*, Hodder & Stoughton, London, 1982.

Santoli, Al, *Everything We Had*, Ballantine Books, New York, 1981.

Scarne, J., *Complete Guide to Gambling*, Simon & Schuster, New York, 1967.

Sciascia, Leonardo, *Mafia Vendetta*, Jonathan Cape, London, 1963.

Shem, Samuel, *The House of God*, Corgi Paperbacks, London, 1978.

6,000 Words: A Supplement to Webster's Third New International Dictionary, G. and C. Merriam, Springfield, Mass., 1976.

Spencer, Donald D., *Computer Dictionary for Everyone*, Charles Scribner's Sons, New York, 1979.

Sunday Times 'Insight' Team, *The Falklands War*, Sphere Books, London, 1982.

Timms, N. and R., *Dictionary of Social Welfare*, Routledge & Kegan Paul, London, 1982.

Toffler, Alvin, *The Third Wave*, Collins, London, 1980.

Uris, Leon, *Battle Cry*, Panther Books, London, 1953.

Versand, K., *The Polyglot's Lexicon*, Links Books, London, 1973.

Walker, John A., *Glossary of Art, Architecture and Design since 1945*, 2nd rev. edn, Clive Bingley, London, 1977.

Wasey Campbell Ewald, Ltd., *Ad Jargon Dictionary*, Wasey Campbell Ewald, London, 1980.

Waterhouse, Keith, *Daily Mirror Style*, Mirror Books, London, 1981.

Webb, James, *Fields of Fire*, Granada Publishing, St Albans, Herts, 1978.

Webster's Third New International Dictionary, G. Bell & Sons, London, 1966.

Wentworth, Harold, and Flexner, Stuart Berg, *Dictionary of American Slang*, 2nd supplemented edn, Thomas Y. Crowell, New York, 1975.

Whitaker, Ben, *The Police in Society*, Methuen, London 1980.

Whiteside, T., 'The Blockbuster Complex', *New Yorker*, New York, 1981.

Wilczynski, Josef, *An Encyclopedia of Marxism, Socialism and Communism*, Macmillan, London, 1981.

Witherow, John, and Bishop, Patrick, *The Winter War*, Quartet Books, London, 1982.

Wodehouse, P. G., *The Clicking of Cuthbert*, Herbert Jenkins, London, 1922.

Wodehouse, P. G., *The Heart of a Goof*, Herbert Jenkins, London, 1926.

Wolfe, Tom, *The Right Stuff*, Farrar, Straus & Giroux, New York, 1979.

Wynn, Dilys, *Murder Ink*, Workman Publishing, New York, 1977.

Zuckermann, Solly (Lord), *Nuclear Illusion and Reality*, Collins, London, 1982.